THE HISTORY & HERITAGE HANDBOOK

2015/16

H
heritagehunter

First published in 2015

Heritage Hunter® is an imprint and registered trademark of
Prepare to Publish Ltd, Charlbury
www.heritagehunter.co.uk

Editor: Andrew Chapman
© Prepare to Publish Ltd 2015
All rights reserved

British Library Cataloguing in Publication Data
A catalogue record for this book is available from the British Library

Paperback edition ISBN 9781905315581
Hardback edition ISBN 9781905315598

Information in this book is edited from text supplied by the venues listed
to www.Culture24.org.uk, and thence to Prepare to Publish Ltd.

While making every effort to ensure all information provided is correct,
Prepare to Publish Ltd and Culture24 cannot be held responsible for the quality
and accuracy of the venue data supplied. Venues listed are encouraged to update their
records in the Culture24 Direct Data Entry system.

Culture24 operates independently on a not-for-profit basis and receives government
funding. Culture24 publishes a number of websites including www.Culture24.org.uk,
and supports others with technical infrastructure and data provision.

Culture24 is committed to furthering the cultural sector's digital agenda and
helping to deliver better information on cultural opportunities to the public.
Culture24 is a registered charity and is governed by a Board of Trustees.

CONTENTS

INTRODUCTION

I s there anywhere in the world with as much history and heritage as the British Isles, crammed into such a relatively small geographical area? From hillforts to henges, stately homes to workhouses, mottes to mills, there are thousands of sites which recall 5000 years or more of human occupation and activity.

Not only that, but there are legions of archives and libraries, societies and institutions which are devoted to unearthing, exploring and sharing that history and heritage. From small, volunteer-run museums to major institutions such as the National Trust, they are vital to the survival and accessibility of our cultural inheritance for posterity.

The purpose of this book is to celebrate all of these diverse locations and organisations, and to offer a user-friendly finding aid which is hopefully more comprehensive than any other available in print. In these pages you will find almost 3500 museums, heritage sites, archives, libraries, societies and other places and groups.

Perhaps you are tracing your family history: if so, you will find most family history societies and regional record offices here – as well as a huge number of museums, many of which may have information about local families. If you are exploring local, social or military history, again you will find museums, libraries and archives which can help. Or perhaps you simply want a good day out, or some historical places to see while on holiday: once again, these pages are packed with them.

Despite the huge number of listings that follow, it should be said we've had to miss some things out simply for space. Local public libraries are generally not here, unless they have significant local studies collections (try www.findalibrary.org.uk if you need more). Nor are registration offices (other than the national ones for England/Wales, Scotland and Northern Ireland) – find those via www.gov.uk/register-offices. We've left out most art galleries and science discovery centres, unless they include collections or displays on historical subjects. We could never hope to include every single parish church (www.findachurch.co.uk), listed building (www.britishlistedbuildings.co.uk) or standing stone (www.megalithic.co.uk) across the richness of these islands – although you'll find many of the most notable ones at least. We have to leave some things for you to find by serendipity!

Most of the listings here have been kindly supplied from the venues themselves to the amazing online resource that is www.Culture24.org.uk, which should be your first port of call when looking up details of events and exhibitions across the UK; and we're hugely grateful to them for supplying information for this book in turn.

With the above caveats borne in mind, we hope you haven't found significant errors and omissions in these pages, but we actively welcome information via **www.heritagehunter.co.uk/update**, which we will use to make the next edition even bigger and better. Overleaf you will find a few notes for getting the most of the pages that follow – in the meantime, we hope you enjoy exploring history and heritage as much as we do. Keep an eye on **www.heritagehunter.co.uk** and **@heritagehunter** on Twitter for details of out other projects and publications coming soon.

USING THIS BOOK

A note on counties

The listings in this book are primarily organised by county – but that familiar word hides a great deal of complication. In England, for example, there are 'historic counties', which are generally those which have their origins in the shires of Anglo-Saxon times and represent one of the longest-surviving land divisions in the world. Nonetheless, their boundaries often changed, and over time there have been many anomalies such as 'exclaves', where a bit of one county was entirely surrounded by another. There are also 'ceremonial counties' (or 'geographic counties'), a concept which began in Victorian times and has been tinkered with numerous times since. They relate closely to many of the historic counties, but also include relatively modern definitions of conurbations such as the West Midlands or Tyne & Wear. There are even postal counties, part of the Post Office system from 1974-1996. Today, there are also many unitary authorities for local government.

In Wales, there are also historic counties, and the 'preserved counties' (ceremonial, and in some cases based on ancient kingdoms) of Gwynedd, Powys etc – and then the current 'principal areas' of local government, which include some of each but also smaller geographic divisions in certain areas. In Scotland, similar changes have occurred over time, with the ceremonial regions known as 'lieutenancy areas'; Northern Ireland's counties have been more consistent, but after 1972 it has had 26 unitary authorities.

All in all, the subject is a minefield. For further details and history, see www.en.wikipedia.org/wiki/List_of_counties_of_the_United_Kingdom and www.county-wise.org.uk from the Association of British Counties, which has an agenda to restore historic counties to the forefront but is also very informative. In this book, we have used historic counties where they make sense in modern times, but also used ceremonial or other areas in certain cases, most notably for the conurbations around London, Manchester, Liverpool, Newcastle/Gateshead/Sunderland, Birmingham, Bristol, Cardiff, Glasgow, Edinburgh and Belfast. So, for example:
• Oxfordshire represents the modern county, although before 1974 much of it (including Abingdon and areas of what are now part of Oxford) was in Berkshire
• Peterborough appears under Cambridgeshire, although in the past the 'Soke of Peterborough' was associated with Northamptonshire; and is today a unitary authority
• likewise, Goole was historically in West Yorkshire but now in East Yorkshire, so we have included it in the latter
• in Scotland, Banffshire and Kincardineshire are now mostly part of Aberdeenshire.

For the avoidance of any doubt, see the Appendix for a full list of past and present county and unitary authority names and which sections of this book they map to.

Finally, each section begins with an edited extract of John Bartholomew's 1887 *Gazetteer of the British Isles* for general interest and a historical perspective. For the complete gazetteer and other fascinating topographical resources, see www.visionofbritain.org.uk.

Opening times and admission prices

It was a difficult decision but we have omitted details of opening times and admission prices in this directory, principally because they are frequently subject to change, especially in these times of cuts to the heritage sector. Where we have received clear information, we have used icons (see below) to indicate that a site or organisation definitely charges or is believed to be free.

What the icons mean

▦ SOCIETY/ASSOCIATION/CAMPAIGN ■ HERITAGE SITE ▣ MUSEUM
▦ ARCHIVE/LIBRARY ★ FREE ENTRY £ CHARGE FOR ENTRY

UK-WIDE

UK-wide

130th (St John) Field Ambulance Research Group

www.130thstjohnfieldambulance.co.uk

contact@130thstjohnfieldambulance.co.uk

A group dedicated to the history of the 130th (St John) Field Ambulance RAMC.

Anglo-German Family History Society

82 Hillside Grove

Chelmsford CM2 9DB

www.agfhs.org.uk

gwendolinedavis@aol.com

Anglo-German Family History Society is for those who are interested in researching the genealogy or family history of people from the German-speaking parts of Europe who have emigrated over the centuries and settled in England, Scotland, Wales and Ireland (North and South), and the neighbouring islands.

Anglo-Italian Family History Society

Yew Cottage, Shurton

Bridgewater TA5 1GF

01278 733874

www.anglo-italianfhs.org.uk

The Anglo-Italian Family History Society website pulls together membership details, recommended reading, Italian surname database, indexes, Latin and Italian record translators, links and other resources for people tracing their Italian immigrant roots in Britain.

Army Children Archive (TACA), The

www.archhistory.co.uk

claregibson@f2s.com

A virtual, not-for-profit archive in the form of a website that chronicles the history of British army children from the 17th century to date. It aims to collect, record and preserve relevant information and also to raise awareness of the unique aspects of growing up as the child of a serving soldier in the British Army.

Baptist Historical Society, The

www.baptisthistory.org.uk

Founded in 1908, the society seeks to advance awareness of Baptist history and principles by promoting lectures, summer schools and publications; by offering an advice and information service and by bringing heritage issues to the attention of the Baptist Union of Great Britain and its member churches. One important aim of the society is to make widely available material about Baptist history written by Baptists.

Battlefields Trust, The

60 Seymour Road

St Albans AL3 5HW

01727 831413

www.battlefieldtrust.com/resource-centre

national.coordinator@battlefieldtrust.com

The UK Battlefields Resource Centre's website is an invaluable education resource and contains important information for those investigating or conserving battlefields. Included are maps, images, air photos, walking and driving tours, resources for teachers and much more.

British Architectural Library

RIBA, 21 Portman Square

London W1H 9HF

020 7580 5533

http://goo.gl/sGS8C8

info@riba.org

The British Architectural Library at the RIBA is the largest and most comprehensive resource in the United Kingdom for research and information on all aspects of architecture. The Library was established in 1834 as part of the RIBA, and today its architectural collections are one of the top three in the world and the finest in Europe.

British Association for Local History

PO Box 6549, Somersal Herbert

Ashbourne DE6 5WH

www.balh.co.uk

mail@balh.co.uk

Our purpose is to encourage and assist the study of local history throughout Great Britain as an academic discipline, and as a rewarding leisure pursuit for both individuals and groups. To achieve this the Association serves as the national body representing local and regional historians.

British Aviation Preservation Council

19 Action Place, High Heaton

Newcastle upon Tyne NE7 7RL

0191 266 2049

www.bapc.org.uk

secretarybapc@btconnect.com

The British Aviation Preservation Council links national, local authority, independent and service museums with private collections, voluntary groups and other organisations in the advancement of aviation preservation.

British Cartoon Archive at University of Kent

Templeman Library, The University of Kent
Canterbury CT2 7NU
01227 823 127
www.cartoons.ac.uk
info@cartoons.ac.uk

The British Cartoon Archive holds the principal collection of British cartoons of social and political comment. Established at the University of Kent at Canterbury in 1973, as the centre for the Study of Cartoons and Caricature, it holds 140,000 original drawings and 85,000 cuttings, representing the work of 350 different cartoonists.

British Commission for Military History (BCMH)

c/o Department of War Studies, King's College London
London WC2R 2LS
020 7848 2112
www.bcmh.org.uk
secgen@bcmh.org.uk

The British Commission for Military History (BCMH) promotes the discussion of military history in the broadest sense, across all periods and regions. Membership comes primarily from those working in military history in universities, museums and archives, defence and the armed forces as well as the media, heritage and cultural studies.

British Deaf History Society

11-13 Wilson Patten Street,
Warrington WA1 1PG
01925 632463
www.bdhs.org.uk
info@bdhs.org.uk

The British Deaf History Society (BDHS) is a recognised voluntary and charitable organisation with its own Constitution. The BDHS's objectives include: to encourage the study of and foster an interest in deaf history; to encourage the preservation of records and material related to the deaf and of historical value. Deaf History Journal is issued and distributed among members three times annually.

British Film Institute

London
020 7255 1444
www.bfi.org.uk

We're the British Film Institute. We promote greater understanding of and access to film and television culture.

British Horological Institute

Upton Hall, Upton
Newark NG23 5TE
01636 813 795
www.bhi.co.uk
info@bhi.co.uk

The BHI was founded in the Clerkenwell district of London in 1858. A group of watchmakers joined together in an attempt to combat the large quantity of clocks and watches flooding into the country from abroad, and to raise the standards of British horology. See the BHI website for details of the museum and archive.

British Library

96 Euston Road
London NW1 2DB
020 7412 7332
www.bl.uk
visitor-services@bl.uk

The British Library is the national library of the United Kingdom, and one of the world's greatest libraries. The John Ritblat Gallery: Treasures of the British Library, PACCAR Gallery of Living Words and the Workshop of Words, Sound and Images offer permanent displays and a changing programme of special thematic exhibitions.

Collections: The British Library is custodian of the most important research collection in the world, spanning almost 3,000 years and every continent. This covers books, journals, manuscripts, stamps, patents, sound recordings, printed music and maps.

British Library Newspapers

96 Euston Road
London NW1 2DB
020 7412 7353
www.bl.uk/collections/newspapers.html
newspapers@bl.uk

British Library Newspapers, the national archive collections in the United Kingdom of British and overseas newspapers. We are the only large, integrated national newspaper service in the world, combining facilities for the collection, preservation, and use of newspapers. See the website for details of the newspaper reading rooms at St Pancras, London and Boston Spa, Leeds.

British Library of Political & Economic Science

Library, London School of Economics & Political Science, 10 Portugal Street
London WC2A 2HD
020 7955 7229
www.lse.ac.uk/library

The working Library of the London School of Economics and Political Science and one of the largest libraries in the world devoted to the economic and social sciences. Its collections are significant to the study of economics, statistics, political science and public administration, international law and in the economic, political, social and international aspects of history and anthropology.

British Museum

Great Russell Street
London WC1B 3DG
020 7323 8299
www.britishmuseum.org
information@britishmuseum.org

Founded in 1753, the British Museum's remarkable collection spans over two million years of human history. Enjoy a unique comparison of the treasures of world cultures under one roof, centred around the magnificent Great Court. World-famous objects such as the Rosetta Stone, Parthenon sculptures, and Egyptian mummies are visited by up to six million visitors per year.

British Red Cross Society

44 Moorfields
London EC2Y 9AL
020 7877 7058
www.redcross.org.uk/museumandarchives
enquiry@redcross.org.uk

The British Red Cross Museum and Archives are based at the society's UK Office in London. The collection contains a fascinating portrait of the humanitarian work of the British Red Cross, from its beginnings in 1870 to its vital contribution in today's society.

Collections: Includes material from the society's national headquarters, regions, branches and centres and items from people who served with, or received assistance from, the British Red Cross since its foundation in 1870. Highlights include the Changi Quilt and Loyd-Lindsay's flag.

Catholic Family History Society

9 Snows Green Road, Shotley Bridge
Consett DH8 0HD
www.catholic-history.org.uk/cfhs
margaretbowery@aol.com

Membership of the society entitles you to attend any of the meetings organised by the Catholic FHS (though a small entrance fee is usually charged), receive copies of 'Catholic Ancestor', have your research interests listed and generally join in the activities of the society.

Chapels Heritage Society - CAPEL

5 Cuffnell Close, Liddell Park
Llandudno LL30 1UX
www.capeli.org.uk
obadiah1@btinternet.com

Capel encourages the study and preservation of the Nonconformist heritage of Wales, and offers information and advice on ways to maintain and preserve their buildings. It records and studies chapel architecture and encourages chapels to safeguard their records.

Costume Society, The

www.costumesociety.org.uk
info@costumesociety.org.uk

Formed 40 years ago it pioneered the exploration of all aspects of clothing and personal appearance within a like-minded membership which now includes collectors, curators, designers, lecturers, students and informed enthusiasts.

Council for British Archaeology

St Mary's House, 66 Bootham
York YO30 7BZ
01904 671417
www.britarch.ac.uk
info@britarch.ac.uk

The CBA is an educational charity working across the UK. We have been campaigning for the better care of Britain's archaeology for more than 60 years.

Culture24

Office 4, 28 Kensington Street
Brighton BN1 4AJ
01273 623266
www.culture24.org.uk
info@culture24.org.uk

News, listings and features from 4,000+ museums, galleries, libraries, archives and heritage sites.

Families in British India Society (FIBIS)

4 Lichfield House, Bishops Walk
Aylesbury HP21 7LE
www.fibis.org

FIBIS is a self-help organisation devoted to members researching their ancestors and the background against which they led their lives in British India.

First World War Walks in Britain

🏛 ⭐

www.worldwaronewalks.com

Britain's famed Blue Badge tourist guides are bringing the home front alive with guided walks, all over the country. There is no better way to appreciate the issues behind the Great War, and learn how they impacted directly on your local area.

Folklore Society

🏛 ⭐

Warburg Institute, Woburn Square

London WC1H 0AB

020 7862 8564

www.folklore-society.com

thefolkloresociety@gmail.com

The Folklore Society (FLS) is a learned society, based in London, devoted to the study of all aspects of folklore and tradition, including: ballads, folktales, fairy tales, myths, legends, traditional song and dance, folk plays, games, seasonal events, calendar customs, childlore and children's folklore, folk arts and crafts, popular belief, folk religion, material culture, vernacular language, sayings, proverbs and nursery rhymes, folk medicine, plantlore and weather lore.

Heraldry Society

🏛

PO Box 772

Guildford GU3 3ZX

01483 237 373

www.theheraldrysociety.com

honsec_heraldry@excite.co.uk

The Heraldry Society exists to increase and extend interest in and knowledge of heraldry, armory, chivalry, genealogy and allied subjects. The society is nonprofit making and is registered as an educational charity.

Heritage Alliance, The

🏛

Camelford House, 89 Albert Embankment

London SE1 7TP

020 7233 0500

www.theheritagealliance.org.uk

toks.ferguson@theheritagealliance.org.uk

The Heritage Alliance, established in 2002 as Heritage Link, is the biggest alliance of heritage interests in the UK and was set up to promote the central role of the non-Government movement in the heritage sector. The Heritage Alliance has 90 members; national and major regional organisations including The National Trust, the Council for British Archaeology, the Campaign to Protect Rural England (CPRE) and The society for the Protection of Ancient Buildings (SPAB) as well as many smaller and more specialised heritage groups.

Heritage Lottery Fund

🏛 ⭐

7 Holbein Place

London SW1W 8NR

020 7591 6000

www.hlf.org.uk

enquire@hlf.org.uk

The Heritage Lottery Fund supports projects that make a lasting difference for heritage, people and communities in the UK. Heritage includes many different things from teh past that we value and want to pass on to future generations, for example people's memories and experiences, historic buildings, cultural traditions, collections of objects, books or docuements, and natural heritage.

Heritage Railway Association

🏛

New Romney TN28 8PL

www.heritagerailways.com

david.woodhouse@hra.gb.com

The Heritage Railway Association represents the majority of heritage and tourist railways and railway preservation groups within both the U.K, and Ireland. There are also several overseas members.

Historic Houses Association

🏛

2 Chester Street

London SW1X 7BB

020 7259 5688

www.hha.org.uk

info@hha.org.uk

The Historic Houses Association represents 1,500 historic houses, castles and gardens throughout the UK, of which a third are open to the public and many offer educational opportunities for people of all ages. Visit our website: www.hha.org.uk and click on Properties to Visit.

Historic Newspapers

🏛 ⭐

23 Vaughan Road

Harpenden AL5 4EL

01582 464829

http://goo.gl/ziDzk4

thomas.walker@historic-newspapers.co.uk

Archive of original newspapers with free educational resources - including our latest: WW1 100th Anniversary Newspaper Book..

Historical Association, The

59a Kennington Park Road
London SE11 4JH
020 7735 3901
www.history.org.uk
enquiry@history.org.uk

The Historical Association produces a wide range of resources both online and within its 3 quarterly journals for Primary and Secondary history teachers and for the general history enthusiast..

Historypin

71 St John Street
London EC1M 4NJ
www.historypin.com

Historypin is a way for millions of people to come together, from across different generations, cultures and places, to share small glimpses of the past and to build up the huge story of human history. We host a website and mobile apps, partnering with hundreds of libraries, archives and museums worldwide. Historypin was created and supported by We Are What We Do, not-for-profit behaviour change company that creates ways for millions of people to do more small, good things.

Huguenot Society of Great Britain & Ireland, The

The Huguenot Library, UCL, Gower Street
London WC1E 6BT
020 7679 5199
www.huguenotsociety.org.uk
library@huguenotsociety.org.uk

In 1885 the society was founded by directors of the The French Hospital (founded in 1718) to promote the publication and interchange of knowledge about the Huguenots in Great Britain and Ireland, a good deal of which, over the passage of time was unknown to many of their descendants. They also aimed to form a bond of fellowship of those who, whether or not of Huguenot descent, respect and admire the Huguenots and seek to perpetuate their memory.

Collections: The Library (incorporating the Library of the French Hospital) forms the most complete body of Huguenot literature in this country. It contains the archives of the French Hospital since its creation in 1718, which are vital to the Hospital's continuing work today.

Jewish Genealogical Society of Great Britain

33 Seymour Place
London W1H 5AU
020 7724 4232
www.jgsgb.org.uk
chairman@jgsgb.org.uk

The Jewish Genealogical Society of Great Britain - JGSGB - was founded in 1992 for beginners and experienced researchers: * To help one another to learn and discover more about genealogy * To encourage genealogical research * To promote the preservation of Jewish genealogical records and resources * To share information amongst members The society is open to all interested in Jewish genealogy and is constituted on a secular basis.

Mass Observation Archive, The

The Keep, Woollards Way
Brighton & Hove BN1 9BP
01273 6337515
www.massobs.org.uk
library.specialcoll@sussex.ac.uk

This Archive specialises in material about everyday life in Britain. It contains papers generated by the original Mass Observation social research organisation (1937 to early 1950s), and newer material collected continuously since 1981.

Collections: This archive provides a written record of everyday life in the 20th and 21st centuries. This collection is a unique social document of the lives of ordinary people in the UK in the 20th and 21st centuries.

Mausolea & Monuments Trust

70 Cowcross Street
London EC1M 8EJ
020 7608 1441
www.mausolea-monuments.org.uk
mausolea@btconnect.com

The Mausolea and Monuments Trust is a charitable trust founded in 1997 for the protection and preservation of mausolea and funerary monuments situated in the United Kingdom of Great Britain and Northern Ireland. Mausolea need protection because, exposed to the ravages of plants and vandals, they are all too often abandoned and friendless.

National Archives, The

Kew TW9 4DU
020 8876 3444
www.nationalarchives.gov.uk
enquiry@nationalarchives.gov.uk

The National Archives is the UK government's official archive, guaranteeing public access to over 1000 years of history with records ranging from parchment and paper scrolls through to digital files and archived websites. We are also at the heart of government information policy, to ensure the survival of today's information for the future.

Collections: Archives of the British government covering over a thousand years of world history and all seven continents from Arctic explorers and Middle Eastern embassies to papal bulls and the photographic collections of Colonial administrations.

Ordnance Society

ordnancesociety.org.uk
ordnance.society@virgin.net

The Ordnance Society was formed in June 1986 to promote, encourage and co-ordinate the study of all aspects of the history of ordnance and artillery. It is today, an international society with members from more than 20 countries and all walks of life.

Parks & Gardens UK

Parks and Gardens Data Services, The Carley Partnership, St James's House, 8 Overcliffe
Gravesend DA11 0HJ
www.parksandgardens.org
info@parksandgardens.org

Parks & Gardens UK is a leading online resource dedicated to historic parks and gardens across the whole of the United Kingdom. The information on the website is available free of charge.

Quaker Family History Society

3 Sheridan Place
Hampton TW12 2SB
www.qfhs.co.uk
info@qfhs.co.uk

The Quaker Family History Society was formed in 1993 and is a member of the Federation of Family History Societies. Our aim is to encourage and assist anyone interested in tracing the history of Quaker families in the British Isles.

Register of One-Place Studies

82 Edwina Drive -
Poole BH17 7JG
www.register-of-one-place-studies.org.uk

Organisation promoting one-place studies.

Religious Archives Group

c/o Tim Powell, The National Archives, Kew
Richmond TW9 4DU
www.religiousarchivesgroup.org.uk
tim.powell@nationalarchives.gsi.gov.uk

The Religious Archives Group is a voluntary association for anybody interested in the collection, preservation and use of religious archives, and personal papers of religious leaders, in the UK. This includes archives created and used by private organisations and individuals and those in public repositories.

Romany & Traveller Family History Society

7 Park Rise, Nonchurch
Berkhamstead HP4 3RT
www.rtfhs.org.uk

We're a friendly crowd who like nothing better than bringing together other like-minded people and helping them to research their family trees, find out about their heritage and share know-how and information.

Romany & Traveller Family History Society

c/o Flat 53, 41 Provost Street
London N1 7NB
www.rtfhs.org.uk
enquiries@rtfhs.org.uk

A non-political non-profit making self help group. Member of the Federation of Family History Societies.

Royal Institute of British Architects

66 Portland Place
London W1B 1AD
020 7580 5533
www.architecture.com/
library.education@riba.org

The Royal Institute of British Architects champions better buildings, communities and the environment through architecture and our members.

Royal Society, The

6-9 Carlton House Terrace
London SW1Y 5AG
020 7451 2500
www.royalsociety.org

The Royal Society is the independent scientific academy of the UK and the Commonwealth dedicated to promoting excellence in science. The society plays an influential role in national and international science policy and supports developments in science, engineering and technology in a wide range of ways. The society is also the world's oldest scientific academy in continuous existence and has been at the forefront of scientific enquiry and discovery since its foundation in 1660.

Science & Society Picture Library

The Science Museum, Exhibition Road
London SW7 2DD
0207 942 4400
www.nmsi.ac.uk/piclib
piclib@nmsi.ac.uk

We provide transparencies, prints and digital images on loan to our clients for reproduction. A small service fee is charged for the loan of the images.

Collections: BTF Collection: Over 10,000 photographs taken by the British Transport Films Unit which document life and work in Britain from the mid - 1940s to the 1960s. Daily Herald Collection: Photographs documenting every aspect of life as reflected in the work of some of Britain's finest news photographers.

Society for Name Studies in Britain & Ireland

22 Peel Park Avenue
Clitheroe BB7 1ET
01200 423771
www.snsbi.org.uk

A society devoted to the study of names (place-names, personal names, and other names) from linguistic, historical, and sociological perspectives.

Society for One-Place Studies

c/o Devon Heritage Centre, Great Moor House, Bittern Road, Sowton
Exeter EX2 7NL
one-place-studies.org
info@one-place-studies.org

There are many individuals, societies and groups across the globe researching the people of a community within the context of the place they live. The vision of this Society is to bring together those like-minded people and provide a platform for members to share good practice, ideas and methodology in one place, as well as promote the research being undertaken on their study area. Read more at http://one-place-studies.org/#JGxi6k3tkiv1xw5U.99.

Society of Brushmakers Descendants Family History Society

13 Ashworth Place
Church Langley CM17 9PU
01279 629392
www.brushmakers.com
s.b.d.@lineone.net

Do you have brushmaking ancestors, or are you just interested in discovering more about the brushmaker's trade? The SBD is a historical society/family history society that specialises in the brush/broom making trades and those who have worked therein for the past few hundred years.

Strict Baptist Historical Society, The

www.strictbaptisthistory.org.uk
thesecretary@sbhs.org.uk

The Strict Baptist Historical Society was formed in 1960 to promote an interest in the history of Strict Baptists; and also to bring into being a central repository where books, documents and other things of historical interest connected directly or indirectly with the rise and growth of Strict Baptists may be preserved for the benefit of present and future generations.

Victorian Military Society

PO Box 5837
Newbury RG14 7FJ
01635 48628
www.victorianmilitarysociety.org.uk
vmsdan@msn.com

The Victorian Military Society (VMS) was founded in 1974, by the late John Crouch RIBA, to foster interest in the military aspects of the Victorian period. This was later extended to include the campaigns of the early part of the 20th century.

Waterways Archive

7th Floor, Llanthony Warehouse, The Docks
Gloucester GL1 2EH
01452 318224
precedent.com/museums/archives.shtml
bwarchive@thewaterwaystrust.org.uk

The Waterways Archive collects, preserves and makes publicly available rich and diverse records in many forms, including plans, drawings, accounts, photographs and audio-visual recordings. At its core are the archives of British Waterways and the early canal companies, which trace the history of Britain's inland waterways back to its very roots. It is an archival resource covering the history of canals from the 17th century to the near present day.

Collections: The collection covers the records of British Waterways and its predecessors the pre-nationalisation navigation companies.

Young Archaeologists' Club

St Mary's House, 66 Bootham
York YO30 7BZ
01904 671417
www.britarch.ac.uk/yac
yac@britarch.ac.uk

The first element of the Young Archaeologists' Club is our UK-wide club. This is based around subscription to our magazine, Young Archaeologist, which is packed with news, features, competitions, letters and pictures from members, and hands-on activities to try at home.

ENGLAND

National

Anglo-Sikh Heritage Trail

2 Victoria Mews
Walsall WS4 2DZ
0845 600 1893
www.asht.info
info@asht.info

The Anglo Sikh Heritage Trail is a groundbreaking initiative that aims to promote a greater understanding of the shared heritage between the Sikhs and Britain.

Archives & Records Association

Prioryfield House, 20 Canon Street
Taunton TA1 1SW
01823 327 077
www.archives.org.uk
ara@archives.org.uk

On 1 June 2010 the Archives and Records Association (ARA) was officially formed as a result of a merger of the National Council on Archives; the Association of Chief Archivists in Local Government (ACALG) and the society of Archivists (SoA). With the creation of ARA, the National Council on Archives ceased to operate as an independent group. Ongoing NCA activities are now continued by the new organisation, further information about which can be found at www.archives.org.uk The website of the National Council on Archives continues to serve as a resource for professional literature.

Children's Society Records & Archive Centre, The

Records and Archives Centre, The Children's Society, Edward Rudolf House, Margery Street
London WC1X 0JL
020 7232 2966
www.hiddenlives.org.uk
archives@childrenssociety.org.uk

The Children's Society was founded in 1881 by Edward Rudolf, who wanted to help the vulnerable children he saw around him in Victorian Britain. In its early history, The Children's Society (then known as The Waifs and Strays Society) did this by running a network of children's homes for poor and disadvantaged children. The Hidden Lives Revealed website has information on children's homes up to the 1980s, and focuses on the period 1881-1918. It includes unique archive material about poor and disadvantaged children cared for by The Waifs and Strays' Society.

Church of England Church Buildings Council

Church House, Westminster
London SW1P 3AZ
www.churchcare.co.uk

Providing support, advice and guidance to The Church of England's 16,000 churches and 43 cathedrals.

Churches Conservation Trust

Society Building, 8 All Saints Street
London N1 9RL
0800 206 1463
www.visitchurches.org.uk
central@tcct.org.uk

The Churches Conservation Trust is the leading body conserving England's most beautiful and historic churches which are no longer needed for regular worship. It promotes public enjoyment of these churches, and encourages their use as an educational and community resource.

Durand Group

26 Park Place
Arundel BN18 9BE
07768 061625
www.durandgroup.org.uk
Mark.khan@durandgroup.org.uk

An association of individuals who have voluntarily undertaken to work together to further research and investigation of military-related subterranean features.

Ecclesiological Society

38 Rosebery Avenue
New Malden KT3 4JS
www.ecclsoc.org
info@ecclsoc.org

The society is for those who love churches. As well as our website which is packed with information and images, we organise tours, lectures, and conferences, and publish a journal twice a year.

England's Past for Everyone

Institute for Historical Research, University of London, Senate House, Malet Street
London WC1E 7HU
www.englandspastforeveryone.org.uk
info@epe.org.uk

England's Past for Everyone is a local history project run by the Victoria County History. Volunteers throughout the country are working alongside authors and researchers to produce a whole range of new resources.

English Folk Dance & Song Society, The

Cecil Sharp House, 2 Regent's Park Road
London NW1 7AY
020 7485 2206
www.efdss.org
info@efdss.org

The English Folk Dance and Song Society (EFDSS) is one of the leading folk development organisations in the UK with a history dating back to 1898. It is custodian of the Vaughan Williams Memorial Library, an internationally renowned library and archive of the folk arts. Through its work, the EFDSS aims to place the indigenous folk arts of England at the heart of our cultural life.

English Heritage Central Office

1 Waterhouse Square, 138 - 142 Holborn
London EC1N 2ST
020 7973 3000
www.english-heritage.org.uk
customers@english-heritage.org.uk

English Heritage cares for over 400 historic buildings, monuments and sites - from world-famous prehistoric sites to grand medieval castles, from Roman forts on the edges of the empire to a Cold War bunker. Through these, we bring the story of England to life for over 10 million people each year.

English Heritage National Monuments Record

Swindon SN2 2EH
01793 414 600
www.english-heritage.org.uk/NMR
nmrinfo@english-heritage.org.uk

The National Monuments Record, the public archive of English Heritage, holds over 12 million photographs, plans, drawings, reports, records and documents linked to England's archaeology, architecture, social and local history. Over 2 million photographs and records are now available online for free.

Eureka. The National Children's Museum

Discovery Road
Halifax HX1 2NE
01422 330069
www.eureka.org.uk
info@eureka.org.uk

Eureka. The National Children's Museum is a magical place where children play to learn and grown-ups learn to play. Everything at Eureka. has been designed to inspire children to find out about themselves and the world around them.

Family & Community Historical Research Society

Pilcot House, Pilcot
Dogmersfield RG27 8SY
01252 617884
www.fachrs.com
HonSec@fachrs.org.uk

The society embraces research topics such as Victorian social history, migration, Victorian social classes & history, local history projects, research projects for pre - Victorian England, plus many more aspects of UK 18th, 19th & 20th century family & community history research. Our new topic is The Home Front, 1914 - 1915.

Federation of Family History Societies

PO Box 8857
Lutterworth LE17 9BJ
01455 203 133
www.ffhs.org.uk
info@ffhs.org.uk

The Federation of Family History Societies (FFHS) is an educational charity. We support, inform and advise our membership, which consists of family history societies and similar bodies across the world.

General Register Office (GRO)

PO Box 2
Southport PR8 2JD
0300 123 1837
www.gro.gov.uk
certificate.services@gro.gsi.gov.uk

The General Register Office is part of Her Majesty's Passport Office and oversees civil registration in England and Wales. We maintain the national archive of all births, marriages and deaths dating back to 1837.

Great War Society, The

c/o Secretary GWS, 15 Wyatt Court, Drews Park
Devizes SN10 5FF
07747 634118
www.thegreatwarsociety.com
helencognitio@aol.com

The Great War Society is a non-profit living history organisation based in the UK. The society's volunteer members seek to commemorate and honour the sacrifices of the men and women of the Great War period.

Heritage Explorer

Heritage Explorer Project Team, The Engine House, Firefly Avenue
Swindon SN2 2EH
www.heritage-explorer.co.uk
heritage.explorer@english-heritage.org.uk.

Teachers can pick and mix from our database of over 10,000 images and find curriculum related resources, for all key stages, to use or adapt for their pupils. Create your own worksheet or presentation. Go to any image - click on the thumbnail to get the medium sized image - select the 'Create' button above it to automatically drop the image into a ready-made template.

Historic England

1 Waterhouse Square, 138 - 142 Holborn
London EC1N 2ST
020 7973 3700
www.historicengland.org.uk
customers@HistoricEngland.org.uk

We're the public body that champions and protects England's historic places. We look after the historic environment, providing expert advice, helping people protect and care for it and helping the public to understand and enjoy it. The Historic England Archive is located within our Swindon office. We hold over 12 million photographs, drawings, reports and publications from the 1850s to the present day, covering the whole country. You can use our collections to: find out about your home's history; learn about your local area; research individual buildings and archaeological sites; discover England's changing urban and rural landscape.

Hungry for History

114 Ramsgate Road
Broadstairs
www.hungryforhistory.info
info@hungryforhistory.info

Hungry for History is a collaborative venture for all schools nationwide. It aims to instil a love of history in children of all ages and to encourage renewed passion and enthusiasm in the teaching and learning of the subject that is the greatest teacher of us all.

Institute of Historic Building Conservation, The

Jubilee House High Street
Tisbury SP3 6HA
01747 873133
www.ihbc.org.uk
admin@ihbc.org.uk

Charity supporting specialists working in built and historic environment conservation with substantial web resources freely available to public.

Institute of Historical Research

University of London, Senate House, Malet Street
London WC1E 7HU
020 7862 8740
www.history.ac.uk
ihr.reception@sas.ac.uk

The Institute of Historical Research is one of ten member Institutes of the School of Advanced Study, part of the University of London. Its mission is to promote the study of history and an appreciation of the importance of the past among academics and the general public, in the UK and internationally, and to provide institutional support and individual leadership for this broad historical community.

Institution of Civil Engineers

1 Great George Street
London SW1P 3AA
020 7665 2251
www.ice.org.uk/Information-resources/Library
library@ice.org.uk

The Institution of Civil Engineers (ICE) is a registered charity that strives to promote and progress civil engineering. We believe that civil engineers are 'at the heart of society, delivering sustainable development through knowledge, skills and professional expertise.' With this in mind, we are a qualifying body, a centre for the exchange of specialist knowledge, and a provider of resources to encourage innovation and excellence in the profession. The ICE was founded in 1818 and granted a royal charter in 1828.

Collections: The library, archive, and works of art are Designated Collections of national importance. The Institution of Civil Engineers.

Institution of Engineering & Technology

2 Savoy Place
London WC2R 0BL
020 7344 8436/8407
www.theiet.org
archives@theiet.org

The Institution of Engineering and Technology is one of the world's leading professional societies for the engineering and technology community. Founded in 1871 as the society of Telegraph Engineers, the IET now has more than 150,000 members in 127 countries and offices in Europe, North America and Asia-Pacific.

Collections: The entire collection of this Institution is a Designated Collection of international importance. The IET Library is a world-class collection of digital and printed resources on all areas of engineering and technology. We specialise in electrical, electronic, control and manufacturing engineering, telecommunications, computing and IT.

Institution of Mechanical Engineers

Birdcage Walk, Whitehall
London SW1H 9JJ
www.imeche.org/knowledge/library/archive
archive@imeche.org

Charitable professional membership organisation run by and for Mechanical Engineers. Archives include collections on mechanical engineering, as well as records of the Institution.

JTrails - National Anglo-Jewish Heritage Trail

c/o Oxford Centre for Hebrew and Jewish Studies, Yarnton Manor
Yarnton, Kidlington OX5 1PY
01865 377946
www.jtrails.org.uk
najht@ochjs.ac.uk

The history of the Jewish community in England stretches back well over 1,000 years. JTrails, is working to raise awareness of this rich, but often unknown, history and heritage among both Jews and non-Jews alike, and to encourage individuals to understand their own roots as well as the fascinating origins of the community and its contribution to the history of England.

Locomotion: The National Railway Museum at Shildon

Shildon DL4 1PQ
01388 777999
www.nrm.org.uk/locomotion
locomotion@nrm.org.uk

We're home to over 300 years of history and over a million wonderful objects. Visit us and you can marvel at iconic locomotives, watch engineering work in progress in the Workshop and browse our object-filled Warehouse.

Museum of English Rural Life

Museum of English Rural Life (MERL), University of Reading,
Redlands Road
Reading RG1 5EX
0118 378 8660
www.reading.ac.uk/merl
merlevents@reading.ac.uk

The museum was founded in 1951 by the University of Reading. It was the first specialist museum of farming and rural life to be established in England and so was able to acquire large collections of high quality material at a time when mechanisation was bringing great changes to the countryside.

Museum on the Move

01905 3261821
www.museumonthemove.org.uk
spope@worcestershire.gov.uk

The Museum on the Move buses contain changing exhibitions and acitivities to engage all age groups. They are ideal for schools, community groups and residential homes. They operate across Herefordshire, Staffordshire, Warwickshire and Worcestershire.

National Army Museum

Royal Hospital Road
London SW3 4HT
020 7730 0717 x2535
www.nam.ac.uk
pr@nam.ac.uk

Discover the impact the British Army has had on the story of Britain, Europe and the world, and see how the actions of a few can affect the futures of many. The National Army Museum tells the story of the British, Indian Army up to 1947 and the Commonwealth armies.

National Arts Education Archive Trust

Lawrence Batley Centre, Bretton Hall, West Bretton
Wakefield WF4 4LG
01924 832020
www.artsedarchive.org.uk
s.kielty@leeds.ac.uk

The National Arts Education Archive was established in 1985 at Bretton Hall College to provide a documentary trace of the development of Arts Education, in the UK and worldwide. It is based in the Lawrence Batley Centre, and now holds some 100 collections of children's and students' work in the Arts.

National Badminton Museum

National Badminton Centre, Bradwell Road, Loughton Lodge
Milton Keynes MK8 9LA
01908 268400
www.badmintonengland.co.uk/homepage.asp
museum@baofe.co.uk

Examples of early racquets, battledores and shuttlecocks are displayed in wall cabinets which can be easily accessed by those visiting the facilities in Milton Keynes. In addition, two free standing cabinets display other items such as old rule books, magazines etc.

National Brewery Centre, The

Horninglow St Horninglow
Burton on Trent DE14 1NG
01283 532 880
www.nationalbrewerycentre.co.uk
info@nationalbrewerycentre.co.uk

The museum celebrates the social history of the development of brewing - the real life experiences and stories of the people who helped to build Burton's world-renowned brewing reputation. Experienced guides take visitors through each step of the brewing process and explain the fascinating roles that the steam engines and vintage vehicles on show played in the development of the industry.

National Co-operative Archive

Co-operative College, Holyoake House, Hanover Street
Manchester M60 0AS
0161 246 2925/2937/2945
www.archive.coop
archive@co-op.ac.uk

Located in central Manchester, the National Co-operative Archive is home to a wide array of records relating to the history of the worldwide co-operative movement. The collections (rare books, periodicals, manuscripts, films, photographs and oral histories) are an unrivalled resource for the development of the co-operative movement from the initial ideas of the 18th century to today.

National Coal Mining Museum for England

Caphouse Colliery, New Road, Overton
Wakefield WF4 4RH
01924 848806
www.ncm.org.uk
info@ncm.org.uk

The National Coal Mining Museum for England is a great day out and offers visitors the unique opportunity to travel 140 metres underground, down one of Britain's oldest working mines, where models and machinery depict methods and conditions of mining from the early 1800s to the present. Experienced local miners guide parties around the underground workings, delivering one of the most engaging and memorable days out.

National Conservation Centre

Whitechapel
Liverpool L1 6HZ
0151 478 4999
www.liverpoolmuseums.org.uk/conservation
conservation@liverpoolmuseums.org.uk

National Museums Liverpool's award-winning Conservation Centre is the first national conservation centre in the UK, and the only one of its kind open to the public.

Collections: The exhibition shows how conservators uncover the secrets within objects and how they keep the ravages of time at bay. Discover how our world class conservators preserve and restore everything from fine art and sculpture to space suits and ancient archaeological treasures, meet a conservator at work via a live video link, take part in a hands-on activity or a behind-the-scenes tour, get an expert's opinion on looking after your heirlooms.

National Emergency Services Museum

West Bar
Sheffield S3 8PT
0114 2491 999
www.emergencymuseum.org.uk
info@emergencymuseum.org.uk

The museum houses over 40 emergency service related vehicles spread across 3 floors of the Victorian combined Police, Fire and Ambulance Station on West Bar in the heart of Steel City Sheffield. Take the time to explore our police cells, jump into police vehicles and get kitted up in the uniform used.

National Fairground Archive at University of Sheffield

Western Bank Library, University of Sheffield, Western Bank
Sheffield S10 2TN
0114 222 7231
www.shef.ac.uk/nfa
nfa@sheffield.ac.uk

The National Fairground Archive (NFA) was inaugurated by the Vice Chancellor of the University of Sheffield in 1994, with the support of the Showmen's Guild of Great Britain and the Fairground Association of Great Britain. Housed in the Main Library, it is a unique collection of photographic, printed, manuscript and audiovisual material covering all aspects of the culture of travelling showpeople, their organisation as a community, their social history and everyday life; and the artefacts and machinery of fairgrounds.

Collections: The NFA collections are continuing to grow: there are now over 80,000 images in the photographic collection, in addition to audio and video material, journals and magazines, and nearly 3,000 monographs. The collection also includes a unique body of fairground ephemera (programmes, handbills, posters, charters and proclamations, plans and drawings).

National Football Museum

Cathedral Gardens
Manchester M4 3BG
0161 605 8200
www.nationalfootballmuseum.com
info@nationalfootballmuseum.com

The National Football Museum in Manchester is the world's biggest and best football museum. An essential part of any visit to the city, the national celebration of the national game offers free entry, and is open 7 days a week.

National Gallery

Trafalgar Square
London WC2N 5DN
020 7747 2885
www.nationalgallery.org.uk
information@ng-london.org.uk

One of the greatest collections of European painting in the world. These pictures belong to the public and admission to see them is free.

National Gas Museum

195 Aylestone Road
Leicester LE2 7QJ
0116 250 3190
www.nationalgasmuseum.org.uk
nationalgasmuseum@gmail.com

The Gas Museum tells the story of gas at home and work. For light, for heat, for cooking - for 200 years gas has been essential energy.

National Glass Centre

Liberty Way
Sunderland SR6 0GL
0191 515 5555 Option 9
www.nationalglasscentre.com
info@nationalglasscentre.com

National Glass Centre at the University of Sunderland is a cultural attraction and venue with a difference. With glass at the heart of everything they do, they celebrate Sunderland's glass making heritage and explore the creative potential of this extraordinary material. Discover the origins, growth and legacy of glass making in Sunderland with their permanent exhibition, Stories of Glass in Sunderland.

National Horseracing Museum

99 High Street
Newmarket CB8 8JL
01638 667333
www.nhrm.co.uk

The story of the people and horses involved in racing from its Royal origins to Lester Piggott, Frankie Dettori and other modern heroes. Highlights include: the head of Persimmon, a great Royal Derby winner in 1896; a special display about Fred Archer, the late Victorian jockey who committed suicide, which features the pistol he used to take his life; and the colourful jackets of 'Prince Monolulu', the 1950s tipster.

National Library for the Blind

National Library for the Blind, Far Cromwell Road
Stockport SK6 2SG
0161 355 2094
www.nlb-online.org
angela.ginger@nlbuk.org

Library of material in alternative formats for blind or partially sighted people. Operates a free loan service to members throughout the UK. Largest collection of books in Braille and Moon in Europe.

National Maritime Museum Cornwall

Discovery Quay
Falmouth TR11 3QY
01326 313388
www.nmmc.co.uk
enquiries@nmmc.co.uk

The multi-award winning National Maritime Museum Cornwall has 15 galleries, over five floors beautifully illustrating the past, present and future of this island nation. The museum features a number of stunning exhibitions dedicated to the sea, boats and Cornwall.

Collections: National Small Boat collection of about 140 boats and other objects and collectables.

National Media Museum

Princes Way
Bradford BD1 1NQ
0844 856 3797
www.nationalmediamuseum.org.uk
talk@nationalmediamuseum.org.uk

The museum's renowned collection includes more than three million items of historical, social and cultural value. These include three key 'firsts': the world's first negative, the earliest television footage and what is regarded as the world's first example of moving pictures.

National Meteorological Library & Archive

Met Office, FitzRoy Road
Exeter EX1 3PB
01392 884841
www.metoffice.gov.uk/learning/library
metlib@metoffice.gov.uk

The National Meteorological Library and Archive has become one of the most comprehensive collections of material on meteorology anywhere in the world. As the national collection on all aspects of the weather and climate and the approved Place of Deposit for UK meteorological records, we are the custodians of the 'public memory of the weather' and a major resource for scientific and historical research.

Collections: The library collection contains books, journals, conference proceedings, reports and data, covering meteorology, climatology and related sciences. It includes all the key published writing on these subjects over the last 200 years from the UK, and a selection of writing and data from around the world.

National Motor Museum, The

Beaulieu
Brockenhurst SO42 7ZN
01590 614650
www.nationalmotormuseum.org.uk
info@beaulieu.co.uk

The world renowned National Motor Museum at Beaulieu has over 250 vehicles from every motoring era. Exhibits include some of the earliest examples of motoring to legendary World Record Breakers like Bluebird, 'TV Star' cars like Del Boy's Reliant Regal and rare oddities like the giant orange on wheels.

National Motorcycle Museum

Coventry Road, Bickenhill
Solihull B92 0EJ
01675 443311
www.nationalmotorcyclemuseum.co.uk

The National Motorcycle Museum opened its doors in October 1984, with a collection of more than 350 motorcycles on display. The award winning conference and banqueting facilities grew out of interest in the museum and followed on in 1985.

National Museum of Computing, The

Block H, Bletchley Park
Bletchley MK3 6EB
01908 374708
www.tnmoc.org
info@tnmoc.org

The National Museum of Computing, located at Bletchley Park, is an independent charity housing the largest collection of functional historic computers in Europe, including a rebuilt Colossus, the world's first electronic computer and the WITCH, the world's oldest working digital computer. The museum enables visitors to follow the development of computing from the ultra-secret pioneering efforts of the 1940s through the large systems and mainframes of the 1950s, 60s and 70s, and the rise of personal computing in the 1980s and beyond.

National Museum of the Royal Navy at Portsmouth Historic Dockyard

HM Naval Base
Portsmouth PO1 3NH
02392 839766
www.historicdockyard.co.uk
enquiries@historicdockyard.co.uk

The National Museum of the Royal Navy, in Portsmouth's Historic Dockyard, is one of Britain's oldest maritime museums. The museum's mission is to preserve and present the history of the 'Fleet' - the ships and the men and women who manned them.

National Piers Society

c/o Honorary Secretary, 4 Tyrrell Road
Benfleet SS7 5DH
01268 757291 or 01472 350404
www.piers.co.uk
timmickleburgh2002@yahoo.co.uk

The National Piers Society exists to promote and sustain interest in the preservation and continued enjoyment of Seaside Piers. The seaside piers around the coast of Britain stand as a powerful reminder of the achievements of Victorian engineers and entrepreneurs.

National Printing Heritage Trust, The

National Printing Heritage Trust, c/o Department of Typography & Graphic Communication, The University of Reading, 2 Earley Gate, Whiteknights, PO Box 239 Reading RG6 6AU
www.npht.org.uk
secretary@npht.org.uk

Over the last five hundred years the printing trade has shown itself to be crucial to the development of society. Despite the recent digital revolution in communication, it continues to play a vital role in our lives by providing information, encouraging debate and stimulating the mind and imagination.

National Railway Museum

Leeman Road
York YO26 4XJ
08448 153 139
www.nrm.org.uk
nrm@nrm.org.uk

For a fantastic free day out in York visit the award winning National Railway Museum. Explore our three giant halls full of trains and railway legends including the majestic Duchess of Hamilton, the iconic Japanese Bullet Train a stunning collection of Royal Trains and the towering Chinese locomotive. With daily demonstrations, loads of interactive exhibits, a special event programme and FREE museum admission, there is something for everyone to enjoy.

National Space Centre

Exploration Drive
Leicester LE4 5NS
0845 605 2001
www.spacecentre.co.uk
info@spacecentre.co.uk

The award winning National Space Centre is the UK's largest attraction dedicated to space. From the minute you catch sight of the Space Centre's futuristic Rocket Tower, you'll be treated to hours of breathtaking discovery and interactive fun. Think you'll never see the whole universe close-up? Then take a seat in our high-tech full domed Space Theatre and prepare to be amazed. The National Space Centre hosts many exciting weekend events - see our website for full details.

National Stone Centre

Porter Lane
Wirksworth DE4 4LS
01629 824833
www.nationalstonecentre.org.uk

Telling the Story of Stone - history, science, technology, art, environment - in the heart of the Derbyshire Dales on the edge of the Peak District. A dramatic site steeped in industrial history, ecology, displaying 330 million year old fossil tropical reefs.

National Theatre Archive

NT Studio, 83-101 The Cut
London SE1 8LL
020 7452 3135
www.nationaltheatre.org.uk/archive
archive@nationaltheatre.org.uk

Theatre is an ephemeral art; but the material collected in a theatre archive can help one to re-imagine a production and gain an insight into the working methods of the performers and the production team. The NT Archive is open to anyone with an interest in the National's history..

Collections: The National Theatre Archive has a broader collecting policy than most theatre archives: it is our constant effort to document the history of both the administrative and creative aspects of the institution. By reference to the various series of records held at the Archive one can trace the lifecycle of any NT production from conception to design to marketing to Stage Manager.

National Trust

Heelis, Kemble Drive
Swindon SN2 2NA
0344 800 1895
www.nationaltrust.org.uk
enquiries@nationaltrust.org.uk

With your help, we protect some of the most important spaces and places in England, Wales and Northern Ireland. We take care of historic houses, gardens, mills, coastline, forests, woods, fens, beaches, farmland, moorland, islands, archaeological remains, nature reserves, villages and pubs - and then we open them up for ever, for everyone.

National Waterways Museum

South Pier Road
Ellesmere Port CH65 4FW
0151 355 5017
www.nwm.org.uk
ellesmereport@thewaterwaystrust.org.uk

At the National Waterways museum at Ellesmere Port we bring Britain's canal history back to life. Come and explore the exhibitions in the historic dock complex and experience life aboard our collection of canal and river craft.

Collections: This collection includes objects painted by boatmen, costumes worn by boating families, waterways souvenirs, along with photographic and archive material.

Royal Photographic Society

Fenton House, 122 Wells Road
Bath BA2 3AH
01225 325733
www.rps.org
reception@rps.org

The Royal Photographic Society was founded in 1853 'to promote the Art and Science of Photography', a mission it continues to this day in the United Kingdom and through its considerable overseas membership. The Royal Photographic Society is responsible for staging three major touring photographic exhibitions.

Seven Stories, National Centre for Children

Seven Stories, 30 Lime Street, Ouseburn Valley
Newcastle & Gateshead NE1 2PQ
0845 271 0777
www.sevenstories.org.uk
info@sevenstories.org.uk

At the heart of Seven Stories is a treasure trove of original artwork and manuscripts which records the creative process involved in making a children's book and provides an insight into the working lives of authors and illustrators. Seven Stories is the only place in the UK which is actively collecting original artwork by British writers and illustrators for children.

Society for Court Studies, The

Canterbury
www.courtstudies.org
admin@courtstudies.org

The society for Court Studies was founded in London in September 1995 with the aim of stimulating and co-ordinating the study of royal and princely courts and households from antiquity to the present. It examines courts from a multi-disciplinary and international perspective, bringing together political, cultural, architectural, military, art, environmental and diplomatic history, and gender studies. The society organises regular seminars and conferences in London throughout the year.

Society for the Protection of Ancient Buildings

[icons]

37 Spital Square
London E1 6DY
020 7377 1644
www.spab.org.uk
info@spab.org.uk

The society for the Protection of Ancient Buildings was founded by William Morris in 1877 to counteract the highly destructive 'restoration' of medieval buildings being practised by many Victorian architects. Today it is the largest, oldest and most technically expert national pressure group fighting to save old buildings from decay, demolition and damage.

Society of Genealogists

[icons]

14 Charterhouse Buildings, Goswell Road
London EC1M 7BA
020 7553 3290
www.sog.org.uk
events@sog.org.uk

The society of Genealogists offers a unique combination of research material, guidance and support for those interested in family history. It is a charity whose objects are to promote, encourage and foster the study, science and knowledge of genealogy.

Sporting Heritage Community Interest Company

[icons]

49 Wesley Road
Leeds LS28 6EJ
nationalsportingheritageday.co.uk
sportingheritagelearninggroup@outlook.com

We aim to support the preservation and access to sporting heritage using a practical, pro-active approach. We manage the National Sporting Heritage Day.

20th Century Society

[icons]

70 Cowcross Street, Farringdon
London EC1M 6EJ
020 7250 3857
www.c20society.org.uk
website@c20society.org.uk

The Twentieth Century Society was founded as the Thirties Society in 1979, and exists to safeguard the heritage of architecture and design in Britain from 1914 onwards. The Society's prime objectives are conservation and education.

United Reformed Church History Society

[icons]

Westminster College, Madingley Road

Cambridge CB3 0AA
01223 741300
http://goo.gl/R6giyv
mt212@cam.ac.uk

The Journal of the society is published twice a year – subscription details from the Administrator. Back copies are usually available. The Library is particularly rich in Presbyterian history and theology, and includes an extensive collection of Civil War sermons and pamphlets.

Victorian Society

[icons]

1 Priory Gardens
London W4 1TT
020 8994 1019
www.victoriansociety.org.uk
admin@victoriansociety.org.uk

The Victorian Society is the champion for Victorian and Edwardian buildings in England and Wales. Our aims are: Conserving: to save Victorian and Edwardian buildings or groups of buildings of special architectural merit from needless destruction or disfigurement. Involving: to awaken public interest in, and appreciation of, the best of Victorian and Edwardian arts, architecture, crafts and design. Educating: to encourage the study of these and of related social history and to provide advice to owners and public authorities in regard to the preservation and repair of Victorian and Edwardian buildings.

Wartime Memories Project, The

[icons]

7 Dunlin Close
Stockton-on-Tees TS20 1SJ
www.wartimememoriesproject.com
remember@wartimememories.co.uk

The Wartime Memories Project is the original WW1 and WW2 commemoration website. Run as a community group by volunteers, our website has been running for almost 15 years and receives in excess of a million hits per month.

Western Front Association, The

[icons]

PO BOX 1918
Stockport SK4 4WN
0161 443 1918
www.westernfrontassociation.com
office@westernfrontassociation.com

The Western Front Association (WFA) was formed with the aim of furthering interest in The Great War of 1914-1918. We aim to perpetuate the memory, courage and comradeship of those who served their countries in France and Flanders and their own countries during The Great War. Through the work of the Association we do not seek to justify or glorify war.

Bedfordshire

*Bedfordshire, or Beds, a midland county of England,
bounded by the counties of Northampton, Cambridge,
Herts, and Bucks. Greatest length, N. and S., 30 miles;
greatest breadth, E. and W., 20 miles; area, 29,983
acres; population 149,473. The surface is mostly flat,
varied in the S. by a spur of the Chiltern Hills, and in
the NW. by a range of chalk hills. The chief river is the
Great Ouse, with its affluent the Ivel. The country
along the banks of the Ouse and other streams is
highly verdant and luxuriant. The greater part of the
surface is under tillage; indeed, agriculture, it is said,
is further advanced here than in any other English
county. On the heavy soils the principal crops are
wheat and beans. The sandy and chalky soils of the
middle districts are well adapted for horticultural
husbandry, and vegetables are extensively grown for
the markets of London, Cambridge, &c. There is
excellent grazing ground in the SE., this co. being
noted for its breeds of sheep and cattle. The principal
manufactures are agricultural implements and
straw-plait for hats. Bedfordshire contains 9 hundreds,
134 parishes and 2 parts, the parliamentary and
municipal borough of Bedford (1 member), and the
municipal boroughs of Dunstable and Luton. It is
almost entirely in the diocese of Ely.*

– John Bartholomew, *Gazetteer of the British Isles* (1887)

Ascott - National Trust

Ascott, Wing
Leighton Buzzard LU7 0PR
01296 688242
www.nationaltrust.org.uk/ascott
ascott@nationaltrust.org.uk

Jacobean House remodelled in the 19th century with superb
collections and gardens. Originally a half-timbered
farmhouse, Ascott was bought in 1876 by the de Rothschild
family and considerably transformed and enlarged by them.

Bedford Physical Education Archive

University of Bedfordshire
Bedford MK41 9EA
https://goo.gl/ZOrORL
bpea@beds.ac.uk

The Bedford Physical Education Archive is home to the archive
of the former Bedford College of Physical Training founded in
1903 (later the Bedford College of Physical Education and now
the University of Bedfordshire). It provides a unique insight
into the early development of women's physical education,
charting the importance of Bedford locally, nationally and
internationally in shaping physical education.

Bedfordshire & Luton Archives & Record Service

Beds & Luton Archives & Records Service, Riverside
Building, Borough Hall, Cauldwell Street
Bedford MK42 9AP
01234 228833
http://goo.gl/mrJl2b

We are the County Record Office for Bedfordshire, based in
Riverside Building, Borough Hall, Bedford, where visitors
are welcome to come in and use the archives for research.

Bedfordshire Family History Society

PO Box 214
Bedford MK42 9RX
www.bfhs.org.uk
bfhs@bfhs.org.uk

The society was formed in 1977 to encourage the study of
Family History, Genealogy and Heraldry, primarily within
the County of Bedfordshire.

Bromham Mill & Gallery

Bridge End
Bromham MK43 8LP
01234 824330
http://goo.gl/o7oe6w

The present mill is an 18th or early 19th century rebuilding in brick, timber and stone on the site of earlier mills. It had two waterwheels, one wooden and undershot driving three pairs of stones, and the other iron and breastshot driving two.

Higgins Bedford, The

Castle Lane
Bedford MK40 3XD
01234 718618
www.thehigginsbedford.org.uk
thehiggins@bedford.gov.uk

The Higgins Bedford reopened in June 2013 following a major redevelopment. The Higgins showcases wonderful and varied collections including the Cecil Higgins Collection of fine and decorative arts, with its world-class watercolour and print collections and unique groups of work by the designers William Burges and Edward Bawden.

John Bunyan Museum & Library

Bunyan Meeting, Mill Street
Bedford MK40 3EU
01234 270303
www.bunyanmeeting.co.uk/museum
curator@bunyanmeeting.co.uk

The John Bunyan Museum tells the story of John Bunyan (1628 -1688), the renowned author, pastor and preacher. Visitors to the museum are able to take a walk through Bunyan's life and times.

Leighton Buzzard Railway

Page's Park Station, Billington Road
Leighton Buzzard LU7 4TN
01525 373888
www.buzzrail.co.uk
station@lbngrs.org.uk

The Leighton Buzzard Railway is one of the few surviving narrow-gauge light railways in England. It was built in 1919, using materials and equipment that were surplus from the War Department Light Railways that had supplied the battlefields in World War 1. Originally built to serve the local sand quarrying industry, the railway has carried a passenger service, mostly hauled by historic steam engines, since 1968.

Luton Culture

Wardown Park Museum, Old Bedford Road
Luton LU2 7HA
01582 546719
www.lutonculture.com
museum.gallery@lutonculture.com

Luton Culture is an independent charity which looks after cultural provision in Luton, managing 12 venues and providing cultural services across Luton and surrounding

area. We were set up in March 2008 and we employ nearly 300 people working across 12 sites.

Military Intelligence Museum, The

Defence Intelligence and Security Centre, Chicksands
Nr Shefford SG17 5PR
01462 752 340
www.militaryintelligencemuseum.org/about-us

The Military Intelligence Museum displays key elements of the history of British Military Intelligence from the Boer War forwards. The central Collection in the museum is the Intelligence Corps Collection, which includes artefacts and special exhibits about the history and activities of the Corps as well as two specific displays: one recording the Honours and Awards received by members of the Corps and the other 'In the Name of the Rose,' a memorial to Corps members who have paid the ultimate sacrifice in the service of their Sovereign and their country.

Moot Hall

Elstow Green, Church End
Elstow MK42 9XT
01234 266 889
http://goo.gl/9ICIYG
moot.hall@bedscc.gov.uk

Moot Hall is a medieval market house, originally built for the nuns of Elstow Abbey on the village green. Restored in 1950 by Bedfordshire County Council, Moot Hall is now a small, but beautiful museum.

Museum of the Bedfordshire & Hertfordshire Regiment Association

Wardown Park
Luton LU2 7HA
01582 546723
http://goo.gl/rHcRks

The Collection is on two sites, and family history and other researchers are recommended to contact Nigel Lutt first at Nigel.Lutt2@virginmedia.com or if urgent on mobile 0750 4015313 for advice. The response will be prompt (within one to three days) with the exception of holidays, which will not be notified in advance, and which will result in a delay of a week or two at most.

Panacea Museum, The

9 Newnham Road
Bedford MK40 3NX
01234 353178
www.panaceatrust.org
museum@panaceatrust.org

The Panacea Museum tells the story of the Panacea Society, a remarkable religious community that existed in Bedford for almost a century. In the main museum building you can discover how the society was formed, what they believed and how they lived. You can also find out about Joanna Southcott and her sealed box of prophecies and why the Panacea Society campaigned tirelessly for the box to be opened.

Priory House Heritage Centre

33 High Street South
Dunstable LU6 3RZ
01582 891420
www.dunstable.gov.uk
prioryhouse@dunstable.gov.uk

Located within a 13th century building, Priory House Heritage Centre boasts a range of things to see and do. Take in a snapshot of a historical era, enjoy a delicious snack, lunch or afternoon tea in the award winning tea rooms.

Shuttleworth Collection, The

Old Warden Park
Biggleswade SG18 9EP
01767 627927
www.shuttleworth.org
marketingevents@shuttleworth.org

The Shuttleworth Collection – A Celebration of Flight was founded in 1928 by Richard Ormonde Shuttleworth. It is in a quiet countryside setting, actually on an old fashioned all grass aerodrome with eight hangars.

Stockwood Discovery Centre

London Road
Luton LU1 4LX
01582 548600
www.stockwooddiscoverycentre.com
museumsluton@lutonculture.com

Stockwood Park Museum has been transformed into Stockwood Discovery Centre, a visitor and discovery centre with brand new facilities such as a cafe shop, extensive gardens, a children's outdoor discovery play area, changing exhibitions, and corporate venue hire. The new centre has an environmental theme running through it and host the current collections: the Mossman carriages, the biggest museum collection of this kind on display in the UK and fascinating displays about the history of the area including the former Stockwood House.

Stotfold Watermill

Mill Lane
Stotfold SG5 4NU
01462 734541
www.stotfoldmill.com
enquiries@stotfoldmill.com

Stotfold Watermill, in its idyllic setting on the River Ivel, is

unique. Having burnt down in 1992 it is now a Grade II listed watermill that has been completely rebuilt with three fully accessible floors to view.

Wardown Park Museum

Old Bedford Road
Luton LU2 7HA
01582 546722
www.wardownparkmuseum.com
museum.gallery@luton.gov.uk

The museum is situated in a beautiful landscaped park and contributes to its charm by telling the story of Luton and its people such as the hat production and car industry, through displays, objects and old photographs. Home of the Bedfordshire and Hertfordshire regiment museum and the many changing exhibitions. There is free parking at the museum and good disabled access including a lift to the first floor.

Woburn Abbey & Gardens

Woburn Park
Woburn MK17 9WA
01525 290666
www.woburnabbey.co.uk
admissions@woburn.co.uk

Woburn Abbey first opened to the public in 1955 and has welcomed visitors from all over the globe. There are 22 rooms that you can experience, which house one of the most significant private art collections in the world. The many individual rooms of Woburn Abbey, house 18th century French and English furniture, magnificent silver and gold collections, a marvellous range of porcelain and many items treasured by generations of the Russell family. Over 28 acres of gardens, inspired by the designs of landscape gardener, Humphry Repton and developed by our dedicated gardens team.

Wrest Park - English Heritage

Silsoe
Luton MK45 4HR
01525 860152
http://goo.gl/VRf7DM
customers@english-heritage.org.uk

After decades behind virtually closed doors, its treasures overgrown and largely unknown, English Heritage is reviving one of Britain's largest and most important 'secret gardens' - Wrest Park. This is a wonderful 90-acre historic landscape and French-style mansion which will take its rightful place among the country's great garden attractions - and give locals and visitors to Bedfordshire a superb new day out.

Berkshire

Berkshire, one of the inland counties of England, lying between Hants and the river Thames, bounded on the N. by Gloucestershire, Oxfordshire, and Bucks, E. by Surrey, S. by Herts, and W. by Wilts; greatest length, E. and W., 53 miles; greatest breadth, N. and W., 30 miles; area 462,210 acres, population 218,363. It is intersected in a westerly direction by a line of chalk hills, a continuation of the Chilterns, the highest elevation being White Horse Hill, altitude 893 ft. N. of this is the White Horse Vale (so called from the figure of a horse cut out on the hill-side), and to the S. lies the Vale of Kennet, watered by the Kennet stream. These tracts are well cultivated, and produce good crops of grain, &c., especially in the Vale of the White Horse. Dairy farms and commons abound; much of the surface is under woods, chiefly of oak and beech. Windsor Forest, covering upwards of 50,000 acres, lies in the E. The Thames flows along the entire N. boundary (100 miles in extent); its tributaries are the Kennet, Lambourn, Ock, and Loddon. The manufactures are unimportant, being chiefly agricultural implements and malt. The Great Western Railway, the Thames, and 2 canals are the chief means of transit. The county contains 20 hundreds, 193 parishes with parts of 4 others, the parliamentary and municipal boroughs of Reading (1 member) and New Windsor (1 member), the municipal boroughs of Maidenhead, Newbury, and Wallingford, and the greater part of the municipal borough of Abingdon. It is almost entirely in the diocese of Oxford.

– John Bartholomew, *Gazetteer of the British Isles* (1887)

Note: the Vale of the White Horse south of the River Thames, originally in Berkshire, has been in Oxfordshire since 1974.

Ashdown House - National Trust

Lambourn
Newbury RG17 8RE
01793 762leighton209
www.nationaltrust.org.uk/ashdown-house
ashdownhouse@nationaltrust.org.uk

17th-century house perched on the Berkshire Downs. This extraordinary Dutch-style house is famous for its association with Elizabeth of Bohemia ('The Winter Queen'), Charles I's sister, to whom the house was 'consecrated'.

Basildon Park - National Trust

Lower Basildon
Reading RG8 9NR
0118 984 3040
www.nationaltrust.org.uk/basildon-park
basildonpark@nationaltrust.org.uk

This beautiful Palladian mansion was built in 1776-83 by John Carr for Francis Sykes, who made his fortune in India. The interior is notable for its original delicate plasterwork and elegant staircase as well as the unusual Octagon Room.

Berkshire Family History Society

161 St Peter's Road, Earley
Reading RG6 1PG
0118 966 3585
www.berksfhs.org.uk/cms
webmaster@berksfhs.org.uk

Berkshire Family History Society for genealogists living in the Royal County and those with ancestors in the pre-1974 county.

Berkshire Library & Museum of Freemasonry, The

Sindlesham Court Ltd., Mole Road
Sindlesham RG41 5EA
0118 9795104
http://goo.gl/F24OEu
robin@berkspgl-adsl.demon.co.uk

The Berkshire Library and Museum of Freemasonry houses an extensive range of books and a fascinating collection of masonic artefacts.

Berkshire Medical Heritage Centre

Level 4, Main Entrance, Royal Berkshire Hospital
Reading RG1 5AN
0118 322 7298
Louise.Griffiths@royalberkshire.nhs.uk

The Heritage Centre was founded in 1997. Our aim is to preserve and display items of historical medical interest particularly those with a local connection.

Berkshire Record Office

9 Coley Avenue
Reading RG1 4QN
0118 9375132
www.berkshirerecordoffice.org.uk
arch@reading.gov.uk

The Berkshire Record Office is the archives of the Royal County of Berkshire. We look after nearly nine hundred years of the county's history. On our website you can discover more about our holdings and how to use us, as well as see some of the treasures from our collections.

Berkshire Yeomanry Museum

Territorial Army Centre, Bolton Road
Windsor SL4 3JG
01753 860600
http://goo.gl/JzmpCf

The museum contains a well displayed and comprehensive collection tracing the history of the regiment since its beginnings in 1794.

Cliveden - National Trust

Taplow
Maidenhead SL6 0JA
01628 605069
www.nationaltrust.org.uk/cliveden
cliveden@nationaltrust.org.uk

Grade I listed garden, extensive woodlands and Italianate mansion. This spectacular estate overlooking the River Thames has a series of gardens, each with its own character, featuring topiary, statuary, water gardens, a formal parterre, Octagon temple, informal vistas, woodland and riverside walks.

Cole Museum of Zoology

School of Animal and Microbial Sciences, University of Reading
Reading RG6 6AJ
0118 378 7024
www.colemuseum.rdg.ac.uk
colemuseum@reading.ac.uk

The Cole Museum is a remarkable collection in that it was built up in the period 1907 to 1939 by three main people. Professor Cole, Dr Nellie B Eales and Mr Stoneman.

Dorney Court

Windsor SL4 6QP
01628 604638
www.dorneycourt.co.uk

Dorney Court is a Grade I Listed Tudor Manor House with the added accolade of being of outstanding architectural and historical interest. The house contains a fine collection of family portraits dating from the 16th century, many tapestries and good English furniture.

Eton College Collections & Museum of Eton Life

c/o Eton College
Windsor SL4 6DB
www.etoncollege.com/moel.aspx

The museum of Eton Life tells the story of the foundation of the College in 1440 and provides a glimpse into the world of the Eton schoolboy past and present. Find out about work, games (including the famous Eton Wall Game), punishment, and some of the colourful customs of the past. Discover well-known Old Etonians, from poets to prime ministers.

Highclere Castle

Highclere Park
Newbury RG20 9RN
01635 253 210
www.highclerecastle.co.uk/index.html
theoffice@highclerecastle.co.uk

Highclere Castle is a beautiful building and a warm, welcoming home to visitors and guests at events and celebrations held here. Apart from exploring the castle, the Egyptian Exhibition fascinates adults and children, whilst the surrounding Grounds and Gardens provide peace and tranquillity.

Maidenhead Heritage Centre

18 Park Street
Maidenhead SL6 1SL
01628 780555
www.maidenheadheritage.org.uk
info@maidenheadheritage.org.uk

Maidenhead Heritage Centre is where local history comes alive - from the stone age to the age of aviation and computers. Our exhibitions celebrate the past and help our visitors understand how and why Maidenhead and the surrounding villages developed. We are also Maidenhead's community memory bank, collecting and preserving artefacts, photographs, documents and tape recordings which all illustrate our local history.

Museum of Berkshire Aviation

Mohawk Way (off The Bader Way)
Woodley, Nr. Reading RG5 4UE
0118 944 8089
home.comcast.net/~aero51/html/index.htm
MuseumofBerkshireAviation@fly.to

Berkshire's dynamic contribution to aviation history is graphically re-captured at the museum. Run as a charitable trust, the museum is at the historic site of Woodley Airfield, near Readin.

Reading Museum

Town Hall, Blagrave Street
Reading RG1 1QH
0118 937 3400
www.readingmuseum.org.uk
mail@readingmuseum.org.uk

At the Reading Museum you can explore the social and natural history of Reading and surrounding area, including: The Biscuit Town: Uncover the story behind biscuit makers Huntley & Palmers Learn about the daily life and fascinating history of the once-splendid Reading Abbey. Explore what the Romans did for us in the Silchester Gallery of Roman Life. Britain's copy of the Bayeux Tapestry - displayed in its magnificent 70 metre entirety in a purpose-built gallery.

REME Museum of Technology

Isaac Newton Road, (off Biggs Lane)
Arborfield RG2 9NH
0118 976 3375
www.rememuseum.org.uk
enquiries@rememuseum.org.uk

South of Reading in rural Berkshire, the REME Museum of Technology tells the history of the Corps of Electrical and Mechanical Engineers. The Corps was formed in 1942 and still undertaking its original function of keeping the army's machines and weapons fitting fit.

Riverside Museum at Blake's Lock

off Kenavon Drive
Reading RG1 3DH
0118 9399800
http://goo.gl/u2PmAB
mail@readingmuseum.org.uk

The museum is sited on the banks of the River Kennet in the centre of Reading. The displays tell the story of the Reading's two rivers – the Kennet and the Thames.

Collections: Objects on display include a spectacular gypsy caravan and a medieval mill wheel. There are waterside views of the town centre and occasional summertime art exhibitions in the Turbine House.

Runnymede - National Trust

Runnymede Estate Office, North Lodge, Windsor Road
Old Windsor SL4 2JL
01784 432891
www.nationaltrust.org.uk/runnymede
runnymede@nationaltrust.org.uk

Riverside site of the sealing of the Magna Carta. Runnymede's diverse natural landscapes provide a backdrop for its unique history. The ancient 'meeting meadow' witnessed King John's sealing of the Magna Carta in 1215.

Shaw House

Newbury RG14 2DR
01635 279279
www.westberks.gov.uk/shawhouse
shawhouse@westberks.gov.uk

Shaw House is a large Elizabethan house; it was built in 1581 by the Dolman family. It was a family home until the 20th century.

Slough Museum

Ground Floor, Slough Central Library, 85 High Street
Slough SL1 1EA
01753 526422
www.sloughmuseum.co.uk
info@sloughmuseum.co.uk

The collection covers a period of around 10,000 years - from when mammoths roamed the area to the present day multi-cultural trading town. This includes the growth of Slough in the 17th and 18th centuries as a coaching town (ideally placed 20 miles outside of London for resting along the Bath road), the Victorian brick and horticultural industries (supplying the growing capital) and the foundations and growth of Slough Trading Estate (attracting workers from around the United Kingdom, the Commonwealth and Europe) which today continues to attract a growing population from around the world.

Thames Valley Police Museum

Thames Valley Police Training Centre, Sulhamstead
Nr Reading RG7 4DU
0118 932 6748
http://goo.gl/dLJQWC

Exhibits include items from the Great Train Robbery, a Triumph Saint Motorbike, an old control room desk, old uniforms and various photographs, helmets, truncheons, whistles and charge books.

University of Reading Special Collections

Special Collections Services, The University of Reading,
Redlands Road
Reading RG1 5EX
0118 378 8660
www.reading.ac.uk/special-collections
specialcollections@reading.ac.uk

The University has a large number of special collections of
rare books, archives, manuscripts and other materials
including the Beckett Collection and the Archive of British
Publishing and Printing. They may be consulted by
members of the public as well as members of the university.
Our collections, which include rare books, archives and
manuscripts, are substantial and varied, particularly for a
university of this age and size.

Ure Museum of Greek Archaeology

University of Reading, Department of Classics, Humanities
Building, Whiteknights
Reading RG6 6AA
0118 378 6990
www.rdg.ac.uk/Ure
ure@reading.ac.uk

The Ure Museum started life in the 1920s as a small
collection of fragmentary pottery by the first Professor of
Classics at the University, Percy Ure. It has now grown due
to the generosity of various donors, and is recognised as the
fourth largest collection of Greek ceramics in Britain. The
museum has recently undergone a massive renewal and
artefacts are now displayed thematically. It is located on the
Whiteknights campus at the University of Reading, where
there are also several other important museums.

West Berkshire Museum

The Wharf
Newbury RG14 5AS
01635 519562 direct 42400 general
www.westberkshiremuseum.org.uk
museum@westberks.gov.uk

Established in 1904, the museum houses various artworks
and collections. The museum is housed in two of
Newbury's most historic buildings. The Cloth Hall was
built in 1626-1627 by Richard Emmes, a master carpenter
of Speenhamland for the Newbury Corporation as a cloth
factory. Originally part of a larger range of buildings with a
courtyard in the centre, the building was subsequently used
as a workhouse, hospital and school before being used for
storing corn from 1829 until its conversion to a museum.

Windsor & Royal Borough Museum

The Guildhall, High Street
Windsor SL4 1LR
01628 685 686
www.rbwm.gov.uk/web/museum.htm
museum@rbwm.gov.uk

Windsor & Royal Borough Museum is a
Registered/Accredited Museum which comprises the local
history collection for the borough, comprising over 7,000
objects including Saxon artefacts from Old Windsor,
prehistoric tools, manuscripts, paintings and Victorian
objects.

Windsor Castle

Windsor SL4 2AP
020 7766 7304
www.royalcollection.org.uk/visit/windsorcastle
information@royalcollection.org.uk

Windsor Castle is an official residence of The Queen and
the largest occupied castle in the world. A royal palace and
fortress for over 900 years, the castle remains a working
palace today.

Bristol

Bristol, city, municipal and parliamentary borough, seaport, and county of itself, chiefly in Gloucestershire but partly in Somerset, at the confluence of the rivers Avon and Frome, 6 miles from the Bristol Channel at Avonmouth and 120 miles W. of London by rail, the port being 29 miles from Cardiff, 70 from Swansea. 245 from Dublin, 255 from Cork, and 325 from Liverpool; municipal borough, 4632 acres, population 206,874; parliamentary borough, population 253,906. Bristol is built on a number of eminences, and has a fine appearance. It contains important institutions, religious, educational, and charitable. It has several fine churches, notably the Cathedral (1142-1160), and the church of St Mary Redcliffe. It includes the suburbs of Clifton, Redland, and Cotham. At Clifton Down a magnificent suspension bridge spans the river Avon, having an elevation of 245 ft. above high-water mark. From an early date Bristol has been a sealport of great importance, its position being very favourable to commerce. In the reign of Henry II. it carried on trade with the N. of Europe, and between 1239 and 1247 there was occasion for enlarging and improving the accommodation for the shipping. There are now extensive docks, not only within the city itself, but also at Avonmouth on the N. side of the mouth of the river, and at Portishead on the S. side; both these harbours being in direct communication with the city by railway. The coasting trade is of great magnitude, steamers plying regularly between Bristol and Cardiff, Swansea, London, Cork, Dublin, Liverpool, and Glasgow; while the foreign trade extends to nearly all parts of the world. Bristol has manufacturers of glass, soap, and earthenware; shipbuilding, tanning, and sugar-refining; and extensive chemical and engineering works.

– John Bartholomew, *Gazetteer of the British Isles* (1887)

Acton Court

Latteridge Road, Iron Acton
Bristol BS37 9TL
01454 228 224
www.actoncourt.com

A beautifully conserved Tudor House built by Nicholas Poyntz for the pleasure of Henry VIII, at Iron Acton, Bristol.

Arnos Vale Cemetery Trust

West Lodge, Bath Road
Bristol BS4 3EW
0117 9719117
www.arnosvale.org.uk
info@arnosvale.org.uk

Arnos Vale Cemetery is one of the earliest and most important working Victorian cemeteries in the UK.

Avon Valley Railway

Bitton Station, Bath Road, Bitton
Bristol BS30 6HD
0117 932 5538
www.avonvalleyrailway.org
info@avonvalleyrailway.org

The Avon Valley Railway is more than just a train ride, offering a whole new experience for some or a nostalgic memory for others. The AVR now offers a six mile return train ride along the former Mangotsfield to Bath Green Park branch of the old Midland Railway, and the chance to see the River Avon valley from an aspect that cars cannot reach.

Blaise Castle House Museum

Henbury Road, Henbury
Bristol BS10 7QS
0117 903 9818
http://goo.gl/xDevmG
heritage.estates @bristol.gov.uk

The museum is situated in an 18th century house and holds most of the museums Service's 30,000 social history collection. Blaise has famous connections - it was immortalised by Jane Austen who described it as 'the finest place in England' in her book Northanger Abbey. The museum contains exhibits of everyday life from centuries past including an impressive domestic equipment gallery, a Victorian toy room including the museum's popular model train collection, old period costumes, other items of everyday life and a beautiful picture gallery.

Bristol & Avon Family History Society

50 Russell Grove
Westbury Park BS6 7UF
www.bafhs.org.uk
secretary@bafhs.org.uk

Formed in 1975, the Bristol & Avon Family History Society aims to provide contacts between members by regular meetings and through a quarterly Journal to assist members with problems encountered during research work. The society also works to promote and encourage the public study of family history, genealogy and associated interests.

Bristol Aero Collection Trust

PO BOX 77
Bristol BS34 7QH
0117 9365350
www.bristolaero.com
enquries@bristolaero.com

The Bristol Aerospace Centre is a new heritage museum and learning centre being planned for Filton, to the north of Bristol. It tells the story of the region's world-class aerospace industry - past, present and future.

Collections: Aircraft, guided missiles, spacecraft and aero engines produced by the Bristol Aeroplane Company and its successors centred on the Filton works north of Bristol. Also some products of the related Bristol Tram and Carriage Co.

Bristol Cathedral

College Green
Bristol BS1 5TJ
0117 926 4879
www.bristol-cathedral.co.uk
reception@bristol-cathedral.co.uk

A church has probably stood on this site for over a thousand years but it came to prominence in 1140 when Robert Fitzhardinge founded the Abbey of St Augustine.

Bristol Museum & Art Gallery

Queen's Road
Bristol BS8 1RL
0117 922 3571
http://goo.gl/g4wBxZ
general.museum@bristol.gov.uk

Bristol's premier museum and art gallery houses important collections of minerals and fossils, natural history, eastern art, world wildlife, Egyptology, archaeology and fine and applied art. Among the applied art collections with a strong Bristol connection are important collections of delftware and glass.

Bristol Museums, Galleries & Archives

Bristol Museum & Art Gallery, Queen's Road
Bristol BS8 1RL
www.bristolmuseums.org.uk

Bristol Museums, Galleries and Archives is the main museum and archives service for the city. It comprises several sites including Bristol Museum & Art Gallery, M Shed, Blaise Castle House Museum, The Red Lodge Museum, The Georgian House Museum, Bristol Records Office and Archives.

Bristol Record Office

'B' Bond Warehouse, Smeaton Road
Bristol BS1 6XN
0117 922 4224
www.bristolmuseums.org.uk/bristol-record-office
bro@bristol.gov.uk

Our goal is to preserve and make available for research records and photographs relating to the history of Bristol. This Record Office has Designated Collections of national importance.

Brunel's ss Great Britain

Great Western Dockyard, Gas Ferry Road
Bristol BS1 6TY
0117 926 0680
www.ssgreatbritain.org
admin@ssgreatbritain.org

The brainchild of our most famous Bristolian, Isambard Kingdom Brunel; this iconic steam ship is the heart of a multi-award winning visitor attraction. Rescued from rust and wreckage in 1970, and since lovingly restored to her Victorian hey-day, a visit to the ss Great Britain allows you to step back in time and explore true stories from the opulent First-Class to the cramped and quarrelsome Steerage.

Clifton Cathedral

Cathedral Church of SS Peter and Paul, Clifton Cathedral House, Clifton Park
Bristol BS8 3BX
0117 973 8411
www.cliftoncathedral.org.uk
Cathedral@CliftonDiocese.com

The Cathedral Church at Clifton is the mother church of the Diocese of Clifton which covers the neighbouring counties of North Somerset, Bath, North and South Gloucester, Wiltshire, South Somerset, and the City and County of Bristol. Construction began in March 1970.

Clifton Rocks Railway

Princes Buildings, Clifton
Bristol BS8 4LD
www.cliftonrocksrailway.org.uk
maggie.shapland@gmail.com

Thousands of people pass the bottom entrance to the Clifton Rocks Railway as they drive along Bristol's Portway, with most not knowing what secret is buried in the rock of the Avon Gorge. Constructed with great difficulty inside the cliffs of the Avon Gorge in order to reduce its visual impact on the picturesque surroundings, this water powered 'funicular' railway opened on 11 March, 1893 and operated for 40 years against diminishing trade. Includes original turnstiles, regenerative gas light, artefacts left by war-time users.

Clifton Suspension Bridge Visitor Centre

Clifton Suspension Bridge Trust, Bridgemaster's Office, Leigh Woods
Bristol BS8 3PA
0117 974 4664
www.cliftonbridge.org.uk
visitinfo@cliftonbridge.org.uk

The Clifton Suspension Bridge is a world famous icon of the city of Bristol. Designed in the 1830s by the Victorian engineer, Isambard Kingdom Brunel, it was not completed until 1864.

Garrison Living History Group, The

93 Poplar Road, Warmley
Bristol BS30 5JS
0117 961 5016
www.thegarrison.org.uk
furey-king@blueyonder.co.uk

Living history group working with the Royal Artillery and veterans associations, based at Larkhill School of Artillery.

Geology Collection, University of Bristol

University of Bristol, School of Earth Sciences, Wills Memorial Building, Queen's Road
Bristol BS8 1RJ
0117 928 9000
http://goo.gl/TFp6qJ
gely-geologycollection@bristol.ac.uk

The Geology Collection at the University of Bristol safeguards a diverse range of over 100,000 geological specimens, maps and archival documents in support of the wider scholarly community and the general public. Visitors are welcome to view our public displays or book an appointment to access the collection.

Georgian House Museum, The

The Georgian House, 7 Great George Street
Bristol BS1 5RR
0117 921 1362
www.bristolmuseums.org.uk/georgian-house-museum
general.museum@bristol.gov.uk

The Georgian House is an 18th century, six storey townhouse that has been restored and decorated to its original glory. The house was built in 1790 for John Pinney, a wealthy slave plantation owner and sugar merchant, it was also where the enslaved African Pero lived. It is displayed as it might have looked in the 18th century and provides an insight into life above and below stairs.

Collections: Part of Bristol Museums.

Glenside Hospital Museum

Glenside Museum, University of the West of England
Glenside Campus, Stapleton
Bristol BS16 1DD
0117 9652829
www.glensidemuseum.pwp.blueyonder.co.uk
glensidemuseum@hotmail.com

A collection on the history of Bristol Psychiatric hospitals and Learning Disability hospitals. Dr Donal Early was the main founder of the museum and was a consultant psychiatrist at Glenside from the 1950s. He and his volunteers collected memorabilia and stored them on the balcony of the dining hall of Glenside.

Collections: Highlights include an array of medications and remedies, drawings by patient Denis Reed, a fully operational church organ, ECT machines, padded cell, straight jacket, mortuary equipment, ophthalmic instruments, an undercarriage door of a Messerschmitt Bomber from WW2, and dioramas of an everyday ward, operating theatre, and GP's surgery.

Kings Weston Roman Villa

Long Cross, Lawrence Weston
Bristol BS11 0LP
01179 506789
http://goo.gl/ezyGyw
gail_boyle@bristol-city.gov.uk

Kings Weston Villa was discovered during the construction of Lawrence Weston housing estate in 1947; the construction of a road partially destroyed it, but a full excavation was carried out in 1948-50. The villa may have been the centre of an estate associated with farming.

Kingswood Heritage Museum

🏛️ 💷

Windmill Tower building, Tower Lane
Warmley BS30 8XT
0117 967 5711
www.kingswoodmuseum.org.uk

Interpretation of the Champion site at Warmley. Displays on local industries and religious history.

M Shed

💷 ⭐

Wapping Road
Bristol BS1 4RN
0117 352 6600
www.bristolmuseums.org.uk/m-shed
general.museum@bristol.gov.uk

M Shed is an exciting and innovative new museum for Bristol that tells the story of our city. Located on the historic dockside, Bristol's flagship museum has been designed to retain the character of the former 1950s transit shed.

Matthew of Bristol

🏛️ 💷

Gas Ferry Road
Bristol BS1 6TY
0117 927 6868
www.matthew.co.uk
info@matthew.co.uk

Over 500 years ago John Cabot and his crew set sail for Asia aboard the original Matthew hoping to trade goods and commodities with the people who lived there. However, he finally arrived on the coast of Newfoundland and therefore was the original discoverer of North America, not Christopher Columbus as most people believe. In 1997 the replica Matthew followed the same course as John Cabot in 1497 and sailed across to Newfoundland. It carried the same number of crew members as the original and took the same amount of time to complete the crossing. Today The Matthew is based in Bristol Harbour during the autumn and winter months and is open to the public as well as undertaking short cruises around the harbour.

Müller House

💷 ⭐

c/o The George M
Bristol BS6 6DA
0117 924 5001
www.mullers.org
admin@mullers.org

Our museum contains photographs and artefacts from the 'Homes' (both the Ashley Down homes and later 'scattered' homes), as well as papers and personal effects which belonged to George Müller. The Trust is also home to archives of the original homes and records of all the orphans – over 17,000 of them. These can be viewed by

arrangement by contacting the Trust office. We regularly receive visitors by appointment from around the world as well as from local groups and schools around Bristol.

New Room - John Wesley's Chapel

36 The Horsefair
Bristol BS1 3JE
0117 926 4740
www.newroombristol.org.uk

The New Room in Bristol is the oldest Methodist Chapel in the world (originally built in 1739) and the cradle of the early Methodist movement. It was built and used by John Wesley and the early Methodists as a meeting and preaching place and the centre for helping and educating the needy members of the community. The chapel itself is on the ground floor (where there is also a shop) and is accessible from either the Broadmead or Horsefair courtyards. Upstairs, are the Preachers' Rooms where the MLA accredited museum is located.

Penguin Archive

🏛️ ⭐

Special Collections, Arts and Social Sciences Library, University of Bristol, Tyndall Avenue
Bristol BS8 1TJ
0117 928 8014
http://goo.gl/5TNS0B
special-collections@bristol.ac.uk

The Penguin Archive contains the archives of Penguin Books Ltd. from its foundation in 1935 to the 1980s.

Recording the Crafts

NEVAC, University of the West of England, Bower Ashton Campus, Kennel Lodge Road, Off Clanage Road
Bristol BS3 2JT
0117 328 4746
www.uwe.ac.uk/sca/research/rtc
matthew.partington@uwe.ac.uk

The National Electronic and Video Archive of the Crafts - NEVAC - gathers materials which will act as a resource for those researching the nature of the Crafts. These materials are characteristically in the form of digital video and sound recordings of people who have been intimately associated with the development of the Crafts in Britain.

Collections: There are currently 261 hours of interviews with 118 people, (including ceramists, textile artists, wood-workers, print-makers, enamel artists and curators).

Red Lodge Museum, The

The Red Lodge, Park Row
Bristol BS1 5LJ
0117 921 1360
www.bristolmuseums.org.uk/red-lodge-museum
general.museum@bristol.gov.uk

The Red Lodge is often described as Bristol's 'hidden treasure' because of its magnificent Tudor rooms. The house, built in 1580, is furnished in Elizabethan, Stuart and Georgian styles and contains the impressive Great Oak Room, with its original Elizabethan plasterwork ceiling, oak panelling and carved chimneypiece.

Rolls-Royce Heritage Trust

c/o Brian Whatley, Rolls-Royce Heritage Trust (Bristol Branch), EW6-18, PO Box 3, Filton
Bristol BS34 7QE
0117 979 5494
http://goo.gl/4XDT7I
brian.whatley@rolls-royce.com

The Bristol branch owns the heritage of the Bristol Engine Company, its predecessors Brazil Straker and Cosmos Engineering, later the Bristol Siddeley company and, ultimately, the heritage of the site during the Rolls-Royce era. Its display reflects the leadership given to the development of the air-cooled radial piston engine by Sir Roy Fedden, to the development of the gas turbine engine for V/STOL and supersonic flight.

Sodbury Vale Family History Group

36 Westcourt Drive, Oldland Common
Bristol BS30 9RU
0117 932 4133
https://goo.gl/Q6IFLx
secretary@bafhs.org.uk

Are you interested in your family history and would like to meet with like minded people? Then Sodbury Vale Family History Group is the place for you.

University of Bristol Theatre Collection

University of Bristol Theatre Collection, Department of Drama, Cantocks Close
Bristol BS8 1UP
0117 331 5086
www.bris.ac.uk/theatrecollection
theatre-collection@bristol.ac.uk

The Theatre Collection is an accredited museum and one of the world's largest archives of British theatre and Live Art. Founded in 1951 to serve the newly formed Drama Department (the first in any UK university), we are now an internationally renowned research facility open to all. Our collections cover all aspects of theatre history to the present day and our visitors include everyone from international scholars to family historians.

Collections: The Theatre Collection covers the period 1572 to the 21st century. The collections encompass a wide range of formats including documents, photographs, artwork, artefacts, costumes, audio-visual and digital media.

University of Bristol, Special Collections

Arts and Social Sciences Library, Tyndall Avenue, University of Bristol
Bristol BS8 1TH
0117 928 8014
http://goo.gl/i1WhFm
special-collections@bristol.ac.uk

The Special Collections of the University Library comprise a rich and diverse range of printed books and journals, archival resources and artefacts in support of the academic work of the University and the wider scholarly community.

Winterbourne Medieval Barn

Church Lane
Winterbourne BS36 1SE
www.winterbournebarn.org.uk/index.html
robert.beetham@phonecoop.coop

Winterbourne Medieval Barn is a building of national importance. Built in 1342, just a few years before the great plagues swept across England, the barn is a unique survival of the medieval agrarian economy.

Buckinghamshire

Buckinghamshire, or Bucks, an inland county of England, bounded N. by Northamptonshire, E. by Bedfordshire, Herts, and Middlesex, S. by Surrey (for the distance of about 1 mile) and Berks, and W. by Oxfordshire; greatest length, N. and S., 50 miles; greatest breadth, E. and W., 24 miles; average breadth, 17 miles; area 477,151 acres, population 176,323. It is intersected by the chalk range of the Chiltern Hills, which extend NE. from Oxfordshire to Bedfordshire, the highest point being Wendover Hill, 905 ft. The country here is beautifully wooded, chiefly with oak and beech. To the S. there is much excellent grazing land. The fertile 'Vale of Aylesbury' lies in the centre of the county, verdant with rich meadows and pasturage. Further N. the heavy arable land is now being brought under steam cultivation, and excellent crops of wheat, beans, &c., are produced. Farms are generally of small size, and are leased on a yearly tenure. Pigs and calves are largely reared on the numerous dairy-farms, and great numbers of ducks are sent yearly to the metropolis from the neighbourhood of Aylesbury. The quantity of butter, besides cream cheese, &c., sent annually to the London market, averages between 4,000,000 and 5,000,000 lbs. The making of wooden spades, brush-handles, bowls, &c., from beech is a considerable industry. Numbers of the female population are employed in the manufacture of thread-lace and straw-plaiting. The county is traversed by the London and North-Western Railway and its branches; the Grand Junction Canal extends about 24 miles through the NE. B. comprises 8 hundreds, – those of Stoke, Burnham, and Desborough being called the 'Chiltern Hundreds'; – 224 parishes; and the municipal boroughs of Buckingham and Chipping Wycombe. It is almost entirely in the diocese of Oxford.

– John Bartholomew, Gazetteer of the British Isles (1887)

Amersham Museum

🏛 £

49 High Street
Amersham HP7 0DP
01494 723700
www.AmershamMuseum.org
Curator@AmershamMuseum.org

This award-winning museum is located in part of a 15th century timber-framed hall house in the centre of Old Amersham with a herb garden running down to the river.

Collections: The collection illustrates Amersham's history from the Romans to the 20th century when the arrival of the railway created Metroland. There are displays on local crafts including chairmaking, lace making and straw plait, Amersham's industries from Weller's Brewery to World War II barrage balloons, local buildings and everyday objects.

Bletchley Park

🏰 🏛 £

The Mansion, Bletchley
Milton Keynes MK3 6EB
01908 640404
www.bletchleypark.org.uk
info@bletchleypark.org.uk

During WW2 the German armed forces top secret codes were broken at Bletchley Park, providing the allies with vital information towards their war effort. The world's first programmable computer and other technologies we take for granted today were initiated at Bletchley Park.

Bradenham Village - National Trust

🏰 ★

Nr High Wycombe HP14 4HF
01494 755573
www.nationaltrust.org.uk/bradenham-village
bradenham@nationaltrust.org.uk

The church and 17th-century manor house (not open) provide an impressive backdrop to the sloping village green. A network of paths provides easy access for walkers to explore the delightful surrounding countryside – which includes hills, farmland and classic Chilterns beech woods.

Buckingham Old Gaol Museum

🏛 £

Market Hill
Buckingham MK18 1JX
01280 823020
www.buckinghamoldgaol.org.uk
info@buckinghamoldgaol.org.uk

Located in the heart of historic market town of Buckingham, the iconic Old Gaol was built in 1748 in the style of a castle, with later additions in 1839 by the famous local architect George Gilbert Scott. The Old Gaol Museum tells the story of Buckingham and rural life, including the Flora Thompson Collection (Lark Rise to Candleford author) and Buckinghamshire Military Trust exhibits.

Buckinghamshire County Museum

Church Street
Aylesbury HP20 2QP
01296 337889
www.buckscc.gov.uk/museum
museumwebsiteenquiries@buckscc.gov.uk

Our award winning County Museum is in the attractive old town area of Aylesbury in beautifully restored buildings, some dating from the 15th century. The museum showcases the County's rich heritage alongside a changing programme of exhibitions in the Buckinghamshire Art Gallery and we also have the Roald Dahl Children's Gallery. Our collections include Archaeology - all the prehistoric, Roman and medieval finds from Bucks and Milton Keynes; Wildlife - plants and animals, birds and insects; Fossils, rocks and minerals; Clothing from Georgian times right up to the 21st century; Textiles - lace, needlework, patchwork and quilts; Buckinghamshire social history of every shape and size; Contemporary studio pottery; Pictures - paintings, drawings and prints.

Buckinghamshire County Museum Resource Centre

Tring Road
Halton HP22 5PJ
01296 624519
www.buckscc.gov.uk/museum
museum@buckscc.gov.uk

Part of Buckinghamshire County Museum. The public galleries are in Aylesbury.

Buckinghamshire Family History Society

PO Box 403
Aylesbury HP21 7GU
www.bucksfhs.org.uk
society@bucksfhs.org.uk

Founded in 1976, we are a group of over 1,500 family historians who have been helping each other with their research. Have a look around and see if we can help with your genealogy.

Buckinghamshire Genealogical Society

Varneys, Rudds Lane
Haddenham HP17 8JP
01844 291631
www.bucksgs.org.uk
eve@varneys.org.uk

The BGS was founded in 1992 to assist members living outside the county with their Bucks research, and to help those living within the county with all aspects of their family history.

Buckinghamshire Military Museum

The Old Gaol, Market Hill
Buckingham MK18 1EW
01280 823 020
www.bmmt.co.uk
info@bmmt.co.uk

The Buckinghamshire Military Museum Trust preserves the heritage of the local military units raised in the historic county of Buckinghamshire in England from the 1500s onwards, including the Militia, Yeomanry, Volunteers, Territorials, and Home Guard.

Buckinghamshire Railway Centre

Quainton Road Station, Quainton
Aylesbury HP22 4BY
01296 655720
www.bucksrailcentre.org
bucksrailcentre@connect.com

Founded in 1969 by the London Railway Preservation Society, the Buckinghamshire Railway Centre is one of the leading steam museums in the country; covering 25 acres, the collection of steam locomotives and other railway vehicles is one of the largest outside the National Railway Museum.

Centre for Buckinghamshire Studies

County Hall, Walton Street
Aylesbury HP20 1UU
01296 382587
www.buckscc.gov.uk/archives
archives@buckscc.gov.uk

County Archives and Local Studies Library for Buckinghamshire offering a range of resources to support research in family, local and house history in the county.

Chesham Museum

15 Market Square
Chesham HP5 1HG
01494 792549
www.cheshammuseum.org.uk
info@cheshammuseum.org.uk

Chesham is one of the largest towns in Buckinghamshire and has a unique history of industry and social reform. The museum is in the town's historic Market Square and houses a collection of objects and photographs illustrating Chesham's history and especially its various industries.

Collections: The permanent exhibition has five main themes: Made in Chesham, Remember Chesham, Chesham at War, Coming to Chesham and Digging up the Past.

Chiltern Open Air Museum

Newland Park, Gorelands Lane
Chalfont St Giles HP8 4AB
01494 871117
www.coam.org.uk
enquires@coam.org.uk

An outstanding collection of historic buildings, rescued from destruction and rebuilt in 45 acres of beautiful Chilterns landscape. Explore the buildings including a 1940s Prefab from Amersham, a Victorian Vicarage Room from Thame, and a 19th-century earth cottage from Haddenham.

Claydon - National Trust

Middle Claydon
Buckingham MK18 2EY
01296 730349
www.nationaltrust.org.uk/claydon
claydon@nationaltrust.org.uk

The extraordinary architecture of the house includes extravagant rococo and chinoiserie decoration, other features include the unique Chinese Room and parquetry Grand Stairs. In continuous occupation by the Verney family for over 380 years. All Saints Church (not NT) in the grounds, is also open to the public.

Collections: Mementoes of Florence Nightingale, a relation of the family who was a regular visitor.

Cowper & Newton Museum, The

The Cowper and Newton Museum, Orchard Side, Market Place
Olney MK46 4AJ
01234 711516
www.cowperandnewtonmuseum.org.uk
house-manager@cowperandnewtonmuseum.org.uk

The museum celebrates two great men who lived in Olney: the leading 18th century poet and letter writer William Cowper and his friend, John Newton who wrote the hymn 'Amazing Grace'. Newton was instrumental in persuading William Wilberforce to campaign in Parliament for the abolition of the slave trade.

Ford End Watermill

Station Road
Ivinghoe LU7 9EA
01442 825421
www.fordendwatermill.co.uk
millman@fordendwatermill.co.uk

This little mill, recorded in 1767 but certainly very much older, was in use until 1963. Restored by volunteers, and now maintained and run by Ford End Watermill Society, it is the only remaining working watermill in Buckinghamshire with original machinery.

Hughenden - National Trust

Thames and Solent Region, Hughenden Manor
High Wycombe HP14 4LA
01494 755573
www.nationaltrust.org.uk/hughenden
hughenden@nationaltrust.org.uk

Queen Victoria's trusted prime minister Benjamin Disraeli lived here from 1848 until his death in 1881. Most of his pictures, furniture and books remain in this, his private retreat from the rigours of parliamentary life.

John Milton's Cottage

Deanway
Chalfont St Giles HP8 4JH
01494 872313
www.miltonscottage.org

Milton's Cottage is the only extant home of John Milton, the great English poet and parliamentarian, in Chalfont St Giles, Buckinghamshire.

Collections: The cottage contains one of the finest collections of 17th century and other early editions of Milton's poetic and prose works.

King's Head - National Trust

King's Head Passage, Market Square
Aylesbury HP20 2RW
01296 381501
www.nationaltrust.org.uk/kings-head
kingshead@nationaltrust.org.uk

Set in the heart of this historic market town, the King's Head is one of England's best preserved coaching inns. Dating back to 1455, the building has many fascinating architectural features – including stained-glass windows, exposed wattle and daub and the original stabling for the inn.

Marlow Museum

Court Garden, Pound Lane
Marlow SL7 2AE
https://marlowmuseum.wordpress.com
marlowmuseum@tiscali.co.uk

After an absence of some sixty years, Marlow has its own Museum again. It is located outside Court Garden Leisure Centre in Marlow, but serves the communities of Bisham, Great Marlow, Little Marlow, Marlow Bottom, Marlow Town and Medmemham.

Milton Keynes Museum

McConnell Drive, Wolverton
Milton Keynes MK12 5EL
01908 316222
www.mkmuseum.org.uk
info@mkmuseum.org.uk

Welcome to Milton Keynes Museum, where we preserve the history of Britain's newest city. Housed in a beautiful Victorian farmstead, our large and constantly changing selection of displays have something for all the family.

Newport Pagnell Historical Society

Chandos Hall, Silver Street
Newport Pagnell MK16 0EW
www.mkheritage.co.uk/nphs
don@hurst1137.fsnet.co.uk

Newport Pagnell Historical Society was founded in 1984 by a small group interested in the buildings and people of the town and surrounding area and concerned in preserving the past for the future.By the 1990s the thriving society, by its own fund raising efforts and with the generous help of the Harry Middleton Gift, was able to purchase and refurbish Chandos Hall and open it both as a Museum and the society's headquarters.

Pitstone Green Museum

Vicarage Road, Pitstone
Leighton Buzzard LU7 9EY
01582 605464
www.pitstonemuseum.co.uk

Set in the Buckinghamshire countryside and housed in the buildings of a 1831 farm, the museum offers a fascinating and inexpensive day out for the family with many interesting displays and artefacts to see. The museum is run by volunteers from the Pitstone & Ivinghoe Museum Society.

Projected Picture Trust

Enigma Cinema
Sherwood Drive MK3 6EB
07747 193447
www.ppttrust.org
contactppt1@gmail.com

The wanton destruction of projectors and related professional film equipment prompted a few like minded preservationists to form The Projected Picture Trust (PPT) in 1978. The aims were to not only locate the equipment being destroyed, but to renovate, preserve and exhibit it for the enjoyment of the public.

Roald Dahl Children's Gallery

Church Street
Aylesbury HP20 2QP
01296 331 441
http://goo.gl/myB9M

Step into the magical world of Roald Dahl with a visit to this exciting hands-on gallery for children.

Roald Dahl Museum & Story Centre, The

Roald Dahl Museum and Story Centre, 81-83 High Street
Great Missenden HP16 0AL
01494 892192
www.roalddahlmuseum.org
admin@roalddahlmuseum.org

This great little Museum has two fun and fact-packed biographical galleries and a fantabulous Story Centre. In Boy and Solo, visitors can learn about the events that shaped Roald Dahl as a writer, from his illicit motorbike outings at school to his time as a World War Two fighter pilot.

Stowe - National Trust

Stowe Landscape Gardens
Buckingham MK18 5EH
01280 822850
www.nationaltrust.org.uk/stowe
stowegarden@nationaltrust.org.uk

Stowe is a 100ha (250 acre) work of art, both beautiful and full of meaning. With its ornamental lakes, glorious open spaces and wooded valleys, adorned with over 40 temples and monuments, it is one of the supreme creations of the Georgian era.

Stowe House

Stowe House Preservation Trust, Stowe House
Buckingham MK18 5EH
01280 818229
www.shpt.org
amcevoy@stowe.co.uk

Since the 18th century, Stowe has welcomed monarchs, poets, politicians and high society to delight in its Neo-classical splendour. The house is now part of a major public school, since 1923 and has been owned by Stowe House Preservation Trust since 2000.

Telephone Museum

Milton Keynes Museum, McConnell Drive, Wolverton
Milton Keynes MK12 5EL
01525 237676
www.mkheritage.co.uk/ttm
thetelephonemuseum@btinternet.com

The Telephone Museum houses an extensive collection of telephones, exchanges, switchboards, and associated items & equipment. Many working displays enable the visitor to try things out for themselves.

Waddesdon Manor - National Trust

Waddesdon
Nr Aylesbury HP18 0JH
01296 653226
www.nationaltrust.org.uk/waddesdon-manor
waddesdonmanor@nationaltrust.org.uk

Waddesdon Manor is a magnificent French Renaissance-style château housing the Rothschild Collection of art treasures. The garden is renowned for its seasonal displays, colourful shrubs and mature trees.

West Wycombe Park - National Trust

West Wycombe Park
West Wycombe HP14 3AJ
01494 513569
www.nationaltrust.org.uk/west-wycombe-park
westwycombe@nationaltrust.org.uk

Perfectly preserved rococo landscape garden surrounding a neo-classical mansion. The garden was created in the mid-18th century by Sir Francis Dashwood, founder of the Dilettanti Society and the Hellfire Club.

Wycombe Museum

Priory Avenue
High Wycombe HP13 6PX
01494 421895
www.wycombe.gov.uk/museum
museum@wycombe.gov.uk

Friendly local museum set in an 18th century house with attractive grounds. Collections include historic Windsor chairs from the Chilterns traditional furniture industry, local history objects from Wycombe District and an art collection including oils, watercolours and sculpture.

Cambridgeshire

Cambridgeshire, inland eastern county of England; bounded N. by Lincolnshire, E. by Norfolk and Suffolk, S. by Essex and Herts, W. by Bedfordshire, Huntingdonshire, and Northamptonshire; greatest length, N. and S., 48 miles; greatest breadth, E. and W., 28 miles; average breadth, 16 miles; area, 524,935 acres; population 185,594. The N. section of the county, including the Isle of Ely and part of the Great Bedford Level, is a large flat expanse of country, which, for the most part, formerly consisted of fen and marsh. It is now intersected in all directions by wide trenches or canals. The land, thus drained and reclaimed, is a rich, black soil, and bears excellent crops. From this tract the pleasant vale of the Cam stretches away to the SW., and contains a great number of excellent dairy farms. Cambridgeshire comprises 17 hundreds, 172 parishes with parts of 7 others, the parliamentary and municipal borough of Cambridge (1 member, and Cambridge University 2 members), and the municipal borough of Wisbech. It is almost entirely in the diocese of Ely.

– John Bartholomew, *Gazetteer of the British Isles* (1887)

Note: the former county of Huntingdonshire has been part of Cambridgeshire since 1974:

Huntingdonshire, Huntingdon, or Hunts, inland county, South Midland District, England; is bounded W. and N. by Northamptonshire, E. by Cambridgeshire, and S. by Bedfordshire; greatest length, N. and S., 30 miles; greatest breadth, E. and W., 23 miles; 229,515 acres; population 59,491. About a fourth of the county (in the NE.) forms a portion of the great 'fen' district, the remainder consisting of a succession of gentle hills and dales. Huntingdonshire is almost wholly devoid of trees, and may be described as an agricultural and pastoral county… Green crops, also of excellent quality, are obtained, while market gardening and cattle rearing form profitable employments. Willows are the chief product of the fen district. The Nen, in the N. and NW., annd the Ouse, in the interior, are the chief rivers; both are navigable for barges. With the exception of papermaking and the preparation of parchment, there are no manufactures of more than local importance. The county is almost entirely in the diocese of Ely. It contains 4 hundreds; 103 parishes, with parts of 6 others; the munincipal boroughs of Huntingdon, Godmanchester, and St Ives; and a part of the city of Peterborough.

– John Bartholomew, *Gazetteer of the British Isles* (1887)

Anglesey Abbey, Gardens & Lode Mill - National Trust

Lode
Cambridge CB25 9EJ
01223 810080
www.nationaltrust.org.uk/anglesey-abbey
angleseyabbey@nationaltrust.org.uk

A passion for tradition and impressing guests inspired one man to transform a run-down country house and desolate landscape. At the age of 30, the future Lord Fairhaven began to create his first home. Wanting to inspire and surprise visitors, he created a spectacular garden with planting for all seasons and a cosy house in which to entertain.

Burwell Museum of Fen Edge Village Life

Mill Close
Burwell CB25 0HL
01638 605 544
www.burwellmuseum.org.uk
museum@burwellmuseum.org.uk

A museum (reg.charity No.290431), run entirely by volunteers, depicting village life on the edge of the Cambridgeshire Fens from the Saxons to the 60s. The displays are housed in various attractive buildings including an 18th century timber framed barn. Stevens' Mill, a Grade II* Listed windmill next to the museum site, is part of the museum but is awaiting full restoration.

Cambridge Museum of Technology

The Old Pumping Station, Cheddars Lane
Cambridge CB5 8LD
01223 500 652
www.museumoftechnology.com
info@museumoftechnology.com

Sited on the bank of the River Cam, the museum is housed in the Old Pumping Station which was built to pump Cambridge's sewage out to the sewage works at nearby Milton. A major feature of the museum is the two Hathorn Davey pumping engines installed in 1894 to pump the sewage from the well beneath the engines. These are the only engines of this type still running in the world. There is also a display of objects produced by local industries including Pye and Cambridge Instrument Company.

Cambridge University Heraldic & Genealogical Society

c/o Crossfield House, Dale Road, Stanton
Bury St Edmunds IP31 2DY
01359 251050
www.cam.ac.uk/societies/cuhags
derekpalgrave@btinternet.com

The Cambridge University Heraldic and Genealogical Society was formed as the result of the merger in 1957 of a previous society of the same name (founded 1950) with the Cambridge University Society of Genealogists (founded 1954). Four speaker meetings are held in each of the Michaelmas and Lent terms and a ninth at the beginning of the Easter term.

Cambridge University Library

Cambridge University Library, West Road
Cambridge CB3 9DR
01223 333000
www.lib.cam.ac.uk
library@lib.cam.ac.uk

Cambridge University Library is a legal deposit library, meaning that it is entitled to claim a copy of every publication in printed form published in the UK and Ireland. Almost all of this material is claimed and can be consulted in the Library.

Cambridgeshire Archives

Box RES 1009, Shire Hall, Castle Hill
Cambridge CB3 0AP
01223 699399
http://goo.gl/sZPUHp

Our aim is to identify, collect, preserve and actively promote the use of historical records relating to Cambridgeshire, including the former counties of Huntingdonshire and the Isle of Ely.

Cambridgeshire Association for Local History

PO BOX 1112
Cambridge CB21 4WP
01223 892430
www.calh.org.uk
michelle.bullivant@talk21.com

One of our aims is to provide an umbrella service for all the local, family and social history societies, groups and clubs in Cambridgeshire. We also act as a central information hub taking in all the latest news of events or what is happening or affecting the history community both locally and nationally and disseminating that information out to the many history based societies, groups and clubs via our various networking facilities. we have a thriving individual and family membership.

Cambridgeshire Family History Society

43 Eachard Road
Cambridge CB3 0HZ
01223 853273
www.cfhs.org.uk
secretary@cfhs.org.uk

Cambridgeshire Family History Society (CFHS) supports family historians researching their ancestry in Cambridgeshire and beyond. Through transcription projects, CFHS helps to preserve original records by making them readily available to everyone.

Centre for Computing History

Rene Court, Coldhams Road
Cambridge CB1 3EW
01223 214446
www.computinghistory.org.uk
events@computinghistory.org.uk

Established in 2006, the centre for Computing History is a pioneering educational charity. Its core purpose is to increase understanding of developments in computing over the past 50 years through exploring the social, cultural and historical impact of the Information Age.

Churchill Archives Centre

Churchill College
Cambridge CB3 0DS
01223 336087
www.chu.cam.ac.uk/archives
archives@chu.cam.ac.uk

The Churchill Archives Centre was purpose-built in 1973 to house Sir Winston Churchill's Papers - some 3000 boxes of letters and documents ranging from his first childhood letters, via his great war-time speeches, to the writings which earned him the Nobel Prize for Literature. They form an incomparable documentary treasure trove. The Churchill Papers served as the inspiration and the starting-point for a larger endeavour - the creation of a wide-ranging archive of the Churchill era and after, covering those fields of public life in which Sir Winston played a personal role or took a personal interest.

Clare Cottage

12 Woodgate, Helpston
Peterborough PE6 7ED
www.clarecottage.org
team@clarecottage.org

Tucked away between Stamford and Peterborough lies the village of Helpston, the birthplace and home of John Clare (1793-1864). He is widely regarded as one of the greatest English poets, and lived in the village for his first forty years

Cromwell Museum

Grammar School Walk, Huntingdon
Huntingdon PE29 3LF
01480 375 830
www.cambridgeshire.gov.uk/cromwell
cromwellmuseum@cambridgeshire.gov.uk

Located in a fragment of a medieval monastic building and the former town Grammar School attended by Oliver Cromwell. The museum marks the life and legacy of Oliver Cromwell 1599-1658, who rose to prominence during the English Civil Wars of the mid 17th century, and became the head of state, the Lord Protector, during England's only experiment with Republicanism.

Ely Cathedral

The Gallery
Ely CB7 4DL
01353 667735
www.elycathedral.org
receptionist@cathedral.ely.anglican.org

Thousands of visitors come to Ely Cathedral each year, from all over the world. Few are ever disappointed, for there is something here for everyone. Lovers of architecture will rejoice in the many different styles, blending to make the whole.

Ely Museum

The Old Gaol
Ely CB7 4LS
01353 666655
www.elymuseum.org.uk
admin@elymuseum.org.uk

Ely Museum is housed in one of the oldest buildings in Ely, dating from the 13th century, it has been a private house, a Tavern, a Registry Office & the Bishop's Goal. Sensitively renovated in 1997, much of the buildings history can still be seen, including prisoners' graffiti, hidden doorways and original planking on the walls.

Collections: The displays include fossils from marine dinosaurs, prehistoric tools and weapons, Roman pottery and Anglo Saxon jewellery. An archive film shows methods of farming in the past, and the Debtors and Condemned Cells show visitors what the Bishops' Gaol was really like.

Farmland Museum & Denny Abbey

Denny Abbey, Ely Road, Waterbeach
Cambridge CB25 9PQ
01223 860988
www.farmlandmuseum.org.uk
info@farmlandmuseum.org.uk

Explore the rural life of Cambridgeshire and discover the fascinating story of the Benedictine monks, Knights Templar and Franciscan nuns who lived in Denny Abbey. Peel away the layers of history in the abbey - from the Victorian farmhouse to the Norman interiors of the 12th century church and the 14th century Franciscan refectory. Find out about farming in the past by visiting the farm buildings including a 17th century thrashing barn, explore the craft workshops, which include a wheelwright and blacksmith.

Collections: Agricultural objects relating to Cambridgeshire, mostly 19th and 20th century which demonstrate the transition from hand tools to the mechanisation of farming. Domestic social history collection related to living in rural Cambridgeshire.

Fenland & West Norfolk Aviation Museum

Fenland & West Norfolk Aircraft Preservation Society, Old Lynn Road
West Walton, nr Wisbech PE14 7DA
http://goo.gl/KPRDvO

One of the finest and most interesting collections of aviation archaeology in the United Kingdom. All the exhibits (except the aircraft) are housed in purpose built premises comprising of three large themed halls, with interactive displays, well lit cabinets and structured themes.

Collections: A splendid collection of memorabilia, mostly associated with aviation past and present, including the second world war, Falklands conflict and Desert Storm. We have the cockpit from one of the two MiG 29's which collided at RAF Fairford (both pilots escaped injury) - the only MiG 29 cockpit in the UK.

Fenland Family History Society

Rose Hall, Walpole Bank, Walpole St Andrew
Wisbech PE14 7JD
www.fenlandfhs.org.uk
judy.green@farming.me.uk W:

The Fenland Family History Society was founded in 2001 to promote and encourage the study of family, local and social history with particular reference to persons having lived in, or having been associated with, the historical area now known as Fenland. Fenland comprises the former Isle of Ely, parts of South Lincolnshire and West Norfolk.

Fitzwilliam Museum

Trumpington Street
Cambridge CB2 1RB
01223 332900
www.fitzmuseum.cam.ac.uk
fitzmuseum-enquiries@lists.cam.ac.uk

From Egyptian coffins to Impressionist masterpieces – the Fitzwilliam Museum's world-class collections of art and antiquities span centuries and civilizations.

Flag Fen Archaeology Park

The Droveway, Northey Road
Peterborough PE6 7QJ
01733 313414
http://goo.gl/UdpZaV
info@flagfen.org

Flag Fen is the site of a 3500 year old ritual causeway and ceremonial platform. Made from wood it contains 60,000 upright timbers and has yielded one of the best collections of

Bronze Age Celtic swords, jewellery and tools in the country.

Collections: The museum of the Bronze Age at Flag Fen contains artefacts found on site, including the oldest wheel in England on permanent display.

Huntingdonshire Archives & Local Studies

Princes Street
Huntingdon PE29 3PA
01480 372738
http://goo.gl/EBikSS

Huntingdonshire Archives holds records relating to the former county of Huntingdonshire, which is roughly the area covered by the current Huntingdonshire District Council, as well as including Alwalton, Stanground, the Ortons and Fletton, which today form part of Peterborough City Council.

Huntingdonshire Family History Society

42 Crowhill, Godmanchester
Huntingdon PE29 2NR
01480 390476
www.huntsfhs.org.uk
secretary@huntsfhs.org.uk

Huntingdonshire Family History Society (HFHS) was founded in 1985 to help people to find out about their family history. The county reorganisation in 1974 saw Huntingdonshire become part of a greater Cambridgeshire.

IWM Duxford

IWM Duxford
Duxford CB22 4QR
01223 835 000
www.iwm.org.uk/visits/iwm-duxford
duxford@iwm.org.uk

IWM Duxford tells the story of the impact of aviation on the nature of war and on people's lives. Set within Britain's best-preserved Second World War fighter station, seven impressive hangars filled with extraordinary collections and state-of-the-art exhibitions take you on an unforgettable journey through times of war and peace.

Collections: The Normandy Experience looks at the dramatic invasion of Europe on D-Day, June 1944, and the events that followed in Normandy and NW Europe until the end of the war. 'Monty' reveals one of the men behind the events shown in The Normandy Experience - Field Marshal Montgomery. The British Aircraft Collection: A selection of military and civil aircraft for you to browse. The Naval Collection: A fascinating range of exhibits from midget submarines to naval helicopters. The Land Warfare Hall houses Duxford's collection of tanks, trucks and artillery. The Battle of Britain Exhibition looks at the people and machines involved in the Battle of Britain and the Blitz of 1940-1941. The American Air Museum houses the finest collection of historic American combat aircraft outside the United States. 'The Forgotten War' Exhibition highlights the political, military and the personal aspects of the Second World War in the Far East, the Pacific

and in particular, Burma between 1941 and 1945. The history of the Royal Anglian Regiment Museum from 1958 - 1960. Includes The Cambridgeshire Regiment Collection. AirSpace houses the finest collection of aircraft including iconic Concorde, the Lancaster and much more.

Kimbolton Castle

Kimbolton
Huntingdon PE28 0EA
01480 860 505
www.kimbolton.cambs.sch.uk/castle
Ncb@kimbolton.cambs.sch.uk

Kimbolton Castle, Katherine of Aragon's last residence, was largely rebuilt as the 18th century country house of the Earls and Dukes of Manchester, owners for nearly 350 years. Although the castle is now the home of Kimbolton School, there are outstanding Pellegrini murals and a fine collection of portraits. Architectural features include state rooms and exterior refacing by Vanbrugh and Hawksmoor, an inner courtyard probably by Henry Bell, and an Adam gatehouse.

Longthorpe Tower

Thorpe Road, Longthorpe
Peterborough PE1 1HA
01733 864663
www.vivacity-peterborough.com
longthorpe.tower@vivacity-peterborough.com

Longthorpe Tower was built around AD 1300. It is a very well preserved example of a solar tower, containing the private apartments of the owner of the fortified house.

March & District Museum

High Street
March PE15 9JJ
01354 655300
www.marchmuseum.co.uk
info@marchmuseum.co.uk

Set up as a local folk museum, there are a number of displays showing the life and times of the late 19th and early 20th Centuries and ongoing to the present day. Room arrangements represent a kitchen, parlour and nursery bedroom while the outside exhibits include a reconstructed working forge, a Fenland cottage and privy.

Museum of Archaeology & Anthropology

Downing Street
Cambridge CB2 3DZ
01223 333 516
maa.cam.ac.uk/maa
admin@maa.cam.ac.uk

Founded in 1884, the museum of Archaeology and Anthropology holds world-class collections of art and artefacts from all over the world, representing cultures and histories over millennia.

Museum of Cambridge - formerly Cambridge & County Folk Museum

🖾 £

2/3 Castle Street
Cambridge CB3 0AQ
01223 355159
www.museumofcambridge.org.uk
events@museumofcambridge.org.uk

Housed in the former White House Inn, this warm-hearted museum was founded in 1936 and has recently been renovated. Fun and interactive, the museum displays the everyday life of Cambridgeshire people.

Collections: Eight rooms to see, including The Inn Bar, The Kitchen, Domestic Crafts, University & City, Childhood and Fens & Folklore.

Museum of Classical Archaeology

🖾 ★

Sidgwick Avenue
Cambridge CB3 9DA
01223 335153
www.classics.cam.ac.uk/museum
museum-education@classics.cam.ac.uk

The museum of Classical Archaeology is one of nine University of Cambridge museums and collections. Why not leave the hustle and bustle of the city centre behind to discover a whole new way of seeing ancient art? Our cast gallery houses over 450 plaster casts of Greek and Roman sculpture, each of which has its own story to tell.

Nene Valley Railway Museum

🏠 🖾

Wansford Station, Stibbington
Peterborough PE8 6LR
01780 784444
www.nvr.org.uk
nvrorg@nvr.org.uk

Nene Valley Railway is the UK's leading international steam attraction, based at Wansford Station, and covering the stations of Ferry Meadows, Orton Mere, Yarwell Junction, and Peterborough. As both a living heritage railway, which is tended to by its loyal band of volunteers, and a thriving attraction for the public to enjoy all year round, Nene Valley Railway offers the chance to experience the thrill of riding a steam engine; learn about the railway's history; and explore the picturesque surroundings of the Nene Valley area.

Norris Museum, The

🖾 ★

The Broadway
St Ives PE27 5BX
01480 497314

www.norrismuseum.org.uk
info@norrismuseum.org.uk

The Norris Museum is a gem of a museum, telling the story of Huntingdonshire's past from the earliest times. We are located just down the road from Market Hill (the main shopping street) and we have an attractive garden which looks out onto the river.

Octavia Hill's Birthplace House Museum

🏠 🖾 🎪 ⅲ £

8 South Brink
Wisbech PE13 1JB
01945 476358
www.octaviahill.org
info@octaviahill.org

The Birthplace House was built in about 1740 on Wisbech's South Brink. As a Grade II* listed building, it is particularly important as a building of outstanding architectural or historic interest. The house was home to James and Caroline Hill as they undertook the social reform activities on which their daughter's life work was based.

Peckover House & Garden - National Trust

🏠 £

North Brink
Wisbech PE13 1JR
01945 583463
www.nationaltrust.org.uk/peckover-house
peckover@nationaltrust.org.uk

Georgian merchant's brick town house with walled garden. Many fine Victorian garden features, an orangery, summerhouses and fernery.

Peterborough & District Family History Society

ⅲ

7 Teasels, Deeping St James
Peterborough PE6 8SJ
01778 341 290
www.peterborofhs.org.uk
secpdfhs@btopenworld.com

We can help with genealogical resources when researching in the Soke of Peterborough and the cathedral areas.

Peterborough Museum

🏠 🖾 ★

Priestgate
Peterborough PE1 1LF
01733 864663
www.vivacity-peterborough.com
museum@vivacity-peterborough.com

Peterborough Museum is a fascinating and fun place to visit for all the family, right in the heart of the city centre. There are over 212,000 objects, which have been collected over 130 years.

Polar Museum, The

Scott Polar Research Institute, Lensfield Road
Cambridge CB2 1ER
01223 336540
www.spri.cam.ac.uk/museum
enquiries@spri.cam.ac.uk

The Scott Polar Research Institute was established in 1920 by Frank Debenham as a memorial to Scott and his companions. Debenham was a geologist on Captain Scott's British Antarctic (Terra Nova) Expedition 1910-13.

Collections: The museum holds an unrivalled collection of artefacts, paintings, drawings, photographs (including cinematographic film, lantern slides, and Daguerreotypes), and other material relating to polar exploration, history and science. The museum displays feature items from Scott's last expedition, including farewell letters to friends and family, diaries, the sleeping bag of Captain Oates, and the black flag left by Amundsen.

Prickwillow Drainage Engine Museum

Main Street, Prickwillow
Ely CB7 4UN
01353 688360
www.prickwillow-engine-museum.co.uk
enquiries@prickwillow-engine-museum.co.uk

The museum is housed in the original Prickwillow Engine House in a picturesque setting on the banks of the River Lark just a few miles from Ely, Lakenheath and Mildenhall. The original building has been extended in recent years to provide modern visitor facilities to cater for families and tourists, as well as the enthusiast of Britain's industrial heritage.

Railworld

Oundle Road
Peterborough PE2 9NR
01733 344240
www.railworld.net

Railworld has a superb 'OO' gauge Model Railway layout, with a number of features. We have refurbished the layout over the last 18 months, with new scenery, track layout alterations.

Ramsey Rural Museum

The Woodyard, Ramsey
Huntingdon PE26 2XE
01487 815715
www.ramseyruralmuseum.co.uk
dyardley@talk21.com

Ramsey Rural Museum is housed in a variety of 18th century farm buildings. The collections include a wide variety of agricultural implements and tools used by local craftsmen.

Royal Anglian Regiment Museum

Imperial War Museum, Duxford
Cambridge CB2 4QR
01223 497298
www.royalanglianmuseum.org.uk
info@royalanglianmuseum.co.uk

The museum is designed to inform the public about the regiment's history and accomplishments by collecting, recording and conserving items associated with the regiment in attractive, up-to-date displays. The Royal Anglian Regiment is the regiment of the ten Counties of East Anglia and the East Midlands and was the first Large Regiment of Infantry in the British Army. The museum covers the history of the East and Royal Anglian Regiments since the amalgamations of the former County Regiments from 1958-60.

Sedgwick Museum of Earth Sciences

University of Cambridge, Department of Earth Sciences, Downing Street
Cambridge CB2 3EQ
01223 333456
www.sedgwickmuseum.org
sedgwickmuseum@esc.cam.ac.uk

The Sedgwick Museum of Earth Sciences is the oldest of the University of Cambridge museums, having been established in 1728 as the Woodwardian Museum. Since then the collection has grown from about 10,000 fossils, minerals and rocks, to at least 2 million.

St Neots Museum

The Old Court, 8 New Street
St Neots PE19 1AE
01480 388921
www.stneotsmuseum.org.uk
stneotsmuseum@tiscali.co.uk

A lively local museum tells the story of this busy market town on the River Ouse, from prehistoric times to the present day.

Stained Glass Museum, Ely Cathedral

The South Triforium, Ely Cathedral
Ely CB7 4DL
01353 660347
www.stainedglassmuseum.com
info@stainedglassmuseum.com

The Stained Glass Museum's main aim is to help people understand and enjoy stained glass. Our Gallery exhibition illustrates over eight hundred years of the history and beauty of this ancient craft. Founded in the early 1970s the museum is located inside Ely Cathedral and is the only museum in the United Kingdom completely dedicated to stained glass.

Thorney Heritage Museum

🏛 🖼 🎢 ⭐

The Tankyard, Station Road
Thorney, Peterborough PE6 0QE
01733 270908
www.thorney-museum.org.uk
enquiry@thorney-museum.org.uk

The Thorney Heritage Museum is an independent museum operated by The Thorney Society. Our main aim is the preservation of the heritage of Thorney and to be a point of contact for education, research and general interest.

University Museum of Zoology

🖼 ⭐

Downing Street
Cambridge CB2 3EJ
01223 336650
www.museum.zoo.cam.ac.uk
umzc@zoo.cam.ac.uk

The museum of Zoology, part of Cambridge University's Department of Zoology, is home to a huge variety of recent and fossil animals. Displays trace the evolution of animal life, with intricately beautiful shells, a comprehensive collection of British birds, and many large skeletons of mammals. Our collections rival those of the major university museums world-wide, and are used for academic study by researchers within and beyond the University.

Collections: The museum's collections date back to 1814, and draw many of the earlier specimens from the great collecting expeditions of the 19th century, including Charles Darwin's 'Beagle' voyage.

University of Cambridge Museums

🎢 ⭐

Cambridge
01223 761067
www.cam.ac.uk/museums
museums@hermes.cam.ac.uk

University of Cambridge Museums is a consortium of the eight University Museums, which works in partnership with Cambridge University Botanic Garden. The University's collections are a world-class resource for researchers, students and members of the public representing the country's highest concentration of internationally important collections, all within walking distance of the City Centre.

Whipple Museum of the History of Science

🖼 ⭐

Department of History and Philosophy of Science, Free School Lane
Cambridge CB2 3RH
01223 330906
www.hps.cam.ac.uk/whipple
hps-whipple-museum@lists.cam.ac.uk

The Whipple Museum holds a pre-eminent collection of scientific instruments and models, dating from the Middle Ages to the present. The Main Gallery of the museum is housed in a large hall with Jacobean hammer-beam roof-trusses, built in 1618 as the first Cambridge Free School.

Whittlesey Museum

🖼

Town Hall, Market Street, Whittlesey
Peterborough PE7 1BD
07706 132437
http://goo.gl/UNHAA

Whittlesey Museum, housed on the ground floor of the 19th century Town Hall in Market Street, was opened in 1976. The Costumes Room was once used to house the town's horse drawn fire engine.

Wimpole Estate - National Trust

🏛 £

Old Wimpole Road, Arrington
Royston SG8 0BW
01223 206000
www.nationaltrust.org.uk/wimpole-estate
wimpolehall@nationaltrust.org.uk

Mrs Elsie Bambridge, daughter of Rudyard Kipling, bequeathed Wimpole Estate in Cambridgeshire, including the Grade I listed landscaped parkland, to the National Trust in 1976. Wimpole had a succession of owners from Lord Harley (1711-1740) to the Earls of Hardwicke (1740-1894) and Viscount's Clifden, before being bought by Elsie Bambridge in 1930s and has a roll-call of celebrated architects and landscape designers who have worked on it, each contributing their own layer to its varied history. Wimpole Home Farm set amidst 18th century thatched farm buildings is the largest rare breeds centre in East Anglia.

Wisbech & Fenland Museum

🖼 🏤 ⭐

Museum Square
Wisbech PE13 1ES
01945 583817
www.wisbechmuseum.org.uk
info@wisbechmuseum.org.uk

Wisbech & Fenland Museum is one of the oldest purpose-built museums in the country. The original Museum Society was formed in 1835, and the present building dates from 1847.

Collections: Thomas Clarkson and the Transatlantic Slave Trade: Wisbech is the home town of slavery abolitionist Thomas Clarkson and the museum holds documents, letters, books and artefacts relating to his work.

Cheshire

Cheshire, or Chester, county palatine and maritime county of England, bounded on the NW. by the Irish Sea, and bordering on the counties of Lancaster, York, Derby, Stafford, Salop, Denbigh, and Flint; extreme length, NE and SW., 58 miles; extreme breadth, 40 miles; average breadth, 18 miles; area, 657,123 acres; population 644,037. Cheshire forms, towards the Irish Sea, a flat peninsula, the Wirrall (12 miles by 7 miles), between the estuaries of the Mersey and the Dee, and inland a vast plain separating the mountains of Wales from those of Derbyshire. This plain is diversified with fine woods of oak, &c., and is studded with numerous small lakes or meres. A low ridge of sandstone hills runs N. from Congleton, near the E. border, and another extends from the neighbourhood of Malpas to Frodsham, near the estuary of the Mersey. The chief rivers are the Mersey with its affluent the Bollin, the Weaver, and the Dee. The soil consists of marl, mixed with clay and sand, and is generally fertile. There are numerous excellent dairy farms, on which the celebrated Cheshire cheese is made; also extensive market gardens, the produce of which is sent to Liverpool, Manchester, and the neighbouring towns. Salt has been long worked; it. is obtained from rock salt and saline springs; the principal works are at Nantwich, Northwich, and Winsford. Coal and ironstone are worked in the districts of Macclesfield and Stockport. There are mfrs. of cotton, silk, and ribbons, carried on chiefly in the towns of the E. division; and shipbuilding, on the Mersey. Cheshire contains 7 hundreds, 503 parishes and a part, the parliamentary and municipal borough of Birkenhead (1 member), the greater part of the parliamentary and municipal boroughs of Chester (1 member), Stalybridge (1 member), and Stockport (2 members), and the municipal boroughs of Congleton, Crewe, Hyde, and Macclesfield. It is mostly in the diocese of Chester.

– John Bartholomew, *Gazetteer of the British Isles* (1887)

Note: some of the former county of Cheshire has been in Merseyside since 1974.

Anderton Boat Lift

Lift Lane, Anderton
Northwich CW9 6FW
01606 786777
www.andertonboatlift.co.uk
info@andertonboatlift.co.uk

The Anderton Boat Lift is an incredible edifice, perched on the banks of the River Weaver like some giant three-storey-high iron spider. It was built by Edwin Clark in 1875 to lift cargo boats the 50 feet from the River Weaver to the Trent & Mersey Canal. Like all great things, the concept is simple: two huge water tanks, each with watertight sealable doors carry boats up and down. The original counter-balanced system was replaced in 1908 by electric operation, but the lift now works hydraulically again. The Operations Centre offers interactive displays and educational facilities.

Anson Engine Museum

Anson Road
Poynton SK12 1TD
01625 874426
www.enginemuseum.org
enquiry@enginemuseum.org

The main building houses a large collection of engines, maintained in running order ranging from early Crossley gas engines through to more modern diesels. Other buildings house specialist collections such as Gardner engines, Atmospheric engines, etc.

Beeston Castle & Woodland Park - English Heritage

Beeston Castle
Tarporley CW6 9TX
01829 260464
http://goo.gl/SVjftp

Climb to the top of the formidable Castle of the Rock with incredible views over eight counties, from the Pennines to the Welsh mountains. Excavations indicate that a Bronze Age settlement and Iron Age hill fort occupied the site long before Beeston Castle was begun in 1225.

Catalyst - Science Discovery Centre

Gossage Building, Mersey Road
Widnes WA8 0DF
0151 4201121
www.catalyst.org.uk
info@catalyst.org.uk

Catalyst is an interactive science centre and museum devoted to chemistry and how the products of chemistry are used in everyday life. Our key aim is to make science exciting and accessible to people of all ages and to inform them about science based industries and their role in our lives, past present and future.

Collections: The collection consists of nearly 7,050 individually numbered items and groups including objects, archive material and photographs. The objects range from test tubes to a 20 ton cast iron caustic soda finishing vessel and the archives include company documents of all kinds, product brochures and general ephemera.

Cheshire Archives & Local Studies Service

Cheshire Record Office, Duke Street
Chester CH1 1RL
01244 977195
archives.cheshire.gov.uk
recordoffice@cheshiresharedservices.gov.uk

The Service collects and preserves historical records relating to both the ancient and modern county of Cheshire, the diocese and the city of Chester. It makes the records available for study free of charge by members of the public.

Cheshire Military Museum

The Castle
Chester CH1 2DN
01244 403933
www.cheshiremilitarymuseum.co.uk
enquiries@cheshiremilitarymuseum.co.uk

In this museum we remember The Cheshire Regiment, The Cheshire Yeomanry, The 3rd Carabiniers, The 5th Royal Iniskilling Dragoon Guards, the Eaton Hall Officer Cadet School and several other small Cheshire units - some now long retired (often from bigger corps of the Army). We also remember the important role of the women of the regiments and the lives of those who were left behind when the men left home to fight.

Chester Cathedral

12 Abbey Square
Chester CH1 2HU
01244 324756
www.chestercathedral.com
events@chestercathedral.com

Chester Cathedral's history spans almost two thousand years. According to legend, a prehistoric Druid temple existed on this site, succeeded by a Roman temple dedicated to Apollo.

Chester History & Heritage

St Michael's Church, Bridge Street Row
Chester CH1 1NW
01244 972210
www.cheshirewestandchester.gov.uk/visiting
Elaine.Pierce-Jones@cheshirewestandchester.gov.uk

Chester History & Heritage is a local & family history resource centre sited in the heart of Chester. We offer free internet access via the popular People's Network and operate a family history advice service provided by research group experts - again - free to all customers.

Chester Roman Amphitheatre

Vicars Lane, Newgate
Chester CH1 1QX.
www.chester.gov.uk/amphitheatre/index.html

The largest Roman amphitheatre in Britain, partially excavated. It was used for entertainment and military training by the 20th Legion, based at the fortress of Deva.

Congleton Museum

Market Square
Congleton CW12 1BT
01260 276360
www.congletonmuseum.co.uk
info@congletonmuseum.co.uk

Displays featuring four main areas of the town's history: prehistoric times, including a log boat found at Astbury; the English Civil War, featuring John Bradshaw, who signed the death warrant of Charles I; the heyday of the textile industry; the Second World War.

Dewa Roman Experience

Pierpoint Lane, Off Bridge Street
Chester CH1 1NL
01244 343407
www.dewaromanexperience.co.uk
info@dewaromanexperience.co.uk

The actual Dewa Roman fortress is now buried under modern day Chester, but it lives on through the Dewa Roman Experience. Most museums have exhibits that are available to the visitor, but here we have an approach that is completely different. On entering, you go into the Roman Galley where there are exhibits of Roman Chester, many of which are 'hands on' type, where you can handle items such as pottery, try on a suit of Roman armour, fire the catapult and design mosaics.

Dunham Massey - National Trust

Dunham Massey
Altrincham WA14 4SJ
0161 941 1025
http://goo.gl/jPaSQH
dunhammassey@nationaltrust.org.uk

Until November 2015 Dunham Massey Hall is open as the Stamford Military hospital. During the First World War, this Georgian house, set in a magnificent deer-park, was transformed into a military hospital, becoming a sanctuary from the trenches for 282 soldiers.

Englesea Brook Chapel & Museum

Museum of Primitive Methodism, Englesea Brook
Crewe CW2 5QW
01270 820836
www.engleseabrook-museum.org.uk
engleseabrook-methodist-museum@supanet.com

A museum telling the story of a predominantly
working-class religious denomination (Primitive
Methodism) in a manner that raises questions about faith
and identity in the contemporary world. Much of the
museum is housed in a chapel dating to 1829.

Family History Society of Cheshire

Little Trees, Gawsworth Road, Gawsworth
Macclesfield SK11 9RA
01625 426173
www.fhsc.org.uk
info@fhsc.org.uk

The Family History Society of Cheshire (FHSC) was
founded in 1969 to advance the study of family history and
genealogy, and we now have around 3000 members
worldwide. As well as helping people with ancestors in
Cheshire, we also assist members living locally whose
ancestors originated elsewhere.

Football & the First World War

3 Standingwood Road Ellesmere Port
Ellesmere Port CH65 3AG
www.footballandthefirstworldwar.com
iainmcmullen@gmail.com

The Football and the First World War Centenary Project is
working in partnership with the National Football Museum
and the Institute of Education's Legacy 110 programme to
create a comprehensive and detailed record of association
football during the Great War.

Grosvenor Museum

27 Grosvenor Street
Chester CH1 2DD
01244 972197
westcheshiremuseums.co.uk
ruth.marshall@cheshirewestandchester.gov.uk

The Grosvenor Museum was founded in 1885 and its
origins are linked to the Chester Society of Natural Science
Literature & Art founded by Charles Kingsley in 1871, and
to Chester Archaeological Society. The museum holds an
internationally important collection of Roman Stones,
found in the City walls in the 19th century.

Hack Green Secret Nuclear Bunker

c/o P.O. Box 127
Nantwich CW5 8AQ
01270 629219
www.hackgreen.co.uk
coldwar@hackgreen.co.uk

Discover the secret world of nuclear government For over
50 years this vast underground complex, remained secret,
hidden on the outskirts of a sleepy Cheshire town.
Declassified in 1993, the 35,000 sq ft underground bunker
would have been the centre of Regional Government had
nuclear war broken out. Built in the 1950s as part of a vast
secret radar network codenamed 'ROTOR'.

King Charles Tower

City Walls
Chester CH1 2DD
01244 402008
www.chestertourist.com/charles.htm

Standing on the North-East corner of the city walls over
looking the canal, is the tower called 'King Charles's Tower'.
Called so because legend (incorrectly) has it on the 24th of
September 1645. King Charles stood on the tower and
watched his army defeated in the battle of Rowton Moor.

Knutsford Heritage Centre

90a King Street
Knutsford WA16 6ED
01565 650 506
www.knutsfordheritage.com

Knutsford Heritage Centre is housed in a reconstucted 17th
timber-framed building which was originally the town's
blacksmiths. It is set amongst secluded courtyard gardens
behind the bustling streets of Knutsford. The centre is most
famously home to the Knutsford Millennium Tapestry, a
40ft masterpiece which was created by over 3,000 members
of the local community to celebrate Knutsford in the
Millennium Year. The centre also houses a temporary
exhibitions gallery with a range of displays throughout the
year, a permanent display on the story of Knutsford and a
well-stocked gift shop.

Lion Salt Works

Ollershaw Lane, Marston
Northwich CW9 6ES
01606 41823
westcheshiremuseums.co.uk
info@lionsaltworkstrust.co.uk

In 1986 the Lion Salt Works closed after the collapse of the
West African salt market. It was purchased by Vale Royal
Borough Council to prevent its demolition. Salt-making in
Cheshire dates back over 2,000 years, when the salt towns
of Cheshire were first established by the Romans.

Little Moreton Hall - National Trust

Congleton CW12 4SD
01260 272018
www.nationaltrust.org.uk/little-moreton-hall
littlemoretonhall@nationaltrust.org.uk

Moated manor house – the icon of English Tudor domestic architecture. This is Britain's most famous and arguably finest timber-framed manor house.

Liverpool Scottish Regimental Museum

c/o Major IL Riley TD FSA Scot, The Shambles, 51a Common Lane, Culcheth
Warrington WA3 4EY
01925 766157
www.liverpoolscottish.org.uk
ilriley@liverpoolscottish.org.uk

A permanent physical museum to hold the collection of objects and archival material is longer feasible. However modern technology does allow the Trust to fulfill its remit in other ways. To this end a series of programmes and projects to digitize the collection before disposal and preserve the archive are underway.

Collections: The museum collection includes the uniforms and other military artefacts covering 100 years of the history of a kilted Scottish volunteer infantry regiment established in Liverpool. The collection of photographs and other documentary information is extensive.

Lyme Park, House & Garden - National Trust

Lyme Park, Disley
Stockport SK12 2NX
01663 762023
www.nationaltrust.org.uk/lyme-park
lymepark@nationaltrust.org.uk

Great estate with lavishly decorated house and fine gardens. Originally a Tudor house, Lyme was transformed by the Venetian architect Leoni into an Italianate palace.

Museum of the South Lancashire Regiment

Peninsula Barracks
Warrington WA2 7BR
01925 33563
http://goo.gl/268hRi

The South Lancashire Regiment was formed in 1881 as a result of the Cardwell reforms of the British Army. With its Regimental Depot at Peninsula Barracks, Warrington, the regiment initially consisted of two battalions, with the 1st formed from the former 40th Regiment of Foot, and the 2nd from the former 82nd (Prince of Wales's Volunteers). The regiment recruited primarily from that area of South Lancashire which is centred on the townships of Warrington and St Helens. During World War I the regiment expanded to a total strength of 21 battalions. They served on the Western Front, at Gallipoli, and in Macedonia, Egypt, Mesopotamia (modern-day Iraq) and India.

Nantwich Museum

Pillory Street
Nantwich CW5 5BQ
01270 627104
www.nantwichmuseum.org.uk
enquiries@nantwichmuseum.org.uk

The fascinating history of one of Cheshire's most attractive and historic towns is brought to life by Nantwich Museum. Located in Pillory Street, at the heart of the town, the museum has main galleries telling the story of Nantwich through the ages - Roman salt making, Tudor Nantwich's Great Fire, the Civil War Battle of Nantwich (1644) and the more recent shoe and clothing industries.

Nether Alderley Mill - National Trust

Congleton Road, Nether Alderley
Macclesfield SK10 4TW
01625 527468
www.nationaltrust.org.uk/nether-alderley-mill
netheralderleymill@nationaltrust.org.uk

15th-century mill beside a tranquil mill pool: * Original Victorian water wheel is a unique tandem design * Mammoth 200 ton stone roof supported by a fine timber frame * Restored to full working order, with regular flour-grinding demonstrations.

North Cheshire Family History Society

9 Kitts Moss Lane, Bramhall
Stockport SK7 2BG
0161 439 2635
www.ncfhs.org.uk
liz.demercado@ntlworld.com

The aim of the society, which was founded in 1976, is to bring together those who are interested in the study of their family history, to give lectures about the availability of records and how to use them; to hold discussion meetings at which more experienced members can help beginners; to further genealogy and co-ordinate research and the transcription of records. We cover all areas in and around Stockport, Hazel Grove, Bramhall, Hyde, Stalybridge, Mottram in Longdendale, Sale, Wilmslow, Altrincham, Knutsford and Macclesfield.

Norton Priory Museum & Gardens

[icons]

The Norton Priory Museum Trust, Tudor Road, Manor Park
Runcorn WA7 1SX
01928 569895
www.nortonpriory.org
info@nortonpriory.org

Norton Priory Museum & Gardens is an award winning museum, excavated medieval ruins, the spectacular St Christopher statue, the lovely Walled Garden and the extensive woodland and sculpture trail.

Paradise Mill

[icons]

Park Lane
Macclesfield SK11 6TJ
01625 618288
www.silk-macclesfield.org
info@macclesfield.silk.museum

Paradise Mill, situated a short distance from the Silk Museum, was a working silk mill until 1981. Today, Paradise Mill is a living museum.

Quarry Bank Mill & Styal Estate - National Trust

[icons]

Styal
Nr Wilmslow SK9 4LA
01625 527468
www.nationaltrust.org.uk/quarry-bank
quarrybankmill@nationaltrust.org.uk

Quarry Bank Mill is a first generation water powered cotton mill built in 1784: see the waterwheel, steam engines and cotton machinery working daily. Guided tours of the Apprentice House show what life was like for the pauper children who worked in the Mill.

Collections: Greg business and family papers dating from 1784 to 1959, Quarry Bank Mill archive, general social history and cotton industry collection.

Silk Museum

[icons]

Heritage Centre
Macclesfield SK11 6UT
01625 613210
www.silkmacclesfield.org.uk
info@macclesfield.silk.museum

The Silk Museum within the Heritage Centre follows the story of silk from its origins in China, along the silk route to Britain and its establishment in Macclesfield. An award winning audio-visual presentation tells of the development of the industry in the town from the perspective of various people involved in the silk industry. The story of silk comes to an end as we consider how silk is used in fashion. Costume, textiles and accessories from both the 19th and 20th century help to show how silk is used for some of the most important occasions in both the social calendar and family life.

Stretton Watermill

[icons]

Mill Lane, Stretton
Nr Farndon SY14 7HS
01606 271640
www.strettonwatermill.org.uk
cheshiremuseums@cheshire.gov.uk

A small working water mill set in beautiful countryside only ten miles from Chester. Visitors see the two waterwheels driving the ancient wooden mill machinery and turning the millstones.

Tatton Park - National Trust

[icons]

Tatton Park
Knutsford WA16 6SG
01625 374400
www.nationaltrust.org.uk/tatton-park
tatton@cheshireeast.gov.uk

Magnificent estate with mansion, grand garden, deer park, farm and Tudor old hall. * Neo-Classical mansion, home to a grand array of antiques and furniture * Fine Victorian arboretum, including a fernery, orangery and Japanese garden.

Trafford Local Studies Centre

[icons]

Sale Library, Sale Waterside
Sale M33 7ZF
0161 912 3013
http://goo.gl/fNVul7
trafflocals@trafford.gov.uk

The Local Studies Centre collects and preserves material relating to the towns and rural areas which now make up the Metropolitan Borough of Trafford. In addition to general local history material, the library also houses a great deal of information which is of interest to anyone researching his or her own family tree.

Warrington Museum & Art Gallery

[icons]

Museum Street
Warrington WA1 1JB
01925 442733
www.warringtonmuseum.co.uk
museum@culturewarrington.org

One of the oldest municipal museums in the country, Warrington Museum & Art Gallery recently celebrated its 150th anniversary. Much of the quintessential character of the building has been preserved and its original glass cabinets are crammed with treasures from all around the world.

Water Tower

City Walls
Chester CH1 2DD
01244 402008
www.chester.gov.uk/main.asp?page=924

The Water Tower stands at the north-west corner of the medieval walled city of Chester, and is now one of the best-preserved features of its defences.

Waterways Archive (CRT), The

Canal and River Trust, National Waterways Museum, South Pier Road
Ellesmere Port CH65 4FW
0151 373 4378
https://goo.gl/0HCZST
archives@canalrivertrust.org.uk

Archive Collection for British Waterways (now Canal & River Trust) and private collections initiated by The Boat Museum, Ellesmere Port;The Canal Museum, Stoke Bruerne and National Waterways Museum, Gloucester Covers mainly early 1700s to late 1900s. Also specialist Canal interest library.

Weaver Hall Museum & Workhouse

162 London Road
Northwich CW9 8AB
01606 271640
www.fowhm.org.uk
cheshiremuseums@cheshire.gov.uk

The Salt Museum works to conserve and promote the history of the Cheshire salt industry and the communities of the Cheshire salt towns. Roughly 200 million years ago, in the Triassic era vast, salt deposits were laid down under what is now the county of Cheshire in England.

Collections: Through original artefacts, models, re-constructions, old photographs, paintings and interactive exhibits Weaver Hall Museum, housed in the old Northwich Workhouse, tells the story of the mid Cheshire area. Students and local history researchers are welcome to make use of a range of resource material by appointment.

West Park Museum

West Park, Prestbury Road
Macclesfield SK10 3BJ
01625 613210
http://goo.gl/3jGc9t
info@macclesfield.silk.museum

Founded in 1898 by the Brocklehurst family. A small, but significant collection of Egyptian antiquities and a range of fine and decorative arts and objects. West Park Museum's Collections comprise a wide range of fine and decorative art material and objects relating to local history.

Cornwall

Cornwall – maritime county of England, forming its SW. extremity; is bounded by Devon on the E., and washed on all the other sides by the sea; length, NE. and SW., 75 miles; average breadth, 22 miles; coastline, about 200 miles; area, 863,665 acres, population. 330,686. The S. coast is much and deeply indented, and has some good harbours. The principal openings from W. to E. are Mounts Bay, Falmouth Bay and Harbour, St Austell Bay, Fowey Harbour, Whitsand Bay, and Plymouth Sound. Falmouth is one of the finest harbours in Britain. The indentations on the N. consist of shallow bays with few or no harbours. The chief promontories are Land's End, where the granite cliffs are about 60 ft. high; and the Lizard, the most S. point of England. The Isles of Scilly lie off Land's End, 25 miles to the SW. The Devonian range extends NE. and SW., rising in Brown Willy to an altitude of 1368 ft. The streams are numerous, but small. The principal are the Tamar (which forms the boundary with Devon), Lyhner, Fowey, and Camel. There is much barren moorland, but the soil in the valleys is fertile. The prevailing rock is granite, of a grey or bluish-grey colour, which often rises above the surface in huge, rugged masses; clay slate also abounds. The tin and copper mines of Cornwall have been celebrated from remote ages, having been known, it is supposed, to the Phoenicians. Some of them are of very great depth, and have been carried beneath the sea. Silver, lead, zinc, arsenic, antimony, and bismuth are also found in considerable quantities. The fisheries, especially of pilchard and mackerel, are extensive and valuable. The county comprises 9 hundreds, the Isles of Scilly, 219 parishes, the parliamentary borough of Penryn and Falmouth (1 member), and the municipal boroughs of Bodmin, Falmouth, Helston, Launceston, Liskeard, Penryn, Penzance, St Ives, and Truro. It is entirely in the diocese of Truro.

– John Bartholomew, *Gazetteer of the British Isles* (1887)

Barbara Hepworth Museum & Sculpture Garden - Tate

Barnoon Hill
St Ives TR26 1AD
01736 796 226
http://goo.gl/mjjmJQ

Barbara Hepworth's studio and garden have been run by the Tate since 1980, and are now an integral part of Tate St Ives. Hepworth, who died in 1975, asked in her will that Trewyn Studios and the adjacent garden, with a group of her sculptures placed as she wished, be permanently open to the public. Visiting the museum and Garden is a unique experience, which gives remarkable insight into the work and outlook of one of Britain's most important 20th-century artists.

Bodmin Town Museum

Mount Folly
Bodmin PL31 2HQ
01208 77067
http://goo.gl/PXjOAx
info@bodmintownmuseum.plus.com

Interesting local history museum using photographs, text and artefacts in displays showing rocks and minerals, WWI and WWII showcases, model forge, agricultural implements, a Cornish kitchen (Victorian), Bardic items, law and order, wildlife, railways, local worthies, medieval church exhibits, Victoriana and fire service including 1770 fire engine.

Bodrifty Iron Age Settlement

Bodrifty Farm, Newmill
Penzance TR20 8XT
01736 361217
www.bodrifty.co.uk
mustill@bodrifty.co.uk

In this area of enclosed moorland are the remains of an Iron Age (600 BC - AD 43) settlement, consisting of the ruins of eight roundhouses within a low enclosing bank. The site was excavated in the 1950s and a wider area surveyed in 1985. Some Bronze Age pottery was found indicating occupation.

Caerhays

Gorran
St Austell PL26 6LY
01872 501310
www.caerhays.co.uk

The imposing edifice of Caerhays Castle has at first glance the appearance of a Norman stronghold. In fact the building was in fact built by the famous architect, John Nash during the 19th century for John Bettesworth Trevanion.

Callington Heritage Centre

Liskeard Road
Callington PL17 7HA
01579 389506
http://goo.gl/W6TLj5
enquiry@callingtonheritage.org.uk

Callington Heritage Centre is situated in the former chapel building on Liskeard Road, Callington. Our interests span all aspects of the social and economic history of Callington and all the surrounding parishes.

Caradon Hill Area Heritage Project

Minions Heritage Centre, Minions
Liskeard PL14 5LJ
01579 362 350
www.chahp.blogspot.co.uk
CHAHP@cornwall.gov.uk

The Caradon Hill Area Heritage Project is a Living Landscape Project funded by the Heritage Lottery Fund, the RDPE and local partners.

Castle Bude, The

Lower Wharf
Bude EX23 8LG
01288 357302
www.thecastlebude.org.uk
pwright@bude-stratton.gov.uk

Bude-Stratton Museum was established in 1974 by the Town Council in an old blacksmith's forge once owned by Bude Canal. By 1994 it had become the first north Cornwall museum to gain MGC Certification status. In 2007 it was renamed 'heritage centre' and re-housed in the Council's newly renovated building, The castle.

Charlestown Shipwreck & Heritage Centre

Quay Road, Charlestown
St Austell PL25 3NJ
01726 69897
www.shipwreckcharlestown.com

The centre tells the history of diving, salvage and shipwrecks from the earliest times to the present day. Originally a dry house for china clay on underground tunnels that visitors can explore.

Chysauster Ancient Village - English Heritage

Gulval
Penzance TR20 8XA
07831 757934
http://goo.gl/Er4tU9

This Iron Age settlement was originally occupied almost 2,000 years ago. The village consisted of stone-walled homesteads known as 'courtyard houses', found only on the Land's End peninsula and the Isles of Scilly.

Constantine Heritage Collection

The Tolmen Centre, Fore Street
Constantine TR11 5AA
01326 341353 / 340279
www.constantinecornwall.com/heritage

From mining and quarrying, music and farming, bowling, and bands to cricket, art and religion, Constantine has a fascinating past. The museum reflects the life and times of this vibrant community near the Helford River.

Cornish Studies Library

The Cornwall Centre, Alma Place
Redruth TR15 2AT
01209 216760
www.cornwall.gov.uk
cornishstudies.library@cornwall.gov.uk

Local Studies library dealing with all things Cornish.

Cornwall Council

http://goo.gl/YK7mah
cro@cornwall.gov.uk

Cornwall Council's Archives and Cornish Studies Service is made up of Cornwall Record Office (in Truro) and the Cornish Studies Library (in Redruth). Together, they are home to hundreds of thousands of manuscripts, maps, photographs and books related to Cornwall's history.

Cornwall Family History Society

5 Victoria Square
Truro TR1 2RS
01872 264044
www.cornwallfhs.com
secretary@cornwallfhs.com

Since its beginning in 1976, the society has aimed to become a 'centre of excellence' by encouraging Cornish family history research. This is being achieved by publishing a quarterly Journal, co-ordinating the transcription and indexing of over 5 million original records, maintaining a research library in Truro for members and the general public and offering a means of worldwide contact and exchange of information between members.

Cornwall Record Office

Old County Hall
Truro TR1 3AY
01872 323127
www.cornwall.gov.uk/cro
cro@cornwall.gov.uk

Cornwall Record Office provides a professional archive service for Cornwall. Its main purpose is to ensure that the archives relating to the people, places and organisations of Cornwall are preserved for the future and made available, where possible, for public consultation.

Cornwall's Regimental Museum

The Keep
Bodmin PL31 1EG
01208 72810
www.cornwalls-regimentalmuseum.org
enquiries@cornwalls-regimentalmuseum.org

Cornwall's Regimental Museum is recognized as probably the finest Military Museum in the South West of England. Housed in 'The Keep' at Bodmin, which is a Grade II listed building, constructed at the time of the Napoleonic threats, the collection tells the story of the County Regiment from 1702 until the present date. The displays cover the story of the Duke of Cornwall's Light Infantry, the volunteers and volunteer militia and the successor Regiment, The Light Infantry.

Cotehele - National Trust

St Dominick
Saltash PL12 6TA
01579 351346
www.nationaltrust.org.uk/cotehele
cotehele@nationaltrust.org.uk

Medieval house with superb collections of textiles, armour and furniture, set in extensive grounds.

Cotehele Mill - National Trust

St Dominick
Saltash PL12 6TA
01579 351346
www.nationaltrust.org.uk/cotehele-mill
cotehele@nationaltrust.org.uk

Restored working watermill and agricultural workshops. Flour produced is regularly available for sale.

Davidstow Airfield Cornwall at War Museum

Nottles Park, Davidstow
Camelford PL32 9YF
07799 194918
www.cornwallatwarmuseum.co.uk

The Davidstow Airfield Cornwall at War Museum has a wide remit, dedicated primarily to RAF Davidstow moor from its opening on 1st October 1942 until its closure at the end of 1945. It also covers all the other airfields along the North Cornwall coast, the Royal Navy in and around the county, the Army civilian services, home front etc.

East Pool Mine - National Trust

Pool
Near Redruth TR15 3ED
01209 315027
www.nationaltrust.org.uk/east-pool-mine
eastpool@nationaltrust.org.uk

At the very heart of the Cornish Mining World Heritage Site sit two great beam engines, originally powered by high-pressure steam boilers introduced by local hero Richard Trevithick. Preserved in their towering engine houses, they are a reminder of Cornwall's days as a world-famous centre of industry, engineering and innovation.

Elliotts Grocery Store

27 Lower Fore Street
Saltash PL12 6JQ
01752 843388/ 07767 444816
http://goo.gl/gSqsq0

Elliott's Store was closed in the 1970s and remains as it was when closed, although the fixtures and fitings predate this by many decades. An exhibition concentrates on the history of the family, the building and local social history.

Fowey Museum

Town Hall, Trafalgar Square
Fowey PL3 1AT
01726 833513
www.museumsincornwall.org.uk/museums/fowey-museum

Housed in the old Fowey Borough Council Chamber the collection illustrates the past social and civic history of the town. Includes mayoral regalia, costumes, old photographs, models of old sailing ships postcards, etc.

Geevor Tin Mine Museum & Heritage Centre

Pendeen
Penzance TR19 7EW
01736 788662
www.geevor.com
bookings@geevor.com

Geevor, situated amid the dramatic scenery of Cornwall's Atlantic coast, is the largest mining history site in the UK. Here you can see how tin was mined and then processed.

Gerrans Heritage Centre

The Old Forge,
Tregassick Road TR2 5EF
01872 580274
www.gerransheritage.co.uk/index.htm

The history of Gerrans Parish is represented in the Heritage Centre through displays depicting farming through the ages, the fishing industry, education, Domesday Book entries and much more. Displays are illustrated with photographs, tithe maps and other documents.

Godolphin - National Trust

Godolphin Cross
Helston TR13 9RE
01736 763194
www.nationaltrust.org.uk/godolphin
godolphin@nationaltrust.org.uk

A historic house and medieval garden all set within an ancient and atmospheric estate Discover Godolphin, one of the most fashionable houses in Cornwall in the 17th century. Long since abandoned, you can soak up the atmosphere of peace and antiquity as you explore this romantic home. Wander around the 16th century garden, one of the most important historic gardens in Europe.

Grampound with Creed Heritage Centre

Old Town Hall,
Fore Street TR2 4QS
01726 883214
www.grampound.org.uk/?q=heritage-centre

The Grampound with Creed Heritage Project has opened a Heritage Centre. It is accommodated in the Old Town Hall at Grampound and comprises a listening post for oral histories, a digital photo-archive, wall banners showing the history of the area and a short film about the locality.

Harveys Foundry Trust / Hayle Heritage Centre

John Harvey House, 24 Foundry Square
Hayle TR27 4HH
01736 757683
Hayleheritagecentre.org.uk
enquiries@harveysfoundrytrust.org.uk

Hayle Heritage Centre is run by Harvey's Foundry Trust - a charity that has for over 20 years been working to protect and promote Hayles rich heritage. The centre is based at Harvey's Foundry site renowned for its contribution to major engineering projects of the 19th century and is associated with great engineers of the Industrial Revolution.

Helston Folk Museum

Old Butter Market, Market Place
Helston TR13 8TH
01326 564027
http://goo.gl/yxYKZx
Helston.museum@kerrier.gov.uk

Housed in the former butter and meat markets, now also the Drill Hall, the museum was established in 1949. The collection is mainly Victorian and covers all aspects of life on the Lizard Peninsula.

Holywell & Crantock - National Trust

North Cornwall coast
near Newquay TR8 5RN
0191 2557610
www.nationaltrust.org.uk/holywell-and-crantock
northcornwall@nationaltrust.org.uk

The Holy Jesus Hospital is a hidden Gem in the centre of Newcastle upon Tyne with over 700 years of history to explore. Home to an Augustinian Friary, an alms house, a soup kitchen and a Tudor tower, the site covers a wide period of history.

Hypatia Trust

Trevelyan House, 16 Chapel Street
Penzance TR18 4AW
01736 366597
www.hypatia-trust.org.uk
info@hypatia-trust.org.uk

The Hypatia Trust has been created to collect, and make available, published and personal documentation about the achievements of women in every aspect of their lives. Central to the Trust's activities is the care and development of the Hypatia Collection, a unique collection of books, artefacts, and archives, by and about women. The Hypatia Library was set up in 1996, with registered offices at the Jamieson Library, Newmill, Penzance, Cornwall to protect and develop the extensive collections of archives

(scrapbooks, diaries, letters), books, periodicals, artefacts and ephemera, and audio-visual materials formed over a 30 year period by Melissa Hardie, who now serves as the company secretary and one of the Trustees.

Isles of Scilly Museum

Church Street
St Mary's, Isles of Scilly TR21 0JT
01720 422337
www.iosmuseum.org
info@iosmuseum.org

Following the severe gales in the winter of 1962, Nornour (Eastern Isles) yielded up some remarkable Romano-British finds, causing some St Mary's residents to establish a local museum. After much fundraising and thanks to huge volunteer enthusiasm, the present Museum was built.

King Edward Mine Museum

Troon
Camborne TR14 9HW
01209 714681
www.kingedwardmine.co.uk
info@kingedwardmine.co.uk

The award-winning King Edward Mine Museum specialises in the mining history of Cornwall. It tells the remarkable story of how this mine has survived almost unaltered for over 100 years.

Lanhydrock - National Trust

Lanhydrock
Bodmin PL30 5AD
01208 265950
www.nationaltrust.org.uk/lanhydrock
lanhydrock@nationaltrust.org.uk

One of the most fascinating and complete late 19th-century houses in England, Lanhydrock is full of period atmosphere. Although the gatehouse and north wing (with magnificent 32yd-long gallery with plaster ceiling) survive from the 17th century, the rest of the house was rebuilt following a disastrous fire in 1881.

Launceston Castle - English Heritage

Launceston PL15 7DR
01566 772365
http://goo.gl/r0PJkR

Set on a large natural mound, Launceston Castle dominates the surrounding landscape. Begun soon after the Norman Conquest, its focus is an unusual keep consisting of a 13th-century round tower built by Richard Earl of Cornwall, inside an earlier circular shell-keep.

Lawrence House - National Trust

9 Castle Street
Launceston PL15 8BA
01566 773277
www.nationaltrust.org.uk/lawrence-house
lawrencehousemuseum@yahoo.co.uk

Lawrence House, Launceston, is a fine Georgian house built in 1753, located in a street which John Betjeman described as 'having the most perfect collection of 18th century townhouses in Cornwall'. It is owned by the National Trust and leased to Launceston Town Council, who use it to house the town museum, and for the Mayor to host small gatherings.

Leach Pottery

Higher Stennack
St Ives TR26 2HE
01736 799703
www.leachpottery.com
office@leachpottery.com

The Leach Pottery in St Ives was established by Bernard Leach and Shoji Hamada in 1920. One of the great figures of 20th century art, Leach played a crucial pioneering role in creating an identity for artist potters in Britain and around the world. Today, following a restoration and rebuild project which was completed in 2008, the Leach Pottery includes the historic workshop and kilns, a dedicated museum space, contemporary gallery and shop and working production studios where the new range of Leach tableware is made by a small international team of potters and apprentices.

Levant Mine & Beam Engine - National Trust

Trewellard Pendeen
near St Just TR19 7SX
01736 786156
www.nationaltrust.org.uk/levant-mine
levant@nationaltrust.org.uk

Part of the Cornwall and West Devon Mining World Heritage Site, this is the only Cornish beam engine anywhere in the world that is still in steam on its original mine site. The famous Levant engine is housed in a small engine house perched on the edge of the cliffs.

Liskeard & District Museum

Foresters Hall, Pike Street
Liskeard PL14 3JE
01579 346087
www.liskeardmuseum.org
enquiries@liskeardmuseum.org

The Caradon mining area is a magnet for industrial heritage enthusiasts. The remains of engine houses on the south eastern edge of Bodmin Moor tell of 19th century mines producing copper, tin and other minerals.

Lost Gardens of Heligan, The

Pentewan
St.Austell PL26 6EN
01726 845100
www.heligan.com
info@heligan.com

Lying at the heart of one of the most mysterious estates in England, Heligan, the former seat of the Tremayne family, is now the site of the largest garden restoration in Europe. Its extraordinary plant collection together with a range of exotic glasshouses, working buildings, romantic structures and designed landscapes reflect the past passions and interests of the family.

Lostwithiel Museum

16 Fore Street
Lostwithiel PL22 0AS
01208 873341
http://goo.gl/espEiw

12th century Lostwithiel was an important town and major port, becoming the capital of Cornwall in the 13th century. Today's fully accredited museum is a registered charity run by volunteers.

Marazion Museum

Town Hall, Market Place
Marazion TR17 0AP
http://goo.gl/H1R57w

A very small museum run by enthusiastic volunteers. The museum houses many artefacts - around 90% of which come from Marazion - and the collections depict life in the town of last century.

Mary Newman's Cottage

48 Culver Road,
Saltash PL12 4DS
01752 848466
http://goo.gl/5imYk7

The cottage gives an insight into Tudor life for the majority of Elizabethans. The interior has a kitchen and bedroom and the garden is a replica of Elizabethan style and includes many plants of the age and information on their uses.

Mevagissey Museum

East Wharf,
Inner Harbour PL26 6QR
01726 843568
www.mevagisseymuseum.co.uk

History's first mention of Mevagissey is in 1313, but its fine, harbourside museum suggests it is much older. Older even than the two 6th century Irish missionaries who gave it its name, or the archaeologically attested trade with Phoenicians in copper and tin.

Mount Edgcumbe House

Cremyll
Torpoint PL10 1HZ
01752 822 236
www.mountedgcumbe.gov.uk
mt.edgcumbe@plymouth.gov.uk

Mount Edgcumbe House is the former home of the Earls of Mount Edgcumbe. Set in Grade I Cornish Gardens within 865 acres Country Park on the Rame Peninsula, South East Cornwall.

Murdoch House

Cross Street, Redruth, United Kingdom
Redruth TR15 2BU
01209 215736
www.murdochhouse.org
dennis.mrtn@googlemail.com

In the late 18th century, the home of William Murdoch, the Scottish Engineer who erected steam engines in the Cornish copper and tin mines and where he perfected the technique of gas lighting. Also the home of the Cornish Global Migration Project.

Museum of Witchcraft

The Harbour
Boscastle PL35 0HD
01840 250 111
www.museumofwitchcraft.com
museumwitchcraft@aol.com

The museum of Witchcraft houses the world's largest collection of witchcraft related artefacts and regalia. The museum has been in Boscastle since 1960 and is one of Cornwalls most popular museums. Attached to the museum is library which has over 5500 occult related titles, and can be accessed by appointment, and is free of charge for members of 'Friends of the Boscastle museum of Witchcraft' - a charity created to support the museum.

Newquay Old Cornwall Society

Secretary, 11, St Aubyn Crescent
Newquay TR7 2RQ
01637 873976
www.newquay.oldcornwall.org.uk
shinner.chris@gmail.com

The object of the society is to advance the education of the public in Cornish pre-history, history, traditions, folklore, music, industries and in the Cornish language. The society arranges lectures, exhibitions, seminars and visits and participates in the activities of the Federation of Old Cornwall Societies.

Old Guildhall & Gaol at East Looe

Old Guildhall and Gaol, Higher Market Street
East Looe PL13 1BP
01503 262070
www.eastlooetowntrust.co.uk/looe-museum.php

The museum features the socioeconomic history of the town since Norman times. Later history, illustrated in over 600 photographs which date from the 1870s, featuring fishing boats, lifeboats, the railway & canal used to transport ore & materials to the mining district around Caradon are all featured.

Padstow Museum

The Institute, Market Place
Padstow PL28 8AL
01841 532752
www.padstowmuseum.co.uk
museum@chynoweth.co.uk

This small but interesting museum is situated just 20 metres from the harbour side in the port of Padstow on the North Cornish Coast. Initially set up in 1971 by an enthusiastic group of local residents headed by retired boat builder Bill Lindsey, it holds an interesting collection of artefacts giving an insight into the history of the Port of Padstow over the past two centuries.

Pendennis Castle - English Heritage

Falmouth TR11 4LP
01326 316594
http://goo.gl/KoE0Xr

Discover the wartime secrets of Cornwall's greatest fortress. Pendennis Castle was built by King Henry VIII to defend against possible attack by Spain and France.

Penlee House Gallery & Museum

Morrab Road
Penzance TR18 4HE
01736 363625
www.penleehouse.org.uk
info@penleehouse.org.uk

Penlee House is the only Cornish public gallery specialising in the Newlyn School artists (c.1880 - c.1940) including Stanhope and Elizabeth Forbes, Walter Langley, Harold Harvey and Laura Knight. Set in an elegant Victorian house and park, Penlee House also covers West Cornwall's archaeology and social history, and offers an excellent café and well-stocked shop.

Penryn Museum

Town Hall,
Higer Market Street TR10 8LT
01326 372158
http://goo.gl/bSiVwi

Our small museum encompasses interesting objects from the vast span of unique history of Penryn and gives an insight into the people who created our past.

Perranzabuloe Museum

Oddfellows Hall, Ponsmere Road
Perranporth TR6 0BW
01872 573321
www.perranzabuloemuseum.co.uk
perranzabuloemuseum.enquiries@gmail.com

Perranzabuloe, meaning 'Perran in the sands', is one of the largest parishes in Cornwall. The biggest centre of population is Perranporth where the museum is located.

Polperro Heritage Museum of Smuggling & Fishing

The Warren
Polperro PL13 2RB
01503 273 005
www.polperro.org/museum.html
blackmore@polperroharbour.freeserve.co.uk

A small, friendly museum situated in the old Pilchard Factory right on the harbour of the historic fishing village of Polperro. Exhibits depict the history of fishing and smuggling as well as local and family history, and include a fascinating photographic collection dating back to the 1860s.

Port Eliot

Port Eliot Estate Office, St Germans
Saltash PL12 5ND
01503 230211
www.porteliot.co.uk
info@porteliot.co.uk

Port Eliot has the rare distinction of being a Grade 1 listed house with a Grade 1 listed park and garden.

Porthcurno Telegraph Museum

Eastern House, Porthcurno
Penzance TR19 6JX
01736 810966
www.porthcurno.org.uk
info@porthcurno.org.uk

Porthcurno in Cornwall is one of the UK's most important historic communications sites and home to the award-winning Porthcurno Telegraph Museum, housed in an underground Second World War building. In 1870 when the beautiful valley of Porthcurno first became a communications centre, pioneering engineers were just beginning to create their own 'Victorian Internet'.

Collections: The core collection of submarine telegraphy objects and the historic archive collections of key international telegraph cable companies tell the story of the development of international communication that changed the world.

Redruth Museum & Treasure Park

Tolgus Tin, Treasure Park
New Portreath Road TR16 4HN
01209 215084
www.redrutholdcornwall.org/museum.htm

Built on the site of an old tin mine and set amidst breath-taking gardens, the Treasure Park is a major family attraction in Cornwall. Redruth Town Museum is on site – find out more about the real mine, view the mining artefacts, tools, maps and tin ingots and transport yourself back with the photographs and displays lovingly cared for by the Redruth Old Cornwall Society.

Restormel Castle - English Heritage

Lostwithiel PL22 0EE
01208 872687
http://goo.gl/4xUAuE

The great 13th-century circular shell-keep of Restormel still encloses the principal rooms of the castle in remarkably good condition. It stands on an earlier Norman mound surrounded by a deep dry ditch, atop a high spur beside the River Fowey.

Royal Cornwall Museum

River Street
Truro TR1 2SJ
01872 272205
www.royalcornwallmuseum.org.uk
enquiries@royalcornwallmuseum.org.uk

Discover Cornwall's unique culture from the ancient past to the present day along with art and artefacts from around the world. Explore magnificent minerals, archaeology and natural history, along with our impressive collection of Newlyn School paintings, old masters and decorative art.

Saltash Heritage

Saltash Heritage Museum and Local History Centre, 17 Lower Fore Street
Saltash PL12 6JQ
01752 848466
www.saltash-heritage.org.uk
info@saltash-heritage.org.uk

Saltash Heritage was formed in 1986 by the late Cornelius 'Corny' Hearl and a group of like minded local people who wanted to see the formation of a permanent museum for Saltash.

St Agnes Parish Museum

Penwinnick Road
St Agnes TR5 0PA
01872 553228
www.stagnesmuseum.org.uk
info@stagnesmuseum.org.uk

An award-winning volunteer-run Museum and Interpretative Centre, comprising information, artefacts and curios relating to the Parish of St Agnes.

St Hilary Church & Heritage Centre

St Hilary Churchtown, St Hilary
Penzance TR20 9DQ
01736 710229
sthilarychurch.org.uk

A small Heritage Centre in a newly-restored Old School building beside St Hilary Church, displaying the rich culture and heritage of the area. Descriptive panels tell the story under various themes and other small artefacts and documents are on view.

St Ives Archives

Upper Parish Room, St Andrew's Street
St Ives TR26 1AH
01736 796408
www.stivestrust.co.uk

We are an archive study centre that collects information on all aspects of St Ives and district history: includes art, fishing, folklore, industry, genealogy, maritime, mining, social history, wartime, buildings, writers, musicians etc.

St Ives Museum

Wheal Dream,
St Ives TR26 1PR
01736 796005
http://goo.gl/ouWC2b

The museum, situated in the old fishing quarter of the town and overlooking St Ives Bay, contains many varied displays and collections relating to the St Ives locality. It is St Ives's best kept secret, so there is plenty for all ages to discover and learn.

St Mawes Castle - English Heritage

Falmouth TR2 5DE
01326 270526
http://goo.gl/uOw2lJ

St Mawes Castle is among the best-preserved of Henry VIII's coastal artillery fortresses, and the most elaborately decorated of them all. One of the chain of forts built between 1539 and 1545 to counter an invasion threat from Catholic France and Spain, it guarded the important anchorage of Carrick Roads, sharing the task with Pendennis Castle on the other side of the Fal estuary.

St Michael's Mount - National Trust

Marazion
Penzance TR17 0EF
01736 710507
www.nationaltrust.org.uk/st-michaels-mount
stmichaelsmount@nationaltrust.org.uk

Rocky island crowned by medieval church and castle, home to a living community, one of England's most famous and dramatic coastal attractions. An enchanting medieval castle and church perched upon a craggy island.

Stuart House Trust

Barras Street
Liskeard PL14 6AB
01579 347347
www.stuarthouse.org.uk
info@stuarthouse.org.uk

Stuart House is a Tudor town house where in 1644 Charles I stayed whilst he mustered his troops for his campaign in Cornwall. It now houses an exhibition about this time in the houses history, as well as being a thriving art and heritage gallery, with refreshments and a wonderful secret garden.

Tintagel Castle - English Heritage

Tintagel Castle
Tintagel PL34 0HE
01840 770328
http://goo.gl/nRqLdc

For a magical day out in Cornwall, visit Tintagel Castle. The wonderful location, set high on the rugged North Cornwall coast, offers dramatic views out to sea, and its fascinating ruins and stunning beach cafe make it a perfect day trip, ideal for those on holiday in the South West.

Tintagel Old Post Office - National Trust

Fore Street
Tintagel PL34 0DB
01840 770024
www.nationaltrust.org.uk/tintagel-old-post-office
tintageloldpo@nationaltrust.org.uk

One of the Trust's most delightful medieval buildings, enhanced by a cottage garden. Contains a fine collection of Victorian postal memorabilia, 19th century samplers and furniture dating from the 17th century.

Torpoint Archives

Council Offices, 3 Bullers Road
Torpoint PL11 2LQ
07530 976981
http://goo.gl/AelyVY

The Torpoint Archives have a great deal of useful information to help those researching their Torpoint ancestry. Such information includes the Torpoint Censuses 1841-1911, local parish records (baptisms, marriages and burials), Trade Directories from 1830 and, for the late 18th century, extracts from the Antony Estate records noting many residents in Torpoint in the 1770s and 1780s.

Trerice - National Trust

Trerice, Kestle Mill
Newquay TR8 4PG
01637 875404
www.nationaltrust.org.uk/trerice
trerice@nationaltrust.org.uk

Elizabethan manor house with fine interiors and delightful garden, famed for its 'barrel-roofed' Great Chamber. Unique lawnmower collection. Additional garden area open, including experimental Tudor plant beds.

Truro Cathedral

Truro Cathedral Office, 14 St Mary's Street
Truro TR1 2AF
01872 245007
www.trurocathedral.org.uk
colin@trurocathedral.org.uk

Truro Cathedral was the first cathedral to be built on a new site since Salisbury was started in 1220. Who else but the Victorians would have had the audacity to contemplate a building feat that colossal? They adapted the classic pointed arches of the gothic style and used modern building techniques to create the wonderful building you see around you.

Wayside Museum & Trewey Watermill

Zennor
Nr St Ives TR26 3DA
01736 796945
http://goo.gl/gjRyq9

An evocative collection of 5000+ artefacts collected over the past 75 years, vividly portraying the lives of the people who lived and worked this ancient landscape in and around Zennor in the far west of Cornwall from 3000BC to the 1950s, all set in areas within the garden of a 16th century Miller's cottage. The granite watermill has been painstakingly restored to full working order, using traditional materials and skills.

Wheal Martyn Museum & Country Park

Carthew
St Austell PL26 8XG
01726 850362
www.wheal-martyn.com
info@wheal-martyn.com

Set within 26 acres of woodland and nature trails Wheal Martyn Museum and Country Park is the UK's only heritage centre which tells the story of Cornwall's billion pound China Clay industry and the lives of the people who lived and worked in the shadows of the white pyramids.

Collections: Industrial archaeology, photographs, archives and social history items relating to the china clay industry and the St Austell area.

County Durham

*Durham – county palatine and maritime county, in
N. of England; is bounded N. by the Derwent and the
Tyne, beyond which is Northumberland; E. by the
North Sea; S. by the Tees, beyond which is Yorkshire;
and W. by Cumberland and Westmorland; greatest
length, 48 miles; greatest breadth, 40 miles; length of
coast line, 32 miles; area, 647,592 acres; population
867,258. The western portion of the co. consists of
hill-ranges, enclosing fertile valleys; the eastern
portion, in which the prevailing rocks are magnesian
limestone and new red sandstone, is more level; in the
central districts are the coal measures. In the valleys,
and in the neighbourhood of the rivers, especially the
Tees, the soil is very fertile. The chief corn crops are
wheat and oats; the chief green crops are potatoes and
turnips. A hardy breed of horses is raised on the
moors in the west, and in the fertile pastures of the
valleys a breed of cattle which is unsurpassed for
dairy purposes. The principal mineral products are
lead, iron, millstone, and coal. The coalfields are the
most important in the kingdom. The principal
manufactures. are chemicals, glass, and earthenware;
shipbuilding and sail-making; paper-making; woollen
and worsted stuffs, &c. There are also large ironworks
and machine factories. Durham has great facilities of
transport. The county comprises 4 wards, 269
parishes, the parliamentary and municipal boroughs
of Darlington, Durham, Gateshead, Hartlepool,
South Shields (1 member each), and Sunderland (2
members), the greater part of the parliamentary and
municipal borough of Stockton (1 member), and the
municipal borough of Jarrow. It is entirely in the
diocese of Durham.*

– John Bartholomew, *Gazetteer of the British Isles* (1887)

Note: see Tyne & Wear for Gateshead, South Shields
and Sunderland.

Anker's House Museum

St Mary and St Cuthbert's Church
Chester-le-Street DH3 3QB
0191 388 3295
http://goo.gl/JIK6Sk

The Anker's House adjoining the Parish Church was the
residence of an Anker/Anchorite - a religious recluse from
the 14th to the 16th century and was probably established
sometime around 1350 - 1380. Up until 1547 it was the
residence of six anchorites who in turn were walled up in
the house for life to spend their time in prayer and
contemplation.

Auckland Castle

Auckland Castle, Market Place
Bishop Auckland DL14 7NR
01388 743750
www.aucklandcastle.org
enquiries@aucklandcastle.org

Set within 200 acres of beautiful parkland above the River
Wear, Auckland Castle has been home to the Bishop of
Durham for over 900 years. After the Norman Conquest,
the Bishop of Durham was granted exceptional powers to
act as a political and military leader. As England's one and
only Prince-Bishop, he was the second most powerful man
in the country and effectively ruled the area between the
Tyne and the Tees.

Aycliffe & District Bus Preservation Society

110 Fewston Close
Newton Aycliffe DL5 7HF
www.aycliffebus.org.uk

The North East of England has a rich and varied industrial
heritage. Public transport is part of that heritage and has
affected everyday life in this northern region. The
preservation of selected local vintage buses is an
opportunity to bring the public at large the transport of
yesteryear - an opportunity to ride, to touch, smell and to
see that which has now left the modern day scene.

Barnard Castle - English Heritage

Barnard Castle DL12 8PR
01833 638212
http://goo.gl/IhTDmy
customers@english-heritage.org.uk

Set on a rock high above the River Tees, imposing Barnard
Castle was the stronghold of the Balliol family. Taking its
name from Bernard de Balliol, who rebuilt it in the 12th
century, it includes a fine great hall and a dominating
round-towered keep.

Beamish - The Living Museum of the North

Beamish Museum
Beamish DH9 0RG
0191 370 4000
www.beamish.org.uk
museum@beamish.org.uk

Experience a real sense of your past at Beamish, and discover what life was like in North East England in Georgian, Victorian and Edwardian times. Beamish is a living, working museum, set in 300 acres of County Durham countryside. Founded in 1970 to illustrate the development of industry, agriculture and the way of life in the North East of England, Beamish is situated in 300 acres of woodland and farmland. Home Farm, a fine 19th century model farmstead, and Pockerley Old Hall, with its medieval stronghouse dating to the 1400s, are both listed buildings preserved in situ.

Binchester Roman Fort

Bishop Auckland DL14 8DJ
01388 663089
www.durham.gov.uk/binchester
archaeology@durham.gov.uk

Binchester Fort was built during the 1st century AD to protect the point where Dere Street (an important road that ran from York to Scotland) crossed the River Wear. There were as many as 1,000 soldiers here at a time.

Bowes Museum, The

Barnard Castle
Durham DL12 8NP
01833 690606
www.thebowesmuseum.org.uk
info@thebowesmuseum.org.uk

Founded over 100 years ago, by John and Joséphine Bowes, the magnificent building contains the greatest collection of European fine and decorative arts in the North of England.

Collections: This collection contains paintings, ceramics, items of woodwork and objects d'art.

Cleveland Family History Society

4 North Park North, Sedgefield
Stockton-on-Tees TS21 3AH
01740 623 175
www.clevelandfhs.org.uk
christinedunn48@yahoo.co.uk

The society is more formally known as The Cleveland, North Yorkshire and South Durham Family History Society. The long title more accurately describes the area of coverage of the society, which is rather larger than that of the county of its title.

Cleveland Ironstone Mining Museum

Deepdale
Skinningrove TS13 4AP
01287 642877
www.ironstonemuseum.co.uk
visits@ironstonemuseum.co.uk

The museum offers visitors an opportunity to discover the skills and customs that built Cleveland's ironstone heritage. It is the only museum in the UK which tells the story of ironstone mining; a key part of the local history of the social and industrial development of Cleveland and Teesside.

Durham Cathedral

The College
Durham DH1 3EH
0191 386 4266
www.durhamcathedral.co.uk
enquiries@durhamcathedral.co.uk

A UNESCO World Heritage Site with breathtaking Romanesque architecture, exquisite stained glass, the Shrine of St Cuthbert and the resting place of St Bede. Things to do include climbing the Cathedral Tower, exploring the monks' dormitory, guided tours and special exhibitions.

Durham County Record Office

County Hall
Durham DH1 5UL
03000 267619
www.durhamrecordoffice.org.uk
record.office@durham.gov.uk

Durham County Record Office is responsible for collecting and preserving documents relating to County Durham and Darlington and for making those records available to as wide an audience as possible. You can visit the record office in person, or make use of our enquiry service.

Durham Heritage Centre & Museum

St Mary-le-Bow, North Bailey
Durham DH1 3ET
0191 384 5589
www.durhamheritagecentre.org.uk
durhamheritagecentre@hotmail.co.uk

Durham Heritage Centre and Museum tells the story of the City of Durham from medieval times to the present day. The museum is situated in the redundant Church of St Mary-le-Bow, close to the World Heritage Site of the Cathedral and Castle.

Durham Light Infantry Museum & Durham Art Gallery

Aykley Heads
Durham DH1 5TU
03000 266590
www.dlidurham.org.uk
dli@durham.gov.uk

The museum tells the proud story of County Durham's own Regiment The Durham Light Infantry from 1758 to 1968, with particular emphasis on WW1 & WW2. The displays focus on the experience of war, using letter & diary extracts, plus the actual voices of DLI WW2 soldiers.

Finchale Priory

Brasside DH1 5SH
0191 - 386 3828
www.english-heritage.org.uk

The very extensive remains of a 13th century priory, founded on the site of a retired pirate's hermitage. Part of it later served as a holiday retreat for the monks of Durham Cathedral. Beautifully sited by the River Wear with delightful riverside walks nearby.

Hartlepool Arts & Museum Service

Sir William Gray House, Clarence Road
Hartlepool TS24 8BT
01429 523438
www.teesmuseums.com/hartlepool.htm

Hartlepool Arts and Museums Service began in 1920 with the opening of the Gray Art Gallery & Museum, the building and the original collection of paintings given by Captain W. Gray, as a thank-offering for the safe return of his son from the 1914-18 War. Since then the collections have been built upon areas of social and maritime history, Asian art, natural history and decorative arts.

Head of Steam - Darlington Railway Museum

North Road Station
Darlington DL3 6ST
01325 460 532
www.head-of-steam.co.uk
headofsteam@darlington.gov.uk

Head of Steam - Darlington Railway Museum was first opened in 1975 and is housed within North Road Station, built in 1842 for the Stockton & Darlington Railway. The Stockton & Darlington Railway was the first steam hauled public railway and was opened on September 27th 1825.

Heugh Battery Museum

Moor Terrace, The Headland
Hartlepool TS24 0PS
01429 272 814
www.heughbattery.com

The Heugh Gun Battery is situated on the Headland in Hartlepool. This area of the North East coast is rich in history and the museum aims to educate its visitors on part of that history.

HMS Trincomalee Trust

Jackson Dock
Hartlepool TS24 0SQ
01429 223193
www.hms-trincomalee.co.uk

For the preservation of the 1817 frigate HMS Trincomalee (formerly Foudroyant). The site is now marketed as Hartlepool Historic Quay.

Killhope - The North of England Lead Mining Museum

Near Cowshill, Upper Weardale
Co Durham DL13 1AR
01388 537505
www.killhope.org.uk
Info@killhope.org.uk

Killhope, The North of England Lead Mining Museum, is a multi award winning museum. Killhope is the only lead mine in the North-east open to the public.

M Bowman Vintage Commercial Vehicle Museum

Unit 2, Dabble Duck Industrial Estate
Shildon DL4 2RA
01388 778582
www.vintagecommercials.co.uk

The museum houses a range of vehicles that have been lovingly restored. Many of which, have been in the Bowman family for generations as true workhorses of industry. The aim of the museum is to allow people to see the progression of a family business over the years from horse and cart through to modern diesel engine lorries which, were to be seen as an everyday part of local life throughout the North East of England.

Museum of Hartlepool, The

Jackson's Docks, Maritime Avenue
Hartlepool TS24 0XZ
01429 860077
www.destinationhartlepool.com

This award-winning museum is the finest free show in town. You'll enjoy the hundreds of exhibits which include the restored paddle steam ship Wingfield Castle; a real 'fishing coble' to climb aboard; the finest 'gas illuminated lighthouse'; sea monsters and monkey fish.

North East War Memorials Project

14 Park Road North
Chester-le-Street DH3 3SD
www.newmp.org.uk

NEWMP records all known War Memorials from the Tweed to the Tees ie Northumberland, Tyne and Wear and Durham and makes them accessible to the public via our website.

Old Fulling Mill Museum of Archaeology

The Banks
Durham DH1 3EB
0191 334 1823
https://www.dur.ac.uk/archaeology.museum
archaeology.museum@durham.ac.uk

Highlights include outstanding Roman collections together with Anglo-Saxon, Medieval and Tudor finds from Durham City and the local area.

Oriental Museum

Durham University, Elvet Hill
Durham DH1 3TH
0191 334 5694
www.durham.ac.uk/oriental.museum
oriental.museum@durham.ac.uk

The Oriental Museum is the only museum in the North of Britain devoted solely to the art and archaeology of the Orient. The remarkable collections reveal the great cultures of Asia; the Near and Middle East; and North Africa.

Palace Green Library

Durham University Library, Palace Green
Durham DH1 3RN
0191 334 2932
www.dur.ac.uk/library
pg.library@durham.ac.uk

Founded in 1833 and occupying listed buildings within the Durham World Heritage site, the Palace Green Library of

Durham University houses archives, early printed books and other special collections. The Library has two exhibition spaces: the Wolfson Gallery, which regularly exhibits treasures from all of the university's heritage collections and the Dunelm Gallery.

Preston Park Museum & Grounds

Preston Hall, Yarm Road
Stockton-on-Tees TS18 3RH
01642 527375
www.prestonparkmuseum.co.uk/
prestonhall@stockton.gov.uk

Nestled alongside the River Tees, Preston Hall, a former Georgian gentleman's residence and former home of industrial magnate Robert Ropner, houses a varied collection of Teesside's treasures. Walk through the impressive doors to find out more about those who lived there, the varied museum collection, the vital role the mighty River Tees has played throughout history and the leisure time pursuits that were just as popular then as they are today.

Tees Cottage Pumping Station

Coniscliffe Road
Darlington DL3 8TF
www.teescottage.com

From 1849, Tees Cottage Pumping Station revolutionized water supply in Darlington and Teeside by supplying cleaner, piped water to inhabitants who had previously relied on wells and rainwater tubs. On Open Days you can experience the 1902 Lancashire Boilers, 1904 steam Beam Engine and 1914 Gas engine, all operated and explained by a group of dedicated volunteers. We also have a working Blacksmith's Shop and a Miniature Railway- a favourite with children.

Teesdale Heritage Group

9-11 Chapel Row, Middleton-in-Teesdale
Barnard Castle DL12 0SN
www.durhamintime.org.uk/teesdale
TeesdaleHG@gmail.com

Local Heritage group; we collect images and information on the local area, holding exhibitions/events and research.

Weardale Museum at High House Chapel

Ireshopeburn
Weardale DL13 1HD
01388 517 433
www.weardalemuseum.co.uk
dtheatherington@ormail.co.uk

This Small Folk Museum was formed in 1985 by a group of volunteers in their third age. It is housed in the former Manse to High House Chapel, which is now the oldest

Methodist Chapel in the World which has been in continuous weekly use since its foundation in 1760.

Collections: A 19th century period kitchen depicting life for leadminer/farming families; the Wesley Room which houses Methodist artefacts from the Wesleyan and Primitive traditions from 1760 and the 13 visits of John Wesley to High House Chapel; the 1788 Westgate Subscription Library; a superb collection of crystalized minerals and fossils; the complete census for Stanhope Parish 1841-1901 and other genealogical resources.

Wheatley Hill Heritage Centre

🏛️ ⭐

Cemetery Road, (in the old chapel of rest)
Wheatley Hill DH6 3JZ
820 01429 824402
www.wheatley-hill.org.uk
history.club2@btinternet.com

The Heritage Centre in Wheatley Hill is a great place to visit to obtain a flavour of the village and its life and times.

Collections: Mostly related to the industrial background of the village but also acknowledging the earlier agricultural traditions which still exist.

Cumbria

Cumberland – a maritime and border county of England; length, NE. and SW., 75 miles; extreme breadth, E. and W., 45 miles; average breadth, 22 miles; coast line, about 75 miles; area, 970,161 acres, population 250,647. The coast on the Solway is low and sandy, but on the Irish Sea it is lofty and rugged; chief promontory, St Bees Head. In the NW. the country is open and flat; it is watered by the Eden and other streams, and consists chiefly of verdant meadows and good arable land. From this plain the surface rises towards the E. and S. into a region with deep denies or dales, which form the mountainous district of 'The Lakes', which attracts great numbers of tourists. The Eden and the Derwent are the two longest rivers. The Esk passes through the co. before entering the Solway Firth, and its affluent, the Liddell, runs for some distance along the Scottish border. Coal and iron are extensively worked in the W., the coalfield stretching from the neighbourhood of Whitehaven to that of Maryport. Numerous blast furnaces are constantly at work. Plumbago or black lead is obtained in considerable quantities near Keswick. Slate, limestone, and sandstone are abundant. Copper, cobalt, antimony, manganese, and gypsum are also found. The cultivation of the soil is less attended to than the rearing of sheep and cattle. The dairy produce is very considerable. Woollen manufacture is carried on to some extent at Carlisle and some other places. The county comprises 5 wards, 208 parishes, the boroughs of Carlisle and Whitehaven. It is mostly in the diocese of Carlisle.

Westmorland, county in N. of England; greatest length, N. and S., 32 miles; greatest breadth, E. and W., 40 miles; area, 500,906 acres, population 64,191. Westmorland presents a continuous succession of mountain, moor, and fell, intersected by deep winding vales, traversed by numerous streams. The principal of these are the Eden, Lowther, Lune, and Kent. The western part of the county is within the Lake District. The climate is moist. The arable land is mostly confined to the valleys, where the soil usually consists of a dry gravelly loam, well adapted for turnips, but the greater part of the county is natural pasture. A few tracts of woodland remain of the forests which formerly clothed all the hills. The mineral productions include graphite, marble, roofing slate, and some coal, lead, and copper. The only manufactures of any consequence are the coarse woollens of Kendal. The county has good communications by railway. It comprises 4 wards, 109 parishes, the municipal borough of Kendal, and the towns of Ambleside, Appleby (the county town), Brough, Kirkby Lonsdale, Kirkby Stephen, and Orton. It is entirely in the diocese of Carlisle.

– John Bartholomew, *Gazetteer of the British Isles* (1887)

A World in Miniature Museum

Houghton Hall Garden Centre
Houghton, Carlisle CA6 4JB
01228 400388
www.aworldinminiature.com/world-miniature
info@aworldinminiature.com

This truly amazing museum contains of one the world's top three collections of quality miniatures, from remarkable 1/12 scale copies of antique furniture, paintings and china in beautiful room settings, to everyday items at sizes you just won't believe..

Acorn Bank - National Trust

Temple Sowerby
nr Penrith CA10 1SP
017683 61893
www.nationaltrust.org.uk/acorn-bank
acornbank@nationaltrust.org.uk

Delightful sheltered garden, renowned for its herbs and orchards growing old English fruit varieties. Ancient oaks and high enclosing walls keep the extremes of the Cumbrian climate out of the garden, resulting in a spectacular display of shrubs, roses and herbaceous borders.

Allan Bank & Grasmere - National Trust

Allan Bank, Grasmere
Ambleside LA22 9QB
015394 35143
www.nationaltrust.org.uk/allan-bank-and-grasmere
allanbank@nationaltrust.org.uk

Opened to the public for the first time ever in March 2012, Allan Bank is a place to relax in front of a warm fire with a cup of tea while the children play. Once home to William Wordsworth and National Trust founder Canon Rawnsley, Allan Bank was rescued from the ravages of fire in 2011.

Armitt Library & Museum

Armitt Library and Museum Centre, Rydal Road
Ambleside LA22 9BL
01539 431212
www.armitt.com
info@armitt.com

The Armitt is a unique place combining Gallery, Museum and Library. It is a treasure-house for scholarship and fun, art and entertainment.

Barrow Archive & Local Studies Centre

Cumbria Archive and Local Studies Centre, Barrow, 140 Duke Street
Barrow-in-Furness LA14 1XW
01229 407377
http://goo.gl/xs43Jh

Original historical documents relating to the area of Furness (Lancashire North of the Sands) and South West Cumberland, particularly for Barrow, Ulverston and Millom.

Beacon Museum, The

West Strand
Whitehaven CA28 7LY
01946 592302
www.thebeacon-whitehaven.co.uk
thebeacon@copelandbc.gov.uk

The Beacon Museum, situated on Whitehaven's beautiful Georgian harbourside, tells the story of the rich history of this fascinating corner of the Western Lake District. There is a fantastic interactive exhibition which tells the story of the nuclear industry in West Cumbria, past, present and future. Beginning at the top of the museum, visitors can expect to enjoy the best view in town in our viewing gallery, looking out across the Solway.

Beatrix Potter Gallery - National Trust

Main Street
Hawkshead LA22 0NS
015394 36355
www.nationaltrust.org.uk/beatrix-potter-gallery
beatrixpottergallery@nationaltrust.org.uk

Gallery showing original watercolours by world famous author Beatrix Potter and displays on her life & work. 2008 features The Tale of Jemima Puddle-duck and The Tale of Samuel Whiskers - which are celebrating their 100th birthday - as well as displays on the major film 'Miss Potter'. This 17th-century building was once the office of her husband, William Heelis.

Birdoswald Roman Fort - English Heritage

Gilsland
Carlisle CA8 7DD
016977 47602
http://goo.gl/r01oLP
customers@english-heritage.org.uk

Birdoswald Roman Fort stands high above a meander in the River Irthing, in one of the most picturesque settings on Hadrian's Wall. A Roman fort, turret and milecastle can all be seen on this excellent stretch of the Wall.

Blackwell: The Arts & Crafts House

Blackwell
Bowness-on-Windermere LA23 3JT
015394 46139
www.blackwell.org.uk
info@blackwell.org.uk

When the architect MH Baillie Scott built a holiday home overlooking Windermere for his client Sir Edward Holt he created Blackwell, a masterpiece of twentieth-century design; a perfect example of the Arts & Crafts Movement. Enjoy a lovingly crafted day out at one of the most enchanting historic houses in the Lake District.

Border & King's Own Royal Border Regiment Museum

Queen Mary's Tower, The Castle
Carlisle CA3 8UR
01228 532774
www.cumbriasmuseumofmilitarylife.org
korbrmuseum@aol.com

The museum founded in 1932 is located in Queen Mary's Tower a 16th century building in Carlisle Castle. This superb medieval fortress founded in 1092, houses the military barracks of the Border Regiment's Depot, the regiment's home since 1873.

Collections: Includes a wide range of uniforms, equipment, badges and insignia, firearms, artillery and edged weapons, personal items, silver, china, musical instruments, medals including those of six of the Border Regiment's Victoria Cross winners, pictures and paintings, and a large archive of photographs, and documents relating to Regular, Volunteer, Militia, Territorial and Home Guard units of the regiment and other military units from Cumbria. Archive and items not on display can be viewed by prior arrangement.

Borrowdale - National Trust

Head of Colesdale, above Braithwaite
Keswick CA12 5UP
017687 74649
www.nationaltrust.org.uk/borrowdale
borrowdale@nationaltrust.org.uk

Last mineral mine processing mill to operate in the lake district. The last operating mineral mine in the lake district.

Brantwood House

Brantwood Trust, Brantwood
Coniston LA21 8AD
015394 41396
www.brantwood.org.uk
enquiries@brantwood.org.uk

The former home of John Ruskin, Brantwood is the most beautifully situated house in the Lake District. Brantwood is both a treasure house of historical importance and a lively centre of contemporary arts and the environment, welcoming in the region of 30,000 visitors a year. Displays and activities in the house, gardens and estate reflect the wealth of cultural associations associated with Ruskin's legacy – from the Pre Raphaelites and Arts and Crafts Movement to the founding of the National Trust and the Welfare State.

Brougham Castle - English Heritage

Penrith CA10 2AA
01768 862488
http://goo.gl/T0l00i
customers@english-heritage.org.uk

Picturesque Brougham Castle was begun in the early 13th century near the site of a Roman fort guarding the crossing of the River Eamont. It was reinforced in the 14th century but was in poor condition by the time of the Civil War.

Carlisle Archive Centre

Lady Gillford's House, Petteril Bank Road
Carlisle CA1 3AJ
01228 227285
http://goo.gl/e22aX8

Sources available at this Archive Centre include original documents from the 12th century to the present day, relating to the part of the historic county of Cumberland which is north of the River Derwent. The areas around Carlisle, Keswick, Penrith and Maryport are amongst those for which material is available.

Carlisle Castle - English Heritage

Carlisle CA3 8UR
01228 591922
http://goo.gl/RfGY9X
customers@english-heritage.org.uk

Wander the passages of this medieval fortress and discover nine centuries of bloody warfare across the Anglo-Scottish border. Learn about its role in sieges, and its connections with Mary Queen of Scots and Bonnie Prince Charlie.

Carlisle Cathedral

7 The Abbey
Carlisle CA3 8TZ
01228 548151
www.carlislecathedral.org.uk
office@carlislecathedral.org.uk

Carlisle Cathedral is one of the jewels of North West England and, after standing on the border with Scotland for almost 900 years, it has a lively story to tell. It may not be the best known medieval Cathedral in England, it is certainly not the biggest, but it delights its many visitors.

Castlerigg Stone Circle

National Grid Reference: NY 292 236

www.english-heritage.org.uk

Castlerigg Stone Circle is one of the most visually impressive prehistoric monuments in Britain, and is the most visited stone circle in Cumbria. Every year thousands of people visit it to look, photograph, draw and wonder why and when and by whom it was built.

Castlesteads Fort

Brampton

www.roman-britain.org/places/banna.htm

Castlesteads was a Roman fort. It was the 12th fort on Hadrian's Wall counting from the east, between Banna (Birdoswald) to the east and Uxelodunum (Stanwix) to the west.

Cumbria Archive & Local Studies Library

Scotch Street

Whitehaven CA28 7NL

01946 852920

www.cumbria.gov.uk/libraries/localstudies

Cumbria's archives are here for everyone, a unique, exciting and inspiring resource documenting life in our area over previous centuries. This Archive Centre has custody of a wealth of archives relating to West Cumbria.

Cumbria Archive Centre

Lady Gillford's House, Petteril Bank Rd

Carlisle CA1 3AJ

http://goo.gl/e22aX8

Cumbria Archive Centre, Carlisle cares for parish registers and other church records, wills, electoral registers, maps and plans, poor law records, title deeds, and photographs. The archives of families, businesses, local authorities, solicitors, societies and schools also help to form a fascinating record of all aspects of life in the county.

Cumbria Family History Society

Rose Villa, 25 Eden Street, Stanwix

Carlisle CA3 9LS

01228 535 228

www.cumbriafhs.com

laarltrev@aol.com

Helping members carry out genealogy research in Cumbria (old counties of Cumberland and Westmorland + parts of Lancs & Yorks).

Cumbria's Museum Of Military Life

Alma Carlisle Castle

Carlisle CA3 8UR

01228 532774

www.cumbriasmuseumofmilitarylife.org

enquiries@cmoml.org

Cumbria's Museum of Military Life is located right in the heart of historic Carlisle Castle. Telling the story of how ordinary people did extraordinary things serving with the local infantry regiments and how they affected the county and the world.

Dalton Castle - National Trust

Market Place

Dalton-in-Furness LA15 8AX

015395 60951

www.nationaltrust.org.uk/dalton-castle

daltoncastle@nationaltrust.org.uk

14th-century tower, containing a local history exhibition organised by Friends of Dalton Castle. Also houses a display about painter George Romney, a native of Dalton.

Derwent Island House - National Trust

Derwent Island, Lake Road

Keswick CA12 5DJ

015394 35599

www.nationaltrust.org.uk/article-1356397015261

borrowdale@nationaltrust.org.uk

18th-century house on an idyllic woodland island in Derwentwater. The house has a restrained classical interior and restored garden.

Dock Museum, The

North Road

Barrow-in-Furness LA14 2PW

01229 876400

www.dockmuseum.org.uk

dockmuseum@barrowbc.gov.uk

Set in a dry dock, the Dock Museum tells the fascinating story of Barrow, the Victorian boom town and 20th century centre of innovation including airships and submarines. A new archaeology gallery explores the area's rich prehistory from stone circles to Viking booty.

Dove Cottage, The Wordsworth Museum & Art Gallery

Dove Cottage, Town End
Grasmere LA22 9SH
015394 35544
www.wordsworth.org.uk
enquiries@wordsworth.org.uk

Visit the traditional Lakeland cottage and home of the poet William Wordsworth, who in 1799 went on a walking tour of the Lake District and fell in love with Grasmere and Dove Cottage, and within a few months had set up home here with his sister, Dorothy.

Collections: The museum covers not only the lives and works of Wordsworth and his circle, but the wider phenomenon of British Romanticism, and the role of the Lake District in inspiring writers and artists of the Romantic Movement.

Farfield Mill, Arts & Heritage Centre

Garsdale Road
Sedbergh LA10 5LW
01539 621958
www.farfieldmill.org
exhibitions@farfieldmill.org

Set in the shadow of the glorious Howgills near Sedbergh and restored from a Victorian woolen mill, Farfield Mill provides an excellent visit for arts and heritage enthusiasts alike. Take your time to discover a programme of top-quality exhibitions; a unique range of fine art and crafts created by resident and visiting artists; fascinating displays telling the history of the Mill.

Furness Abbey - English Heritage

Barrow-in-Furness LA13 0PJ
01229 823420
http://goo.gl/KC5kT7

The impressive remains of an abbey founded by Stephen, later king of England, including much of the east end and west tower of the church, the ornately decorated chapter house and the cloister buildings. Set in the 'vale of nightshade', the romantic ruins were celebrated by Wordsworth in his Prelude of 1805. An exhibition on the history of the abbey, with a display of elaborately carved stones, can be seen in the visitor centre.

Furness Family History Society

64 Cowlarns Road, Hawcoat
Barrow-in-Furness LA14 4HJ
01229 830942
www.furnessfhs.co.uk
julia.fairbairn@furnessfhs.co.uk

The Furness Family History Society is a group of people having an interest in family history (in Furness or elsewhere) and pursuing their own researches while also helping each other in the subject.

Guildhall Museum

Greenmarket
Carlisle CA3 8JE
01228 534781
http://goo.gl/7PR8nX

The Guildhall Museum can be found in Carlisle's only medieval house. Each of the Guild Rooms has its own attractions. - ranging from the ship's cabin-like atmosphere of the Shoemakers room to the Victorian character of the Butcher's room. There are displays of objects relating to the history of the Guilds throughout the museum, including items of Guild silver dating back to the early 18th century.

Haig Colliery Mining Museum

Solway Road, Kells
Whitehaven CA28 9BG
01946 599949
https://haigpit.wordpress.com
museum@haigpit.com

Haig Colliery Mining Museum is situated high on the cliffs above Whitehaven with magnificent views across to the Scottish Hills and the Isle of Man. The museum is a twenty minute detour from the famous Coast to Coast Walk and within yards of the Cumbria Coastal Way.

Hawkshead Grammar School Museum

Hawkshead Grammar School
Hawkshead LA22 0NT
015394 36735
www.hawksheadgrammar.org.uk
ecdavidshaw@aol.com

The museum in the Old Grammar School building in the village of Hawkshead, Cumbria, houses a unique collection of historic artefacts relating to the ancient school, some of which date back to the 16th century. The museum operates a guided tour which brings the school to life. You can feel the atmosphere and almost believe you are in a working schoolroom of 200 years ago.

Helena Thompson Museum

Park End Road
Workington CA14 4DE
01900 64040
helenathompson.org.uk
whghtm@hotmail.co.uk

The Helena Thompson Museum, originally known as Park End, was the home of Helena Thompson, MBE, JP, for over seventy years and it was her gift to the people of

Workington upon her death, on the condition that it be made into a museum for Workington and the surrounding district. Miss Thompson's family had been associated with the house since the late 18th century.

Heron Corn Mill & Mill Barn

Heron Corn Mill, Mill Lane, Beetham,
Milnthorpe LA7 7PQ
01539 564271
www.heronmill.org
info@heronmill.org

Heron Corn Mill is on the banks of the River Bela, in South Cumbria close to the Lancashire border, and is one of the few working mills left in Cumbria. Evidence shows that a mill existed on the site prior to 1096.

Hill Top - National Trust

Near Sawrey
Hawkshead LA22 0LF
015394 36269
www.nationaltrust.org.uk/hill-top
hilltop@nationaltrust.org.uk

Beatrix Potter wrote many of her famous children's stories in this little 17th-century house which she owned for 38 years, and scenes from the house, garden, farm and village appear in them. It has been kept exactly as she left it, complete with her furniture and china. There is a traditional cottage garden attached.

Holker Hall & Gardens

Cark-in-Cartmel
Grange-over-Sands LA11 7PL
01539 558328
www.holker.co.uk

Holker Hall is the home of the Cavendish family who welcome visitors of all ages to one of the best-loved stately homes in Britain. Magnificently situated only a short distance from Grange-over-Sands and the expanse of Morecambe Bay. Holker Hall is set in exceptionally beautiful countryside with gardens that merge into parkland framed by the Lakeland Hills.

Kendal Archive Centre

Cumbria Archive Centre, Kendal, Kendal County Offices
Kendal LA9 4RQ
01539 713540
http://goo.gl/a4Navl

Records relating to the historic county of Westmorland, and also some for the Sedbergh-Dent district (formerly in the West Riding of Yorkshire) and for the Cartmel district (formerly in Lancashire North of the Sands).

Kendal Museum of Natural History & Archaeology

Station Road
Kendal LA9 6BT
01539 815597
www.kendalmuseum.org.uk
info@kendalmuseum.org.uk

Kendal is situated on the edge of the English Lake District and is home to one of the country's oldest museums. Founded in 1796, Kendal Museum's fascinating collections include local archaeology, history, geology and a natural history collection from around the globe.

Keswick Museum & Art Gallery

Fitz Park, Station Road
Keswick CA12 4NF
017687 73263
www.allerdale.gov.uk/default.aspx?Page=16
info@keswickmuseum.co.uk

The museum tells the story of Keswick and the surrounding area. Keswick has a unique history, with lots of firsts, including the first pencils, some very famous residents, and lots of beautiful scenery. It was purpose built in 1897 of local green volcanic state and St Bees sandstone and is set in the beautiful Fitz Park.

Lakeland Motor Museum

Old Blue Mill, Backbarrow,
Newby Bridge LA12 8TA
015395 30400
www.lakelandmotormuseum.co.uk
info@lakelandmotormuseum.co.uk

The Lakeland Motor Museum has a fascinating collection of over 30,000 cars, motorcycles, scooters, cycles and auto memorabilia and is housed in a restored mill and ultramarine pigment factory in the heart of The Lake District. Highlights of the museum include a Campbell Bluebird Exhibition with replicas of the record-breaking machines that saw the famous Campbell family break 21 world and land speed records. In addition to the fascinating exhibits from the world of motoring, the museum also features displays about the local Lakeland motoring heritage, period shopping displays, electric cars and cycles and the history of Old Blue Mill that now houses the collection.

Lancaster Military Heritage Group

c/o 1 Brae Cottages, Staveley
Kendal LA8 9PL
01539 821977
www.lmhg.org
lmhg@live.com

The Lancaster Military Heritage Group is a voluntary association with a small subscription and with members from all walks of life who have interest in our military heritage. The group works with others in and around Lancaster to promote an understanding of the Armed Forces and arranges talks on military, naval and air subjects.

Lanercost Priory - English Heritage

Lanercost
Brampton CA8 2HQ
01697 73030
http://goo.gl/Mq8DP8
customers@english-heritage.org.uk

Standing close to Hadrian's Wall, the Augustinian priory of Lanercost was much involved in the Anglo-Scottish wars. The abbey suffered terribly from Scottish raids, being sacked at least four times.

Laurel & Hardy Museum

4c Upper Brook St
Ulverston LA12 7BH
01229 582292
www.laurel-and-hardy.co.uk

The museum started life as one man's collection stemming from his lifelong love of 'the boys'. Starting out as a few scrapbooks of photos, the collection grew over time until it filled this museum.

Levens Hall & Topiary Garden

Kendal LA8 0PD
01539 560321
www.levenshall.co.uk
houseopening@levenshall.co.uk

Levens Hall is an Elizabethan House with ten acres of world famous topiary gardens laid out by Monsieur Guillaume Beaumont in 1694. The garden still retains many of its original features including a unique collection of ancient and extraordinary topiary characters sculpted from box and yew.

Maryport Maritime Museum

1 Senhouse Street, Shipping Brow
Maryport CA15 6AB
01900 813738
http://goo.gl/vQ0Jns

The museum houses a wealth of objects, pictures, models and paintings that illustrate Maryport's proud maritime and painting tradition. The collection at the museum was initially based on the donations of items by local resident Miss Annie Robinson, and consisted almost entirely of artefacts from or linked to the Town of Maryport.

Millom Heritage Museum & Visitor Centre

Station Building, Station Road
Millom LA18 5AA
01229 772555
millomdiscoverycentre.co.uk
information@millomfolkmuseum.co.uk

Millom Folk Museum Society was founded in 1973, some five years after the Ironworks closed down. Its founders were a handful of local people all with a shared passion to preserve the town's mining heritage.

Museum of Lakeland Life & Industry

Abbot Hall
Kendal LA9 5AL
01539 722464
www.lakelandmuseum.org.uk
info@lakelandmuseum.org.uk

The museum takes you back through time to explore the story of the Lake District and its inhabitants. Isolated before the arrival of the railway and motorcar, this area developed its own unique customs and traditions. Recreated period rooms and workshops reveal how rural people lived and worked and played and how different life was before the introduction of machinery.

Nenthead Mines Heritage Centre

Nenthead
Alston CA9 3PD
01434 382037
www.nentheadmines.com
info@npht.com

A museum dedicated to both showing and telling the 'story' of the mineral mining past of the North Pennines. Prepare to launch on a voyage of discovery at Nenthead Mines, learning more about the people, places, tools, lifestyle, and legacy of the mining industry that at one time completely dominated the landscape of the North Pennines.

Pencil Museum

Southey Works, Greta Bridge
Keswick CA12 5NG
017687 73626
www.pencilmuseum.co.uk
alex.spencer@acco.com

The first pencil factory in Keswick opened in 1832. The second and current factory was started in the 1920s and completed in 1950. The museum opened in 1981. Discover the colourful world that is home to a giant, an escape artist's pencil, art adventures and the world's longest colour pencil.

Pendragon Castle

Mallerstang

www.visitcumbria.com/pen/pendragon.htm

Just the ruined base of a great tower remains at Pendragon Castle, which according to legend is the place where Uther Pendragon, King Arthur's father, died. The castle was built next to the River Eden in the Vale of Mallerstang in the late 12th century, probably by Hugh de Morville.

Penrith & Eden Museum

Robinson's School, Middlegate

Penrith CA11 7PT

01768 865105

www.eden.gov.uk/museum

museum@eden.gov.uk

Penrith and Eden Museum is located at the heart of the bustling market town of Penrith. The museum is housed in Robinson's School, an Elizabethan building dating from 1670 and used as a school until the early 1970s.

Quaker Tapestry Museum

Friends Meeting House, Stramongate

Kendal LA9 4BH

01539 722975

www.quaker-tapestry.co.uk

info@quaker-tapestry.co.uk

The award-winning Quaker Tapestry is a masterpiece of storytelling and a celebration of life, revolutions, and remarkable people.. Often compared with the Bayeux Tapestry, this modern, internationally created exhibition, made by 4,000 people, reveals a myriad of stories within 77 captivating and colourful embroidery panels.

Ravenglass Railway Museum

The Ravenglass and Eskdale Railway

Ravenglass CA18 1SW

01229 717171

www.ravenglass-railway.co.uk

steam@ravenglass-railway.co.uk

The railway runs for seven miles (11.3 kilometres) from the Lake District National Park's only coastal village of Ravenglass in the Western Lake District, through hidden Miterdale, to the grandeur of the Eskdale valley. The terminus at Dalegarth for Boot - home to our new visitor centre - nestles at the foot of England's highest mountains. The story of the Railway is outlined in the Railway Museum, situated in Ravenglass Station car park.

Ruskin Museum, The

Yewdale Road

Coniston LA21 8DU

01539 441164

www.ruskinmuseum.com

information@ruskinmuseum.com

Ruskin gave a collection of minerals/crystals to Coniston Mechanics' Institute in 1884. Local objects were added.

Sellafield Visitor Centre

Sellafield

Seascale CA20 1PG

www.sellafield.com

Sellafield is probably BNFL's most well known site, and is home to the Sellafield Visitors Centre. The Visitors Centre presents a unique educational experiene and contains interesting and innovative exhibitions providing an insight into the world of BNFL and Sellafield.

Senhouse Roman Museum

The Battery, Sea Brows

Maryport CA15 6JD

01900 816168

www.senhousemuseum.co.uk

senhousemuseum@aol.com

Dramatically sited on cliffs overlooking Maryport harbour and the Scottish coast, this unique and award-winning Museum is next to the site of the Roman fort built at the centre of Hadrian's coastal defences on the Solway. It is housed in a Royal Naval Reserve Battery building, and a new display covers the history of the building and of the military units associated with it.

Sizergh - National Trust

Sizergh

Kendal LA8 8AE

015395 60951

www.nationaltrust.org.uk/sizergh

sizergh@nationaltrust.org.uk

Medieval house extended in Elizabethan times, with handsome gardens. Originally built in the Middle Ages by the Strickland family, who still live here, this imposing house has an exceptional series of oak-panelled rooms culminating in the Inlaid Chamber.

Solway Aviation Museum

Aviation House, Carlisle Airport, Crosby-on-Eden
Carlisle CA6 4NW
01228 573823
www.solway-aviation-museum.co.uk
info@solway-aviation-museum.co.uk

The Solway Aviation Museum is run by volunteers from the Solway Aviation Society, with a theme of British Military Aircraft manufactured in the North West of England between the 1950s and 1960s. With the kind permission of the Carlisle Airport management, and with help from sponsors the collection is housed in 'Aviation House' to the right of the main Airport entrance.

St Martin's Church, Brampton

Front Street
Brampton CA8 1SH
07586 906368
www.stmartinsbrampton.org.uk
wendy.912@tiscali.co.uk

St Martin's Church is a splendid example of the work of the Pre-Raphaelites. This is the only church built by the architect Philip Webb and is adorned by an exquisite set of stained glass windows designed by Sir Edward Burne-Jones and manufactured by William Morris.

Stott Park Bobbin Mill

Finsthwaite, Newby Bridge
Nr Ulverston LA12 8AX
01539 531087
www.english-heritage.org.uk/stottpark
customers@english-heritage.org.uk

This extensive working mill was begun in 1835 to produce the wooden bobbins vital to the Lancashire spinning and weaving industries. Although small compared to other mills, some 250 men and boys (some drafted in from workhouses) worked here in often arduous conditions to produce a quarter of a million bobbins a week.

Townend - National Trust

Townend, Troutbeck
Windermere LA23 1LB
015394 32628
www.nationaltrust.org.uk/townend
townend@nationaltrust.org.uk

Fine example of Lake District vernacular architecture. Largely 17th-century, the solid stone and slate house is an exceptional survival.

Tullie House Museum & Art Gallery

Castle Street
Carlisle CA3 8TP
01228 618718
www.tulliehouse.co.uk
enquiries@tulliehouse.co.uk

Discover, explore and enjoy award winning Tullie House, where historic collections, contemporary art and family fun are brought together in one impressive museum and art gallery. Set in beautiful gardens, Old Tullie House is a Grade 1 listed building, and is home to a nationally important collection of Pre-Raphaelite art.

Whitehaven Archive & Local Studies Centre

Cumbria Archive and Local Studies Centre, Whitehaven, Scotch Street
Whitehaven CA28 7NL
01946 506420
http://goo.gl/F4yQQe

Original historical documents dating from the 12th century to the present day relating to the area of West Cumbria bounded by the River Derwent in the North and the River Duddon in the South.

Windermere Steamboat Museum

Rayrigg Road
Bowness-on-Windermere LA23 1BN
015394 46139
www.lakelandartstrust.org.uk
info@steamboats.org.uk

The Lakeland Arts Trust has embarked upon an ambitious project to redevelop the Windermere Steamboat Museum.

Collections: The collection of historic vessels at the Windermere Steamboat Museum is one of the most important in the world, telling the story of boating in the Lake District from early mediaeval log boats to record-breaking speed boats of the 1960s and 70s.

Wordsworth House & Garden - National Trust

Main Street
Cockermouth CA13 9RX
01900 820884
www.nationaltrust.org.uk/wordsworth-house
wordsworthhouse@nationaltrust.org.uk

Living Georgian town house where William Wordsworth was born in 1770. Costumed servants are on duty every day in the working Georgian kitchen.

Derbyshire

Derbyshire, midland county of England, having Yorkshire on the N., Notts on the E., Leicestershire, Warwickshire, and Staffordshire on the S., and Staffordshire and Cheshire on the W.; length, N. and S., 52 miles; greatest breadth, 35 miles; average breadth, 20 miles; area, 658,624 acres; population 461,914. The surface in the S. is either flat or undulating, irregular in the middle and NE., and picturesquely mountainous in the NW. or Peak district. The principal rivers are the Trent, Derwent, Dove, and Wye; river communication is supplemented by the Erewash and Grand Trunk Canals. The road and railway systems are highly developed. The soil in the Vale of the Trent is alluvial and very productive. In the hilly districts the land is mostly in pasture; much of it is rocky and unproductive. Oats, barley, potatoes, and wheat are cultivated; and there are many excellent dairy-farms. Warm mineral springs are numerous, the most popular being those at Buxton, Matlock, and Bakewell. Coal is abundant; iron ore and lead are worked; among the other mineral products are zinc, manganese, and barytes. There are numerous and extensive quarries of limestone and marble; fluor-spar is found in the caverns, and is manufactured into a great variety of ornamental articles. Silk, cotton, and lace are the chief manufactures, but malting and brewing are also carried on, and there are some extensive iron foundries. The county comprises 6 hundreds, 314 parishes, with parts of 8 others, the parliamentary and municipal borough of Derby (2 members), and the municipal boroughs of Chesterfield and Glossop. It is mostly in the diocese of Southwell.

– John Bartholomew, *Gazetteer of the British Isles* (1887)

Bakewell Old House Museum

🏠 £

Cunningham Place, Off North Church Street
Bakewell DE45 1DD
01629 813 642
www.oldhousemuseum.org.uk
bakewellmuseum@googlemail.com

This enchanting museum houses 10 beamed rooms with massive Tudor fireplaces. The building incorporates a Victorian kitchen, Tudor Parlour and Houseplace.

Barlborough Heritage & Resource Centre

🏛 ⊞ ★

1 Ward Lane, Barlborough
Chesterfield S43 4JD
01246 810100
www.barlboroughrc.btck.co.uk
linda@barlboroughrc.co.uk

A Village Heritage Centre. Exhibitions and displays of the local history and heritage of this agricultural and mining area.

Barrow Hill Roundhouse Railway Centre

🚂 🏠

Campbell Drive, Barrow Hill
Chesterfield S43 2PR
01246 472450
www.barrowhill.org.uk
project_man@barrowhill.org.uk

We have over 60 diesel, steam and electric locomotives on the site, and more are brought in for the Steam and Diesel galas. Our archive room is full of books, videos, magazines, photographs and much more, which have all been kindly donated to the Barrow Hill Engine Shed Society.

Bolsover Castle - English Heritage

🚂 🏠 £

Castle Street, Bolsover
Chesterfield S44 6PR
01246 822844
http://goo.gl/hSRBeQ
Gareth.Gwilt@english-heritage.org.uk

Bolsover is a 17th century house built on the site of a Norman fortress and is a wonderful place to meander and muse. See the fairytale house, designed as a fantasy house for entertaining, of rooms stacked on top of one another to create the 'Little Castle' with its range of charming and spectacular interiors.

Bolsover Cundy House

Bolsover S44 6BQ
01246 822844
http://goo.gl/i1YdiC
andrea.hill@english-heritage.org.uk

This 17th-century conduit house used to supply water to Bolsover Castle. It has recently been restored, with a solid stone-vaulted roof.

Buxton Museum & Art Gallery

Terrace Road
Buxton SK17 6DA
01629 533540
www.derbyshire.gov.uk/leisure/buxton_museum
buxton.museum@derbyshire.gov.uk

Founded in 1893, the museum houses geology and archaeology of the Peak District, including the archives and collections of Sir William Boyd Dawkins and Dr JW Jackson. A busy programme of temporary exhibitions provides opportunities for contemporary artists and access to the museum's own fine art and photographic collections.

Calke Abbey - National Trust

Calke
Ticknall DE73 1LE
01332 863 822
www.nationaltrust.org.uk/calke-abbey
calkeabbey@nationaltrust.org.uk

Vivid example of a great country house in decline, with extraordinary contents, historic park and restored garden. * Baroque mansion with unique collections of curiosities * Invisible corridors, underground tunnels and a secret garden.

Caudwell's Mill & Craft Centre

Bakewell Road, Rowsley
Matlock DE4 2EB
01629 733185
www.caudwellscrafts.co.uk
info@caudwellscrafts.co.uk

Caudwell's Mill Craft Centre is set in the most beautiful surroundings and the relaxing and informal atmosphere make it a unique place for an interesting day out. Whether you are just stopping to shop and have a coffee with friends or planning a family day trip, taking in the Mill and workshops, you will enjoy a friendly welcome and marvel at the stunning Derbyshire countryside.

Chatsworth

Bakewell DE45 1PP
01246 565300
www.chatsworth.org
visit@chatsworth.org

The 'Palace of the Peak' contains one of Europe's finest private collections of treasures, displayed in more than 30 rooms, from the grandeur of the 1st Duke's painted hall and state apartments with their rich decoration and painted ceilings, to the 19th century library, great dining room and sculpture gallery. Throughout the house, there are magnificent displays of paintings, including work by Rembrandt, Van Dyck, Gainsborough and Freud, furniture, silver, tapestries and porcelain and a gallery of neo-classical sculptures.

Chesterfield & District Family History Society

2 Highlow Close, Loundsley Green
Chesterfield S40 4PG
01246 231900
www.cadfhs.org.uk
cadfhs@aol.com

CADFHS was founded in 1989 and is based in Chesterfield, Derbyshire, England. The society covers the area of North East Derbyshire previously known as the Scarsdale Hundred.

Chesterfield Museum & Art Gallery

St Mary's Gate
Chesterfield S41 7TD
01246 345727
www.chesterfieldmuseum.co.uk
museum@chesterfield.gov.uk

The museum tells the story of Chesterfield from its origin as a Roman fort to the present day. It is located in the Stephenson Memorial Hall, built in 1879 as a mechanics institute, and named in honour of the town's most famous Victorian resident, railway pioneer George Stephenson.

Crich Tramway Village/National Tramway Museum

Crich Tramway Village, Crich
Matlock DE4 5DP
01773 854321
www.tramway.co.uk
enquiries@tramway.co.uk

Take a tram ride through time. Step aboard a vintage tram and travel back in time along a recreated village street complete with working pub.

Collections: Home to over 70 trams and a host of associated equipment, the museum has sought to acquire an example of each important stage in the evolution of the

British tramcar, a vehicle that dramatically influenced the growth of towns and cities. Significant foreign tramcars are also included.

Derby Cathedral

Iron Gate
Derby DE1 3GP
01332 341201
www.derbycathedral.org
office@derbycathedral.org

Like all other Cathedrals, Derby is much more than a beautiful building. It is, as its constitution states, 'the seat of the Bishop and a centre of worship and mission'.

Derby Museum & Art Gallery

The Strand
Derby DE1 1BS
01332 641901
www.derbymuseums.org
info@derbymuseums.org

A museum featuring collections relating to the history, culture and natural environment of Derby and Derbyshire. Visit the museum and Art Gallery to discover the fantastic recently refurbished Joseph Wright Gallery as well as our vibrant contemporary exhibition spaces. Discover Derby's thriving local history in our Nature and Origins galleries alongside favourite exhibits such as The Mummies, 1001 Objects and The Soldier's Story.

Derbyshire Ancestral Research Group

86 High Street, Loscoe
Heanor DE75 7LF
01773-604916
darg.gukutils.org.uk

The group comprises enthusiasts mainly in the fields of family history and local history and is involved in recording monumental inscriptions in churches, churchyards and cemeteries throughout Derbyshire, with occasional visits over the county border.

Derbyshire Family History Society

Bridge Chapel House, St Mary⊠s Bridge, Sowter Road
Derby DE1 3AT
01332 363876
www.dfhs.org.uk

For over 25 years the society has linked together people researching their family history in Derbyshire. During that time we have built up an extensive library and assembled a team of expert volunteers.

Derbyshire Record Office

New Street
Matlock DE4 3AG
01629 580000 Ext 35201
www.derbyshire.gov.uk/leisure/record_office
record.office@derbyshire.gov.uk

The Derbyshire Record Office provides the archive service for the county. It is approved by the Lord Chancellor and Master of the Rolls as the recognised record office for Derbyshire holding official public archives which come from the county.

Collections: You can see original archives from the mediaeval period to modern times at the record office. They include records of more than 250 Church of England Parishes, 600 Methodist and other nonconformist chapels, 500 schools, 200 societies and voluntary organisations and 350 businesses.

Diseworth Heritage Trust

Lady Gate
Diseworth DE74 2QF
01332 853647
www.diseworthcentre.org
info@diseworthcentre.org

Heritage Centre, villages archive, museum, training and exhibition centre.

Donington Grand Prix Collection

Donington Park, Castle Donington
Derby DE74 2RP
01332 811027
http://goo.gl/ZUD4ko
enquiries@doningtoncollection.co.uk

The Donington Grand Prix Exhibition is, quite simply, the largest collection of Grand Prix racing cars in the world. Five halls, with over 130 exhibits, illustrate the history of motor sport from the turn of the 20th century.

Erewash Museum

High Street
Ilkeston DE7 5JA
0115 9071141
www.erewashmuseum.co.uk
museum@erewash.gov.uk

Housed in a grade II listed Georgian town house with a Victorian extension. We are a community led museum, focusing on our geographical area, and exhibit for several local societies. We also have a collection of paintings by local artists and pottery from the art potters at West Hallam in the 1920s.

Eyam Hall & Craft Centre - National Trust

Main Street
Eyam S32 5QW
01433 639565
http://goo.gl/9aBROP
eyam@nationaltrust.org.uk

Nearly 350 years ago the community village of Eyam made the ultimate sacrifice to prevent the spread of the deadly plague – their own lives. To help you explore some of these stories we've created a number of walks starting from Eyam Hall. The centre, built in the Hall's former stable yard, offers a vibrant hub from which to explore the wider village of Eyam and its captivating stories.

Eyam Museum

Hawkhill Road, Eyam
Hope Valley S32 5QP
01433 631371
www.cressbrook.co.uk/eyam/museum

When plague struck the village of Eyam in 1665, the villagers made the extraordinary sacrifice of isolating themselves in order to prevent the spread of this terrible disease. The harrowing story is the central theme of Eyam Museum, which also tells the story of the village from prehistory to the present.

Hardwick Hall - National Trust

Doe Lea
Chesterfield S44 5QJ
01246 850430
www.nationaltrust.org.uk/hardwick
hardwickhall@nationaltrust.org.uk

One of the most splendid houses in England. Built by Bess of Hardwick in the 1590s, and unaltered since: yet its huge windows and high ceilings make it feel strikingly modern.

Kedleston Hall - National Trust

Kedleston
Quarndon DE22 5JH
01332 842 191
www.nationaltrust.org.uk/kedleston-hall
kedlestonhall@nationaltrust.org.uk

Neo-classical mansion with Adam interiors, landscape gardens and park Masterpiece of neo-classical architecture, designed by Robert Adam. * Eastern Museum filled with the collections of Lord Curzon, Viceroy of India * Lovely gardens, with celebrated displays of azaleas and rhododendrons (June).

Kegworth Village Association & Museum

52 High Street
Kegworth DE74 2DA
01509 670137
www.kegworthmuseum.org.uk
info@kegworthmuseum.org.uk

Kegworth village association and museum forms a centre for researching, recording and preserving Kegworth life, past present and future, as evidenced through artefacts, photographs, records and presonal memories.

Little Chester Heritage Centre

St Paul's Church, Chester Green, Mansfield Road
Derby DE1 3RA
01332 363354
www.beehive.thisisderbyshire.co.uk/lchc
jdarcy@qcinternet.co.uk

The centre shows the history of Little Chester (Chester Green) from Roman to recent industrial times by means of artefacts, models and photographs.

Living in the Past Community Archaeology Project

1 West Park Road
Derby DE22 1GG
01332 233961
www.livinginthepast.org.uk
liparchaeology@gmail.com

Community project examining domestic life in the Midlands (specifically Derby) during the 19th and early 20th centuries, through archaeology and social history.

Measham Museum

56 High Street, Measham
Swadlincote DE12 7HZ
01530 273956
www.meashammuseum.btck.co.uk/Visitorinformation

Central to the museum is the Dr Hart collection, a treasury of artefacts, pictures, letters and documents recording the history of a Midland village through the eyes of two local doctors – father and son – over nearly a century. Linked to the Hart Collection are items recalling the coal mining, terracotta and pottery traditions of this area, where mining was first recorded in the 13th century.

Midland Railway Centre

Butterley Station
Ripley DE5 3QZ
01773 570 140
www.midlandrailway-butterley.co.uk
info@midlandrailway-butterley.co.uk

Butterley Station is the entrance to the Midland Railway –
Butterley and everything that you see has been built since
the Midland Railway Trust arrived in 1973. At that time the
railway was derelict and all the buildings had been
bulldozed.

Moira Furnace Museum & Country Park

Furnace Lane Moira
Swadlincote DE12 6AT
www.moirafurnace.org
moirafurnace@hotmail.co.uk

Moira Furnace is an early 19th century blast furnace built
to manufacture iron. Unfortunately, the furnace was not a
great success and by 1811 it had closed down and been
converted into housing for miners.

New Mills Heritage & Information Centre

Rock Mill Lane, New Mills
High Peak SK22 3BN
01663 746904
www.newmillstowncouncil.org.uk/heritage.php

The centre is on the track leading down into the 'Torrs', a
dramatic gorge above which the town perches and which
includes mills and the ruined foundations of mills and
weirs lying in the bottom of the gorges, attracted to the site
at the end of the 18th century by the water power potential.

North East Midland Photographic Record - Picture the Past

c/o Derbyshire County Council, Heanor Library, Ilkeston
Road
Heanor DE75 7DX
01773 716967
www.picturethepast.org.uk
admin@picturethepast.org.uk

The libraries and museums of Derby, Derbyshire,
Nottingham and Nottinghamshire have in their collections,
hundreds of thousands of historic photographs, slides,
negatives, glass plates, postcards and engravings recalling
the history of the local communities over the last hundred
years and more. In the past, these treasures were held in
filing cabinets and anyone who wanted to see them would
have to make a trip to the library or museum - perhaps to
several different locations. Now thousands of them are
available online.

Peak District Mining Museum

The Pavilion
Matlock Bath DE4 3NR
01629 583834
www.peakmines.co.uk
mail@peakmines.co.uk

Visit a museum where you can experience and wonder at
the forgotten world of a Derbyshire lead miner. For
centuries, men have toiled underground in cramped and
hazardous conditions to earn a meagre living by extracting
the mineral galena (lead ore). See the tools they used,
clothes they wore, the advances in technology and the
importance of this metal in our modern day lives. Crawl
and climb through a maze of twisted tunnels and shafts to
feel for yourself the cramped conditions of a Derbyshire
lead miner.

Peveril Castle - English Heritage

Market Place, Castleton
Hope Valley S33 8WQ
01433 620613
http://goo.gl/a7mlE1

Perched high above the pretty village of Castleton, the
castle offers breathtaking views of the Peak District.
Founded soon after the Norman Conquest of 1066 by
William Peverel, one of King William's most trusted
knights, it played an important role in guarding the Peak
Forest area. Following extensive conservation work on the
keep, a walk-way erected at first floor level enables visitors
to enter two chambers previously inaccessible: a medieval
garderobe, and a small room with beautiful views of the
surrounding countryside.

Pickford's House Museum of Georgian Life & Costume

41 Friar Gate
Derby DE1 1DA
01332 715181
www.derby.gov.uk/museums
Louise.Hilland@derby.gov.uk

You can see the ground floor dining room, drawing room
and morning room as they might have been in Joseph
Pickford's time. A Georgian bedroom and dressing room
have been recreated on the first floor, while on the top floor
there is a servant's bedroom complete with straw mattress.

Princess Royal Class Locomotive Trust, The

The Princess Royal Class Locomotive Trust's West Shed
Museum, Midland Railway - Swanwick Junction site
Ripley DE5 3QZ
01773 743986
www.prclt.co.uk
westshed6233@btconnect.com

The West Shed is home to The Princess Royal Class
Locomotive Trust - a voluntary organisation formed in
1993 to look after and promote the historic locomotives in
its care. The West Shed houses a collection of historic steam
locomotives and railway coaches, whose history is told
through display boards, audio commentary domes,
animatronic figures and a mini-cinema with short films.

Red House Stables Working Carriage Museum

Old Road, Darley Dale
Matlock DE4 2ER
01629 733583
www.workingcarriages.com

Red House Stables Working Carriage Museum has one of
the finest collections of original horse drawn vehicles and
equipment in Britain. Established in 1946.

Regimental Museum of the 9th/12th Royal Lancers - Prince of Wales

The Strand
Derby DE1 1BS
01332 716656
www.derbymuseums.org/the-soldiers-story

Dedicated to the history of the 9th/12th Royal Lancers, The
Sherwood Foresters and the Derbyshire Yeomanry. In
Soldiers Story you will follow the story of Derby's and
Derbyshire's soldiers from the days of muskets and swords
at the Battle of Waterloo to the present day conflicts of Iraq
and Afghanistan.

Renishaw Hall

Renishaw Park
Renishaw S21 3WB
01246 432310
www.renishaw-hall.co.uk
enquiries@renishaw-hall.co.uk

Renishaw Hall is rightly celebrated for its stunning
Italianate gardens, laid out in 1895 by Sir George Sitwell
(1860 - 1943), great-grandfather of Alexandra Sitwell, the
current owner. The gardens boast several 'rooms' each with
their own names such as the ball room and secret garden,
which house species of hellebores, delphiniums and
camellias among many others. The Hall is beautifully
decorated by generations of Sitwell's yet visitors will still
find evidence of the Hall as a modern family home.

Revolution House

61 High Street, Old Whittington
Chesterfield S41 9LA
01246 345727
www.chesterfieldmuseum.co.uk
museum@chesterfield.gov.uk

The Revolution House, in the Derbyshire village of Old
Whittington, three miles north of Chesterfield, takes its
name from the Revolution of 1688. Three hundred years
ago, this cottage was an alehouse, the 'Cock and Pynot'
('Pynot' is a dialect word for magpie), and it was here, as
history and tradition relate, that three local noblemen- the
Earl of Devonshire (from nearby Chatsworth), the Earl of
Danby and Mr John D'Arcy met to begin planning their
part in the overthrow of James II.

Royal Crown Derby Museum

194 Osmaston Road
Derby DE23 8JZ
www.royalcrownderby.co.uk/visiting

Royal Crown Derby houses the most comprehensive
collection of Derby Porcelain to be seen anywhere in the
world. It includes pieces from all three of the factories in
our history.

Shardlow Heritage Centre

London Wharf, London Road, Shardlow
Derby DE72 2GA
homepages.which.net/~shardlow.heritage
shardlow.heritage@which.net

Visit Shardlow and its Heritage Centre for a fascinating
insight into this 18th century canal transhipment port.
Follow the village trail, on sale at the Heritage Centre..

Sharpe's Pottery Museum

West Street
Swadlincote DE11 9DG
01283 222 600
www.sharpespotterymuseum.org.uk
sdcollections@btconnect.com

A sensitive conversion of a 19th century pottery. The
Visitor Centre is a small registered museum centred around
a bottle kiln, with artefacts, models, film clips and
imaginative computer interactives where people can
explore the rich industrial and cultural heritage of the area.

Silk Mill, The

🏛 ✉ ⭐

Silk Mill Lane, Off Full Street

Derby DE1 3AF

01332 255308

www.derby.gov.uk/museums

info@derbymuseums.org

The Silk Mill, Derby's Museum of Industry and History, is on the site of the world's oldest factories, the Silk Mills built by George Sorocold in 1702 and 1717. The foundations and parts of the tower from the 1717 mill are still visible.

Sir John Moore Heritage Centre

🏛 ✉ 🏤 ⭐

Appleby Magna DE12 7AH

01530 273629

www.sirjohnmoore.org.uk

deana@sirjohnmoore.org.uk

17th century school building, designed by Sir Christopher Wren and Sir William Wilson. Many original architectural features from the seventeeth, 18th and 19th centuries remain.

Sir Richard Arkwright's Masson Mills

🏛 £

Derby Road

Matlock Bath DE4 3PY

01629 581001

www.massonmills.co.uk

Sir Richard Arkwright's 1783 showpiece Masson Mills on the River Derwent at Matlock Bath are the finest and best preserved example of an Arkwright cotton mill. The Masson Mill pattern of design was influential in nascent British and American cotton mill construction.

Collections: The collection contains diverse items from the British textile industry from its foundations in the late 18th century and illustrates the Legacy of Sir Richard Arkwright.

Strutt's North Mill

🏛 ✉ £

Derwent Valley Visitor Centre, North Mill, Bridgefoot

Belper DE56 1YD

01773 880474

www.belpernorthmill.org.uk

manager@belpernorthmill.org.uk

Jedediah Strutt began building mills in Belper in 1776. The North Mill was rebuilt after a fire in 1803 to a 'fire-proof' design by Jedediah's son William.

Collections: Some original and some replica machines displays the evolution of cotton spinning from cottage industry to factory system, from drop spindle and spinning wheel through to Hargreaves jenny, water-frame and Crompton.

Sudbury Hall & the National Trust Museum of Childhood

🏛 ✉

Sudbury Hall and The Museum of Childhood

Sudbury DE6 5HT

01283 585305

www.nationaltrust.org.uk/sudburyhall

sudburyhall@nationaltrust.org.uk

Sudbury Hall is a 17th century house situated in the picturesque village of Sudbury in Derbyshire. It was built by the Vernon family and contains exquisite examples of craftsmanship, including an impressive wood carving by Grinling Gibbons.

Sutton Scarsdale Hall

🏛 ⭐

Sutton cum Duckmanton

Chesterfield S44 5UR

01246 822844

www.english-heritage.org.uk

andrea.hill@english-heritage.org.uk

Work has recently been carried out by English Heritage to make the ruins of this 16th-century house safe. Visitors can now see the fragments of its former rich plaster decoration.

Wirksworth Heritage Centre

🏛 ✉ £

Market Place

Wirksworth DE4 4ET

01629 825225

www.storyofwirksworth.co.uk

enquries@storyofwirksworth.co.uk

Wirksworth Heritage Centre tells the 'story of Wirksworth' a unique town set in the heart of Derbyshire. From a prehistoric woolly rhino to the history of lead mining and quarrying, Wirksworth has a fascinating history - words, pictures and memories bring this history to life.

Devon

Devon – maritime county in SW. of England; is bounded N. by the Bristol Channel, E. by Somerset and Dorset, S. by the English Channel, and W. by Cornwall; length, 69 miles; breadth, 65 miles; coast-line, about 143 miles; area, 1,655,208 acres, population 603,595. The surface is richly diversified; the prevailing scenery is beautiful; the climate is mild and salubrious. The coast-line is rocky and precipitous. In the S. is the fertile district called South Hams; in the centre is the bleak and rugged tract of Dartmoor, rising to a mean elevation of 1700 ft., and the rich and beautiful Vale of Exeter; in the N. of the co. moorland prevails. The principal rivers are the Taw and the Torridge, flowing into the Bristol Channel, and the Exe, Axe, Teign, Dart, Avon, and Tamar, flowing into the English Channel. The estuaries of all these rivers afford good harbours. The prevailing rocks are – granite on Dartmoor, Devonian limestone in the N. and S., millstone grit in the centre and W., and new red sandstone, &c., in the E. The minerals are tin, copper, lead, iron, granite, limestone, marble, slate, &c. Potter's clay and pipeclay are also worked. Devon is celebrated for its orchards and dairy farms; butter, cheese, cider, and live stock are largely exported. The manufactures are coarse woollen goods, lace, paper, gloves, and shoes. The fisheries are considerable. The county comprises 33 hundreds, 481 parishes, with 2 parts, the parliamentary and municipal boroughs of Devonport (2 members), Exeter (1 member), and Plymouth (2 members), and the municipal boroughs of Barnstaple, Bideford, Dartmouth, Honiton, South Molton, Tiverton, Torrington, and Totnes. It is mostly in the diocese of Exeter.

– John Bartholomew, *Gazetteer of the British Isles* (1887)

A la Ronde

Summer Lane
Exmouth EX8 5BD
01395 265514
www.nationaltrust.org.uk/a-la-ronde
alaronde@nationaltrust.org.uk

This unique sixteen-sided house was described by Lucinda Lambton as having 'a magical strangeness that one might dream of only as a child'. It was built for two spinster cousins, Jane and Mary Parminter, on their return from a grand tour of Europe in the late 18th century. It contains many objects and mementoes of their travels. The extraordinary interior decoration includes a feather frieze, gathered from native game birds and chickens, laboriously stuck down with isinglass. There is also a fragile shell-encrusted gallery, said to contain nearly 25,000 shells, which can be viewed in its entirety using a touch screen 360 degree virtual tour.

Allhallows Museum of Lace & Antiquities

Allhallows Museum, High Street
Honiton EX14 1PG
01404 44966
www.honitonmuseum.co.uk
info@honitonmuseum.co.uk

In the town famous for lace-making Allhallows Museum has one of the most comprehensive collections of Honiton Lace in the world. Lace-making demonstrations are given daily by volunteers throughout the months of June, July and August.

Arlington Court & the National Trust Carriage Museum - National Trust

Arlington
Barnstaple EX31 4LP
01271 850296
www.nationaltrust.org.uk/arlington-court
arlingtoncourt@nationaltrust.org.uk

Arlington Court is an impressive Regency house with a vast collections of artefacts from paintings to pewter and ships to shells. Set in grounds of 2700 acres with formal gardens and woodland.

Ashburton Museum

1 West Street
Ashburton TQ13 7AB
www.ashburton.org

No visit to Ashburton would be complete without a visit to the Town's Museum. Originally started in a private house, it moved to the tower of St Lawrence Chapel and, when it outgrew that, in 1962, to the old blacksmith's shop behind the chapel (part of the old grammar school site).

Axe Valley Heritage Museum

Town Hall, Fore Street
Seaton EX12 2LD
01297 24227
www.seatonmuseum.co.uk

The museum is situated on the top floor of Seaton Town Hall in Fore Street. Of particular interest is the large collection of photographs and documents illustrating life in Seaton in past days. Displays illustrate the history of the Axe Valley, including archaeology, natural history and geology.

Axminster Museum

Church Street
Axminster EX13 5AQ
01297 34668
http://goo.gl/qZ2J5U

Originally the Old Police Station and Courthouse, the museum is opposite St Mary's Church in the centre of Axminster.

Collections: Visitors can discover old police cells, see displays in the former courtroom, and view collections ranging from agricultural tools to Axminster carpets, archaeology to old photographs.

Bampton Heritage & Visitor Centre

c/o 21, Briton Street, Bampton
Tiverton EX16 9LN
01398 331482
www.bampton.org.uk
kenmills22@talktalk.net

You can visit the Heritage and Visitor Centre to read and hear about Bampton's history and you can also take a guided town trail to see Bampton's history!

Barnstaple Heritage Centre

The Strand
Barnstaple EX31 1EU
01271 373003
http://goo.gl/9XO3km

On your journey through time, you can experience Saxon life in Barnstaple, find out what was on offer in the medieval market, listen to merchants trading at the Tome Stone, and make sure the enemy does not surround you as the Civil War reaches town! Escape the battles to reach the genteel 18th century, and tread the boards with John Gay's Beggar's Opera.

Barometer World Museum

Quicksilver Barn
Merton EX20 3DS
01805 603443
www.barometerworld.co.uk
barometers@barometerworld.co.uk

The Barometer World Exhibition is bound to be of interest to many visitors, with an incredible variety of weather predictors from conventional mercury and aneroid barometers, rare and strange instruments from the past to unusual natural weather forecasters including sharks, frogs and leeches.

Berry Pomeroy Castle - English Heritage

Totnes TQ9 6LJ
01803 866618
http://goo.gl/WW1u0Y

Tucked away in a steep wooded valley, Berry Pomeroy Castle is the perfect romantic ruin. Within the 15th-century defences of the Pomeroy family castle, still displaying a wall painting of the Three Kings in its gatehouse chamber, looms the dramatic ruined shell of its successor, the great Elizabethan mansion of the Seymours.

Bill Douglas Centre for the History of Cinema & Popular Culture

University of Exeter, Old Library Building, Prince of Wales Road
Exeter EX4 4SB
01392 264321
www.exeter.ac.uk/bill.douglas
bdc@exeter.ac.uk

The Bill Douglas Centre opened in 1997 as part of the University of Exeter's developing film studies programme. The museum is dedicated to the history of the moving image.

Collections: The centre houses one of the largest collections of film- and cinema-related memorabilia in the UK, including Disney toys, posters, film stills, sheet music, postcards, campaign material and an extensive library. The collections also represent the wealth of Victorian optical entertainments, including shadow puppets, magic lanterns, panoramas, zoetropes and peepshows.

Bishopsteignton Museum of Rural Life

Shute Hill
Bishopsteignton TQ14 9QL
01626 775308
www.devonmuseums.net
bishopsteignton@devonmuseums.net

Our museum is quite small but contains a wealth of exhibits relating to the history of the village and its inhabitants. We have a large collection of documents relating to the population over the years and our curator is happy to help visitors seeking family information.

Bradley - National Trust

Bradley
Newton Abbot TQ12 6BN
01803 661907
www.nationaltrust.org.uk/bradley
bradley@nationaltrust.org.uk

Unspoilt and fascinating medieval manor house, still a relaxed family home, in a green haven of riverside meadows and woodland.

Branscombe - National Trust

Branscombe
Seaton EX12 3DB
01752 346585
www.nationaltrust.org.uk/branscombe
branscombe@nationaltrust.org.uk

Nestling in a valley that reaches down to the sea on east Devon's dramatic Jurassic Coast, the village of Branscombe is surrounded by picturesque countryside with miles of tranquil walking through woodland, farmland and beach. Branscombe's charming thatched houses, working forge and restored watermill add to the timeless magic of the place. An easy graded trail winds up from the beach to the village passing Manor Mill, the Old Bakery tearooms and the working forge.

Braunton & District Museum

The Bakehouse Centre, Caen Street
Braunton EX33 1AA
01271 816688
www.explorebraunton.org
brauntonmuseum@yahoo.co.uk

The Bakehouse Centre was specially converted from a former bakehouse and two cottages to house today's Museum. Museum Staff are pleased to welcome visitors and offer a guided tour if requested. A printed guide to the collection is also available.

Britannia Royal Naval College Museum & Archives

The Britannia Museum, Britannia Royal Naval College
Dartmouth TQ6 0HJ
01803 677233
http://goo.gl/r85CEG
britanniamuseum@hotmail.co.uk

This small yet fine museum has collected together many pictures and artefacts showing the history of BRNC from its beginnings in 1863 as two vessels moored in the River Dart, through the opening in 1905 of today's College.

Brixham Heritage Museum

The Old Police Station, New Road
Brixham TQ5 8LZ
01803 856267
www.brixhamheritage.org.uk
mail@brixhamheritage.org.uk

Brixham Museum & History Society was founded in 1957 to record, save and display the heritage of the historic town and fishing port. The museum moved to its present location, the 1902 Police Station and Sergeant's House, in 1976.

Buckfast Abbey

Buckfast Road
Buckfastleigh TQ11 0EE
01364 645550
www.buckfast.org.uk
education@buckfast.org.uk

The Buckfast monks are pleased to invite visitors to their abbey. We seek to provide a stimulating learning environment for all ages and ability levels.

Buckland Abbey, Garden & Estate - National Trust

Buckland
Yelverton PL20 6EY
01822 853607
www.nationaltrust.org.uk/buckland-abbey
bucklandabbey@nationaltrust.org.uk

700-year-old building with fine 16th-century great hall, associated with Elizabethan seafarers Drake and Grenville. Tucked away in its own secluded valley above the River Tavy, Buckland was originally a small but influential Cistercian monastery.

Burton Art Gallery & Museum

Kingsley Road
Bideford EX39 2QQ
01237 471455
www.burtonartgallery.co.uk

The Burton Art Gallery and Museum consists of Bideford Museum display area, temporary exhibition spaces and a craft gallery.

Castle Drogo - National Trust

Drewsteignton
near Exeter EX6 6PB
01647 433306
www.nationaltrust.org.uk/castle-drogo
castledrogo@nationaltrust.org.uk

Castle Drogo was built for self-made millionaire Julius Drewe by architect Sir Edwin Lutyens. Unfortunately the castle, with its flat roof, has suffered from serious water penetration from the start, and is now undergoing a 5 year conservation project that will last until 2017 to make it watertight.

Coldharbour Mill Trust

Working Wool Museum, Uffculme
Collompton EX15 3EE
01884 840960
www.coldharbourmill.org.uk
info@coldharbourmill.org.uk

Welcome to Coldharbour Mill, a 200 year old spinning mill set in the tranquil Devon village of Uffculme. Built by Thomas Fox to spin woollen and later worsted yarns in 1799, Coldharbour Mill is a rare example of surviving Georgian architecture, industry and enterprise. Since reopening as a museum in 1982 the mill has continued to produce high quality worsted knitting yarn on its period machinery.

Coleton Fishacre - National Trust

Brownstone Road
Kingswear TQ6 0EQ
01803 752466
www.nationaltrust.org.uk/coleton-fishacre
coletonfishacre@nationaltrust.org.uk

Travel back in time to the Jazz Age at the holiday home of the D'Oyly Carte family. You can lose yourself in the magical 12-hectare (30-acre) garden: viewpoints give enticing glimpses out to sea, paths weave through glades past tranquil ponds, and tender plants from the Mediterranean, South Africa and New Zealand thrive in the moist and sheltered valley.

Combe Martin Museum & Tourist Information Point

Cross Street
Combe Martin EX34 0DH
01271 889301
www.combe-martin-museum.co.uk
mail@visitcombemartin.com

A volunteer run museum which gained Heritage Lottery and Devon Rennaisance funding in 2008 to relocate to newly renovated premises in historic Cross Street.

Compton Castle - National Trust

Marldon
Paignton TQ3 1TA
01803 661906
www.nationaltrust.org.uk/compton-castle
comptoncastle@nationaltrust.org.uk

Built between the 14th and 16th centuries, the castle has been home to the Gilbert family for most of the last 600 years. Sir Humphrey Gilbert (1539–1583) was coloniser of Newfoundland and half-brother to Sir Walter Raleigh.

Crediton Area History & Museum Society

The Old Town Hall, High Street
Crediton EX17 3LF
01363 773919
creditonhistory.org.uk
info@creditonhistory.org.uk

Local museum & history society for Crediton and surrounding villages in Mid-Devon. Exhibitions are usually based on local themes and use the society's archive of documents and photographs.

Dartmoor Trust & Archive

Ford Farm, Sticklepath
Okehampton EX20 2NS
01822 600100
www.dartmoortrust.org
tonyclark@dartmoortrust.org

The Dartmoor Trust works closely with the National Park Authority on projects that benefit Dartmoor. At the core of the Dartmoor Trust is our archive project. The Dartmoor Trust Archive is home to 20,000 images dating back over 100 years.

Dartmouth Castle - English Heritage

Castle Road
Dartmouth TQ6 0JN
01803 833588
http://goo.gl/MDD6BQ

One of the most picturesquely-sited fortresses in England. For over 600 years Dartmouth Castle has guarded the narrow entrance to the Dart Estuary and the busy, vibrant port of Dartmouth.

Dartmouth Museum

6 The Butterwalk, Duke Street
Dartmouth TQ6 9PZ
01803 832923
www.dartmouthmuseum.org
dartmouth@devonmuseums.net

A small and unusually interesting Museum housed in an old Merchant's House, dated 1640. The museum houses marine and local artefacts, including a superb collection of ships in bottles and an extensive photographic archive of the local area, shipbuilding and shipping on the Dart.

Dawlish Museum Society

The Knowle, Barton Terrace
Dawlish EX7 9QH
01626 888557
www.devonmuseums.net/dawlish
dawlish@devonmuseums.net

Knowle House was built as a gentleman's residence in 1805, and has been used for various purposes since. It now houses Dawlish Museum.

Devon & Cornwall Constabulary Heritage & Learning Resource

Okehampton Police Station, Exeter Road
Okehampton EX20 1NN
01837 658414
http://goo.gl/UrAA8q

Previously known as the Force Museum, Devon & Cornwall Constabulary's Heritage & Learning Resource is now based in Okehampton. One of our long-term aims is to open as a Police Heritage Centre which will illustrate aspects of police history as well as policing today.

Devon Family History Society

PO Box 9
Exeter EX2 6YP
01392 433212
www.devonfhs.org.uk
enquiries@devonfhs.org.uk

The society's objects are to promote the study of genealogy and history, especially of Devon families and places, to educate the public therein through advice and instruction, and, for the public benefit, to encourage the preservation and transcription of relevant documents and records, especially for the county of Devon.

Devon Record Office

Great Moor House, Bittern Road, Sowton
Exeter EX2 7NL
01392 384253
www.devon.gov.uk/record_office.htm
devrec@devon.gov.uk

The Devon Record Office exists to collect and preserve the historical records of Devon and to make them available to all who wish to study them. There are three record offices which share this task. The Devon Record Office at Exeter houses all types of historical records relating to the county of Devon, the city of Exeter, and East, Mid and South Devon, including Torbay.

Devon Rural Archive

Shilstone, Nr Modbury
Plymouth PL21 0TW
01548 830832
www.devonruralarchive.com
office@dra.uk.net

The Devon Rural Archive was launched in 2006 to promote a greater understanding of the county's rural domestic architecture. Our growing reference library is open to the public two days a week for private research and provides the perfect place to explore Devon's architectural heritage.

Dingles Fairground Heritage Centre

The Fairground Heritage Trust, Milford
Lifton PL16 0AT
01566 783425
www.fairground-heritage.org.uk
info@fairground-heritage.org.uk

The Fairground Heritage Trust, formed in 1986, is a charity which is committed to saving, conserving and sharing historic fairground equipment. Our aim is to establish Dingles Fairground Heritage Centre as a remarkable and fascinating experience; a place to visit offering fun, enjoyment and learning for a broad range of audiences. In addition to our other collections, the Trust also has access to an extensive collection of ephemera and a large photographic archive.

Exeter Cathedral

Exeter EX1 1HS
www.exeter-cathedral.org.uk

Pilgrims and visitors have been making their way to Exeter Cathedral since medieval times. It is one of the most visited places in the west country.

Exeter Synagogue

Exeter Hebrew Congregation, Synagogue Place, Mary
Arches Street
Exeter EX4 3BA
01392 251529
www.exetersynagogue.org.uk
webmaster@exetersynagogue.org.uk

Jews have lived and worshipped in Exeter for over 250
years. The synagogue, which was built in 1763, is small,
beautiful and, happily, still used regularly for services.

Exeter's Underground Passages

Romangate Passage, Off High Street
Exeter EX4 3PZ
01392 665887
www.exeter.gov.uk/index.aspx?articleid=2914
undergroundpassages@exeter.gov.uk

A visit to Exeter's Underground Passages is a most unusual
event and one of the most exciting things available for
young people in the City of Exeter. The passages welcome
bookings from schools, student groups, clubs and societies.

Exmouth Museum

Sheppards Row, Exeter Road
Exmouth EX8 1PW
07768 184127
www.devonmuseums.net/exmouth
exmouthmuseum@aol.com

Exmouth Museum was first opened in 1985, and is housed
in a 19th century building which was the Council Stables
together with the adjoining foreman's cottage. It is now
divided into three galleries, two on the ground floor and
one on the first floor.

Fairlynch Museum & Arts Centre

27 Fore Street
Budleigh Salterton EX9 6NP
01395 442666
www.devonmuseums.net/fairlynch
admin@fairlynchmuseum.co.uk

The town of Budleigh Salterton possesses one of the
important costume collections in the country. For this
reason alone a call at the museum is a must for visitors to
the town.

Finch Foundry - National Trust

Finch Foundry, Sticklepath
Nr Okehampton EX20 2NW
01837 840046
www.nationaltrust.org.uk/finch-foundry
finchfoundry@nationaltrust.org.uk

Set amid beautiful Dartmoor countryside in the village of
Sticklepath, this last remaining water-powered forge in
England gives a unique insight into village life in the 19th
century. In its heyday the foundry made 400 tools a day,
including sickles, scythes and shovels for West Country
farmers and miners. Don't miss the demonstrations and
tours of the machinery every hour.

Greenway - National Trust

Greenway Road
Galmpton, nr Brixham TQ5 0ES
01803 843235
www.nationaltrust.org.uk/greenway
greenway@nationaltrust.org.uk

Glorious woodland garden on the banks of the Dart
estuary. From 1938-1959, Greenway was the holiday home
of Mrs Mallowan – Agatha Christie – and her husband.

Grimspound

Challacombe Farm, Dartmoor
Postbridge, Yelverton PL20 6TD
http://goo.gl/RPKXsq

Late Bronze Age settlement featuring the remains of 24
huts within an area of over 6,000 square metres (four
acres), enclosed by a massive stone wall, some 9 feet thick.
This was the model for the prehistoric hut in which
Sherlock Holmes spent the night in The Hound of the
Baskervilles.

Holsworthy Museum

Manor Offices
Holsworthy EX22 6DJ
01409 259337
www.devonmuseums.net/holsworthy
holsworthymuseum@btinternet.com

The museum is housed in part of a building which is in
itself a museum piece; a small manor house dating from the
17th century which was used as a parsonage in 1724. There
are five separate rooms, individually themed, which cover
the history of Holsworthy, local tradesmen's tools, medical
and apothecary items, World War II and a kitchen with its
original cobbled floor, copper and fireplace.

Ilfracombe Museum

Wilder Road
Ilfracombe EX34 8AF
01271 863541
www.ilfracombemuseum.co.uk
info.ilfracombemuseum@gmail.com

Delve into the treasure trove that is Ilfracombe Museum. Overflowing with curiosities and memorabilia, this historic building houses unimaginable finds from a shrunken head to pickled bats, and marvellous insect, spider and butterfly specimens to explore.

Kennaway House

Coburg Road
Sidmouth EX10 8NG
01395 515551
www.kennawayhouse.org.uk
mail@kennawayhouse.co.uk

Built in 1805, the year of Trafalgar, Kennaway House is a handsome Regency mansion standing in its own grounds in the heart of Sidmouth.

Collections: There is a permanent display illustrating the history of the house and its significance within the architectural context of Sidmouth. There is a permanent display of the work of influential Sidmouth architect, RW Sampson, to which entry is free but by application. The restored Regency rooms are worth visiting in their own right and include exhibition space for the work of both established and new artists in the south west.

Kents Cavern Prehistoric Caves

Kents Cavern, Cavern House, Ilsham Road
Torquay TQ1 2JF
01803 215136
www.kents-cavern.co.uk
caves@kents-cavern.co.uk

Kents Cavern is one of the most important Stone Age cave sites in Europe, making it Britain's premier prehistoric cave. For thousands of years the cave was home to ancient humans, sheltering from extreme weather, making fires, shaping stone tools and hunting wild Ice Age predators.

Killerton - National Trust

Killerton, Broadclyst
Exeter EX5 3LE
01392 881345
www.nationaltrust.org.uk/Killerton
killerton@nationaltrust.org.uk

Fine 18th-century house with costume collection, hillside garden and estate. Delightful hillside garden featuring rhododendrons, magnolias, and rare trees. Home to the 'Paulise de Bush' costume collection, with over 9,000 outfits.

Kingsbridge Cookworthy Museum

The Old Grammar School, 108 Fore Street
Kingsbridge TQ7 1AW
01548 853235
www.kingsbridgemuseum.org.uk
wcookworthy@kingsbridgemuseum.org.uk

The Kingsbridge Cookworthy Museum is an independent museum, founded in 1971. It is housed in the Grade II listed 17th century former Grammar School, a well-known landmark in Kingsbridge.

Knightshayes Court - National Trust

Bolham
Tiverton EX16 7RQ
01884 254665
www.nationaltrust.org.uk/knightshayes-court
knightshayes@nationaltrust.org.uk

When pioneer lace-maker John Heathcoat was chased out of Loughborough by the Luddites in 1816, his relocation to Tiverton led eventually to one of the finest surviving Gothic Revival houses being built in the lush landscape of mid Devon. In 1869 his grandson employed the architect and decorator William Burges – a passionate Gothic enthusiast – to build Knightshayes Court.

Lyn & Exmoor Museum

St Vincent's Cottage, Market Street
Lynton EX35 6HJ
01598 752317
www.devonmuseums.net/lynton
lynexmuseum@yahoo.co.uk

A charming, rural museum with a collection of agricultural and domestic tools from Lynton and Exmoor. Housed in Lynton's oldest surviving domestic dwelling, it even includes its own ghost. Cottage kitchen with large stone fireplace, bread oven and pots and pans and domestic clutter.

Merchant's House

33 St Andrew Street
Plymouth PL1 2AX
01752 304774
www.plymouth.gov.uk/museums
museum@plymouth.gov.uk

See four mini museums under one roof in this former home of famous Elizabethan privateer, William Parker. Old curiosities, a Victorian schoolroom, Blitz room and Edwardian pharmacy provide a fascinating snapshot of Plymouth's recent past.

Morwellham Quay Museum

Morwellham
Tavistock PL19 8JL
01822 832766
www.morwellham-quay.co.uk
info@morwellham-quay.co.uk

An award-winning, evocative museum and visitor centre in the heart of the Cornwall and West Devon Mining Landscape World Heritage Site and Tamar Valley Area of Outstanding Natural Beauty. Just four miles west of Tavistock the historic port, mine workings and estate border the beautiful River Tamar.

Museum of Barnstaple & North Devon

The Square
Barnstaple EX32 8LN
01271 346 747
http://goo.gl/0hzT9I
museum@northdevon.gov.uk

A visit to the museum of Barnstaple and North Devon is the perfect way to get to know the area's landscape, wildlife, history and culture. In The Story of North Devon special effects and hands on activities help you find out about life from prehistoric to Victorian times.

Museum of British Surfing

Caen Street car park
Braunton EX33 1AA
01271 815155
www.museumofbritishsurfing.org.uk
contact@museumofbritishsurfing.org.uk

Historic British surfboards and associated memorabilia dating back to the time when Captain James Cook and his crew first discovered surfing in 1769. We have a large range of surfing publications dating back 200 years, plus photographs, films and interviews with pioneer surfers.

Museum of Dartmoor Life

3 West Street
Okehampton EX20 1TG
01837 52295
www.museumofdartmoorlife.eclipse.co.uk

Rural life on Dartmoor 100 years ago: Could you live without electricity? Could you cope without central heating? Where would you get food and clothes if there were no supermarkets or clothes shops? Find out how people survived at the museum of Dartmoor Life, Okehampton.

Newton Abbot Town & Great Western Railway Museum

2a St Pauls Road
Newton Abbot TQ12 2HP
01626 201121
www.museum-newtonabbot.org.uk
museum@newtonabbot-tc.gov.uk

The museum collections are focused on the Great Western Railway and the social history of the town. The working signal box takes pride of place within the GWR Room, a hands-on connection with the great days of the Great Western Railway. An audio system enables you to hear ex-GWR men talking about their lives as railwaymen.

North Devon Maritime Museum

Odun House, Odun Road
Appledore EX39 1PT
01237 474852
www.devonmuseums.net/appledore
maritime.mus@btinternet.com

This Museum covers all aspects of North Devon's history from the invasion of the Danes in 878 to present day shipbuilding. Subjects include our seafaring past and present, with models and photographs of sail, steam and motor ships, the Tudor period of Grenville and the Armada, the Newfoundland fishing trade, emigration, smuggling, shipbuilding, rope making, coopering, wreck & rescue and World War II activities in North Devon. Large archive of reference books, copies of Custom House records for Bideford, Barnstaple and Ilfracombe from 1786 to 1900, Mariners Mirror and Sea Breezes, documents, several photographic collections - all available by appointment only.

Okehampton Castle - English Heritage

Castle Lodge
Okehampton EX20 1JA
01837 52844
http://goo.gl/DhvFB3

The remains of the largest castle in Devon, in an outstandingly picturesque setting on a wooded spur above the rushing River Okement. Begun soon after the Norman Conquest as a motte and bailey castle with a stone keep, it was converted into a sumptuous residence in the 14th century by Hugh Courtenay, Earl of Devon, much of whose work survives.

Otterton Mill Centre & Working Museum

Nr Budleigh
Salterton EX9 7HG
01395 568521
www.ottertonmill.com

here has been a working mill at Otterton since at least Norman times, when King William the Conqueror granted all the local land hereabouts to the abbots of St Michel of Normandy. The earliest written record of the mill is in the Domesday survey in 1068, which confirmed its status as one of the largest and most productive of the seventy mills in Devon.

Overbeck's - National Trust

Sharpitor
Salcombe TQ8 8LW
01548 842893
http://goo.gl/h9Ns98
overbecks@nationaltrust.org.uk

A hidden paradise of subtropical gardens and eclectic collections.. With a climate more like the Mediterranean Riviera than the British mainland, Overbeck's is home to an astonishing plant collection.

Plymouth & West Devon Record Office

Unit 3, Clare Place
Plymouth PL4 0JW
01752 305940
www.plymouth.gov.uk/archives/

The Plymouth and West Devon Record Office is the principal archive repository within Plymouth and the West Devon area. It exists to collect and preserve the historical records of the area and to promote and encourage their use by all who want to study them.

Plymouth City Museum & Art Gallery

Drake Circus
Plymouth PL4 8AJ
01752 304774
www.plymouthmuseum.gov.uk
museum@plymouth.gov.uk

A visit to the City Museum and Art Gallery gives you a chance to see thousands of objects in our permanent galleries. Our ground floor displays include fascinating objects from Asia, Africa, Oceania and Europe. You can learn about life and death in Ancient Egypt, discover more about Plymouth's distant and more recent past and see a variety of natural specimens. On our first floor you can see highlights from our large decorative art collection and discover the story of porcelain. You can also see our Cottonian Collection, which offers a glimpse into the achievements of an 18th century gentleman.

Royal Albert Memorial Museum & Art Gallery

Queen Street
Exeter EX4 3RX
01392 665858
www.rammuseum.org.uk
ramm@exeter.gov.uk

Fully refurbished after a multimillion pound redevelopment, the new displays showcase the collections and collectors that have helped RAMM to become one of Britain's finest regional museums. They tell the story of Exeter and Devon from the prehistoric to the present but, more than a local museum, its internationally important world cultures and natural history collections also tell a story of global exploration and collecting in the 18th and 19th centuries. Original architectural features have been revealed allowing visitors to experience the splendour of the original Victorian spaces.

Salcombe Maritime & Local History Museum

Basement, The Old Council Hall, Market Street
Salcombe TQ8 8DE
http://goo.gl/pFVK3I
salcombemuseum@ship.eclipse.co.uk

When in Salcombe do find time to visit our museum. It is one of the town's few wet weather attractions and has, in recent years, been much upgraded.

Sidmouth Museum

Hope Cottage, Church Street
Sidmouth EX10 8IY
01395 516139
www.sidvaleassociation.org.uk
sidmouth@devonmuseums.net

Situated alongside the lych gate of the parish church, Sidmouth Museum celebrates 240 million years of history. It offers something for everyone with an interest in the World Heritage Jurassic Coast, local history and archaeology. There are permanent displays of fine prints, paintings and old photographs illustrating the history of Sidmouth from a fishing village, through its Regency period to the current time.

South Devon Railway Museum

South Devon Railway Trust, The Station
Buckfastleigh TQ11 0DZ
0845 345 1466
www.southdevonrailway.co.uk/museum
trains@southdevonrailway.org

The South Devon Railway Museum can be found in the former goods shed at Buckfastleigh station. Part has been closed while new displays and artefacts have been prepared, whilst the infrastructure has been greatly improved.

South Molton & District Museum

The Guildhall, The Square
South Molton EX36 3AB
01769 572951
www.southmoltonmuseum.org
info@southmoltonmuseum.org

The museum is located on the ground floor of the town's 18th century Guildhall, which was completed in 1743 and is situated on the town square. Discover the true spirit of the characters from South Molton's past, through the exhibits and interactive displays.

South West Image Bank

25 The Parade Barbican
Plymouth PL1 2JN
01752 665445
www.southwestimagebank.com
info@southwestimagebank.com

The South West Image Bank (SWiB) is a community based specialist photography archive managed by our Archivist, and a full time Outreach Officer. SWiB is supported by a team of volunteers who undertake cataloguing and digitisation of the unique photographic archives deposited by members of the public, photographers and local businesses.

St Nicholas Priory

The Mint, off Fore Street
Exeter EX4 3BL
01392 665858
www.exeter.gov.uk/priory
priory@exeter.gov.uk

Originally part of a medieval monastery, this splendid Grade 1 listed building later became the Tudor home of a wealthy merchant family. Now presented as their richly furnished Elizabethan town house adorned with beautifully crafted replica furniture and bright paint and textiles of the period. Also displayed are some of Exeter's original Tudor artefacts from the collection at the Royal Albert Memorial Museum.

Tavistock Museum

Court Gate, Guildhall Square
Tavistock PL19 0AE
www.tavistockmuseum.co.uk

Tavistock Museum is a town museum located in the historic Court Gate. The entrance is in Guildhall Square.

Teignmouth & Shaldon Museum

29 French Street
Teignmouth TQ14 8ST
01626 777041
www.teignmuseum.org.uk
enquiries@teignmuseum.org.uk

Two wonderful permanent galleries which have been carefully designed to appeal to both adults and children. The centre also houses a roof terrace, a large meeting and events space, the Teign Room, a small shop, dedicated research area and archive room.

Tiverton Museum of Mid Devon Life

Beck's Square
Tiverton EX16 6PJ
01884 256295
www.tivertonmuseum.org.uk
education@tivertonmuseum.org.uk

Tiverton Museum is a vibrant, award-winning and much loved museum that provides extensive displays on local history. It runs a lively events programme, including temporary exhibitions (on anything from the history of underwear to local farming memories), guided walks, talks, holiday craft activities, themed days and lots more.

Topsham Museum

25 The Strand
Topsham, Exeter EX3 0AX
01392 873244
http://goo.gl/bYBlel
museum@topsham.org.uk

Topsham Museum is housed in one of a group of late 17th century buildings overlooking the Exe Estuary. Part of the museum's focus is on Topsham's maritime history – one particular showpiece is the River Gallery, featuring unique historic river craft. Visitors can also enjoy the furnished period rooms of the original house and the Sail Loft with its historical timeline of the town's general history. Other interesting exhibits include wildlife of the Exe Estuary, local trades and organisations and memorabilia of the film star Vivien Leigh.

Torquay Museum

🖼 🏛 ⏣ £

529 Babbacombe Rd
Torquay TQ1 1HG
01803 293975
www.torquaymuseum.org
enquiries@torquaymuseum.org

Torquay Museum is Devon's oldest established Museum still operating, founded in 1845 and still owned and run by Torquay Museum Society. The museum holds collections that are exceptional for a Museum of this size, with over 300,000 objects, some of which are of international importance. The museum is home to the second oldest anatomically modern human fossil in Europe, along with a large collection of stone tools and animal remains from the nearby Kents Cavern - one of the most important prehistoric sites in Europe.

Torre Abbey Historic House & Gallery

🖼 🖵 £

The King's Drive
Torquay TQ2 5JE
01803 293 593
www.torre-abbey.org.uk
torreabbeyenquiries@torbay.gov.uk

Torre Abbey was founded in 1196 as a monastery for the Premonstratensian order of Canons. By the 15th century it was the richest monastery of the order in the whole of the UK.

Collections: Torre Abbey contains a regionally important collection of oil paintings and watercolours. It is particularly strong in 19th century portraits and landscapes, especially the work of the Pre-Raphaelites.

Torrington Museum

🖵 ⭐

14 South Street
Great Torrington EX38 8AA
01805 624 324
www.torringtonmuseum.org.uk

Torrington Museum is a small, friendly and free museum, which possesses or holds on loan many fascinating exhibits and reflects the diverse history of this ancient market town.

Totnes Castle - English Heritage

🖼 £

Totnes TQ9 5NU
01803 864406
http://goo.gl/edT9b7

A classic Norman motte and bailey castle, founded soon after the Conquest to overawe the Saxon town. A later stone shell-keep crowns its steep mound, giving sweeping views across the town rooftops to the River Dart.

Totnes Elizabethan House Museum

🖼 🖵 £

70 Fore Street
Totnes TQ9 5RU
01803 863821
www.devonmuseums.net/totnes
info@totnesmuseum.co.uk

The Totnes Elizabethan House Museum collection is contained in a magnificent Tudor house, built in 1575. There are 13 rooms on three floors covering over 5000 years of history from Totnes and District.

Collections: In Saxon times Totnes was a minting Burgh, a fortified town which produced its own coinage. The museum houses a collection of coins minted in Totnes during the Saxon period, which are currently on display in the Archaeology Gallery.

Totnes Fashion & Textiles Museum

🖵 £

Bogan House, 43 High Street
Totnes TQ9 5NP
www.devonmuseums.net/57/1043/museum.html
costumemuseum@yahoo.co.uk

The Devon Collection of Period Costume contains clothing for men, women and children from the 18th century to the end of the 20th century. A themed exhibition, which is changed annually, is displayed in the most intact Tudor Merchant's House in Totnes.

Valiant Soldier, The

🖵

79/80 Fore Street
Buckfastleigh TQ11 0BS
www.valiantsoldier.org.uk
Valiantsoldierbuckfastleigh@gmail.com

The Valiant Soldier was an active pub in Buckfastleigh which closed in the late 1960s and never re-opened. Everything was literally left as it was and today, it's open as a museum, giving visitors a glimpse of the past.

Whimple Heritage Centre

🖵

Lockyers Linhay, Church Road
Exeter EX5 2SQ
01404 822499
www.whimple.org/heritage.htm

Whimple Heritage Centre is concerned with the history and heritage of Whimple and the surrounding area. Our Centre has numerous artefacts on display and many records and photographs of life in the village including much to do with the Whiteways Cyder Factory which was based in the village.

Dorset

Dorset, maritime county, on S. coast of England; is bounded N. by Somerset and Wilts, E. by Hants, S. by the English Channel, and W. by Devon; length, E. and W., 52 miles; breadth, N. and S., 37 miles; coastline, 75 miles; area, 627,265 acres; population 191,028. The main features of the coast are Poole Harbour, St Alban's Head, and the singular projection called the Isle of Portland. The principal streams are the Stour and the Frome. Great part of the county is traversed by the two ranges of chalk hills called the North and South Downs, and the soil consists mainly of chalk, gravel, and sand, but is very fertile in the valleys. Wheat and barley are grown in the W. and N. Immense flocks of sheep are pastured on the Downs. Dairy farms are generally large, and dairy husbandry is carried to a very high point of perfection. The only mineral of any importance is Portland stone, quarried in the Isle of Portland. There are manufactures, to some extent, of sailcloth, sacking, nets, paper, silk, &c., with malting and brewing, and iron-founding. The fisheries, especially of mackerel, are considerable, and ships and yachts are built at Poole. The county comprises 34 hundreds, 22 liberties, 290 parishes, and a part, and the municipal boroughs of Blandford, Bridport, Dorchester, Lyme Regis, Poole, Shaftesbury, and Weymouth and Melcombe Regis. It is mostly in the diocese of Salisbury.

– John Bartholomew, *Gazetteer of the British Isles* (1887)

Ancient Technology Centre

Damerham Road, Cranborne
Wimborne BH21 5RP
01725 517618
www.ancienttechnologycentre.co.uk
atc@dorsetcc.gov.uk

The Ancient Technology Centre's activities and buildings are based on archaeological evidence from a range of periods including the Neolithic, Iron Age (Celtic), Roman, Anglo Saxon and Viking eras. These have all been built with the help of thousands of visiting school children, using authentic methods and locally-sourced materials where possible.

Beaminster Museum

Old Congregational Chapel, Whitcombe Road
Beaminster DT8 3NB
01308 863623
https://beaminstermuseum.wordpress.com

Beaminster Museum is a local history museum covering Beaminster and the surrounding villages. Its collection covers past local families of importance, which includes the Hine family who formed the Hine Cognac Dynasty; past local trades and schools; a fine collection of agricultural tools and a working church turret clock.

Blandford Fashion Museum

Lime Tree House, The Plocks, Blandford
Forum DT11 7AA
01258 453006
www.theblandfordfashionmuseum.com

Lime Tree House was opened to the public as a home for the fashion collection in 1995. This beautiful Georgian house was was built by John and William Bastard after the great fire of Blandford in 1731. Conservation and dating of costumes is of the utmost importance and archives are kept up to date .

Blandford Forum Museum

Bere's Yard, Market Place
Blandford Forum DT11 7HQ
01258 450388
www.blandfordtownmuseum.org

The museum houses artefacts illustrating the history of Blandford Forum and the surrounding area. Our collections include railway memorabilia, artefacts from World War I and II, material from the local fire and police services over the last 200 years, musical instruments, palaeontological finds including a fossil Ichthyosaur, the Durden Collection of archaeological discoveries, a cobbler's shop, a forge, and a Victorian child's playroom.

Bournemouth Aviation Museum

Hangar 600, Bournemouth International Airport
Christchurch BH23 6SE
01202 473141
www.aviation-museum.co.uk
admin@aviation-museum.co.uk

Bournemouth Aviation Museum is the only UK charitable museum dedicated to preserving and presenting to the public at large, amongst others, operational examples of historic military jets. Bournemouth Aviation Museum occupies a 30,000 sq ft hanger at Bournemouth International Airport.

Bridport Museum

25 South Street
Bridport DT6 3NR
01308 422116
www.bridportmuseum.co.uk
office@bridportmuseum.co.uk

From Romans to ropemaking - Bridport Museum tells the unique history of the town in this Tudor building. The story of Bridport's world famous rope and net making industries is told.

Cerne Giant - National Trust

Cerne Abbas Giant
Cerne Abbas
01297 489481
www.nationaltrust.org.uk/cerne-giant
westdorset@nationaltrust.org.uk

The striking giant of Cerne Abbas is a 180 foot high figure of a man bearing a 121 foot long club, incised into the chalk of the hillside. It has been speculated that the giant may have carried a cloak over his left arm and gripped a severed head in his left hand.

Christchurch Priory & St Michael's Loft Museum

Christchurch Priory Church, Quay Road
Christchurch BH23 1BU
01202 488645
www.christchurchpriory.org
parishoffice@christchurchpriory.org

Christchurch Priory Church (the parish church) is very much a living church. It is open every day not only for the usual daily services of Matins and Evensong, but from 10.00am to 5.00pm for pilgrims, tourists and visitors for personal prayer, relaxation or just viewing.

Corfe Castle - National Trust

The Square, Corfe Castle
Wareham BH20 5EZ
01929 481294
www.nationaltrust.org.uk/corfe-castle
corfecastle@nationaltrust.org.uk

Thousand-year-old castle, rising above the Isle of Purbeck. One of Britain's most majestic ruins, the castle controlled the gateway through the Purbeck Hills and has been an important stronghold since the time of William the Conqueror.

Corfe Castle Museum

Corfe Castle Town Hall, West Street
Corfe Castle BH20 5HA
www.corfecastletowntrust.co.uk/the-museum

The museum has images and artefacts taken from Corfe's past with the clay, stone and Purbeck Marble industries and snapshots of why and how the village became what it is today. The museum is housed on the ground floor of the smallest Town Hall in England and so it is quite small too, but well worth a visit.

Dinosaur Museum, The

Icen Way
Dorchester DT1 1EW
01305 269880
www.thedinosaurmuseum.com
info@thedinosaurmuseum.com

Britain's original Dinosaur Museum combines fossils, skeletons and life-size dinosaur reconstructions with hands-on, interactive and cinematic displays to inform and entertain. Reconstructions include the newly interpreted T rex, deinonychus, stegosaurus and triceratops.

Dorset County Museum

High West Street
Dorchester DT1 1XA
01305 262735
www.dorsetcountymuseum.org
enquiries@dorsetcountymuseum.org

The Dorset County Museum is where the story of Dorset's rich landscape unfolds in a range of fascinating displays. The museum was founded in 1846 to help protect and record the county's unique historical and natural environment.

Dorset Family History Society

Treetops Research Centre, Suite 5 Stanley House, 3 Fleets Lane
Poole BH15 3AJ
01202 785623
www.dorsetfhs.org.uk
contact@dorsetfhs.org.uk

Dorset Family History Society is for people who are interested in tracing their family history, beginners or experts. Dorset FHS caters for people in the UK or overseas with family interests in Dorset, as well as Dorset residents whose families may have lived in other counties or countries.

Dorset History Centre

Bridport Road
Dorchester DT11RP
01305 250550
www.dorsetforyou.com/dorsethistorycentre
archives@dorsetcc.gov.uk

Home to the archives of Dorset, Bournemouth and Poole.

Gillingham Museum

Chantry Fields
Gillingham SP8 4UA
01747 854018
www.gillinghammuseum.co.uk

The museum tells the story of the town, the immediate parishes and their people. Many generations have seen this corner of the Blackmore Vale grow from a Neolithic settlement to the bustling Gillingham of today.

Gold Hill Museum

Gold Hill
Shaftesbury SP7 8JW
01747 852157
www.shaftesburyheritage.org.uk
enquiries@goldhillmuseum.org.uk

Gold Hill Museum is housed in two historic buildings, themselves a feature of the collection. You'll see a squint into the adjacent St Peter's Church in the medieval Priest's House. A blocked entry from the 1700s cottage into a cellar under the old church is adorned with a mural depicting the beer kegs it once held. The cottage once functioned as a doss house for the important weekly market held outside on Gold Hill. Collections include ancient and Roman archaeology, Saxon roots, agricultural and market heritage, local traditions, domestic life, cottage industries and politics.

Keep Military Museum, The

Bridport Road
Dorchester DT1 1RN
01305 264066
www.keepmilitarymuseum.org
info@keepmilitarymuseum.org

The Keep Military Museum respresents the honour, service and traditions of the following Regiments; Devonshire, Dorsetshire, Dorset, Devonshire & Dorset, and the associated Yeomanry of Devonshire and Dorset. The Keep is a Grade 2 listed building, built in 1879 to resemble a Norman gatehouse.

Kingston Lacy - National Trust

Kingston Lacy
Wimborne BH21 4EA
01202 883402
www.nationaltrust.org.uk/kingston-lacy
kingstonlacy@nationaltrust.org.uk

Home of the Bankes family for more than 300 years, this striking 17th-century house was radically altered in the 19th century by Sir Charles Barry. The house is noted for its lavish interiors, including William Bankes's dramatic Spanish Room, with its gilded leather walls.

Langton Matravers Parish Museum

Swanage BH19 3HE
01929 423 168
www.langtonia.org.uk
localhistory@langtonia.org.uk

For some years the Langton Matravers Local History and Preservation Society has been amassing a collection of over 24,000 items from the parish which illustrate the local history and life of the village. These are all properly documented and stored, but owing to limited accommodation, have been seen only at occasional short exhibitions, generally in the Village Hall.

Lyme Regis Museum

Bridge Street
Lyme Regis DT7 3QA
01297 443370
www.lymeregismuseum.co.uk
info@lymeregismuseum.co.uk

Built on the site of the home of Lyme's renowned fossilist Mary Anning, the museum is one of the architectural gems of the town and is packed with fascinating displays.

Maiden Castle - English Heritage

Nr Dorchester

http://goo.gl/iXf2Ys

This is the finest and largest Iron Age hillfort in Europe. Its banks enclose an area the size of 50 football pitches, which would have been home to about 200 families.

Max Gate - National Trust

Alington Avenue

Dorchester DT1 2AB

01305 262538

www.nationaltrust.org.uk/max-gate

maxgate@nationaltrust.org.uk

Max Gate, home to Dorset's most famous author and poet, Thomas Hardy, was designed by the writer himself in 1885. This atmospheric Victorian home is where Hardy wrote some of his most famous novels including Tess of the d'Urbervilles and Jude the Obscure, as well as most of his poetry.

Nothe Fort

Barrack Road

Weymouth DT4 8UF

01305 766626

www.nothefort.org.uk

museum@nothefort.force9.co.uk

The Nothe Fort, a grade II* listed scheduled ancient monument, comprises over 70 rooms on three levels (Ramparts, Courtyard and Magazines). It was built between 1860 and 1872 as part of the defences of the new naval base at Portland and was designed and constructed by the Royal Engineers for a 12-gun battery of massive cannons.

Collections: The collection illustrates Victorian and WW2 life in a military garrison, history as seen from the Nothe headland, and the part played by the people of Weymouth in the Second World War. The collection is particularly strong in military uniforms, rifles, equipment, cap badges and general WW2 militaria.

Old Crown Court & Cells

Stratton House, High West Street

Dorchester DT1 1UZ

01305 252241

http://goo.gl/Tu5WTB

tourism@westdorset-dc.gov.uk

Famous for the trial of the Tolpuddle Martyrs in 1834. The courtroom only is open all year free of charge.

Poole Museum

4 High Street

Poole BH15 1BW

01202 262600

www.boroughofpoole.com/museums

museums@poole.gov.uk

Poole Museum is housed in a 19th century quayside mill, extended in 2007. Poole's rich history is revealed in four floors of galleries, with displays and exhibitions ranging from archaeology to art and pirates to potteries.

Portland Castle - English Heritage

Mulberry Avenue

Portland DT5 1AZ

01305 820539

http://goo.gl/n2s88x

The history of this fortress, which overlooks Portland harbour, is diverse and fascinating. Built by Henry VIII to defend the anchorage against possible French and Spanish invasion, its squat appearance is typical of the artillery forts built in the early 1540s. Unusually for a fortress of this period, the castle has seen much interior alteration, though the exterior remains largely unchanged.

Portland Museum

217 Wakeham

Portland DT5 1HS

01305 821804

www.portlandmuseum.co.uk

The museum is based in two thatched 17th century cottages above Church Ope, one of which was a known location from Thomas Hardy's novel, 'The Wellbeloved'. There are exhibitions on shipwrecks, the history of stone, local archaeology, and Dr Marie Stopes, the famous birth control pioneer, who gifted the cottages to the people of Portland in 1930.

Priest's House Museum & Garden, The

23-27 High Street

Wimborne Minster BH21 1HR

01202 882 533

www.priest-house.co.uk

priestshouse@eastdorset.gov.uk

The Priest's House is an historic town house dating from the 16th century, located in the heart of Wimborne Minster. This Grade II* listed building retains many original architectural features.

Purbeck Mineral & Mining Museum

Norden Park and Ride BH20 5DW

01292 481461

www.pmmmg.org

chairman@pmmmg.org

The Purbeck Mineral and Mining Museum Group was formed to consider establishing a permanent mining museum at Norden to exhibit artefacts primarily connected to the mining of ball clay in Dorset and other significant minerals extracted in Purbeck, which were intimately connected with the growth and history of the Swanage Railway. The museum is to enhance the visitor experience when visiting the Swanage Railway.

Purbeck Stone Museum

St George's Close, Langton Matravers

Swanage BH19 3HZ

01929 423 168

www.langtonia.org.uk

Purbeck Limestone has been used from Roman times to the present day for walls, roofs and floors of buildings, from humble homes to great cathedrals. Its history is displayed here in a former Coach House, which with the village itself, is a living illustration of the uses of stone.

Red House Museum & Gardens

Quay Road

Christchurch BH23 1BU

0845 6035 635

www3.hants.gov.uk/redhouse

heritage@hants.gov.uk

A charming Georgian building (originally the town's workhouse) filled with a rich variety of displays and objects with a local theme.

Collections: Displays include the archaeological material from Christchurch and the surrounding area; a large social history & bygones gallery featuring Victorian and Edwardian objects on many themes; the Herbert Druitt Costume Gallery (currently displaying wedding dresses 1820s-1960s) and a 1930s room setting with furniture by local Arts & Crafts maker Arthur Romney Green.

Roman Town House

Colliton Park

Dorchester DT1 1XJ

01305 224283

www.romantownhouse.org

roman town house@dorsetcc.gov.uk

Find out more about Romano-British urban life at the best preserved example of a Roman town house in the country. Roman Town House was discovered, almost by chance in 1937 during an archaeological dig.

Royal Signals Museum

Blandford Camp

Blandford Forum DT11 8RH

01258 482248

www.royalsignalsmuseum.com

info@royalsignalsmuseum.com

The Royal Corps of Signals Museum is located in Blandford Camp in the beautiful Dorset countryside, only a stone's throw from the scenic and interesting Georgian Town of Blandford Forum. It is the national museum of Army communications and the exhibits and displays show the part that communications have played in the many wars and campaigns of the last 150 years.

Russell-Cotes Art Gallery & Museum

East Cliff

Bournemouth BH1 3AA

01202 451858

www.russell-cotes.bournemouth.gov.uk

r-c.enquiries@bournemouth.gov.uk

This Grade II* seaside villa is the former home of Sir Merton and Lady Annie Russell-Cotes, who designed it to house their art collection and objects from their world travels. It was gifted to the borough in 1908 and opened as a museum in 1922.

Scaplen's Court: Poole Museums Service

Scaplen's Court, Sarum Street

Poole BH15 1JW

01202 262600

http://goo.gl/i4FtZ0

museums@poole.gov.uk

Scaplen's Court is Poole's most complete mediaeval domestic building and has undergone many changes over the centuries. During the Civil War it was known as the 'George Inn' and was probably occupied by troops, as many initials and dates from that period are scratched on the old stone fireplaces.

Shaftesbury Abbey Museum & Garden

Park Walk

Shaftesbury SP7 8JR

01747 852910

www.shaftesburyheritage.org.uk

user@shaftesburyabbey.fsnet.co.uk

Shaftesbury Abbey Museum & Garden is set on the site of Saxon England's foremost Benedictine nunnery founded by King Alfred in 888AD. The Abbey was to act as the catalyst for the prosperity of the town and surrounding area for over 650 years. The excavated foundations of this once important and influential Abbey lie in a peaceful walled garden - a lasting reminder of the Abbey's eventful past. The story of the Abbey and its inhabitants has been vividly brought to life in a new, state-of-the-art museum.

Sherborne Abbey

Acreman Street
Sherborne DT9 3LQ
01935 812452
www.sherborneabbey.com
ParishSecretary@sherborneabbey.com

Founded by St Aldhelm in AD 705, the Abbey has developed from Saxon Cathedral to the worshipping heart of a monastic community, and, finally, to one of the most beautiful of England's parish churches.

Sherborne Museum

Abbey Gate House, Church Lane
Sherborne DT9 3BP
01935 812252
www.sherbornemuseum.co.uk
info@sherbornemuseum.co.uk

Sherborne Museum was founded in 1968 and occupies what was the gatehouse and almonry associated with the original Benedictine monastery, currently a Grade II listed building. From the outset it was dedicated to the preservation of the heritage of Sherborne town and its surrounding villages and is still very much community oriented and run entirely by local volunteers.

Sherborne Old Castle - English Heritage

Sherborne DT9 3SA
01935 812730
http://goo.gl/Gs64Th

After two sieges during the Civil War, visitors to the castle today see it in its more recent role as a romantic ruin in the grounds of the 'new' Sherborne Castle. Only the Southwest Gatehouse and parts of the castle including the Great Tower and the North Range survived.

Somerset & Dorset Family History Society

PO Box 4502
Sherborne DT9 6YL
01935 389611
www.sdfhs.org
society@sdfhs.org

Situated in a 17th century building next to Sherborne Museum our Family History Centre is the first port of call for our many visitors. Here you will find an informed and dedicated group of volunteers, on hand to help you at whatever level you are with your family history research. If you are unable to visit the centre in person our volunteers can also undertake research for you.

Sturminster Newton Museum

1, Old Market Cross House, Market Cross
Sturminster Newton DT10 1AN
01258 817116
www.sturminsternewton-museum.co.uk
sylviadenham564@btinternet.com

Sturminster's small museum is housed in an historic, thatched 16th C building in a conservation area in the centre of town. The museum is managed by the Sturminster Newton Museum & Mill Society, which, as the name implies, also managed the town's historic 17th C Mill which, regularly, still grinds corn. The collection mainly contains objects, photographs and printed ephemera relating to Sturminster Newton and outlying villages.

Swanage Museum

The Square
Swanage BH19 2LJ
01929 475836
www.swanagemuseum.co.uk
swanagemuseum@swanagemuseum.plus.com

A fascinating insight into the history and heritage of this unique town and its residents: the museum specialises in local and family history. Our permanent interpretive panels tell the story of Swanage from dinosaurs to the Second World War. The quarrying of Purbeck stone and the local stone trade are included in the displays.

Swanage Railway

Station Approach
Swanage BH19 1HB
01929 425800
www.swanagerailway.co.uk

Swanage Railway is a six-mile heritage railway running from Swanage past Corfe Castle to a park & ride at Norden. It is primarily a steam-hauled service.

Tank Museum, The

The Tank Museum
Bovington BH20 6JG
01929 405096
www.tankmuseum.org
info@tankmuseum.org

The Tank Museum in Dorset holds the world's largest collection of tanks and armoured fighting vehicles. From the first tank ever built to the modern Challenger II, the museum houses examples from 28 different countries; Our definitive collection comprises over 250 vehicles dating back to 1909. In our bursting programme of live action displays, you can witness the awesome power of tanks in action.

Teddy Bear Museum

🖼 £

Eastgate, Corner of High East Street & Salisbury Street
Dorchester DT1 1JU
01305 266040
www.teddybearmuseum.co.uk
info@teddybearmuseum.co.uk

The Teddy Bear Museum is a unique family museum, with Edward Bear and his family of people-sized bears arranged around their Edwardian style 'home'. There is plenty of nostalgia with teddy bears from the very earliest antique bears to today's TV favourites.

Terracotta Warriors Museum

🖼 £

Eastgate, corner of High East Street & Salisbury Street
Dorchester DT1 1JU
01305 266040
www.terracottawarriors.co.uk

The Terracotta Warriors Museum in Dorchester, Dorset, is one of the few museums outside China exclusively dedicated to the amazing Terracotta Warriors. All the terracotta warriors displayed in the museum have been specially made for exhibition by the technicians of the Lintong Museum Cultural Relic Workshop, Xian, China, as well as workshops of the China National Arts & Crafts Corporation, Xian.

Tolpuddle Martyrs Museum

🖼 ★

TUC Memorial Cottages, Tolpuddle
Dorchester DT2 7EH
01305 848237
www.tolpuddlemartyrs.org.uk
jpickering@tuc.org.uk

The Tolpuddle Martyrs Museum tells the harrowing tale of the Martyrs' arrest, trial and punishment, leading to the foundation of modern day trade unionism. The museum has been re-designed into a modern, informative, and educational exhibition, using interactive touch screen displays new graphic panels telling the story in text and images.

Tutankhamun Exhibition

🖼 £

High West Street
Dorchester DT1 1UW
01305 269571
www.tutankhamun-exhibition.co.uk
info@tutankhamun-exhibition.co.uk

The Tutankhamun Exhibition features Tutankhamun's major treasures meticulously recreated, wherever possible, in their original materials. In addition, the ante-chamber and burial chamber Tutankhamun's tomb have been accurately recreated together with all the tomb furniture and treasures.

Wareham Museum

🖼 ★

3 East Street
Wareham BH20 4NN
01929 553 448
www.wtm.org.uk

Wareham Town Museum tells the story of the Wareham area from prehistoric times to the present day. It has a special section on Lawrence of Arabia and is regularly updated with new exhibits.

Weymouth Museum

🖼 ★

Brewers Quay, Hope Square
Weymouth DT4 8TR
01305 777622
www.weymouthmuseum.org.uk
collectionmanager@weymouthmuseum.org.uk

Weymouth Museum, which is located on the first floor of Brewers Quay, is home to the Borough Collection, which reflects the physical, cultural and economic history of the area. Entry to the museum is free, but donations are welcome, and are used to purchase new exhibits and to finance new displays and exhibitions.

East Sussex

Sussex, maritime county in SE. of England, bounded N. and NE. by Surrey and Kent, SE. and S. by the English Channel, and W. and NW. by Hants; greatest length, N. and S., 27 miles; greatest breadth, E. and W., 76 miles; area, 933,269 acres, population 490,505. From the Hants border, near Petersfield, to Beachy Head, the county is traversed by the South Downs; to the N. of this range of chalk hills is the valley of the Weald, rising into the Forest Ridge on the NE., and sinking 011 the SE., towards the sea, into wide marshes. The rivers are not important; they are the Arun, Adur, Ouse, and Rother, all flowing S. to the English Channel. The principal means of communication are the railways; these belong chiefly to the London, Brighton, and South Coast system, which has steamers running daily between Newhaven and Dieppe. The most fertile soil is the low land along the coast, which yields heavy crops of grain and hay; the South Downs are chiefly pastoral, and support a well-known breed of sheep to which they give name; the Weald consists generally of sandy or tenacious clays of a very indifferent description, but the clays produce a stiff soil, remarkably favourable to the growth of forest trees, particularly the oak, and about 150,000 acres are under wood; hops are grown in the eastern part of the county, which borders on the hop districts of Kent. Ironstone is abundant, and so long as wood only was used for smelting the county was one of the chief seats of the British iron trade. The manufactures include woollens, paper, gunpowder, bricks and tiles, &c., but are not extensive. The seaports are now small and comparatively unimportant, but the mildness of the climate along the sea coast has led to the growth of numerous watering and bathing places and health resorts, including Brighton, Hastings, Eastbourne, Seaford, Littlehampton, and Bognor. Sussex was the scene of much of the early history of the country, and is rich in archaeological remains. The county contains 6 rapes, which comprise 68 hundreds, 2 liberties, the parliamentary and municipal boroughs of Brighton (2 members) and Hastings (1 member), and the municipal boroughs of Arundel, Chichester, Eastbourne, Lewes, and Rye. It is almost entirely in the diocese of Chichester.

– John Bartholomew, *Gazetteer of the British Isles* (1887) [The above description refers to East and West Sussex combined.]

Alfriston Clergy House - National Trust

The Tye, Alfriston
Polegate BN26 5TL
01323 870001
www.nationaltrust.org.uk/alfriston-clergy-house
alfriston@nationaltrust.org.uk

The Clergy House is remarkable as a surviving example of a typical thatched Wealden Hall House dating back to the 14th century. It was probably built for a yeoman farmer and later passed into the possession of the church.

Anne of Cleves House

52 Southover High Street
Lewes BN7 1JA
01273 474610
www.sussexpast.co.uk
anne@sussexpast.co.uk

Henry VIII granted this beautiful timber-framed house to his fourth wife, Anne of Cleves, as part of her divorce settlement. Let your imagination take you back to the 16th century as you wander through the kitchen or gaze at the rafters in the high roof of the hall.

Collections: The Lewes Gallery tells the story of Lewes from the 15th century to modern times, the role of local resident Tom Paine, Lewes bonfire night traditions and the story of the Snowdrop Inn. Another gallery illustrates the important Wealden iron industry.

Bateman's - National Trust

Burwash
Etchingham TN19 7DS
01435 882 302
www.nationaltrust.org.uk/batemans
batemans@nationaltrust.org.uk

Jacobean house, home of Rudyard Kipling: * Left just as he left it, reflecting the author's exotic oriental tastes * Original illustrations for The Jungle Book, drawn by Detmold brothers * Delightful gardens run down to the River Dudwell and a working water mill.

Battle Abbey - English Heritage

Battle TN33 0AD
01424 773792
www.english-heritage.org.uk/battleabbey

Stand at the centre of the landscape where England's future was fought. Imagine the battle as you follow in the footsteps of King Harold and William the Conqueror. Uncover the stories of the day, all vividly brought to life in the exhibition and audio tour. Start planning your attack on the country's most famous battlefield and abbey ruins, and experience the atmosphere for yourself.

Battle Museum of Local History

🖂 🏛 £

The Almonry, High Street
Battle TN33 0EA
01424 775955
www.battlemuseum.co.uk
info@battlemuseum.co.uk

The Battle Museum was born from the preparations to celebrate the 'Festival of Britain' in 1951. From this 'Battle District Historical Society' was formed. Artefacts were given to the society who set up a small permanent museum in 1953. Various venues housed the museum until it moved to Langton House in 1965.

Bayham Old Abbey - English Heritage

🖼 £

Bayham Road (B2169), Little Bayham
Lamberhurst TN3 8DE
01892 890381
http://goo.gl/42ssl5

Enjoy a wonderful family day out and explore the impressive ruins of 13th century Bayham Old Abbey. A perfect picnic site with plenty of space for children play whilst adults relax and take in the romantic setting.

Bexhill Museum

🖂 £

Bexhill Museum, Egerton Road
Bexhill on Sea TN39 3HL
01424 787950
www.bexhillmuseum.co.uk
museum@rother.gov.uk

The Bexhill museum was started in 1914 by a small group of dedicated enthusiasts who specialised in natural history, archaeology and ethnography. It has since developed into a fascinating and comprehensive collection. Fossil dinosaur and teeth bones and foot prints are on display at the museum and new examples are still regularly being found in and around Bexhill.

Bluebell Railway

🖼 £

Sheffield Park Station, Sheffield Park
Nr Uckfield TN22 3QL
01825 720825
www.bluebell-railway.co.uk
info@bluebell-railway.co.uk

Steam railway running for 9 miles From Sheffield Park to Kingscote in East and West Sussex. Over 30 steam locomotives with several in use each running day.

Bodiam Castle - National Trust

🖼 🖂 £

Bodiam
Nr Robertsbridge TN32 5UA

01580 830196
www.nationaltrust.org.uk/bodiam-castle
bodiamcastle@nationaltrust.org.uk

When you think of a castle, you think Bodiam. Built by Sir Edward Dalyngrigge in 1385, Bodiam is one of the most beautiful and iconic medieval castles left in Britain today.

Booth Museum of Natural History

🖂 ★

194 Dyke Road
Brighton & Hove BN1 5AA
03000 290900
boothmuseum.org
visitor.services@brighton-hove.gov.uk

Over half a million specimens, natural history literature and data extending back over three centuries are housed in this fascinating museum, including hundreds of British birds displayed in recreated natural settings. Plus butterflies, skeletons, a whale and dinosaur bones.

Brede Steam Engine Society - Giants of Brede

🖼 ★

Reg. Office 42 Chyngton Way
Seaford BN25 4JD
01323 897310
www.bredesteamgiants.co.uk
bsesgiantsofbrede@btinternet.com

A collection of heritage water pumping engines dating from 1889 and extensively restored. They depict the development of pumping technology through the steam period and into the diesel and electrical eras.

Brighton Fishing Museum

🖂

201 King's Road Arches
Brighton & Hove BN1 1NB
01273 723064
www.brightonfishingmuseum.org.uk

The main museum arch is the focal point of Brighton's fishing quarter. It contains a 27ft beach boat, prints, photographs and memorabilia of Brighton seafront life from the Regency days to the post-war boom in pleasure boat operations.

Brighton Museum & Art Gallery

🖂 ★

Royal Pavilion Gardens
Brighton & Hove BN1 1EE
03000 290900
www.brighton-hove-museums.org.uk
visitor.services@brighton-hove.gov.uk

Brighton Museum & Art Gallery, with its rich and diverse collections, creates a vibrant cultural centre in and around the Royal Pavilion estate in the heart of the city of Brighton & Hove. Dynamic and innovative galleries provide greatly improved access to the museum's nationally and locally important collections. Objects are displayed in stimulating contexts with a wide range of interpretative techniques, including interactive information technology.

Brighton Toy & Model Museum

52-55 Trafalgar Street
Brighton & Hove BN1 4EB
01273 749 494
www.brightontoymuseum.co.uk
info@brightontoymuseum.co.uk

Brighton Toy and Model Museum is a treasure trove of toys and models that extends over four thousand square feet of floorspace, through four of the Early Victorian arches supporting Brighton Railway Station's forecourt. Founded in 1991, it has over ten thousand toys and models in its catalogue, including priceless model train collections and many period antique toys.

British Engineerium

Nevill Road
Brighton & Hove BN3 7QA
01273 554070
www.britishengineerium.org
info@britishengineerium.com

A beautifully restored working Victorian pumping station and museum of mechanical antiquities.

Charleston

Near Firle
Lewes BN8 6LL
01323 811265
www.charleston.org.uk
info@charleston.org.uk

'It is not so much a house as a phenomenon' Quentin Bell once said of Charleston. It was in 1916 that the phenomenon came into being, as Duncan Grant, Vanessa Bell and David Garnett made the move from Suffolk to Charleston, where Clive Bell and Maynard Keynes were also to be regular visitors.

Collections: Charleston is the only surviving complete example of the decorative work of Bell and Grant, with walls, doors and furniture painted in their exuberant style. The house shows an evolution in decorative style throughout its different rooms.

Ditchling Museum of Art & Craft

Lodge Hill Lane
Ditchling BN6 8SP
01273 844744
www.ditchlingmuseumartcraft.org.uk
enquiries@ditchlingmuseumartcraft.org.uk

The rich collection of art, craft, and applied art reflects the important place that Ditchling holds in the tradition of 20th century art and craft. Famous artists and craftsmen represented in the museum include Sir Frank Brangwyn, Ethel Mairet (weaver) and Edward Johnston (calligrapher). Unique collection of work from the arts and crafts community established by Eric Gill and Hilary Pepler.

Eastbourne & District (Family Roots) Family History Society

8 Park Lane
Eastbourne BN212 2UT
01323 502 432
www.eastbournefhs.org.uk
johnandvalmai@talktalk.net

Our aim is to promote and encourage the public study of family history and genealogy with particular reference to persons living in or associated with the Eastbourne area and the preservation, security and accessibility of archival material.

Eastbourne Heritage Centre

2 Carlisle Road
Eastbourne BN21 4BT
01323 411189
www.eastbourneheritagecentre.co.uk
services@eastbourneheritagecentre.co.uk

The Eastbourne Heritage Centre is housed in a delightful Grade II Listed Victorian tower house, 2 Carlisle Road Eastbourne. It was fomerly the residence of the Devonshire Park and Baths Manager.

Firle Place

Firle
Lewes BN8 6LP
01273 858307
www.firle.com
gage@firleplace.co.uk

Firle Place, set in an ancient park, has been the home of the Gage family for over 500 years. The estate is now owned by the 7th Viscount Gage.

Grange, The

The Green, Rottingdean
Brighton & Hove BN2 7HA
01273 301004
http://goo.gl/L7Xqtd
rps.grange@gmail.com

The Grange Museum has a wide range of exhibitions and displays of interest to all ages. Old Rottingdean is captured in the large collection of photographs showing how the village has changed over time.

Great Dixter

Northiam
Rye TN31 6PH
01797 252878
www.greatdixter.co.uk
office@greatdixter.co.uk

Great Dixter is the family home of Christopher Lloyd, who devoted his lifetime to creating one of the most experimental, exciting and constantly changing gardens of our time. Incorporating many medieval buildings, the gardens surround the house, each complementing the other. There is a wide variety of interest from yew topiary, carpets of meadow flowers, the colourful tapestry of mixed borders (including the famous Long Border), natural ponds, a formal pool and the exuberant Exotic Garden.

Hastings & Rother Family History Society

355 Bexhill Road
St Leonards on Sea TN38 8AJ
01424 437493
www.hrfhs.org.uk
enquiries@hrfhs.org.uk

The society was formed in 1986 to encourage the study and research of family history in Hastings and Rother.

Hastings Fishermen's Museum

Rock-a-Nore Road
Hastings TN34 3DW
01424 461446
www.hastingsfish.co.uk/museum.htm
hastingsfishermensmuseum@ohps.org.uk

The Hastings Fishermen's Museum is one of the biggest attractions in Hastings. Over 140,000 people come through the doors every year to see the many photographs, paintings and historic objects - and to climb aboard the last of the local sailing luggers, built in 1912.

Hastings Museum & Art Gallery

Johns Place, Bohemia Road
Hastings TN34 1ET
01424 451052
www.hmag.org.uk
museum@hastings.gov.uk

Hastings Museum contains a rich and varied mixture of local history, Sussex pottery, paintings, dinosaurs and British wildlife. There are displays on local personalities such as Grey Owl, John Logie Baird and Robert Tressell, and on seaside holidays, Mods and Rockers and Native Americans.

Hastings Old Town Hall Museum of Local History

High Street, Old Town
Hastings TN34 3EW
01424 781166
www.hmag.org.uk

The Old Town Hall Museum provides an introduction to the history of the Old Town of Hastings. The museum reopened in 1999 following a major refurbishment project supported by the Heritage Lottery Fund.

Hove Museum & Art Gallery

19 New Church Road
Brighton & Hove BN3 4AB
03000 290900
http://goo.gl/sdVQZt
visitor.services@brighton-hove.gov.uk

Permanent collections of toys, film, local history, paintings and contemporary craft. The collections of decorative arts include the Regency furniture and silver-gilt displayed in the Royal Pavilion, the Macquoid furniture at Preston Manor, the Willett Collection of ceramics illustrating popular history, and outstanding holdings of British and European 20th century decorative design and craft.

Hurstpierpoint Museum

Village Centre, Trinity Road
Hurstpierpoint, Hassocks BN6 9UY
07985 201335
www.sussexmuseums.co.uk/find/museum.asp%3FID%3D11

Hurstpierpoint Museum consists of two unmanned display cabinets in the foyer of the Hurstpierpoint Village centre, Trinity Road, Hurstpierpoint. Themed displays, usually with a local connection, in the large free standing cabinet are changed about four times a year, and that in the wall mounted cabinet to the left of the main display is of a more permanent nature.

Keep, The (East Sussex Record Office)

Woollards Way
Brighton BN1 9BP
01273 482349
www.thekeep.info
thekeep@eastsussex.gov.uk

The Keep is a world-class centre for archives that opens up access to all the archive collections of the East Sussex Record Office (ESRO), the Royal Pavilion & Museums and the internationally significant University of Sussex Special Collections. It is also a centre of excellence for conservation and preservation and represents the new generation of archive buildings in the UK.

Lamb House - National Trust

West Street
Rye TN31 7ES
01797 229 542
www.nationaltrust.org.uk/lamb-house
lambhouse@nationaltrust.org.uk

Fine brick-fronted house with literary associations: * House dates from 18th century * Home to writer Henry James from 1898-1916 * Later home of authors EF Benson and Rumer Godden * Some of James's personal possessions on display * Charming walled garden.

Lewes Castle & Barbican House Museum

Barbican House, 169 High Street
Lewes BN7 1YE
01273 486290
www.sussexpast.co.uk
castle@sussexpast.co.uk

Lewes Castle is one of the oldest castles in England, built soon after the Norman Conquest of 1066. Over the years it was extended and altered and its high keep and towers still dominate the town. Barbican House Museum, which stands opposite the castle, tells the story of Sussex from the Stone Age to the end of the medieval period. Displays include stone axes, Roman pottery and beautiful Saxon jewellery.

Lewes Priory of St Pancras

Cockshut Road Southover
Lewes BN7 1HP
01273 812296
www.lewespriory.org.uk
enquiries@lewespriory.org.uk

Founded in the 11th century by the Norman nobleman William de Warenne and his wife Gundrada, the Priory of St Pancras was the largest monastic establishment of its day. It was demolished at the Dissolution but is still one of the most important heritage sites in Sussex.

Long Man of Wilmington

Windover Hill
Wilmington
01273 487188
www.sussexpast.co.uk

The Long Man of Wilmington, mysterious guardian of the South Downs, has baffled archaeologists and historians for hundreds of years.

Michelham Priory

Upper Dicker
Hailsham BN27 3QS
01323 844224
www.sussexpast.co.uk
adminmich@sussexpast.co.uk

Michelham Priory is an historic house, gardens, forge and watermill with 800 years of history and the longest water filled moat in England. The museum explores rural life in Sussex as a Medieval religious house, through the Tudor period and into the 20th century.

Mill Toy & Pedal Car Museum, The

The Mill, Station Road
Northiam TN31 6QT
01797 253803
www.themilltoymuseum.com
kathy@themilltoymuseum.com

The Mill was built between 1900 and 1910 and operated for many years as a gas powered flour mill, 100 years later the building has been lovingly restored and converted into a toy and pedal car museum which is widely considered the largest and finest collection of pedal cars in Europe. With exhibits dating from Victorian times, visitors of all ages will enjoy a trip down memory lane as a world in miniature awaits discovery.

Monk's House - National Trust

The Street, Rodmell
near Lewes BN7 3HF
01273 474760
www.nationaltrust.org.uk/monks-house
monkshouse@nationaltrust.org.uk

Country retreat of the novelist Virginia Woolf. This small weather-boarded house was the home of Leonard and Virginia Woolf until Leonard's death in 1969.

Museum of the Royal National Lifeboat Institution

King Edward Parade
Eastbourne BN21 4BY
01323 730717
www.eastbournernli.org/museum

Housed in the 1898 RNLI William Terris Memorial Boathouse, King Edwards Parade, at the western end of Eastbourne Seafront. The boathouse was built from public donations collected by the Daily Telegraph, to commemorate the life of the well known actor, William Terriss, who was assassinated outside the Adelphi Theatre in 1897. The museum, completely refurbished in November 2011, houses collections and displays showing the history of the Eastbourne lifeboats since 1822, when the first lifeboat came on the scene at Eastbourne. It was given by the well known local eccentric John 'Mad Jack' Fuller. The lifeboat variously known as 'samaritan' or 'The Rose' served until 1863. Various lifeboats served in this boathouse until 1924, when the retiring lifeboat 'James Stevens N06" was placed within as an exhibition piece. In 1936 it was sold to a local fishing family and became a beach pleasure boat. In 1937 the boathouse became the first RNLI museum in the country. After the war a souvenir shop was incorporated which has now become one of the top performing outlets selling gifts and souvenirs in support of the RNLI. Whilst in the museum read about 'The 'New Brunswick' service in 1833 when due to storms, the lifeboat had to be towed by relays of horses to Birling Gap, some 8 miles away, before it could be launched. The' Jane Holland' at Dunkirk.

Musgrave Collection, The

77 Seaside Road
Eastbourne BN22 3PL
01323 648106
www.musgravemuseum.co.uk

The Musgrave Collection is a small, independent museum and art gallery dedicated to the works and the collections of George Musgrave. It comprises hundreds of paintings, mini-sculptures, Roman and British coin collections, newspapers from the era of the Battle of Trafalgar, a diorama depicting the changing seasons, cabinets depicting the evolution of writing systems and visuaal aids, ancient Egyptian artefacts and Victoriana.

Newhaven Fort

Fort Road
Newhaven BN9 9DS
01273 517 622
www.newhavenfort.org.uk
info@newhavenfort.org.uk

Newhaven Fort is an award winning attraction and a fine example of an English fortification, Newhaven Fort has the sights and sounds of the past, offering a truly unforgettable day out for the whole family. Newhaven Fort's on-site military museum demonstates its role through the First and Second World Wars, offering exciting glimpses into England's dramatic wartime past.

Newhaven Local & Maritime Museum

Paradise Family Leisure Park, Avis Road
Newhaven BN9 0NY
01273 612530
www.newhavenhistoricalsociety.org.uk

A vast collection of photographs of local people / events/ places. Family history records (census, school records, port workers etc).

Observatory Science Centre, The

Wartling Road, Herstmonceux
Hailsham BN27 1RN
01323 832731
www.the-observatory.org
info@the-observatory.org

The Observatory Science Centre is one of the UK's leading science centres. Explore science, space and astronomy with over 100 exhibits, both inside and out, amongst the domes and telescopes of a world-famous astronomical observatory.

Old Courtroom, The

118 Church Street (side entrance)
Brighton BN1 1UD
03000 290900
www.brighton-hove-museums.org.uk
visitor.services@brighton-hove.gov.uk

This historic Victorian building, situated just opposite the Royal Pavilion estate in the heart of Brighton's cultural quarter, was used as a County Court until 1967. It has been fully refurbished, retaining many original features, and is now available for day and evening hire for all kinds of functions.

Old Police Cells Museum, The

Brighton Town Hall, Bartholomews
Brighton BN1 1JA
www.oldpolicecellsmuseum.org.uk
info@oldpolicecellsmuseum.org.uk

The Old Police Cells Museum is housed in the basement of Brighton Town Hall and offers visitors a unique insight into the history of policing in Sussex and is both educational and entertaining. It provides an opportunity to visit Brighton Borough main police station for the period 1830 to 1967 and learn about the murder of Chief Constable Henry Solomon in 1844 by a prisoner. See some of the old cells with their graffiti from the Mods and Rockers era, the policemans wash room and uniform store areas, police memorabilia and artefacts. The museum also houses a unique collection of trunchions and tipstaves, one of the largest in the country.

Pevensey Castle - English Heritage

Pevensey Castle
Pevensey BN24 5LE
01323 762604
http://goo.gl/63U44t

Pevensey Castle is a great family day out in East Sussex, encompassing rich history and fun things to do and see for adults and children. With a history stretching back over 16 centuries, Pevensey Castle chronicles more graphically than any other fortress the story of Britain's south coast defences.

Beginning in the 4th century as one of the last and strongest of the Roman 'saxon Shore' forts, two-thirds of whose towered walls still stand.

Planet Earth & Dinosaur Museum

Paradise Park, Avis Road
Newhaven BN9 0DH
01273 512123
http://goo.gl/TPwd4h
enquiries@paradisepark.co.uk

This is the extraordinary life story of our planet from its earliest beginnings. The exhibition is one of the finest of its type in the country and is home to a unique collection of fossils and minerals.

Polegate Windmill

Polegate BN26 5LB
www.sussexmillsgroup.org.uk/pole1.htm

An early method of grinding grain into meal was by using the rotary quern, and a working example can be seen at Polegate Mill.

Preston Manor

Preston Drove
Brighton & Hove BN1 6SD
03000 290900
http://goo.gl/zbMPdv
visitor.services@brighton-hove.gov.uk

Delightful Manor House, powerfully evoking the atmosphere of an Edwardian gentry home both 'Upstairs' and 'Downstairs'. Explore over twenty rooms on four floors, from the superbly renovated servants' quarters in the basement to the attic bedrooms on the top floor.

Redoubt Fortress & Military Museum

Royal Parade
Eastbourne BN22 7AQ
01323 410300
www.eastbournemuseums.co.uk
redoubtmuseum@eastbourne.gov.uk

For nearly 200 years, the Redoubt Fortress has defended the Eastbourne coast. Formerly a barracks and store depot, it formed part of the chain of Martello Towers which stretched from Folkestone to Seaford. Today this magnificent building provides the perfect setting for the largest military museum on the south coast.

Collections: The museum consists of several collections, primarily those of two distinguished regiments of the British Army, The Royal Sussex Regiment and The Queen's Royal Irish Hussars. The other major collection is that of the Sussex Combined Services Museum, which records all military ties with the county.

Regency Town House, The

13 Brunswick Square
Brighton & Hove BN3 1EH
01273 206 306
www.rth.org.uk
jules@rth.org.uk

The Regency Town House is a Grade 1 listed, 5 storey town house, built in the 1820s. It is currently under restoration and once complete will be open on a daily basis as a museum and heritage centre.

Collections: Our archive focuses mainly on Brunswick Town and the greater area of Brighton & Hove between 1790 - 1840. It includes a number or books, prints, plans and drawings from this area and includes a number of works by the architect Charles Augustin Busby.

Robertsbridge Aviation Society

Bush Barn
Robertsbridge TN32 5PA
01424 773428
https://goo.gl/nX6nR9

Robertsbridge Aviation Society founded their collection in 1973. Exhibits cover civil and military aviation, particularly World War II.

Royal Pavilion

4-5 Pavilion Buildings
Brighton & Hove BN1 1EE
03000 290900
www.brightonmuseums.org.uk/royalpavilion
visitor.services@brighton-hove.gov.uk

Experience the extraordinary at the Royal Pavilion, an exotic palace in the centre of Brighton. Built as a seaside pleasure palace for George IV, this historic house mixes Regency grandeur with the visual style of India and China. The Royal Pavilion's lavish interiors combine Chinese-style decorations with magnificent furniture and furnishings.

Rye Castle Museum

Gungarden
Rye TN31 7HH
01797 226728
www.ryemuseum.co.uk
info@ryemuseum.co.uk

Rye Castle Museum has two sites: the Ypres Tower and East Street. The Ypres Tower is one of the oldest buildings in Rye, being built in 1249 as part of the town's defences.

Rye Heritage Centre

Strand Quay
Rye TN31 7AY
01797 226696
www.ryeheritage.co.uk
ryeheritagectre@btconnect.com

The Rye Heritage Centre provides an ideal introduction to the town bringing together the Story of Rye set within the Rye Town Model, Audio Walking Tours of Rye including Ghost Walks in the restored Old Sail Loft building.

Screen Archive South East

University of Brighton, Grand Parade
Brighton & Hove BN2 0JY
01273 643213
www.brighton.ac.uk/screenarchive
screenarchive@brighton.ac.uk

Screen Archive South East is a public sector moving image archive serving the South East of England. Established in 1992 at the University of Brighton, this regional archive locates, collects, preserves, provides access to and promotes screen material related to the South East and of general relevance to moving image history.

Seaford Museum & Heritage Society

P.O. Box 2132, The Esplanade, BN25 9BH
Seaford BN25 1JH
01323-898222
www.seafordmuseum.co.uk
info@seafordmuseum.co.uk

Seaford Museum is housed in Martello Tower no. 74, which is situated at the eastern end of Seaford seafront.

Collections: Contains records of Seaford's history from its days as a Cinque Port and has many displays including shops, tableaux, collections of domestic appliances and office machinery and a particularly large collection of radios and television sets. The museum has a reference archives of pictures, articles etc.

Shipwreck Museum

Rock-a-Nore Road
Hastings TN34 3DW
01424 437452
www.shipwreck-heritage.org.uk
info@shipwreck-heritage.org.uk

The Shipwreck Heritage Centre, opened in 1986, is acknowledged as one of the best of its kind in the United Kingdom. It contains an interesting and varied collection of artefacts from several wrecks, and has on display a unique collection of wooden rudders from the 15th to 18th Centuries.

Stanmer Rural Museum

Stanmer Park
Brighton & Hove BN1 9SE
01273 509563
www.stanmer.org.uk

The Stanmer Rural Museum displays an amazing variety of rural artefacts, with a reconstructed blacksmith's forge, one of the last remaining horse traves and all sorts of agricultural working and craft equipment. You can also visit the nearby donkey wheel house, where water was drawn to supply the village. Location: Behind Stanmer House.

Sussex Archaeological Society

Bull House, 92 High Street
Lewes BN7 1XH
https://sussexpast.co.uk

We are a registered charity whose charitable aims are to enable people to enjoy, learn about and have access to the heritage of Sussex. We do this by opening six historic sites in Sussex to visitors old and young, providing research facilities in our library, running excavations, providing a finds identification service and offering a variety of walks, talks and conferences on the archaeology and history of Sussex.

Sussex Farm Museum

Horam Manor
Horam, Heathfield TN21 0JB
01435 813352
www.horammanorfarm.co.uk
vfmroberts@tiscali.co.uk

Sussex Farm Museum at Horam manor is not just a collection of agricultural items, but is representative of all aspects of farming life over the last 100 years. Around the farmyard are carts, ploughs and other machinery; the large drying barn (an interesting building in itself) houses iron and brick items and a stagecoach. The main barn is divided into farmhouse room settings plus cabinets showing hobbies, toys, medicines, wartime relics and much more.

Towner

Devonshire Park, College Road
Eastbourne BN21 4JJ
01323 434660
www.townereastbourne.org.uk
towner@eastbourne.gov.uk

Towner is the award-winning contemporary art museum for South East England. We present major exhibitions of UK and international contemporary art – and as a museum, we also have a nationally significant collection of art from across the ages.

Collections: An internationally renowned collection of around 4000 historical, modern and contemporary works. the Towner Collection is best known for its modern British art.

West Blatchington Windmill

Holmes Avenue
Brighton & Hove BN3 7LE
01273 776017
www.sussexmillsgroup.org.uk/blatchington.htm
museums@brighton-hove.gov.uk

West Blatchington Windmill was built circa 1820 on a tall flint and brick tower to which abutted barns on the north, south and west side. It was beautifully illustrated by John Constable in a watercolour dated 5th November 1825. The design is of the style known as a 'smock' mill due to the resemblance in silhouette to the garment worn by the millers and shepherds of that period.

West Pier Trust, The

Kings Road
Brighton & Hove BN1 2FL
01273 321 499
www.westpier.co.uk
info@westpier-trust.demon.co.uk

Brighton's West Pier, opened in 1866, is England's finest seaside pier and the only one to be Grade I listed. Although closed since 1975 and ravaged by the elements, it has survived as a magical and enduring part of seaside England and an essential feature of the Brighton seafront.

Whitehawk Primary School Air-raid Shelter

Whitehawk Road
Whitehawk BN2 5FL
01273 681377
www.culture24.org.uk/am22934
suzylking@hotmail.com

An air-raid shelter sited inside school grounds. Benches, lighting and an exhibition of artefacts and transcripts available for visits from schools and other groups.

Collections: Artefacts from WW2. Gas masks, old toilets, manufactured objects and old wrappings found in the shelter when re-opened.

Winchelsea Museum

Court Hall, High Street
Winchelsea TN36 4EA
01797 229 525
www.winchelsea.com/museum.html
j.leb@btopenworld.com

Inside the Court Hall museum, displays illustrate the history of the Antient Town, since it was built by Edward I as a medieval 'New Town' over 700 years ago, and about Winchelsea's position as Head Port of the Confederation of Cinque Ports. The Court Hall is certainly one of the oldest buildings in the town.

East Yorkshire

Yorkshire, East-Riding, in the SE. of the county; is separated from the North-Riding by the Derwent, and from the West-Riding by the Ouse; on the E. it is bounded by the North Sea, and on the S. by the Humber; area, 750,828 acres, population 315,460. The principal industries are the agricultural. Fine crops of wheat, beans, and hay are grown on the level tracts of Holderness and the banks of the Humber, and of barley and turnips on the Wolds, where the soil is a light, friable, calcareous loam. Industries other than agricultural are carried on principally at Beverley and Hull, the latter of which is a great seaport. The East-Riding comprises 6 wapentakes; 352 parishes, with part of another; the parliamentary and municipal borough of Kingston upon Hull (3 members); and the municipal boroughs of Beverley and Hedon. It is entirely in the diocese of York.

– John Bartholomew, *Gazetteer of the British Isles* (1887)

Arctic Corsair

Wilberforce House, 36 High Street
Hull HU1 1NQ
01482 658838
www.hullcc.gov.uk/museums/arctic/index.php

Come aboard Hull's last sidewinder trawler the Arctic Corsair and let the crew take you on a guided tour (access is limited). You'll hear all about life at sea and the dangers deep sea trawlermen faced in the Icelandic fishing grounds. You can also find out more about the Arctic Corsair at the museum, which is free to enter and you do not need to book.

Bayle Museum

Bayle Gate, Old Town, Bridlington
Bridlington YO16 4PZ
01262 674308
www.baylemuseum.moonfruit.com
bayle@lordsfeoffees.com

The Bayle Museum is situated in a monastic gatehouse over 800 years old, which was once the entrance to Bridlington Priory, among the wealthiest monasteries in Yorkshire in the 15th century.

Collections: The museum has varied collections including: local social history, Green Howards Military History, agricultural objects, photographs, medieval manuscripts and much more.

Beverley Guildhall & Community Museum

Beverley Guildhall, Register Square
Beverley HU17 9XX
01482 392783
www.museums.eastriding.gov.uk
fiona.jenkinson@eastriding.gov.uk

The Guildhall was the traditional seat of government in Beverley from 1501 until the late 20th century. The building has splendid rooms, including a courtroom with stucco ceiling and panels by Guiseppe Cortese dating from 1762, and historic furniture that has been in place since it was acquired in the 17th and 18th centuries.

Burton Constable Hall

Burton Constable
Skirlaugh, Hull HU11 4LN
01964 562 400
www.burtonconstable.com
enquiries@burtonconstable.com

Burton Constable Hall is set in 300 acres of natural parkland landscaped by Capability Brown and has been the home of the Constable family for over 400 years. This truly hidden gem offers unrivalled access to more than 30 rooms and its interiors of faded grandeur are filled with collections of exquisite furniture, paintings and sculpture, a library of 5,000 books and a remarkable 18th century 'cabinet of curiosities', which contains fossils, natural history specimens and the most important collection of scientific instruments to be found in any country house.

East Riding Archives & Local Studies Service

County Hall
Beverley HU17 9BA
01482 392790
http://goo.gl/C1Vzxz

The archives and local studies service collects and looks after documents and local studies books about the East Riding of Yorkshire so that people can look at them and enjoy them. You can see collections in the archives and local studies research room of the Treasure House building in Beverley.

East Yorkshire Family History Society

Carnegie Heritage Centre, 342 Anlaby Road
Hull HU3 6JA
www.eyfhs.org.uk
secretary@eyfhs.org.uk

The East Yorkshire Family History Society is the only society for those with roots in eastern Yorkshire.

Fort Paull

Fort Paull Museum, Battery Road
Paull nr. Kingston Upon Hull HU12 8FP
01482 896236
www.fortpaull.com
echo@tinyworld.co.uk

10 Acre Napoleonic Fortress on the banks of the Humber Estuary dating back to 1542 when the first fort was built in the reign of Henry VIII. Containing underground rooms and tunnels and a large events arena.Exhibits have a strong local content and the site also contains exhibits of the world's only Blackburn beverley aircraft and the berliner railcar.

Goole Museum

Carlisle Street
Goole DN14 5AA
01482 393777
www.museums.eastriding.gov.uk/goole-museum
debbie.hardy@eastriding.gov.uk

Community museum celebrating the history and culture of the port and town of Goole and its surrounding area. Permanent exhibition plus temporary exhibition gallery.

Hands on History

Old Grammar School, South Church Side
Hull HU1 1RR
01482 613902
www.hullcc.gov.uk/museums
museums@hullcc.gov.uk

The Hands on History Museum is housed in Hull's old Grammar School, built in the late 16th century. William Wilberforce studied here, and current displays explore the Story of Hull, including a fascinating 'hands on' glimpse into Victorian childhood.

Hedon Museum

Town Hall Complex, St Augustine Gate
Hedon HU12 8EX
01482 890908
https://goo.gl/V9Zedg

Aspects of the history of the town displayed, including civic life, trades, inns, education, the church & war memorabilia.The story of Hedon's medieval street names and the growth and decline of the port, once the 11th largest in England.

Hornsea Museum

11-17 Newbegin
Hornsea HU18 1AB
01964 533443
www.hornseamuseum.com
hornseamuseum@tiscali.co.uk

Farmhouse occupied by the Burn family for nearly 300 years. Come and see how the family lived, worked and played here during the later Victorian era - farmhouse kitchen, parlour, bedroom, dairy and wash-house.

Collections: Includes domestic and local history collections & photographs centred on Hornsea and north Holderness. There are currently over 2000 pieces of Hornsea Pottery on display in the new buildings opened in 2008.

Hull & East Riding Museum

Museums Quarter, High Street
Hull HU1 1NQ
01482 613902
www.hullcc.gov.uk/museums

Located in the attractive Museums Quarter, Hull and East Riding Museum has seen a series of major developments since the 1980s. Highlights of the collections include the only dinosaur bones to have been found in East Yorkshire, mysterious Bronze Age warriors, and spectacular treasures from the Middle Ages.

Hull City Archives

Hull History Centre, Hull City Council, Worship Street
Hull HU2 8BG
01482 317500
http://goo.gl/GRA2JW

If you are interested in the history of Hull, Hull City Archives holds a wealth of information, covering the rich and varied fortunes of the city, dating from the 13th century to the present day.

Hull Guildhall Collection & the Hull Tapestry

Hull City Council, Guildhall
Hull HU1 2AA
01482 613902
www.hullcc.gov.uk/museums/guildhall/index.php

The Guildhall houses a fascinating and high quality public collection that includes fine art, sculpture, furniture, civic insignia and silver.

Hull History Centre

Worship St
Hull HU2 8BG
01482 317500

www.hullhistorycentre.org.uk
hullhistorycentre@hullcc.gov.uk

The History Centre brings together the material held by the City Archives and Local Studies Library with those held by the University of Hull and includes: - the City's borough archives, dating back to 1299 - records relating to the port and docks of Hull - papers of companies and organisations reflecting Hull's maritime history - papers of notable individuals including Andrew Marvell, Philip Larkin and Amy Johnson - records relating to local and national politics and pressure groups - over 100,000 photographs, illustrations; maps and plans and newspapers The centre is open to everyone, free of charge.

Hull Maritime Museum

Queen Victoria Square
Hull HU1 2AA
01482 610 610
www.hullcc.gov.uk/museums/maritime/index.php

The museum is housed in the Victorian Dock Offices in Queen Victoria Square. These nautical themed offices were designed by Christopher G Wray and originally opened in 1871. Now they display Hull's maritime activities from the late 18th century to present. Discover the whaler's craft of Scrimshaw and see a full-sized whale skeleton, alongside superb ship models and stunning artefacts from Hull's whaling, fishing and merchant trade.

Hull Remembers

22 Whitefriargate
Hull HU1 2EX
07856 178885
www.hull-remembers.co.uk
info@hull-remembers.co.uk

Our hands-on exhibition centre displays images of Hull at war, artefacts from WW1 & II and a number of real, deactivated, weapons which may be handled by our visitors. We also offer a free military research service and can help to decypher complicated military records. Visits from schools, college, youth groups, clubs and societies are always welcome and we are also happy to bring a selection of our favourite artefacts along to you.

Maister House

160 High Street
Hull HU1 1NL
01723 879900
www.nationaltrust.org.uk/maister-house
maisterhouse@nationaltrust.org.uk

18th-century merchant's house. Rebuilt in 1743 after a fire, this merchant's house survives from Kingston-upon-Hull's international trading heyday.

Museum of Club Culture, The

10 Humber Street
Hull HU1 3HB
www.museumofclubculture.com

The world's first and only Museum of Club Culture spearheads the establishment of a creative and cultural quarter in Hull's idiosyncratic and historic Fruitmarket. The museum looks behind the stereotypes and champions the cultural significance of nightclubs and streetstyle and the important role that they have played in shaping modern culture. The museum's specialist and extensive archival collections include dress styles, artefacts, music, memorabilia, articles, books,international case studies,oral histories from clubbers, databases, illustrations, film, video and reportage photography chronicling the subterranean world of night-clubs throughout history.

RAF Holmpton Bunker Tours

Rysome Lane, Holmpton
Withernsea HU19 2RG
01964 630208
www.rafholmpton.com
info@rafholmpton.com

The station started life in 1952 as a construction site and became operational as a 'Rotor' Radar Station in 1953. The technical site at Holmpton housed an R3 bunker comprising some 30,000sq ft of space set about 100ft below ground with the associated radars located directly above the bunker on a 36 acre secure site. RAF Holmpton offers public tours and an exhibition depicting over 50 years service of this major UK command centre. The exhibiton covers the first 25 years of radar, the subsequent use of the site for RAF Support Command and its current use today. Note: the bunker is currently closed to the public and will reopen in March 2016.

Sewerby Hall & Gardens

Church Lane, Sewerby
Bridlington YO15 1EA
01262 677874
www.sewerbyhall.co.uk
sewerby.hall@eastriding.gov.uk

Formerly gatehouses and lodge to the Grade 1 listed Georgian House of Sewerby Hall, these period properties have been carefully renovated to a very good standard, resulting in three unique detached holiday cottages. Visitors can enjoy access to Sewerby Hall and Gardens (hall open Easter to September) with its impressive historic interiors, collection of memorabilia once owned by the famous local aviator Amy Johnson and a frequently changing exhibition programme.

Skidby Windmill & Museum of East Riding Rural Life

Skidby
Cottingham HU16 5TF
01482 848405
www2.eastriding.gov.uk/find-menu/a-z
jane.bielby@eastriding.gov.uk

Yorkshire`s last working windmill, a Grade ll listed four-sailed tower mill built in 1821 and and commanding magnificent views over the beautiful East Yorkshire Wolds. Two galleries in the attached warehouses illustrate the agricultural and rural history of the area at the East Riding Museum of Rural Life.

Spurn Lightship

Hull Marina
Hull HU1 1TJ
01482 613902
www.hullcc.gov.uk/museums
museums@hullcc.gov.uk

The Spurn Lightship guided ships safely through the treacherous River Humber for almost 50 years. Step aboard to discover how it was used as a navigational aid and find out what life was like on board.

Streetlife Museum of Transport

Museums Quarter, High Street
Hull HU1 1NQ
01482 613902
www.hullcc.gov.uk/museums
museums@hullcc.gov.uk

Climb aboard at the Streetlife Museum of Transport and enjoy all the sights, sounds and smells of the past. Experience 200 years of transport history as you walk down a 1940s high street, board a tram or enjoy the pleasures of our carriage ride.

Treasure House

East Riding Archives and Local Studies, Champney Road
Beverley HU17 9BA
01482 392790
http://goo.gl/S5pqUV
archives.service@eastriding.gov.uk

In its role as the museum of the East Riding, the Treasure House acts as a repository for artefacts, documents and photographs relating to the archaeology, geology and social history of the East Riding. Notable holdings include the South Cave Weapons Cache, a unique group of Iron age swords/speaheads and a collection of First World War uniforms, photographs and documents relating to the East Riding Yeomanry.

Wilberforce House Museum

Wilberforce House, 25 High Street
Hull HU1 1NQ
01482 613902
www.hullcc.gov.uk/museums
museums@hullcc.gov.uk

Wilberforce House Museum explores the history of slavery, abolition and the legacy of slavery today. It is the birthplace of slavery abolitionist William Wilberforce.

Withernsea Lighthouse Museum

Hull Road
Withernsea, Holderness HU19 2DY
01964 614 834
www.withernsealighthouse.co.uk
info@withernsealighthouse.co.uk

Withernsea Lighthouse is an inland lighthouse standing in the middle of the town. The base features RNLI and HM Coastguard exhibits with models and old photography recording the history of shipwrecks and the Withernsea lifeboats and crews who saved 87 lives between 1862 and 1913 and the history of the Spurn lifeboats. The local history room has Victorian and Edwardian photos including the pier and railway.

Yorkshire Quaker Heritage Project

Archives and Special Collections, Brynmor Jones Library, University of Hull
Hull HU6 7RX
01482 465265
www.hull.ac.uk/oldlib/archives/quaker
archives@hull.ac.uk

The aims of this project were to increase awareness of and broaden access to Quaker archives and printed collections held in Yorkshire, and beyond, relating to the region. Finding aids include an online database describing and locating Yorkshire Quaker collections (known as a location register); a name index database to the records of several Yorkshire Monthly Meetings; and a research guide.

Yorkshire Waterways Museum

Yorkshire Waterways MuseumDutch River Side
Goole DN14 5TB
01405 768730
www.waterwaysmuseum.org.uk
info@waterwaysmuseum.org.uk

The museum tells the story of the Aire and Calder Navigation in Yorkshire, England, and of the origins and development of the Port of Goole.

Essex

Essex, maritime county in SE. of England; is bounded N. by Cambridgeshire and Suffolk, E. by the North Sea, S. by the river Thames, and W. by Middlesex and Herts; greatest length, N. and S., 44 miles; greatest breadth, E. and W., 57 miles; 987,032 acres; population 576,434. On the coast are several marshy islands, such as Canvey, Foulness, Wallasea, Mersea, &c. Essex is one of the Metropolitan shires, or 'Six Home Counties', and took its name from the East Saxons. It rests upon the London clay, and is watered by the Stour, Colne, Chelmer, Crouch, Thames, Roding, and Lea; the surface, flat near the coast and the rivers, is undulating and sometimes hilly towards the NW.; the soil is generally fertile. Wheat and barley of fine quality are largely grown in the NW. and the centre; the marshes on the coast have for the most part been drained and converted into fertile grazing lands. Essex had at one time a great extent of forest, which has almost entirely disappeared. Hainault Forest was disforested in 1851; Epping Forest was preserved by the Act of 1871. The county has no mineral wealth, with the exception of chalk for lime, septaria for Roman cement, and clay for bricks. Its manufactures are of no great extent -- ironworks for the local supply of agricultural implements; crape, damasks and satins, &c. The Barking fishing smacks carry on an active industry; and there are very productive oyster beds in the estuaries of the Crouch, the Blackwater, and the Colne. Essex comprises 19 hundreds, 1 liberty, and 413 parishes, with parts of 3 others, the parliamentary and municipal borough of Colchester (1 member), the parliamentary borough of West Ham (2 members), and the municipal boroughs of Harwich, Maldon, and Saffron Walden. It is mostly in the diocese of St Albans.

– John Bartholomew, *Gazetteer of the British Isles* (1887)

Audley End House & Gardens - English Heritage

Audley End
Saffron Walden CB11 4JF
Disabled access: Tel 01799 522842
http://goo.gl/r4G9f

Audley End House and Gardens is one of England's grandest 17th century country homes with over 30 lavishly decorated rooms and magnificent grounds.

Bata Reminiscence & Resource Centre

East Tilbury Library, Princess Avenue
East Tilbury RM18 8ST
www.batamemories.org.uk
fred@batamemories.org.uk

A self-funding organisation set up to collect the memories of people who have lived and worked within the British Bata Community at East Tilbury in Essex over the past 70 years. The collection has grown at an enormous rate and we now have a very large collection of artefacts and photographs dealing with this unique community.

Braintree District Museum

Manor Street, Braintree, Essex, CM7 3HW
Braintree CM7 3HW
01376 328868
www.braintreemuseum.co.uk
info@braintreemuseum.co.uk

At Braintree District Museum the story of the district and its diverse industrial and commercial history unfolds. The Main Galleries examine the development of the area from prehistory to the 20th century, focusing upon the textile and manufacturing industries of Courtaulds, Warners and Crittalls, as well as displays of Castle Hedingham pottery, the work of the Great Bardfield artists and Essex straw and lace.

Brentwood Museum

Cemetery Lodge, Lorne Road, Warley Hill
Brentwood CM14 5HH
01277 224012
www.brentwoodmuseum.org.uk

Brentwood Museum is housed in a picturesque 19th century building once a sexton's cottage, and although small it offers a fascinating insight into Brentwood life in the early part of this century, with an exciting collection of social and domestic objects dating from around 1840-1950.

Brightlingsea Museum

1 Duke Street
Brightlingsea CO7 0EA
01206 303286
www.brightlingsea-town.co.uk/history/museum.htm

A major display gives an insight into how the people of Brightlingsea lived in Roman times. From the evidence of central heating, glass in windows, decorated walls and the wide range of of kitchen and tableware found locally it would seem local residents enjoyed comfortable living.

Burnham-on-Crouch & District Museum

Coronation Road
Burnham-on-Crouch CM0 8HW
01621 783444
www.burnhammuseum.co.uk
info@burnham.org.uk

The Burnham on Crouch and District Museum is situated on the Quay at the junction with Coronation Road. It is devoted to the history of the Dengie Hundred area.

Chelmsford Cathedral

New Street
Chelmsford CM1 1TY
01245 294489
www.chelmsfordcathedral.org.uk
office@chelmsfordcathedral.org.uk

This is one of the smallest cathedrals in England in one of the largest dioceses. The first church on the site of the present cathedral was founded (as was the town of Chelmsford itself) 800 years ago.

Chelmsford Museum

Oaklands Park, Moulsham Street
Chelmsford CM2 9AQ
01245 605700
www.chelmsford.gov.uk/museums
museums@chelmsford.gov.uk

Chelmsford Museum first opened in 1835 in the governor's parlour in Chelmsford Gaol, it has had a long and interesting history. The museum was taken over by Chelmsford Borough Council in 1906 and in 1930 it moved to a Victorian house, Oaklands, which is still its home.

Coggeshall Grange Barn - National Trust

Village Hall, Stoneham Street
Coggeshall CO6 1UH
01376 563003
www.nationaltrust.org.uk/coggeshall-grange-barn
coggeshall@nationaltrust.org.uk

A small local independent museum located in the centre of an historic market town.It is housed in the annexe to the village hall (formerly St Peter's Hall) which was once a Coggeshall brewery.

Collections: The collection gives a good insight into the social history and local characters of this charming and ancient market town, from prehistoric times to modern day. There is a working wool weaving loom, a fine collection of Coggeshall lace and some of the earliest post-Roman bricks in Britain.

Colchester & Ipswich Museums

Museum Resource Centre, 14 Ryegate Road
Colchester CO1 1YG
01206 282931
www.cimuseums.org.uk
museums@colchester.gov.uk

Local Authority Museum Service serving Colchester and Ipswich.

Colchester Castle Museum

Castle Park
Colchester CO1 1TJ
01206 282939
www.cimuseums.org.uk
museums@colchester.gov.uk

A visit to Colchester Castle Museum takes you through 2000 years of some of the most important events in British history. Once capital of Roman Britain, Colchester has experienced devastation by Boudica (Boadicea), invasion by the Normans and siege during the English Civil War. Since the 16th century, the castle has been a ruin, a library and a gaol for witches.

Colchester Natural History Museum

All Saints Church, High Street
Colchester CO1 1DN
01206 282939
http://goo.gl/4tXzpa
museums@colchester.gov.uk

Did you know there was an earthquake in Colchester in 1884? Or that mammoths and hippos used to roam around here? If you didn't and you want to find out more, come to the Natural History Museum. Housed in the unique setting of the former All Saints Church in 1957, the museum focuses on the rich natural heritage of north-east Essex.

Travel from the open through the salt marshes and beaches to the more familiar urban environments of the park.

Colne Valley Postal History Museum

In the grounds of: The Laurels, 109 Head Street
Halstead CO9 2AZ
www.cvphm.org
curator@cvphm.org

A privately owned postal history museum in the heart of East Anglia. The collection has been built up over a number of years by one man and now comprises more than 70 ex-British Post Office letter boxes together with Stamp Vending Machines, documents and associated artefacts.

Combined Military Services Museum

Station Road, Maldon
Chelmsford CM9 4LQ
01621 841826
www.cmsm.co.uk
a.bliss@cmsm.co.uk

The Combined Military Services Museum is a state registered charity, which houses an independent collection of British military artefacts, from 16th century to present date. It contains key items from the Navy, RAF, Army and Special Forces.

Copped Hall Trust, The

Stables Courtyard, Copped Hall, Crown Hill
Epping CM16 5HS
www.coppedhalltrust.org.uk

Copped Hall is a fine Georgian mansion that is currently under restoration. It is superbly sited on a ridge overlooking its landscaped parkland.

Cressing Temple

Witham Road
Braintree CM77 8PD
01376 584903
www.cressingtemple.org.uk
cressing.temple@essex.gov.uk

Cressing Temple is a scheduled ancient monument in Essex, UK. The site has its origins in the 12th century, when it was the first grant land of land given to the Knights Templar in England.

East Anglian Railway Museum

Chappel Station
Wakes Colne CO6 2DS
01206 242524
www.earm.co.uk

information@earm.co.uk

The East Anglian Railway Museum is a living heritage site based at Chappel railway station. We are situated on the edge of breathtaking Constable Country and adjacent to one of the largest railway viaducts in Eastern England.

East Essex Aviation Society & Museum

Martello Tower, Point Clear
St Osyth, nr. Clacton-on-Sea CO16 8NG
07899 917144
www.stosyth.gov.uk/default.asp?calltype=museum

The East Essex Aviation Society and Museum has been housed in the historic Martello Tower at Point Clear since it opened in the summer of 1986. The Tower is one of the first built in 1805 to repel a Napoleonic invasion expected from France which never materialised. It is also one of the few Martello Towers still open to the public along the Essex coast.

Epping Forest District Museum

39 - 41 Sun Street
Waltham Abbey EN9 1EL
01992 716882
www.eppingforestdc.gov.uk/museum
museum@eppingforestdc.gov.uk

The museum, which opened in 1981, is located in a Grade 2 listed Tudor town house in the historic market town of Waltham Abbey. The service provides a range of exhibitions for the public.

Epping Ongar Railway

Station Road
Ongar CM5 9BN
01277 365200
www.eorailway.co.uk
enquiries@eorailway.co.uk

Essex's longest heritage railway and the closest to London, running from Ongar to North Weald and into Epping Forest. We run a fleet of former mainline steam and diesel locomotives which haul a range of period coaches between our beautifully restored period stations.

Essex Fire Museum

Grays Fire Station, Hogg Lane
Grays RM17 5QS
01375 379167
www.essex-fire.gov.uk/pages/index.asp?area=48

The Essex Fire Museum gives visitors the opportunity to take a fascinating look at the history of the Fire Service here in Essex. Housing a collection featuring historic fire engines, firefighting equipment, uniforms and photographs.

Essex Police Museum

PO Box 2, Essex Police Headquarters, Springfield
Chelmsford CM2 6DA
01245 457150
www.essex.police.uk/museum
museum@essex.pnn.police.uk

The museum tells the story of the history of the police in Essex from the Victorians to modern day. Our aim is to preserve the history of Essex Police and expand public knowledge and awareness of the history of our police force by collecting, preserving, and displaying material relevant to the history of Essex Police.

Essex Record Office

Wharf Road
Chelmsford CM2 6YT
01245 244644
http://goo.gl/qxcPX0

The Essex Record Office (ERO) is the county's central repository for resources about the history of the county, its people and buildings. Information includes, contacts, opening hours on Wharf Road, research (genealogy), SEAX, and Searchroom.

Essex Regiment Museum

Oaklands Park, Moulsham Street
Chelmsford CM2 9AQ
01245 605700
www.chelmsford.gov.uk/museums
museums@chelmsford.gov.uk

Two exciting permanent displays tell the story of the proud County Regiment of Essex.

Essex Society for Family History

c/o Essex Record office
Chelmsford CM2 6YT
01245 244670
www.esfh.org.uk
secretary@esfh.org.uk

Aims to promote and encourage the public study of British family history, genealogy, heraldry, and local history with particular reference to Essex. Also to promote the preservation, security and accessibility of archival material.

Halstead Heritage Museum

Mill House, The Causeway
Halstead CO9 1ET
www.halsteadhistory.org.uk/halsteadmuseum.html
info@halsteadhistory.org.uk

Current displays include transport through the ages, the history of Courtaulds, a look at the famous Victorian stove manufacturers Portway and various artefacts from Halstead and surrounding villages.

Harlow Museum

Muskham Road
Harlow CM20 2LF
01279 454959
www.science-alive.co.uk
info@science-alive.co.uk

The museum is located in the former Mark Hall stables, linked with the Mark Hall Manor House – visited on three occasions by Queen Elizabeth 1 and her retinue. It is surrounded by the beautiful Walled Gardens which were originally the kitchen gardens for the great house and the famous families which lived there. Our four main Galleries tell the story of Harlow over four periods: from recent times and the story of how modern Harlow was designed and built, through the Victorians, Stuart and Tudor times, reaching back through the middle ages to the remarkable Roman finds in the local area.

Haven Plotlands Museum

Essex Wildlife Trust Langdon Third Avenue, Lower Dunton Road
Basildon SS16 6EB
01268 419103
http://goo.gl/f0cuU1
langdon@essexwt.org.uk

Our museum is located at the Essex Wildlife Trust Langdon Nature Reserve. The Haven Plotlands Museum is a 1930s bungalow and garden that shows what life was like for resident Plotlanders before the building of Basildon New Town.

Hollytrees Museum

High Street
Colchester CO1 1UG
01206 282 940
www.cimuseums.org.uk
museums@colchester.gov.uk

Enjoy 300 years of history through hands-on exhibits and displays. Look out for the dolls' house, it's a model of Hollytrees House.

Hylands House & Estate

Hylands Park, London Road
Chelmsford CM2 8WQ
01245 605500
www.chelmsford.gov.uk/hylands
hylands@chelmsford.gov.uk

Hylands Estate is a fantastic place to go in Essex. It is a stunning Heritage Venue set in 574 acres of parkland.

Jaywick Martello Tower

The Promenade, Belsize Avenue
Jaywick CO15 2LF
01255 822783
www.jaywickmartellotower.org
jaywickmartellotower@hotmail.co.uk

Jaywick Martello Tower is an arts, heritage and community space. The ground floor houses an exhibition on the history of the Tower, the first floor is a temporary arts space and the roof provides a reading room and replica cannon to help bring the tower to life.

Kelvedon Hatch Secret Nuclear Bunker

To contact the bunker's owners: Crown Buildings, Kelvedon Hall Lane, Brentwood CM14 5TL
Manningtree CM15 0LA
01277 364 883
www.secretnuclearbunker.com
bunkerinfo@japar.demon.co.uk

The address above is a contact address for the owners of the bunker: Full directions to the site itself are on the Secret Nuclear Bunker website. The tour is self guided by personal handsets. This is included in admission price.

Maldon District Museum

47 Mill Road
Maldon CM9 5HX
01621 842688
www.maldonmuseum.org.uk
enquiries@maldonmuseum.org.uk

Maldon Museum exhibits items directly related to the district, whether they are domestic, industrial, natural or manufactured, discovered locally or collected from afar. We hold a vast archive of artefacts from Maldon's history.

Manningtree Museum

The Public Library, High Street
Manningtree CO11 1AB
01206 395548

www.manningtree-museum.org.uk

pwg02@tiscali.co.uk

A small local history museum covering Manningtree, Mistley, Lawford and Brantham in Suffolk as well as the lower River Stour.

Mersea Island Museum

High Street

West Mersea, Colchester CO5 8QD

01206 385191

www.merseamuseum.org.uk

info@merseamuseum.org.uk

The Mersea Island Museum is an independent museum established in 1976 and occupying purpose-built premises in the centre of West Mersea, just to the east of the parish church. The traditional local activities of fishing, oystering, wild fowling and boat building are represented.

Munnings Collection at Castle House, The

Castle Hill, Dedham

Colchester CO7 6AZ

01206 322127

www.siralfredmunnings.co.uk

enquiries@siralfredmunnings.co.uk

Castle House, is the former home of artist Sir Alfred Munnings (1878-1959) and his wife Violet. The house, grounds, studio and garden café are set in forty acres of beautiful countryside in the Dedham Vale on the borders of Essex and Suffolk. This elegant Tudor and Georgian building is now home to the largest collection of paintings by the artist, who was President of the Royal Academy 1944-1949.

Museum of Power

Steam Pumping Station, Hatfield Road, Langford

Maldon CM9 6QA

01621 843183

www.museumofpower.org.uk

enquiries@museumofpower.org.uk

The museum of Power, set in seven acres of grounds and housed in the Steam Pumping Station at Langford in Essex, exhibits and demonstrates working examples of power sources of all types and chronicles the major roles that they have played in history. The museum aims to provide an entertaining and educational environment in which to explore our use of power.

Naze Tower

The Naze, Old Hall Lane

Walton-on-the-Naze CO14 8HH

07966 776417

www.nazetower.co.uk

mail@nazetower.co.uk

A truly unique visitor attraction located on an attractive stretch of coastline at Walton-on-the-Naze, Essex. This impressive 86ft octagonal tower, constructed in 1720 by Trinity House as a navigational mark to aid shipping is grade II* listed for unusual architectural interest.

North Weald Airfield Museum

Merlin Way

North Weald Bassett CM16 6AA

01992 523010

www.nwamuseum.co.uk

bryn.e.elliott@gmail.com

The museum will give you an insight into the history of this great airfield, the importance it played during wartime, the people involved, the planes etc.

Nottage Maritime Institute

The Quay

Colchester CO7 9BX

01206 824142

www.nottagemaritimeinstitute.org.uk

admin@nottagemaritimeinstitute.org.uk

Institute for maritime skills and museum of local maritime heritage.

Old Chapel, The

Sacred Heart of Mary Girls' School, St Mary's Lane

Upminster RM14 2QR

01708 222660

www.theoldchapelupminster.co.uk

gsmith@mary.havering.sch.uk

The Old Chapel was built in 1800 by Protestant Dissenters. It has been beautifully restored and is open for public to learn more about the history of the building and the local area with regular events and talks.

Paycocke's - National Trust

West Street, Coggeshall

Colchester CO6 1NS

01376 561305

www.nationaltrust.org.uk/paycockes

paycockes@nationaltrust.org.uk

Merchant's house, dating from c.1500: * The finest variety of domestic Tudor architecture * Uncommonly intricate carved woodwork and panelling * Display of the renowned Coggeshall lace * Peaceful and attractive cottage garden.

Prittlewell Priory Museum

Priory Park, Victoria Avenue
Southend-on-Sea SS2 6NB
01702 342878
www.southendmuseums.co.uk/page/Visit-Priory

Prittlewell Priory was founded in the 12th century, and subsequently underwent a fascinating history under different owners before being presented to the town as a museum.

Rayleigh Windmill

Bellingham Lane
Rayleigh SS6 7ED
01702 318120
www.rochford.gov.uk/windmill
leisure@rochford.gov.uk

The Rayleigh Windmill is an award-winning tourist and educational attraction, and popular venue for weddings and civil ceremonies. It is a Grade II listed building more than 200 years old and contains an accredited museum, an exhibition space and information about Rayleigh Mount.

Redbridge Museum

Central Library, Clements Road
Ilford IG1 1EA
020 8708 2317
www.redbridge.gov.uk/museum
gerard.greene@redbridge.gov.uk

Redbridge Museum was opened in 2000. It is the community museum for the London Borough of Redbridge and explores the many different places, people and events in over 150,000 years of Redbridge history. It is particularly evocative of the development of Ilford, Wanstead and Woodford from 1850s - 1950s.

Royal Gunpowder Mills

Beaulieu Drive
Waltham Abbey EN9 1JY
01992 707370
www.royalgunpowdermills.com
info@royalgunpowdermills.com

Set in 170 acres of natural parkland and boasting 20 buildings of major historic importance, the site mixes fascinating history, exciting science and beautiful surroundings to produce a magical day out for all the family.

Saffron Walden Museum

Museum Street
Saffron Walden CB10 1JL
01799 510333
www.saffronwaldenmuseum.org
museum@uttlesford.gov.uk

Discover a world of surprises in one of Britain's oldest museums, founded in 1835. From local archaeology to cultures of distant lands, from fossils to today's wildlife, from Tudor beds to fine ceramics to Ancient Egypt, Saffron Walden Museum owes the scope and depth of its collections to its long history and many generous benefactors. It stands beside the ruins of the 12th century Walden Castle.

Sandford Mill Museum - The Engine House Project

Sandford Mill Road, Chelmer Village
Chelmsford CM2 6NY
01245 475498
www.chelmsford.gov.uk/sandfordmill

The Engine House project is based at Sandford Mill, Chelmsford's old waterworks, where the museum's industrial collections are stored. In our science sessions we use the museum collections and our own purpose built interactive exhibits to give children exciting hands-on experiences.

Social History Museum

Colchester CO1 1YG
01206 282935
www.cimuseums.org.uk/article/10337/Social-History

Social history covers all aspects of domestic and social life from 1600 to the present day. Our collections include a wide range of items from art, costume, community history, world cultures and oral history.

Southchurch Hall Museum

Victoria Avenue
Southend-on-Sea SS0 8AD
01702 215130
www.southendmuseums.co.uk

A short walk from Southend on Sea's busy seafront and High Street, the house, gardens and archaeology are a green oasis caputred in time. Interesting interiors are laid out in a series of period rooms including a great open hall reflecting life in the later middle ages, a Tudor kitchen with magnificent fireplace, and a solar wing displaying rooms in late Tudor and Stuart style.

Southend Central Museum & Planetarium

Victoria Avenue
Southend-on-Sea SS2 6EW
01702 434449
www.southendmuseums.co.uk
museums@southend.gov.uk

The Central Museum is situated in Victoria Avenue, and houses the main offices of the museums Service, together with the Planetarium and principal artefact store.

Southend Pier Museum

Southend Pier, (Under the pier- Shore End), Marine Parade
Southend-on-Sea SS1 1EE
01702 611214
www.southendpiermuseum.co.uk
Info@SouthendPierMuseum.co.uk

If you walk along Southend-on-Sea's High Street, towards the sea, your eye will be drawn in a straight line towards the longest pleasure Pier in the world. Standing for over a century it extends 2.158 metres (1.341 miles) into the Thames Estuary, and is a well loved and recognised symbol of Southend and the pleasures of the English seaside.

Collections: Exhibits include many items of memorabilia such as an original restored working Pier signal box, a restored ex-Pier Toast Rack tram circa 1890 and train carriages circa 1949 and extensive informative pictorial displays featuring the Pier from 1830. We also have a small collection of working antique penny slot machines and much more.

Stables Centre

Hylands House, Hylands Park, London Road
Chelmsford CM2 8WQ
01245 605500
www.chelmsford.gov.uk/stables-visitor-centre

Hylands House is a fascinating and beautifully restored country house, dating from 1730. Originally built as a modest red brick Queen Anne style house, Hylands House has changed and developed considerably throughout its history.

Stow Maries WW1 Aerodrome

Hackmans Lane
Nr Maldon CM3 6RN
www.stowmaries.org.uk

Stow Maries Aerodrome is an functioning airfield with most of its Great War brick buildings still intact and is currently being restored to its 1918 condition. It is Europe's largest surviving World War I aerodrome.

Thurrock Museum

Orsett Road
Grays RM17 5DX
01375 382555
http://goo.gl/FcHoMK

The extensive museum gallery is housed within the Thameside Complex along with the Thameside Theatre and Thurrock Main Library in Orsett Road, Grays. Here you can explore the history of Thurrock through 40 permanent display cases and 20 temporary display cases, containing over 1,500 objects, interpreting 250,000 years of Thurrock's past.

Tilbury Fort - English Heritage

No. 2 Office Block, The Fort
Tilbury RM18 7NR
01375 858489
http://goo.gl/hpefdv

The artillery fort at Tilbury on the Thames estuary protected London's seaward approach from the 16th century through to World War II. Henry VIII built the first fort here, and Queen Elizabeth famously rallied her army nearby to face the threat of the Armada.

Upminster Tithe Barn Museum of Nostalgia

Hall Lane
Upminster RM14 1AU
01708 447535
www.upminstertithebarn.co.uk
ean23@btopenworld.com

The Upminster Tithe Barn houses a collection of artefacts of nostalgic origin and is located in Hall Lane, Upminster in the London Borough of Havering. It is owned by Havering London Borough Council and run in partnership with the Hornchurch and District Historical Society.

Valentines Mansion & Gardens

Emerson Road
Ilford IG1 4XA
020 8708 8100
www.valentinesmansion.com
valentines@redbridge.gov.uk

Discover a beautiful 300 year old country house and gardens in the heart of Ilford. Visit the recreated Victorian kitchen and Georgian rooms, with gorgeous views over surroundling parkland.

Waltham Abbey Gardens

Abbey View
Waltham Abbey EN9 1XD
08456 770 600
www.leevalleypark.org.uk/gardensandheritage

Once one of the largest Augustinian Abbeys in the country, founded by King Henry II in 1177 and reputed to be the site of King Harold's grave after the Battle of Hastings in 1066. These gardens have a Green Flag Award.

Walton-on-the-Naze Maritime Museum

The Old Lifeboat House, East Terrace
Walton-on-the-Naze CO14 8PY
www.fwheritage.co.uk/waltoninfo.aspx
info@walton-on-the-naze.com

A 120-year-old former lifeboat house, carefully restored with exhibitions of local interest particularly maritime, urban, geological and seaside and development. Currently restoring a 100-year-old Norfolk and Suffolk-type lifeboat, James Stevens no.14, which is the oldest surviving motorised lifeboat in the world.

Warner Textile Archive

Warners Mill, Silks Way
Braintree CM7 3GB
01376 557741
www.warnertextilearchive.co.uk
info@warnertextilearchive.co.uk

Located in the heart of Braintree, Essex, the Warner Textile Archive is the country's second largest collection of flat textiles, and narrates the rich history of a great British industry from its roots in the late 18th century to the flourishing success of Warner & Sons in the 20th century. The collection contains nearly 100,000 textile and wallpaper samples, paper designs, documents and other industry records representing two centuries of creativity and commerce.

Gloucestershire

Gloucestershire, a west midland county, situated upon the estuary of the Severn and bounded N. and NE. by Herefordshire, Worcestershire, and Warwickshire; E. by Oxfordshire; S. by Berks, Wilts, and Somerset; and W. by Monmouthshire, Herefordshire, and the estuary of the Severn; greatest length, SW. to NE., 54 miles; greatest breadth, NW. to SE., 33 miles; area, 783,699 acres; population 572,433. The face of the county shows varied aspects, of which the most distinctive are the Cotswold Hills, in the E.; the valley of the Severn, in the middle; and the Forest of Dean, in the W. Besides the Severn there are numerous important rivers, such as the Avon, Lower Avon, Wye, Thames, and Windrush. The canal system has been largely developed, and several important water-ways of that description pass through the county. Agriculture forms the leading occupation of the rural population; in the hills sheep-farming receives attention; while the rich valley of the Severn has long been famed for the superiority of its products. Its luxuriant pastures especially have originated and supported a great industry in the shape of dairy farms which produce the celebrated Glo'ster cheese. In the W. of the county are 2 great coal-fields -- the Forest of Dean on the N., and the Bristol coal-field on the W. Other minerals are gypsum, barytes, quartz, limestone, and freestone. The manufactures are mostly woollen and cotton stuffs, but at Bristol there are also large hardware manufactures. Gloucestershire comprises 29 hundreds, 387 parishes and parts of 4 others, the greater part of the parliamentary and municipal borough of Bristol (4 members), the parliamentary and municipal boroughs of Cheltenham (1 member) and Gloucester (1 member), and the municipal borough of Tewkesbury. It is mostly in the diocese of Gloucester and Bristol.

– John Bartholomew, *Gazetteer of the British Isles* (1887)

Artemis Archery research collection

Yew Corner
Oldland N/A
0117 9323276
www.artemisarchery.com

Extensive representative collection of traditional
recreational bows, arrows and other artefacts. Associated
badges, medals, prints and ephemera.

Chavenage House

Chavenage
Tetbury GL8 8XP
01666 502329
www.chavenage.com

16th century, grey Cotswold stone manor house with many
Civil War associations including the tapestry-lined rooms
stayed in by Cromwell and his second-in-command,
General Ireton, in 1648. The house was added to at the turn
of the last century and features the Edwardian Ballroom.

Chedworth Roman Villa - National Trust

Yanworth
Nr Cheltenham GL54 3LJ
01242 890256
www.nationaltrust.org.uk/chedworth-roman-villa
chedworth@nationaltrust.org.uk

The remains of one of the largest Roman villas in Britain
provide a fascinating insight into the period. The site was
discovered in 1864 by a local gamekeeper and subsequently
excavated.

Cheltenham Synagogue

Synagogue Lane, St James's Square
Cheltenham GL50 3PU
01242 578893
www.cheltenhamsynagogue.org.uk
info@cheltenhamsynagogue.org.uk

Our Grade 2* listed Synagogue is over 150 years old and
unique in Gloucestershire. It provides a focus for both
Jewish education in the region and the appreciation of
Regency architecture.

Cirencester Lock-up

Trinity Road
Cirencester GL7 1BR
01285 623000
www.cirencester.co.uk/attractions
museums@cotswold.gov.uk

A two-celled lock-up built in 1804 and moved to its present
site in 1837. Display panels tell the story of lock-ups in
general and the history of this building & the Cirencester
workhouse.

Clearwell Caves - Ancient Iron Mines

Nr Coleford
Royal Forest of Dean GL16 8JR
01594 832535
www.clearwellcaves.com
info@clearwellcaves.com

The show caves are a part of an extensive natural cave
system, mined for iron ore to make one of Britain's most
complex and oldest mine workings; dating back well over
4,500 years, when Neolithic miners dug for ochre pigments.
Nine atmospheric ancient caverns are open to visitors, that
have an exciting and intriguing past.

Corinium Museum

Park Street
Cirencester GL7 2BX
01285 655611
www.coriniummuseum.org
CoriniumMuseum@slm-ltd.co.uk

Discover the treasures of the Cotswolds at the Corinium
Museum. Two years and five million pounds in the making,
the Corinium Museum has been transformed into the
must-see visitor attraction of the Cotswolds. Corinium was
the second largest city in Roman Britain.

Cotswold Motoring Museum & Toy Collection

The Old Mill, Sherbourne Street, Bourton-on-the-Water
Cheltenham GL54 2BY
01451 821255
www.cotswold-motor-museum.com
museum@cotswoldmotormuseum.co.uk

The museum has seven galleries - overflowing with vintage
and classic cars, caravans, precarious looking motorcycles,
original enamel signs, a unique toy collection and an
intriguing array of motoring curiosities. It provides a
nostalgic journey through history, complete with sounds,
smells and stories from the eras.

Court Barn Museum

Church Street
Chipping Campden GL55 6JE
01386 841951
www.courtbarn.org.uk
admin@courtbarn.org.uk

Court Barn Museum celebrates the talented designers and
craftspeople who have worked in Chipping Campden and
the north Cotswolds since the beginning of the 20th
century. This is a story of the Arts and Crafts movement

and its legacy, a story of how a small town in a beautiful setting became a gathering place for designers and craftspeople of national and international reputation.

Collections: There is a permanent exhibition of silver, jewellery, ceramics, sculpture, industrial design, bookbinding, printing, and stained glass. The entire working archive of Robert Welch is also there.

Dean Forest Railway Museum

Dean Forest Railway, Norchard Railway Centre, Forest Road
Lydney GL15 4ET
01594 845840
www.dfr.co.uk
dfr.museum@virginmedia.com

Spend a moment of your visit to the Dean Forest Railway to look around with artefacts from the former Severn & Wye Joint Railway and associated Great Western & Midland Railways.

Dean Heritage Centre, Forest of Dean

Camp Mill, Soudley, Cinderford
Forest of Dean GL14 2UB
01594 822170
www.deanheritagecentre.com
info@deanheritagecentre.com

Set across a stunning and fully interactive five acre site, the centre protects and preserves the unique history and heritage of the beautiful Forest of Dean.

Collections: Includes archaeology, natural history, geology, industrial history, coal and iron mining, agriculture, costume, social history, friendly societies, library and archives.

Dr Jenner's House & Garden

The Chantry
Berkeley GL13 9BH
01453 810631
www.jennermuseum.com
info@edwardjenner.co.uk

It was from this house in 1796 that Edward Jenner pioneered a vaccination against smallpox and it changed the world. During his life he was also fascinated by geology, ballooning, poetry and natural history. Find out about Dr Jenner's life, his hopes, the setbacks and how he changed the world.

Dyrham Park - National Trust

Dyrham Park, Dyrham
near Bath SN14 8ER
0117 9375201
www.nationaltrust.org.uk/dyrham-park
dyrhampark@nationaltrust.org.uk

Explore 270 acres (110 hectares) of ancient parkland, where a historic herd of fallow deer roams freely and magnificent trees and breathtaking views abound. Inside the impressive mansion, built by hard-working civil servant William Blathwayt, discover fascinating interiors little changed in 300 years, as well as a rich collection that includes superb Dutch art and ceramics of the period.

Forest of Dean Local History Society

45 Allaston Road
Lydney GL15 5SS
01594 842164
www.forestofdeanhistory.org.uk
cecilehunt@btinternet.com

To advance education for the benefit of the public by the study of local history, in particular the local history of the Forest of Dean and its surrounding area.

Frenchay Village Museum

Begbrook Park
Frenchay BS16 1SZ
0117 957 0942
www.frenchay.org/museum.html
frenchaymuseum@hotmail.com

A few miles northeast of Bristol, in South Gloucestershire, Frenchay Village Museum gives an insight into an unusual village that, from the 17th century, was a community largely made up of non-conformist Quakers and Unitarians.

Gloucester Cathedral

Gloucester GL1 2LR
01452 508211
www.gloucestercathedral.org.uk
lin@gloucestercathedral.org.uk

The Cathedral today is much more than just an ancient monument - it is a living church open 365 days a year.

Gloucester City Council Culture, Learning & Leisure

Learning and Leisure, Heritage and Museums, Herbert Warehouse, The Docks
Gloucester GL1 2EQ

01452 396620
http://goo.gl/O3a7pZ
city-museum@gloucester.gov.uk

Heritage and Museums service responsible for museums, collections, archaeological planning advice, and monuments in Gloucester.

Gloucester City Museum & Art Gallery

Brunswick Road
Gloucester GL1 1HP
01452 396131
www.gloucestermuseums.co.uk
museums@gloucester.gov.uk

Treasures from all over Gloucestershire reveal the county's early history - dinosaur bones and diorama; life of early man; the beautiful Bronze age Birdlip Mirror; life and death in Roman Gloucestershire; the amazing Gloucester Tables Set (early backgammon) and an intricate Mediaeval closing ring from a local church. Discover beautiful antique furniture, clocks and decorative arts and paintings by well known artists such as Turner and Gainsborough.

Gloucester Folk Museum

99-103 Westgate Street
Gloucester GL1 2PG
01452 396868
http://goo.gl/27CGPP
folk.museum@gloucester.gov.uk

Museum displays on three floors of three half-timbered buildings of c.1500-1650 plus new extensions at the rear of the site - dairy, ironmonger's shop, wheelwright and carpenter workshops.

Collections: Collections cover the social history, trades, crafts and industries from the City & County of Gloucester from the mid-16th.century to the present.

Gloucester Waterways Museum

Llanthony Warehouse, Gloucester Docks
Gloucester GL1 2EH
01452 318200
https://goo.gl/fbIQHp
gloucester@thewaterwaystrust.org.uk

The award-winning Gloucester Waterways Museum (part of The Waterways Trust) is housed in a splendid Victorian warehouse at the historic Gloucester Docks. The collections include objects painted by boatmen, costumes worn by boating families, and waterways souvenirs, along with photographic and archive material.

Gloucestershire Archives

Clarence Row, Alvin Street
Gloucester GL1 3DW
01452 425295
www.gloucestershire.gov.uk/archives
archives@gloucestershire.gov.uk

Gloucestershire Archives aims to preserve historical records relating to Gloucestershire, and to make them available for research. Gloucestershire Archives holds over 8 million documents dating from the 12th century to the present day and reflecting all aspects of life in Gloucestershire.

Gloucestershire Family History Society

Clarence Row, Alvin Street
Gloucester GL1 3AH
01452 524344
www.gfhs.org.uk
secretary@gfhs.org.uk

The society provides free online research facilities and friendly volunteers to help you find your ancestors in Gloucestershire and beyond.

Hailes Abbey - National Trust

Near Winchcombe
Cheltenham GL54 5PB
01242 602398
www.nationaltrust.org.uk/hailes-abbey
hailesabbey@nationaltrust.org.uk

The Cistercian abbey of Hailes was founded in 1246 in Gloucestershire by the Earl of Cornwall in thanks for surviving a shipwreck. Though never housing large numbers of monks, it held a renowned relic, 'the Holy Blood of Hailes' – allegedly a phial of Christ's own blood.

Hidcote - National Trust

Hidcote Bartrim
near Chipping Campden GL55 6LR
01386 438333
http://goo.gl/0GVCb5
hidcote@nationaltrust.org.uk

Hidcote is an Arts and Crafts garden in the north Cotswolds, a stone's throw from Stratford-upon-Avon. Created by the talented American horticulturist, Major Lawrence Johnston, its colourful and intricately designed outdoor 'rooms' are always full of surprises.

Holst Birthplace Museum

🏛 £

4 Clarence Road
Cheltenham GL52 2AY
01242 524846
www.holstmuseum.org.uk
curator@holstmuseum.org.uk

The Holst Birthplace Museum aims to celebrate the life and works of Gustav Holst, composer of The Planets. The museum was opened by Holst's daughter Imogen in 1975.

Collections: Holst's piano, family items and extensive printed archive of photographs and ephemera.

John Moore Countryside Museum & Merchant's House

🏛 £

41 Church Street
Tewkesbury GL20 5SN
01684 297174
www.johnmooremuseum.org
curator@johnmooremuseum.org

The John Moore Museum is nestled in a row of historic timber-framed buildings close to the Abbey in Tewkesbury, Gloucestershire. The museum was established in 1980 in memory of the writer and naturalist John Moore. Today it is also home to an extensive natural history collection featuring specimens of the mammals and birds native to our countryside, woodlands, wetlands and farmland. A few doors away is The Merchant's House, a two storey building which has been beautifully restored and furnished to show the construction of a 15th century shop and dwelling. The museum has also recently taken over the management of the Old Baptist Chapel, originally a late Medieval Hall house which was later converted for use as a Nonconformist meeting house.

Living Memory Historical Association, The

The Living Memory Historical Association Exhibition and Study Centre
Cirencester GL7 1QW
0128 565 5650
www.livingmemory.btik.com
peter@thegraces.co.uk

The LMHA is a registered charitable trust founded in 1989, dedicated to the study of local history within living memory. It holds a considerable archive of artefacts and ephemera, mainly of the Second World War period.

Museum in the Park, The

Stratford Park, Stratford Road
Stroud GL5 4AF
01453 763394
www.museuminthepark.org.uk
museum@stroud.gov.uk

Family-friendly museum in beautiful parkland setting. Featuring colourful displays relating to the history, people and places of Stroud District and a varied programme of temporary exhibitions and events.

Nature in Art

Wallsworth Hall, A38, Tewkesbury Road
Twigworth, near Gloucester GL2 9PA
01452 731422
www.nature-in-art.org.uk
enquiries@nature-in-art.org.uk

The museum and art gallery dedicated to art inspired by nature from around the world. The collection spans 1500 years, from 60 countries by 600 artists and craftspeople.

Newark Park - National Trust

Ozleworth
Wotton-under-Edge GL12 7PZ
01453 842644
www.nationaltrust.org.uk/newark-park
jenny.rogers@nationaltrust.org.uk

This unusual and atmospheric property was built c.1550 as a hunting lodge and added to in the 1790s. It stands high on the edge of a 40-ft cliff with outstanding views.

Snowshill Manor & Garden - National Trust

Snowshill Road
nr Broadway WR12 7JU
01386 852410
www.nationaltrust.org.uk/snowshill-manor
snowshillmanor@nationaltrust.org.uk

Snowshill is no ordinary manor, as Charles Paget Wade was no ordinary Edwardian gentleman. Mr Wade embodied his family motto 'Let nothing perish', spending his life and inherited wealth amassing a spectacular collection of everyday and extraordinary objects.

Soldiers of Gloucestershire Museum

Custom House, The Docks
Gloucester GL1 2HE
01452 522 682
soldiersofglos.com
curator@sogm.co.uk

The Soldiers of Gloucestershire is a small military museum, which tells the story of the Gloucestershire Regiment and the Royal Gloucestershire Hussars over the last three hundred years. Located in Gloucester Docks, galleries are on two floors of the old Custom house, which is listed grade two.

South Gloucestershire Mines Research Group

www.sgmrg.co.uk

This area has a rich mining history. The date of the earliest mines is unknown, while the last coal mine closed as recently as 1963. South Gloucestershire Mines Research Group (SGMRG) was set up by local people to understand, record and where appropriate preserve the remains, of what was once an extensive industry, for the present community and future generations.

Stroudwater Textile Trust

www.stroud-textile.org.uk

imack@btopenworld.com

The Stroudwater Textile Trust began its life in 1999 as successor to the Friends of Stroud Museum Textile Group as the result of the wish of a group of local people to recognise and interpret the importance of the woollen industry in the Stroud Valleys at all levels from the local to the international. An essential aspect of the Trust's work is that it considers the present and future of working with wool in the area to be an important part of its purpose as well as that of the past.

Sudeley Castle

Winchcombe GL54 5JD

01242 602308

www.sudeleycastle.co.uk

Set against the backdrop of the beautiful Cotswold Hills, Sudeley Castle is steeped in history. With royal connections spanning a thousand years, it has played an important role in the turbulent and changing times of England's past. The castle was once home to Queen Katherine Parr, the last and only surviving wife of Henry VIII.

Swinford Museum

Fox House, Filkins, Nr Lechlade

Gloucester GL7 3JQ

01367 860209

www.filkins.org.uk/swinford_museum.html

Domestic agricultural and building crafts from a Cotswold village.

Tetbury Police Museum

The Old Court House, 63 Long Street

Tetbury GL8 8AA

01666 504670

www.visittetbury.co.uk/police-museum

The original police office and cells contain a most interesting array of exhibits and memorabilia which is well worth a visit, including the world renowned Alex Nichols collection of Handcuffs and Restraints. The centre is primarily dedicated to the history of the Gloucestershire Constabulary.

Tewkesbury Abbey

Church Street

Tewkesbury GL20 5RZ

01684 850959

www.tewkesburyabbey.org.uk

office@tewkesburyabbey.org.uk

Tewkesbury Abbey was founded in 1087, but the building of the present Abbey did not start until 1102. Two styles of architecture dominate the Abbey; the Norman piers and arches of the Nave and the Decorated-style 14th century chancel, imposed on the previous work.

Tewkesbury Museum

64 Barton Street

Tewkesbury GL20 5PX

01684 292901

www.tewkesburymuseum.org

info@tewkesburymuseum.org

Social history and archaeology collections illustrating the history of Tewkesbury and its people. A fun learning experience for children and adults alike.

Thornbury & District Museum

c/o The Town Hall, 35 High Street

Thornbury BS35 2AR

01454 857774

www.thornburymuseum.org.uk

enquiries@thornburymuseum.org.uk

The Trust's collection includes objects, a document archive, photographs and digital images which all help tell the story of Thornbury and its surrounding parishes. Some of the collection is placed in store and can be accessed by arrangement for research, as well as being used to create exhibitons and displays.

Wellington Aviation Museum

British School House, Broadway Road

Moreton-in-Marsh GL56 0BG

01608 650323

www.wellingtonaviation.org

Some years ago Gerry Tyack opened his small museum dedicated to all those who served or who passed through RAF Moreton-in-Marsh, on one of the many training courses for RAF bomber command. Though the airfield is now a fire training station Gerry keeps the memory of the base alive in the museum with his vast range of artefacts from the war years and beyond.

Wilson, The - Cheltenham Art Gallery & Museum

Clarence Street
Cheltenham GL50 3JT
01242 237431
www.cheltenham.artgallery.museum
ArtGallery@cheltenham.gov.uk

Gallery spaces allow visitors to explore highlights from the museum's collections - including a new gallery space dedicated to the internationally renowned Arts & Crafts collection, open archives showing tales of local heroes, including the great Edward Wilson (one of Scott's key men on his 1912 expedition to Antarctica) and temporary exhibition spaces filled with varied programming including fun shows for families.

Winchcombe Folk & Police Museum

Old Town Hall, Winchcombe
Cheltenham GL54 5LJ
01242 609151
www.winchcombemuseum.org.uk

Our police collection is a small part of the Simms Collection which was founded in 1953. Winchcombe's Police Collection opened in 1983 in the Old Court Room of the Town Hall. On display we have British and International police uniforms, caps, helmets, badges, truncheons, handcuffs and other equipment.

Wotton Heritage Centre

The Chipping
Wotton-under-Edge GL12 7AD
01453 521541
www.wottonheritage.com
info@wottonheritage.com

Located in a converted fire station in the Chipping, Wotton-under-Edge, the museum provides visitors with an excellent introduction to this historic wool town and its surrounding area of outstanding natural beauty. Visit the Wotton Heritage Centre and discover intriguing artefacts from Wotton-under-Edge's crafts and industry; changing exhibition displays; photographs, postcards, documents, maps and books of local interest; microfiches of parish registers; card indexes of family and local history and a variety of databases for family history research.

Yate & District Heritage Centre

Church Road
Yate BS37 5BG
01454 862200
www.yateheritage.co.uk
yate.heritage@southglos.gov.uk

At present, the centre controls the two major local history collections in the area and these are both available to the public on open days and through appointment. There are over 3,000 objects in the centre.

Greater London

Middlesex, south-midland county of England, bounded N. by Herts, E. by Essex, W. by Bucks, and S. by the river Thames, which separates the county from Surrey; greatest length, NE. to SW., 24 miles; greatest breadth, N. to S., 18 miles; area, 181,317 acres; population 2,920,485. Excepting Rutland, this is the smallest of the English counties; but as it contains the greater part of London, its population is second only to Lancashire, which has the highest position in point of numbers. It is the metropolitan county of England. The appearance of the country is generally flat, with slight elevations on the Herts border and in the N. suburbs of London. The Thames, and its affluents the Colne, Lea, and Brent, are the only rivers, although there are several smaller streams in the county Middlesex is likewise traversed by the Grand Junction, Paddington, and Regent Canals, also by the New River, an artificial watercourse constructed in the reign of James I in connection with the water supply of the metropolis. The London clay forms the greater part of the soil, so that it is generally poor for farming operations except in some places on the banks of the Thames. Farming is carried on with much spirit, and with scientific attention. A large number of market-gardens, in connection with the metropolitan supplies are to be found in the county. The county comprises 6 hundreds, 222 parishes, the parliamentary boroughs of London City, Bethnal Green, Chelsea, Finsbury, Fulham, Hackney, Hammersmith, Hampstead, Islington, Kensington, Marylebone, Paddington, St Pancras, Shoreditch, Tower Hamlets, and Westminster. It is mostly in the diocese of London.

– John Bartholomew, *Gazetteer of the British Isles* (1887)

Note: Greater London consists of most of Middlesex, along with parts of Kent, Surrey, Essex and Hertfordshire (and the former County of London).

18 Stafford Terrace

18 Stafford Terrace
London W8 7BH
020 7602 3316
www.rbkc.gov.uk/subsites/museums.aspx
museums@rbkc.gov.uk

In 1874 Edward Linley Sambourne married Marion Herapath, the daughter of a wealthy stockbroker. Helped by Marion's father, the couple paid £2,000 for an 89-year lease on 18 Stafford Terrace. A hidden gem in the heart of London, remarkably well-preserved and complete with its original interior decoration and contents.

2 Willow Road - National Trust

2 Willow Road, Hampstead
London NW3 1TH
020 7435 6166
www.nationaltrust.org.uk/2-willow-road
2willowroad@nationaltrust.org.uk

The architect Erno Goldfinger designed and built this unique Modernist house as his family home in 1939. The central house of a terrace of three, it is one of Britain's most important examples of Modernist architecture.

Alexander Fleming Laboratory Museum

St Mary's Hospital, Praed Street
London W2 1NY
020 7886 6528
http://goo.gl/f0451w
Kevin.Brown@imperial.nhs.uk

Founded in 1993, the museum features Fleming's laboratory restored to its condition in 1928 when he discovered penicillin in that very room.

Collections: Material relating to Alexander Fleming, penicillin, antibiotics, 20th-century microbiology/bacteriology and St Mary's Hospital.

Alexander Kerensky Museum

2nd Floor, 145-157 St.John Street
London EC1V 4PY
www.kerensky.org.uk

Alexander Fyodorovich Kerensky (1881-1970) was the last President of Russia before the Bolshevik coup d'état of October 1917.

All Hallows by the Tower

Byward Street
London EC3R 5BJ
020 7481 2928
www.ahbtt.org.uk
parish@ahbtt.org.uk

All Hallows By The Tower church was founded in 675 AD and, throughout London's history, has played a key part in almost every important event. A Roman pavement, Saxon stonework, Mediaeval paintings and statues, and the glorious Grinling Gibbons font cover are all on show.

Anaesthesia Heritage Centre

21 Portland Place
London W1B 1PY
020 7631 1560
www.aagbi.org
heritage@aagbi.org

All the collections (museum, library and archive) relate to the history of anaesthesia, pain relief and resuscitation and celebrate the people who helped the specialty to develop.

Apsley House - English Heritage

Apsley House
London W1J 7NT
020 7499 5676
http://goo.gl/pHMnxu
joseph.saunders@english-heritage.org.uk

Apsley House, home of the 1st Duke of Wellington, is one of the capital's finest residences. Famously known as No.1 London, it was designed and built by Robert Adam between 1771-1778.

Archives for London

c/o London Metropolitan Archives, 40 Northampton Road
London EC1R 0HB
020 7332 3816
www.archivesforlondon.org
enquiries@archivesforlondon.org

Archives for London is the independent voice for archives in the Capital. We are a membership organisation for people who use and work with historic documents, films and photographs in or about London. AfL brings together people who are passionate about archives of the UK's capital city to sharing news and ideas and different perspectives on how archives can benefit and contribute to all our lives.

Arsenal Football Club Museum

Arsenal Museum, Highbury House, 75 Drayton Park
London N5 1BU
0207 704 4504
www.arsenal.com/history/the-arsenal-museum
tours@arsenal.co.uk

The spectacular Arsenal museum at Emirates Stadium is now open in the Northern Triangle Building. Arsenal supporters can still expect their favourite exhibitions, including Michael Thomas' boots from Anfield '89 and Charlie George's FA Final Cup shirt from 1971, along with a whole array of newly donated memorabilia.

Bank of England Museum

Bartholomew Lane
London EC2R 8AH
020 7601 5545
www.bankofengland.co.uk/museum
museum@bankofengland.co.uk

The Bank of England Museum tells the story of the Bank from its foundation in 1694 to its role in today's economy. Ineractive programmes with graphics and video help explain its many and varied roles.

Banqueting House

Whitehall
London SW1A 2ER
0844 482 7777
www.hrp.org.uk
banquetinghouse@hrp.org.uk

Walk in the footsteps of a dazzling company of courtiers who once danced, drank and partied beneath the magnificent Rubens painted ceiling. This revolutionary building was created for court entertainments, but is probably most famous for the execution of Charles I in 1649.

Baring Archive, The

60 London Wall
London EC2M 5TQ
020 7767 6021
www.baringarchive.org.uk
baring.archive@uk.ing.com

The Baring Archive is one of the finest archives of a financial institution anywhere in the world. It contains material from the establishment in 1762 of the London merchant house of John & Francis Baring & Co, later known as Baring Brothers, through to the firm's acquisition by ING in 1995. The documents illustrate the range of Barings' business activities.

Barking & Dagenham Archives & Local Studies Centre

Archives and Local Studies Centre, Valence House Museum,
Becontree Avenue
Dagenham RM8 3HT
020 8227 2033
https://goo.gl/FcoSC4

We collect, preserve and make available historical records, photographs and films on Barking and Dagenham and its people. They inspire an understanding of our rich history, pride in the borough and contribute to the development of cultural identity.

Barnet Local Studies & Archives

80 Daws Lane
London NW7 4SL
020 8959 6657
http://goo.gl/RcxGfA
library.archives@barnet.gov.uk

The centre holds the records of the Borough of Barnet and its predecessors for the areas of Barnet, Edgware, Finchley Golders Green and Hendon. Explore the history of this huge Borough covering 8,663 hectares and a population of 314,564.

Barts Pathology Museum

3rd Floor, Robin Brook Centre, West Smithfield
London EC1A 7BE
020 7882 8766
www.facebook.com/BartsPathologyMuseum
c.connolly@qmul.ac.uk

Opened in 1879 by The Prince of Wales (who later became Edward VII), the Pathology Museum is a vast space made up of 3 mezzanine levels each around 8 metres high, all linked by a beautiful spiral staircase. It contains some 5000 anatomical specimens, including forensic and historical examples, as well as corresponding archive information.

BBC Heritage Collections

c/o BBC Heritage, Room B027, Main Block, Television Centre, Wood Lane
London W12 7RJ
www.bbc.co.uk/heritage

The BBC heritage collection is a fascinating collection of arts, artefacts and historic technology from the earliest days of the BBC up to the present. We currently have items from the collection on loan to the National Media Museum in Bradford.

Ben Uri Gallery & Museum

108a Boundary Road
London NW8 0RH
020 7604 3991
benuri.org.uk
info@benuri.org.uk

Ben Uri is an Art Museum and educational charity, founded in July 1915 in Whitechapel, East London. Known as 'The Art Museum for Everyone' the museum collection and programming both focus on the universal themes of Art, Identity and Migration.

Collections: The collection is internationally recognised and encompasses over 1300 works, principally from the start of the 20th century, by some 385 artists originating from 35 different countries.

Benjamin Franklin House

36 Craven Street
London WC2N 5NF
0207 839 2006
www.benjaminfranklinhouse.org
info@benjaminfranklinhouse.org

Home to Benjamin Franklin between 1757 and 1775, 36 Craven Street is the location where the famous US statesman conducted numerous important experiments such as measuring the effects of the Gulf Stream, exploring Daylight Saving Time and inventing bi-focal lenses.

Bentley Priory Museum

Mansion House Drive
Stanmore HA7 3FB
020 8950 5526
www.bentleypriory.org
enquiries@bentleypriory.org

Famous for its pivotal role as the Headquarters of Fighter Command during the Battle of Britain in 1940 a trust has been set up to ensure that Bentley Priory is retained as a permanent living memorial to those who served in the Royal Air Force and fought in the Battle. The Bentley Priory Museum is situated within a beautiful Georgian mansion, which was once home to John James Hamilton, the first Marquess of Abercorn who employed Sir John Soane to make various structural additions to the house which still stand today.

Berkshire & Westminster Dragoons Museum

Cavalry House, Duke of Yorks HQ, Kings Road, Chelsea
London SW3 4SC
020 8856 7995
http://goo.gl/hpdPFV

The Westminster Dragoons have a long and distinguished history. That history is recorded mainly in privately-published books and pamphlets with only limited circulation.

Bevis Marks Synagogue

Bevis Marks
London EC3A 5DQ
020 7626 1274
www.sandp.org/opening.htm

Situated in a secluded courtyard, Britain's oldest synagogue was opened in 1701 to serve the Spanish & Portuguese Jews' Congregation. Today it is one of the best-preserved houses of worship of its period still in regular use.

Bishopsgate Institute

230 Bishopsgate
London EC2M 4QH
020 7392 9200
www.bishopsgate.org.uk
enquiries@bishopsgate.org.uk

Bishopsgate Institute is based in a beautiful Grade II* listed building in central London. Since 1895, we have provided an independent meeting place for people with shared interests to learn about a vast array of subjects. Explore our world-renowned collections on London history, labour and socialist history, freethought and humanism, co-operation, and protest and campaigning.

Black Cultural Archives

1 Othello Close
London SE11 4RE
020 7582 8516
www.bcaheritage.org.uk
info@bcaheritage.org.uk

Founded in 1981, Black Cultural Archives began collecting materials which would seek to redress the historical imbalance of the representation of Black people in Britain. Our reference library currently contains around 6,000 books and independently published literature. We have also recently acquired the Runnymede Collection Library which is one of the most important libraries on race relations in the country.

Brent Archives

Willesden Green Library Centre, 95 High Road
Willesden Green NW10 2SF
020 8937 3541
www.brent.gov.uk/archives
kate.jarman@brent.gov.uk

Brent Archives holds collections related to the London Borough of Brent and its residents. We hold the records of Brent Council and its predecessors, including council minutes and building plans, as well as historical maps and street directories, electoral registers, school records, and an extensive collection of old photographs and postcards.

Brent Museum

Willesden Green Library Centre, 95 High Road, Willesden
Green
London NW10 2SF
020 8937 3600
www.brent.gov.uk/heritage.nsf
museum@brent.gov.uk

The collection consist of objects relating to the local Brent
area and the communities who live there. The museum is
encouraging all people from the many diverse communities
in Brent to donate a part of their history, either through
objects or oral history, to ensure that they make their mark
and history known to future generations.

British Airways Speedbird Heritage Centre

Waterside, PO Box 365
Harmondsworth UB7 0GB
0208 562 5777
www.ba.com/heritage
ba.1.museum@ba.com

British Airways Speedbird Heritage Centre's collection has
existed since the formation of British Airways. It was
formed to preserve the records and artefacts of British
Airways predecessor companies BOAC, BEA, BSAA and
the pre-war Imperial Airways and British Airways Ltd.

Collections: The Collection comprises an extensive
document archive recording the formation, development
and operations of the above companies and British Airways
as well as memorabilia and artefacts. Over 130 uniforms
from the 1930s to the present day are preserved as well as a
large collection of aircraft models and pictures. An
historically important collection of thousands of
photographs is also available as well as probably the most
complete set of aviation posters in the UK.

British Dental Association Museum

British Dental Association, 64 Wimpole Street
London W1G 8YS
020 7563 4549
www.bda.org/museum
museum@bda.org

The British Dental Association (BDA) Museum has one of
the largest collections of dental heritage in the UK telling
the story of how dentistry has developed from a
marketplace spectacle to the complex procedures and
treatment of today.

Collections: The collections of the BDA Dental Museum
comprise over 30,000 objects, archives and images relating
to the history of dentistry in the UK, and is of international
importance.

British Music Experience

The O2, Peninsula Square
London SE10 0DX
020 8463 2000
www.britishmusicexperience.com
help@britishmusicexperience.com

The British Music Experience is the new national museum
of popular music. It opened at The O2 on the Greenwich
Peninsula in March 2009 and fills a void by acting as a
cultural provider and giving people the opportunity to both
learn and celebrate the history of British popular music.

British Optical Association Museum

The College of Optometrists, 42 Craven Street
London WC2N 5NG
020 7766 4353
www.college-optometrists.org/museum
museum@college-optometrists.org

Now in its second century, The British Optical Association
Museum, founded 1901, is a collection comprising over
13,000 outstanding items of ophthalmic and optical
interest, covering the history of opticians and vision aids.
The museum was entrusted to the care of the College of
Optometrists in 1980 and continues to be recognised as the
oldest and one of the best specialist optical collections in
the world.

Collections: The collection includes over 2000 pairs of
spectacles, from the 17th century through to the 21st, as
well as historic examples of other optical devices and aids
to vision including scissor spectacles, folding eyeglasses,
pince-nez, lorgnettes, magnifiers, quizzing glasses and
monocles.

British Postal Museum & Archive, The

Freeling House, Phoenix Place
London WC1X 0DL
020 7239 2570
www.postalheritage.org.uk
info@postalheritage.org.uk

The British Postal Museum & Archive cares for the visual,
written and physical records of over 400 years of postal
development. We are responsible for managing The Royal
Mail Archive on behalf of Royal Mail Group plc.

Collections: The archives relate to the operation, policy,
development and social impact of the British Post Office
from 1636 to the present day.

Bromley Local Studies Library & Archives

Bromley Central Library, High Street
Bromley BR1 1EX
020 8461 7170
http://goo.gl/Cgh87v

The Local Studies Library in Bromley Central Library offers resources going back hundreds of years, on topics related to the London Borough of Bromley and its environs. It has specialist collections on The Crystal Palace, Walter de la Mare and HG Wells.

Bromley Museum

The Priory, Church Hill
Orpington BR6 0HH
01689 873826
bromley.museum@bromley.gov.uk

Bromley Museum is situated in the Orpington Priory, an important historic building set in attractive gardens. Throughout the year the museum holds a number of temporary exhibitions and events.

Brooking Collection of Period Architectural Detail, University of Greenwich

University of Greenwich, 30 Park Row
London SE10 9LS
020 8331 9309
www.gre.ac.uk/schools/a-and-c
P.J.Wall @ gre.ac.uk

The University of Greenwich houses a proportion of the Brooking Collection of Period Architectural Detail at the Avery Hill Campus near Eltham, London SE9. This is not open to the public but is accessible through CPD short courses.

Bruce Castle Museum

Lordship Lane
London N17 8NU
020 8808 8772
http://goo.gl/Uf7myB
museum.services@haringey.gov.uk

Bruce Castle is a Grade I listed 16th century manor house in 20 acres of parkland. William Compton - a member of Henry VIII's court - built the oldest surviving parts of the building. Since then the building has been modified several times by new owners including the Coleraine family.

Brunel Museum

Brunel Engine House, Railway Avenue
London SE16 4LF
0207 231 3840
www.brunel-museum.org.uk
robert.hulse@brunel-museum.org.uk

Isambard Kingdom Brunel's first and last projects are on the River Thames. The Thames Tunnel with his father Sir Marc Brunel is now an International Landmark Site and the oldest section of tunnel in the London Underground.

Collections: An exhibition in the restored Engine House tells the story of the men who worked in the dark, dodging flames and showered with raw sewage every day. Watercolours, peep-shows, engravings, and models, explain this epic feat of engineering.

Brunel University Archives

Brunel University, Kingston Lane
Uxbridge UB8 3PH
http://goo.gl/97RlIn
archivesandrecords@brunel.ac.uk

The University Archives chart the history of Brunel University from Acton Technical College in 1928 through Brunel College of Technology in 1957 and finally to Brunel University in 1966 and the merger with West London Institute for Higher Education in 1995. The holdings include Council and Senate and other University committee minutes and papers, student administrative papers, annual reports, prospectuses, photographs, and staff and student magazines.

BT Archives

Holborn Telephone Exchange, 268-270 High Holborn
London WC1V 7EE
020 7440 4220
www.bt.com/archives
archives@bt.com

BT Archives preserves the historical information of British Telecommunications plc and its predecessors from the early part of the 19th century up to the present day, effectively the history of telecommunications services in the United Kingdom and from the UK to overseas.

Collections: Near complete set of telephone directories for the whole country produced not only by BT, but also by its predecessors.

Buckingham Palace

London SW1A 1AA
020 7766 7300
www.royalcollection.org.uk
bookinginfo@royalcollection.org.uk

Buckingham Palace has served as the official London residence of Britain's sovereigns since 1837. It evolved from a town house that was owned from the beginning of the 18th century by the Dukes of Buckingham.

Building Exploratory, The

8 Orsman Road
London N1 5QJ
020 7729 2011
www.buildingexploratory.org.uk
mail@buildingexploratory.org.uk

Exhibition charts the development of London, with a special focus on Hackney. Takes in ideas of finding sense of place, different housing styles and their implications, and how events such as bomb damage have shaped our built environment.

Camden Local Studies & Archives

Holborn Library, 32-38 Theobalds Road
London WC1X 8PA
020 7974 6342
http://goo.gl/VyoG0b
localstudies@camden.gov.uk

Whether you are tracing the history of a building, undertaking a GCSE project, discovering the history of your family or just interested in the local history of the area where you live, the Camden Local Studies and Archives Centre is the place to start. The centre contains about 180,000 items on the history of the borough and we aim to keep anything that helps reflect life in Camden past and present.

Cannizaro Park

Cannizaro Park, West Side Common, Wimbledon
London SW19 4UE
020 8946 7349
www.cannizaropark.com

The grounds of Cannizaro House have become a public park - and perhaps the best public example of a type of large garden which London mansions had in the 19th century. It has a 'formal garden', with excellent summer bedding, a pool and a woodland garden.

Carew Manor Dovecote

Church Road
Beddington SM6 7NH
020 8770 4781
www.sutton.gov.uk
valary.murphy@sutton.gov.uk

There has been a dovecote at Carew Manor from late medieval times which stood in Pigeon House Meadow, to the east of the present site. It was probably demolished and replaced by the existing large octagonal brick building between 1707 and 1727, when the first Baronet, Sir Nicholas Carew, reorganised the grounds around the house.

Collections: Inside is a Roman Coffin on the ground floor which was found in the 1930s when a pipe trench was dug on the east side of Church Road just south of the churchyard. Tours of the Dovecote include a visit to Carew Manor Great Hall, with its late medieval arch-braced hammer-beam roof, listed Grade 1; and a tour of the Manor's cellars with a visible chalk and flint construction dating to earlier houses on this site.

Carlyle's House - National Trust

24 Cheyne Row, Chelsea
London SW3 5HL
020 7352 7087
www.nationaltrust.org.uk/carlyles-house
carlyleshouse@nationaltrust.org.uk

A classic Queen Anne house, this was the home of the writer Thomas Carlyle from 1834 until his death in 1881. A tall townhouse in Cheyne Row, close to the River Thames, Carlyle's House was built in 1708 as part of a terrace of London homes.

Carshalton Water Tower & Historic Garden Trust

West Street
Carshalton SM5 3PN
020 8669 1546
www.carshaltonwatertower.co.uk

The Water Tower is a unique Grade II-listed early 18th century garden building, sited in the grounds of Carshalton House in Surrey. As the name suggests, this contained a water-powered pump, which supplied water to Carshalton House and the fountains in its garden. However, the building was and is much more than this as it contains a suite of rooms such as the Saloon, the Orangery and a splendid early 18th century bathroom with tile-lined plunge bath.

Cartoon Museum

35 Little Russell Street
London WC1A 2HH
0207 580 8155
www.cartoonmuseum.org
info@cartoonmuseum.org

The Cartoon Museum exhibits the very finest examples of British cartoons, caricature, and comic art from the 18th century to the present day. There is also a shop, an archive and a reference library.

Charles Dickens Museum

48 Doughty Street
London WC1N 2LX
020 7405 2127
www.dickensmuseum.com
info@dickensmuseum.com

Number 48 Doughty Street is the only remaining London home of eminent Victorian author Charles Dickens. Dickens described the terraced Georgian dwelling as 'my house in town' and resided here from 1837 until 1839 with his wife and young family.

Collections: The collection ranges from paintings by well-known Victorian artists such as Maclise and Frith to manuscripts, personal items, memorabilia and reconstructed rooms.

Charlton Library

Charlton Road, Greenwich
London SE7 8RE
0208-319-2525
www.gll.org/libraries

Charlton House is regarded as the best-preserved
ambitious Jacobean house in Greater London. It was built
in 1607-12 of red brick with stone dressing, and has an
'E'-plan layout.

Chelsea Physic Garden

66 Royal Hospital Road
London SW3 4HS
020 7352 5646
www.chelseaphysicgarden.co.uk
enquiries@chelseaphysicgarden.co.uk

Situated in the heart of Chelsea, this 'secret Garden' is a
centre of education, beauty and relaxation. Founded in
1673 by the Worshipful Society of Apothecaries, it
continues to research the properties, origins and
conservation of over 5000 species.

Collections: The Garden holds approximately 5000 taxa,
the collection concentrates on medicinal plants and those
of ethnobotanical interest, as well as rare and endangered
species. We also grow plants named or introduced by
people associated with the Garden's history.

Chiswick House & Gardens Trust

Chiswick House and Gardens
London W4 2RP
020 8742 3905
www.chgt.org.uk
info@chgt.org.uk

Chiswick House is a pioneering example of neoclassical
architecture inspired by ancient Rome. It was designed by
the third Earl of Burlington, 1694-1753.

Chocolate Museum, The

187 Ferndale Road, Brixton
London SW9 8BA
07723 434235
www.TheChocolateMuseum.co.uk
info@TheChocolateMuseum.co.uk

The Chocolate Museum's mission is to inspire a passion for
learning about quality chocolate and its history both in
Britain and worldwide. Britain, one of the three largest
consumer of chocolate in the world, is indeed where solid
chocolate was invented, and the first country to give
chocolate to its army: chocolate helped sailors and soldiers
from the 1780s to World War I and II.

Collections: Our collection encompasses a range of objects
and memorabilia acquired over many years from different
merchants and collectors. Our oldest artefact dates back to
the 18th century.

Churchill War Rooms

Clive Steps, King Charles Street
London SW1A 2AQ
020 7930 6961
www.iwm.org.uk/visits/churchill-war-rooms
cwr@iwm.org.uk

Visit Churchill War Rooms to discover the original Cabinet
War Rooms, the wartime bunker that sheltered Churchill
and his government during the Blitz. Explore the historic
rooms to experience the secret history that lives on
underground.

Cinema Museum

The Master's House, 2 Dugard Way, off Renfrew Road
London SE11 4TH
020 7840 2200
www.cinemamuseum.org.uk
info@cinemamuseum.org.uk

The Cinema Museum is a charitable organisation founded
in 1986. The content of The Cinema Museum ranges from
items relating to film production to film exhibition and the
experience of cinema going.

City of Westminster Archives Centre

10 St Ann's Street
London SW1P 2DE
020 7641 5180
www.westminster.gov.uk/archives
archives@westminster.gov.uk

Westminster Archives Centre is a vast source of information
on family, local, business and community history. Our local
government records date back to 1460 and we have
extensive collections of visual material, including over
60,000 prints and photographs. Special collections include
the William Blake Collection and a Theatre Collection. The
centre holds archives of Liberty & Co, Jaeger, and Gillow.

Clarence House

London SW1A 1AA
020 7766 7303
www.royal.gov.uk/output/page2262.asp
information@royalcollection.org.uk

Clarence House, which stands beside St James's Palace, was
built between 1825 and 1827 to the designs of John Nash
for Prince William Henry, Duke of Clarence, who resided
there as King William IV from 1830 until 1837. During its
history, the house has been altered, reflecting the changes
in occupancy over nearly two centuries.

Clockmakers' Museum, The

Guildhall Library, Aldermanbury
London EC2P 2EJ
020 7332 1865
www.clockmakers.org
keeper@clockmakers.org

The museum was founded in 1813 and is the oldest collection specifically of clocks, watches and marine timekeepers in the world. It has been open to the public (free) since 1873.

Constance Howard Resource & Research Centre in Textiles

Visual Arts Department, Goldsmiths College, University of London, High Street, New Cross
London SE14 6NW
020 7717 2210
www.goldsmiths.ac.uk/constance-howard
connitex@gold.ac.uk

The orginal collection was formed in the 1980s and reflected the pedagogic principals of Constance Howard and Audrey Walker, two former Heads of Textiles at Goldsmiths College, University of London.

Collections: The contents of the material archive is an eclectic, international treasure trove of textiles which are extraordinarily rich in breadth and diversity, ranging from full-scale quilts to tiny fragments of embroidery and lace. There is a special archive of techno-fabrics from Nuno in Japan and donations by ex-graduates from the 1980s and 1990s.

Corps of Army Music Museum

Kneller Hall
Twickenham TW7 2DU
020 8744 8635
www.army.mod.uk/music/23294.aspx
camus.curator@gmail.com

The Corps of Army Music Museum is dedicated to preserving the history of British military music.

Crossness Pumping Station

Thames Water Crossness Works, Belvedere Road, Abbey Wood
London SE2
020 8311 3711
www.crossness.org.uk

The Crossness Pumping Station was built by Sir Joseph Bazalgette as part of Victorian London's urgently needed main sewerage system.

Croydon Airport Visitor Centre

Airport House, Purley Way
Croydon CR0 0XZ
www.croydonairportsociety.org.uk
info@croydonairportsociety.org.uk

Built in 1928, it's official title was Air Port of London, Croydon. This was the UK's international airport through the 1920s and 30s. Exhibition space includes displays located in the world's oldest Air Traffic Control Tower in Airport House. Features include interactive display, exhibits and visual images charting the history of Croydon Airport from World War I airfield, London's international airport, Battle of Britain airfield and closure in 1959.

Croydon Local Studies Library

Local Studies Library, Level 3, Central Library, Croydon Clocktower, Katharine Street
Croydon CR9 1ET
020 8726 6900
https://goo.gl/N7RteU

We collect books, photographs, maps, newspapers and other items that are of value in the study of the past, present and future of Croydon.

Croydon Natural History & Scientific Society Museum

Chipstead Valley Primary School
Coulsdon CR5 3BW
020 8668 6909
http://goo.gl/dKzafX

The Croydon Natural history & Scientific Society was founded in 1870, as The Croydon Microscopical Club, to encourage the study of the sciences, local history and archaeology of the Croydon area. The museum is a small collection of archives dealing with the society, open for research by appointment with the curator only.

Crystal Palace Museum

Anerley Hill
London SE19 2BA
020 8676 0700
www.crystalpalacemuseum.org.uk

The history of the Crystal Palace is kept alive by the Crystal Palace Museum which tells the story of the Hyde Park and Sydenham Crystal Palaces. With photographs and displays of documents, handbills and ceramics.

Cuming Museum

The Old Town Hall, 151 Walworth Road
London SE17 1RY
020 75252332
www.southwark.gov.uk/cumingmuseum
cuming.museum@southwark.gov.uk

The Cuming Museum is temporarily closed following the fire at Walworth Road Town Hall in 2013. The museum's onsite services remain temporarily suspended. See the website for details of online exhibitions.

Collections: The Cuming Museum comprises the worldwide and local collections of the Cuming family as well as local and social history collected by the borough during the 20th century. We also care for an extensive art collection.

Cutty Sark

King William Walk, Greenwich
London SE10 9HT
020 8858 2698
www.rmg.co.uk

The existing collections consist principally of the 1869 composite clipper ship Cutty Sark, and her contents. In addition the Trust possesses a collections of artefacts relating to the ship and her history, designers, builders, owners, crews, cargoes, the clipper ship genre, the Merchant Navy and Robert Burns.

De Morgan Centre, The

38 West Hill
London SW18 1RX
020 8871 1144
www.demorgan.org.uk
info@demorgan.org.uk

The De Morgan Foundation owns a large collection of the work of the Victorian ceramic artist William De Morgan and his wife, the painter Evelyn De Morgan. The ceramics collection includes vases, tiles and panels.

Dennis Severs' House

18 Folgate Street
London E1 6BX
020 7247 4013
www.dennissevershouse.co.uk
info@DennisSeversHouse.co.uk

Dennis Severs was an artist who lived in the house in much the same way as its occupants in the 18th century would have done. He used his visitors' imagination as his canvas while they are taken on an historical tour around the house.

Design Museum

28 Shad Thames
London SE1 2YD
020 7403 6933
www.designmuseum.org
info@designmuseum.org

The Design Museum is one of the world's leading museums of modern and contemporary design. Since its foundation in 1989, the museum has become the cultural champion of UK design and won international acclaim for exhibitions of modern design history and contemporary design innovation.

Dilston Grove

Southwest Corner of Southwark Park
London SE16 2UA
020 7237 1230
www.cgplondon.org
admin@cgplondon.org

Dilston Grove is the former Clare College Mission Church on the Southwest corner of Southwark Park and is Grade II listed. Designed by architects Sir John Simpson and Maxwell Ayrton, it was built in 1911 and is one of the earliest examples of poured concrete construction. Today, Dilston Grove represents London's only large-scale raw space regularly available to artists.

Dorich House Museum

Kingston University, 67 Kingston Vale
London SW15 3RN
0208 417 5515
www.dorichhousemuseum.org.uk
B.Martin@Kingston.ac.uk

Dorich House was the studio, gallery and home of the sculptor Dora Gordine (1895-1991) and her husband the Hon. Richard Hare (1907-1966), a Professor of Russian Literature. Dorich House holds the largest single collection of Gordine's bronze and plaster sculptures, as well as many of her paintings and drawings. The Russian art collection includes icons, paintings, ceramics, glassware, metalwork, folk art and furniture dating from the early 18th century to the early 20th century. The archive consists of photographs, architectural drawings, press cuttings, books, correspondence and taped interviews.

Dr Johnson's House

17 Gough Square
London EC4A 3DE
020 7353 3745
www.drjohnsonshouse.org
curator@drjohnsonshouse.org

Dr Johnson's House is a charming 300-year-old townhouse,

nestled amongst a maze of courts and alleys in the historic City of London. Samuel Johnson, the writer and wit, lived and worked here in the middle of the eighteenth century, compiling his great Dictionary of the English Language in the Garret. Today, the house is open to the public with a collection relating to Johnson, a research library, restored interiors and a wealth of original features.

Ealing Local History Centre

103 Ealing Broadway Centre (first floor), The Broadway
London W5 5JY
020 8825 8194
http://goo.gl/KH8V1q
localhistory@ealing.gov.uk

Are you working on a school project? Did your family come from Ealing? Did any famous people live in Ealing? What is the story of that interesting building you pass every day? If you are looking for the answers to these questions, then Ealing Library is a good place to start. We have a wide range of local history resources and can offer you help and advice on researching local and family history.

East of London Family History Society

46 Brights Avenue
Rainham RM13 9NW
www.eolfhs.org.uk

The society's geographic area of interest is that part of Greater London, north of the Thames, east of the old City of London gates of Aldgate and Bishopsgate, and through the modern day London Boroughs of Tower Hamlets, Hackney, Newham, Barking and Dagenham through Redbridge to the edge of Metropolitan Essex at Havering.

Eastbury Manor House - National Trust

Eastbury Square, Barking
London IG11 9SN
0208 227 2946
www.nationaltrust.org.uk/eastbury-manor-house
eastburyhouse@lbbd.gov.uk

Welcome to Eastbury Manor House, a beautiful Grade 1 listed Tudor mansion. It is owned by the National Trust and managed by the London Borough of Barking and Dagenham.

Eltham Palace - English Heritage

London SE9 5QE
020 8294 2548
http://goo.gl/GO7Zd4

Immerse yourself in 1930s Art Deco decadence at Eltham Palace, one of the most enchanting visitor attractions in London. Built by the wealthy Courtauld family next to the remains of Eltham Palace, childhood home of Henry VIII, it's among the finest examples of Art Deco architecture in England. The stunning entrance hall, marvellous panelled dining room, luxurious bathroom, and the magnificent medieval Great Hall, are just some of the highlights.

Emery Walker Trust

7 Hammersmith Terrace
London W6 9TS
020 8741 4104
www.emerywalker.org.uk
admin@emerywalker.org.uk

No 7 Hammersmith Terrace is a tall terraced house on the River Thames at Hammersmith in west London. Its sober Georgian exterior hides a secret – the decoration and furnishings preserved as they were in the lifetime of the printer Emery Walker (1851-1933), a great friend and mentor to William Morris.

Enfield Local Studies Library & Archive

Thomas Hardy House (1st floor), 39 London Road
Enfield EN2 6DS
0208 379 2724
http://goo.gl/ujwfnE

Enfield Library and Museum service has a dedicated Local Studies Library and archive at Thomas Hardy House in Enfield Town. Archive material includes records relating to the three former local authorities of Edmonton, Enfield and Southgate.

Enfield Museum

Dugdale Centre, Thomas Hardy House, 39 London Road
Enfield, Middlesex EN2 6DS
020 8379 1469
www.enfield.gov.uk/museum
jan.metcalfe@enfield.gov.uk

Enfield Museum Service aims to reflect the history and cultural diversity of Enfield through advancing an understanding of our collective past and shared future. It is responsible for the care, display and interpretation of collections through temporary exhibitions and events, which aim to make the collections accessible to all the people of Enfield.

Faber Archive

The Archive, Faber and Faber Ltd, Bloomsbury House, 74-77
Great Russell Street
London WC1B 3DA
www.faber.co.uk/faqs
archiveenquiries@faber.co.uk

With a distinguished history stretching back to the mid-1920s, and featuring many of the greatest literary and artistic figures of the 20th century, Faber and Faber has preserved a unique publishing archive. This is still an integral part of the company, and is used to support new editions, but is a great potential resource for anyone interested to learn more about the firm and its great authors.

Fan Museum, The

□ £

12 Grooms Hill, Greenwich
London SE10 8ER
020 8305 1441
www.thefanmuseum.org.uk
info@thefanmuseum.org.uk

The Fan Museum is the only museum in the UK entirely dedicated to the subject. The museum is housed in two early Georgian townhouses in the heart of Maritime Greenwich.

Fashion & Textile Museum

□ £

83 Bermondsey Street
London SE1 3XF
020 7407 8664
www.ftmlondon.org
info@ftmlondon.org

The Fashion and Textile Museum (FTM) lies at the heart of the Fashion quarter of London's artistic Bermondsey Village. A remarkable building designed by Mexican architect, Ricardo Legoretta, the FTM is now a part of Newham College and is being redeveloped as an up to the minute education, exhibition and visitor centre for contemporary fashion, textiles and jewellery.

Fenton House & Garden - National Trust

Windmill Hill, Hampstead
London NW3 6SP
020 7435 3471
www.nationaltrust.org.uk/fenton-house
fentonhouse@nationaltrust.org.uk

Handsome 17th century merchant's house with delightful walled garden with fine displays of roses, an orchard and a working kitchen garden. The house has connections with the actress Mrs Jordan and the painter William Nicholson.

Collections: The Benton Fletcher collection of early keyboard instruments, most of which are in working order; an outstanding collection of porcelain; 17th century needlework pictures and Georgian furniture.

Firepower, The Royal Artillery Museum

□ □ □ £

Firepower, Royal Artillery Museum, Royal Arsenal
London SE18 6ST
020 8855 7755
www.firepower.org.uk
info@firepower.org.uk

The museum tells the story of the Gunners – the 2.5 million men and women of the Royal Artillery, the part they have played in history and their role in today's British Army. Tales of extraordinary heroism and endeavour are presented alongside explanations the technological and scientific advances driven by the development of artillery from Roman times to the present day.

Fitzroy House

□ ★

37 Fitzroy Street
London W1T 6DX
0207 255 2422
www.fitzroyhouse.org
info@fitzroyhouse.org

Fitzroy House is an original 1791 building imitating the designs of Robert Adam, the famous Georgian period architect who along with his brother designed Fitzroy Square. The house is one of the last remaining structures on the block that retains its original external architecture and now shows the life and work of L Ron Hubbard. Steeped in nostalgic memorabilia, Fitzroy House will take you on a trip down memory lane, with its faithfully restored communications office equipment including Adler typewriters, Grundig tape recorder and a Western Union Telefax.

Flanders Fields Memorial Garden

□ ★

Guards Museum, Wellington Barracks,, United Kingdom
Bird Cage Walk SW1E 6HQ
020 7125 0519
www.memorial2014.com
garden@flandersfieldappeal.com

The Flanders Fields Memorial Garden is an initiative of the Guards Museum, in conjunction with Flanders House in London, the Commonwealth War Graves Commission, and the Belgian-Luxembourg Chamber of Commerce in the UK.

Florence Nightingale Museum

□ £

2 Lambeth Palace Road, South Bank
London SE1 7EW
020 7620 0374
www.florence-nightingale.co.uk
info@florence-nightingale.co.uk

Discover the woman behind the legend. It includes artefacts owned or used by Florence Nightingale, including her pet owl Athena and the medicine chest she took with her to the Crimea.

Forty Hall & Estate

Forty Hill
Enfield EN2 9HA
020 8363 8196
www.fortyhallestate.co.uk
forty.hall@enfield.gov.uk

A trip to Forty Hall & Estate is a memorable day out for all of the family. Forty Hall is a Grade 1 listed Jacobean Manor House, nestled in leafy Enfield and set amidst pleasure gardens, ancient royal parkland, majestic trees, lakes and watercourses. Our permanent exhibition tells the story of Forty Hall & Estate throughout the ages and looks at the life and times of Sir Nicholas Rainton and life in the 17th century.

Foundling Museum, The

40 Brunswick Square
London WC1N 1AZ
020 7841 3600
www.foundlingmuseum.org.uk
enquiries@foundlingmuseum.org.uk

The Foundling Museum explores the history of the Foundling Hospital, the UK's first children's charity and first public art gallery, established in 1739 by the philanthropist Captain Thomas Coram.

Collections: Poignant social history gallery telling the story of London's first home for abandoned children, including personal histories, artefacts, photographs and recordings; London's first art gallery featuring works by Hogarth, Rysbrack, Gainsborough, Reynolds, Roubiliac, Hudson, Ramsay and Wilson; Fine 18th-century, Rococo and Georgian interiors; and Gerald Cook Handel collection of Handel memorabilia.

Freud Museum London

20 Maresfield Gardens
London NW3 5SX
020 7435 2002
www.freud.org.uk
info@freud.org.uk

Listed house in Hampstead where Sigmund Freud and his family lived after fleeing the Nazis in 1938.

Collections: Sigmund Freud's large collection of Egyptian, Greek, Roman and Oriental antiquities and his library. His study with the psychoanalytic couch preserve his working environment.

Fulham Palace

Bishop's Avenue
London SW6 6EA
020 7736 3233
www.fulhampalace.org
mail@fulhampalace.org

Fulham Palace is a truly remarkable place. For centuries, this Grade I Listed building, situated in extensive grounds by the River Thames, was a country residence of the Bishops of London.

Collections: Includes paintings, textiles, books and artefacts illuminating daily life of the Bishops of London, their families and local workers, in and around Fulham Palace over the centuries. Strong social history collection reflects local culture, trades and everyday life.

Fusilier Museum London, The

RRF, HM Tower of London
London EC3N 4AB
0203 166 6912
www.fusiliermuseumlondon.org
stephanie@fusiliermuseumlondon.org

The Fusilier Museum tells the story of a British army regiment, formed at the Tower of London in 1685 by King James II. The museum is housed in a building originally built as army Officers' quarters. The building still houses the Royal Regiment of Fusiliers' Regimental Headquarters and the Officers' Mess, which is used for formal dinners and ceremonial occasions.

Galton Collection, UCL

Galton Collection, University College London, Wolfson House, 4 Stephenson Way
London NW1 2HE
020 7679 2647
www.ucl.ac.uk/museums/galton
n.mcenroe@ucl.ac.uk

The Galton Collection comprises the scientific instruments, papers, and personal memorabilia left to University College London on the death of Sir Francis Galton (1822-1911). Galton set up a Eugenics Laboratory at UCL, and is chiefly remembered for inventing fingerprinting, and for his work in eugenics, statistics, biometry, composite photography, and meteorology.

Collections: The collection contains Galton's fingerprinting kits, craniometers, numerous other measuring instruments, his desk, bookcase, bust, curios from his travels as a young man, his personal possessions, and research papers.

Garden Museum

5 Lambeth Palace Road
London SE1 7LB
020 7401 8865
www.gardenmuseum.org.uk
info@gardenmuseum.org.uk

The Garden Museum explores and celebrates British gardens and gardening through its collection, temporary exhibitions, events, symposia and garden. Whether you are an enthusiastic amateur gardener, more of a specialist or someone with a passion for museums, history or even architecture the museum has something for you. Situated on the South Bank of the Thames, opposite the Houses of Parliament, the museum has a spectacular home in the former St Mary-at-Lambeth Parish Church, which itself its steeped in history and has some interesting stories to tell. For example, the tomb of the John Tradescants, gardeners to Charles I and adventurous plant hunters, can be found in the museum Garden.

Geffrye Museum of the Home, The

136 Kingsland Road, Shoreditch
London E2 8EA
020 7739 9893
www.geffrye-museum.org.uk
info@geffrye-museum.org.uk

The Geffrye explores the home from 1600 to the present day, focusing on the urban living rooms and gardens of the English middle classes. Our collections show how homes have been used and furnished over the past 400 years, reflecting changes in society and behaviour as well as style, fashion and taste. A series of period rooms lead visitors on a walk through time from 17th century oak furniture and panelling, past muted Georgian elegance and eclectic Victorian style, to 20th century modernity and contemporary living. These rooms are complemented by a sequence of period gardens and an award-winning walled herb garden which illustrate the role of the garden in home life (open April - October).

Geology Collections, University College London

Geology Rock Room, Room 4, First Floor, South Wing,
University College London, Gower Street
London WC1E 6BT
020 7679 7900
www.geology.museum.ucl.ac.uk
j.dunn@ucl.ac.uk

The Geology Collection contains a wealth of rocks, minerals and fossils collected from all over the world during the 150 year history of the department.

Collections: Primarily a teaching and research resource, some of the 40,000 specimens are on display to the public. One of the highlights is the Johnston-Lavis volcanological collection of minerals, rocks, photographs and gouaches collected from 1880- 1912. The collection also contains the NASA archive of thousands of images housed in the new Planetary Science suite, and the internationally important micropalaeontological collections.

George Padmore Institute

76 Stroud Green Road, Finsbury Park
London N4 3EN
020 7272 8915
www.georgepadmoreinstitute.org
info@georgepadmoreinstitute.org

The GPI is an archive, educational research and information centre housing materials relating to the black community of Caribbean, African and Asian descent, in Britain and continental Europe.

Gilwell Park

Bury Road
London E4 7QW
0845 300 1818
scouts.org.uk
info.centre@scout.org.uk

Gilwell Park, the Headquerters of the UK Scout Association has three areas of intrest for the visitor. Gilwell is a large wooded campsite and activity centre that has many historical Scouting artefacts distributed around the site. Scouting visitors can visit these sites using a self guided tour and map.

Golden Hinde Living History Museum

The Golden Hinde, St Mary Overie Dock, Cathedral Street
London SE1 9DE
020 7403 0123
www.goldenhinde.co.uk
info@goldenhinde.co.uk

The Golden Hinde is a full scale reconstruction of the notorious 16th century warship that Sir Francis Drake circumnavigated the world between 1577 and 1580. Now berthed in St Mary Overie Dock, near Southwark cathedral, the Golden Hinde is a living history museum offering the opportunity to see what life as a 16th century sailor would have really been like.

Goldsmiths' Company, The

Goldsmiths' Hall, Foster Lane
London EC2V 6BN
020 7606 7010
www.thegoldsmiths.co.uk

The Goldsmiths' Company is one of the Twelve Great Livery Companies of the City of London with its roots in the trade guilds of the Middle Ages. The collection of archives (dating from the 14th century), books, journals, negatives and slides is a most valuable resource enjoyed by historians, students, designers and picture researchers. It is available, by appointment, to members of the Company and the general public interested in the subjects of silver, jewellery, regalia, assaying and hallmarking.

Government Art Collection

Queens Yard, 179a Tottenham Court Road
London W1T 7PA
020 7211 2425
www.gac.culture.gov.uk
gac@culture.gov.uk

Works of art from the collection are displayed in British Government buildings both in the United Kingdom and around the world.

Collections: Dating from 1898, the Government Art Collection now holds approximately 12,000 works of art by British artists in a variety of media, including paintings, sculpture, prints, drawings, photographs, textiles and video works, from the 16th century to the present day.

Grant Museum of Zoology

UCL Rockefeller Building, 21 University Street
London WC1E 6DE
020 3108 2052
www.ucl.ac.uk/museums/zoology
zoology.museum@ucl.ac.uk

Dating back to 1828, the museum houses a diverse natural history collection covering the whole of the animal kingdom. Retaining an air of the avid Victorian collector, the museum contains cases packed full of skeletons, mounted animals and specimens preserved in fluid.

Greek Orthodox Cathedral of Saint Sophia with Museum

Moscow Road, Bayswater
London W2 4LQ
020 7229 7260
www.stsophia.org.uk
mail@stsophia.org.uk

The Greek Orthodox Church of St Sophia in Bayswater opened a small museum in its crypt in 2006. It shows various treasures donated to the cathedral by wealthy 19th century patrons, as well as a rotating display of material from the archives of the Greek community in London, stretching back to the 18th century.

Greenwich Heritage Centre

Artillery Square, Royal Arsenal, Woolwich
London SE18 6ST
020 8854 2452
http://goo.gl/Qvp9PR
heritage.centre@greenwich.gov.uk

The Heritage Centre brings together the former Borough Museum and Local History Library to offer a wealth of information and fascinating displays about the history of Greenwich.

Collections: A free exhibition, 'Inside the Arsenal' tells the amazing story of the Royal Arsenal and the surrounding area through the lives of the people who lived and worked there.

Guardian News & Media Archive

Kings Place, 90 York Way
London N1 9GU
020 3353 3304
www.guardian.co.uk/gnm-archive
archives@guardian.co.uk

The GNM Archive preserves and promotes the histories and values of the Guardian and Observer newspapers by collecting and making accessible archive material that provides an accurate and comprehensive history of the papers. It holds the Guardian Archive, the Observer Archive and personal collections of journalists, cartoonists and photographers associated with the papers.

Guards Museum

Wellington Barracks, Birdcage Walk
London SW1E 6HQ
020 7414 3271
www.theguardsmuseum.com
guardsmuseum@aol.com

The museum contains a wealth of information and artefacts relating to the five regiments of Foot Guards namely Grenadier, Coldstream, Scots, Irish and Welsh Guards. Along with the two regiments of Household Cavalry they make up Her Majesty's Household Division and enjoy the treasured privilege of guarding The Sovereign and the Royal Palaces.

Guildhall Art Gallery

Guildhall Yard
London EC2V 5AE
020 7332 3700
www.guildhallartgallery.cityoflondon.gov.uk
guildhall.artgallery@corpoflondon.gov.uk

The collections are mainly comprised of British works of art. Included are fascinating views of London & London life from the 16th century to the present day, & Victorian paintings & sculpture including well-known Pre-Raphaelite works.

Guildhall Library

Aldermanbury
London EC2V 7HH
020 7332 1868
www.cityoflondon.gov.uk/guildhalllibrary
guildhall.library@cityoflondon.gov.uk

Guildhall Library, the library of London history, holds the

world's largest collection of material devoted to a single city. With titles from the 13th century to the present day, it tells the remarkable story of 2,000 years of life in the capital and covers all aspects of life in London, past and present. Our free temporary exhibitions focus on the library's collections and the history of London, from the history of the City Livery Companies to Shakespeare and the Great Plague.

Gunnersbury Park & Museum

Gunnersbury Park, Pope's Lane, Acton
London W3 8LQ
020 8992 1612
http://goo.gl/8SnCno
gp-museum@carillionservices.co.uk

The local history museum for the London Boroughs of Ealing and Hounslow, housed in a Grade II* listed mansion which was the home of the first English Rothschilds.

Hackney Archives

2nd floor, Dalston CLR James Library and, Dalston Square
London E8 3BQ
020 8356 8925
www.hackney.gov.uk/archives
archives@hackney.gov.uk

Hackney Archives looks after the archives of the London Borough of Hackney - the administrative records of the borough council and its predecessors back to 1700, together with the records of organisations and individuals with links to the area of the modern London borough.

Hackney Museum

Technology and Learning Centre, 1 Reading Lane, Hackney
London E8 1GQ
020 8356 2509
www.hackney.gov.uk/hackneymuseum
hmuseum@hackney.gov.uk

This exciting museum explores the reasons why people have moved to Hackney from all over the world for more than 1000 years. The museum displays include objects, interactives, computer programmes and the stories of real people.

Hall-Carpenter Archives

Archives Division, Library of the London School of Economics & Political Science, 10 Portugal Street
London WC2A 2HD
020 7955 7223
http://goo.gl/g9LQYH
Document@lse.ac.uk

The Hall-Carpenter Archives (HCA) founded in 1982 are

the largest source for the study of gay activism in Britain which followed the publication of the Wolfenden Report in 1958.

Collections: Archives of gay organisations and activists, and a periodicals collection which includes complete runs of most British and Irish gay serials including Gay News and Capital Gay, and many newsletters from lesbian and gay groups throughout the UK.

Ham House & Garden - National Trust

Ham Street
Richmond-upon-Thames TW10 7RS
020 8940 1950
www.nationaltrust.org.uk/ham-house
hamhouse@nationaltrust.org.uk

Ham House, set on the banks of the river Thames near Richmond, is perhaps the most remarkable Stuart House in the country. Built in 1610 and enlarged in the 1670s by the influential Duke and Duchess of Lauderdale, Ham was a centre for court intrigue throughout most of the 17th century.

Hammersmith & Fulham Archives & Local History Centre

The Lilla Huset, 191 Talgarth Road
London W6 8BJ
020 8741 5159
http://goo.gl/o6ipQf
archives@lbhf.gov.uk

The work of the archives covers the history of the borough of Hammersmith & Fulham. We are particularly concerned with its administrative history but our collection illustrates other aspects too.

Hampstead Museum - Burgh House

Hampstead Museum, Burgh House, New End Square, Hampstead
London NW3 1LT
020 7431 0144
www.burghhouse.org.uk
info@burghhouse.org.uk

Burgh House is a grade I listed house built in 1703/4. The Hampstead Museum is incorporated in the House on the first floor and offers permanent displays on Hampstead history.

Collections: Permanent displays on the history of Hampstead; John Constable, Helen Allingham and on the Isokon flats and furniture.

Handel House Museum

25 Brook Street, Mayfair
London W1K 4HB
020 7495 1685
www.handelhouse.org
mail@handelhouse.org

Handel House Museum at 25 Brook Street, London was home to the great baroque composer George Frideric Handel. He lived here from 1723 until his death in 1759, and composed some of the greatest music in history.

Collections: Portraits of Handel and his contemporaries, early Georgian furniture, musical instruments, manuscripts.

Haringey Archive Service

Archivist, Bruce Castle Museum, Lordship Lane
London N17 8NU
020 8808 8772
http://goo.gl/s9IJLq

The service holds the archives and the local history library and collections of the borough of Haringey.

Harrow Civic Centre Reference Library

Civic Centre Reference Library, P.O. Box 4, Civic Centre, Station Road
Harrow HA1 2XY
020 8424 1055
http://goo.gl/XLP9MY

If you are tracing your family history, researching the history of a building, or just have an interest in the local area, please come in and use our resources.

Harrow Museum & Heritage Centre

Headstone Manor, Pinner View
Harrow, Middlesex HA2 6PX
020 8861 2626
www.harrow.gov.uk
harrow.museum@harrow.gov.uk

Harrow Museum was founded in 1986. It is located in the historic buildings and grounds of Headstone Manor.

Headstone Manor Museum

Headstone Manor, Pinner View
Harrow HA2 6PX
020 9963 6720
www.harrow.gov.uk/museum
Harrow.Museum@harrow.gov.uk

Headstone Manor Museum is a complex of four historic buildings set in beautiful grounds, including the medieval moat. Entry is free to this tranquil oasis hidden away in the middle of a London suburb.

Highgate Cemetery

Swains Lane
London N6 6PJ
020 8341 1834
www.highgatecemetery.org
info@highgate-cemetery.org

Highgate Cemetery is a haven of beauty and tranquillity, a place of peace and contemplation where a romantic profusion of trees, memorials and wildlife flourish in the heart of London. The East Cemetery is where Karl Marx is buried. Visitors may roam freely on this side, but there is an entrance charge. Admission to the West Cemetery is by guided tour only.

Hillingdon Family History Society

20 Moreland Drive
Gerrards Cross SL9 8BB
01753 885602
www.hfhs.co.uk
gillmay@dial.pipex.com

Hillingdon Family History Society was founded in 1988 and exists to promote and encourage family history, local history and genealogy. We are affiliated to the Federation of Family History Societies.

Hillingdon Local Studies, Archives & Museum Service

Central Library, 14-16 High Street
Uxbridge, Middlesex UB8 1HD
01895 250 702
www.hillingdon.gov.uk/history
archives@hillingdon.gov.uk

Hillingdon Local Studies, Archives and Museum Service exists to: take care of the Borough's collections of historic material, help local people find out about their heritage, promote responsible care for all historic items, old and new, and work for the establishment of a Borough Museum in Hillingdon. The Service is Hillingdon's museum and records service.

HMS Belfast

The Queen's Walk
London SE1 2JH
020 7940 6300
www.iwm.org.uk
hmsbelfast@iwm.org.uk

Explore HMS Belfast's nine decks to discover the stories of

life on board this warship during Arctic convoys, D-Day and beyond. Imagine sleeping in one of the tightly packed hammocks during duties in Arctic waters, or being stationed deep in the bowels of the ship when she opened fire in support of Allied troops on D-Day.

Hogarth's House

Hogarth Lane, Great West Road
London W4 2QN
020 8994 6757
www.hounslow.info/arts/hogarthshouse/index.htm
info@cip.org.uk

Hogarth's House, built around 1700, was the country home of the great painter, engraver and satirist William Hogarth (1697-1764) from 1749 until his death. Hogarth's House holds an extensive collection of the artist's 18th century prints, of which a selection will always be on display and a set of his engraving plates. The panelled rooms also house some replica pieces of 18th century furniture.

Honeywood Museum

Honeywood Walk
Carshalton SM5 3NX
020 8770 4297
www.sutton.gov.uk
honeywoodmuseum@sutton.gov.uk

Honeywood is a fine late Victorian and Edwardian house, incorporating part of an earlier 17th century building, overlooking the picturesque town ponds.

Collections: Displays tell the history of the people of the Borough of Sutton from the days of early settlement to the present, including Tudor life, the mills and country houses linked to the River Wandle, the Victorian and Edwardian eras and the Second World War. Period rooms include the Edwardian Billiards Room with its original fixtures and fittings.

Honourable Artillery Company

Armoury House, City Road
London EC1Y 2BQ
020 7382 1537
www.hac.org.uk
hac@hac.org.uk

The Honourable Artillery Company's private museum is now open to members of the HAC. Members of the general public may be able to visit by appointment only.

Honourable Company of Master Mariners, The

HQS Wellington, Temple Stairs, Victoria Embankment
London WC2R 2PN
020 7836 8179
www.hcmm.org.uk/
info@hcmm.org.uk

The Honourable Company of Master Mariners is a City of London Livery Company open to British and Commonwealth Master Mariners from the Merchant and Royal Navies. Its livery hall is the ship HQS Wellington, on board which exhibitions periodically are staged.

Horniman Museum & Gardens

100 London Road, Forest Hill
London SE23 3PQ
020 8699 1872
www.horniman.ac.uk
enquiry@horniman.ac.uk

The Horniman has a unique range of exhibitions, events and activities which illustrate the cultural and natural world. Our collections of anthropology, natural history and musical instruments provide the inspiration for our programme of permanent and temporary exhibitions and events and activities.

House Mill

Three Mill Lane
London E3 3DU
0208 980 4626
www.housemill.org.uk

The House Mill was built in 1776 as a timber framed building with a brick facade. It was rebuilt after a fire in 1804. The House Mill is a grade 1 listed 18th century tidal mill set in a beautiful riverside location in the heart of London's East End. It is the largest existing tidal mill in the world.

House of Illustration

2 Granary Square, King's Cross
London N1C 4BH
020 7936 1280
www.houseofillustration.org.uk

The House of Illustration is the place to see past and present illustration, both British and international. It will be the world's first centre dedicated to the art of illustration in all its forms. Our aim is to put illustration centre stage and give it the attention it deserves, revealing the creative processes behind illustration and the way in which it impacts on our daily lives.

Household Cavalry Museum

Horseguards Parade, Whitehall
London SW1A 2AX
020 7414 2392
www.householdcavalrymuseum.co.uk
museum@householdcavalry.co.uk

The Household Cavalry Museum is a living museum about real people doing a real job in a real place. You can see troopers working with horses in the original 18th century stables and hear first hand accounts of their rigorous and demanding training. The experience comes alive with compelling personal stories, interactive displays and stunning rare objects – many on public display for the first time.

Houses of Parliament

London SW1A 0AA
020 7219 4496
www.parliament.uk
hcinfo@parliament.uk

The Palace of Westminster is the home of the UK's Houses of Parliament, including the House of Commons and the House of Lords. Parliament is responsible for making and changing the laws of the United Kingdom and checking the work of the Government. he Parliamentary Archives provides access to the archives of the House of Lords, the House of Commons and to other records relating to Parliament. We also provide a records management service for both Houses of Parliament.

HQS Wellington & the Wellington Trust

HQS Wellington, Temple Stairs, Victoria Embankment,
London WC2R 2PN
020 7836 8179
www.thewellingtontrust.com
info@thewellingtontrust.com

Launched in 1934, the HQS Wellington is the last surviving member of the Royal Navy's Grimsby class of sloops. After 4 years of duty in the South Pacific, the ship served with distinction in the Second World War.

Collections: Historic charts, silver and gold, ship models, paintings and maritime artefacts.

Hunterian Museum at the Royal College of Surgeons

Hunterian Museum at the Royal College of Surgeons of England, 35-43 Lincoln
London WC2A 3PE
020 7869 6560
www.hunterianmuseum.org
museums@rcseng.ac.uk

The Hunterian Museum collections, brought together over four centuries by a cast of colourful characters including John Hunter (1728-1793), are a fascinating mix of comparative anatomy and pathology specimens; complete skeletons, bones, skulls and teeth; dried preparations, corrosion casts and wax teaching models; historical surgical and dental instruments together with modern surgical instruments and technologies; as well as paintings, drawings and sculpture.

Inns of Court & City Yeomanry Museum

10 Stone Buildings, Lincoln's Inn
London WC2A 3TG
020 7405 8112
www.iccy.org.uk/museum.html

A small collection housed in a classical George II building (1760 approx) in Lincoln's Inn recording the most unusual history of the regiment and its predecessor units going back to 1584 when the members, all lawyers, were formed to defend London against the threat of a Spanish invasion. Subsequently members took part in the English Civil War and the defence of the City during the Gordon Riots.

Island History Trust

Dockland Settlement, 197 East Ferry Road
London E14 3BA
020 7987 6041
www.islandhistory.org.uk
eve@islandhistory.org.uk

The Island History Trust is a community history project dedicated to recording and preserving the history of the Isle of Dogs and the people who live there. The Isle of Dogs lies in a loop in the River Thames in the East End of London between Limehouse and Blackwall, opposite Greenwich on the South Bank.

Islington Local History Centre & Museum

245 St John Street, Islington
London EC1V 4NB
020 7527 2837
http://goo.gl/GOPsdx
islington.museum@islington.gov.uk

The New Islington Museum opened its doors in May 2008. Using its collection it explores the boroughs history through a number of exciting ways.

Collections: Islington Museum.

IWM London (part of Imperial War Museums)

Lambeth Road
London SE1 6HZ
020 7416 5000
www.iwm.org.uk
mail@iwm.org.uk

IWM London tells the stories of those whose lives have been shaped by war through the depth, breadth and impact of our Galleries, displays and events. Our new First World War Galleries tell the story of the war – how it started, why it continued and its global impact – through the lives of those who experienced it.

Collections: 20th century collections, include: art, documents, film and video archive, printed books, photograph archive, sound archive, exhibits and firearms.

Jewel Tower - English Heritage

Abingdon Street, Westminster
London SW1P 3JX
020 7222 2219
http://goo.gl/txjqSX

The Jewel Tower dates back over 700 years and is an intriguing visitor attraction in the heart of Westminster. It was built around 1365 to house Edward III's treasures and was known as the 'King's Privy Wardrobe'.

Jewish East End Celebration Society - JEECS

Jewish East End Celebration Society, 85- 87 Bayham Street
London NW1 0AG
www.jeecs.org.uk
enquiries@jeecs.org.uk

Our aim is to increase awareness of the history and culture of London's Jewish East End, to preserve what remains and record what has now gone. Our magazine - The Cable - contains a wealth of articles and photos that will interest all who wish to rediscover the rich history of our immigrant forefathers. We organise walks, talks, film shows and more to celebrate the Jewish story.

Jewish Military Museum

Shield House, Harmony Way, (off Victoria Road), Hendon
London NW4 2BX
020 8202 2323
www.thejmm.org.uk/home
headoffice@ajex.org.uk

Illustrating British Jewry's contribution to the Armed Forces of the Crown from the Crimea to the present day. The museum commemorates the contribution made by British and other Jewish men and women over the last two centuries who have taken part in the various military struggles, though it inevitably focuses on the two world wars. The museum receives memorabilia donated by veterans and their families.

Jewish Museum London

Jewish Museum, Raymond Burton House, 129-131 Albert Street, Camden Town
London NW1 7NB
020 7284 7384
www.jewishmuseum.org.uk
admin@jewishmuseum.org.uk

The Jewish Museum London celebrates Jewish life and cultural diversity. The collections held by The Jewish Museum are unique in the UK for their rich representation of items of Judaica, in particular with an English provenance.

John Wesley's House & the Museum of Methodism

Wesley's Chapel, 49 City Road
London EC1Y 1AU
020 7253 2262
www.wesleyschapel.org.uk
museum@wesleyschapel.org.uk

Step back into 18th century London with a visit to Wesley's House. Discover the day-to-day running of a small Georgian town house.Built by Wesley, the founder of Methodism, in 1779, he lived here the last eleven winters of his life, when not touring to visit and preach to his Methodist societies round the country.

Keats House

Keats Grove, Hampstead
London NW3 2RR
020 7332 3868
www.cityoflondon.gov.uk/keats
keatshouse@cityoflondon.gov.uk

Keats House is where the poet John Keats (1795-1821) lived from 1818 to 1820. Here he wrote some of his best known poetry, including 'Ode to a Nightingale'.

Collections: The Keats House Collection consists of books, manuscripts, letters, prints, paintings and artefacts relating to the life of the poet John Keats (1795-1821), his circle and the English Romantic movement. The Keats House Collection, including the Keats Memorial Library, is currently available for consultation by appointment only.

Kelmscott House

26 Upper Mall, Hammersmith
London W6 9TA
020 8741 3735
http://goo.gl/dG9bsu
info@williammorrissociety.org.uk

Kelmscott House was William Morris's home from 1878-96 and is close to the premises of his Kelmscott Press, founded in 1890.

Kempton Park Pumping Station & Steam Museum

Kempton Park Waterworks, Snakey Lane
Hanworth, Middlesex TW13 6XH
01932 765328
www.kemptonsteam.org
info@kemptonsteam.org

Home of the world's largest operating triple expansion steam engine.

Kensington & Chelsea Local Studies

Kensington Central Library, Phillimore Walk
London W8 7RX
020 7361 3010
http://goo.gl/cVKHB

The Kensington and Chelsea Local Studies collection is housed at Kensington Central Library. It contains all the borough's material on the history of both Kensington and Chelsea, including books, newspapers, illustrations (these include prints, photographs, paintings and drawings: we also hold a large collection of maps including Ordnance Survey, parish and general maps of London), census returns, electoral registers, manuscripts, ephemera and other archive material.

Kensington Palace

Kensington Gardens
London W8 4PX
0844 482 7777
www.hrp.org.uk
kensingtonpalace@hrp.org.uk

Kensington Palace is not a traditional heritage experience - our approach is tradition with a twist, and we apply this to the four routes that your ticket includes: Victoria Revealed - an exhibition exploring the life and reign of one of the palace's most famous residents Queen Victoria, in her own words; the King's State Apartments which tell the grand stories of the Hanoverian court; the Queen's State Apartments which has a more modern and theatrical display to tell the story of William and Mary through to George I; and Fashion Rules: Dresses from the collections of HM The Queen, Princess Margaret and Diana, Princess of Wales.

Kenwood House - English Heritage

London NW3 7JR
020 8348 1286
http://goo.gl/uFQ4pR

Set in splendid grounds beside Hampstead Heath, this outstanding neoclassical house holds one of the most important collections of paintings ever given to the nation. Works by Rembrandt, Vermeer, Turner, Reynolds and Gainsborough all hang against a backdrop of sumptuous rooms.

Kew Palace & Queen Charlotte's Cottage

Royal Botanic Gardens Kew
Richmond TW9 3AB
0870 751 5179
www.hrp.org.uk
tim.powell@hrp.org.uk

Step into this tiny doll's house of a palace and sense the joys and sorrows of past royal lives in intimate detail, as King George III and his family come to life.

Kingston Local History Room

Room 46, North Kingston Centre, Richmond Road
Kingston upon Thames KT2 5PE
020 8547 6738
http://goo.gl/KLYPxQ

The Kingston Museum and Heritage Service manages the museum, the Local History Room and our archives.

Kingston Museum & Heritage Service

Kingston Museum, Wheatfield Way
Kingston upon Thames KT1 2PS
020 8547 6460
www.kingston.gov.uk/museums
kingston.museum@rbk.kingston.gov.uk

Kingston Museum was built in 1904. The museum has three permanent galleries: Ancient Origins, Town of Kings (telling the story of the Borough from Saxon times) and Eadweard Muybridge. There is also an art gallery for special exhibitions.

Kirkaldy Testing Museum, The

99 Southwark Street
London SE1 0JF
020 7828 0401
www.testingmuseum.org.uk
info@testingmuseum.org.uk

A museum which preserves a unique Victorian Materials Testing Machine in working order in the premises built to house it. It tells the story of the Kirkaldy family who ran the business for almost 100 years and the wider history of materials testing. The museum occupies the ground floor and basement of 99 Southwark Streeet.

Lambeth Archives

Minet Library, 52 Knatchbull Road
London SE5 9QY
020 7926 6076
www.lambeth.gov.uk/places/lambeth-archives
archives@lambeth.gov.uk

Lambeth Archives is the borough's record office and local history library and is open to the public, free of charge. Whether you want to trace a house history, discover the origins of your neighbourhood, trace your family history, or look at the records of Lambeth Council staff will guide and assist you through our collections of historical material.

Lambeth Palace Library

Lambeth Palace Road
London SE1 7JU
020 7898 1400
www.lambethpalacelibrary.org
archives@churchofengland.org

Lambeth Palace Library is the historic library of the
Archbishops of Canterbury and the principal library and
record office for the history of the Church of England. The
Library focuses on ecclesiastical history, but its rich
collections are important for an immense variety of topics
from the history of art and architecture to colonial and
Commonwealth history, and for innumerable aspects of
English social, political and economic history.

Lea Valley Experience Museum Project, The

10 South Access Road, Walthamstow
London E17 8AX
0208 531 2897
www.leavalleyexperience.co.uk
lindsey.collier1@ntlworld.com

TThe concept of the museum is based around the
industrial transport achievements of the Lea Valley
Corridor since the 1800s, and the coming of the railways to
the valley. We currently have a collection of many types of
artefacts both large and small.

Leighton House Museum

12 Holland Park Road
London W14 8LZ
020 7602 3316
www.rbkc.gov.uk/subsites/museums.aspx
museums@rbkc.gov.uk

Leighton House Museum is the former studio-house of the
great Victorian artist Frederic, Lord Leighton (1830-1896).
Located on the edge of London's Holland Park, the house is
one of the most extraordinary buildings of the 19th
century.

Lesbian & Gay Newsmedia Archive

LAGNA, Bishopsgate Library, Bishopsgate Institute, 230
Bishopsgate
London EC2M 4QH
020 7392 9270
www.lagna.org.uk
enquiries@lagna.org.uk

LAGNA consists primarily of a collection of 200,000 press
cuttings covering all aspects of lesbian and gay life from the
1930s to the present. The Lesbian and Gay Newsmedia
Archive is open to anyone with an interest in lesbian, gay,
bisexual or transgender history.

Lewisham Heritage

199-201 Lewisham High Street
London SE13 6LG
020 8314 8501
http://goo.gl/IVwcMC
local.studies@lewisham.gov.uk

Lewisham Heritage is responsible for the archives, local
history, museum and art collections of the London
Borough of Lewisham. The Local History and Archives
Centre holds historic materials for the borough of
Lewisham and is situated in Lewisham Library.

Liberal Democrat History Group

54 Midmoor Road
London SW12 0EN
020 8673 8101
www.liberalhistory.org.uk
journal@liberalhistory.org.uk

The Liberal Democrat History Group promotes the
discussion and research of topics relating to the histories of
the British Liberal Democrats and its predecessor parties,
the Liberal Party and the SDP, and of liberalism more
broadly.

Library & Museum of Freemasonry, The

Freemasons' Hall, Great Queen Street
London WC2B 5AZ
020 7395 9257
www.freemasonry.london.museum
libmus@freemasonry.london.museum

One of the finest publicly available collections of Masonic
material in the world. The collections illustrate the
international, social and ethnic diversity of the
membership including royalty, public figures, scientists and
writers as well as the many millions of members from all
walks of life. The museum contains an extensive collection
of objects with Masonic decoration including pottery and
porcelain, glassware, silver, furniture and clocks, jewels and
regalia.

Lindley Library - Royal Horticultural Society, The

80 Vincent Square
London SW1P 2PE
020 7821 3050
http://goo.gl/xuKa4l
library.london@rhs.org.uk

The RHS Lindley Libraries are the largest visual and written
resource on horticulture in the world. Collections,
including books, art, photographs, and archives span 500
years of Britain's gardening history.

Little Holland House

40 Beeches Avenue
Carshalton SM5 3LW
020 8770 4781
www.sutton.gov.uk
valary.murphy@sutton.gov.uk

The former home of artist, designer and craftsman Frank Dickinson (1874-1961). Designed and built by Dickinson between 1902-04, the Grade II* listed interior was created entirely by him, inspired by the ideals of Ruskin, Carlyle & Morris, in an eclectic mix of Arts and Crafts, Art Nouveau and Glasgow School style.

Local Studies, Richmond upon Thames

Old Town Hall, Whittaker Avenue
Richmond TW9 1TP
020 8734 3309
www.richmond.gov.uk/local_studies_collection
localstudies@richmond.gov.uk

Archive for London Borough of Richmond upon Thames.

London Canal Museum

12-13 New Wharf Road, King's Cross
London N1 9RT
020 7713 0836
www.canalmuseum.org.uk
info@canalmuseum.org.uk

London Canal Museum tells the story of London's canals, their people, cargoes, and the horses which pulled their boats.

Collections: Centrepiece is the narrowboat Coronis with a reconstructed cabin into which visitors can step, listening to the sound of a family having their meal and discussing their lives. Our collection includes 'roses and castles' canal art and other decorative art, lifting, handling and weighing equipment for cargo, horse care equipment, and the working Bantam IV tug which is moored outside.

London Film Museum

1st Floor, Riverside Building, County Hall
London SE1 7PB
020 7202 7040
www.londonfilmmuseum.com
info@londonfilmmuseum.com

Here at the London Film Museum we celebrate all aspects of the British Film Industry. Since we started in 2008 we have been collecting and displaying items both historical and contemporary from major films.

London Fire Brigade Museum

Winchester House, 94a Southwark Bridge Rd
London SE1 0EG
020 7587 2894
http://goo.gl/gAfpxO
museum@london-fire.gov.uk

Visit our museum in Southwark and see how firefighting has developed over the last 340 years. It holds a wealth of information and exhibits depicting the history of firefighting in London from the Great Fire of London in 1666 to the present day.

London Metropolitan Archives

40 Northampton Road
London EC1R 0HB
020 7332 3820
www.cityoflondon.gov.uk/lma
ask.lma@cityoflondon.gov.uk

LMA holds archives about the administrative, social and family history of London. Over 105km of shelving store records of schools, churches, hospitals, businesses, local government and much more.

London Motor Museum

3 Nestles Avenue, Hayes, Middlesex
London UB3 4SB
07894 495817
www.londonmotormuseum.co.uk
info@londonmotormuseum.co.uk

The London Motor Museum is the only custom car museum in Europe and home to a unique collection of privately owned American and European classic cars of the automobile era ranging from the 50s, 60s, 70s and 80s. The London Motor Museum has a fantastic collection of over 100 classic and custom cars, including hot rods, film cars like the Batmobile, Delorean (Back To The Future), a signed Ford Torino (Starsky and Hutch) and a range of beautiful cars from the 1930s to the present day, creating a unique blend of classic and custom cars which are unique and breathtakingly stunning.

London Motorcycle Museum

Ravenor Farm, Oldfield Lane South
Greenford, Middlesex UB6 9LB
0208 575 6644
www.london-motorcycle-museum.org
thelmm@hotmail.com

The LMM - London's only motorcycle museum - is the capital's friendly focus for Britain's biking history and heritage. We have some 80 machines and other exhibits on permanent display.

London Museum of Water & Steam

Green Dragon Lane
London TW8 0EN
020 8568 4757
www.kbsm.org

Housed in a Grade I listed water pumping station built in the 19th century to supply Londoners with water, the museum is recognised as the most important historic site of the water industry in Britain. The museum's architecture ranges from late Georgian to Italianate with a thriving community of artists housed in the site's external workshop buildings. There is also an excellent 'Water for Life' gallery which describes the provision of water to London from Roman times to the present day.

London Pearly Kings & Queens Society

London
www.pearlysociety.co.uk
lpkqs@yahoo.co.uk

The London tradition of the Pearly Kings and Queens began in 1875, by a small lad named Henry Croft. The Pearly tradition has survived for over 125 years and hopefully it will continue for many more to come. We still have a few families who can be traced back to the original generation of Pearlies.

London Sewing Machine Museum, The

308 Balham High Road
London SW17 7AA
020 8682 7916
www.sewantique.com
wimbledonsewingmachinecoltd@btinternet.com

Approximately 600 sewing machines on display including Queen Victoria's and Charlie Chaplin's sewing machines.

London South Bank University Archives Centre

London South Bank University, 103 Borough Road
London SE1 0AA
www.lsbu.ac.uk/archives
archives@lsbu.ac.uk

An archive service holding the corporate and historic records of London South Bank University and its predecessor bodies. The University Archives Centre collects and makes accessible the institutional archives of London South Bank University (LSBU) and its amalgamated institutions.

Collections: We hold material tracing LSBU's history from its foundation as the Borough Polytechnic Institute in 1892 to the present day.

London Transport Museum

Covent Garden Piazza
London WC2E 7BB
020 7565 7299
www.ltmuseum.co.uk
bookings@ltmuseum.co.uk

Lively new galleries tell the story of London's transport system and how it shaped the lives of people living and working in London. The Design for Travel gallery showcases original artworks and advertising posters.

London, Westminster & Middlesex Family History Society

57 Belvedere Way, Kenton
Harrow HA3 9XQ
020 8204 5470
www.lwmfhs.org.uk
william.pyemont@virgin.net

The society's area now comprises the City of London, the City of Westminster and the London Boroughs of Barnet, Brent, Camden, Enfield, Haringey, Harrow and Islington, together with parts of Ealing and Hillingdon. We aim to bring together all those family historians with ancestors in the area or who live in the area.

Magic Circle Museum at the Centre for the Magic Arts

Centre for the Magic Arts, 12 Stephenson Way
London NW1 2HD
0845 006 2500
www.magiccirclevenue.co.uk/venue/TheMuseum.htm
mail@magiccirclevenue.co.uk

Priceless treasures that bring the history of mystery vividly to life. Accompanied by expert guides, you'll see the actual handcuffs used by Harry Houdini and the props used by HRH Prince Charles when he took his examination to become a member of The Inner Magic Circle. Learn how the great illusionist, Chung Ling Soo was shot dead during a performance an 1918. Discover how the British army used a famous magician to make the Suez Canal invisible to enemy bombers in 1941 and, if you look very closely, you might even see how a rabbit appears in a top hat.

Magna Carta Trust

c/o Govnet Communications 22 Long Acre
London WC2E 9LY
http://goo.gl/fSjd4d

Magna Carta Trust's 800th Commemoration Committee.

Marble Hill House - English Heritage

Twickenham, Middlesex TW1 2NL
020 8892 5115
http://goo.gl/HdbwHf

A magnificent Palladian villa set within lush riverside grounds. Visitors to Marble Hill House can catch a glimpse of the lavish entertaining that took place here, in these extravagantly gilded rooms, when it served as the Thames-side retreat for Henrietta Howard, mistress of King George II.

Maritime Archaeology Sea Trust

9 Avondale Park Gardens
London W11 4PR
www.thisismast.org

Mast is a charitable company whose aim is to investigate our maritime past through archaeology, research, study and dissemination.

Markfield Beam Engine & Museum

Markfield Road, South Tottenham
London N15 4RB
01707 873628
www.mbeam.org
info@mbeam.org

The Markfield Beam Engine and Museum is located in a Victorian Engine House which has in situ the original Beam Pumping Engine and was part of the original Tottenham Sewage Works. The site has recently been landscaped, the engine renovated and the engine restored to steam operation.

Marylebone Cricket Club Museum

Marylebone Cricket Club, Lord's Cricket Ground
London NW8 8QN
020 72891611
http://goo.gl/hSid05
communications@mcc.org.uk

The oldest sports museum in the world, the MCC is housed by the most famous cricket ground in the world, Lord's.

Collections: From the original Ashes urn, kit used by the greatest players in the history of the sport to a changing gallery of cricket portraits.

Metropolitan Police Historical Collection

Empress State Building Lillie Road
Fulham SW6 1TR
020 7161 1234
www.met.police.uk/history

The Collection has a display of historical artefacts relating to the history of the Metropolitan Police. This includes old records, uniforms, truncheons, and equipment.

Monument, The

Monument Street
London EC3R 8AH
0207 626 2717
www.themonument.info
enquiries@towerbridge.org.uk

The Monument stands at the junction of Monument Street and Fish Street Hill in the City of London. It was built between 1671 and 1677 to commemorate the Great Fire of London (1666) and to celebrate the rebuilding of the City.

Museum No 1, Royal Botanic Gardens, Kew

Richmond TW9 3AB
020 8332 5655
www.kew.org
info@kew.org

Located within Kew Gardens, Museum No 1 houses the Plants+People exhibition. This shows the many fascinating ways in which we depend on plants, including products from the Amazon to Australia; the artistry of Japanese papers and lacquerware; plant-based medicines like quinine and vincristine that helped revolutionise human healthcare; and examples of the raw materials that make our music and feed, clothe and invigorate us.

Museum of Asian Music

Bradford Road
London W3 7SP
020 8742 9911
www.amc.org.uk/museum
info@amc.org.uk

The museum of Asian Music is an innovative learning resource with a busy calendar of recitals, events and exhibitions. Opened by the Prince of Wales in 2008, the museum offers an interactive way to discover the diversity of Asian music in a hands-on environment.

Museum of Brands, Packaging & Advertising

111-117 Lancaster Road, Notting Hill
London W11 1QT
020 7908 0880
www.museumofbrands.com
info@museumofbrands.com

200 years of consumer culture, reflected through packaging design, brand development, poster and TV advertising from the collection of Robert Opie. Over 12,000 items including toys, magazines, branded goods, social ephemera, postcards and fashions.

Museum of Croydon

Croydon Clocktower, Katharine Street
Croydon CR9 1ET
020 8253 1022
www.museumofcroydon.com
museum@croydon.gov.uk

The museum of Croydon is built on the fascinating objects and stories of the people who have lived, loved and worked in Croydon. The displays cover the history of Croydon from 1800 to the present day, with changing exhibitions in our Croydon NOW area and temporary exhibition gallery.

Museum of Domestic Design & Architecture - MoDA

Middlesex University, 9 Boulevard Drive, Beaufort Park
Colindale NW9 5HF
020 8411 5244
www.moda.mdx.ac.uk
moda@mdx.ac.uk

The museum of Domestic Design & Architecture's (MoDA) collections are available online, on tour and on request. The collections include wallpapers, textiles, designs, books, catalogues and magazines from the late 19th to the late 20th century.

Collections: The Silver Studio collection at MoDA is a Designated Collection of national importance. This is the archive of one of Britain's leading commercial design studios active between 1880 and 1963, and comprises over 40,000 designs on paper, samples, pattern books and an archive of the Studio's letters, diaries, visual reference material, trade cards and other printed ephemera.

Museum of Immigration & Diversity, The

19 Princelet Street
London E1 6QH
020 7247 5352
www.19princeletstreet.org.uk
information@19princeletstreet.org.uk

The exhibition 'suitcases and Sanctuary', made largely by local schoolchildren, is a genuinely innovative celebration of immigration housed in a magical Grade II* listed building that combines a remarkable unrestored 1719 Huguenot master silk weaver's house with a rare Victorian synagogue illuminated by a pastel coloured stained glass ceiling. The complementary exhibition 'Leave to Remain' by 3 refugee artists takes a wry look at asylum in today's Britain.

Museum of London

London Wall
London EC2Y 5HN
020 7001 9844
www.museumoflondon.org.uk
info@museumoflondon.org.uk

The Museum of London charts the history of the capital and its people from the prehistoric period to the present day. Its galleries and exhibitions make sensitive use of both traditional and modern interactive techniques, and the museum has long been committed to educational and outreach services.

Museum of London Docklands

No. 1 Warehouse, West India Quay, Hertsmere Road
London E14 4AL
020 7001 9844
www.museumoflondon.org.uk/docklands
info@museumoflondon.org.uk

From Roman settlement to the development of Canary Wharf, this 200 year old warehouse reveals the long history of the capital as a port through stories of trade, migration and commerce.

Collections: The collection consists of objects reflecting the social history of the Thames and London's port, including archaeological finds, works of art, scale models, contemporary tools and many miscellaneous items that would have been traded through the port. Collections also include the Sainsbury Archive, a collection of documents, artefacts and photographs relating to the history of the food retailing company founded by John James and Mary Ann Sainsbury in 1869.

Museum of Richmond

Old Town Hall, Whittaker Avenue
Richmond TW9 1TP
020 8332 1141
www.museumofrichmond.com
museumofrichmond@btconnect.com

The museum of Richmond celebrates the rich and diverse social heritage of the borough of Richmond which has been a centre of fashion, the arts and the intellect for centuries. The intimate display spans from the prehistoric times to the present day.

Museum of Soho (mosoho)

St Anne's Tower, 55 Dean Street
London W1D 6AF
www.mosoho.org.uk
info@themuseumofsoho.org.uk

The museum was started c1990 by a group of amateurs, keen to preserve any material relating to the history of

Soho. Initially, it was hoped that a traditional museum could be established, but we have gradually come round to the idea that a 'virtual' museum would actually be more feasible. We now have a large interactive touch-screen situated in Sherwood St where you can access illustrations, galleries and articles about Soho from the street.

Museum of the Order of St John

St John's Gate, St John's Lane
London EC1M 4DA
020 7324 4005
www.museumstjohn.org.uk
museum@nhq.sja.org.uk

The Museum of the Order of St John tells a unique and fascinating story — the story of the Order of St John — from its origins in 11th century Jerusalem, through to its role today with St John Ambulance and the St John Eye Hospital in Jerusalem.

Museum of the Royal Pharmaceutical Society

1 Lambeth High Street
London SE1 7JN
020 7572 2210
www.rpharms.com/about-pharmacy/our-museum.asp
museum@rpsgb.org

The museum of the Royal Pharmaceutical Society was founded in 1842, as a scientific collection of materia medica for use by pharmacy students in the society's school of pharmacy. It only began to collect historical material in the 1930s.

Collections: The 45,000 objects in the Royal Pharmaceutical Society's collections cover all aspects of British pharmacy history, from traditional dispensing equipment to 'Lambeth delftware' drug storage jars, and from proprietary (brandname) medicines to medical caricatures.

Musical Museum, The

The Musical Museum, 399 High Street
Brentford TW8 0DU
020 8560 8108
www.musicalmuseum.co.uk
Fred.stone@musicalmuseum.co.uk

The Musical Museum contains one of the world's foremost collections of self-playing musical instruments. From the tiniest of clockwork music boxes to the 'Mighty Wurlitzer' the collection embraces an impressive and comphrehensive array of sophisticated reproducing pianos, orchestrions, orchestrelles, residence organs and violin players.

Myddelton House Gardens

Bulls Cross
Enfield, Middlesex EN2 9HG
http://goo.gl/S1XYL3
info@leevalleypark.org.uk

Created by E.A. Bowles (1865-1954), Myddelton House Gardens have been refurbished and offer an impressive range of flora, fauna and historical artefacts.

Natural History Museum

Cromwell Road
London SW7 5BD
020 7942 5000
www.nhm.ac.uk
information@nhm.ac.uk

Dinosaurs, volcanoes, precious gems, creepy crawlies - as a visitor to The Natural History Museum you will be amazed by the diversity of our natural world. The Natural History Museum is home to the nation's finest collections of natural history specimens and is one of the UK's top visitor attractions. The museum's collection now runs to 70 million plants, animals, fungi, bacteria, fossils, rocks and minerals - many of which are displayed through its fascinating exhibitions and more than you could ever see in one day.

Newham Archives & Local Studies Library

Stratford Library, Stratford
London E15 1EL
020 3373 6881
www.newhamstory.com

London Borough of Newham's Heritage & Archives service's aims are to preserve, promote and interpret the rich diversity of the heritage of Newham, and make it accessible to all.

Old Operating Theatre Museum

9A St Thomas' Street
London SE1 9RY
020 7188 2679
www.thegarret.org.uk
curator@thegarret.org.uk

Hidden in the roof of a church, a 300-year old herb garret houses Britain's only surviving 19th century operating theatre. This museum, one of London's most intriguing historical interiors, contains the Operating Theatre, in use between 1821 and 1862 in the days before anaesthetic and antiseptic surgery.

Collections: The museum has a diverse collection of medical, surgical and herbal objects, including amputation sets, bloodletting instruments, pharmaceutical jars, and nursing and obstetric instruments and items.

Old Royal Naval College

King William Walk
Greenwich SE10 9NN
020 8269 4799
www.ornc.org
boxoffice@ornc.org

Welcome to the Old Royal Naval College (ORNC), Sir Christopher Wren's twin-domed riverside masterpiece and one of London's most famous landmarks. The ORNC is open daily and is a breathtaking place to visit – whether you have an hour or a day. The iconic buildings stand on the site of Greenwich Palace, Henry VIII's favourite royal residence and include the Discover Greenwich Visitor Centre, Painted Hall and Chapel.

Old Speech Room Gallery, Harrow School

Church Hill, Harrow on the Hill
London HA1 3HP
020 8872 8205
www.harrowschool.org.uk/default.aspx?id=97
crl@harrowschool.org.uk

The Old Speech Room was built in 1819-21 as a chamber in which to encourage public speaking. It was converted into a gallery by Alan Irvine in 1976 as a repository for the School's varied and distinguished collection of antiquities and fine art.

Collections: The collections comprise Egyptian and Greek antiquities, English watercolours, Modern British paintings, some sculpture, printed books and natural history. There is also a set of Stuart Devlin's parcel gilt Easter eggs, designed in the tradition of Fabergé.

On the Record

123a Paulet Road
London SE5 9HW
07583 656 338
on-the-record.org.uk
info@on-the-record.org.uk

We are a small, not for profit cooperative Community Interest Company. We work to uncover untold stories, using oral history, digital storytelling and heritage projects.

Orleans House Gallery

Riverside
Twickenham, Middlesex TW1 3DJ
020 8831 6000
http://goo.gl/9aIZMl
artsinfo@richmond.gov.uk

Orleans House has a rich and vibrant history, from the baroque Octagon room, which was designed by renowned architect James Gibbs, to a main gallery which hosts five temporary exhibitions each year - ranging from the historical to the contemporary.

Collections: Orleans House Gallery looks after the prestigious Richmond Borough Art Collection. The collection of over 2,700 paintings, watercolours, drawings, prints, photographs and objects primarily comprises local topographical views of the Twickenham and Richmond riverside, dating from the late 18th century to the present day.

Osterley Park & House - National Trust

Jersey Road, Isleworth
Osterley, Middlesex TW7 4RB
020 8232 5050
www.nationaltrust.org.uk/osterley-park
osterley@nationaltrust.org.uk

Surrounded by gardens, park and farmland, Osterley is one of the last surviving country estates in London. Once described by Horace Walpole as 'the palace of palaces', Osterley was created in the late 18th century by architect and designer Robert Adam for the Child family to entertain and impress their friends and clients. Today the house is presented as it would have looked in the 1780s; enter the house as the family's guests would have via the impressive stone steps leading up to the portico. Stroll through the colourful formal gardens, transformed during our six year long project from an overgrown wilderness back to their 18th century grandeur of herbaceous borders, roses and ornamental vegetables beds.

Our Democratic Heritage

B142 Paul Robeson House 1 Penton Rise
Greater London WC1X 9EH
07712 833909
www.odh.org.uk
democraticheritage@gmail.com

Our charity aims to strengthen the popular celebration of democratic heritage in the British cultural mainstream. While the history of the monarchy is a highly visible part of our cultural memory, democratic history is significantly less so, and ODH believes that it is important to recognize those who did so much to create the freedoms we enjoy today.

Parliamentary Archives

Houses of Parliament
London SW1A 0PW
0207 219 3074
www.parliament.uk/archives
archives@parliament.uk

Parliamentary records are at the heart of our democracy. They have embodied our liberties, rights and responsibilities for over five hundred years.

Collections: The Parliamentary Archives holds several million historical records relating to Parliament, dating from 1497 to present day. These include: Records of the House of Commons and House of Lords, including Acts of Parliament, Journals, Committee papers, papers laid before both Houses, and plans of roads, railways, canals and other public works desposited in relation to private bills; other collections relating to Parliament; private political papers, including those of David Lloyd George, Andrew Bonar Law and Lord Beaverbrook; records about the Palace of Westminster.

Petrie Museum of Egyptian Archaeology

University College London, Malet Place
London WC1E 6BT
020 7679 2884
www.petrie.ucl.ac.uk
petrie.museum@ucl.ac.uk

The Petrie Museum houses an estimated 80,000 objects, making it one of the greatest collections of Egyptian and Sudanese archaeology in the world. It illustrates life in the Nile Valley from prehistory through the time of the pharaohs, the Ptolemaic, Roman and Coptic periods to the Islamic period. It is largely based on the artefact collections gathered by the pioneering archaeologist Sir Flinders Petrie on his many excavations, and includes his own detailed documentation.

Pollock's Toy Museum

1 Scala Street
London W1P 1LT
020 7636 3452
www.pollocksmuseum.co.uk
info@pollockstoymuseum.com

Pollock's Toy Museum occupies two houses joined together in the heart of Fitzrovia, one 18th century, one 19th; the rooms are small and connected by narrow winding staircases. The whole place exudes atmosphere and evocations of those special times of childhood.

Poverest Road Bath House & Anglo-Saxon Cemetery

Poverest Road
Orpington BR5 2DH
01689 873826
bromley.museum@bromley.gov.uk

The bath-house is situated in Poverest Road, Orpington and was excavated between 1971 and 1975. It consists of three rooms, the walls of which stand up to 600mm high. Used from about AD270 to AD400 it probably served a small settlement or farm complex that extended southwards towards Fordcroft Road.

Priory Church of St Bartholomew the Great

West Smithfield
London EC1A 9DS
020 7606 5171

www.greatstbarts.com
admin@greatstbarts.com

The ancient Priory Church of St Bartholomew the Great was founded by a courtier of Henry I (son of William the Conqueror). It is a stunning example of Norman architecture which has survived the numerous transformations and upheavals London has undergone over the past 900 years, including the Great Fire and the air raids of two world wars.

Queen Elizabeth's Hunting Lodge

Rangers Road, Chingford
London E4 7QH
020 8529 6681
http://goo.gl/9Kzig1
epping.forest@cityoflondon.gov.uk

Queen Elizabeth's Hunting Lodge is a unique timber-framed Tudor hunt standing built by Henry VIII in 1543. It has magnificent views of Epping Forest from its upper floors and permanent displays in its Tudor kitchen.

Queen Square Library, Archive & Museum

UCL Institute of Neurology, 1st floor, 23 Queen Square
London WC1N 3BG
020 3448 4709
www.queensquare.org.uk/archives
neuroarchives@ucl.ac.uk

The Queen Square Archive and Museum collections are housed in and managed by the Queen Square Library. They comprise the archives belonging to the National Hospital for Neurology and Neurosurgery (NHNN) and those of UCL Institute of Neurology (IoN).

Ragged School Museum

46-50 Copperfield Road
London E3 4RR
020 8980 6405
www.raggedschoolmuseum.org.uk
chris@raggedschoolmuseum.org.uk

The award-winning Museum is housed in three Victorian canalside warehouses, converted by Dr Barnardo into a ragged school. Visitors to the museum today can take a journey through the history of the region as well as experience what it was like to be taught over one hundred years ago by 'stepping back in time' to the atmospheric recreated Victorian classroom.

Reminiscence Centre, The

11 Blackheath Village, Blackheath
London SE3 9LA
020 8318 9105
www.age-exchange.org.uk/htm/reminiscence.htm

administrator@age-exchange.org.uk

The Reminiscence Centre in Blackheath, south-east London, is our base. Opened in 1987, the centre is visited by over 30,000 visitors each year.

Collections: On the other side of our brass handled door, visitors find a 1930s shop full of authentic articles which can be handled freely and which are highly effective memory triggers. We also display many fascinating objects and documents from the first half of the 20th century, including hats and dresses, a wind-up gramophone and large collection of records, a Victorian kitchen range and wartime memorabilia, such as gas masks and ration books.

RIBA Library Photographs Collection

66 Portland Place
London W1B 1AD
020 7307 3684
www.ribapix.com
photo@inst.riba.org

The Royal Institute of British Architects is the UK body for architecture and the architectural profession, supporting 40,500 members worldwide through training, publications and events, and setting standards for architectural education in the UK and overseas. The RIBA Trust manages the RIBA's cultural assets and activities including a collection of over four million items in the British Architectural Library and an extensive programme of awards, talks, exhibitions and education events.

Richmond Local Studies Collection

Local Studies, Old Town Hall, Whittaker Ave
Richmond TW9 1TP
020 8734 3309
www.richmond.gov.uk/local_studies_collection

The Local Studies Collection is based at the Old Town Hall, Richmond and provides access to material relating to the history of the London Borough of Richmond upon Thames. It contains the collections previously held by the former boroughs of Barnes, Richmond and Twickenham.

Rose Theatre

56 Park Street
London SE1 9AR
020 7902 1500
www.rosetheatre.org.uk
info@rosetheatre.org.uk

Built in 1587 by Philip Henslowe, the Rose was the first theatre on London's Bankside. In 1989 its remains were discovered and partially excavated amidst a blaze of international press coverage.

Royal Academy of Music Museum

Royal Academy of Music, Marylebone Road
London NW1 5HT
020 7873 7373
www.ram.ac.uk/museum
museumandcollections@ram.ac.uk

The museum displays material from the Academy's world renowned collection of instruments, manuscripts, objects and images. An integral part of Academy life, the museum regularly hosts exhibitions and events including daily live demonstrations on our historic pianos. We welcome all members of the public, students and families. The Royal Academy of Music is Britain's senior conservatoire, founded in 1822.

Collections: The collections contain early printed and manuscript music and books dating from the 16th century to the present day.

Royal Air Force Museum

Grahame Park Way, Colindale
London NW9 5LL
020 8205 2266
www.rafmuseum.org/london
groups@rafmuseum.org

Wing your way over to a wonderful collection of aircraft, interactives, medals, uniforms, film shows and memorabilia on display and trace the story of the RAF and aviation itself. Visit the awe-inspiring sound and light show that takes you back in time to the Battle of Britain.

Royal Armouries at HM Tower of London

HM Tower of London
London EC3N 4AB
020 7488 5658
www.armouries.org.uk

The Royal Armouries is located in the White Tower, the central keep of the Tower of London, which is its historical home. The Armouries is one of the ancient institutions of the Tower of London. Its origins may be traced back to the working armoury of the medieval kings of England. The first recorded paying visitor to the Armouries was in 1545 when a visiting foreign dignitary viewed the personal armoury of Henry VIII in the White Tower. The Restoration of Charles II in 1660 saw the establishment of two permanent public displays: the Line of Kings and the Spanish Armoury. All these displays can still be seen in the White Tower, along with more modern weapons and armours.

Royal Botanic Gardens, Kew

🏛 🎫 £

Kew Gardens
Richmond TW9 3AB
020 8332 5655
www.kew.org
info@kew.org

Explore glasshouses, landscapes and 250 years of history at the world's most famous garden. Climb to the treetops on the Xstrata Treetop Walkway, delve into rainforest inside the iconic Palm House or discover more on a guided tour.

Royal College of Music Museum of Instruments

📷 £

Prince Consort Road
London SW7 2BS
020 7591 4346
www.rcm.ac.uk/visit/museum
museum@rcm.ac.uk

The RCM Museum is full of musical treasures dating from the 15th century onwards. On display you will find highlights from the collection of over 1,000 instruments including the anonymous clavicytherium, believed to be the earliest surviving stringed keyboard instrument, remarkable and unfamiliar instruments such as the contrabassophon, division viol and serpent, plus trombones owned and played by Elgar and Holst. Alongside these are some of the most significant portraits from the RCM collection, including oil paintings of Haydn, Boyce and Farinelli, as well as manuscripts, early printed edition, photographs, letters and many other objects from the Library and Special Collections.

Royal College of Nursing Library & Heritage Centre

📷 🎫 ⚌ ★

20 Cavendish Square
London W1G 0RN
0345 337 3368
http://goo.gl/Fydc3K
rcn.library@rcn.org.uk

The Royal College of Nursing Library and Heritage Centre is home to Europe's largest nursing specific collection of materials. In 2013 we opened an exciting new space which includes publicly accessible exhibitions, a cafe and a shop within the Library space. Also publicly accessible is a new space celebrating our Nursing History Collection – enabling visitors to browse nursing history texts, access some of our historic printed collection and to browse smaller exhibitions curated with the RCN History of Nursing Society.

Collections: The Collection dates mainly from the 1850s onwards, though some earlier items are held. It comprehensively collects English language materials, focusing on nursing in the UK: .

Royal College of Obstetricians & Gynaecologists

🎫 ⚌ ★

27 Sussex Place, Regent's Park
London NW1 4RG
020 7772 6385
https://goo.gl/F7lpDc
museum@rcog.org.uk

The College museum comprises a unique collection of obstetric, midwifery, surgical and gynaecological instruments and artefacts spanning over four hundred years. This collection has been built up from a series of gifts and acquisitions since the foundation of the College. 500 Years: The Birth of Modern Obstetrics and Gynaecology is a semi-permanent exhibition of objects, together with items from the library and archive collections, which has been mounted in the Education Centre of the College.

Royal College of Physicians

🏛 📷 🎫 ★

11 St Andrews Place, Regent's Park
London NW1 4LE
0203 075 1543
www.rcplondon.ac.uk/museum-and-garden
history@rcplondon.ac.uk

The Royal College of Physicians is the oldest medical college in England. Since our foundation by royal charter of Henry VIII in 1518, the RCP has built up magnificent collections of books, manuscripts, portraits, silver, and medical artefacts. Visit us to experience extraordinary historical and ceremonial spaces set inside a radically modern building created by Sir Denys Lasdun in 1964.

Royal College of Veterinary Surgeons Trust

🎫 ⚌

The RCVS Trust, Belgravia House, 62-64 Horseferry Road
London SW1P 2AF
020 7202 0741
www.rcvstrust.org.uk
trust@rcvs.org.uk

The Trust's principal aims are to provide and maintain a library, to encourage education and training in veterinary medicine at all professional levels, and to promote veterinary research.

Royal Greenwich Heritage Trust

⚌ ★

Artillery Square, Royal Arsenal Woolwich
Greenwich
020 8854 2452
www.greenwichheritage.org/site
info@greenwichheritage.org

At Greenwich Heritage Centre you can find out about the fascinating history of Royal Borough of Greenwich, from earliest times to the present day. Whether you are researching your family history or want to know more about an area, our friendly, welcoming and knowledgeable staff can help you make the most of your visit. With Charlton House, Greenwich Heritage Centre is part of Royal Greenwich Heritage Trust.

Royal Hospital Chelsea

Royal Hospital Road
London SW3 4SR
020 7881 5246
www.chelsea-pensioners.co.uk
info@chelsea-pensioners.org.uk

The Royal Hospital Chelsea was founded in 1682 by King Charles 11 as a home for old or wounded soldiers. The King was inspired by Louis XIV's 'Hotel des Invalides' in Paris and wanted to create an equally splendid home for his veteran soldiers.

Collections: Pictures, documents and artefacts relating to the history of The Royal Hospital. Medals and other items left by In-Pensioners.

Royal Institution, The

The Royal Institution of Great Britain, 21 Albemarle Street, Mayfair
London W1S 4BS
020 7409 2992
www.rigb.org
ri@ri.ac.uk

For over 200 years, the RI has been 'diffusing science for the common purposes of life'.

Collections: Includes the original apparatus and papers of many of those who have researched, lectured and lived at the Royal Institution including Humphry Davy, Michael Faraday, John Tyndall, James Dewar, William Bragg, Lawrence Bragg and George Porter. The collection also includes important collections of iconographical material in various media, scientific instruments, as well as a large administrative archive, covering all aspects of the work of the Royal Institution.

Royal London Hospital Archives & Museum

Church of St Augustine with St Philip, Newark Street
London E1 1BB
020 7377 7000

The museum is located in the former crypt of a fine, late 19th century, early English style church, designed by Arthur Cawston, which has been extensively restored. The building also accommodates the Library of the School of Medicine and Dentistry at Whitechapel.

Royal Mews, The

Buckingham Palace, Buckingham Palace Road
London SW1A 1AA
020 7766 7302
www.royal.gov.uk
information@royalcollection.org.uk

The Royal Mews houses the State vehicles, both horse-drawn carriages and motor cars, used for coronations, State Visits, royal weddings, the State Opening of Parliament and official engagements. Visitors can see the Gold State Coach which was last used during The Queen's Golden Jubilee in 2002 to carry Her Majesty and Prince Philip to the Service of Thanksgiving at St Paul's Cathedral.

Royal Museums Greenwich

Park Row
Greenwich SE10 9NF
020 8858 4422
www.rmg.co.uk
bookings@rmg.co.uk

Royal Museums Greenwich comprises of three linked sites: the National Maritime Museum, the Royal Observatory Greenwich and the 17th-century Queen's House. Set among the beautiful scenery and architecture of Maritime Greenwich World Heritage Site, Royal Museums Greenwich incorporates the world's largest maritime museum, the Prime Meridian of the world and London's only planetarium.

Royal Parks, The

The Old Police House, Hyde Park
London W2 2UH
020 7298 2000
www.royalparks.org.uk
hq@royalparks.gsi.gov.uk

Millions of Londoners and tourists visit the eight Royal Parks for free each year. The 5,000 acres of historic parkland provide unparalleled opportunities for enjoyment, exploration and healthy living in the heart of the capital.

Salvation Army International Heritage Centre

William Booth College
London SE5 8BQ
020 7326 7800
www.salvationarmy.org.uk/uki/heritage
heritage@salvationarmy.org.uk

The Salvation Army International Heritage Centre tells the story of The Salvation Army from its origins in the 1860s to the present, both in the UK and overseas. The Heritage Centre includes a library, archive and museum.

SAVE Britain's Heritage

70 Cowcross Street
London EC1M 6EJ
020 7253 3500
www.savebritainsheritage.org
office@savebritainsheritage.org

SAVE has been campaigning for historic buildings since its formation in 1975 by a group of architects, journalists and planners. SAVE is a strong, independent voice in conservation, free to respond rapidly to emergencies and to speak out loud for the historic environment.

Science Museum

Exhibition Road
London SW7 2DD
0870 870 4868
www.sciencemuseum.org.uk
info@sciencemuseum.ac.uk

Where else can you find life-changing objects from Stephenson's Rocket to the Apollo 10 command module, take in a science show, catch an immersive 3D movie, enjoy the thrills of a special effects simulator, introduce children to science with fun, hands-on interactives and encounter the past, present and future of technology in seven floors of galleries? At the Science Museum you can find all this and more..

Collections: The Science Museum has over 300,000 objects in its care, with particular strengths in the history of western science, technology and medicine since 1700. It has been uniquely placed to acquire objects recording the Industrial Revolution, and now holds unrivalled collections in this area. Medical artefacts from all periods and cultures also form an important part of its holdings.

Shakespeare's Globe

21 New Globe Walk, Bankside
London SE1 9DT
0207 902 1500
www.shakespeares-globe.org
info@shakespearesglobe.com

Founded by the pioneering American actor and director Sam Wanamaker, Shakespeare's Globe is a unique international resource dedicated to the exploration of Shakespeare's work and the playhouse for which he wrote, through the performance and education. Together, the Globe Theatre Company, Shakespeare's Globe Exhibition and Globe Education seek to further the experience and international understanding of Shakespeare in performance through three central and inter-dependent activities: 1) The faithfully reconstructed Globe Theatre hosts an extensive exhibition about Shakespeare and the theatre of his day. 2) Producing excellent performances through productions of stimulating classic and new plays at the Globe Theatre.

Sherlock Holmes Museum

221B Baker Street
London NW1 6XE
0207 224 3688
www.sherlock-holmes.co.uk
curator@sherlock-holmes.co.uk

Sherlock Holmes and Doctor John H. Watson lived at 221b Baker Street between 1881-1904, according to the stories written by Sir Arthur Conan Doyle. The house is protected by the government due to its 'special architectural and historical interest', while the 1st floor study overlooking Baker Street is still faithfully maintained for posterity as it was kept in Victorian times.

Sikorski Museum

20 Princes Gate
London SW7 1PT
020 7589 9249
www.sikorskimuseum.co.uk

The Sikorski Museum was established at the end of World War II by the exiled Polish community in London who did not wish to return home to a Russian controlled homeland. The exhibition consists of 10,000 military objects, and the Enigma Ciphering Machine which was cracked by Polish mathematicians. Exhibits are marked in Polish, but for non-Polish speakers there is an English language tour.

Sir John Soane's Museum

13 Lincoln's Inn Fields
London WC2A 3BP
020 7405 2107
www.soane.org
pwaite@soane.org.uk

The architect Sir John Soane's house, museum and library at No. 13 Lincoln's Inn Fields has been a public museum since the early 19th century.

Collections: Sir John Soane's Museum comprises his collections and personal effects, acquired between the 1780s and his death in 1837. The museum's collections contain many important works of art and antiquities, including Hogarth's A Rake's Progress and An Election, Canaletto's Riva degli Schiavoni looking West, the alabaster sarcophagus of Seti I, 30,000 architectural drawings, 6,857 historical volumes, 252 historical architectural models as well as important examples of furniture and decorative arts.

Society of Antiquaries of London

Burlington House, Piccadilly, London
London W1J 0BE
020 7479 7080
www.sal.org.uk
admin@sal.org.uk

The society of Antiquaries of London is charged by its Royal Charter of 1751 with 'the encouragement, advancement and furtherance of the study and knowledge of the antiquities and history of this and other countries'. It celebrated its Tercentenary in 2007. The society's 2,900 Fellows include many distinguished archaeologists and art and architectural historians.

Somerset House

Strand
London WC2R 1LA
020 7845 4600
www.somersethouse.org.uk
info@somersethouse.org.uk

Somerset House is a spectacular neo-classical building in the heart of London, sitting between the Strand and the River Thames. During summer months a 'grove' of 55 fountains dance in the courtyard, and in winter you can skate on London's favourite outdoor ice rink.

Southside House

3-4 Woodhayes Road, Wimbledon Common, Wimbledon
London SW19 4RJ
020 8946 7643
www.southsidehouse.com
info@southsidehouse.com

Southside House, on Wimbledon Common, was rebuilt by Robert Pennington in the William & Mary style, after the Great Plague of London in 1665. One of the oldest houses in Greater London, it is still used as a private residence by descendants of the Pennington family, and the house remains largely unchanged.

Collections: Behind the long facade are the old rooms, still with much of the furniture that Pennington brought here. The house also has connections with Anne Boleyn, Frederick Prince of Wales, Marie Antoinette, Admiral Lord Nelson, Lady Hamilton and Lord Byron.

Southwark Cathedral Education Centre

Southwark Cathedral, London Bridge
London SE1 9DA
020 7367 6715
http://goo.gl/hvlnen
edcentre@southwark.anglican.org

The Cathedral lies on the South Bank of the River Thames close to London Bridge on a site occupied by a Church for over one thousand years. The main structure of today's church was built between 1220 and 1420.

Collections: The Cathedral does not have either an archivist or an archive department although our Visitors' Officer is willing to receive any enquiries of a more general nature relating to the Cathedral and its history to assist you in your researches. We would be delighted to receive copies of old guidebooks, articles, photographs and prints relating to the Cathedral although please write giving details of items held before despatching them to us. If you are interested in searching our parish records please note that they are held at London Metropolitan Archives.

Southwark Council Libraries, Arts & Heritage Service

Environment Department, Libraries, Arts and Heritage Division, Southwark Council, 160 Tooley Street
London SE1
020 7525 2169
www.southwark.gov.uk
Judy.aitken@southwark.gov.uk

Southwark Council is responsible for the Cuming Museum, Southwark Local History Library and Archive, Kingswood House, the grade 2 listed house near Sydenham and currently cares for the now-closed Livesey Museum.

Southwark Local History Library

John Harvard Library, 211 Borough High Street
London SE1 1JA
020 7525 0232
http://goo.gl/ZV8i30

Southwark's range of historical experience is a story vividly told through surviving documents. We have gathered these historical sources at Southwark Local History Library and Archive along with information on changes in Southwark today.

Spelthorne Museum

1 Elmsleigh Road
Staines, Middlesex TW18 4PN
01784 461804
www.spelthornemuseum.org.uk
staff@spelthorne.free-online.co.uk

Woolly mammoths tusks from the Ice Age, tools from the Stone Age, a large collection of Roman artefacts, a 1738 fire engine and Victorian memorabilia – Spelthorne Museum has the whole history of this area.

Spencer House

27 St James Place
London W14 9DT
0207 499 8620
www.spencerhouse.co.uk

From its conception, Spencer House was recognised as one of the most ambitious aristocratic town houses ever built in London and is, today, the city's only great 18th-century private palace to survive intact. Spencer House was built in 1756-66 for John, first Earl Spencer, an ancestor of Diana, Princess of Wales (1961-97). Situated in the heart of St James's, Spencer House is a short distance from St James's Palace, Buckingham Palace and the Palace of Westminster, and has a splendid terrace and garden with magnificent views of Green Park.

SS Robin, The

SS Robin, 2D/2E Royal Victoria Place
London E14 1UQ
020 7998 1343
www.ssrobin.org
info@ssrobin.com

SS Robin is a precious diamond, a national treasure and one of London's best kept secrets. She's the world's oldest complete steamship and the last of her type in the world.

Collections: SS Robin Gallery seeks to challenge perceptions by illustrating and exploring our lives and planet through extraordinary documentary images.

St Bartholomew's Hospital Archives & Museum

North Wing, St Bartholomew
London EC1A 7BE
020 3465 5798
www.bartshealth.nhs.uk/bartsmuseum
barts.archives@bartshealth.nhs.uk

Set in the historic North Wing of St Bartholomew's Hospital, the museum tells the story of this renowned institution, celebrates its achievements and explains its place in history. A video relates the foundation of the hospital and life-size models bring the history of Barts to life.

St Bride Foundation

Bride Lane, Fleet Street
London EC4Y 8EQ
020 7353 3331
sbf.org.uk
info@sbf.org.uk

In 1891, St Bride Foundation was established to provide a social, cultural and recreational centre for London's Fleet Street and its burgeoning print and publishing trade. Now, this historic site is a living and breathing community once again, with new projects, facilities and programmes expanding its central mission: to excite and inspire. At the heart of the Foundation is an unparalleled library of print, media, communications and design, believed to be the largest in the world – but its remit is becoming even more broad and exciting.

St Paul's Cathedral

St Paul's Churchyard
London EC4M 8AD
020 7236 4128
www.stpauls.co.uk
chapter@stpaulscathedral.org.uk

A Cathedral dedicated to St Paul has overlooked the City of London since 604AD, a constant reminder to this great commercial centre of the importance of the spiritual side of life. The current Cathedral – the fourth to occupy this site – was designed by the court architect Sir Christopher Wren and built between 1675 and 1710 after its predecessor was destroyed in the Great Fire of London.

Stephens Collection

Avenue House, East End Road, Finchley
London N3 3QE
www.london-northwest.com/sites/Stephens

The Stephens Collection aims to show aspects of the life of Henry Stephens; the history of the Stephens Ink Company; the history of Avenue House; the development of writing.

Strawberry Hill

268 Waldegrave Road
Twickenham, Middlesex TW1 4ST
0208 744 1241
www.strawberryhillhouse.org.uk
jenny.mayer@strawberryhillhouse.org.uk

Created by Horace Walpole in the 18th century, Strawberry Hill is internationally famous as Britain's finest example of Georgian Gothic revival architecture. It also inspired the first gothic novel The castle of Otranto.

Sutton Archives

Central Library, St Nicholas Way
Sutton SM1 1EA
020 8770 4747
www.sutton.gov.uk
local.studies@sutton.gov.uk

Sutton Local Studies & Archives Service holds primary and secondary records relating to the London Borough of Sutton and its predecessor authorities, local people, organisations and businesses.

Sutton House - National Trust

2 & 4 Homerton High Street, Hackney
London E9 6JQ
020 8986 2264
www.nationaltrust.org.uk/sutton-house
suttonhouse@nationaltrust.org.uk

Built in 1535 by Sir Ralph Sadleir, Principal Secretary of State to Henry VIII, Sutton House is the oldest brick house in East London. Surviving for over 450 years, Sutton House is fascinating for its visible layers of change - from the original Tudor linenfold panelling and stone fireplaces, through the 17th-century painted staircase, to the Victorian Study and the more recent squatter's mural painted during the 1980s.

Syon House & Park

Syon Park
Brentford, Middlesex TW8 8JF
020 8560 0881
www.syonpark.co.uk
info@syonpark.co.uk

Syon Park has been home to the family The Duke of Northumberland for over four hundred years and still owned and looked after by them. It is full of beauty and magnificence, of great paintings and furniture, with perhaps the finest Robert Adam interior in the country. Surrounded by its own parkland, with Kew Gardens across the Thames, it is hard to believe that Syon is barely 10 miles from central London.

Thames Discovery Programme

LAARC, Mortimer Wheeler House, 46 Eagle Wharf Road
London N1 7ED
0207 566 9310
www.thamesdiscovery.org
enquiries@thamesdiscovery.org

When the tide is out, the Thames is the longest open-air archaeological site in London, and much of the foreshore is freely accessible to the public. The Thames Discovery Programme is a community archaeology project designed to monitor the exposed archaeological sites of the inter-tidal area of the Thames with volunteer support.

Thames Ironworks Heritage Trust

London
https://www.facebook.com/TIHTUK
tihtorg@gmail.com

The Thames Ironworks Heritage Trust's goal is to revive the shipbuilding and wider manufacturing heritage of east London. The charity aims to do this primarily through the restoration of a number of Thames Ironworks-made lifeboats close to the place where they were originally built over 100 years ago, creating employment and new skills for apprentices in the process.

Thomas Layton Memorial & Museum Trust

CIP, Treaty Centre, High Street
Hounslow, Middlesex TW3 1ES
0845 456 2800
www.thomaslayton.org.uk
layton@cip.org.uk

The Trust celebrates the legacy of Thomas Layton, who lived in Brentford, Middlesex, between 1826 and 1911. He was committed to Brentford and served on various local bodies for over 45 years, helping to develop many new buildings and services for the growing town. Thomas Layton was also an avid collector of books, prints, maps and archaeological artefacts.

Tower Bridge

London SE1 2UP
020 7403 3761
www.towerbridge.org.uk
enquiries@towerbridge.org.uk

Tower Bridge has stood over the River Thames in London since 1894 and is one of the finest, most recognisable bridges in the World. At the Tower Bridge Exhibition you can enjoy breath-taking views from the high-level Walkways and learn about the history of the Bridge and how it was built.

Tower Hamlets Local History Library & Archives

Tower Hamlets Local History Library and Archives, 277 Bancroft Road
London E1 4DQ
020 7364 1290
http://goo.gl/q75gpq
localhistory@towerhamlets.gov.uk

Tower Hamlets local history library and archives covers the area of the present-day London Borough of Tower Hamlets; the original East End of London which, until 1965, comprised of the Boroughs of Bethnal Green, Poplar and Stepney. If you are interested in a building in the borough, tracing your ancestors who lived here, doing a school or college project on some aspect of the borough or are just feeling nostalgic, we may well be able to help you.

Tower of London

The Tower of London
London EC3N 4AB
0203 166 6654
www.hrp.org.uk
towereducation@hrp.org.uk

The ancient stones reverberate with dark secrets, priceless jewels glint in fortified vaults and ravens strut the grounds. The Tower of London, founded by William the Conqueror in 1066-7, is one of the world's most famous fortresses, and one of Britain's most visited historic sites.

Collections: The Tower of London has been home to the Crown Jewels since the 14th century and the Jewel House is an essential part of any visit to the Tower today. Marvel at some of the world's largest and most historic diamonds set in the regalia used to crown the sovereigns of England. The Martin Tower houses a special exhibition, Crowns & Diamonds: the making of the Crown Jewels, which explains the evolution of British crowns and the role that diamonds played in their decoration.

TUC Library Collections

Learning Centre, London Metropolitan University, North Campus, 236-250 Holloway Road, London, N7 6PP
London N7 6PP
020 7133 2260
http://goo.gl/p3cCp0
tuclib@londonmet.ac.uk

The TUC Library Collections, established in 1922 for the use of the Trades Union Congress and affiliated trade unions, moved to the London Metropolitan University in 1996. They are a major research resource for the study of all aspects of trade unions, lifelong learning and people at work.

Collections: The Collections hold books, pamphlets, periodicals and ephemera relating to political and labour history from the mid 19th century to the present day. There are also archival collections, the largest of which is the Workers' Educational Association Library and Archive.

Turner's House, Twickenham

40 Sandycoombe Road
Twickenham TW1 2LR
www.turnerintwickenham.org.uk
info@turnerintwickenham.org.uk

It's been a well-kept secret that Britain's greatest landscape painter, JMW Turner, designed his own house in Twickenham 200 years ago, as a country retreat for himself and his father.

Collections: As part of his bequest to Turner's House Trust Prof. Harold Livermore left a large collection of watercolours, prints, drawings - and a few oil paintings - which are of great value in interpreting Turner's own work and contemporary art and literature.

Twickenham Museum, The

25 The Embankment
Twickenham, Middlesex TW1 3DU
020 8408 0070
www.twickenham-museum.org.uk

The history centre for Twickenham, Whitton, Teddington and the Hamptons. These villages, situated by the River Thames to the south-west of London, have a rich history going back thousands of years.

Two Temple Place

2 Temple Place
London WC2R 3BD
020 7836 3715
www.twotempleplace.org

Two Temple Place is one of London's architectural gems, an extraordinary late Victorian mansion built by William Waldorf Astor on Embankment. The house is owned by registered charity, The Bulldog Trust and supports the charitable activities of the Trust through exhibitions and events hosted in the building. It also provides a unique setting for both corporate and private events, from weddings to conferences.

UCL Art Museum

South Cloisters, University College London, Gower Street
London WC1E 6BT
020 7679 2540
www.ucl.ac.uk/museums/uclart
college.art@ucl.ac.uk

Over 10,000 works of art make up the collections of UCL Art Museum, from the 1500s to the present day. Works separated by centuries are linked by a desire to experiment with new materials, theories, and reproduction techniques in order to produce new meanings, share ideas and inspire.

Collections: The College Art Collections contains over 10,000 objects including paintings, drawings, prints and sculpture from 1490 - present. Founded in 1847 when sculpture models by the neo-classical artist John Flaxman were given to UCL.

UCL, Institute of Archaeology

31-34 Gordon Square, London WC1H 0PY
London WC1H 0PY
020 7679 7495
www.ucl.ac.uk/museums/archaeology
c.frearson@ucl.ac.uk

The Institute of Archaeology houses fine teaching and reference collections. They include prehistoric ceramics and stone artefacts from many parts of the world as well as collections of Classical Greek and Roman ceramics.

UCL Library Special Collections

c/o National Archives, Kew
Richmond TW9 4DU
www.ucl.ac.uk/Library/special-coll

UCL Library Special Collections is one of the foremost university collections of manuscripts, archives and rare books in the UK. It includes fine collections of medieval manuscripts and early printed books, notably from the CK Ogden Collection and Graves Library, as well as significant holdings of 18th century works, and highly important 19th and 20th century collections of personal papers, archival material, and literature, covering a vast range of subject areas, notably Latin American archives, Jewish collections and the George Orwell Archive.

University College London Museums & Collections

University College London, Gower Street
London WC1E 6BT

020 7679 2000
www.ucl.ac.uk/museums
s.washington@ucl.ac.uk

UCL is the first university to be established in England after Oxford and Cambridge. It was also the first to admit students regardless of class, race, gender or religion.

Collections: UCL is home to four museums and eleven collections. These were gathered and developed from the 1820s to assist UCL's academic staff in their teaching and research.

Untold London

c/o The Museum of London
London online
www.untoldlondon.org.uk

Join us as we hunt through London's museums, galleries and archives for the hidden histories of a multicultural city.

V&A Museum of Childhood

Cambridge Heath Road
Bethnal Green E2 9PA
020 8983 5200
www.museumofchildhood.org.uk
moc@vam.ac.uk

Welcoming over 400,000 visitors through its doors every year, the V&A Museum of Childhood in London's Bethnal Green houses the Victoria and Albert Museum's collection of childhood-related objects and artefacts, from the 1600s to the present day. The collection features toys - including dolls, dolls' houses, puppets and teddy bears - games, childcare, clothing, furniture and art and photography.

Vestry House Museum

Vestry Road
London E17 9NH
020 8496 4391
www.walthamforest.gov.uk/vestry-house
vhm.enquiries@walthamforest.gov.uk

Only a few minutes walk from Walthamstow's busy shopping centre, Vestry House Museum is waiting to unlock the story of the people of Waltham Forest. The museum is housed in Walthamstow's original workhouse, built in 1730 as a home for local paupers.

Collections: As well as having a large social history collection of objects, the museum holds approximately 80,000 historic photographs of the Borough, is the home for the Local Studies Library and also houses the Borough Archives.

Valence House Museum

Becontree Avenue
Dagenham RM8 3HT
020 8227 2034
https://goo.gl/J2edGX
valencehousemuseum@lbbd.gov.uk

Valence House is a Medieval and later timber-framed and partially moated building situated in parkland.

Collections: The collection includes items from Prehistoric to modern times representing the lives of the inhabitants of the Essex parishes of Barking and Dagenham. The display areas include a reconstruction council 1945 living room and kitchen, a Victorian Servants Parlour of the 1890s and a Barking chemists shop.

Victoria & Albert Museum

Cromwell Road, South Kensington
London SW7 2RL
020 7942 2211
www.vam.ac.uk
vanda@vam.ac.uk

The Victoria and Albert Museum (V&A) is the world's greatest museum of art and design.

Collections: The Victoria and Albert Museum's collections span two thousand years of art in virtually every medium, from many parts of the world, and visitors to the museum encounter a treasure house of amazing and beautiful objects.

Wallace Collection

Hertford House, Manchester Square
London W1U 3BN
020 7563 9551
www.wallacecollection.org
booking@wallacecollection.org

The Wallace Collection is a national museum which displays the wonderful works of art collected in the 18th and 19th centuries by the first four Marquesses of Hertford and Sir Richard Wallace, the son of the 4th Marquess. It was bequeathed to the British nation by Sir Richard's widow, Lady Wallace, in 1897. Displayed at Hertford House, the main London townhouse of its former owners, the Wallace Collection presents its outstanding collections in a sumptuous but approachable manner which is an essential part of its charm. It is probably best known for its paintings by artists such as Titian, Rembrandt, Hals (The Laughing Cavalier) and Velázquez and for its superb collections of 18th-century French paintings, porcelain, furniture and gold boxes, probably the best to be found anywhere outside France. But there are also splendid medieval and Renaissance objects, including Limoges enamels, maiolica, glass and bronzes, as well as the finest array of princely arms and armour in Britain, featuring both European and Oriental objects.

Waltham Forest Archives & Local Studies Library

Vestry House Museum, Vestry Road, Walthamstow
London E17 9NH
020 8496 4381
http://goo.gl/GeV1Yv

We can help you if you are interested in researching the following: your family history; the history of your house or street; the development of the local area and local communities; subjects for a school project or for academic research.

Wandsworth Heritage Service

Battersea Library, 265 Lavender Hill
London SW11 1JB
020 7223 2334
www.better.org.uk/libraries/areas/wandsworth
heritage@gll.org

Archives and local history service for Wandsworth.

Wandsworth Museum

38 West Hill, Wandsworth,
London SW18 1RX
020 8870 6060
www.wandsworthmuseum.co.uk
Contact@wandsworthmuseum.co.uk

The Wandsworth Museum houses exhibitions and objects that tell the story of the region we know today as the Borough of Wandsworth, from 25,000 years ago to the present day. Throughout its history, people from all over the world have made their homes in Wandsworth. Take a walk through the centuries and uncover how they lived their lives and how your own story links you to this rich legacy. Wandsworth Museum is a private charity and as such receives no direct support from any governmental funding bodies to operate its facilities.

Wellcome Collection

183 Euston Road, London
London NW1 2BE
020 7611 2222
www.wellcomecollection.org
info@wellcomecollection.org

Wellcome Collection is the free visitor destination for the incurably curious. Located at 183 Euston Road, London, it explores the connections between medicine, life and art in the past, present and future.

Wellcome Library

183 Euston Road
London NW1 2BE
020 7611 8722
wellcomelibrary.org
library@wellcome.ac.uk

The Wellcome Library is one of the world's greatest collections of books, manuscripts, pictures and films around the meaning and history of medicine from the earliest times to the present day.

Wellington Arch - English Heritage

London W1J 7JZ
020 7930 2726
http://goo.gl/4VIT3g

The neoclassical arch, England's answer to the Arc de Triomphe, was first erected in 1826 as a grand entrance to Buckingham Palace. From 1846, it was topped with a huge equestrian statue of the Duke of Wellington but a major road widening of Piccadilly in 1882, due to the increasing demands of Victorian traffic, was used as an excuse to remove the oversized statue to Aldershot.

West Ham United Football Club Museum

Boleyn Ground
London E13 9AZ
020 85482700
www.whufc.com

The official museum of the history of the West Ham United Football Club from Thames Ironworks roots to the Premier League.

Collections: Memorabilia and photographs from the early days right up to the present, including the Champions Collection of medals, caps and shirts worn and won by England's World Cup winners Bobby Moore, Sir Geoff Hurst and Martin Peters.

West Middlesex Family History Society

1 Camellia Place, Whitton
Twickenham TW2 7HZ
www.west-middlesex-fhs.org.uk
secretary@west-middlesex-fhs.org.uk

West Middlesex Family History Society aims to encourage and assist those involved in the study of family history and genealogy in the western part of the ancient English county of Middlesex.

Westminster Abbey

20 Dean's Yard Westminster
London SW1P 3PA
020 7222 5152
www.westminster-abbey.org
info@westminster-abbey.org

Westminster Abbey is one of the world's great churches, with a history stretching back over a thousand years. A royal church from its first beginnings, it still has the shrine of its principal founder, the Anglo-Saxon king and saint, Edward the Confessor, at the heart of the building.

Westminster Cathedral

42 Francis Street
London SW1P 1QW
020 7798 9055
www.westminstercathedral.org.uk

Westminster Cathedral is one of the greatest secrets of London; people heading down Victoria Street on the well-trodden route to more famous sites are astonished to come across a piazza opening up the view to an extraordinary facade of towers, balconies and domes. The architecture of Westminster Cathedral certainly sets it apart from other London landmarks. It was designed in the Early Christian Byzantine style by the Victorian architect John Francis Bentley.

White Lodge Museum & Ballet Resource Centre

The Royal Ballet School, White Lodge, Richmond Park
London TW10 5HR
020 8392 8440, option 7
www.royalballetschool.org.uk/the-school/museum
museum@royalballetschool.co.uk

White Lodge Museum and Ballet Resource Centre is the first dedicated ballet museum in the UK. It is housed within White Lodge - a Grade I listed building, which is now the home of The Royal Ballet Lower School.

Whitehall

1 Malden Road
Cheam Village SM3 8QD
020 8643 1236
www.sutton.gov.uk/index.aspx?articleid=1909
whitehallmuseum@sutton.gov.uk

An attractive weather-boarded house in the heart of the Cheam Village conservation area. Whitehall has stood on this site since about 1500, and opened to the public in 1978.

Collections: Discover 500 years of living history; original timbering with wattle and daub plus carpenter's marks visible on roof structure; inglenook fireplace with cooking pots, baking oven and ashpit; medieval Cheam Pottery display - story of Henry VIIIs nearby Nonsuch Palace; learn about the Killick family who lived here for over 250 years; furnished Victorian schoolmaster's study bedroom; rear garden with medieval well.

Wiener Library, The

29 Russell Square
London WC1B 5DP
020 7636 7247
www.wienerlibrary.co.uk
info@wienerlibrary.co.uk

The Wiener Library for the Study of the Holocaust & Genocide is one of the world's leading and most extensive archives on the Holocaust and Nazi era. The Library's unique collection of over one million items includes published and unpublished works, press cuttings, photographs and eyewitness testimony.

William Morris Gallery

Lloyd Park, Forest Road
London E17 4PP
020 8496 4390
www.wmgallery.org.uk
wmg.enquiries@walthamforest.gov.uk

The William Morris Gallery is the only public gallery devoted to the life and legacy of William Morris: designer, craftsman, socialist.

Wimbledon Lawn Tennis Museum & Tour

Wimbledon Lawn Tennis Museum, Museum Building, The All England Lawn Tennis & Croquet Club, Church Road, Wimbledon
London SW19 5AE
020 8946 6131
www.wimbledon.com/museum
museum@aeltc.com

The collection dates from 1555, and is widely seen as the world's greatest tennis collection open to the public. New items are added each year from the current Champions.

Wimbledon Society Museum of Local History

22 Ridgeway, Wimbledon
London SW19 4QN
0208 296 9914
www.wimbledonmuseum.org.uk
wimbledonmuseum@yahoo.co.uk

A small intimate museum in which you're shown, in pictures, words and objects, the three thousand year history of Wimbledon. The staff you'll meet are friendly local people who are proud of our history and will gladly help you in any way they can.

Wimbledon Windmill Museum

🏛 ⌂ £

Windmill Road, Wimbledon Common
London SW19 5NR
020 8947 2825
www.wimbledonwindmill.org.uk

Wimbledon Windmill Museum is a museum of windmills housed in the windmill on Wimbledon Common. It depicts the history of windmills and milling using working models and the machinery and tools of the trade, with hands-on milling for children. In the entrance to the museum is a diorama showing how the windmill was built, with some of the early types of tools used in its construction.

Winston Churchill's Britain At War Experience

🏛 ⌂

Churchill House, 64 - 66 Tooley Street, London Bridge
London SE1 2TF
020 7403 3171
www.britainatwar.co.uk
info@britainatwar.org.uk

Britain at War Experience offers a glimpse of what life was like for the civilians in war-torn Britain during WW2. This is a unique museum of interest to all ages, featuring evacuation, rationing, shelters, weddings, bomb disposal, gasmasks and a walk through the London Blitz.

World Rugby Museum & Twickenham Stadium Tours

🏛 ⌂ 🏛 £

Twickenham Stadium, Rugby Road
Twickenham, Middlesex TW1 1DZ
020 8892 8877
http://goo.gl/Uk4HSF
museum@rfu.com

There is nowhere in England more important to rugby union than Twickenham Stadium. Home to England Rugby and the World Rugby Museum (WRM) – this is the ultimate experience for the rugby enthusiast. The World Rugby Museum gives a unique insight into this magnificent sport. People of all ages and nationalities can follow the history of the game from its origins in Rugby School to the present day.

Greater Manchester

Manchester, parliamentary and municipal borough, city, parish, and township, SE. Lancashire, on rivers Irk, Irwell, and Medlock, 31 miles E. of Liverpool and 186 miles NW. of London by rail - parish (including the greater part of the sister town of Salford, separated from Manchester by the Irwell), 35,248 acres, population 720,481; township, 1646 acres, population 118,794; municipal borough, 4293 acres, population 341,414; 12 newspapers. When the woollen manufactures were introduced into England during the reign of Edward III (1327-1377) Lancashire became the centre of the industry, and from that period the prosperity of Manchester may be dated. The cotton trade, with which the city is peculiarly and lastingly identified, was in its early days the cause of two deplorable pestilences (1605 and 1645) arising from infected imports of the material from Smyrna. Three circumstances especially gave power and direction to the trade of the city: (1.) The success of the great work of the Duke of Bridgwater (assisted by James Brindley), who in 1758 began the system of inland navigation, and gave Manchester a splendid waterway for traffic; (2.) the introduction of machinery in cotton spinning, which occurred late in the 18th century; and (3.) the opening of the Manchester and Sheffield Railway in 1830 - the second in the kingdom. The town has played an important part in modern politics, having been intimately associated with the initial proceedings connected with the great reform agitation, while it was also the headquarters of action in the struggle for the repeal of the corn laws. Great distress prevailed in the city, and in fact throughout Lancashire, during the civil war in America, at which time the dearth of raw material paralysed the staple trade in cotton. Central Manchester now consists of immense piles of warehouses and offices, their extent unequalled by any in the world. Nearly all the factories have been removed to the outskirts of the city, and to the villages and towns in the environs. It is estimated that there are 250 cotton factories in the neighbourhood. Cotton, however, does not constitute the sole great industry of the city. Woollen and silk fabrics are manufactured in vast quantities. Engineering, and the making of machinery of all descriptions, employ thousands of the people, as also do various large chemical works. Manchester has extensive railway facilities, the largest stations being Victoria, London Road, and the Central. Power from Parliament to connect the city with the sea by means of a ship canal has now been obtained.

– John Bartholomew, *Gazetteer of the British Isles* (1887)
Note: Greater Manchester comprises parts of the historic counties of Lancashire, Cheshire and the West Riding of Yorkshire.

Aeroplane Collection

7 Mayfield Avenue
Stretford M32 9HL
0161 866 8255
www.theaeroplanecollection.org

TAC focuses on single aeroplane restoration projects either for Hooton Park or for other museums and groups who have the space and facilities to look after them properly but lack the necessary skills or work space for restorations.

Alexandra Park Pavilion

Alexandra Park
Manchester M16 8PJ
07816 683171
www.alexandra-arts.org.uk
hello@alexandra-arts.org.uk

Alexandra Park is regarded as of national importance and is a Grade 2-listed landscape on the English Heritage Register of Parks and Gardens. It has recently reopened following a restoration project funded by Manchester City Council, Heritage Lottery Fund and various sports bodies.

Archives+ at Manchester Central Library

Central Library, St Peter's Square
Manchester M2 5PD
0161 234 1979
archivesplus.org
info@archivesplus.org

Archives+ is an exciting City Centre showcase and repository for archives and family history. Situated in the magnificent Manchester Central Library, this purpose-built centre brings together a partnership of amazing regional and national collections of documents, photographs and films, and helps to satisfy a growing demand for accessible community history and personal heritage.

Astley Green Colliery Museum

Higher Green Lane, Astley, Tyldesley
Manchester M29 7JB
www.agcm.org.uk
info@agcm.org.uk

On the edge of Chat Moss, in an area once full of collieries, lies the picturesque village of Astley Green. In the heart of the village stands Astley Green Colliery Museum. The museum houses Lancashire's only surviving headgear and engine house, both of which now have listed building status. The museum houses many exhibits, not least of which is the collection of 28 colliery locomotives, the largest collection of its type in the United Kingdom.

Bramall Hall

Bramhall Park, Bramhall
Stockport SK7 3NX
0161 488 4248
http://goo.gl/7p210h
bramall.hall@stockport.gov.uk

Bramall Hall is a magnificent black and white timber-framed Tudor manor house, with Victorian additions, spanning six centuries and set within 70 acres of parkland. It gives a unique insight into the families and servants who have lived and worked here.

Bury Archives Service

Archives Service, Bury Museum and Archives Moss Street
Bury BL9 0DR
0161 253 6782
www.bury.gov.uk/index.aspx?articleid=3535

Bury Archives Service was established in 1985 to collect the records, papers and photographs which are of cultural and historic value relating to the Borough of Bury and make them available free of charge to the public. The collections of records we hold relate all aspects of life in the Borough and are donated by the Council, local businesses, schools, churches, various clubs, societies, organisations and individuals dating from 1675 to the present day.

Bury Art Museum

Moss Street
Bury BL9 0DR
0161 253 5878
www.bury.gov.uk/index.aspx?articleid=2537
artgallery@bury.gov.uk

Housed in a distinctive Edwardian building, Bury Art Museum offers a welcoming, warm and friendly setting for visitors to enjoy art, (old and new), and discover the rich history of Bury and the surrounding area. Highlights from the art collection include 'Calais Sands' and 'Ehrenbreitstein' by JMW Turner.

Bury Transport Museum

Castlecroft Goods Shed, Castlecroft Road, Bury
Bury BL9 0LN
0161 764 7790
www.east-lancs-rly.co.uk/?m=52&p=btm
transport.museum@east-lancs-rly.co.uk

This new-look museum is the essential fun attraction for all the family and tells the story of transport in the local area. It's full of exciting exhibits and interactive hands-on galleries that will keep both adults and children entertained.

Chetham's Library

Long Millgate
Manchester M3 1SB
0161 834 7961
www.chethams.org.uk
librarian@chethams.org.uk

Chetham's Library was founded in 1653 and is the oldest public library in the English-speaking world. It is an independent charity and remains open to readers and visitors free of charge. The Library began acquiring books in August 1655, and has been adding to its collections ever since.

Collections: The Library holds over 100,000 volumes of printed books, of which 60,000 were published before 1851. These include particularly rich collections of 16th- and 17th-century printed works, periodicals and journals, broadsides and other ephemera.

Church of St John the Divine

186, Brooklands Road
Brooklands Sale, M33 3PB
0161 962 0051
www.stjohnsbrooklands.org.uk
bryan.hackett@btinternet.com

The Grade II listed Anglican parish church was built thanks to the generosity of wealthy Manchester banker Samuel Brooks. He commissioned Alfred Waterhouse, one of the greatest architects of Victorian England, to design the building, and the 'church in the fields' was consecrated in 1868.

Elizabeth Gaskell's House

84 Plymouth Grove
Manchester M13 9LW
0161 273 2215
www.elizabethgaskellhouse.co.uk
enquiries@elizabethgaskellhouse.co.uk

The House, a Grade II* listed property, was built between 1835-1841 and is a rare example of the elegant Regency-style villas once popular in Manchester. Elizabeth Gaskell was one of the 19th century's most important writers, and she lived here from 1850-65.

Ellenroad Engine House

Elizabethan Way, Newhey
Rochdale OL16 4LE
07789 802632
www.ellenroad.org.uk
enquiry@ellenroad.org.uk

The Ellenroad Trust Ltd was established in 1985 to ensure the preservation of the Ellenroad Engine House and Engines. The Trust arranged the refurbishment of the boiler house and the engines and started to run the site as a steam museum.

Fusilier Museum, The

Fusilier Museum, Moss Street
Bury BL9 0DF
0161 763 8950
www.fusiliermuseum.com
enquiries@fusiliermuseum.com

The Fusilier Museum is home to the collections of The Lancashire Fusiliers and the Royal Regiment of Fusiliers. Together they record over 300 years of history and heritage of the people who served in the regiments.

Collections: A wonderful collection of medals, including VC's, uniforms and other militaria, along with personal effects of former soldiers.

Gallery of Costume

Manchester, Platt Hall, Wilmslow Road, Rusholme
Manchester M14 5LL
0161 245 7245
www.manchestergalleries.org
galleryofcostume@manchester.gov.uk

The Gallery of Costume houses one of the finest collections of clothing and fashion accessories in the country. Two floors of themed displays give a fascinating insight into fashion over the centuries.

Collections: The collection consists of more than 21,000 items from the 17th century to the present day, including rare examples of the everyday dress of working people.

Gallery Oldham

Greaves Street
Oldham OL1 1AL
0161 770 4742
www.galleryoldham.org.uk
galleryoldham@oldham.gov.uk

Gallery Oldham has been collecting artworks and objects since 1883 and is still collecting today. The current collections include: over 12,000 social and industrial history items, more than 2,000 works of art, about 1,000 items of decorative art, more than 80,000 natural history specimens, over 1,000 geological specimens, about 3,000 archaeological artefacts, 15,000 photographs and a large number of books, pamphlets and documents.

Greater Manchester Fire Service Museum

Maclure Road
Rochdale OL11 1DN
01706 901227 Answerphone
www.manchesterfire.gov.uk/museum
museum@manchesterfire.gov.uk

The official Museum of GMC Fire Service is situated at Rochdale Fire Station, in the north-east of the county, and opened in 1983. The many and varied exhibits include several full- size fire appliances, along with equipment, uniforms, models, photographs, medals and insignia, which together portray the history of fire fighting in general, but particularly within Greater Manchester. Parts of the museum are laid out to form period tableaux, including a Victorian street (with fire station, insurance office and fire equipment suppliers) and a World War II Blitz scene.

Greater Manchester Police Museum & Archives

57a Newton Street
Northern Quarter, Manchester M1 1ET
0161 856 3287
s367873952.websitehome.co.uk
police.museum@gmp.police.uk

Explore Manchester's hidden past - a labyrinth of alleyways and slums, interrupted only by the huge mills casting shadows below. An eerie underworld, lit by gas lamps where police officers were kept busy apprehending unsavoury characters of all ages. The Greater Manchester Police Museum and Archives enables you to experience what life was really like for these officers in a busy Victorian police station.

Collections: The collection dates from c.late 19th century onwards and ranges from vehicles, costume and memorbilia to restored cells, a charge office (1879) and magistrates court (1895 from Denton).

Hat Works

Wellington Mill, Wellington Road South
Stockport SK3 0EU
0161 474 2400
www.stockport.gov.uk/hatworks
bookings.hatworks@stockport.gov.uk

Hat Works is the UK's first and only museum dedicated to the hatting industry, headwear and hats. It is home to a fantastic collection of hats and headgear with some hats dating as far back as the 18th century. There are hats for every occasion, contemporary hats from today's top milliners, hats from all over the world and the worlds tallest top hat. The museum also houses a vast collection of Victorian millinery machinery which has been restored back to full working order.

Heaton Hall

Heaton Park, Prestwich
Manchester M25 2SW
0161 773 1231 Thurs-Sun
www.manchestergalleries.org

There has been a house on the site of the present Heaton Hall since the late 17th century, but the building would have been quite old-fashioned by the time Sir Thomas Egerton, the seventh baronet and later first Earl of Wilton, inherited it in 1756. On his marriage to the heiress Eleanor Assheton of Middleton in 1772, that Sir Thomas decided to commission architect James Wyatt to re-model the house.

IWM North (Imperial War Museum)

The Quays, Trafford Wharf Road
Manchester M17 1TZ
0161 836 4000
www.iwm.org.uk/visits/iwm-north
iwmnorth@iwm.org.uk

This multi-award winning IWM North is a great free day out for all ages. Designed by world-renowned architect Daniel Libeskind to represent a globe shattered by conflict, it reveals how war shapes lives through powerful exhibitions, the Big Picture (a 360 degree light and sound show), tours, object handling sessions, and family activities all available daily.

Collections: The museum charts world events from 1900 to the present day, examining war and its effect on people and places; from photographs to film, artefacts, weapons and souvenirs the entire experience of war is explored.

John Rylands Library, The

150 Deansgate
Manchester M3 3EH
0161 306 0555
www.manchester.ac.uk/library/rylands/
uml.special-collections@manchester.ac.uk

The Library became part of The University of Manchester in 1972 and currently holds the Special Collections of The University of Manchester Library. Mrs Rylands' memorial to her husband is now part of the third largest academic library in the United Kingdom, and the Deansgate building houses over 250,000 printed volumes, and well over a million manuscripts and archival items.

Lancashire County Cricket Club Museum

Lancashire County Cricket Club, Old Trafford
Manchester M16 0PX
0161 2824000
www.lccc.co.uk/index.php?p=news&id=37
enquiries@lccc.co.uk

The rich history of Lancashire Cricket is exhibited in the club museum at Old Trafford. Manchester Cricket Club was formed at the beginning of the 1800s and moved to the present Old Trafford in 1857.

Collections: On show are some of the finest trophies in the cricket world presented by players from the 1820s, some silver tankards from 1738, paintings, scores, rules of the game and some memorabillia from the early development of cricket, including some of the earliest cricket statistics in existence. Lancashire County Cricket Club was formed in 1864 and amongst the displays are early team photographs, silver trophies, scrapbooks, caps, and cncket balls belonging to famous players who performed memorable feats for their county.

Manchester & Lancashire Family History Society

Clayton House, 59 Piccadilly
Manchester M1 2AQ
0161 236 9750
www.mlfhs.org.uk
office@mlfhs.org.uk

Manchester & Lancashire FHS was formed in 1964 and is now one of the largest family history societies in the world. Although the society is united by a common interest in genealogy and family history, members also pursue interests in closely related fields.

Manchester Cathedral

Cathedral Yard
Manchester M3 1SX
0161 833 2220
www.manchestercathedral.org
office@manchestercathedral.com

Manchester Cathedral now has a stunning Visitor Centre in which we aim to make your visit a really enjoyable experience. The hi-tech, interactive displays in our exhibition area are a magnet for young and old alike. Perhaps the greatest feature is the historic Hanging Bridge, a 15th century bridge which connected the Mediaeval Town with the Church.

Collections: The Archives of Manchester Cathedral date from 1421 to the current day. Housed in a purpose built strong-room above the North Porch, the collection contains a wealth of documents with great potential for historical research; these include records concerning the cathedral.

Manchester Centre for Regional History

Department of History and Economic History, Manchester Metropolitan University, Room 122, Geoffrey Manton Building, Rosamond St West
Manchester M15 6LL
0161 247 6491
www.mcrh.mmu.ac.uk
m.tebbutt@mmu.ac.uk

The Manchester Centre for Regional History was formally set up in 1998 with the aim of building upon established strengths within Manchester Metropolitan University in the history of Manchester and the north west of England. It is an umbrella for a number of scholars within the Department of History and Economic History whose work has a distinctively local or regional emphasis. The centre is strongly rooted in the history of its region, but is also concerned with broader historical questions which explore the significance of regions, regional identity and the relationship between regions and the nation state.

Manchester City FC Museum & Stadium Tour

Etihad Stadium, Etihad Campus
Manchester M11 3FF
0870 062 1894 option 8
http://goo.gl/Y0GxUn
tours@mcfc.co.uk

Museum displays are themed around events or significant stories such as the Supporters, the FA Cup, Grounds, Kits, Players, League Championship etc. Key items on display include trophies & medals from the Club's earliest years to present day; shirts from 1934 to the modern era etc.

Manchester Jewish Museum

190 Cheetham Hill Road
Manchester M8 8LW
0161 834 9879
www.manchesterjewishmuseum.com
education@manchesterjewishmuseum.com

Manchester Jewish Museum tells the story of the Jewish community in Manchester over the last 200 years. Through photographs, objects, documents and room settings, visitors gain an insight into the lives of the individuals who came to the city in different waves of Jewish immigration.

Manchester Masonic Museum

Freemasons' Hall 36 Bridge Street
Manchester M3 3BT
0161 832 6256
www.pglel.co.uk/Museum/Museum.asp

The Manchester Masonic Museum is a non-profit organisation dedicated to promoting the values of, and stimulating debate about the heritage of Freemasonry in the North West of England. The collection has been held at Freemasons' Hall in Manchester since the building opened in 1929 and holds many varied artefacts dating back to the mid 1700s.

Manchester Metropolitan University Special Collections

Sir Kenneth Green Library, All Saints
Manchester M15 6BH
0161 247 6107
www.specialcollections.mmu.ac.uk
lib-spec-coll@mmu.ac.uk

Manchester Metropolitan University Special Collections is a museum, gallery and reading room and is open to the public to browse or research the unique collections, attend an event or to see our exhibitions. The Special Collections Gallery features 2-3 exhibitions a year, showcasing our collections and artwork by regional and internationally acclaimed artists.

Manchester Military History Society

Knivton Street, Godley
Hyde SK14 2PU
mcrmilhist.org.uk/
info@mcrmilhist.org.uk

We are an informal group united by a common interest in military history. All are welcome regardless of age, sex or ethnicity.

Manchester Museum

The University of Manchester, Oxford Road
Manchester M13 9PL
0161 275 2648
www.manchester.ac.uk/museum
museum@manchester.ac.uk

Encounter Manchester Museum's assortment of treasures from the natural world and the many cultures it is home to. Visitor favourites include dinosaurs, mummies and live amphibians and reptiles.

Manchester Postal Museum

Manchester Southern Cemetery, Remembrance Lodge, 212 Barlow Moor Rd,
Manchester M21 7GL
https://goo.gl/BPrrsO
david.mcrpost.harrop@googlemail.com

A large private collection of postal memorabilia/history, currently setting up a permanent display in Stockport

Manchester United Museum & Tour Centre

Sir Matt Busby Way, Old Trafford
Manchester M16 0RA
0161 868 8000
http://goo.gl/7XzRUj
museum.enquiries@manutd.co.uk

Only at the Old Trafford Museum & Tour Centre, Manchester tourism award's large visitor attraction of the year, can you see the stadium through the eyes of Manchester United greats themselves. Or get even closer to the world of Manchester United and share 130 years of football.

Museum of Science & Industry

Liverpool Road, Castlefield
Manchester M3 4FP
0161 832 2244
www.mosi.org.uk
marketing@mosi.org.uk

Uncover Manchester's industrial past and learn about the fascinating stories of the people who contributed to the history and science of a city that helped shape the modern world. Located on the site of the world's oldest surviving passenger railway station and only minutes from Manchester's City Centre, the museum's action-packed galleries, working exhibits and costumed characters tell the amazing story of revolutionary discoveries and remarkable inventions both past and present - a memorable day out for everyone.

Museum of the Manchester Regiment

The Town Hall
Ashton-under-Lyne OL6 6DL
0161 343 2878
www.tameside.gov.uk/museumsgalleries/mom
garry.smith1@tameside.gov.uk

The museum tells the story of generations of soldiers, from the raising of the regiment in 1756 through to Regimental life today. The museum's Ladysmith Gallery (re-developed in 2002) tells our story chronologically, covering major actions such as the American War of Independence, New-Zealand, the Crimea, South Africa, both World Wars and the Malayan Emergency. The Gallery also houses over 2000 medals including 6 Victoria Cross Groups as well as a reconstruction of a First World War trench.

Museum of Transport

Boyle Street, Cheetham
Manchester M8 8UW
0161 205 2122
www.gmts.co.uk
email@gmts.co.uk

Find out about Greater Manchester's transport history with the museum of Transport in Manchester. Opened in 1979, the museum has a large and varied collection of exhibits, charting the development of public transport in the county, ranging from a Victorian horse-drawn bus to a full size prototype for Greater Manchester's Metrolink.

Collections: Includes buses, trams, trolleybuses, coaches and other vehicles which formerly provided public transport services in Greater Manchester. Also includes historical records relating to public transport in the county, such as company records, photographs and films and a large collection of objects ranging from street furniture to ticketing equipment.

Museum of Wigan Life

Library Street
Wigan WN1 1NU
01942 828128
www.wlct.org/wigan/museums-archives/mowl
heritage@wlct.org

We hold over 30,000 objects relating to life in Wigan Borough, past and present. Our collections include fine art, archaeology, social history, natural history, coins, decorative art and industrial history. The museum of Wigan Life is housed in Wigan's first public library and first public building with electric lighting.

North West Film Archive

Manchester Metropolitan University, Manchester Central Library, Albert Square
Manchester M60 2LA
0161 247 3097
www.nwfa.mmu.ac.uk
n.w.filmarchive@mmu.ac.uk

The Archive cares for over 38,000 items from the pioneer days of film in the mid 1890s to video production of the present day. The work of both the professional and the amateur is collected. Local residents and groups can take advantage of the NWFA's free research, viewing and loan services.

Oldham Local Studies & Archives

Local Studies & Archives, 84 Union Street
Oldham OL1 1DN
0161 770 4654
http://goo.gl/sCLMJM

Oldham's archives date from 1597 and cover an enormous range of subjects and activities.

Ordsall Hall Museum

322 Ordsall Lane, Ordsall
Salford M5 3AN
0161 872 0251
http://goo.gl/DAVSdt
ordsall.hall@scll.co.uk

Ordsall Hall - Salford's Grade 1 listed Tudor manor house - was first recorded in 1177. Since then, it has been home to medieval gentry, Tudor nobility, Catholics loyal to the crown, butchers, farmers, an Earl, an artist, priests, scout troops, mill workers, cows and several ghosts. Today, it is an engaging heritage site open to visitors 5 days a week throughout the year.

Pankhurst Centre, The

60 - 62 Nelson Street, Chorlton on Medlock
Manchester M13 9WP
0161 273 5673
www.thepankhurstcentre.org.uk
admin@thepankhurstcentre.org.uk

The Pankhurst Centre provides a museum area open to all and a women only space that is a unique environment in which women can learn together, work on projects and socialise. The centre is of historical significance as it was the home of Emmeline Pankhurst and her daughters Sylvia, Christabel and Adela who were centrally involved in the campaign for Votes for Women.

People's History Museum

Left Bank, Spinningfields
Manchester M3 3ER
0161 838 9190
www.phm.org.uk
info@phm.org.uk

There have always been ideas worth fighting for. Join a march through time at the People's History Museum following Britain's struggle for democracy over two centuries.

Collections: The collections of the People's History Museum contain items relating to the working people of Britain, and cover ceramics, prints, posters, banners, ephemera and photographs. The museum (registered as the National Museum of Labour History) is the national centre for the collection, conservation, interpretation and study of material relating to the history of working people in Britain.

Portland Basin Museum

Heritage Wharf, Portland Place
Ashton-under-Lyne OL7 0QA
0161 343 2878
portland.basin@mail.tameside.gov.uk

Portland Basin is an award winning museum housed in a reconstruction of the historic 1834 Ashton canal warehouse. Discover the life and work experiences of the people of Tameside.

Rochdale Pioneers Museum

31 Toad Lane
Rochdale OL12 0NU
01706 524920
www.rochdalepioneersmuseum.coop
museum@co-op.ac.uk

On 21 December 1844 the Rochdale Pioneers opened their store selling pure food at fair prices and honest weights and measures. The business revolution that started here now involves a billion co-operators as members of 1.4 million co-operative societies across the world. The Rochdale Pioneers Museum exists to preserve the original store of the Rochdale Pioneers and to generate an understanding of the ideals and principles of the co-operative movement.

Royal Northern College of Music Archives

124 Oxford Road
Manchester M13 9RD
0161 907 5211
www.rncm-archive.rncm.ac.uk
maryann.davison@rncm.ac.uk

The RNCM was established in 1973 following the merger of the Royal Manchester College of Music (1893-1973) and the Northern School of Music (1920-1973). Today the Archive acquires materials relating to the RNCM and its predecessors, and the papers of individuals with significant RNCM connections.

Collections: Key collections include: Organisational archives of the Northern School of Music and The Royal Manchester College of Music; the performing archive of the Philip Jones Brass Ensemble; personal papers covering the entire careers of the violinists Adolph Brodsky and Philip Newman, the soprano Elizabeth Harwood, and Walter and Ida Carroll; the correspondence of Sir Charles Halle; the compositions of Arthur Butterworth, Arnold Cooke, John Golland, John Ogdon, Thomas Pitfield and Alan Rawsthorne.

Saddleworth Museum & Art Gallery

High Street, Uppermill
Nr Oldham OL3 6HS
01457 874093
www.saddleworthmuseum.co.uk
curator@saddleworthmuseum.co.uk

The museum opened in 1962 and is situated in one of the outbuildings of the 19th century Victoria Mill. Saddleworth Museum is full of intriguing objects from the past and tells the story of the people who have created Saddleworth's landscape and character.

Salford Museum & Art Gallery

Peel Park, The Crescent
Salford M5 4WU
0161 778 0800
http://goo.gl/ly4al5
salford.museum@scll.co.uk

Our permanent attractions include a Picture Gallery where you can relax and enjoy the splendour of the Victorians' passion for painting and the decorative arts, or stroll down the Victorian Street and marvel through shop windows displaying their original 19th century wares. Salford Museum and Art Gallery was the UK's 'first free public library' and today, still houses the city's Local History Library and archive.

Salford War Memorials Project

67 Sutherland Street, Winton
Salford M30 8BR
www.salfordwarmemorials.co.uk
salfordwarmemorials@talktalk.net

A project to record all war memorials in the City of Salford, Greater Manchester, and research the names inscribed. The Salford War Memorial Project was founded in September 2010 with the aim of finding, recording and cataloguing all of Salford's war memorials for posterity. The sacrifices made by the men and women of Salford to protect our freedom both deserve and demand our attention.

Staircase House

30-31 Market Place
Stockport SK1 1ES
0161 474 2388
http://goo.gl/mmDyPb
staircasehouse@stockport.gov.uk

Staircase House is a beautifully restored townhouse situated in Stockport's historic market place. The house is famous for its rare cage newell staircase dating back to 1618. Journey through time from its humble beginnings as a medieval cruck framed building in 1460 to the splendour of the 17th century townhouse, concluding in WWII.

Stockport Air Raid Shelters

61 Chestergate
Stockport SK1 1NE
0161 474 1940
www.airraidshelters.org.uk
bookings.hatworks@stockport.gov.uk

Step back in time to 1940s wartime Britain and experience the sights and sounds of Britain's homefront. Stockport Air Raid Shelters were carved into the natural sandstone cliffs in Stockport Town Centre.

Stockport Museum

Vernon Park, Turncroft Lane, Offerton
Stockport SK1 4AR
0161 474 4460
www.stockport.gov.uk/stockportstory

Visit this fascinating museum, one of the first purpose built museums in the country. It is situated in the beautiful surroundings of Vernon Park, which has been renovated to its original Victorian splendour.

Stockport Story Museum

30/31 Market Place
Stockport SK1 1ES
0161 480 1924
www.stockportstory.org.uk
staircasehouse@stockport.gov.uk

Experience 10,000 years of Stockport's history, as you travel through time from prehistoric Stockport to present day. Discover the fantastic finds from Mellor, life in medieval Stockport, the thriving textile industry of the Victorian era, the impact of WWII, concluding with an insight into modern day Stockport.

Tameside Local Studies & Archives Centre

Central Library Old Street
Ashton-under-Lyne OL6 7SG
0161 342 4242
www.tameside.gov.uk/localstudies
localstudies.library@tameside.gov.uk

The Local Studies and Archives Centre holds local and family history material for the towns of Tameside - Ashton-under-Lyne, Audenshaw, Denton, Droylsden, Dukinfield, Hyde, Longdendale, Mossley and Stalybridge.

Touchstones Rochdale

The Esplanade
Rochdale OL16 1AQ
01706 924492
www.link4life.org/touchstones
touchstones@link4life.org

The borough's award winning arts and heritage centre offers a museum, four art galleries, heritage gallery, tourist information centre, café and shop with regular events and workshops.

Victoria Baths

Hathersage Road, Chorlton on Medlock
Manchester M13 0FE
0161 224 2020
www.victoriabaths.org.uk
info@victoriabaths.org.uk

Victoria Baths is the most intact Edwardian Baths in Britain. It is an architectural gem, rich in stained glass, mosaic floors and decorative tiling.

Collections: We hold an archive of material relating to the history of Victoria Baths, swimming in Manchester and some other historic pools. Some of this material is on display at our Open Days. We provide access to our archive for researchers.

Wigan Archives Service

Leigh Town Hall
Wigan WN7 1DY
01942 404 430
heritage@wlct.org

The Wigan Archives Service's mission is to make Wigan's Archives accessible to all for learning and enjoyment, and to foster a sense of belonging and pride in local heritage through the collection and preservation of archive records. We hold collections of records for Wigan's people, places, businesses, churches, societies and all manner of other organisations, preserving the history of the entire Borough. We look after millions of documents, from paper records and digital archives, to maps, plans and photographs.

Working Class Movement Library

51 The Crescent
Salford M5 4WX
0161 736 3601
www.wcml.org.uk
enquiries@wcml.org.uk

Working people have always struggled to get their voices heard. The Working Class Movement Library records over 200 years of organising and campaigning by ordinary men and women.

Collections: There are important collections on Thomas Paine, Peterloo, Chartism, rise of trade unionism, Socialism, Labour Party, Communist Party of Great Britain, Ireland, Spanish Civil War, General Strike, CND, suffragettes and suffragists, Co-operative movement.

Wythenshawe Hall

Wythenshawe Park, Northenden
Manchester M23 0AB
0161 998 2331 Thurs-Sun
www.manchestergalleries.org

Wythenshawe Hall was a family home for nearly four hundred years. The original Hall was built around 1540 by Robert Tatton, possibly on the site of an earlier medieval building.

Hampshire

Hampshire, Hants, or Southampton, maritime county, in S. of England; bounded N. by Berks, E. by Surrey and Sussex, S. by the English Channel, and W. by Wilts and Dorset; greatest length, N. to S., 46 miles; greatest breadth, E. to W., 46 miles; 1,037,764 acres, population 593,470. (The figures of ac. and pop. include the Isle of Wight.) Hampshire is undulating, finely wooded, and fruitful. Its coast line is very irregular, the principal indentation being Southampton Water. From Surrey and Sussex, NE. to Wilts and Berks, two ranges of chalk hills, known as the North and South Downs, traverse the co. In the W. is the New Forest, and in the SE. are the Forests of Bere and Waltham Chase. The Avon, Exe, Test, Itching, and Hamble are the chief rivers. The county is noted for its agriculture, the wheat of Hampshire being especially prized. Upon the Downs are reared large flocks of the variety of sheep known as 'Hampshire Downs' or 'short wools'. Pig breeding, and the curing of bacon, have long been large and lucrative branches of the county's industry. The mineral resources are meagre; and, except in large coast towns, such as Portsmouth and Gosport, the manufactures also are unimportant. The shipping, however, is very extensive. Hampshire (with the Isle of Wight) comprises 38 hundreds, 12 liberties, 349 parishes, with parts of 3 others, the parliamentary and municipal boroughs of Portsmouth, Southampton, and Winchester, the parliamentary borough of Christchurch, and the municipal boroughs of Audover, Basingstoke, Lymington, Newport, Romsey, and Ryde. It is almost entirely in the diocese of Winchester.

– John Bartholomew, *Gazetteer of the British Isles* (1887)

Note: Until 1890 the county included the Isle of Wight.

1642 Living History Village

Little Woodham Lane, Howe Road, Rowner
Gosport PO12 2HH
02392 522944.
www.littlewoodham.org.uk

A unique pattern woven in the fabric of time. Within the Parish of Rowner, surrounded by woodland, the village of Little Woodham exists to educate both children and adults about 17th century rural life in the South of England. In the April of 1642 the King of England, Charles Stuart and his Parliament stood on the eve of Civil War. Using extensively researched local events and people the villagers link their families and their lives to national and international events. During your tour you will meet 'villagers', interpreters dressed in period costume. Little Woodham's living history interpreters involve you and your children in their daily lives.

Action Stations at Portsmouth Historic Dockyard

HM Naval Base
Portsmouth PO1 3LJ
02392 839766
www.historicdockyard.co.uk
enquiries@historicdockyard.co.uk

Action Stations is a hi-tech visitor attraction that offers visitors of all ages an insight into the modern day Royal Navy. As well as two climbing exhibits, a laser weapons range, a Merlin Flight Simulator and a 6-axis motion simulator, Action Stations also boasts a 275 seat auditorium for the daily showings of 'Command Approved' (Cert PG.)

Adjutant General's Corps Museum

Peninsula Barracks, Romsey Road
Winchester SO23 8TP
01962 877826
www.winchestermilitarymuseums.co.uk
info@winchestermilitarymuseums.co.uk

The museum seeks to tell the story of personnel administration and pay, policing and detention, education, legal matters and women in the Army by using the collections of the antecedent corps.

Aldershot Military Museum

Queens Avenue
Aldershot GU11 2LG
0845 603 5635
www.hants.gov.uk/aldershot-museum

The museum collections are housed in four historically rich buildings. The two main galleries (which are the only two remaining Victorian Infantry barrack blocks left in Aldershot) tell the military and civilian stories of Aldershot, Farnborough and Cove.

Andover Museum

6 Church Close
Andover SP10 1DP
0845 603 5635
www.hants.gov.uk/andover-museum

Andover Museum tells the rich and fascinating story of Andover and the surrounding area. It displays natural history, archaeology and social history, including the story of the notorious Andover workhouse scandal and the Weyhill Fair, once the largest sheep sale in the country.

Army Medical Services Museum

Keogh Barracks, Ash Vale
Aldershot GU12 5RQ
01252 868612
www.ams-museum.org.uk
armymedicalmuseum@btinternet.com

The four collections of the Royal Army Medical Corps (RAMC), Royal Army Veterinary Corps (RAVC), Royal Army Dental Corps (RADC) and Queen Alexandra's Royal Army Nursing Corps (QARANC) are held at the AMS Museum in Keogh Barracks, Mytchett in Surrey. The museum tells the tale of army medicine and healthcare, human and animal, from the English Civil War to the current day as AMS personnel continue to serve across the globe as part of the British Army.

Army Physical Training Corps Museum

Queen's Avenue
Aldershot GU11 2LB
01252 24431 x 2168
www.rushmoor.gov.uk/index.cfm?articleid=205
regtsec@aptc.org.uk

The Army Physical Training Corps Museum display includes pictorial records, militaria and gymnastic equipment used from the very first Army Physical Training Course held at Oxford University in 1860 to the present day.

Basing House

FREE car park address, Barton's Lane, Old Basing, Basingstoke
Basingstoke RG24 8AE
01256 463965
www.basinghouse.org.uk
basinghouse@hants.gov.uk

Visited by Henry VIII, besieged by Cromwell... Discover the many stories of Basing House, a nationally important historical site that has undergone re-development. See the new Visitor Centre, the Great Barn with audio/ visual presentation, audio guide, refreshments, museum and an exciting events programme.

Bishop's Waltham Museum

The Farmhouse, Bishop's Waltham Palace
Bishop's Waltham SO32 1DH
01489 895428
www.bishopswalthammuseum.org.uk
anita.taylor@tiscali.co.uk

Small local museum, a registered charity run by volunteers. Housed in the Farmhouse at Bishop's Waltham Palace.

Bishop's Waltham Palace - English Heritage

Bishop's Waltham SO32 1DH
01962 854 766
http://goo.gl/wH42oa

The ruins of a medieval palace (together with later additions) used by the Bishops and senior clergy of Winchester as they travelled through their diocese. Winchester was the richest diocese in England, and its properties were grandiose and extravagantly appointed. Much of what can be seen today is the work of William Wykeham, who was bishop from 1367. The ground floor of the farmhouse is occupied by the Bishop's Waltham Town Museum. Other palaces of the Bishops of Winchester include Farnham Castle Keep and Wolvesey Castle (Old Bishop's Palace).

Bitterne Local History Society, Heritage & Research Centre

225 Peartree Avenue, Bitterne
Southampton SO19 7RD
www.bitterne.net
martyn.blhs@btinternet.com

The society was formed in 1981 when a by-pass cut its way through the heart of the old village. Now we offer a museum containing artefacts from some of those shops that sadly met their demise more than 25 years ago. Clearly our interest was centred on Bitterne but we cater for all areas of Southampton east of the Itchen.

Buckler's Hard

Beaulieu
Brockenhurst SO42 7XB
01590 614645
www.bucklershard.co.uk

Buckler's Hard is a picturesque 18th century village on the banks of the Beaulieu River in the heart of the New Forest. Historically, it is famed as the place where some of the ships of Nelson's fleet were built, but whether your interest is as a visitor - as an individual, family, group or educational party - or as a sailor wishing to moor in the River, the things to see and enjoy are as varied as the history of the area itself.

Collections: There is the Buckler's Hard Story and cottage displays to be seen. Visitors can stay in the village at the Master Builders House Hotel, or you can just enjoy the natural beauty of this historic village.

Bursledon Brickworks Industrial Museum

Swanwick Lane, Swanwick
Southampton SO31 7HB
01489 576248
www.bursledonbrickworks.org.uk
admin@busledonbrickwoks.org.uk

The only remaining steam driven brickworks in the country, we show how brick making made the leap from small scale production to 20 million bricks a year.

Collections: Bursledon Brickworks Conservation Centre contains exhibitions and displays covering the history of the brickworks, traditional building materials and conservation practice.

Bursledon Windmill

Windmill Lane, Bursledon
Southampton SO31 8BG
0845 603 5635
www.hants.gov.uk/windmill
enquiries.museum@hants.gov.uk.

Visit this restored 'tower' mill and discover how the windmill works. Explore the other buildings on the site: Chineham Barn, rescued from demolition, houses the ticket office and other visitor facilities. Hiltingbury granary, stores the grain.

Butser Ancient Farm

Chalton Lane, Chalton
Waterlooville PO8 0BG
023 9259 8838
www.butserancientfarm.co.uk
admin@butserancientfarm.co.uk

An experimental archaeological site of worldwide standing, open seven days a week (most of the year) to the public and schools. Displaying on-going constructions of buildings based on real sites, crops from prehistory, and rare breeds of animals. Exploring ancient technologies, and allowing 'hands on' activities for visitors.

Centre for Archaeology - English Heritage

Portsmouth PO4 9LD
023 9285 6700
cfa@english-heritage.org.uk

English Heritage's Centre for Archaeology at Fort Cumberland, near Portsmouth, was established in 1999 by bringing together the Central Archaeology Service, already based in Portsmouth, and the Ancient Monuments Laboratory, relocated from London. CfA was set up with the aim of becoming a national centre of excellence in archaeological practice, integrating work in the field, stratigraphic analysis, finds studies and work in the laboratory; it provides a resource for English archaeology, working in partnership with units, universities and amateur

groups, and a source of help and advice on policy and casework for colleagues within English Heritage.

Challenge at Aldershot - Military & Aerospace Museums

Wavell House, Cavans Road
Aldershot GU11 2LQ
01252 210480

The museum has a collection of vehicles, displayed either in the Montgomery Gallery, or outside the museum. There is an active programme of restoration on the vehicles by the museum's volunteer vehicle group. Most of the vehicles work and some are registered for road use, enabling them to travel to outside events.

Charles Dickens Birthplace Museum

393 Old Commercial Road
Portsmouth PO1 4QL
023 9282 7261
www.charlesdickensbirthplace.co.uk
info@charlesdickensbirthplace.co.uk

The famous writer Charles Dickens was born in this modest house in Portsmouth, England in 1812. The house has miraculously survived and is now preserved as a museum furnished in the style of 1809 which is when John and Elizabeth Dickens set up the first home of their married life there.

Collections: The furniture, ceramics, glass, household objects and decorations faithfully re-create the Regency style which Charles's parents would have favoured, although their actual possessions have long since been dispersed. There are three furnished rooms: the parlour, the dining room and the bedroom where Charles was born.

Chawton House Library

Chawton
Alton GU34 1SJ
01420 541010
www.chawtonhouse.org
info@chawton.net

Chawton House Library is a charity with a unique collection of books focusing on women's writing in English from 1600 to 1830. This specialist collection, set in the home and working estate of Jane Austen's brother, provides the opportunity to study and savour the texts in their original setting and inspires passion in readers of all ages. The Library's mission is to promote study and research in early English women's writing; to protect and preserve Chawton House, an English manor house dating from the Elizabethan period; and to maintain a rural English working manor farm of the late 18th and early 19th centuries, for the benefit of everyone.

City of Portsmouth Preserved Transport Depot

Wicor Farm, Cranleigh Road
Portchester PO16 9DR
https://www.facebook.com/cpptd
friends.cpptd@ntlworld.com

CPPTD is one of three separate and operationally independent bus preservation projects in Hampshire and West Sussex that are administered by the Working Omnibus Museum Project Ltd – the others are the Medstead Depot Omnibus Group and the Stedham Garage Group.

Curtis Museum

01420 82802
www.hants.gov.uk/museum/curtis

One of the finest local history collections in Hampshire, exploring 100 million years of history. Displays include prehistoric tools, Roman pottery reconstruction, Saxon burials, the Battle of Alton 1643, the notorious tale of Sweet Fanny Adams and hop picking and brewing.

D-Day Museum & Overlord Embroidery

Clarence Esplanade, Southsea
Portsmouth PO5 3NT
023 9282 7261
www.ddaymuseum.co.uk
info@ddaymuseum.co.uk

The D-Day Museum was established in 1984 to tell the story of Operation Overlord from its origins in the dark days of 1940 to victory in Normandy in 1944.

Collections: The museum's centrepiece is the Overlord Embroidery. Inspired by the Bayeux Tapestry, it is a moving tribute to the efforts and sacrifices of the Allies in defeating Nazi Germany.

Diving Museum, The

The Diving Museum, No 2 Battery, Stokes Bay Road
Gosport PO12 2QU
02392 602260
www.divingmuseum.co.uk
info@drjohnbevan.com

It is not yet popularly known, but Gosport is the home of the global diving industry. The co-inventor of the diving helmet, John Deane, lived in Gosport from 1835 to 1845 during which time he discovered the Mary Rose.

Eastleigh Museum

25 High Street
Eastleigh SO50 5LF
023 8064 3026
www.hants.gov.uk/museum/eastlmus
sue.tapliss@hants.gov.uk

Eastleigh Museum, housed in the old Salvation Army Citadel, is on High Street in the busy town centre and close to the Swan Shopping Centre. Discover Eastleigh's past, and meet Mr and Mrs Brown, a local locomotive engine driver and his wife.

Eastney Beam Engine House

Henderson Road, Eastney
Portsmouth PO4 9JF
023 92 827261
www.portsmouthmuseums.co.uk
mvs@portsmouthcc.gov.uk

Come, see and feel the powerful and majestic 'James Watt' Beam Engines in full steam. These engines are still housed in their original High-Victorian engine house.

Eling Tide Mill

The Tollbridge, Totton
Southampton SO40 9HF
023 8086 9575
www.elingtidemill.org.uk
info@elingtidemill.org.uk

Eling Tide Mill is a water mill that harnesses the power of the tide to grind wheat into wholemeal flour. Situated on the edge of Southampton Water beside the renowned New Forest, there has been a mill on the site for over 900 years, although it has had to be rebuilt several times, with the current building being some 230 years old. Tide mills were once an important part of the economy of many countries, such as Great Britain and the United States of America - the latter having many hundreds of tide mills on the eastern coast from the 17th to 19th centuries.

Emsworth Museum

10B North Street
Emsworth PO10 7DD
01243 378091
www.emsworthmuseum.co.uk
info@emsworthmuseum.co.uk

The museum, opened in 1988, was formed to archive and display the history of Emsworth and its surroundings, to make the public aware of Emsworth's historical position. The museum is entirely run by volunteers, and has a selection of the area's history displayed in articles, books, pictures, clothing ships models.

Explosion. The Museum of Naval Firepower

Heritage Way, Priddy's Hard
Gosport PO12 4LE
023 9250 5600
www.explosion.org.uk
info@explosion.org.uk

Explosion., The museum of Naval Firepower is a multi-million pound interactive museum set in the historic former Royal Navy armaments depot at Priddy's Hard, on the Gosport side of Portsmouth Harbour. Telling the story of naval firepower from the days of gunpowder to modern missiles with an unique collection which includes the Red Beard atom bomb, the Exocet missile and the Schwartzkopff torpedo.

Fordingbridge Museum

King's Yard, Salisbury Street
Fordingbridge SP6 1AB
01425 655222
www.fordingbridgemuseum.co.uk
info@fordingbridgemuseum.co.uk

Museum was founded in 2000 based on the collection donated by John Shering, a local businessman & benefactor of the town. Located in the middle of town in King's Yard, the museum building was a former granary.

Collections: Artefacts illustrating life in a rural town mainly between 1850 and 1950. A large photographic collection of Fordingbrige and surrounding villages including some of the people who lived there and their way of life.

Fort Brockhurst - English Heritage

Gunners Way, Elson
Gosport PO12 4DS
02392 581059
www.english-heritage.org.uk/fortbrockhurst

Fort Brockhurst is one of five forts known as the Gosport Advanced Lines, built to defend Portsmouth Harbour from a flanking attack by the French.

Collections: Holds archaeological, architectural and historical objects from English Heritage sites in the south of England.

Fort Cumberland - English Heritage

Portsmouth PO4 9LD
02392 856700

Perhaps England's most impressive piece of 18th-century defensive architecture, Fort Cumberland was reconstructed in pentagonal form by the Duke of Cumberland between 1785 and 1810, and designed to protect Langstone Harbour. Southsea beach is nearby.

Gilbert White's House & Garden & the Oates Collection

The Wakes, High Street
Selborne GU34 3JH
01420 511275
www.gilbertwhiteshouse.org.uk
info@gilbertwhiteshouse.org.uk

Discover the fascinating stories of three explorers of the natural world- Gilbert White, 18th century author and naturalist; Frank Oates, Victorian explorer of America and Africa; Captain Lawrence Oates who famously lost his life on Scott's ill fated expedition to Antarctica 1911-1912. Explore the charming house, 25 acres of restored gardens and ancient parkland.

God's House Tower Museum of Archaeology

Museum of Archaeology, Winkle Street
Southampton SO14 2NY
02380 915732
museums@southampton.gov.uk

Built in 1417, God's House Tower is the first purpose built artillery fortification in England. Gunpowder, shot and guns were stored on the ground floor and the main firing platform was on the roof.

Collections: They include spectacular medieval glass, imported pottery collections, and significant Roman, Saxon and medieval material. The size and range of the archaeology collections reflect the importance of Southampton in the past and at present, and the 50 years of systematic archaeological investigations in the city.

Gosport Discovery Centre

High Street
Gosport PO12 1BT
0845 603 5631
www.discoverycentres.co.uk/gosport
gosport@discoverycentres.co.uk

In the centre of Gosport, the Discovery Centre combines the best of traditional libraries with an exciting world of fun, learning and leisure. Whether you want to find the latest blockbuster, dig up information on your ancestors, watch a dance performance, or learn to surf the net, it's all here.

Great Hall & Round Table, Winchester Castle

The Great Hall, The Castle
Winchester SO23 8PJ
01962 846476
www3.hants.gov.uk/greathall
the.great.hall@hants.gov.uk

The first and finest of all 13th century halls, with the greatest symbol of medieval mythology, 'The Round Table of King Arthur'. Winchester Castle dates from the reign of

William the Conqueror (1066-1087). Although now known to have been constructed in the 14th century, and repainted in its present form for King Henry VIII, the table has for centuries been venerated by generations of tourists.

Gurkha Museum

Peninsula Barracks, Romsey Road
Winchester SO23 8TS
01962 842832
www.thegurkhamuseum.co.uk
curator@thegurkhamuseum.co.uk

The Gurkha Museum commemorates the services of the Gurkhas to the British Crown since 1815. Displays cover the Gurkhas' service in the old Indian Army which took them to battlefields across the world. From 1948 onwards the displays cover the story of the four Gurkha regiments transferred to the British Army and the corps which were subsequently raised to join them.

Hampshire Archives & Local Studies

Hampshire Record Office, Sussex Street
Winchester SO23 8TH
01962 846154
www.hants.gov.uk/archives
enquiries.archives@hants.gov.uk

Hampshire Record Office holds parish registers, wills and inventories, school log books, and tithe and enclosure maps, as well as archives of many significant institutions and organisations which have proved key to an understanding of national trends and events. Among these are the records of the medieval bishops of Winchester.

Hampshire Genealogical Society

198A Havant Road, Drayton
Portsmouth PO6 2EH
023 9238 7000
www.hgs-online.org.uk
secretary@hgs-online.org.uk

Helping you explore your family history in Hampshire in the UK and worldwide.

Hampshire Museums & Archives Service

Chilcomb House, Chilcomb Lane
Winchester SO23 8RD
01962 846304
www.hants.gov.uk/museums
musmsw@hants.gov.uk

We are one of the largest and most dynamic museum services managing 19 museums and specialist sites across Hampshire. We care for a wealth of collections representing Hampshire's archaeology, history, natural sciences, art and cultural life.

Hampshire Naval Collection

Gosport Library, High Street
Gosport PO12 1BT
023 9252 3431
clsonav@hants.gov.uk

Hampshire Naval Collection at Gosport Discovery Centre covers the Royal Navy and all aspects of British naval history including the Merchant Navy when there is an involvement in warfare. A substantial amount of material reflects the strong links between Hampshire, particularly Gosport, and the Navy.

Hinton Ampner - National Trust

Hinton Ampner, Bramdean
nr Alresford SO24 0LA
01962 771305
www.nationaltrust.org.uk/hinton-ampner
hintonampner@nationaltrust.org.uk

Hinton Ampner is one of the great gardens of the 20th century and is a masterpiece of design by Ralph Dutton, 8th and last Lord Sherborne. The 5ha (12 acre) garden unites a formal layout with varied and informal plantings in pastel shades. The house contains a fine collection of Regency furniture, Italian paintings and hardstone items.

Historic Environment Centre - HEC

Colebrook Street
Winchester SO23 9LJ
01962 840 222
www.winchester.gov.uk/heritage
museums@winchester.gov.uk

Located in Winchester Guildhall, above the Tourist Information Centre, the Historic Environment Centre is a search room where members of the public can consult aspects of the museums Service collections and meet members of staff by appointment only. Also museums' education service based there and the Historic Environment Record - a database and associated information of all known historic sites and monuments across the district. It replaces the former resources centre based at Hyde, and brings the services formerly provided there into the centre of town for greater convenience.

HMS Victory at Portsmouth Historic Dockyard

HM Naval Base
Portsmouth PO1 3NH
02392 839766
www.historicdockyard.co.uk
groups@historicdockyard.co.uk

HMS Victory is the Royal Navy's most famous warship. Best known for her role in the Battle of Trafalgar, the Victory currently has a dual role as the Flagship of the First Sea Lord and as a living museum to the Georgian Navy.

HMS Warrior 1860 at Portsmouth Historic Dockyard

🏛 📷 £

HM Naval Base
Portsmouth PO1 3LJ
02392 839766
www.historicdockyard.co.uk
enquiries@historicdockyard.co.uk

As you arrive at Portsmouth Historic Dockyard, the stunning sleek, black lines of Britain's first iron-hulled, armoured battleship, take your breath away. The pride of Queen Victoria, Warrior revolutionised warship construction.

Hollycombe - Steam in the Country

🏛 📷 £

Iron Hill, Midhurst Road
Liphook GU30 7LP
01428 724900
www.hollycombe.co.uk
info@hollycombe.co.uk

Steam powered fairground, railways, traction engines, sawmill and farm set in beautiful woodland gardens. Experience the fun of an Edwardian fair, ride on the railways and behind traction engines. A great day out for all the family with a wide variety of attractions to enjoy without the queues usually experienced at more modern theme parks. The collection is of national importance and a registered charity.

Hovercraft Museum Trust, The

🏛 📷 🏠 £

Argus Gate, Chark Lane
Lee-on-Solent PO13 9NY
023 9255 2090
www.hovercraft-museum.org
enquiries@hovercraft-museum.org

The Hovercraft Museum, based in Lee-on-the-Solent, has the only collection in the world of historic hovercraft. There are 60 hovercraft within several hangars on the Daedalus site. Every year we have a major Hovershow event when you can experience the thrill of hovercraft trips, displays of modern and historic craft and see many more on display.

Jane Austen's House Museum

🏛 📷 £

Chawton
Alton GU34 1SD
01420 83262
www.jane-austens-house-museum.org.uk
enquiries@jane-austens-house-museum.org.uk

Jane Austen's House Museum in the village of Chawton in Hampshire is where Jane spent the last eight years of her life. It is of international importance as the place where she did the majority of her mature writing, but at the same time retains the charm of a village home.

Collections: The museum houses an attractive collection of items connected with Jane and her family including the table that she used to write her novels. There is some of her jewellery, and examples of her needlework skill.

King's Royal Hussars Museum in Winchester

📷 £

Peninsula Barracks, Romsey Road
Winchester SO23 8TS
01962 828541
www.horsepowermuseum.co.uk

Visit HorsePower, the museum of The King's Royal Hussars, with its stunning displays of life size models, interactive exhibits, medals, swords, magnificent uniforms and fascinating photographs which show how the Cavalry of horse and sabre developed into the modern armoured regiment of today. Trace the history of three famous regiments over a period of 300 years and marvel at the great heroes who won the Victoria Cross for their valour. The dramatic exploits of men who fought in the Peninsula War, the Charge of the Light Brigade, the two World Wars are revealed and much more besides.

Maritime Archaeology Trust

🏛 📷 🏢 £

Room W1/95, National Oceanography Centre, Empress Dock
Southampton SO14 3ZH
023 8059 3290
www.maritimearchaeologytrust.org
info@hwtma.org.uk

Maritime Archaeology Trust promotes interest, research and knowledge of maritime archaeology and heritage in Great Britain with core activities concentrated in the counties of Hampshire, the Isle of Wight and the adjacent South Coast areas. The Trust run a programme of research led fieldwork involving professional archaeologists, volunteers and students. The results of this work are widely disseminated through our programme of educational initiatives including lectures, seminars and publications.

Collections: Shipwrecks: Artefacts from protected wreck sites in the region such as Pomone and Santa Lucia. Submerged Solent: Artefacts and stratigraphy from Bouldnor Cliff the only submerged mesolithic landscape of its kind in Britain. Large collection of flint tools from lost Stone Age sites beneath the sea.

Maritime Museum, Buckler's Hard, The

📷 £

Buckler's Hard, Beaulieu
Brockenhurst SO42 7XB
01590 614645
www.bucklershard.co.uk

Discover the fascinating story of Montagu Town as it was originally known. Founded as a free port for the trading of sugar from the West Indies, the newly re-designed Maritime Museum tells why the ambitious plans for a new town were never realised and why its name changed to Buckler's Hard.

Mary Rose Museum at Portsmouth Historic Dockyard

🔲 🔲 £

HM Naval Base
Portsmouth PO1 3LJ
02392 839766
www.historicdockyard.co.uk
enquiries@historicdockyard.co.uk

The Mary Rose was one of the earliest ships to carry heavy guns. She was a favourite of King Henry VIII and sank off Portsmouth in 1545 during an engagement with a French invasion fleet, in full view of the King, the screams of the men onboard, ringing in his ears.

Collections: The Mary Rose is the only recovered 16th century warship and is of international significance in maritime archaeology and beyond. Weighing some 300 tons, and standing as high as a four-storey building, the hull is revolutionary in design and provides vital evidence of shipbuilding techniques for a period when ship-plans do not survive.

Medieval Merchant's House - English Heritage

🔲 🔲

58 French Street
Southampton SO1 0AT
02380 221503
http://goo.gl/AKMsxo

The Medieval Merchant's House is tucked away within walking distance from the busy city centre. Escape from city life and take in the history of Southampton's 'old town'. A residence and place of business, it stood on one of the busiest streets in medieval Southampton. Now restored to its mid-14th century appearance by the removal of later additions, it is equipped with replica period furnishings. It stands near the medieval town wall, built to defend Southampton against seaborne attacks.

Mid Hants Railway - the 'Watercress Line'

🔲 £

The Watercress Line, The Railway Station
Alresford SO24 9JG
01962 733810
www.watercressline.co.uk
info@watercressline.co.uk

Formerly part of Britain's national rail network between the towns of Alton and Alresford in Hampshire, this preserved heritage steam railway line is now operated by dedicated volunteers for the enjoyment of all. The railway runs 10 miles from Alresford to Alton, on the way visiting Ropley and Medstead & Four Marks.

Milestones - Hampshire's Living History Museum

🔲 🔲 £

Leisure Park, Churchill Way West
Basingstoke RG22 6PG

01256 477766
www3.hants.gov.uk/milestones
milestones.museum@hants.gov.uk

Step back in time to the late Victorian period and experience Hampshire during the Industrial Revolution. Explore an authentically recreated network of streets, houses and factories, and discover a host of fascinating objects and vehicles from the Victorian era to the 1940s.

Mottisfont - National Trust

🔲

Mottisfont
nr Romsey SO51 0LP
01794 340757
www.nationaltrust.org.uk/mottisfont
mottisfontabbey@nationaltrust.org.uk

Set amidst glorious countryside along the River Test, this 12th century Augustinian priory was converted into a private house after the Dissolution of the Monasteries and still retains the spring or 'font' from which its name is derived. The key attraction is the grounds with magnificent trees, walled gardens and the National Collection of Old-fashioned Roses, at their best in mid-June.

Collections: Drawing room decorated by Rex Whistler and Derek Hill's 20th century picture collection.

Museum of Army Chaplaincy

🔲 ⭐

Amport House, Amport
Andover SP11 8BG
01264 773144 x 4248
www.army.mod.uk/chaplains/23363.aspx
DBlake.afcc@defenceacademy.mod.uk

The Royal Army Chaplain's Department (RAChD) was formed in 1796 to aid the recruitment of clergy serving with the army. However, this isn't the beginning of the story as priests have served with the military for hundreds of years.

Museum of Army Flying, The

🔲 🔲 🔲 🔲 £

Middle Wallop
Stockbridge SO20 8DY
01264 784421
www.armyflying.com
enquiries@flying-museum.org.uk

Historic helicopters, aeroplanes, kites, gliders, dioramas, exhibits, displays, all telling the story of 'soldiers in the air' from 19th century balloons to the present day and attack helicopters. Plus 2 flight simulators, rifle simulators, play park, 1940s house, childrens centre, gift shop, cinema, licensed cafe with airfield views, picnic area and plenty of parking. A343 between Andover and Salisbury; next to busy working airfield.

Museum of the Iron Age

[icons]

6 Church Close
Andover SP10 1DP
0845 603 5635
www.hants.gov.uk/museum-of-the-ironage

The Iron Age Museum tells the story of Danebury Ring, an Iron Age hillfort. It was excavated by Prof Barry Cunliffe between 1969 and 1988 becoming one of the most intensively studied sites of the British Iron Age (750 BC to the Roman invasion 43AD). The museum has life-sized models and reconstructions, as well as finds from the excavations, creating a picture of how people farmed, fought, worshipped and died, more than 2000 years ago. After completing work at the hillfort, Barry Cunliffe set about investigating Iron Age and Roman sites in the vicinity. Finds from some of these, together with the first La Tene mirror from Hampshire, are also displayed in the museum.

New Forest Centre, The

[icons]

New Forest Centre
Lyndhurst SO43 7NY
023 8028 3444
www.newforestcentre.org.uk
office@newforestcentre.org.uk

The New Forest Centre houses a museum of the New Forest, a temporary exhibition gallery, a reference library, shop and VIC. We run an education service that caters to local schools and a lifelong learning programme of exhibitions and events.

Petersfield Museum

[icons]

The Old Courthouse, St Peters Road
Petersfield GU32 3HX
01730 262601
www.petersfieldmuseum.co.uk
curator@petersfieldmuseum.co.uk

The museum was set up in 1999 and is located in the former Magistrates Courthouse.

Collections: The museum holds collections on the social, industrial and agricultural history of Petersfield and the surrounding villages. The collections are made up from artefacts and archives (including maps, oral history accounts, and photographs).

Pompey Pals Project

[icons]

c/o 14 Trevis Road, Milton
Portsmouth PO4 8LY
07751 465723
www.pompeypals.org.uk
pompeypalsmemorial@gmail.com

An organisation to commemorate those men and women from Portsmouth & surrounding area who served during the Great War whether overseas or at home.

Portchester Castle - English Heritage

[icons]

Portchester PO16 9QW
02392 378291
www.english-heritage.org.uk/visit/places/portchester-castle

One of a series of forts from the Solent to the Wash built in the late third century by the Romans to defend against Saxon pirates – a castle was built on the site in 1120. From then on, Portchester became a convenient place of embarkation for successive kings of England departing on journeys or military expeditions abroad.

Portsmouth Cathedral

[icons]

St Thomas's Street, Old Portsmouth
Portsmouth PO1 2HA
02392 892965
www.portsmouthcathedral.org.uk
rachel.richardson@portsmouthcathedral.org.uk

Portsmouth Cathedral welcomes visitors for services, tours or simply a wander around.

Portsmouth City Museum

[icons]

Museum Road
Portsmouth PO1 2LJ
023 9282 7261
www.portsmouthcitymuseums.co.uk
mvs@portsmouthcc.gov.uk

The City is the museum of and for the people of Portsmouth. There are temporary exhibition galleries, which have a frequently changing parade of fascinating shows on a wide range of subjects. The City Museum is dedicated to local history and fine and decorative art.

Collections: Local History, Arthur Conan Doyle, Story of Portsmouth, Portsmouth at Play, No Place Like Pompey.

Portsmouth Historic Dockyard

[icons]

Visitor Centre, Victory Gate, HM Naval Base
Portsmouth PO1 3LJ
02392 839 766
www.historicdockyard.co.uk
enquiries@historicdockyard.co.uk

Featuring the Mary Rose Museum and world famous ships HMS Victory and HMS Warrior 1860, plus HMS Alliance, the only remaining WW2 era British ocean going submarine. Also including the National Museum Royal Navy Portsmouth, Action Stations and Harbour Tours, there's plenty to see and do.

Portsmouth Museums & Records Service

Portsmouth Museums, Portsmouth City Museum
Portsmouth PO1 2LJ
www.portsmouthmuseums.co.uk

Portsmouth's collections cover a vast array of subjects; notably social history, military history, natural history, fine and decorative art and the literary collections pertaining to Charles Dickens and Arthur Conan-Doyle.

Portsmouth Natural History Museum

Eastern Parade, Southsea
Portsmouth PO4 9RF
02392 827261
www.portsmouthnaturalhistory.co.uk
info@portsmouthnaturalhistory.co.uk

The museum tells the story of the wild things of the riverbank, marshes, woods and urban areas of Portsmouth. Have a look for the heron stalking its prey and the brent geese coming into land after their 3000 km flight from the arctic.

Portsmouth Records Office

Portsmouth History Centre, Norrish Central Library,
Guildhall Square
Portsmouth PO1 2DX
023 9268 8046
www.portsmouthrecordsoffice.co.uk/

The Portsmouth History Centre is on the second floor of Portsmouth Central Library and comprises: City Records Office Archive; library resources on family, local and naval history; Arthur Conan Doyle and Charles Dickens collections.

Rifles Collection, The

Peninsula Barracks
Winchester SO23 8TS
01962 828505
www.riflesmuseum.co.uk

The Rifles Collection aims to tell the story of The Rifles, a regiment formed in 2007, drawing on both the heritage of its antecedent regiments and the current Regiment. The museum reflects the experiences of the modern Regiment, showcasing their tales from modern conflicts such as Iraq and Afghanistan as well as their role in British culture such as the role in the 2012 Olympics.

Rockbourne Roman Villa

Rockbourne
Fordingbridge SP6 3PG
0845 603 5635

www.hants.gov.uk/rockbourne-roman-villa

The villa once stood in the centre of a large farming estate, and is the largest known Roman villa in the area. Its history spans the period from the Iron Age through to the 5th century AD. Today you can walk around the remains of the villa and visit the site museum which displays many of the fascinating objects found on the site and shows what life was like for the Roman Britons who lived here over 1600 years ago. The villa site includes bath houses, living quarters, farm buildings and workshops.

Round Tower

Broad Street
Portsmouth PO1 2JD
023 9282 7261
www.portsmouthmuseums.co.uk
mvs@portsmouthcc.gov.uk

One of Portsmouth's oldest permanent fortifications. The Round Tower was built in around 1418 to defend the entrance to Portsmouth Harbour and prevent raids on the city by French ships.

Royal Armouries, Fort Nelson

Portsdown Hill Road
Fareham PO17 6AN
01329 233734
www.armouries.org.uk
fnenquiries@armouries.org.uk

This imposing Victorian fort is home to the Royal Armouries national collection of artillery – The Big Guns. Strategically positioned atop Portsdown Hill, with panoramic views across the Meon Valley and Portsmouth Harbour, Fort Nelson is an historic monument, restored to how it would have been in the 1890s. Visitors can access most areas of the fortifications and see how the Fort would have operated. The museum's displays trace the development of artillery from pre-gunpowder siege machines to modern-day super guns.

Collections: Fort Nelson also houses the world-renowned Royal Armouries collection of historic big guns and cannon, part of the National Museum of Arms and Armour. See the infamous Iraqi Supergun and its ancestor the Great Turkish Bombard of 1464.

Royal Green Jackets - Rifles Museum

Royal Green Jackets Museum, Peninsula Barracks, Romsey Road
Winchester SO23 8TS
01962 828549
www.rgjmuseum.co.uk
museum@royalgreenjackets.co.uk

Situated close to the City Centre and the heart of historic Winchester, with its Great Hall and Cathedral, this excellent Museum records, chronologically, graphically and entertainingly, the history of The Royal Green Jackets and its antecedent Regiments from 1741 to the present day. The museum houses an outstanding collection of uniforms, weapons, silver, paintings and medals, including 34 of the regiment's 59 Victoria Crosses. Amongst nine battle models there is a magnificent diorama of Waterloo, measuring 22' x 11' with 22,000 model soldiers and horses, plus an accompanying sound and light commentary.

Royal Hampshire Regiment Museum

Serle's House, Southgate Street
Winchester SO23 9EG
01962 863658
www.serleshouse.co.uk/index.html

The museum was opened shortly after the Second World War and originally occupied two floors. In 2004 it was reopened in its present site on the ground floor of Serles House. It comprises two large rooms connected by a long corridor which houses the picture gallery. The first room you enter concerns the history of the regiment from 1702 until 1905.

Royal Marines Museum

Southsea PO4 9PX
023 9281 9385
www.royalmarinesmuseum.co.uk
info@royalmarinesmuseum.co.uk

Explore the fascinating history of the Royal Marines. Take a walk through history from 1664 and learn about the lives of the extraordinary people who have become Royal Marines.

Royal Military Police Museum

The RMP Museum, DCPG, PP38, Southwick Park
Nr Fareham PO17 6EJ
023 9228 4372
www.rhqrmp.org/rmp_museum.html
museum_rhqrmp@btconnect.com

Since the 1950s, wherever the RMP have undertaken their training, a collection of historic artefacts has also been housed. Using the past to instil both a shared ethos and pride in the Military Police was, and still is, one of the roles of the museum.

Royal Navy Submarine Museum

Haslar Jetty Road
Gosport PO12 2AS
02392 510354
www.submarine-museum.co.uk
enquiries@submarine-museum.co.uk

Walk through HMS Alliance, the UK's only surviving British WW2 submarine, become a pirate and feel the force in our interactive gallery. Meet the crew, dive into games and discover tales of true heroes of the Submarine Service.

Royal Observer Corps Museum

Abbotts Road
Winchester
www.therocmuseum.org.uk
info@therocmuseum.org.uk

The Royal Observer Corps Museum is the national Museum of the ROC and has an unrivalled collection of photographs, documents, records, equipment, artefacts and memorabilia covering the history of the ROC from its formation in 1925 until final standdown in 1995.

Royal Victoria & Military Cemetery Netley Archive

24 Johns Rd, Woolston
Southampton SO19 9BU
www.netley-military-cemetery.co.uk
jd.green@outlook.com

An archive for anyone interested in the Royal Victoria Hospital and Military cemetery at Netley.

Sammy Miller Motorcyle Museum

Bashley Cross Road
New Milton BH25 5SZ
01425 616446
www.sammymiller.co.uk/museum.htm
info@sammymiller.co.uk

The museum houses the finest collection of fully restored motorcycles in Europe, including factory racers and exotic prototypes, plus memorabilia spanning 7 decades of motorcycling for sport and for pleasure.

Collections: There are over 300 rare and classic motorcycles on display in four galleries.

Sandham Memorial Chapel - National Trust

Harts Lane, Burghclere
nr Newbury RG20 9JT
01635 278394
www.nationaltrust.org.uk/sandham-memorial-chapel
sandham@nationaltrust.org.uk

Chapel containing Stanley Spencer's visionary paintings: * Unique 1920s decorated chapel * Filled with Stanley Spencer's murals inspired by the experience of First World War * Internationally recognised monument of British art * Orchard carpeted with wild flowers, with views of Watership Down * Stanley Spencer educational resources.

SeaCity Museum

Havelock Road
Southampton SO14 7FY
023 8083 3007
www.seacitymuseum.co.uk
museums@southampton.gov.uk

Based at the heart of Southampton, SeaCity Museum tells the story of the people of the city, their fascinating lives and historic connections with Titanic and the sea. Visit SeaCity Museum and Southampton to discover how we bring maritime history to life through an interactive experience designed for all ages.

SEARCH - Hampshire Museums' Hands-On Centre

50 Clarence Road
Gosport PO12 1BU
023 9250 1957
www.hants.gov.uk/museum/search

SEARCH is a hands-on centre for history and natural sciences in Gosport. We offer a range of exciting activity sessions for primary schools using real museum collections.

Solent Sky Aviation Museum

Albert Road South
Southampton SO14 3FR
02380 635830
www.solentskymuseum.org
info@spitfireonline.co.uk

The Hall of Aviation depicts the history of aviation in the Solent area and Hampshire. The museum tells the story of 26 aircraft companies including the Supermarine Aircraft Works where RJ Mitchell's famous aircraft, the Spitfire, was designed and built, also the Schneider Trophy winning aircraft the S6B.

Southampton Archives

Civic Centre, Civic Centre Road
Southampton SO14 7LY
023 8083 2251
www.southampton.gov.uk/archives

Southampton archives services hold a rich variety of material relating to the city and its people dating back to 1199. Whether you are researching your Southampton or merchant seamen ancestors, the history of your house or general topics such as Southampton during the Second World War, we may have sources to help.

Southsea Castle

Clarence Esplanade, Southsea
Portsmouth PO5 3PA
023 9282 7261
www.southseacastle.co.uk
info@southseacastle.co.uk

Built in 1544, Southsea Castle was part of a series of fortifications constructed by Henry VIII around England's coasts to protect the country from invaders. Barely was the work completed when Henry VIII's flagship, the Mary Rose, tragically sank in front of the castle.

Spring Arts & Heritage Centre, The

Old Town Hall, 56 East Street
Havant PO9 1BS
02392 451155
www.thespring.co.uk

The exhibition of local artefacts dates back beyond the original Roman settlements through to recent times. The artefacts include: the stocks and whipping post, Scalextric, St Faith's Church Turret Clock, Stents leather, a 1900s police truncheon and much more.

Square Tower

Broad Street
Portsmouth PO1 2JE
07519 505785
www.squaretower.co.uk
enquiries@squaretower.co.uk

The Square Tower is one of the oldest surviving parts of Portsmouth's fortifications, built to defend the city and the harbour. Built in 1494, it was originally a fortified residence for the governor of Portsmouth.

St Barbe Museum & Art Gallery

St Barbe Museum, New Street
Lymington SO41 9BH
01590 676969
www.stbarbe-museum.org.uk
office@stbarbe-museum.org.uk

St Barbe Museum & Art Gallery tells the story of the coastal strip between the New Forest and The Solent and hosts a changing programme of high quality exhibitions. The area has seen a thriving salt industry, smugglers landing their illegal cargoes on the coast, and has a long tradition of innovative boat building. The museum's aim is to capture the unique flavour of life in the district and to bring first class art exhibitions into the town.

Stansted Park

Standsted Park Foundation

Rowlands Castle PO9 6DX

02392 412265

www.stanstedpark.co.uk

enquiry@stanstedpark.co.uk

Stansted Park, in the South Downs National Park, is a beautiful Edwardian 'Upstairs-Downstairs' house with an ancient private chapel. Set in the middle of a forest, with spectacular views south over the Solent, enjoy walks through the arboretum and picnics in the grounds.

Sutton Mandeville Heritage Trust

Yew Tree Barn, Sutton Mandeville

Wiltshire SP3 5NE

www.sutton-down-badges.com

info@sutton-down-badges.com

Sutton Mandeville Heritage Trust is seeking to reinstate two regimental badges (Royal Warwickshire Regiment; 7th (City of London) Battalion of the London Regiment) cut into the hillside above Sutton Mandeville in the First World War, to carry out historical research and raise awareness of the military camps in the parish, and to commemorate those lost from the camps and the parish.

Tudor House & Garden

Bugle Street

Southampton SO14 2AD

02380 834563

www.tudorhouseandgarden.com

museums@southampton.gov.uk

TSouthampton's most important historic building, Tudor House reveals over 800 years of history in one fascinating location at the heart of the Old Town. The timber-framed building facing St Michael's Square was built in the late 15th Century, with King John's Palace, an adjacent Norman house accessible from Tudor House Garden, dating back a further 300 years. Tudor House gives a unique and atmospheric insight into the lives and times of both its residents through the years, and of Southampton itself.

Twyford Waterworks Trust

Twyford Waterworks, Hazely Road

Twyford SO21 1QA

01962 714716

www.hants.org.uk/twt

TwyfordWater@aol.com

Twyford Waterworks is a preserved Edwardian water pumping station which provides the complete story of water pumping and supply in the area. It is still also an operational site and the two original wells are in regular use by Southern Water Services to produce some five million gallons of water per day, to supply parts of Eastleigh,

Fairoak, Bitterne, West End and Botley. Exhibits include a variety of engines including steam, diesel, petrol gas and water plus the story of water supply.

Vyne, The - National Trust

Sherborne St John

Basingstoke RG24 9HL

01256 883 858

www.nationaltrust.org.uk/vyne

thevyne@nationaltrust.org.uk

Built in the early 16th century for Lord Sandys, Henry VIII's Lord Chamberlain, the house acquired a classical portico (the first of its kind) in the mid 17th century and contains a fascinating Tudor chapel with Renaissance glass, a Palladian staircase and a wealth of old panelling and fine furniture. Attractive grounds feature herbaceous borders and a wild garden with lawns, lakes and woodland walks.

Westbury Manor Museum

Westbury Manor, 84 West Street

Fareham PO16 0JJ

01329 824 895

www.hants.gov.uk/museum/westbury

julie.biddlecombe@hants.gov.uk

Fareham's local museum tells the story of the borough. Set in a fabulous Georgian building, the museum is right in the heart of Fareham.

Westgate Museum

High Street

Winchester SO23 8ZB

01962 840 222

www.winchester.gov.uk/heritage

museums@winchester.gov.uk

Medieval gateway, positioned close to Winchester's Great Hall, with portcullis slot and early gunports. Interesting graffiti from its use as a debtor's prison from the 16th to the 18th century.

Whitchurch Silk Mill

28 Winchester Street

Whitchurch RG28 7AL

01256 892065

www.whitchurchsilkmill.org.uk

info@whitchurchsilkmill.org.uk

Whitchurch Silk Mill was built on the River Test in Hampshire in 1800, during the reign of King George III. Silk has been woven here since the 1820/1830s.

Collections: Includes Victorian winding, warping and weaving machinery; a working water wheel.

Willis Museum & Sainsbury Gallery, The

Old Town Hall, Market Place
Basingstoke RG21 7QD
01256 465 902
www.hants.gov.uk/willis-museum
musmst@hants.gov.uk

Founded by Mr. Willis, a local watch and clock-maker the Willis Museum looks at the last 200 years of Basingstoke and the surrounding area.

Winchester Cathedral

1 The Close
Winchester SO23 9LS
01962 857200
www.winchester-cathedral.org.uk
cathedral.office@winchester-cathedral.org.uk

Explore more than 1000 years of history in Europe's longest medieval Cathedral. Discover the beautiful illuminated Winchester Bible, Morley Library, 12th-century wall paintings, medieval carvings, contemporary art and the awe and wonder of this magnificent building.

Winchester City Mill - National Trust

Bridge Street
Winchester SO23 0EJ
01962 870057
www.nationaltrust.org.uk/winchester-city-mill
winchestercitymill@nationaltrust.org.uk

This water-powered corn mill was first recorded in the Domesday survey of 1086. Rebuilt in 1744, it remained in use until the turn of the last century and has now been restored to full working order.

Winchester City Museum

The Square
Winchester SO23 9ES
01962 863 064
www.winchester.gov.uk/museums
museums@winchester.gov.uk

New displays bring to life Winchester's nationally important story, using the city's rich archaeological and local history collections. Winchester was a major Roman centre, Venta Belgarum, as shown by the many mosaics on view, and became the principal city of King Alfred and later Anglo-Saxon and Norman kings.

Winchester College Treasury

College Street
Winchester SO23 9NA
01962 621 100
www.winchestercollege.co.uk
information@wincoll.ac.uk

Winchester College is unusual in having its own museum, known as Treasury. It houses the Duberly Collection of Chinese art and the College collection of Greek vases.

Winchester Discovery Centre

Jewry Street
Winchester SO23 8SB
0845 603 5631
www.discoverycentres.co.uk/winchester
winchester.discovery.centre@hants.gov.uk

Winchester Discovery Centre is a new generation of libraries, run by Hampshire County Council. It houses a public library, two galleries, a performance hall, cafe and learning spaces.

Winchester Science Centre & Planetarium

Telegraph Way, Morn Hill
Winchester SO21 1HZ
01962 863791
www.winchestersciencecentre.org
info@winchestersciencecentre.org

Winchester Science Centre is a unique hands-on interactive science and technology centre with 100 exhibits to amuse and enthuse the whole family. At Winchester Science Centre you will understand how to bend light, create your own tornado and vortex, create electronic music and see your body through a heat sensitive camera.

World War One Remembrance Centre

Fort Widley, Portsdown Hill Road
Portsmouth PO6 3LS
023 9279 8751

The new centre has been set up to display artefacts, reproduction exhibits and memorabilia from World War One. We have a memorial centre and a walk through trench system.

Herefordshire

Herefordshire, an inland county on the SE. border of Wales, and bounded N. by Shropshire and Worcestershire, E. by Worcestershire and Gloucestershire, S. by Gloucestershire and Monmouthshire, and W. by Monmouthshire, Radnorshire, and Brecknockshire; greatest length N. and S. 38 miles, greatest breadth E. and W. 35 miles; 532,918 acres, population 121,062. The county is almost circular in form, and its surface shows a series of quiet and beautiful undulations. It is watered by the Wye, Lugg, Monnow, Arrow, and Frome, also the Teme, which flows on the NE. boundary. All these streams are well stocked with fish. Of late agriculture has been greatly improved in the county: the soil peculiarly suitable for the growth of timber, which is very abundant. The pear and apple orchards of Herefordshire are famous; while the luxuriant meadow-land affords pasture for a well-known breed of oxen. Marl and clay form the chief part of the soil; the subsoil is mostly limestone. There are no valuable minerals, and the manufactures are insignificant. The county comprises 11 hundreds, 258 parishes, and parts of 3 others, the parliamentary and municipal borough of Hereford, and the municipal borough of Leominster. It is mostly in the diocese of Hereford.

– John Bartholomew, *Gazetteer of the British Isles* (1887)

Berrington Hall - National Trust

Berrington Hall
Nr Leominster HR6 0DW
01568 615721
www.nationaltrust.org.uk/berrington-hall
berrington@nationaltrust.org.uk

Neo-classical mansion with fine interiors, set in landscaped grounds. Amazing painted ceilings and French Regency furniture.

Brockhampton Estate - National Trust

Greenfields
Bringsty WR6 5TB
01885 482077
www.nationaltrust.org.uk/brockhampton-estate
brockhampton@nationaltrust.org.uk

Romantic medieval moated manor house on Herefordshire / Worcestershire borders. 14th-century great hall with an immense, locally-timbered roof. Lovely crooked gatehouse and ruined Norman chapel.

Bromyard Local History Centre

5 Sherford Street
Bromyard HR7 4DL
01885 488755
www.bromyardhistorysociety.org.uk
bromyard.history@virgin.net

The Local History Centre is the headquarters of the Bromyard and District Local History Society. It houses exhibition space, a shop, research room and archive.

Butcher Row Museum

Burgage Hall, Church Lane
Ledbury HR8 1DW
01531 632040
www.ledburycivicsociety.org/butcherrowhouse.html

Butcher Row House Museum features many items of local interest including reproduction helmets and breastplates that would have been worn in the Battle of Ledbury in 1645 and a small collection of musical instruments ranging from a 'hurdy-gurdy' to a Tibetan pipe fashioned from a thigh bone.

Coningsby Museum & St John's Medieval Museum

Widemarsh Street
Hereford HR4 9HN
http://goo.gl/jgJ6T9

Visit the site of The Blackfriars Monastery, which was a Dominican Monastery home of crusaders of the Order of St John and an ex-serviceman's hospital, now within an attractive rose garden. See the stone Preaching Cross set within the garden, one of the last surviving examples of such a cross. Learn about the foundation of the Coningsby Red Coat Hospital, probably the model for The Chelsea Hospital in London. Explore the Museum, which explains the links between the Crusades, the Knights Templar and The Hospitaller Knights. Visitors can view the 13th century chapel, which is still in use today by the Order of St John. The remains of Blackfriars monastery are directly beside the museum.

Croft Castle & Parkland - National Trust

Croft
Leominster HR6 9PW
www.nationaltrust.org.uk/croft-castle
croftcastle@nationaltrust.org.uk

Home of the Croft family for nearly 1,000 years Croft Castle, a place of power, politics and pleasure, nestles in peaceful Herefordshire countryside at the heart of a 607-hectare (1,500-acre) estate of woodlands, farm and parkland. Explore the miles of woodland trails, learn about the family who have made Croft so special.

Eastnor Castle

Eastnor
Ledbury HR8 1RL
01531 633160
www.eastnorcastle.com
enquiries@eastnorcastle.com

Eastnor Castle, in the dramatic setting of the Malvern Hills and surrounded by a deer park, arboretum and lake, is home to the Hervey-Bathurst family. Although built in the Norman style, the castle dates from 1820 when it was built by Earl Somers to demonstrate his political importance and status.

Goodrich Castle - English Heritage

Goodrich HR9 6HY
01600 890538
www.english-heritage.org.uk/visit/places/goodrich-castle

Goodrich stands majestically on a wooded hill commanding the passage of the River Wye into the picturesque valley of Symonds Yat. The castle was begun in the late 11th century, by the English thegn Godric who gave it his name. Goodrich boasts one of the most complete sets of medieval domestic buildings surviving in any English castle.

Grange Court

Pinsley Road
Leominster HR6 8NL
01568 737980
www.grangecourt.org
info@grangecourt.org

Grange Court is a timber framed market house built by John Abel in 1633. It is unique in its design, structure and decoration, giving it a Grade II* Listed status. The building has an eclectic history and its stories are told through interactive interpretation and an innovative Tablet Tour.

Hampton Court Castle

Hampton Court Estate, Hope-Under-Dinmore
Leominster HR6 0PN
01568 797676
www.hamptoncourt.org.uk
ticketoffice@hamptoncourt.org.uk

Welcome to our 15th century medieval castle, award winning gardens and parkland with 1,000 acres of imagination where events take place all season.

Hellens Manor

Much Marcle
Ledbury HR8 2LY
01531 660504
www.hellensmanor.com
info@hellensmanor.com

The site of Hellens has been occupied for nearly a thousand years. A 13th century Tudor/Jacobean manor in pleasant grounds.

Collections: Among paintings of interest here are the Laughing Girl by Reynolds, Lord Whartons's portraits, a fine Van Dyke portrait of Endymion Porter, Charles I's art expert and several good specimens of 17th century woodwork. The Cordova Room contains a simple, balanced and beautifully carved fireplace and the Spanish 17th century leader hangings.

Hereford Cathedral - Mappa Mundi & Chained Library Exhibition

Hereford Cathedral, 5 College Closters, Cathedral Close
Hereford HR1 2NG
01432 374209
www.herefordcathedral.org
exhibition@herefordcathedral.org

Hereford's famous medieval map of the world is displayed alongside the unique Chained Library, with the oldest book dating form the eighth century. Interpretive exhibition featuring original artefacts, models and interactive technology.

Hereford Cider Museum

21 Ryelands Street
Hereford HR4 0EF
01432 354207
www.cidermuseum.co.uk
enquiries@cidermuseum.co.uk

The extensive collection includes cider mills, presses, bottles, old photographs, watercolours, advertising memorabilia and a rare collection of English lead crystal cider flutes. The Archive of Cider Pomology (www.ArchiveOfCiderPomology.co.uk) is sponsored by the National Association of Cider Makers and provides a central depository for documents, books, images, maps and oral histories.

Hereford Museum & Art Gallery

Broad Street
Hereford HR4 9AU
01432 260692
https://www.herefordshire.gov.uk/museums
herefordmuseums@herefordshire.gov.uk

Hereford Museum and Art Gallery, housed in a spectacular Victorian gothic building, has been exhibiting artefacts and works of fine and decorative art connected with the local area since 1874. Although the exterior of the building has changed very little the museum and gallery have kept up with the times.

Collections: The collections are relevant to life in Herefordshire and include nationally important costume and textiles as well as an important collection of fine and decorative art. Although display space is limited there is access to the collections through the museum Store and Resource Centre at Friar Street.

Herefordshire Archive Service

Herefordshire Record Office, Harold Street
Hereford HR1 2QX
01432 260750
www.herefordshire.gov.uk/archives/

Herefordshire Record Office houses archives for the county of Herefordshire, the city of Hereford, the diocese of Hereford, as well as other local bodies and individuals.

Herefordshire Family History Society

17 Whittern Way, Tupsley
Hereford HR1 1PE
01981 250974
www.herefordshirefhs.org.uk

The Herefordshire Family History Society helps and encourages everyone interested in genealogy and family history in the county and Diocese of Hereford.

Herefordshire Museums Service

Museum Resource and Learning Centre, 58 Friar Street
Hereford HR4 0AS
01432 260692
https://www.herefordshire.gov.uk/museums

Herefordshire Museums Service operates five sites across Herefordshire, plus a roving Museum on the Move. They also support independent museums throughout the county via our museum development officer. Admission to all of our sites is free, but small charges may apply for some services and special events.

Kingston Museum

Mill Street
Kington HR5 3AL
01544 231486
www.kingtonmuseum.co.uk
info@kingtonmuseum.co.uk

The museum was opened in June 1986, and is housed in what were the stables of the King's Head Inn that was demolished in 1885, although it has had a somewhat chequered history since that time. Please note the museum is only opened between April and September.

Ledbury Heritage Centre

Church Lane
Ledbury HR8 1DN
01432 260692
aclark@herefordshire.gov.uk

This half-timbered building used to be the grammar school for Ledbury from the 16th century through to the early 19th. The low beams and smoke bay are typical of the timber-framing style and a small part of the wattle and daub has been uncovered to show this simple but effective method of construction.

Collections: The displays trace the history and development of Ledbury through photographs, illustrations and a computer slideshow as well as exploring the literary history of the town. John Masefield and Elizabeth Barrett-Browning both lived in this most picturesque of market towns and the fascinating Edna Lyall has connections with the nearby village of Bosbury.

Leominster Folk Museum

Etnam Street
Leominster HR6 8AQ
01568 615186
www.leominster.co.uk/leominster-museum.htm

Leominster Folk Museum in Etnam Street, Leominster, has collections of many artefacts that illustrate local life. The museum also has on display a burial from the Bronze Age, and a collection of early postage marks and stamps of Leominster. Since opening in 1972 the museum has purchased a Victorian stable which had belonged to the house next door. An extension has also been built to house a complete cider mill which was bequeathed to the museum.

Leominster Museum

Etnam Street
Leominster HR6 8AN
01885 483634
www.leominstermuseum.org.uk
deborah@leominstermuseum.org.uk

Small accredited museum covering the history of the ancient town of Leominster and its surrounding villages. Entirely volunteer run; closed during the winter months.

Mortimers Cross Mill

Mortimers Cross
Nr Aymestrey HR6 9PE
01568 708820

A rare one-man-operated 18th-century water mill in part working order. Nearby there are attractive gardens and woodland walks, a stone weir and the significant Aymestrey Limestone Quarry.

Old House

High Town
Hereford HR1 2AA
01432 260694
jhodges@herefordshire.gov.uk

The Old House is a wonderfully-preserved example of a Jacobean half-timbered building – a startling sight in the middle of a modern shopping precinct in the heart of Hereford. Built in 1621 as part of Butchers' Row, this only remaining house has been has been home to butchers, ironmongers and bankers over the years, but since 1929 has been a fascinating museum giving an insight into daily life in Jacobean times.

Violette Szabo GC Museum

Cartref
Wormelow HR2 8HN
01981 540477
www.violette-szabo-museum.co.uk

The Violette Szabo Museum opened its doors in June 2000 and was the brain child of Rosemary Rigby MBE who was Violette's aunt. Many years of fundraising and collecting artefacts from people who knew Violette or served with her during the war came to fruition on that day in June. The story and life of Violette Szabo is much in evidence at the museum along with life stories of the many resistance workers who sacrificed their lives for our freedom. Visitors can learn about Ravensbruck, the concentration Camp that Violette and many of her compatriots were sent to following their capture.

Waterworks Museum

Broomy Hill
Hereford HR4 0JS
01432 344062
www.waterworksmuseum.org.uk

The museum traces the history of drinking water from the cave-dwellers up to the present day through wonderful working engines, superb display panels, illuminated displays, guidebooks and films. Classified by English Heritage as 'a site of clear national importance", the museum is home to the oldest working triple-expansion steam engine in the UK and probably has the widest range of working pumping engines.

Weobley Museum

Back Lane
Weobley HR4 8SG
01544 340292

Our museum is very small but we hold a wide variety of artefacts and documents relating to the Weobley area. We like to show as much of our material as we can in the space available, and we change our displays each year.

Hertfordshire

Hertfordshire (or Herts), an inland county in SE. of England, bounded N. by Cambridgeshire, E. by Essex, S. by Middlesex, W. by Bucks, and NW. by Bedfordshire; greatest length, NE. and SW., 35 miles; greatest breadth, E. and W., 26 miles: 465,141 acres, population 203,069. In appearance the county is hilly, but interspersed with fine pasture lands, arable farms, and picturesque parks and woods. The Lea, the Colne, and the Ivel are the principal rivers; the Grand Junction Canal likewise passes through a part of the county. A large number of the inhabitants are employed in husbandry, and in addition to grain of choice quality, hay, vegetables, and numerous fruits and flowers are extensively cultivated, especially for the London market. The greater portion of the commerce of the county is supported by the trade in corn and malt. Manufactures are few; paper-making, silk-weaving, and straw-plaiting being the principal industries. Railways penetrate to all parts of the county; no place is at a greater distance than 5 miles from a station. Geologically the greater part of Herts consists of Lower, Middle, and Upper Chalk; in the S. is the London clay. The minerals are of no commercial importance. Herts comprises 8 hundreds, 138 parishes, and parts of 3 others, and the municipal boroughs of Hertford and St Albans. It is almost entirely in the diocese of St Albans.

– John Bartholomew, *Gazetteer of the British Isles* (1887)

Airfield Research Group

9 Milton Road
Ware
www.airfieldinformationexchange.org.uk
wjt@pawnee.co.uk

The airfield Research Group is dedicated to the dissemination of material on the history, architecture, development, current status and use of military, civil and private airfields throughout the United Kingdom.

Apsley Paper Trail

Frogmore Mill, Fourdrinier Way, Apsley, and, Apsley Mills Cottage, London Road, Apsley
Hemel Hempstead HP3 9RY
01442 234600
www.thepapertrail.org.uk
visitors@thepapertrail.org.uk

The world of paper - from its industrial beginnings to its sustainable future. The Paper Trail project is a unique activity-based industrial sustainability 'exploration' centre built around the two sites – Frogmore Mill and Apsley Mills – that were the birthplace of paper's industrial revolution 200 years ago.

Ashridge Estate - National Trust

Ashridge Estate Visitor Centre, Moneybury Hill
Berkhamsted HP4 1LX
01494 755557
www.nationaltrust.org.uk/ashridge-estate
ashridge@nationaltrust.org.uk

Vast swathe of beautiful woodlands and chalk downland at the north end of the Chiltern Hills. Super panoramas from Ivinghoe Beacon and the Duke of Bridgewater Monument. Historical remains from Iron Age to Victorian era.

Ashwell Village Museum

Swan Street, Ashwell
Baldock SG7 5NY
01462 742956
www.ashwellmuseum.org.uk
enquiries@ashwellmuseum.org.uk

Ashwell Museum is full of the everyday objects of life in the village and the surrounding countryside from the Stone Age to the present day. The collection has grown over the years and is still growing through the generosity of many people.

Barnet Museum

31 Wood Street
Barnet EN5 4BE
020 8440 8066
www.barnetmuseum.co.uk

Barnet Museum was opened in March 1938 at 31 Wood Street, to house the collection of the Barnet & District Local History Society . Its building is an attractive early Georgian house in the heart of Chipping Barnet.

Berkhamsted School

Castle Street
Berkhamsted HP4 2BB
www.berkhamstedschool.org

The Archive and Historic Collection of Berkhamsted School preserves and makes available for research and enquiry a permanent establishment of records, memorabilia and artefacts relating to the history of Berkhamsted School (Boys and Girls).

Bishop's Stortford Museum

South Road
Bishop's Stortford CM23 3JG
01279 651746
www.rhodesbishopsstortford.org.uk
museum@rhodesbishopsstortford.org.uk

The Bishop's Stortford Museum was created in 2002 following the merger of the Rhodes Memorial Museum and the Bishop's Stortford Local History Museum. The museum has collections relating to local history, archaeology, Cecil Rhodes and Southern Africa.

Collections: The Rhodes collection includes photographs, portraits, models, costumes, furniture and a selection of ethnographic objects. Exhibits illustrate African cultural traditions from basketry and beadwork to wood carving and weaponry. The major local history archive is that of Sir Walter Gilbey, and contains personal correspondence, documents of the W & A Gilbey Wine Co and the family connections.

British Schools Museum

British Schools Museum, Queen Street
Hitchin SG4 9TS
01462 420144
www.britishschoolsmuseum.org.uk
admin@hitchinbritishschools.org.uk

Today the British Schools Museum celebrates the history of elementary education in Britain from 1798 to the 1960s. The listed buildings include the only surviving Lancasterian School-room (1837) where ONE master taught 300 boys, and the Galleried Classroom (1853) for 110 boys.

Collections: The museum houses the Jill Grey Collection of Childhood and Educational Material. Around 35,000 items

related to education of children from the 17th century collected by Hitchin resident Jill Grey (one-time personal assistant to Frank Whittle).

Bushey Museum & Art Gallery

Rudolph Road
Bushey WD23 3HW
020 8420 4057
www.busheymuseum.org

The museum tells the story of Bushey and its unique artistic history. It has a large collection of works and articles relating to Sir Hubert von Herkomer RA and his world-renowned Art School.

Clock Tower

Market Place
St Albans AL3 5DR
01727 751810
www.stalbansmuseums.org.uk

Built between 1403 and 1412 and is the only medieval town belfry in England. Its fine bell has also survived almost 600 years of use.

Dacorum Heritage Trust

The Museum Store, Clarence Road
Berkhamsted HP4 3YL
01442 879525
www.dacorumheritage.org.uk
curator@dacorumheritage.org.uk

The Dacorum Heritage Trust is the Accredited museum organisation for the borough of Dacorum, based at the museum Store in Clarence Road, Berkhamsted. The museum Store is the home of over 100,000 objects relating to the surrounding areas, including Berkhamsted, Bovingdon, Chipperfield, Flamstead, Hemel Hempstead, Kings Langley, Markyate and Tring.

de Havilland Aircraft Heritage Centre - incorporating the Mosquito Aircraft Museum

de Havilland Aircraft Heritage Centre, Salisbury Hall
London Colney AL2 1BU
01727 822051
www.dehavillandmuseum.co.uk
museum@dehavillandmuseum.co.uk

Welcome to the oldest aviation museum in the UK dedicated to the preservation and display of de Havilland Aircraft. The de Havilland Aircraft Company played an important role in the history of aircraft development in 20th century Britain. We are a 'working museum' where we actively restore de Havilland Aircraft so you are likely to see our volunteers at work, who are always willing to answer your questions.

Forge Museum & Victorian Cottage Garden, The

🏛 £

The Forge, High Street
Much Hadham SG10 6BS
01279 843 301
hadham.museum@btinternet.com

The Forge Museum is set in an attractive Grade II* listed building situated in the picturesque village of Much Hadham. Originally a farmhouse of Moor Place, the earlier parts of the building date from the 15th century, Horseshoe Cottage and Forge Cottage date from the 16th century. The forge and bellows room are part of a 17th century barn conversion, and in 1811 the shoeing room and blacksmith's shop were added when Frederick Page moved in.

Hatfield House

🏛 £

Hatfield Park
Hatfield AL9 5NQ
01707 287010
www.hatfield-house.co.uk
visitors@hatfield-house.co.uk

Hatfield House is the home of the 7th Marquess and Marchioness of Salisbury and their family. The estate has been in the Cecil family for 400 years. We hold documents and collections of local, national and international significance. Our primary aim is to preserve the papers in our care for the benefit of future generations. The collection is used by the owner and managers of the estate but the records are also made available to suitably qualified researchers.

Hertford Museum

🏛 ✉ ★

18 Bull Plain
Hertford SG14 1DT
01992 582686
www.hertfordmuseum.org
hertfordmuseum@btconnect.com

The museum is located in a 17th century town house with an attractive Jacobean style garden.

Collections: Extensive collections from Hertford, Hertfordshire and beyond. Local archaeology, social history, photographs, paintings and prints, plus ethnographic collection and Hertfordshire regiment collection.

Hertfordshire Archives & Local Studies - HALS

🏛 ★

Hertfordshire Archives and Local Studies (HALS), Hertfordshire County Council, CHR002, County Hall, Pegs Lane
Hertford SG13 8EJ
0300 1234 049
www.hertsdirect.org/hals
hertsdirect@hertscc.gov.uk

Hertfordshire Archives & Local Studies (HALS) is the specialist centre of information on the local history of Hertfordshire, covering many aspects of life in the county including the people, the environment, the geography and history etc. Based at County Hall in Hertford, HALS comprises the former Hertfordshire Record Office and the county Local Studies Library, and offers an integrated service providing archives and local studies material, including over 6000 archive collections, 30,000 books, 30,000 images, 10,000 maps, and 200 newspaper and periodical titles.

Hertfordshire Family History Society

👥

30 Blenheim Way
Stevenage SG2 8TE
01438 216785
www.hertsfhs.org.uk
secretary@hertsfhs.org.uk

The society was founded in 1977 and is a member of the Federation of Family History Societies and also a registered charity with a brief to educate and inform the public about genealogy with its focus on the county of Hertfordshire in the United Kingdom.

Hertfordshire Fire Brigade Museum

✉ 🏛 ★

Fire Station, Lower High Street
Watford WD17 2AG
01923 232297
www.watfordmuseum.org.uk/firemuseum
firemuseum@watfordmuseum.org.uk

The museum is based in a purpose-built building at the new Fire Station, Lower High Street, Watford, opened in November 2009. We have a substantial collection of various items of fire service equipment, uniform and documents, old and new, along with a large and varied photographic display of fire appliances, fire/incident scenes and local fire history.

International Garden Cities Exhibition

✉ ★

296 Norton Way South
Letchworth Garden City SG6 1SU
01462 482710
www.letchworthgc.com/first_garden_city
fgchm@letchworth.com

The International Garden Cities Exhibition charts the history of the Garden City Movement, the founding of Letchworth Garden City and the key principles which shaped it, and its influence around the world. Ebenezer Howard, founder of Letchworth Garden City, had a vision that would end the poverty and slums suffered by so many in the late Victorian era.

Knebworth House, Gardens & Park

Estate Office
Knebworth SG1 2AX
01438 812661
www.knebworthhouse.com
info@knebworthhouse.com

The romantic exterior of Knebworth House with its turrets, domes and gargoyles silhouetted against the sky does little to prepare the visitor for what to expect inside. The House has stood for many years longer than the Victorian decoration suggests and the stucco hides from view a red brick house dating back to the Tudor times. Every generation of the Lytton family has left something of its style and taste, making Knebworth an extraordinary walk through 500 years of British history.

Letchworth & District Family History Group

60 Woodland Rise
Welwyn Garden City AL8 7LF
www.ldfhg.org.uk
secretary@ldfhg.org.uk

LDFHG is a group of amateur family historians from in and around Letchworth, most of whom are looking for ancestors further afield than Hertfordshire.

Letchworth Museum & Art Gallery

Broadway
Letchworth Garden City SG6 3PF
01462 685647
letchworth.museum@north-herts.gov.uk

Letchworth Museum & Art Gallery occupies an attractive Edwardian building facing Broadway Gardens, in the centre of Letchworth, beside the Library. The museum has four main galleries.

Lincolnsfields Children's Centre

Bushey Hall Drive
Bushey WD23 2ES
01923 233 841
www.lincolnsfields.co.uk
info@lincolnsfields.co.uk

The Lincolnsfields Children's Centre is located on what was originally the site of Bushey Hall - the wartime location of the USAAF 8th Fighter Command Headquarters - a unique WW2 heritage site. We stage regular historical events within the grounds using the remaining twelve WW2 buildings. Our 1940s house is open on on selected Sundays.

Lowewood Museum

High Street
Hoddesdon EN11 8BH
01992 445 596
museum.leisure@broxbourne.gov.uk

Lowewood Museum is situated in a listed Georgian building and houses an impressive collection of photographs and memorabilia depicting town life in the 19th century, all contributed by the local community. The museum also provides a free identification service, to inform residents about any unusual item they might own.

Mill Green Museum & Mill

Mill Green
Hatfield AL9 5PD
01707 271362
www.welhat.gov.uk/museum
museum@welhat.gov.uk

A local history museum for the Welwyn Hatfield District, housed in the former Miller's House dating back to the 16th century. Three galleries housing local artefacts or temporary exhibitions.

Museum of St Albans

Hatfield Road
St Albans AL1 3RR
01727 819340
www.stalbansmuseums.org.uk
d.broom@stalbans.gov.uk

The story of historic St Albans from the departure of the Romans to the present day. There is an ever changing special exhibitions programme and a small wildlife garden and pond to explore.

Collections: With special Saxon & Medieval galleries. Home to the famous Salaman Collection of trade and craft tools.

Museum of Technology The Great War & WWII

81 High Street
Hemel Hempstead HP1 3AH
01442 262541
www.museumoftechnology.org.uk

The museum of Technology The Great War & WW11 incorporates a very small period in history, in which the technological revolution took place. All the items on display represent the evolution of electrical, electronic, and warfare advances around 1850 - 1980.

Natural History Museum at Tring

Akeman Street
Tring HP23 6AP
020 7942 6171
www.nhm.ac.uk/tring
tring-enquiries@nhm.ac.uk

Discover the fascinating range of animals collected by Lionel Walter Rothschild in our beautiful Victorian Museum. It is home to the world-class research and collections of the Natural History Museum's Bird Group.

North Hertfordshire Museum

Paynes Park
Hitchin SG5 1EH
01462 434476
www.northhertsmuseum.org

North Herts Museum is a completely new museum opening in 2015, amalgamating the collections of the previous Hitchin and Letchworth Museums, as well as displaying material relating to North Hertfordshire which has never before been shown. The museum illustrates life in the area from prehistory to the present day, with thousands of fascinating objects.

Potters Bar Museum

Wyllyotts Centre, Darkes Lane
Potters Bar EN6 2HN
01707 645005

Opened in 1990, the museum is managed and run by volunteers who are members of Potters Bar and District Historical Society. Situated opposite the timber-framed building of what remains of the medieval manor of Wyllyotts, the displays interpret the long history of Potters Bar and its district. Artefacts from archaeological excavations in the area are on display, including medieval finds from Wyllyotts Manor itself, South Mimms motte-and-bailey castle and finds from a Roman tile kiln.

Royston & District Family History Society

60 Beldam Avenue
Royston SG8 9UW
www.roystonfhs.org.uk
membership@roystonfhs.org.uk

Royston and District Family History Society is based in Royston, a market town in Hertfordshire, and serves the district around it which also covers parts of Cambridgeshire and Essex.

Royston & District Museum

Lower King Street
Royston SG8 5AL
01763 242587
www.roystonmuseum.org.uk

Royston is a small market town which grew up at the point where two ancient roads cross—the Icknield Way and Ermine Street. Its history is reflected in the Royston Tapestry at the museum, a project initiated in 1992 by previous curator Jane Vincent and depicting scenes from the town's past.

Runnymede Collection at Middlesex University, The

Middlesex University, Cat Hill
Barnet EN4 8HT
0208 411 6686
j.vaknin@mdx.ac.uk

The Runnymede Collection at Middlesex University is a unique resource for the study of the history of race relations in Britain since the 1960s. It is a specialist collection of books, pamphlets, documents, journals and press cuttings on the development of multiculturalism and cultural diversity.

Rye House Gatehouse

Rye House Quay, Rye Road
Hoddesdon EN11 0EH
08456 770 600
www.leevalleypark.org.uk/gardensandheritage
info@leevalleypark.org.uk

Rye House Gatehouse was one of the first brick built buildings in the country. The house formed the hub of what was a large estate for its time.

Shaw's Corner - National Trust

Ayot St Lawrence
Welwyn AL6 9BX
01438 820307
www.nationaltrust.org.uk/shaws-corner
shawscorner@nationaltrust.org.uk

An Edwardian villa, the home of George Bernard Shaw from 1906 till his death in 1950. A large red-brick detached house, Shaw's Corner was built in 1902 as the New Rectory for Ayot St Lawrence.

Sopwell Nunnery

off Cottonmill Lane, St Albans
St Albans
01727 751810
www.stalbansmuseums.org.uk

Ruins of a Tudor manor house, on the site of a 21st century nunnery.

Speedway Museum

Paradise Wild Life Park, White Stubbs Lane
Broxbourne EN10 7QA
01992 469555
www.speedwaymuseum.co.uk
speedwaymuseum@pwpark.com

The museum offers an insight into the history of speedway racing - the technical developments of the racing machines, the personalities and riders involved with the sport over the years.

St Albans & Hertfordshire Architectural & Archaeological Society

SAHAAS Library, c/o Tourist Information Centre, The Town Hall, Market Place
St Albans AL3 5DJ
www.stalbanshistory.org
ww1mt@stalbanshistory.org

Our society was formed in 1845 to research the archaeology, architectural & local history of St Albans in particular and Hertfordshire in general.

St Albans Cathedral

Cathedral and Abbey Church of St Alban, Sumpter Yard
St Albans AL1 1BY
01727 860780
www.stalbanscathedral.org
mail@stalbanscathedral.org

The Cathedral and Abbey Church of Saint Alban is the seat of the Bishop of St Albans and serves the Diocese of St Albans in the counties of Hertfordshire, Bedfordshire, the Borough of Luton and the London Borough of Barnet. The Cathedral is also a parish church with a large and active congregation.

St Albans Organ Theatre

St Albans Organ Museum, 320 Camp Road
St Albans AL1 5PE
01727 873 896
www.stalbansorgantheatre.org.uk

info@stalbansorgantheatre.org.uk

Remember the good old days? That magical musical atmosphere that has been lost and forgotten in today's digital age. See and hear the fascinating world of mechanical musical instruments at St Albans Organ Theatre. The Theatre is open to the public every Sunday from 2.15pm till 4.30pm during which time there is a live, continuous musical performance of the various instruments, given with a descriptive commentary.

Collections: The museum currently has two theatre organs, four cafe organs worked by punch-card and numerous other instruments including music boxes and a self playing violin.

St Albans Signal Box Preservation Trust

Ridgmont Road
St Albans AL1 3AJ
www.sigbox.co.uk

This is a Midland Railway signal box, erected June 1892, and abandoned by British Railways 1980. Taken on by the Preservation Trust in 2006, it was restored by late 2008, and opened regularly to the public from 2009 onwards. It is the largest preserved Midland Railway signal box in England, and the only one preserved where it originally worked.

Stevenage Museum

St Georges Way
Stevenage SG1 1XX
01438 218881
www.stevenage.gov.uk/about-stevenage/museum
museum@stevenage.gov.uk

Stevenage Museum is a lively community service working with local people and groups to present a full programme of projects, exhibitions and events. Our permanent displays show life in the town from pre-history to the present day.

Tower Museum Bassingbourn

Hangar #3, Bassingbourn Barracks
Royston SG8 5LX
01763 243 500
www.towermuseumbassingbourn.co.uk
towermuseum.121@btinternet.com

The Tower Museum Bassingbourn is housed in the original control tower that dates back to the 1930s when the airbase was constructed. One of the first museums in the country to be housed in an original control tower, the museum opened in 1974; its aim to educate visitors in the history of this world famous base when the RAF and the USAAF were stationed here.

Verulamium Museum

St Michaels
St Albans AL3 4SW
01727 751810
www.stalbansmuseums.org.uk/verulamium
a.coles@stalbans.gov.uk

Verulamium is the award winning museum of everyday life
in Roman Britain. It is on the site of one of the major cities
in Roman Britain set in attractive parkland and near
Roman theatre, walls and hypocaust. There is a new Iron
Age gallery, recreated Roman rooms, discovery areas and
some of the best mosaics outside the Mediterranean.

Ware Museum

Priory Lodge, 89 High Street
Ware SG12 9AL
01920 487 848
www.waremuseum.org.uk

The small museum that brought the Great Bed of Ware home.
The Bed has now returned to the V&A but you can still touch
and feel our full sized replica of one of the bedposts.

Collections: Permanent displays show a timeline of Ware's
Social, Industrial and Archaeological History from
pre-historic times to the Second World War. New displays
on Malting and a Hitch Brick 'window'. The mediaeval well
discovered within the museum grounds is now
incorporated in the new gallery. World War 2 bunker with
interactive display.

Watford Museum

194 Lower High Street
Watford WD17 2DG
01923 232297
www.watfordmuseum.org.uk
info@watfordmuseum.org.uk

Telling the story of Watford past and present, Watford
Museum is housed in the former Benskins Brewery
Mansion. The museum has displays of local history and
industry, including Watford Football Club memorabilia
and the Cassiobury Collection of fine art.

Welwyn Roman Baths

Welwyn Bypass
Welwyn AL6 9HT
01707 271362
www.welhat.gov.uk/museum
c.rawle@welhat.gov.uk

Tunnel through time to the world of the Romans with a
visit to Welwyn Roman Baths. Discover the secrets of the
past in a steel vault deep under the A1(M) motorway,
where you can find the unique remains of a once-luxurious
bathing suite.

Isle of Wight

Wight, Isle of, in the English Channel, and in the county of Hants [until 1890], from which it is separated by Spithead and the Solent; greatest length, E. and W., from Bembridge Point to the Needles, 23 miles; greatest breadth, N. and S., from Cowes to St Catherine's Point, 13 miles; area, 93,341 acres, population 73,633. From E. to W. the island is divided into two parts by a range of downs, which form excellent sheep walks; the northern part is wooded, and the soil is generally a stiff cold clay, while the southern part has far less timber, and the soil is a fertile sandy loam. From S. to N., again, the island is divided by the river Medina into 2 liberties of nearly equal extent, called respectively East Medina and West Medina, the former comprising 14 and the latter 16 parishes. The Isle of Wight was invaded, A.D. 43, by the Romans, who retained possession of it till 530, when it was reduced by Cedric the Saxon. The Conqueror conferred on William Fitz-Osborne the lordship of the island, which continued to be governed by its independent lords till 1293, when the regalities were purchased by Edward I. Since that time it has been governed by wardens, appointed by the Crown, but the office has now become honorary. Cement is manufactured, and largely exported. The mildness of the climate (especially in the district known as the Undercliff), and the beauty of the scenery, have made the Isle of Wight a great resort of invalids, and a favourite place of residence. Newport is the chief town, Cowes is the principal port, and Ryde and Cowes are important yachting centres. The other places of note are Bembridge, Brading, Fresh-water, Sandown, Shanklin, Ventnor, and Yarmouth. The most interesting antiquities are Carisbrooke Castle and the remains of Quarr Abbey. Osborne is a royal residence.

– John Bartholomew, *Gazetteer of the British Isles* (1887)

Appuldurcombe House - English Heritage

Isle of Wight PO38 3EW

01983 852484

http://goo.gl/eejnbz

The shell of Appuldurcombe, once the grandest house on the Isle of Wight and still an important example of English baroque architecture: the 1701 south front has now been restored. It stands in 'Capability' Brown-designed grounds.

Bembridge Windmill - National Trust

High Street

Bembridge PO35 5SQ

01983 873945

www.nationaltrust.org.uk/bembridge-windmill

bembridgemill@nationaltrust.org.uk

This grade I listed building is the only surviving windmill on the Isle of Wight, and is one of its best known landmarks. Built around 1700, its original machinery is still intact.

Brading Roman Villa

Morton Old Road

Brading PO36 0EN

01983 406223

www.bradingromanvilla.org.uk

anthony@bradingromanvilla.org.uk

Brading Villa is an unusual maritime villa sited at the eastern end of the Isle of Wight.

Carisbrooke Castle - English Heritage

Newport PO30 1XY

01983 522107

www.english-heritage.org.uk/visit/places/carisbrooke-castle

Visit Carisbrooke Castle and enjoy over 800 years of history. The Isle of Wight's royal castle is remarkably complete, with battlements to march across, a keep to climb and a museum to explore. Discover why it was famous as a royal prison to Charles I; see the room from which he tried to escape – twice.

Carisbrooke Castle Museum

Carisbrooke Castle

Newport PO30 1XY

01983 523112

www.historicimages.co.uk

info@carisbrookecastlemuseum.org.uk

The museum was founded by Princess Beatrice in 1898 in memory of her husband, Henry, as a museum of Isle of Wight history. It is an independent charitable trust which occupies the former great hall and Governor's residence at Carisbrooke Castle.

Collections: Material on the history of Carisbrooke Castle, including excavated items, and objects and documents relating to King Charles I's imprisonment Local and social history material (now restricted to post-1500) Topographical pictures.

Classic Boat Museum, The

The Classic Boat Museum, The Quay, Newport Harbour
Newport PO30 2EF
01983 533493
www.classicboatmuseum.org
cbmiow@hotmail.com

This collection of classic boats started in 1976 with the purchase of the river launch Flying Spray., but really began to progress with the arrival of the first racing yacht, the Dragon, Mistress, in 1988. Displays include photographs, films, tools, artefacts, models, books and many other items associated with the history of boating and associated industry in the Solent, over the past century. The museum is spread over two sites - the boat collection can be found in Albany Road and other archives and photographic collections can be seen in the Gallery, on Colombine Road, East Cowes PO32 6AA.

Cowes Maritime Museum

Cowes Library, Beckford Road
Cowes PO31 7SG
01983 293394
museums@iow.gov.uk

The museum has a small exhibition area that introduces the rich maritime history of Cowes. The museum has an off site archive of photographs and plans depicting yachting and the shipbuilding industry in Cowes; please make an appointment to view. The museum is situated within Cowes Library, which also houses a collection of maritime related books.

Dimbola Museum & Galleries

Dimbola Lodge, Terrace Lane
Freshwater Bay PO40 9QE
01983 756814
www.dimbola.co.uk
administrator@dimbola.co.uk

Dimbola Museum and Galleries is housed within the former home of Julia Margaret Cameron, the noted Victorian portrait photographer. Dimbola is not only where Cameron began and carried out most of her acclaimed work, but was also a centre of Victorian culture.

Dinosaur Isle

Culver Parade
Sandown PO36 8QA
01983 404344
www.dinosaurisle.com

Discover, Experience and Encounter – Dinosaur Isle is the first purpose built dinosaur attraction in the country where a walk back through geological time takes you to the lost world of the dinosaurs a 120 million years ago. Discover the skeletal remains as they are found by fossil hunters, encounter our palaeontologists working on the latest finds, experience the sounds and smells the dinosaurs may have encountered.

Historic Ryde Society

Ryde District Heritage Centre, Royal Victoria Arcade, Union Street
Ryde PO33 2LQ
01983 717435
www.historicrydesociety.co.uk
Admin@historicrydesociety.com

Ryde District Heritage Centre has been created and is run by Historic Ryde Society volunteers. Its aim is to 'Give Ryde's past to the future'.

Isle of Wight Archaeology & Historic Environment Service

61 Clatterford Road
Newport PO30 1NZ
01983 529963

Safeguarding the future of our Island's past, the Isle of Wight County Archaeology and Historic Environment Service is based in the old infants' school in Clatterford Road, Carisbrooke.

Isle of Wight Bus & Coach Museum

Newport Quay
Newport PO30 2EF
01983 533352
www.iowbusmuseum.org.uk
info@iowbusmuseum.org.uk

The Isle of Wight Bus & Coach Museum was established in 1997 and contains an impressive display of vintage buses and coaches, collected to show the Island's transport heritage. The buses are housed in a former grain storage warehouse, on Newport Quay. They range from a 1889 tram car and a 1927 Daimler, to more recent vehicles.

Isle of Wight Family History Society

13 Britannia Way
East Cowes PO32 6DG
01983 289 599
www.isle-of-wight-fhs.co.uk
val.luter@talktalk.net

Members include people with island ancestry who live on the UK mainland or elsewhere in the world as well as those who live on the Isle of Wight but whose families came from elsewhere.

Isle of Wight Record Office

26 Hillside
Newport PO30 2EB
01983 823820

The Record Office preserves historical documents relating to the Isle of Wight and makes them available to the public for research. Our material spans the 12th - 21st centuries, and includes records of parish churches, estates, families, businesses, schools and local government.

Isle of Wight Shipwreck Centre & Maritime Museum, The

Arreton Barns Craft Village,
Arreton PO30 3AA
01983 533079
www.iowight.com/shipwrecks

The Shipwreck and Maritime Museum was founded in 1978, and had been an ambition of the owner, Martin Woodward, since he first started diving on shipwrecks in the 1960s. Martin, a professional diver by trade, has amassed a huge collection of artefacts personally recovered by him from under the sea, and he is still actively diving on wrecks and archaeological projects worldwide.

Isle of Wight Steam Railway

The Railway Station, Havenstreet
Ryde PO33 4DS
01983 882204
www.iwsteamrailway.co.uk
info@iwsteamrailway.co.uk

For the family and casual visitor, we offer a unique and exciting day out, as you step back to a bygone era when steam power was the order of the day. We are one of Britain's Heritage Railways and a registered educational charity, but we're also much more besides.

Museum of Island History

The Guildhall, High Street
Newport PO30 1TY
01983 823366
www.iow.gov.uk/council/departments/museums
museums@iow.gov.uk

A museum presenting the story of the Isle of Wight from the time of the dinosaurs to the present day. Discover the island through interactive displays.

Needles Old Battery & New Battery, The - National Trust

West High Down
Alum Bay PO39 0JH
01983 754772
needlesoldbattery@nationaltrust.org.uk

The Old Battery, built in 1862 following the threat of a French invasion, is a spectacularly sited fort perched on the extreme westerly edge of the Island. It contains exhibitions about its involvement in both World Wars, plus two original gun barrels displayed in the parade ground.

Newport Roman Villa

Cypress Road
Newport PO30 1HA
01983 529720
museums@iow.gov.uk

Amongst the houses of suburban Newports stands a Roman villa. Visitors can see the extensive remains of hot and cold baths amidst reconstructed rooms.

Newtown Old Town Hall - National Trust

Newtown Old Town Hall
Newtown PO30 4AT
01983 531785
www.nationaltrust.org.uk/newtown-old-town-hall
oldtownhall@nationaltrust.org.uk

17th-century town hall with a fascinating history. The small, now tranquil, village of Newtown once sent two members to Parliament and the Town Hall was the setting for often turbulent elections.

Osborne House - English Heritage

[icons]

Osborne House, York Avenue,
East Cowes PO32 6JX
01983 200022
www.english-heritage.org.uk/osborne
osborne.house@english-heritage.org.uk

Osborne, Queen Victoria's family home, is one of the most popular tourist attractions on the Isle of Wight. After first visiting Osborne, England's longest-reigning monarch wrote: 'It is impossible to imagine a prettier spot'. Visit Victoria and Albert's private apartments, their bathing beach and children's play-cottage for an intimate glimpse of royal family life.

Sunken Secrets: Shipwrecks & Submerged Settlements

[icons]

Fort Victoria
Nr Yarmouth PO41 0RR
01983 761214
www.sunkensecrets.hwtma.org.uk
info@hwtma.org.uk

Come to Sunken Secrets: Shipwrecks and Submerged Settlements at Fort Victoria to learn about our fascinating local maritime heritage. Hear about the unfortunate ships that have been claimed by the treacherous seas around the Island. Learn about the work of maritime archaeologists and the Lost Land that has been discovered beneath the Solent.

Ventnor Heritage Museum

[icons]

11 Spring Hill
Ventnor PO38 1PE
01983 855407
www.ventnorheritage.org.uk
ventnorheritage@tiscali.co.uk

In addition to the items on view in the Exhibition Hall, the museum houses an extensive archive of many thousands of items relating to Ventnor and the surrounding area.

Yarmouth Castle - English Heritage

[icons]

Quay Street
Yarmouth PO41 0PB
01983 760678
www.english-heritage.org.uk/visit/places/yarmouth-castle

This last and most sophisticated addition to Henry VIII's coastal defences was completed after his death in 1547, with the first new-style 'arrowhead' artillery bastion built in England. Displays inside the castle include atmospheric recreations of how the rooms were used in the 16th century, and an exhibition about the many wrecks which occurred in the treacherous stretch of sea which the castle overlooks.

Kent

Kent, an important maritime county in SE. of England, bounded N. by the Thames and the North Sea, E. and SE. by the Strait of Dover, S. by the English Channel, SW. by Sussex, and W. by Surrey; greatest length, W. to E., 65 miles; greatest breadth, N. to S., 35 miles; 995,392 acres, population 977,706. The surface of the county is hilly, being traversed E. and W. by the North Downs, a chalk range from 3 to 6 miles in breadth. On the N., along the shores of the Thames and Medway, there is a belt of marshland, which extends over a mile inland. The greater portion of the seaboard is washed by tidal water. Besides the Thames and Medway, the chief rivers are the Stour and the Darent. The soil is varied and highly cultivated, more especially in the valley of the Medway. All classes of cereals and root produce are abundant, as is also fruit of choice quality, and more hops are grown in Kent than in all the rest of England. The woods are extensive. The chief manufacture of the county is paper, most of the mills being on the banks of the Medway, Cray, and Darent. The Government works and dockyards at Woolwich, Chatham, Sheerness, &c., employ an immense number of the inhabitants. Fishing is extensively prosecuted along the coast and in the estuaries of the rivers Thames and Medway, of which the oyster beds are especially famous. The county contains 5 lathes, 73 hundreds, 435 parishes, and parts of 6 others, the Cinque Port Liberties of Dover, Hythe, and New Romney, the parliamentary and municipal boroughs of Canterbury, Dover, Gravesend, Hythe, Maidstone, and Rochester, the parliamentary boroughs of Chatham, Deptford (part of), Greenwich, Lewisham, and Woolwich, and the municipal boroughs of Deal, Faversham, Folkestone, Margate, Sandwich, and Tenterden. It is almost entirely in the dioceses of Canterbury and Rochester.

– John Bartholomew, *Gazetteer of the British Isles* (1887)

Agricultural Museum

The Street, Brook
Ashford TN25 5PS
01304 824969
www.agriculturalmuseumbrook.org.uk
brianwimsett@hotmail.com

The museum at Brook forms part of an attractive and historic group of buildings consisting of Court Lodge farmhouse, with its medieval moated site, manorial barn and hop oast. The adjacent Church of St Mary is a fine example of Norman and Early English work. In the barn there are most of the items from when the horse was the power round the farm such as turnwrest ploughs, seed drills, reapers and wagons (click thumbnail on right). In the largely intact oast house are items associated with hops and other small items.

Archaeology in Education Service

Canterbury Archaeological Trust, 92a Broad Street
Canterbury CT1 2LU
01227 462062
www.canterburytrust.co.uk/learning/aes
admin@canterburytrust.co.uk

The Archaeology in Education Service (AES) was set up in the late 1980s to support, as a priority, the implementation of the new National Curriculum in Kent's schools. The AES is run by a part-time Education Officer who plans and participates in and/or manages all aspects of the service, engaging other CAT staff as appropriate.

Ashford Borough Museum

The Old Grammar School, The Churchyard
Ashford TN23 1QG
01233 631511
www.ashfordmuseum.org.uk
ashford.museum@ntlworld.com

Built in 1635 by Sir Norton Knatchbull to house the newly founded Ashford Grammar School. On view are photographs of old Ashford, Ashford at War, local archaeological and geological discoveries, artefacts from an old established Ashford pharmacy plus exhibits of everyday life.

Beaney Art Museum & Library, The

18 High Street
Canterbury CT1 2RA
01227 862162
www.thebeaney.co.uk
beaney@canterbury.gov.uk

The Beaney is an art museum and library situated in the heart of the historic city of Canterbury.

Belmont House & Gardens

Belmont House, Belmont Park, Throwley
Faversham ME13 0HH
www.belmont-house.org
events@belmont-house.org

The focus of Belmont is the magnificent neo-classical house, but we also have beautiful gardens and the finest private collection of clocks in Britain to explore.

Bethlem Royal Hospital Archives & Museum

The Bethlem Royal Hospital, Monks Orchard Road
Beckenham BR3 3BX
020 3228 4307
www.bethlemheritage.org.uk
victoria.northwood@slam.nhs.uk

Founded in 1247, Bethlem Royal Hospital is now located in Beckenham, South London, as part of the wider South London and Maudsley NHS Foundation Trust. The Archives and Museum service is dedicated to the history of mental health treatment, and includes historical and archival material as well as a large art collection.

Collections: Collections illustrate aspects of mental health and mental healthcare. They include archives of Bethlem Hospital (the original 'Bedlam') and the Maudsley Hospital (founded in the 20th century, influential in psychiatric teaching and research).

Bexley Local Studies & Archive Centre

Townley Road
Bexleyheath DA6 7HJ
020 8836 7440
www.bexley.gov.uk/archives
archives@bexley.gov.uk

Our collections include the records of the London Borough of Bexley and its predecessors, schools, churches, estates, people, businesses and societies. We have newspapers from 1873 to the present; unique photographs, postcards and illustrations; books and journals on all aspects of Bexley, Kent and London; pamphlets; posters; oral histories; local maps and plans, from around the 18th century to present; census records; street and trade directories and south east London telephone directories from 1940 onwards.

Bexley Museum at Hall Place

Hall Place, Bourne Road
Bexley DA5 1PQ
01322 526574
www.hallplace.org.uk
info@hallplace.org.uk

A fine Grade 1 Listed country house built in 1540 for Sir John Champneis, Lord Mayor of London, and extended in the 17th century. Open to the public with free admission

Hall Place is set in beautiful formal gardens on the banks of the River Cray.

Blue Town Heritage Centre

69 High St Blue Town
Sheerness ME12 1RW
01795 662981
www.thecriterionbluetown.co.uk
bthc@btconnect.com

The Blue Town heritage centre is a mixture of museum, music hall, cinema and educational and research facility. It is adjacent to Sheerness dockyard and its aims are to promote and preserve the history of Blue Town and the Isle of Sheppey.

Brenzett Aeronautical Museum Trust

Ivychurch Road
Brenzett, Romney Marsh TN29 0EE
www.brenzettaero.co.uk

The Romney Marsh Wartime Collection is a unique collection of wartime equipment, remains recovered from aircraft crash sites and memorabilia collected and donated to the museum since its formation in 1972. The exhibition is located within the original buildings used as a Hostel for the Women's Land Army during the war, and part of the exhibition is devoted to those ladies - some of their graffiti is still evident today.

Canterbury Cathedral

Cathedral House, 11 The Precincts
Canterbury CT1 2EH
01227 762862
www.canterbury-cathedral.org
enquiries@canterbury-cathedral.org

Canterbury Cathedral is the Mother Church of the Anglican Communion and seat of the Archbishop of Canterbury. The Cathedral is both a holy place and part of a World Heritage Site.

Canterbury Cathedral Archives

The Precincts
Canterbury CT1 2EH
01227 865330

Canterbury Cathedral Archives holds a wealth of manuscripts, photographs, maps and other records dating back to the late 8th century. These make up an extraordinarily rich resource.

Canterbury Heritage Museum

Stour Street
Canterbury CT1 2NR
01227 475 202
www.canterbury-museums.co.uk
museums@canterbury.gov.uk

Discover Canterbury's history, from millions of years ago to the present, explored through interactive displays in an amazing medieval building. Includes Anglo-Saxon treasures, Oliver Postgate's Thomas Becket story, the Tudors, Joseph Conrad's study, the Blitz gallery, Stephenson's original Invicta railway engine, Rupert Bear and the real Bagpuss. Around the museum are over 30 exciting hands-on activities for families - you can write your name in Viking runes, sniff medieval poo, investigate finds like an archaeologist, try on Elizabethan costume and listen to wartime memories.

Canterbury Roman Museum

Butchery Lane
Canterbury CT1 2JR
01227 785 575
www.canterbury-museums.co.uk
museums@canterbury.gov.uk

Explore the Roman town beneath your feet. Canterbury's underground Roman Museum is built around the remains of a Roman town house with mosaics preserved where excavated.

Canterbury Tales, The

St Margaret's Street,
Canterbury CT1 2TG
01227 454888
www.canterburytales.org.uk
info@canterburytales.org.uk

Ever wondered what it would be like to step back in time and experience the sights, sounds and smells of a bygone era? At The Canterbury Tales you can do just that. Step into medieval Canterbury and accompany Geoffrey Chaucer and his colourful pilgrims on their magical journey from London to the Shrine of St Thomas Becket in Canterbury. Along the way, their stories of love, romance, jealousy and trickery are vividly re-created with all the humour of Chaucer's famous tales. The Canterbury Tale is a fascinating and accurate portrayal of life in medieval England during the 14th century.

Canterbury West Gate Towers

St Peter's Street
Canterbury CT1 1TF
01227 452747
museums@canterbury.gov.uk

After the Cathedral, the West Gate is Canterbury's next eye-catching landmark. It has stood for six centuries on guard over the road to and from London. It is the largest surviving medieval gate in England.

Capel-le-Ferne Memorial

Battle of Britain Memorial, New Dover Road, Capel-le-Ferne
Folkestone CT18 7JJ
01303 249292
www.battleofbritainmemorial.org
battleofbritain@btinternet.com

A striking memorial to those who flew and those who gave their lives in the Battle of Britain stands on the White Cliffs between Dover and Folkestone at Capel le Ferne. It is an ideal location and one which was all too familiar to both the RAF and the Luftwaffe during that desperate summer of 1940.

Centre for Kentish Studies

Sessions House, County Hall
Maidstone ME14 1XQ
01622 694 291

The centre for Kentish Studies is the Headquarters for the Kent Archives Centre for Kentish Studies search room service. It holds manuscript and printed records for the County of Kent.

Chantry Heritage Centre

Fort Gardens, Commercial Place
Gravesend DA12 2BH
01474 337442
http://goo.gl/jLIeJi

The oldest surviving 14th century building in the Borough of Gravesham. The building fell into disuse after the Reformation. The chapel became an inn towards the end of the 17th century, and later became part of the fort and defence works erected on the site. Today the building is promoted as the Chantry Heritage Centre and houses a range of exhibits relating to Gravesend, Northfleet and the nearby villages.

Chartwell - National Trust

Mapleton Road
Westerham TN16 1PS
01732 868381
www.nationaltrust.org.uk/chartwell
chartwell@nationaltrust.org.uk

Bought by Sir Winston Churchill for its magnificent views over the Weald of Kent to Sussex, Chartwell was his home and the place from which he drew inspiration from 1924 until the end of his life.

Chiddingstone Castle

Hill Hoath Road
Edenbridge TN8 7AD
01892 870347
www.chiddingstonecastle.org.uk
events@chiddingstonecastle.org.uk

Home to a fascinating collection of Japanese Samurai armour, Buddhist figures, Ancient Egyptian artefacts,Jacobite and Stuart paintings and memorabilia. All were collected by the last owner of the castle, Denys Bower.

Colonel Stephens Museum

Tenterden Town Station, Station Road
Tenterden TN30 6HE
087 060 060 74
www.hfstephens-museum.org.uk

The Colonel Stephens Museum recording the career of Holman Fred Stephens, light railway promoter, engineer and manager, his family, his railways and his successors.

Cranbrook Local History Museum

Carriers Road
Cranbrook TN17 3JX
01580 715542
www.cranbrookmuseum.org
curator@CranbrookMuseum.org

Cranbook Museum is an engaging local museum with collections spanning te history of Cranbrook Town, its industry, culture and local nature.

Crofton Roman Villa

Crofton Road, Orpington BR6 8AF
01689 860939
www.the-cka.fsnet.co.uk
crofton.roman.villa@gmail.com

Crofton Roman Villa is the only villa open to the public in Greater London. It was inhabited from about AD 140 to 400 and was the centre of a large farming estate.

Dartford Borough Museum

Market Street
Dartford DA1 1EU
01322 224739
www.dartford.gov.uk/museum
museum@dartford.gov.uk

Permanent display of local archaeology, reconstruction of a draper's shop and Dartford during the Second World War. Regular temporary exhibitions on a variety of subjects.

Deal Castle - English Heritage

Victoria Road
Deal CT14 7BA
01304 372762
www.english-heritage.org.uk/visit/places/deal-castle/

For a day out of adventure and exploration, where kids can imagine life as a soldier visit Deal Castle. Dare the whole family to explore the dark passages that wind through the huge bastions and discover the castle's history from the interactive exhibition.

Deal Maritime & Local History Museum

22 St George's Road
Deal CT14 6BA
01304 375816
www.home.freeuk.com/deal-museum
dealmuseum@lineone.net

Exhibits include the Saxon King (the last of the Deal Galleys), many ships models (including the Cutty Sark), colourful figureheads and numerous pictures, prints and memorabilia of the famous Deal Boatmen, the Deal, Walmer, and Kingsdown lifeboat crews and of the Royal Marines stationed at Deal for over 300 years.

Dog Collar Museum at Leeds Castle, The

The Dog Collar Museum, Leeds Castle
Maidstone ME17 1PL
01622 765400
enquiries@leeds-castle.co.uk

A unique collection of historic and fascinating dog collars has been built up over the years and is now the only one of its kind in Great Britain. Mrs. Gertrude Hunt most generously presented her collection of collars to the Leeds Castle Foundation in memory of her husband, John Hunt, the distinguished medievalist. The collection of over 100 collars and related exhibits has since been added to and enhanced by the Foundation itself.

Dover Castle - English Heritage

Dover CT16 1HU
01304 211067
http://goo.gl/XGvTxK

Set high above the famous white cliffs, Dover Castle boasts a colourful and fascinating history. The most iconic of all English fortresses commanding the gateway to the realm for nine centuries. Climb the Great Tower, meet the characters and immerse yourself in vivid medieval interiors. Then delve deep within Dover's White Cliffs to witness the drama in the Secret Wartime Tunnels. Roam through centuries of history at Dover Castle, from the Romans to the Cold War.

Dover Museum

01304 201066

www.dovermuseum.co.uk

museumenquiries@dover.gov.uk

Dover Museum is a local history and archaeology museum situated in the town centre of Dover, Britain's historic port town. It is home to the Dover Bronze Age Boat, the world's oldest known seagoing boat and a fascinating archaeological discovery.

Dover Transport Museum

Willingdon Road, Whitfield

Dover CT16 2JX

01304 822409

www.dovertransportmuseum.org.uk

info@dovertransportmuseum.org.uk

Stroll through the collection of over 50 vehicles housed in two main galleries set in period street scenes of a bygone age, bringing the past, present and future together.

Down House - Home of Charles Darwin

Down House

Downe BR6 7JT

01689 859119

www.english-heritage.org.uk/server/show/nav.14922

An intimate window into the life of England's best known scientist. It was from his study at Down House that Charles Darwin worked on the scientific theories that culminated in a book 'On the Origin of Species by Means of Natural Selection' that both scandalised and revolutionised Victorian Britain.

Drop Redoubt

Drop Redoubt Road

Dover CT17 9AP

www.doverwesternheights.org

rp_doust@yahoo.co.uk

The Drop Redoubt together with the Western Heights, forms the largest Napoleonic fortress in Britain. They are an excellent example of British defence from the Napoleonic period right through to the Second World War.

Eden Valley Museum

Church House, 72 High Street

Edenbridge TN8 5AR

01732 868102

www.evmt.org.uk

curator@evmt.org.uk

An innovative new museum housed in a Grade 2* listed building. This timber framed mediaeval farmhouse helps to tell the story of the people of the Eden Valley.

Collections: Local social history including industry, farming, domestic artefacts, painting and prints, costume Archaeology of the Eden Valley Archives.

Finchcocks

Goudhurst TN17 1HH

01580 211702

www.finchcocks.co.uk

Finchcocks, a fine Georgian manor in Kent, houses Richard Burnett's celebrated collection of over 100 keyboard instruments: harpsichords, pianos, organs and many more. Some forty of them are in full working order, with a staff of professional musicians providing live demonstrations throughout your visit. Finchcocks also invites keyboard players of all ages to play the instruments, and to experience first-hand the sounds that composers such as Handel, Mozart, Beethoven, Chopin and Brahms made as they created their masterpieces, or simply entertained their friends.

Fleur De Lis Heritage Centre

13 Preston Street

Faversham ME13 8NS

01795 534542

www.favershamsociety.org/_museum.html

The Fleur de Lis Heritage Centre comprises three adjoining grade II listed buildings in Preston Street right in the centre of Faversham. The Heritage Centre, or the Fleur, as it is affectionately known, is owned and voluntarily run by the Faversham Society and offers many facilities for the visitor and locals alike.

Folkestone & District Family History Society

Kingsmill Down, Hastingleigh

Ashford TN25 5JJ

01233 750321

www.folkfhs.org.uk

secretary@folkfhs.org.uk

The Folkestone and District Family History Society was founded in 1976 to encourage and promote the study of family history in the South East Kent area. It provides advice and assistance to members with South East Kent ancestry as well as to members whose roots are elsewhere, and welcomes the beginner and the more experienced family historian alike.

Folkestone History Resource Centre

2 Grace Hill

Folkestone CT20 1HD

08458 247200

folkestonelibrary@ kent.gov.uk

Get a glimpse of Folkestone's extensive and diverse collection. From Roman wall plaster and woolly mammoth teeth, to mine detectors and early cameras, not to mention our sixth century skeleton.

Fort Amherst Heritage Trust

Dock Road
Chatham ME4 4UB
01634 84774
www.fortamherst.com
admin@fortamherst.com

Fort Amherst, based in Chatham, Medway, Kent, is Britain's largest Napoleonic Fortress and provides a great day out for all the family. Visitors can enjoy: over 300 years of military history with an amazing network of underground passageways, historic buildings and gun emplacements all set in 20 acres of beautiful parkland.

Gateways to the First World War

School of History, Rutherford College, University of Kent
Canterbury CT2 7NX
www.gatewaysfww.org.uk
gateways@kent.ac.uk

Gateways is an AHRC-funded centre for public engagement with the First World War centenary. The centre is managed by the University of Kent in partnership with the Universities of Brighton, Greenwich, Portsmouth, Leeds and Queen Mary, London.

Grand Shaft Staircase

c/o Dover Town Hall, Biggin Street
Dover CT16 1DL
01304 201200

Triple spiral staircase built 1803-1809 connecting grand shaft barracks on the cliff top with Snargate Street at sea level.

Gravesend Cold War Bunker

Woodlands Park, Wrotham Road
Gravesend DA11 0QF
01474 33 76 00
www.gravesham.gov.uk/index.cfm?Articleid=2807
customer.services@gravesham.gov.uk

Gravesend's secret Cold War bunker was an underground command post, built in 1954, from which Gravesend's rescue and emergency services were to be co-ordinated in the event of a nuclear attack. Its 13 rooms contained power and ventilation plant, communications areas for the command staff and dormitories.

Gravesham Museum (online only)

Windmill Street
Gravesend DA12 1BE
01474 323 159
www.discovergravesham.co.uk

At the click of your mouse you will be able to glimpse the cultural, social and commercial heritage of Gravesend, Northfleet and the nearby villages.

Groombridge Place

Groombridge
Tunbridge Wells TN3 9QG
01892 861444
www.groombridge.co.uk

A visit to Groombridge Place will give you an unforgettable day whether you come as garden enthusiasts to explore and enjoy the sights and scents of the 17th century formal walled gardens; or with your family to discover the secret, quirky and mysterious gardens of the ancient forest where children's imagination will run wild; or for one of our many popular special events.

Guildhall Museum

High Street
Rochester ME1 1PY
01634 333111
guildhall.museum@medway.gov.uk

The Guildhall Museum was built in 1687 and is one of the finest 17th century civic buildings in Kent. The main staircase and principal chamber have magnificently decorated plaster ceilings, given in 1695 by Admiral Sir Cloudsley Shovell who was a Member of Parliament for the city of Rochester at the time.

Collections: At the Guildhall Museum you can look at what people made and used so many years ago. Reach back into the past with the help of evidence - from the huge Roman potteries by the river; from the busy farms scattered through the countryside; and from the important Roman town of Durobrivae itself.

Hall Place & Gardens

Bourne Road
Bexley DA5 1PQ
01322 526574
www.hallplace.org.uk
info@hallplace.org.uk

Hall Place is a Grade I listed Tudor country house originally built in 1537 and also with a 17th century courtyard built by later owner Sir Robert Austen.

Herne Bay Museum & Gallery

12 William Street
Herne Bay CT6 5EJ
01227 367368
www.canterbury-museums.co.uk
museums@canterbury.gov.uk

This coastal museum features the story of the Victorian seaside resort of Herne Bay and its surrounding area, with exciting finds from nearby Reculver Roman fort. Displays include local paintings, prints and photos, mammoth tusks and fossils from local beaches, coastal wildlife and a Barnes Wallis Bouncing Bomb prototype from World War Two. Among display themes are seaside holidays and attractions, the town's piers, clock tower and the development of the resort.

Herne Windmill

c/o 46 Windmill Road
Herne Bay CT6 7DF
01227 361326
www.herne-mill.btck.co.uk

Herne Mill is a Kentish smock windmill dating from 1789. It is Grade I listed and is owned by Kent County Council and cared for by the Friends of Herne Mill. The latest in a long line of mills which have occupied the site for centuries, the windmill is a local landmark on the skyline above the ancient village of Herne in Kent.

Hever Castle & Gardens

Hever Road
Nr Edenbridge TN8 7NG
01732 861710
www.hevercastle.co.uk
mail@hevercastle.co.uk

700 years of history to be discovered at this 13th century double moated romantic castle, once the childhood home of Anne Boleyn and housing an important collection of Tudor portraits, fine furniture, tapestries and artefacts. The natural and formal gardens include Italian Gardens with a magnificent collection of Italian statuary, many of which are over 2000 years old, topiary, grottoes, fountains, boating lake, yew and water maze and adventure playground with Henry VIII tower maze.

Historic Dockyard Chatham

The Historic Dockyard
Chatham ME4 4TZ
01634 823800
www.thedockyard.co.uk
info@chdt.org.uk

A unique, award winning maritime heritage destination with a fantastic range of attractions, iconic buildings and historic ships to explore, plus a fabulous programme of temporary exhibitions at No 1 Smithery. Make rope on the Victorian Ropery Tour; be gripped by stories of life aboard our three historic warships and hear of heroic stories in the RNLI Historic Lifeboat Collection.

Home Front Bus

2 Broadfield Crescent
Folkestone CT20 2PH
01303 779339
www.homefrontbus.com
info@homefrontbus.com

Home Front Bus is a unique Living History Experience. The classic double decker bus houses detailed reconstructions of a 1940s living room, a shop, a bombed out street and an air raid shelter, each containing period features and artefacts replicating the sights and sounds on the Home Front during World War 2.

Huguenot Museum

95 High Street
Rochester ME1 1LX
01634 789347
https://www.facebook.com/huguenotheritagecentre
learning@huguenotmuseum.org

Opening Summer 2015. The Huguenot Museum tells the story of Britain's first refugees: the skills they brought to the UK, their descendants, and relevance to the story of refugees today. 'We help people to better understand the present by learning about the past, enabling us to make connections between Huguenot history and the world around us.'

Hythe Local History Room

Oaklands, Stade Street
Hythe CT21 6BQ
01303 267111
www.hythetc.kentparishes.gov.uk
admin@hythe-kent.com

The Hythe Local History Room was established in the neighbourhood of Oaklands, in 1933, in a house left to the town and Cinque Port of Hythe by Dr Randolph Davis. The collection, including material about archaeology and social history as well as paintings, illustrates the history of the town and the Small Arms School, in three rooms adjoining the public library.

Ightham Mote - National Trust

Ivy Hatch
Sevenoaks TN15 0NT
01732 810378
www.nationaltrust.org.uk/ightham-mote
ighthammote@nationaltrust.org.uk

Superb 14th-century moated manor house: * See the results of the Trust's largest ever conservation project * Tudor chapel with hand-painted ceiling * Grade I listed dog kennel * Lovely gardens, with lakeside and woodland walks, in a secluded valley.

Institute of Heraldic & Genealogical Studies

79 - 82 Northgate
Canterbury CT1 1BA
01227 768664
www.ihgs.ac.uk
ihgs@ihgs.ac.uk

The Institute of Heraldic and Genealogical Studies (IHGS) was the first centre for Family History Studies. Founded in 1961, it offers a wide range of courses on family history, heraldry and related historical subjects.

Kent & Sharpshooters Yeomanry Museum Trust

Hever Castle
Hever, Edenbridge TN8 7NG
01732 865224
www.ksymuseum.org.uk
curator@ksymuseum.org.uk

Commemorating the Royal East Kent Mounted Rifles, Queen's Own West Kent Yeomanry, Kent Yeomanry, 3rd County of London Yeomanry (Sharpshooters), 23rd London Armoured Car Company (Sharpshooters), 4th County of London Yeomanry (Sharpshooters), 3rd/4th County of London Yeomanry (Sharpshooters), Kent and County of London Yeomanry (Sharpshooters).

Kent Battle of Britain Museum

Aerodrome Road, Hawkinge
Folkestone CT18 7AG
01303 893140
www.kbobm.org
kentbattleofbritainmuseum@btinternet.com

The most important collection of Battle of Britain artefacts on show in the country. The museum was lucky to acquire one of the sites of Britain's epic struggle for survival in 1940, in what was the greatest air battle of all time.

Kent County Council Arts & Museums

Springfield
Maidstone ME14 2LH
01622 696434
elizabeth.ritchie@kent.gov.uk

Manages three museums in library buildings at Folkestone, Ramsgate and Sevenoaks.

Kent Family History Society

Bullockstone Farm, Bullockstone Road
Herne Bay CT6 7NL
www.kfhs.org.uk
secretary@kfhs.org.uk

Established in 1974 as the largest and oldest family history society in Kent, with more than 3,200 members worldwide, we are uniquely able to help members to learn how to research their own family tree.

Kent Firefighting Museum

Kent County Council Fire Department, Straw Mill Hill, Tovil
Maidstone ME15 6XB
01622 692 121
www.kentfirefightingmuseum.org.uk

Displays historical firefighting appliances, equipment, artefacts, photographs and documentary records relating to the history of firefighting in Kent.

Kent History & Library Centre

James Whatman Way
Maidstone ME14 1LQ
03000 413131

The Kent History and Library Centre is purpose built to protect and give access to the county's archives. It houses around 14 kilometres of historic material relating to Kent dating back to 699 AD and is the place to come for anyone interested in local history.

Kent Life

Lock Lane, Sandling
Maidstone ME14 3AU
01622 763936
www.kentlife.org.uk
enquiries@kentlife.org.uk

There's so much new to do at Kent's premier heritage farm attraction. Agricultural tools and machinery, social history – domestic life, working life and the life of hop pickers.

Kent Police Museum

The Historic Dockyard
Rochester ME1 3NJ
01634 403260
www.kent-police-museum.co.uk
info@kent-police-museum.co.uk

The Police Museum was started as a collection of police memorabilia in the 1960s by officers who felt there was a need to show our history. The museum also provides a service for any research of family history enquiries. The services are available by contacting the museum curator.

Knole - National Trust

[museum] [£]

Knole House
Sevenoaks TN15 0RP
01732 462100
www.nationaltrust.org.uk/knole
knole@nationaltrust.org.uk

Knole is one of England's most important, complete, yet fragile historic houses, set at the heart of Kent's last remaining medieval deer park. * Rare collection of Royal Stuart furniture * Important portraits by Van Dyke, Gainsborough and Reynolds * Birthplace of novelist and poet Vita Sackville-West * Magnificent 1,000-acre deer park, a Site of Special Scientific Interest.

Lashenden Air Warfare Museum

[mail] [★]

Headcorn Aerodrome, Headcorn
Ashford TN27 9HX
01622 890226
www.lashendenairwarfaremuseum.co.uk
lashendenairwar@aol.com

The museum was formed in 1970 with the aim of preserving the aviation heritage of Kent, with particular emphasis on World War II. Also to promote and develop an aviation awareness in the general public, raising money for RAF and other associated charities.

Collections: The museum has 5 aircraft on display, including two original World War 2 German aircraft. The Focke Achgelis Fa 330 rotor kite & a Fieseler Fi 103R4 Richenberg piloted V1 flying bomb.

Leeds Castle

[museum] [£]

Leeds Castle
Maidstone ME17 1PL
01622 765 400
www.leeds-castle.com
enquiries@leeds-castle.co.uk

Leeds Castle, set on two islands on the River Len in the heart of Kent, has been home to royalty, lords and ladies for more than 900 years. Visitors are transported through the castle's history; an eclectic mix of period architecture, sumptuous interiors and family treasures waiting to be discovered.

Light Vessel 21

[museum] [mail] [building]

Pier Approach Road Gillingham Pier
Gillingham ME7 1RX
07796 177237
www.LV21.co.uk
info@lv21.co.uk

Ahoy. LV21 is a 40 metre steel-hulled lightship being transformed into a floating cultural facility and maritime heritage centre. Designed to provide a range of services promoting and supporting the creative industries in the Medway area and beyond, whilst celebrating and honouring the maritime traditions of the vessel, LV21 is set to become an iconic landmark on the river Medway.

Lullingstone Roman Villa - English Heritage

[museum] [mail]

Nr Swanley DA4 0JA
01322 863467
http://goo.gl/pi00cl

Among the most outstanding Roman villa survivals in Britain, Lullingstone has been vividly re-displayed, providing a unique - and all-weather - opportunity to trace Roman domestic life over three centuries. Set in the attractive surroundings of the Darent Valley, the villa was begun in about AD 100, and developed to suit the tastes and beliefs of successive wealthy owners.

Maidstone Museum & Bentlif Art Gallery

[mail] [★]

St Faiths Street
Maidstone ME14 1LH
01622 602838/9
www.museum.maidstone.gov.uk
museuminfo@maidstone.gov.uk

Maidstone Museum & Bentlif Art Gallery is an award winning museum, housed in a beautiful Elizabethan manor house. Highlights include a 2,500 year old mummy; Maidstone's local history; a fascinating journey through time when dinosaurs walked the earth; one of the finest Japanese collections of Japanese art in the country; magnificent 'Old Master' oil paintings; and the splendour of the Queen's Own Royal West Kent Regimental Museum.

Maison Dieu - English Heritage

[museum] [£]

Maison Dieu
Faversham ME13 8NS
01795 534542
www.english-heritage.org.uk/visit/places/maison-dieu

Originating as a 13th-century wayside hospital, this flint and timber-framed building now displays Roman artefacts from nearby sites.

Margate Museum

[mail] [£]

Market Place, Old Town
Margate CT9 1EU
01843 231213
https://margatemuseum.wordpress.com
friendsofmargatemuseum@gmail.com

Margate Museum is situated in the vibrant Old Town. The building itself was once the town magistrates court and gaol and boasts many original features.

Medway Archives & Local Studies

Medway Archives Office, Civic Centre, Strood
Rochester ME2 4AU
01634 332714
cityark.medway.gov.uk/

We preserve and make available for research the archives of the Medway area of Kent and also the parish records of north-west Kent. Our oldest records date from 604.

Meopham Windmill

Wrotham Road
Meopham, Gravesham DA13 0QA
01474 813518

The Meopham Windmill was built in 1801 by the three Killick brothers reputedly from old ships timbers purchased from Chatham Dockyard. It was built to a 'smock' design similar to the brothers' other mill at Strood; the name derives from the similarity to the garment worn by agricultural workers in earlier times.

New Tavern Fort

Milton Place
Gravesham DA12 2BT
01474 337442
www.gravesham.gov.uk/index.jsp?articleid=960
newtavernfort@gravesham.gov.uk

The New Tavern Fort is the remains of an 18th century fort situated within the Fort Gardens and built in the 1780s to defend the Thames against the threat of a naval attack from France and extensively rebuilt by General Gordon between 1865 and 1879. Come along and venture into the mysterious underground world of the Victorian artilleryman and see the magazines and full size reconstructions of scenes from Gravesend during the Second World War.

North West Kent Family History Society

51 Newbury Avenue Allington
Maidstone ME16 0RG
01322 384 836
www.nwkfhs.org.uk
chairman@nwkfhs.org.uk

The North West Kent Family History Society was formed in 1978 with the object of aiding and encouraging the study of family history and genealogy in South East London and North West Kent.

Old Soar Manor - National Trust

Plaxtol
Borough Green TN15 0QX
01732 810378
www.nationaltrust.org.uk/old-soar-manor

This is all that is left of the manor house of c. 1290 which stood here until the 18th century.

Owletts - National Trust

The Street, Cobham
Gravesend DA12 3AP
01474 813 849
www.nationaltrust.org.uk/owletts
owletts@nationaltrust.org.uk

The former home of Sir Herbert Baker, the architect, famous for his work in India (where he worked with Lutyens) and South Africa, the house has a Carolean staircase and plasterwork ceiling and a large kitchen garden.

Parish Church of St Mary of Charity, The

Parish Church of St Mary of Charity, Church Road
Faversham ME13 8GZ
01795 532592
www.faversham.org/stmaryofcharity
built2inspire@stmaryofcharity.org

The Parish Church of St Mary of Charity is set in the heart of the historic Market Town of Faversham, Kent. It has a wealth of artefacts for visitors to see including a medieval painted column (1306) - one of the finest examples in Britain today; brasses and 16th century misericords; and the likely resting place of King Stephen and Queen Matilda.

Penshurst Place & Gardens

Penshurst Place Penshurst
Tonbridge TN11 8DG
01892 870307
www.penshurstplace.com
contactus@penshurstplace.com

Though at its heart a medieval and Tudor building, the house has been modified and extended over the centuries. Eight architectural styles are evident, with plenty for visitors to explore in it's fascinating history - and still many mysteries to be revealed. Penshurst Place has been owned by the Sidney family since 1552.

Powell-Cotton Museum

Quex Park, Park Lane
Birchington CT7 0BH
01843 842 168
www.quexmuseum.org
enquiries@quexmuseum.org

Museum created by PHG Powell-Cotton (1866-1940) housing his collections from 25 expeditions to Africa and 5 trips to SE Asia between 1889 and 1939 (26 years actually on African soil). Three galleries of amazing animal diorama displays - the finest in this country - depicting more than 250 African and Asian mammals against their natural habitats.

Princess of Wales's Royal Regiment & Queen's Regiment Museum

5 Keep Yard, Dover Castle
Dover CT16 1HU
01304 240121
www.army.mod.uk
pwrrqueensmuseum@btconnect.co.uk

Military history from 1572 to present. Story of 12 Foot and 9 County Infantry regiments.

Quebec House - National Trust

Quebec House
Westerham TN16 1TD
01732 868381
www.nationaltrust.org.uk/quebec-house
quebechouse@nationaltrust.org.uk

Childhood home of General James Wolfe. * Unique collection of Georgian memorabilia * Fascinating Battle of Quebec exhibition * Gabled red brick 17th-century house.

Queen's Own Royal West Kent Regiment Museum

St Faith's Street
Maidstone ME14 1LH
01622 754 497
www.museum.maidstone.gov.uk/information

This independent museum has been housed within Maidstone Museum since 1960. It is packed with fascinating, colourful and thought-provoking exhibits.

RAF Manston Spitfire & Hurricane Memorial Museum

Spitfire and Hurricane Memorial, The Airfield, Manston Road
Ramsgate CT12 5DF

01843 821940
www.spitfire.memorial.museum
spitfire752@btconnect.com

The Memorial Building is situated on one of the very few surviving airfields which participated in the Battle of Britain. RAF Manston was the closest airfield to the enemy coast and bore the brunt of the early Luftwaffe air attacks in the long hot summer of 1940.

Collections: Supermarine Spitfire Mk XVI (LF) - Type 361 - Serial TB752 - Sqn Code KH-Z: TB752 is one of the few surviving Spitfires with a wartime record.

Ramsgate Maritime Museum

The Clock House, Maritime Museum Pier Yard
Ramsgate CT11 8LS
07810 358135
www.ramsgatemaritimemuseum.org
info@ramsgatemaritimemuseum.org

Situated in the Clock House on the quayside at Ramsgate Harbour, Ramsgate Maritime Museum focuses strongly on Ramsgate and its immediate environs, with a brief introduction to the rest of the region's maritime past.

Ramsgate Tunnels

Marina Esplanade
Ramsgate CT11 8NA
01843 588123
www.ramsgatetunnels.org
admin@ramsgatetunnels.org

The tunnels, which were dug prior to the start of WWII, at the behest of the then Mayor ABC Kemp, designed to hold 60,000 people, and spanning some 3 1/4 miles beneath the town of Ramsgate. They incorporate a 3/4 mile long Victorian railway tunnel as well as a labyrinth of chalk tunnels which are 7 x 6ft.

Red House - National Trust

Red House Lane
Bexleyheath DA6 8JF
020 8304 9878
www.nationaltrust.org.uk/red-house
redhouse@nationaltrust.org.uk

Commissioned by William Morris in 1859 and designed by Philip Webb, Red House is of enormous international significance in the history of domestic architecture and garden design. The unique building is constructed of warm red brick, under a steep red-tiled roof, with an emphasis on natural materials and a strong Gothic influence.

Richborough Roman Fort & Amphitheatre - English Heritage

Richborough
Sandwich CT13 9JW
01304 612013
http://goo.gl/vc4BHq

Witnessing both the beginning and almost the end of Roman rule in Britain, Richbourough Roman Fort & Amphitheatre is an inspirational and fascinating day out. With plenty of space for adults to relax and children to play this is the perfect place for a family picnic.

RNLI Historic Lifeboat Collection

Lifeboat., The Historic Dockyard
Chatham ME4 4TZ
01634 823800

Housed in an 1848 covered slip, the Lifeboat Gallery contains 17 historic boats, many of which earned their Coxswains RNLI bravery medals. From an 1897 pulling and sailing lifeboat, to the familiar Arun class and Blue Peter inflatable inshore lifeboats, visitors can explore how lifeboats have evolved over the past century.

Rochester Castle

Castle Hill
Rochester ME1 1SW
01634 402276
http://goo.gl/jVTP9a

Strategically placed astride the London Road, guarding an important crossing of the River Medway, this imposing fortress has a complex history of destruction and rebuilding. Its Norman tower-keep of Kentish ragstone was built about 1127 by William of Corbeil, Archbishop of Canterbury, with the encouragement of Henry I. Consisting of three floors above a basement, it still stands 113 feet high. Attached is a tall protruding forebuilding, with its own set of defences to pass through before the keep itself could be entered at first floor level. In 1215, garrisoned by rebel barons, the castle endured an epic siege by King John. Rebuilt under Henry III and Edward I, the castle remained as a viable fortress until the sixteenth century.

Rochester Cathedral

Chapter Office, Garth House, The Precinct
Rochester ME1 1SX
01634 810073
www.rochestercathedral.org
bookings@rochestercathedral.org

Rochester Cathedral is England's second oldest cathedral, having been founded in 604AD by Bishop Justus. The present building dates back to the work of the French monk, Gundulf, in 1080.

Romney, Hythe & Dymchurch Railway

New Romney Station
New Romney TN28 8LG
01797 362353
www.rhdr.org.uk
enquiries@rhdr.org.uk

First opened to traffic in July 1927 as the 'World's Smallest Public Railway' and now covering a distance of 13.5 miles from the picturesque Cinque Port of Hythe, near the channel tunnel, to the fishermen's cottages and lighthouses at Dungeness.

Royal Engineers Museum, Library & Archive

Prince Arthur Road
Gillingham ME4 4UG
01634 822839
www.re-museum.co.uk
mail@re-museum.co.uk

The Royal Engineers Museum and Library tell the story of the Corps of Royal Engineers and military engineering. It is a story about the Sappers and their courage, creativity and innovation. In peace and war the Corps has been everywhere and involved in everything. The museum holds a particularly comprehensive collection of British medals.

Sandwich Guildhall Museum

Cattle Market
Sandwich CT13 9AH
01304 617 197
www.sandwichtowncouncil.gov.uk
Sandwich-Archivist@lycos.co.uk

The museum is housed in the Guildhall, a listed building, and tells the story of Sandwich from medieval times. There are many well-designed illustrative panels relating to the history of the town with artefacts dating back to the early 13th century.

Scotney Castle - National Trust

Lamberhurst
Tunbridge Wells TN3 8JN
01892 893820
www.nationaltrust.org.uk/scotney-castle
scotneycastle@nationaltrust.org.uk

The moated 14th century castle and landscape of Scotney together make this one of England's most romantic places. Created in the 1830s by Edward Hussey who had the imagination to transform the medieval Scotney Castle from derelict dwelling to quaint ruin, thus forming the focus of his picturesque landscape garden, which he called his pleasure gardens.

Sevenoaks Museum

Sevenoaks Library, Buckhurst Lane
Sevenoaks TN13 1LQ
01732 453118
www.kent.gov.uk
sevenoakslibrary@kent.gov.uk

Sevenoaks Museum is situated inside Sevenoaks Library. The 1980s building was re-developed in 2005/6 and also contains a contemporary art gallery, local studies library and cafe space.

Shoreham Aircraft Museum

13 High Street, Shoreham Village
Sevenoaks TN14 7TB
01959 524416
www.shoreham-aircraft-museum.co.uk
mail@shoreham-aircraft-museum.co.uk

The museum houses hundreds of aviation relics excavated by the group over many years from crashed British and German aircraft, as well as items which have been kindly donated. In addition, there is a fine collection of flying helmets, uniforms and insignia.

Sissinghurst Castle - National Trust

Sissinghurst, nr. Cranbrook
nr. Cranbrook TN17 2AB
01580 710700
www.nationaltrust.org.uk/sissinghurst-castle
sissinghurst@nationaltrust.org.uk

One of the world's most celebrated gardens, the creation of Vita Sackville-West and her husband Sir Harold Nicolson.

Smallhythe Place - National Trust

Smallhythe
Tenterden TN30 7NG
www.nationaltrust.org.uk/smallhythe-place
smallhytheplace@nationaltrust.org.uk

Ellen Terry's early 16th-century house and cottage gardens. The half-timbered house, built for the harbourmaster in the early 16th century when Smallhythe was a thriving shipbuilding yard, was the home of the Victorian actress Ellen Terry from 1899 to 1928 and contains her fascinating theatre collection.

Snodland Millennium Museum

Waghorn Road
Snodland ME6 5BQ
01634-243001
www.snodlandhistory.org.uk/museum/page6.htm

aa0060962@blueyonder.co.uk

The museum is owned and maintained by Snodland Town Council. Admission is free.

South Foreland Lighthouse - National Trust

The Front, St Margaret
Dover CT15 6HP
01304 852463
www.nationaltrust.org.uk/south-foreland-lighthouse
southforeland@nationaltrust.org.uk

A striking landmark on the White Cliffs of Dover, this historic building was the site of Faraday's work in pioneering the use of electricity in lighthouses, and was the first to display an electrically powered signal. South Foreland was also used by Marconi for his successful wireless telegraphy experiments in 1898.

St Augustine's Abbey - English Heritage

Canterbury
01227 767345
www.english-heritage.org.uk/server/show/nav.14831

This great abbey, marking the rebirth of Christianity in southern England, was founded shortly after AD 597 by St Augustine. Originally created as a burial place for the Anglo-Saxon kings of Kent, it is part of the Canterbury World Heritage Site, along with the cathedral and St Martin's Church. The impressive abbey is situated outside the city walls and is sometimes missed by visitors.

St Margaret's Museum

Beach Road, St Margaret's Bay
Dover CT15 6DZ
01304 852764
www.helionix.com/html/museum.html
enquiries@baytrust.org.uk

Directly opposite the main entrance to the Pines Garden is St Margaret's museum and The Garden Café. The museum, created by the Trustees in memory of Fred Cleary CBE, houses a programme of changing displays on environmental themes and local history. Also on display is a tribute to one-time resident of St Margaret's, Noel Coward.

Stoneacre - National Trust

Otham
Maidstone ME15 8RS
01622 862157
www.nationaltrust.org.uk/stoneacre
stoneacre@nationaltrust.org.uk

15th-century half-timbered yeoman's house, featuring a great hall and surrounded by glorious garden, orchard and meadows. A perfect example of a Wealden Hall-House, it is full of beautiful collections of furniture, wood and metal work.

Tenterden & District Museum

Station Road
Tenterden TN30 6HN
01580 764310
www.ukpages.net/kent/museum.htm

The museum is housed in a two-storey weatherboarded building, one of the last representatives in Tenterden of a type of industrial building common in the area in the latter part of the 19th century. It serves as a focus for research and enquiry and provides a repository for artefacts connected with the area.

Timeball Tower

Victoria Parade
Deal CT14 7BP
01304 360987
www.dealtimeball.co.uk
mcarey@talktalk.net

Originally in 1796 a Shutter Telegraph station, the current Tower was built in 1821 as a Semaphore Tower but was later equipped with a Timeball which was raised on a mast on the roof and dropped at 1 pm by a signal fron Greenwich so that the many ships anchored off shore could check their chronometers. There are 4 floors of exhibits, video and interactive displays of signalling, timekeeping & navigation equipment.

Timescapes

On-line virtual organisation
Whitstable
https://timescapeskent.wordpress.com
timescapeskent@gmail.com

Timescapes is a community group committed to involving local people in the history and archaeology of Whitstable and the North Kent Coast. We work closely with other groups and organsations to undertake research and education programmes.

Tunbridge Wells Family History Society

Yew Tree Byre, Yew Tree Lane, Rotherfield
Rotherfield TN6 3QP
www.tunwells-fhs.co.uk
secretary@tunwells-fhs.co.uk

We are a small Society with around 250 members who either live in or have family history connections with the Tunbridge Wells area, which straddles the Kent / East Sussex border.

Tunbridge Wells Museum & Art Gallery

Civic Centre, Mount Pleasant
Tunbridge Wells TN1 1JN
01892 554171
www.tunbridgewellsmuseum.org
museum@tunbridgewells.gov.uk

Tunbridge Wells Museum and Art Gallery shares the special story of the borough of Tunbridge Wells. Enjoy our wonderful collections, visit our major exhibitions and take part in activities for everyone.

Tyrwhitt Drake Museum of Carriages

The Archbishops' Stables, Mill Street
Maidstone ME15 6YE
01622 602838
www.museum.maidstone.gov.uk
museuminfo@maidstone.gov.uk

Maidstone Carriage Museum is home to a unique collection of horse-drawn vehicles and transport curiosities. More than 60 vehicles are displayed, from grand carriages and ornate sleighs to antique sedan chairs and Victorian cabs - even an original ice cream cart.

Upnor Castle - English Heritage

Upnor ME2 4XG
0870 333 1181
www.english-heritage.org.uk/visit/places/upnor-castle/

Set in tranquil grounds adjoining a riverside village, this rare example of an Elizabethan artillery fort was begun in 1559 and redeveloped in 1599-1601, to protect warships moored at Chatham dockyards. Despite a brave attempt, it entirely failed to do so in 1667, when the Dutch sailed past it to burn or capture the English fleet at anchor.

Walmer Castle & Gardens - English Heritage

Kingsdown Road
Walmer CT14 7LJ
01304 364288
http://goo.gl/hPgPT1

Built during the reign of King Henry VIII, Walmer Castle is one of the most fascinating visitor attractions in the South East. Originally designed as part of a chain of coastal artillery defences it evolved into the official residence of the Lord Warden of the Cinque Ports.

White Mill Rural Heritage Centre

Ash Road
Sandwich CT13 9JB
07891 389 675
www.whitemillheritagecentre.org.uk
greg@whitemill.info

White Mill is a smock mill which retains its original wooden machinery and was restored between 1961 and 1981. It is surrounded by the original outbuildings and millers cottage. White Mill was built in 1760 and still has most of its original wooden machinery.

Whitstable Museum & Gallery

Oxford Street
Whitstable CT5 1DB
01227 276998
www.canterbury-museums.co.uk
museums@canterbury.gov.uk

Dive in to maritime history and explore the town. The fascinating displays give townspeople and visitors an idea of why Whitstable is here, how it grew and how it has changed over the years.

Woodchurch Village Life Museum

Susans Hill
Woodchurch, near Ashford TN26 3RE
01233 860240
www.woodchurchmuseum.com

Woodchurch is a picturesque Kent village which is situated 7 miles from the historic market town of Ashford and 5 miles from the Cinque Ports town of Tenterden. The museum is housed in an 18th century oak-framed barn and 17th century cart shed, on a rural site not far from the village centre.

Woolwich & District Family History Society

121 Crofton Avenue
Bexley DA5 3AU
www.woolwichfhs.org.uk
suhiwfhs@tiscali.co.uk

The society covers not just Woolwich but also Greenwich, Woolwich, Charlton, Plumstead, Eltham, Welling, Bexleyheath and Crayford. Many people have ancestors who spent a few years or a few generation in this area.

Lancashire

Lancashire, or Lancaster, county palatine and maritime shire, in NW. of England. bounded N. by Westmorland and Cumberland, E. by Yorkshire, S. by Cheshire, and W. by the Irish Sea; greatest length, 76 miles; greatest breadth, 45 miles; area, 1,208,154 acres; population 3,454,441. A detached part of the county, known as Furness (25 miles long, 23 miles broad), is separated from the main portion by Morecambe Bay and a part of Westmorland county [note: Furness has been part of Cumbria since 1974]. The coast line of Lancashire is very irregular, the chief inlets being Morecambe Bay, Lancaster Bay, and the estuaries of the Mersey and the Ribble. Towards the shore, which comprises great stretches of sand, the land has generally a flat appearance. In the N. and E. it becomes more elevated. The principal rivers are the Mersey, Ribble, Lune, Wyre, Winster, and Leven. Peat prevails in the soil of the upland districts, while much of the low lying land consists of a rich loam. The chief crops are oats, wheat, and potatoes. Carboniferous limestone abounds in the N. part of the co.; on the coast is the old red sandstone. The great coalfield of Lancashire, the existence of which has greatly contributed towards establishing its pre-eminence as a manufacturing co., covers an area of about 217 sq. miles between the Ribble and the Mersey. Iron is abundant in Furness. Lancashire is intersected by an intricate network of canals and railways. Its immense cotton manufactures have a world-wide fame, while other textile fabrics are largely produced. Its manufactures of machinery of all descriptions are also extensive. Lancashire comprises 6 hundreds and 453 parishes. It is comprised in the dioceses of Liverpool, Manchester, Carlisle, and Ripon.

– John Bartholomew, *Gazetteer of the British Isles* (1887)

14th/20th King's Hussars Museum

Stanley Street
Preston PR1 4YP
01772 534075
www.lancashire.gov.uk
stephen.bull@lancashire.gov.uk

The museum of Lancashire contains the museums of two historic regiments. The gallery of the 14th/20th King's Hussars traces the history of the regiment from 1715 and includes two Victoria crosses as well as artefacts from the Napoleonic era and India.

Astley Hall & Coach House

Astley Park, Off Hallgate
Chorley PR7 1NP
01257 515151
www.chorley.gov.uk/astleyhall
astley.hall@chorley.gov.uk

Astley Hall is a museum and art gallery housed within a Grade I listed historic house. The hall is set within the beautiful surroundings of Astley Park which include historic woodland, a lake, a fully renovated Victorian walled garden alongside clean and modern facilities for visitors to enjoy. The hall is perhaps best known for its stunning Jacobean plasterwork ceilings and the house is built around an internal Elizabethan courtyard.

Be Prepared - The Story of Scouting

Story of Scouting Museum, Waddecar Scout Activity Centre, Snape Rake Lane
Goosnargh PR3 2EU
01253 354244
www.storyofscouting.org.uk

The museum, the very first purpose-built Scouting museum in the country is situated at Waddecar Scout Activity Centre. It provides over 160 square metres of display and storage space. There are over 2000 books and publications in the library including all the known reference works.

Blackburn Museum & Art Gallery

Museum St
Blackburn BB1 7AJ
01254 667130
blackburnmuseum.org.uk
museum@blackburn.gov.uk

Blackburn Museum and Art Gallery is housed in a beautiful 'Arts and Crafts' style building in the town centre, near the Town Hall and cinema. It opened in 1874 originally as both a museum and a library, and now offers a lively programme of exhibitions and events for all the family.

Bolton Museum, Aquarium & Archive

Le Mans Crescent
Bolton BL1 1SE
01204 332211
www.boltonmuseums.org.uk
museum@bolton.gov.uk

Bolton is a medium sized regional museum that has its origins in the Chadwick Museum and Mere Hall Art Gallery.

Collections: The museums collection includes archaeology, art, botany, egyptology, entomology, geology, social history, natural history, and zoology.

Bolton Steam Museum

Mornington Road
Bolton BL1 4EU
01204 846490
www.nmes.org
dlewis66@talktalk.net

Over 25 textile mill stationary steam engines have been rescued and restored to working order. These include some very rare and unusual types of engine.

British Commercial Vehicle Museum

King Steet
Leyland PR25 2LE
01772 451011
www.bcvm.co.uk
enquiries@bcvm.co.uk

This is one of Britain's most important heritage collections - a unique display of historic commercial vehicles and buses spanning a century of truck and bus building. Visitors can view an imaginative display of vehicles, which use sound and lighting special effects to give a virtual reality tour for all the exhibits, creating a spectacular and fascinating exhibition.

British Lawnmower Museum

106-114 Shakespeare St
Southport PR8 5AJ
01704 501336
www.lawnmowerworld.com
museum@lawnmowerworld.com

The museum has now become one of the leading authorities on vintage lawnmowers specialises in antique garden machinery, supplying parts, archive conservation of manuscript materials and valuing machines from all over the world.

Carnforth Station Heritage Centre

Warton Road
Carnforth LA5 9TR
01524 735165
www.carnforthstation.co.uk
sdo@carnforth-station.co.uk

After many years of dereliction the Carnforth Station Trust Company restored the derelict station into what has become an award winning Heritage Centre. Attractions include the Brief Encounter Cinema area and Refreshment Room as seen in David Lean's film of 1945, various exhibition areas covering past local industry, the golden age of steam and the Bateman Gallery hosting 'guest' exhibitions throughout the year.

Clitheroe Castle Museum

Castle Hill
Clitheroe BB7 1BA
01200 424568
museum@ribblevalley.gov.uk

Now fully open after a complete makeover, the museum stands high on Castle Hill, in the shadow of the castle Keep, an image which has dominated Clitheroe's skyline for over 800 years. Explore our 'hands-on' galleries, collections and displays which reveal amazing stories and take you on a journey through 350 millions years of history.

Colne Heritage Centre

The Old Colne Grammar School, Church Street
Colne BB8 0AP
01282 871155

Features permanent and changing exhibitions about the ancient market town of Colne. Including a collection of Wallace Hartley memorabilia, the bandmaster who went down with the Titanic in 1912.

Cottage Museum, The

15 Castle Hill
Lancaster LA1 1YS
01524 64637
www.lancashire.gov.uk/museums
cottagemuseum@lancashire.gov.uk

Tiny and intriguing 18th century cottage, offering an intimate glimpse of early Victorian life. Meet our Victorian housekeeper.

Duke of Lancaster's Own Yeomanry Museum

Stanley Street
Preston PR1 4YP
01772 264 075
http://goo.gl/eu0e5J

Re-opened in mid 2011, following a major refurbishment, the museum of Lancashire contains the museums of two historic regiments. The gallery of the 14th/20th King's Hussars traces the history of the regiment from 1715 and includes two Victoria crosses as well as artefacts from the Napoleonic era and India. The Duke of Lancaster's Own Yeomanry collection marks its association with the county with exhibits that include items from World War I in the Middle East, Peterloo, and South Africa.

Earby & District Local History Society

c/o 22 Salterforth Road, Earby
Barnoldswick BB18 6ND
www.earbyhistory.co.uk
info@earbyhistory.co.uk

Our aims are to raise awareness and interest in the history of the Ancient Parish of Thornton-in-Craven, of which Earby was a part. We aim to facilitate research into the heritage of Earby and District, including Thornton-in-Craven, Kelbrook, Sough, Hague, Harden and Salterforth.

Fleetwood Memorial Park

Warrenhurst Road
Fleetwood
01253 891000
www.wyre.gov.uk/memorialpark
kate.baird@wyre.gov.uk

Fleetwood's Memorial Park is a Grade II listed park in the heart of the town. Memorial Park is unique in that the entire grounds were created in commemoration of the First World War, unlike most conventional architectural memorials, and it is one of only a few listed war memorial parks and gardens in the country.

Fleetwood Museum

Queens Terrace
Fleetwood FY7 6BT
01253 876621
www.lancashire.gov.uk/museums
fleetwoodmuseum@lancashire.gov.uk

The museum explores the story of Fleetwood, the Victorian idealism of Fleetwood's founder Sir Peter Hesketh Fleetwood and the architect Decimus Burton, who designed the new Victorian town. Discover Fleetwood's heyday as a Victorian seaside resort, cargo trade, ferry services, lifeboats, about the docks and industrious fishing industry – both inshore and deep sea, trawlers at war, the chemical giant ICI and so much more.

Gawthorpe Hall - National Trust

Padiham
Nr Burnley BB12 8UA
01282 771004
www.nationaltrust.org.uk/gawthorpe-hall
gawthorpehall@lancashire.gov.uk

This imposing house, set in tranquil grounds in the heart of urban Lancashire, resembles the great Hardwick Hall and is very probably by the same architect, Robert Smythson. In the middle of the 19th century Sir Charles Barry was commissioned to restore the house, thereby creating the opulent interiors we see today.

Hall i' th' Wood Museum

Greenway, off Crompton Way
Bolton BL1 8UA
01204 332211
www.boltonmuseums.org.uk
historichalls@bolton.gov.uk

Hall i' th' Wood Museum is a rare surviving example of a Tudor wooden framed house.

Collections: On display are examples of 17th and early 18th century furniture and objects relating to Samuel Crompton and the founder of the museum, Lord Leverhulme.

Harris Museum & Art Gallery

Market Square
Preston PR1 2PP
01772 258248
www.harrismuseum.org.uk
harris.museum@preston.gov.uk

Located in the heart of Preston in a beautiful Grade I listed building, the Harris Museum & Art Gallery hosts a huge range of free exhibitions as well as events and activities for all ages.

Collections: There are three main collection areas - fine art, decorative art and history.

Helmshore Mills Textile Museum

Holcombe Road, Helmshore
Rossendale BB4 4NP
01706 226459
www.lancashire.gov.uk/museums
helmshoremuseum@lancashire.gov.uk

18th century water powered fulling mill and a 19th century condenser cotton spinning mill, both with working machinery.

Hoghton Tower

Hoghton Tower
Hoghton PR5 0SH
01254 85 2986
www.hoghtontower.co.uk
mail@hoghtontower.co.uk

Hoghton Tower is one of Lancashire's gems. A Tudor – Elizabethan manor and the ancestral home of the de Hoghton family, the Tower stands proudly on its hill overlooking the surrounding countryside.

Horwich Heritage Centre

The Resource Centre, Beaumont Road, (off Longworth Road), Horwich
Bolton BL6 7BG
www.horwichheritage.co.uk

The Heritage Centre is the permanent home of Horwich Heritage and a permanent exhibition is on display there. There are several exhibition areas in the new centre, one of them being Horwich Loco Works, which includes a three-quarter scale model of a locomotive footplate. Other areas include a Victorian kitchen, local industry, a Horwich pub, childhood, local sport, Leverhulme's Rivington and transport.

Judges' Lodgings

Church Street
Lancaster LA1 1YS
01524 32808
www.lancashire.gov.uk/museums
judges.lodgings@lancashire.gov.uk

Lancaster's oldest town house, nestled in the shadow of Lancaster Castle. Originally the home of Thomas Covell and later used by judges visiting the Assize Courts, this Grade 1 listed building offers something for all the family. See the splendidly restored period rooms featuring fine furniture by the renowned Gillows of Lancaster. Take a journey through history in the museum of Childhood with our enchanting collection of dolls, toys and games from the 18th century to the present day.

King's Own Royal Regiment Museum

City Museum, Market Square
Lancaster LA1 1HT
01524 64637
www.kingsownmuseum.plus.com
kingsownmuseum@iname.com

The museum covers the history of the King's Own Royal Regiment (4th Regiment of Foot) from its raising in 1680 through to the present day. Displays cover the Napoleonic, Crimean and Abyssinian Campaigns of the 19th century, and the Boer War, Great War and Second World War of the 20th century. The museum's website is a fascinating resource on the history of the regiment.

Lancashire Archives

Lancashire Record Office, Bow Lane, Preston
Lancashire PR1 2RE
01772 533039

Lancashire Archives collects unique, historic records that reflect Lancashire and Lancashire life - past and present.

Lancashire County Council Cultural Services

CH Room, Lancashire Archives, Bow Lane
Preston PR1 2RE
01772 534021
www.lancashire.gov.uk
ch.enquiries@lancashire.gov.uk

We celebrate and bring together the heritage of Lancashire through a wide range of activities showcasing the Local History and Heritage collections held by Lancashire County Council. Collections are housed within these Cultural Services venues.

Lancashire County Council Museum Service

Stanley Street
Preston PR1 4YP
01772 534061
www.lancashire.gov.uk/museums
museums.enquiries@lancashire.gov.uk

The textile industry collections of Lancashire County Museum Service include three former textile mills, textile machinery, photographs, books, catalogues and textile machine manuals. They are located at Helmshore Mills Textile Museum, Rossendale and Queen Street Mill Textile Museum, Burnley.

Lancashire Infantry Museum

Fulwood Barracks
Preston PR2 8AA
01772 260362
www.lancashireinfantrymuseum.org.uk
enquiries@lancashireinfantrymuseum.org.uk

The museum houses the largest military collection in the North West. It covers the history of the County's three infantry regiments from the raising of Lord Castleton's Regiment of Foot in 1689 through the several amalgamations that have resulted in the creation of the current Duke of Lancaster's Regiment.

Collections: The museum houses the largest military collection in the North West. It covers the history of the County.

Lancaster Castle

Shire Hall, Castle Parade
Lancaster LA1 1YJ
01524 64998
www.lancashire.gov.uk/museums
lancastercastle@lancashire.gov.uk

Discover one of the most important historic monuments in the North West.. This fascinating Grade 1 listed building has dominated Lancaster for almost 1000 years and is one of the best preserved and hardest working castles in the country.

Lancaster City Museum

Market Square
Lancaster LA1 1HT
01524 64637
www.lancashire.gov.uk/museums
lancastercitymuseum@lancashire.gov.uk

Lancaster City Museum is housed in an elegant Georgian building situated at the heart of historic Lancaster. Discover Lancaster's past from the time of the Romans to the present day. Trace the history of the Lancaster King's Own regiment. Changing programme of temporary exhibitions.

Lancaster Maritime Museum

St George's Quay
Lancaster LA1 1RB
01524 382264
www.lancashire.gov.uk/museums
lancastermaritimemuseum@lancashire.gov.uk

Lancaster Maritime Museum is an award-winning museum set within the former Port of Lancaster Custom House. Let us take you on a journey to discover all things nautical relating to the Morecambe Bay area.

Lancaster Priory

Castle Hill
Lancaster LA1 1YZ
01524 65338
www.lancasterpriory.org
lancasterpriory@yahoo.co.uk

Lancaster Priory & Parish Church in North West England - just south of the Lake District - dates from the 11th century, though there has been a church on this site from 630 A.D. and maybe in Roman times.

Lewis Textile Museum

Exchange Street
Blackburn BB1 7JN
01254 667 130
blackburnmuseum.org.uk
museum@blackburn.gov.uk

The Lewis Textile Museum on Exchange Street, facing the Town Hall and just around the corner from Blackburn Museum and Art Gallery, tells the story of the town's cotton industry and features a programme of textile based exhibitions.

Littleborough Museum

Littleborough OL15
01706 377 685
www.littleboroughshistory.org/page4.html

This collection has been made up of pieces that are directly or indirectly related to the people of this community. Using the many artefacts that are on display, the collection hopes to bring to life the long and colourful history of the town and its people, taking a particular interest in the way that normal people's lives have changed with the advent of new technology and working practices.

Lytham Windmill Heritage Museum

The Windmill, Lytham Green
Lytham FY8 5LD
01253 794 879
www.lythamwindmill.co.uk
touristinformation@fylde.gov.uk

Built on what is now Lytham Green in 1805, the Windmill is the landmark that everyone sees when they come to Lytham. One of several mills on the Fylde, Lytham Mill was worked until 1919 when a fire destroyed most of the machinery.

Marsh Mill Windmill

76 Barton Street
Thornton-Cleveleys FY5 4AE
01253 860765
www.friends-of-marshmill.com

Marsh Mill itself is the finest, well preserved example of its kind in the north west of England. It was built in 1974 by Ralph Slater who was a Fylde Millwright. It was commissioned by Bold Hesketh, uncle of Peter Hesketh (later Peter Hesketh-Fleetwood) who would go on to play a prominent role in the expansion of Fleetwood.

Museum of Lancashire

Stanley Street
Preston PR1 4YP
01772 534075
www.lancashire.gov.uk/museums
museumoflancashire@lancashire.gov.uk

Explore 2000 years of Lancashire history with our fantastic new range of family friendly, interactive galleries. Explore a range of objects which will introduce you to the story of Lancashire.

North West Sound Archive

Old Steward's Office, Castle Grounds, Clitheroe Castle
Clitheroe BB7 1BA
01200 427897
www.gmcro.co.uk/other/NWSA/nwsa.htm
archives@gmcro.co.uk

The North West Sound Archive has around 50,000 such recordings of BBC Radio Manchester as well as over 110,000 sound recorded items and 2.5 tonnes of 78-rpm gramophone records ranging from George Formby to the Halle Orchestra. There are internationally important collections including the survey of English dialect and solidarity speeches from the Dockyards of Poland.

Ormskirk & District Family History Society

PO Box 213, Aughton
Ormskirk L39 5WT
01695 578780
www.odfhs.org.uk
secretary@odfhs.org.uk

Explores genealogy in south west Lancashire.

Pendle Heritage Centre

Park Hill, Barrowford
Nelson BB9 6JQ
01282 677152
www.htnw.co.uk
pendleheritagecentre@htnw.co.uk

Pendle Heritage Centre, listed grade II buildings, incorporates a museum, art gallery, parlour shop, tea-room, 18th century walled garden, cruck-barn, tourist information centre and conference facilities.

Queen Street Mill Textile Museum

Harle Syke
Burnley BB10 2HX
01282 412555
www.lancashire.gov.uk/museums
queenstreetmill@lancashire.gov.uk

Queen Street Mill Textile Museum is the last remaining operational steam powered weaving mill in the world. The museum collections are designated as being of national importance and the boilerhouse, enginehouse and chimney have Ancient Monument status.

Ribble Steam Railway & Museum

Chain Caul Road
Preston PR2 2PD
01772 728800
www.ribblesteam.org.uk
enquiries@ribblesteam.org.uk

A visit to the Ribble Steam Railway will not only give you the opportunity to travel along the one-and-a half-mile dock and riverside line, but also access our extensive museum and workshop. On site we have over 40 industrial locomotives, including Deltic Prototype currently on loan from The National Railway Museum.

Ribchester Museum of Roman Antiquities

Riverside, Ribchester
Preston PR3 3XS
01254 878 261
www.ribchesterromanmuseum.org
ribchestermuseum@btconnect.com

Roman Ribchester is brought to life by dramatic displays, which contain a life size cavalryman, Roman legionary and exciting interactive exhibits. Columns have been erected for the first time in 2000 years and there are wonderful objects, including weaponry, jewellery and leatherwork alongside favourites like the replica of the Ribchester Parade Helmet and the impressive sculpture of a cavalryman riding down his Celtic adversary.

Roman Bath House

Castle Hill
Lancaster LA1 1YS
01524 64637
http://goo.gl/DtiOu1
lancaster.citymuseum@mus.lancscc.gov.uk

Discovered and excavated in 1973-4, the Roman bath-house in Vicarage Field, Lancaster, formed one end of a large courtyard house, probably the home of a Roman official. It was demolished in about 340AD to make way for a new and massive stone fort. Part of the fort wall, known as the 'Wery Wall', can also be seen.

Rufford Old Hall - National Trust

Rufford
nr Ormskirk L40 1SG
01704 821254
www.nationaltrust.org.uk/rufford-old-hall
ruffordoldhall@nationaltrust.org.uk

One of Lancashire's finest 16th-century buildings. The spectacular Great Hall has an intricately carved 'moveable' wooden screen and dramatic hammer-beam roof.

Samlesbury Hall

Preston New Road
Preston PR5 0UP
01254 812010
www.samlesburyhall.co.uk
enquiries@samlesburyhall.co.uk

Samlesbury Hall is Lancashire's foremost ancestral home offering a variety of facilities ensuring a great day out. Samlesbury Hall boasts three main galleries that show new and exciting exhibitions from a variety of different artistic disciplines.

Smithills Hall

Smithills Dean Road
Bolton BL1 7NP
01204 332377
www.boltonmuseums.org.uk/historic-halls
historichalls@bolton.gov.uk

One of Bolton's original family homes, Smithills Hall is a Grade 1 listed building, full of history and drama.

Collections: Furniture: 17th century;18th century;19th century; Arts and Crafts movement. Decor: from mediaeval to Arts and Crafts. Paintings: mainly from 18th to 19th century.

South Ribble Museum & Exhibition Centre

The Old Grammar School, Church Road
Leyland PR25 3FJ
01772 422041
south-ribble.co.uk/srmuseum
museum@southribble.gov.uk

The Leyland Free Grammar School was established by Henry ffarington in 1524, and the present building was probably erected on this site about 1580. Although extended a century later most of the structure has been changed very little.

Collections: Includes finds from E.E.Pickering's 1946-58 excavations on the Roman supply base at Walton-le-Dale. Small economic and socisl history collections reflect the South Ribble district's economic development (textiles/cloth bleaching etc).

Towneley Hall Art Gallery & Museum

Towneley Park
Burnley BB11 3RQ
01282 424213
www.burnley.gov.uk/residents/towneley-hall
towneleyhall@burnley.gov.uk

Towneley Hall is a council-owned museum and art gallery, offering an intriguing combination of historic art collection alongside a changing programme of contemporary exhibitions.

Turton Tower

Chapeltown Road, Turton
Nr Bolton BL7 0HG
01204 852203
www.turtontower.co.uk
friends@turtontower.co.uk

A delightful Tudor house in woodland gardens. A distinctive 15th century English country house. Set in relaxing woodlands on the edge of the popular walking area of the West Pennine Moors.

Weavers' Triangle Visitor Centre

85 Manchester Road
Burnley BB11 1JZ
01282 452403
www.weaverstriangle.co.uk
weaverstriangle@yahoo.co.uk

Discover what it was like to live in a 19th century Lancashire mill town. From the Visitor Centre, walk through the Weavers' Triangle - a unique Victorian industrial landscape.

Whitaker, The

Whitaker Park, Rawtenstall
Rossendale BB4 6RE
01706 260785
www.lancashire.gov.uk/museums
rossendalemuseum@lancashire.gov.uk

Set within tranquil Whitaker Park. Displays include a late Victorian drawing room, fine arts and furniture.

Leicestershire

Leicestershire, inland county of England, bounded N. by Notts, E. by Lincolnshire and Rutland, SE. by Northamptonshire, SW. by Warwickshire, and NW. by Derbyshire; greatest length, about 44 miles; greatest breadth, about40 miles; area, 511,907 acres, population 321,258. Low undulating hills cover the surface of the county, the highest elevation being Bardon Hill (902 ft.), in the Charnwood range. Charnwood Forest, in the NW., is now nearly destitute of trees. The principal rivers are tributaries of the Trent, which flows in the NW. of the county; these are the Soar, Wreak, Anker, Devon, and Mease. The Avon and Welland flow in the S. Two canals, the Union and the Grand Union, are connected with the Grand Junction Canal. Much of the soil is loamy, and the richest districts are kept in pasture, upon which are reared the varieties of sheep and cattle for which the county is famous. Dairy farms are numerous, especially in the vicinity of Melton Mowbray where the well-known Stilton cheese is largely produced. Leicestershire consists mostly of the new reel sandstone formation. The coal measures have a total area of about 15 square miles, the most productive mines being in the neighbourhood of Ashby de la Zouch. Hosiery is the leading manufacture, the wool employed being that of Leicestershire sheep. The county has 6 hundreds, 332 parishes, and 8 parts, and the parliamentary and municipal borough of Leicester. It is almost entirely in the diocese of Peterborough.

– John Bartholomew, *Gazetteer of the British Isles* (1887)

Abbey Pumping Station

Corporation Road, Abbey Lane
Leicester LE4 5PX
0116 299 5111
www.abbeypumpingstation.org
museums@leicester.gov.uk

The Abbey Pumping Station is Leicester's Museum of Science and Technology. The museum collects and displays the industrial, technological and scientific heritage of Leicester.

Ashby de la Zouch Castle - English Heritage

South Street
Ashby de la Zouch LE65 1BR
01530 413343
http://goo.gl/Mv1Wuu

Ashby Castle forms the backdrop to the famous jousting scenes in Sir Walter Scott's classic novel of 1819, Ivanhoe. Now a ruin, the castle began as a manor house in the 12th century.

Ashby De La Zouch Museum

North Street
Ashby De La Zouch LE65 1HU
01530 560090
www.ashbydelazouchmuseum.org.uk
enquiries@hastyngs.plus.com

The collection is based on the history of the town of Ashby and the surrounding villages of Packington, Blackfordby, Smisby, Staunton Harold, Breedon, Lount and Coleorton. In addition to a huge archive of local photographs and documents, the museum runs a full programme of talks, workshops, walks and evening classes.

Belgrave Hall & Gardens

Church Road, Off Thurcaston Road
Leicester LE4 5PE
0116 229 8181
www.leicester.gov.uk/museumsandgalleries
museums@leicester.gov.uk

Belgrave Hall provides an oasis of peace and quiet in a busy city. It was built in the early 18th century, in what was then a small village three miles from the town of Leicester. Now city traffic passes, almost unnoticed, just beyond the garden walls.

Bellfoundry Museum

John Taylor Bellfounders Limited, The Bellfoundry, Freehold Street
Loughborough LE11 1AR
01509 233414
www.taylorbells.co.uk/web/?q=node/52
museum@taylorbells.co.uk

In this museum, Taylor's Bellfoundry has created a permanent record of the company and the industry, telling the story of bellfounding through the ages. An extensive range of exhibits and memorabilia tells the story of one of the oldest manufacturing industries in the world.

Castle Donington Museum

4 Apiary Gate, Castle Donington
Derby DE74 2JA
01332 812711
www.castledoningtonmuseum.org

The museum occupies the ground floor of a 17th century, stone built house which was originally used as a farm. We have a charming garden with a small outdoor display of artefacts.

Charles Moore Collection of Musical Instruments, University of Leicester

Charles Moore Collection of Musical Instruments, Music Department, University of Leicester, University Road
Leicester LE7 7RH
0116 252 2781
www2.le.ac.uk/institution/music/moore

The Charles Moore Collection is one of the few academic musical instrument collections in British universities. Its particular speciality is 18th and 19th century woodwind and brass instruments.

Charnwood Museum

Granby Street
Loughborough LE11 3DU
01509 233754
www.leics.gov.uk/museums/charnwood/index.htm
charnwood@leics.gov.uk

Charnwood Museum features a wide range of exhibits reflecting the history, geology, archaeology and industries of Charnwood and the surrounding area. Permanent displays include 'Coming to Charnwood', 'The Natural World of Charnwood', 'Living off the Land' and 'Earning a Living'.

De Montfort University

The Gateway
Leicester LE1 9BH
0116 250 6392
http://goo.gl/YpycTc
archives@dmu.ac.uk

De Montfort University is a is a public research and teaching university situated in Leicester. It was originally founded as Leicester School of Art in 1870 and gained university status in 1992. The Archives and Special Collections of De Montfort University are situated in a custom built reading room and store in Room 00.21 on the lower ground floor of the Kimberlin Library.

Donington le Heath Manor House

Manor Road, Donington le Heath
Coalville LE67 2FW
01530 831259
www.doningtonleheath.com
dlhmanorhouse@leics.gov.uk

The museum is based in a Medieval Manor House dating back to 1280. The house has a fascinating history and restored with fine oak furnishings.

East Midlands Oral History Archive

Centre for Urban History, University of Leicester
Leicester LE1 7RH
0116 252 5065
www.le.ac.uk/emoha
emoha@le.ac.uk

The East Midlands Oral History Archive is based on the University of Leicester's satellite campus in Marc Fitch House along with the centre for Urban History and English Local History. It was originally funded by the Heritage Lottery Fund to establish the first large-scale archive of oral history recordings for Leicestershire & Rutland.

Foxton Canal Museum & Inclined Plane Trust

Middle Lock, Gumley Road, Foxton
Market Harborough LE16 7RA
0116 279 2657
www.fipt.org.uk
info@fipt.org.uk

Foxton Canal Museum was opened in 1989 and is situated in the reconstructed Boiler House of the lift. It tells the story of the lift and canals it served for the public. The museum researches the history of the lift and local canals. It holds extensive waterway archives, as well as objects from the site.

Foxton Locks

Gumley Road
Foxton LE16 7RA
01926 626150

Explore a place brimming with history and bursting with wildlife. See elegant brick bridges, a steep staircase of locks, the old canal company stables, lock keeper's cottage and the remains of a gigantic boat lift.

Grace Dieu Priory

Ashby Road
Belton LE67 3FJ
01530 454603
www.gracedieupriory.org.uk
angela.bexton@nwleicestershire.gov.uk

Monastic house for Augustinian Canonesses, 1235-40. The main feature now is a large four-centred arch on corbels.

Great Central Railway

Great Central Station, Great Central Road
Loughborough LE11 1RW
01509 230726
www.gcrailway.co.uk

sales@gcrailway.co.uk

Main line steam trains - every weekend throughout the year. Re-creating the experience of famous expresses of the steam age.

Guildhall, The

Guildhall Lane
Leicester LE1 5FQ
0116 253 2569
www.leicester.gov.uk/museumsandgalleries
museums@leicester.gov.uk

The Guildhall has had many uses and lives. The Great Hall itself was built in about 1390 as a meeting place for the Guild of Corpus Christi (a small but powerful group of businessman and gentry).

Collections: Today, The Guildhall is best known as an excellent performance venue, attracting acts from across the country, and as a museum where visitors can step back in time and come face to face with 'Crankie Gemmie' and 'Emma Smith', two of Leicester's notorious criminals who can be found lurking within the Victorian police cells.

Harborough Museum

Council Offices, Adam & Eve Street
Market Harborough LE16 7AG
01858 821087
museums@leics.gov.uk

Find out about the historic town of Market Harborough and its surrounding area. For many centuries Market Harborough has been a market town, a social centre for the surrounding countryside a hunting centre, and a stagecoach post.

Hinckley & District Museum

Framework Knitters Cottages, Lower Bond Street
Hinckley LE10 1QU
01455 251218
www.hinckleydistrictmuseum.org.uk
hinckleymuseum@hotmail.co.uk

Local history museum housed in a row of half-timbered thatched cottages dating from the 17th century. The museum has been open to the public since 1995.

Collections: Local and social history of Hinckley and district, including the hosiery and boot and shoe industries.

Jewry Wall Museum

St Nicholas Circle
Leicester LE1 4LB
0116 225 4971
www.leicester.gov.uk/museumsandgalleries

museums@leicester.gov.uk

At Jewry Wall Museum you can discover the archaeology of Leicester's past and find out about the people of Leicester from prehistoric times to the medieval period. A special display on the history of archaeology in Leicester, 'Archaeology and Endeavour' explains why our city has such rich and interesting museum collections and includes a stunning display of extremely rare medieval glass from Wygston's House. The museum grounds contain one of Leicester's most famous landmarks, the Jewry Wall, part of the Roman town's public baths.

King Richard III Visitor Centre

4A St Martins,
Leicester LE1 5DB
0300 300 0900
kriii.com
info@kriii.com

Home to the brand new exhibition, King Richard III: Dynasty, Death and Discovery. Using great storytelling, beautiful design and 21st century technology, the centre tells the fascinating and moving story of the king's life and death, and reveals one of the greatest archaeological detective stories ever told.

Kirby Muxloe Castle

Oakcroft Ave
Kurby Muxloe LE9 2DH
www.english-heritage.org.uk

Construction of this picturesque, moated brick castle was begun in 1480 by William, Lord Hastings. He was later beheaded and the castle was left unfinished.

Knitting Together - Leicester City Museums Service

c/o 12th Floor, A Block, New Walk Centre, Welford Place
Leicester LE1 6ZG
www.knittingtogether.org.uk

The Knitting Together website tells the story of the East Midlands knitting industry over the past four hundred years, with a virtual museum, project themes, interactive exhibits and a range of other information. Sound, video, interactive tours, virtual exhibitions, and places to visit will provide an insight to the history of the East Midlands knitting industry.

Leicester Castle

Castle View
Leicester LE1 5WH
0116 253 2569
www.leicester.gov.uk/museumsandgalleries
museums@leicester.gov.uk

The first castle at Leicester was probably built around 1070 either by William the Conqueror or by Hugh de Grandsmesnil, the first Norman lord or castellan of Leicester.

Leicester Cathedral

St Martins House, 7 Peacock Lane
Leicester LE1 5PZ
0116 261 5200
www.leicestercathedral.org
leicestercathedral@leccofe.org

The Cathedral Church for the Diocese of Leicester.

Leicester Royal Infirmary Museum

Knighton Street Nurses Home, Royal Infirmary
Leicester LE1 5WW
0116 254 1414
www.lri.org.uk/museum.htm

Find out all about the Royal Infirmary since it opened in 1771. Look at pictures, prints, manuscripts and memorabilia, including medical equipment showing how medicine has changed through the years.

Leicestershire & Rutland Family History Society

37 Cyril Street
Leicester LE3 2FF
0116 285 7211
www.lrfhs.org.uk
secretary@lrfhs.org.uk

Founded in 1974 by 12 family history enthusiasts, the society, run by volunteers, has gone from strength to strength and in 2014 celebrated its 40th anniversary. From humble beginnings we have grown to a society with currently over 2,000 members UK and worldwide.

Leicestershire County Cricket Club Museum

Leicestershire County Cricket Club, County Ground, Grace Road
Leicester LE2 8AD
0116 2832128
www.leicestershireccc.co.uk
enquiries@leicestershireccc.co.uk

Exhibition of the history of the game of cricket and the Leicestershire County Cricket Club.

Leicestershire Museums

Leicestershire Museums Room 400
Glenfield LE3 8RA
sue.alderman@leics.gov.uk

The County Council Museum Service is responsible for the care and stewardship of over 1 million objects which are held in trust for the people of Leicestershire. These have been collected since 1849 and are cared for by specialist curators.

Loughborough War Memorial Museum

Queens Park, Granby Street
Loughborough LE11 3DU
01509 263370
www.loughborough-rollofhonour.com

Why is the tower here? It was built as a memorial to the Loughborough men who died in the Great War, and looks like to towers of bells built in parts of Europe, particularly Flanders. The ground floor has collections of wartime objects mainly given by local people.

Lutterworth Museum & Historical Society

Wycliffe House, Gilmorton Road
Lutterworth LE17 4DY
01455 284733
lutterworthmuseum.com
Alijgeoff@aol.com

Museum for the area covering local history, family history, displays, events, talks, slide shows, etc. Very large important Sir Frank Whittle collection.

Magazine, The

Oxford Street
Leicester LE2 7BY
0116 225 4980
www.leicester.gov.uk/museumsandgalleries
museums@leicester.gov.uk

The Magazine Gateway was the main entrance into the Newarke precinct and was built around 1400. The gate has no portcullis (sliding iron door) and its main purpose was to impress visitors rather than be defensive.

Melton Carnegie Museum

Thorpe End
Melton Mowbray LE13 1RB
0116 305 3860
www.leics.gov.uk/meltonmuseum
meltonmuseum@leics.gov.uk

Fox hunting, Stilton cheese and pork pies, local history, sporting art and much, much more. Melton Mowbray is a medieval market town, and was the only Leicestershire market recorded in the 1086 Domesday Survey. Find out about the enthralling history of the town at the Melton Carnegie Museum, located in beautiful old Carnegie Library built in 1905.

New Walk Museum & Art Gallery

53 New Walk
Leicester LE1 7EA
0116 225 4900
www.leicester.gov.uk/museumsandgalleries
museums@leicester.gov.uk

On the historic New Walk, Leicester's original museum has collections spanning the natural and cultural world. A family friendly day-out, displays include Dinosaurs, Egyptians, Geology, The Den, Wild Space and World Arts. The art galleries showcase Modern and Old Masters, contemporary art and craft exhibitions and permanent galleries of Arts & Crafts and Picasso Ceramics: The Attenborough Collection.

Newarke Houses Museum & Gardens

The Newarke
Leicester LE2 7BY
0116 225 4980
www.leicester.gov.uk/museumsandgalleries
museums@leicester.gov.uk

Newarke Houses Museum and Gardens incorporating the museum of the Royal Leicestershire Regiment. Newarke Houses Museum is composed of two historic houses, Wygston's Chantry House and Skeffington House and tells the story of contemporary Leicester and the history of the Royal Leicestershire Regiment. The museum displays include a cinema experience, a collection of toys from Tudor to present day and a play area for children to try various games. Find out more about Leicester's famous son Daniel Lambert and visit a 1950s street scene inspired by Wharf Street that includes the Jolly Angler public house, a grocer and a pawnbroker, with sounds and conversations from the times.

Old Rectory Museum

Rectory Place
Loughborough LE11 1UW
01509 843297
www.lrmf.org.uk/m_11_rec.htm

Visit this medieval manor house, that became the rectory to the nearby parish church for 700 years. The museum it now contains holds collections on the history of Loughborough through the ages. Temporary exhibitions and archaeological discoveries from the area can be seen.

Record Office for Leicestershire, Leicester & Rutland

Long Street
Wigston Magna LE18 2AH
0116 257 1080
www.leics.gov.uk/museums
museums@leics.gov.uk

The Record Office is a service provided by Leicestershire County Council in partnership with Leicester City Council and Rutland County Council. The Record Office exists to preserve and provide access to a wide range of Resources which can be used to research the history and culture of Leicestershire, Leicester and Rutland.

Snibston

Snibston Discovery Park, Ashby Road
Coalville LE67 3LN
01530 278444
www.snibston.com
snibston@leics.gov.uk

Leicestershire's award winning all-weather museum. Snibston is one of the largest and most dynamic museums in the Midlands. On the site of a former colliery, the museum displays a rich collection of historic objects telling the story of transport, mining and quarrying, engineering and the fashion industry.

Wigston Framework Knitters Museum

42/44 Bushloe End, Wigston
Leicester LE18 2BA
0116 288 3396
www.lrmf.org.uk/m_26_wig.htm

Come to a hosier's house built in the 1700s, and see the knitting workshop from the 1800s. This has eight original hand knitting frames, and all the equipment once used to make stockings and gloves.

William Carey Museum, The

Central Baptist Church, Charles Street
Leicester LE1 1LA
0116 276 6862
www.central-baptist.org.uk
churchadministrator@central-baptist.org.uk

William Carey was a founder of the Baptist Missionary Movement, and this museum tells his story. Figures show scenes from his life.

Wygston's House

12 Applegate
Leicester LE1 5LD
0116 225 4980
www.leicester.gov.uk/museums
museums@leicester.gov.uk

Wygston's House is the oldest house in Leicester. It has been here since medieval times and the road it stood on was the widest and busiest thoroughfare in the town, High Street. The house comprises a timber hall of around 1490; a brick block of 1796 which replaced an earlier timber shop and chamber and a Victorian (1800s) wing standing on the site of the medieval kitchen.

Lincolnshire

Lincolnshire, maritime county in E. of England, bounded N. by Yorkshire, from which it is separated by the Humber; E. by the North Sea; S. by Northamptonshire, Cambridgeshire, and Norfolk; and W. by Notts, Leicestershire, and Rutland; greatest length, N. to S., 75 miles; greatest breadth, E. to W., 45 miles; area, 1,767,879 acres, population 469,919. Lincolnshire is the second largest county in England. For a very long time it has been divided into 3 'parts' - namely, the Parts of Lindsey, the Parts of Kesteven, and the Parts of Holland. Generally speaking the land is flat and low, especially on the coast, which in some parts requires an embankment to check the encroachments of the sea. The Wolds, or Chalk Hills, in the NE., are about 47 miles long and 6 miles broad. Most of the county is watered by the rivers Trent, Witham, Ancholme, and Welland, with their tributaries. The county is intersected by an intricate network of canals and dykes, the latter being cut for the purposes of drainage. The soil is varied and generally fertile, being especially rich in pasture, upon which splendid breeds of oxen, horses, and sheep are reared. The coast fisheries, especially at Grimsby, are of immense value. Inland the inhabitants are mostly employed in agriculture. Shipbuilding, cordage and net manufacture and machine-making are carried on. Lincolnshire comprises 31 wapentakes, hundreds, liberties, and sokes, 757 parishes, and 4 parts of parishes, the parliamentary and municipal boroughs of Boston, Grantham, Great Grimsby, and Lincoln, and the municipal boroughs of Louth and Stamford (part). It is almost entirely in the diocese of Lincoln.

– John Bartholomew, Gazetteer of the British Isles (1887)

Alford Manor House

🏛️ 📷 ⭐

West Street
Alford LN13 9HT
01507 463073
www.alfordmanorhouse.co.uk
PhlpMs@aol.com

To the rear of the Manor House is the Hackett Barn, which is a museum of memorabilia and bygones: it contains lovingly restored examples of agricultural and other machinery, as well as a fine Victorian hearse, the original Alford town stocks, carts, a horse-drawn fire engine, and many other fascinating exhibits.

Appleby Frodingham Railway Preservation Society

🏛️ £

Scunthorpe DN16 1XA
01652 656661
www.afrps.co.uk
glenn@afrps.co.uk

Steam train rides around the internal railway system of Tata Steel's Scunthorpe site. Our trains take a 7 or 15 mile tour around the 100 mile internal railway system of the Scunthorpe site, while a commentary is given by one of our experienced guides.

Ayscoughfee Hall Museum

🏛️ 📷 ⭐

Churchgate
Spalding PE11 2RA
01775 764555
www.ayscoughfee.org
museum@sholland.gov.uk

Ayscoughfee Hall Museum is set in a Medieval Hall dating back to around 1451. This fascinating grade I listed building includes exhibitions, displays and educational opportunities for all to enjoy.

Battle of Britain Memorial Flight Visitor Centre

🏛️ 📷 £

RAF Coningsby
Coningsby LN4 4SY
01526 344041
www.raf.mod.uk/bbmf/visitorscentre
bbmf@lincolnshire.gov.uk

The Battle of Britain Memorial Flight operates a Lancaster, five Spitfires, two Hurricanes, two Chipmunks, and a Dakota. These aircraft are no museum pieces - they are all still flying and can be seen at a variety of air shows in the summer months. Since 1986, the Visitor Centre has welcomed over 300,000 people, all of whom have received a guided tour.

Baysgarth House Museum

Caistor Road
Barton-upon-Humber DN18 6AN
01652 637568
www.champltd.org/contact.html
info@champltd.org

Located in the heart of historic Barton upon Humber, Baysgarth House is the ancestral home of the prominent Nelthorpe family. Set within 30 acres of parkland this Grade II listed building is a beautiful example of Georgian architecture and is the perfect setting for a family day out.

Collections: Superb Georgian and Victorian Period rooms and a fine collection of 18th and 19th century English and Oriental pottery and porcelain are just a few of the attractions that await you. Discover Barton's rural crafts with reconstructed stonemason, shoemaker and wheelwrights' workshops.

Belton House - National Trust

Belton
Nr Grantham NG32 2LS
01476 566116
www.nationaltrust.org.uk/belton-house
belton@nationaltrust.org.uk

Restoration country house with magnificent interiors, gardens and park. Built in 1685-88 for 'Young' Sir John Brownlow, Belton is undoubtedly one of the finest examples of Restoration country house architecture.

Bolingbroke Castle - English Heritage

Hagnaby Road
Bolingbroke PE23 4HJ
01529 461499
http://goo.gl/QEBhhc

The remains of a 13th-century hexagonal castle - the birthplace, in 1367, of Henry I; Bolingbroke was besieged by Cromwell's Parliamentarians in 1643.

Boston Guildhall

South Street
Boston PE21 6HT
01205 365954
www.bostonguildhall.co.uk
ticboston@boston.gov.uk

Boston's Guildhall of St Mary is one of the oldest and most significant religious guildhalls in the country.

Collections: Items include: Original inventory of the Guildhall mid-16th century (which is 9 feet long), portrait of Sir Joseph Banks, Corporation Regalia, Charter signed by King Henry 8th, original printing of Foxe's Book of Martyrs. Sounds of a busy kitchen of the 18th century and audio re-enactment of banqueting through the ages.

Browne's Hospital

Broad Street
Stamford PE9 1PF
01780 763153

Browne's Hospital was founded by William Browne, a rich wool merchant of Stamford, and built in 1475 in the reign of Edward IV. With his brother, John, William Browne was largely responsible for enlarging and embellishing the Church of All Saints nearby.

Burghley House

Stamford PE9 3JY
01780 752451
www.burghley.co.uk
info@burghley.co.uk

Burghley House was built between 1565 and 1587 by William Cecil, Lord Treasurer to Queen Elizabeth I. Cecil intended Burghley as his family seat; he also owned a London house and the remarkable palace for entertaining the Queen and Court that he built at Theobalds Park in Hertfordshire (sadly no longer standing.) William Cecil was his own architect, basing the design for Burghley on elements of other great houses of the period together with European influences.

Burtey Fen Collection

3 Burtey Fen Lane, off Herring Lane,
Pinchbeck near Spalding, PE11 3SR
01775 766081
www.burteyfen.co.uk
burteyfen@yahoo.co.uk

The Burtey Fen Collection is a privately owned music hall housing three pipe organs - a Compton Cinema Organ, A Wurlitzer Cinema Organ and a classical pipe organ. The collection also features a vast collection of memorabilia associated with entertainment. Organ concerts by top names of the organ world are a monthly feature.

Church Farm Village & Museum

Church Road South
Skegness PE25 2HF
01754 766658
churchfarmvillage.org.uk
info@churchfarmvillage.org.uk

The only open air museum in Lincolnshire, the Village Church Farm offers the chance for visitors to step back in time to a more simple age. See Bob the Traction Engine paired with a Hornsby threshing drum; step inside Withern Cottage, a wonderful example of a Lincolnshire 'mud and Stud' thatched cottage; explore the 18th century Farm House, Barn,Stables and Summer House, relax in the Tea Room Orchard and Gardens and much more..

Collection, The: Art & Archaeology in Lincolnshire

🏛 ✉ ⭐

Danes Terrace
Lincoln LN2 1LP
01522 782040
www.thecollectionmuseum.com
thecollection@lincolnshire.gov.uk

The county museum and gallery for Lincolnshire the Collection incorporates the Usher Gallery and the City and County Museum. The museum part of the enterprise is housed in a new, purpose-built building close to the Usher gallery in the city of Lincoln displaying internationally significant treasures from the area, including a 3-by-3-metre Roman mosaic.

Collections: City and County Museum's currently contain over 2,000,000 objects. Any material from official archaeological excavations in Lincolnshire is eventually deposited at the museum so the collections are growing all the time.

Doddington Hall & Gardens

🏛 £

Doddington
Lincoln LN6 4RU
01522 694 308
www.doddingtonhall.com
info@doddingtonhall.com

Doddington Hall is a superb Elizabethan mansion completed in 1600 by the brilliant architect, Robert Smythson. The Hall stands today exactly as it was built with its walled gardens, gatehouse, and family church. The elegant Georgian interior contains a fascinating collection of pictures, textiles, porcelain and furniture that reflect four centuries of unbroken family occupation.

Ellys Manor House

🏛 £

Dallygate
Great Ponton NG33 5DP
01476 530023
www.ellysmanorhouse.com
ellysmanor@btinternet.com

A unique and magical Tudor wool merchant's house, built in the Flemish style, Ellys Manor House is an architectural gem. The main feature of the house is a fabulous scheme of early 16th century wall paintings in the upper rooms.

Epworth Old Rectory

🏛 ✉

1 Rectory Street
Epworth DN9 1HX
01427 872268
www.epwortholdrectory.org.uk
curator@epwortholdrectory.org.uk

Welcome to Epworth Old Rectory. A visit to this impressive grade 1 listed Queen Anne building set in beautiful gardens will transport you back into early 18th century life and introduce you to the remarkable family who lived here. This is the home in which the rector of the parish of St Andrew, Epworth, Samuel Wesley and his wife Susanna brought up their sons, John and Charles Wesley, who went on to develop the Methodist movement, with their seven sisters and elder brother Samuel.

Fenscape: The Fens Discovery Centre

✉ ⭐

Fenscape, Springfields, Camelgate
Spalding PE12 6EU
01775 764800 - 10am-5pm
nicola@visitthefens.co.uk

Discover the fens through interactive and audio visual displays, interpretive sculptures, theatrical sets, graphic panels and more. Each display brings to life a particular aspect of the Fens' unique past and involves the audience in issues and choices faced by the people that were involved in shaping the fens that we see today.

Gainsborough Old Hall

🏛 £

Parnell Street
Gainsborough DN21 2NB
01427 612669
www.lincolnshire.gov.uk/section.asp?catId=2707
gainsborougholdhall@lincolnshire.gov.uk

Medieval manor house dating from 1460s, original kitchen, great hall etc with additional room settings of the 17th century.

Gordon Boswell Romany Museum

✉ £

Clay Lake
Spalding PE12 6BL
01775 710599
www.boswell-romany-museum.com

The museum houses a wonderful collection of Romany caravans, carts, harnesses and photos and a large and comfortable lecture room for slide-show and talk on the Romany way of life.

Grantham Museum

✉ ⭐

St Peters Hill
Grantham NG31 6PY
01476 568783
www.granthammuseum.org.uk
grantham.museum@lincolnshire.gov.uk

The Grantham Museum was founded by a local dignitary Henry Preston in the early 20th century. The basis of the collection is material provided by Henry Preston, the first Curator and Founder, and 20th century additions included material about Sir Isaac Newton, Edith Smith and Margaret Thatcher. There is also material about the Dambusters raid.

Grimsby Fishing Heritage Centre

Alexandra Dock
Grimsby DN31 1UZ
01472 323345
www.thefishingheritagecentre.com
fhc@nelincs.gov.uk

Discover the sites and sounds of the 1950s fishing heritage. Enjoy a guided tour of the Ross Tiger. Opened in 1991, managed by North East Lincolnshire Council.

Grimsthorpe Castle, Park & Gardens

Grimsthorpe Castle, The Estate Office, Grimsthorpe
Bourne PE10 0LY
01778 591205
www.grimsthorpe.co.uk
ray@grimsthorpe.co.uk

Built for a visit by Henry VIII in 1541, the imposing Castle sits amongst rolling Lincolnshire countryside surrounded by formal gardens, extensive woodland and a 50-acre lake.

Collections: Family portraits from c16 to present day Collection of general paintings Tapestries Assorted items from the Old House of Lords including thrones and fabric hangings Fine giltwood furniture from 18th century.

Gunby Hall & Gardens - National Trust

Gunby
nr Spilsby PE23 5SS
01754 890102
www.nationaltrust.org.uk/gunby-hall
gunbyhall@nationaltrust.org.uk

A homely country house dated 1700 set in Victorian walled gardens at the foot of the Lincolnshire Wolds. With links to Tennyson and Vaughan-Williams there is so much to discover about the family home of the Massingberd family. Explore three floors of the hall full of interesting collection pieces amassed over generations from 1700 until 1963.

Humber Keel & Sloop Preservation Society

c/o Hillside Cottage, 21 Freemans Lane, Bonby
Near Brigg DN20 0PN
01652 618997
www.keelsandsloops.org.uk
sales@keelsandsloops.org.uk

The Humber Keel and Sloop Preservation Society's aim is to preserve and sail examples of the Humber Keel and Humber Sloop in their traditional waters on the River Humber. We have two ships, the Humber Keel 'Comrade', built at New Holland in 1923, and the Humber Sloop 'Amy Howson', built at Beverley in 1914.

Immingham Museum

Civic Centre, Pelham Road
Immingham DN40 1QF
01469 577066
www.imminghammuseum.org
admin@imminghammuseum.org

A fascinating collection of local objects with small exhibitions on the Pilgrim Fathers, Great Central Railway and the Docks, upon which modern Immingham was founded. There are also exhibitions about the life and times of Immingham during the earliest part of the 20th century.

Isle of Axholme Family History Society

Colywell, 43 Commonside, Westwoodside
Doncaster DN9 2AR
01427 752692
www.axholme-fhs.org.uk
secretary@axholme-fhs.org.uk

We are alway happy to greet new members to the society, be they 1 mile or 10,000 miles away from this small corner of the County of Lincolnshire.

Kirton in Lindsey Town Hall

High Street
Kirton in Lindsey DN21 4LZ
01652 648978
www.kirtoninlindseytownhall.co.uk
kirtonclerk@btinternet.com

Built for Queen Victoria's Diamond Jubilee, the Town Hall is a heritage site regularly hosting displays on a variety of local heritage projects and topics.

Lincoln Castle

Castle Hill
Lincoln LN1 3AA
01522 511068
Lincoln_Castle@lincolnshire.gov.uk

By Norman times, Lincoln was the third city of the realm in prosperity and importance. In 1068, two years after the Battle of Hastings, William the Conqueror began building Lincoln Castle on a site occupied since Roman times. For 900 years the castle was used as a court and prison with many being executed on the ramparts. Many original features still remain and the wall walks provide visitors with magnificent views of the Cathedral, the City of Lincoln and the surrounding countryside.

Lincoln Cathedral

Minster yard
Lincoln LN2 1PX

01522 561600
www.lincolncathedral.com
visitors@lincolncathedral.com

Lincoln Cathedral is one of the finest medieval buildings in Europe, which towers above Lincoln, a prominent landmark for miles around. The imposing West Front incorporates the surviving part of the first Romanesque Cathedral dating from 1072.

Lincoln Medieval Bishops' Palace - English Heritage

Minster Yard
Lincoln LN2 1PU
01522 527468
http://goo.gl/R74Crv
charles.rodgers@english-heritage.org.uk

Built in the late 12th century, the palace was one of the most important buildings in England. Its architecture and scale reflect the enormous wealth and power of the medieval bishops as princes of the church.

Lincolnshire Archives

St Rumbold Street
Lincoln LN2 5AB
01522 782040
www.lincolnshire.gov.uk/Archives
lincolnshire.archives@lincolnshire.gov.uk

Lincolnshire Archives is the public archive service for Lincolnshire. The Archives centre in Lincoln offers an accessible search room for researchers investigating the extensive archive and reference library collections. Visit our website to find out more about the collections, research and copying services and guidance on how to get the most out of your search room visits. Intending visitors must book Search Room spaces in advance.

Collections: The Lincoln Episcopal Rolls and Registers are a Designated Collection. The size of the pre-Reformation Diocese of Lincoln makes this a key archive for English history from the mid-13th century onwards, especially up to the Reformation in 1542.

Lincolnshire Aviation Heritage Centre

East Kirkby Airfield, East Kirkby
Nr Spilsby PE23 4DE
01790 763207
www.lincsaviation.co.uk
enquiries@lincsaviation.co.uk

The Lincolnshire Aviation Heritage Centre is a family run museum and was set up over 20 years ago. It is now widely seen as a living memorial to the 55,500 men of Bomber Command who lost their lives during WW2.

Lincolnshire Family History Society

Unit 6, 33 Monks Way, Monks Road
Lincoln LN2 5LN
01522 528088
www.lincolnshirefhs.org.uk
researchcentre@lincolnshirefhs.org.uk

The Lincolnshire Family History Society covers Holland, Kesteven and Lindsey, the three parts of the Historic County of Lincolnshire. Founded in 1990, the society now has over 3000 members worldwide, and in the year 2000 the LFHS leased premises in central Lincoln as a research centre.

Louth Museum

4 Broadbank
Louth LN11 0EQ
01507 601211
www.louthmuseum.org.uk

Louth Museum is a small museum in the beautiful historic market town of Louth in Lincolnshire. It was built in 1910 by the Louth Naturalists' Antiquarian and Literary Society and is still run by them today.

Metheringham Airfield Visitor Centre

Westmoor Farm
Nr Metheringham LN4 3BQ
01526 378604
www.metheringhamairfield.org
foma@btinternet.com

During 1942, around 600 acres of farmland and woods were cleared to create a new airfield for 5 Group, Bomber Command. Situated between the villages of Metheringham and Martin, the airfield opened in October 1943. Today, there are still signs of this once active airfield. On the Communal Site, where many original buildings remain, the former ration store has been restored and now houses a fascinating exhibition of photographs and memorabilia recalling life on an operational Second World War airfield.

Mrs Smith's Cottage Museum

3 East Road, Navenby, Lincoln, Lincolnshire
Lincoln LN5 0EP
07887 928733
www.mrssmithscottage.co.uk
Jennie_Chandler@n-kesteven.gov.uk

Mrs Smith's Cottage Museum in Navenby is a preserved example of a simple, early Victorian, Lincolnshire cottage. With walls only a single brick thick and the only modern innovations an inside toilet, cold water tap and electricity, it offers a glimpse into life in a bygone age. The Cottage and Visitors Centre at the museum display artefacts and information relating the life and times of Mrs Smith in a rural village from the Edwardian period to the late 20th century. Note: the museum is closed in 2015 due to problems with the roof structure.

Museum of Lincolnshire Life

Burton Road
Lincoln LN1 3LY
01522 528448
www.lincolnshire.gov.uk/museumoflincolnshirelife
lincolnshirelife.museum@lincolnshire.gov.uk

The museum of Lincolnshire Life is the largest and most diverse community museum in the county. Just five minutes walk from Lincoln Castle, the museum reflects the culture of the people of Lincolnshire. Be inspired to discover more about the rich heritage of Lincolnshire and gain an insight into local culture today.

Normanby Hall Country Park

Normanby
Nr Scunthorpe DN15 9HU
01724 720588
www.northlincs.gov.uk/normanby
normanby.hall@northlincs.gov.uk

Set in the heart of undiscovered North Lincolnshire, the 300 acres of Normanby Hall Country Park provides the perfect day out for all the family. Return to the elegance of a more leisurely era in the beautiful Regency Hall and learn about Lincolnshire's rich rural heritage in the fascinating Farm Museum.

Normanby Park Farming Museum

Normanby Hall Country Park, Normanby
Scunthorpe DN15 9HU
01724 720588
customerservice@northlincs.gov.uk

Where else can you find a needle in a haystack, man traps and laying out boards for the dead? These are just a few of the unusual, not to mention downright bizarre items you can see in the Farming Museum at Normanby Hall. The Farming Museum is a fascinating microcosm of North Lincolnshire's rural past. Large scale agricultural machinery like binders and reapers are on display here.

North Lincolnshire Museum

Oswald Road
Scunthorpe DN15 7BD
01724 843533
www.northlincs.gov.uk/museums
museum@northlincs.gov.uk

A great day out for all the family. Discover the stories of North Lincolnshire through many interactive exhibits – become a nature detective in Go Wild, step back in time in the Victorian ironstone cottage and relive the Peoples' War.

Oscar Stewart Museum of Medical History

Lincoln County Hospital, Greetwell Road
Lincoln LN2 5QY

The museum was started by surgeon Oscar Stewart in the early 1990s and most of the instruments in the collection were donated by Lincolnshire GPs. It includes a library and archive of the county's medical history.

Royal Air Force Digby Sector Operations Room Museum

Royal Air Force Digby, 'L' Sector Operations Room Museum
Lincoln LN4 3LH
01526 327619
www.raf-lincolnshire.info/digby/digbymuseum.htm
m794evl@hotmail.com

Royal Air Force Digby, Lima Sector Operations Room Museum is dedicated to those who served and fought in support of freedom at home and abroad during World War Two. It also allows later generations to experience how a great victory was achieved.

Collections: The museum has been restored to resemble its appearance at the start of World War Two. The display centres on the main operations room, complete with plotting table, state boards, period furniture, communications equipment and contemporary furnished side offices.

Royal Lincolnshire Regimental Museum

The Old Barracks, Burton Road
Lincoln LN1 3LY
01522 528 448
www.thelincolnshireregiment.org/museum.shtml
postmaster@thelincolnshireregiment.org

Fittingly, the building that this museum resides in, was once the City Barracks. The museum collection contains uniforms, medals, weapons, Regimental Silver, paintings, photographs, archival material and personal effects relating to the history of the Royal Lincolnshire Regiment and the Lincolnshire Yeomanry.

Scawby Hall & Gardens

The Hall, Vicarage Lane
Scawby, Brigg DN20 9LX
01652 654 272
www.scawbyhall.com
info@scawbyhall.com

This early Jacobean manor house was begun in 1605 and has been lived in by members of the Nelthorpe family ever since. The building is Grade-I listed and contains a number of important paintings including five by George Stubbs.

Sibsey Trader Windmill

🏛️ £

Sibsey PE22 0UH

01205 750036

www.english-heritage.org.uk

This six-storey mill, built in 1877, still works today.

Sleaford Museum Trust

🖻 ★

c/o 15 Castle Street

Sleaford NG34 7QE

01526 833964

www.sleafordmuseum.org.uk

sootit@btinternet.com

This is a local history collection covering all aspects of the history and heritage of the rural market town of Sleaford in Lincolnshire. Items range from ceramics, household goods, clothing, medical equipment, military items and archaeological finds to manuscripts, local almanacks, printed documents, maps and photographs.

Society for Lincolnshire History & Archaeology

🎟️ ★

Jews' Court, 2-3 Steep Hill

Lincoln LN2 1LS

01522 521337

www.slha.org.uk

info@slha.org.uk

The Society for Lincolnshire History and Archaeology is a registered charity that aims to promote greater awareness, interest and understanding of all aspects of the cultural heritage of Lincolnshire past and present. The society office and bookshop is located in a wonderful 12th century building in the heart of historic Lincoln.

Spalding Flower Bulb Museum

🖻 ★

Surfleet Road Pinchbeck

Spalding PE11 3XY

01775 680490

www.birchgrovegc.co.uk

george@birchgrovegc.co.uk

The History of Lincolnshires Flower Bulb Industry brought to life. Inspired by memories of the hard working people from the South Holland fens the Spalding flower bulb museum opened in 1995 to preserve the history of the industry for future generations.

Spider T Historic Ship

🏛️ ★

Keadby Lock Station Road

Keadby DN17 3BN

07739 863604

www.spidert.co.uk

m.nicholson4@sky.com

Spider T is a unique Humber Super Sloop which has been restored to an exquisite finish. Launched in 1926 at Warren's Shipyard, the Spider's efficient design allowed her to transport goods at top speeds along the Humber Estuary. In the 70s she fell into disrepair but her current owner rescued the waterlogged ship and made her sea-worthy again, fitting her with a plush Edwardian interior.

St Botolph's Church - The Boston Stump

🏛️

Wormgate

Boston PE21 6NP

01205 354670

www.parish-of-boston.org.uk

parish.office@virgin.net

St Botolph's Church, nicknamed the Boston 'stump', is described by Pevsner as 'a giant among English parish churches.' It has always been a landmark both to seafarers and people travelling across the flat fenland that surrounds the town. Replacing an earlier Norman church, construction of the present building commenced in 1309 at the east end and was completed by 1390.

St Katherine's 900 Years of History

🏛️ ★

Colegrave Street, South Park

Lincoln LN5 8DW

01522 572778

www.visitlincoln.com/things-to-do/st-katherines

info@stkatherineslincoln.co.uk

St Katherine's is a vibrant new tourist destination, cultural resource and heritage and education venue for the local community, the city of Lincoln, the region and beyond. The centre is housed in a fully restored Wesleyan church building, an outstanding, grade II listed 19th century building that stands on the site of the Gilbertine priory of St Katherine, founded in 1148. Interactive displays tell the story of the site.

Stamford Museum

🖻 ★

Broad Street

Stamford PE9 1PJ

01780 766317

www.lincolnshire.gov.uk/pagenotfound.aspx

stamford_museum@lincolnshire.gov.uk

Come to Stamford Museum to find out more about the 'finest stone town in England.' See our unique Stamford Tapestry, fascinating local history collections and chat to our enthusiastic and knowledgeable staff - there is something for everyone..

Tattershall Castle - National Trust

🏛️ £

Sleaford Road, Tattershall

Lincoln LN4 4LR

01526 342543

www.nationaltrust.org.uk/tattershall-castle

tattershallcastle@nationaltrust.org.uk

Dramatic 15th-century red-brick tower, with six floors to explore. This fortified and moated tower was built for Ralph Cromwell, Lord Treasurer of England from 1433 to 1443.

Tattershall College - English Heritage

Tattershall LN4 4LJ

01529 461499

http://goo.gl/nD5bgF

Remains of a grammar school for church choristers, built in the mid-15th century by Ralph, Lord Cromwell, who was the builder of nearby Tattershall Castle.

Thornton Abbey & Gatehouse

Thornton Abbey DN39 6TU

The enormous and ornate fortified gatehouse of Thornton Abbey is among the finest surviving in Britain. An early example of brick building, it proclaimed the prosperity of one of the wealthiest English Augustinian monasteries.

Thorpe Camp Visitor Centre

Woodhall Spa Road

Tattershall Thorpe LN4 4PE

01526 342249

www.thorpecamp.org

mjhodgson@lancfile.demon.co.uk

The Thorpe Camp Visitor Centre was formerly No 1 Communal Site, Royal Air Force Woodhall Spa, a typical World War II bomber airfield and home to four bomber squadrons, including 617, the famous Dambusters Squadron.

Time Trap

Grimsby Town Hall, Town Hall Square

Grimsby DN31 1HX

01472 323345

paul.wisken@nelincs.gov.uk

Discover this surprising attraction within the former police cells of Grimsby Town Hall, it will take you on a time travel journey to uncover the town's colourful past. As you pass through dark, twisting corridors you will be able to explore mysterious nooks and crannies and make your way up and down winding stairs.

Trolleybus Museum at Sandtoft, The

Belton Road, Sandtoft

Nr Doncaster DN8 5SX

01724 711391

www.sandtoft.org

trolleybusmuseum@sandtoft.org

The home of Britain's and the world's largest single collection of preserved trolleybuses. These operate on the specially constructed overhead circuit on open days.

Collections: Houses around 40 trolleybuses formerly used in towns all over the UK, and some from Europe.

Wilderspin National School Museum

Queen Street

Barton-upon-Humber DN18 5QP

01652 635172

www.wilderspinschool.org.uk

enquiries@wilderspinschool.org.uk

Wilderspin National School is one of the most important schools surviving in England. Built in 1844, this Grade II* Listed Building is unique because of its association with the educational pioneer, Samuel Wilderspin, the self-styled founder of the Infant School System.

Woodhall Spa Cottage Museum

The Bungalow, Iddesleigh Road.

Woodhall Spa LN10 6SH

01526 353775

www.cottagemuseum.co.uk

info@cottagemuseum.co.uk

Housed in a rare 19th century corrugated iron prefabricated building, the Cottage Museum tells the fascinating story of the development of Woodhall Spa from its Victorian beginnings through to modern times. Explore the small and unique Cottage Museum which is packed with intriguing stories and exciting displays about Woodhall Spa and the Wield family who lived in the building from 1887 until the 1960s.

Woolsthorpe Manor - National Trust

23 Newton Way, Woolsthorpe-by-Colsterworth

nr Grantham NG33 5NR

01476 860338

www.nationaltrust.org.uk

woolsthorpemanor@nationaltrust.org.uk

Birthplace and family home of Isaac Newton. This 17th century Lincolnshire manor house was home to one of the world's most famous scientists. Newton developed his remarkable work about light and gravity here.

Wrawby Mill

Ivy House Farm, Wrawby

Brigg DN20 8SR

www.wrawby.org.uk

Wrawby post mill was built between 1760 and 1790 to serve the Elsham Hall estate.

Merseyside

Liverpool, parliamentary and municipal borough, city, seaport, and parish, SW. Lancashire, on estuary of river Mersey, 31 miles W. of Manchester and 201 miles NW. of London by rail - parish, 1715 acres land and 755 water, population 210,164; municipal borough, 5210 acres, population 552,508. From the latter part of the 18th century its progress in mercantile and maritime affairs is without a parallel, and justly entitles it to its position in the first rank of British seaports. Commercial intercourse is maintained with every part of the world. Several lines of splendid steamships keep up regular communication with New York; others with Boston, Philadelphia, New Orleans, Halifax, the Canadian ports, and the East and West Indies. Extending along both shores of the Mersey are immense lines of docks, which form the principal feature of the city. On the Liverpool shore they cover fully 6 miles, and on the Cheshire shore, at Birkenhead, 2 miles. Large vessels may proceed up the Mersey as far as the mouth of the Irwell, 35 miles above Liverpool; 5 great lines of railway now enter the city; but by the completion of the Mersey Tunnel, a formidable undertaking, begun in 1872, these facilities have been very materially increased. Inland water communication is kept up with Yorkshire and all parts of Lancashire, chiefly by the Leeds and Liverpool Canal. Cotton is the staple of the imports of Liverpool, which otherwise include goods from all parts of the world. Recently an enormous trade has arisen through the importation of provisions, including live stock, from America and the colonies. The port, too, is the principal place in the kingdom for the departure of emigrants. Manufactures are not extensive. Shipbuilding has fallen off greatly owing to the competition at the Clyde and in the north of England. The manufactures of engines for marine navigation, however, have a worldwide renown. Sugar refining, iron and brass founding, ropemaking, brewing, chemical works, iron chain cable and anchor making, and the distilling of tar and turpentine, form other leading industries. A large source of trade exists in the produce of neighbouring collieries. Liverpool was created a diocese in 1880, at which time it was transformed into a city by royal charter.

– John Bartholomew, *Gazetteer of the British Isles* (1887)
Note: Merseyside was created in 1974 from parts of Lancashire and Cheshire.

20 Forthlin Road

Allerton
Liverpool L24 1YP
0870 900 0256
www.nationaltrust.org.uk/beatles-childhood-homes

20 Forthlin Road is one of the most important houses in the history of popular music. This ordinary terraced house was the family home of Sir Paul McCartney right through the early Beatles years.

Beatles' Childhood Homes, The - National Trust

Mendips, (National Trust)
Liverpool L24 1YP
08457 585702
www.nationaltrust.org.uk/beatles
thebeatleshomes@nationaltrust.org.uk

Mendips was the childhood home of John Lennon, he lived there with his Aunt Mimi and Uncle George and composed early songs in the front porch and in his bedroom. Mendips has been restored to its 1950s period glory.

Bevin Boys Association

General Enquiries to:, Bevin Boys Secretary, D.Elizabeth Todd [Mrs], The Chalet, 24 Oldfield Way, Heswall, Wirral CH60 6RG
0151 342 3703
www.bevinboysassociation.co.uk

The Bevin Boys Association was formed in 1989 with a small membership of 32 in the Midlands area. By 2009 the membership had grown to over 1,800 from all over the United Kingdom and overseas.

Collections: The Imperial War Museum has now become the home for the preservation of Bevin Boy records, documents and photographs.

Birkenhead Priory & St Mary's Tower - The Birkenhead Packet

Priory Street
Birkenhead, Wirral L41 5JH
0151 666 1249
www.birkenheadprioryparish.co.uk

This Benedictine Monastery established 1150 is the oldest building on Merseyside. Much of the original building still remains and other parts have been sympathetically restored to their former stature. First restored over a century ago, the site continues to develop with museum displays, education/meeting/concert space and chapel dedicated to HMS Conway (open by appointment).

Croxteth Hall & Country Park

Croxteth Hall Lane
Liverpool L12 0HB
0151 233 6910
www.croxteth.co.uk
croxtethcountrypark@liverpool.gov.uk

Croxteth Hall Country Park is at the heart of what was once a great country estate stretching hundreds of square miles and was the ancestral home of the Molyneux family, the Earls of Sefton. It is now managed by The City of Liverpool and is one of the major heritage centres of the North West, attracting thousands of visitors every year.

Everton Collection, The

Liverpool Record Office, Central Library, William Brown Street
Liverpool L3 8EW
www.evertoncollection.org.uk
everton.collection@liverpool.gov.uk

The Everton Collection is Heritage Lottery funded to promote the history of football through the story of Everton F.C. The Everton Collection is the most complete collection of football memorabilia in the world relating to a single football club.

Garstang Museum of Archaeology, The

School of Archaeology, Classics and Egyptology, 14 Abercromby Square
Liverpool L69 3BX
0151 794 2467
www.liv.ac.uk/sace/garstang-museum/index.htm
garstang@liverpool.ac.uk

The Garstang Museum of Archaeology, in the School of Archaeology, Classics and Egyptology is named in honour of Professor John Garstang, whose excavations in Egypt, Sudan and the Levant produced the majority of our archaeological collections.

Hardmans' House, The - National Trust

59 Rodney Street
Liverpool L1 9ER
0151 709 6261
www.nationaltrust.org.uk/hardmans-house
thehardmanshouse@nationaltrust.org.uk

Georgian terraced house - the former studio and home of the photographer E. Chambre Hardman. Collections include a selection of Hardman'ss collection of photographs - over 142,000 images.

International Slavery Museum

Albert Dock
Liverpool L3 4AQ
0151 478 4499
www.liverpoolmuseums.org.uk/ism
MMMInfo@liverpoolmuseums.org.uk

The International Slavery Museum highlights the international importance of slavery, both in a historic and contemporary context. Working in partnership with other museums with a focus on freedom and enslavement, the museum provides opportunities for greater awareness and understanding of the legacy of slavery today.

Liverpool & S W Lancashire Family History Society

6 Kirkmore Road
Liverpool L18 4QN
www.liverpool-genealogy.org.uk
secretary@liverpool-genealogy.org.uk

We are an active and forward-looking society that brings together genealogists and historians with an interest in the area covered by the old Hundred of West Derby.

Liverpool Cathedral

Liverpool L1 7AZ
0151 709 6271
www.liverpoolcathedral.org.uk
education@liverpoolcathedral.org.uk

Liverpool Cathedral is an awesome, beautiful building and a vibrant living church attempting to live the Christian Gospel.

Liverpool Central Library, Archive & Record Office

Liverpool Central Library and Archive, William Brown Street
Liverpool L3 8EW
0151 233 5817
recoffice.central.library@liverpool.gov.uk

The largest library is the Central Library in the City Centre. There are smaller community libraries spread across the city.

Collections: Liverpool Record Office's photographic image collection is a Designated Collection of national importance. The photographic collection contains photographs from the City Engineer.

Liverpool Football Club Museum

☐ £

Liverpool FC, Anfield Road
Liverpool L4 0TH
0151 260 6677
www.liverpoolfc.tv/club/tour.htm

Seize your opportunity to gain exclusive access behind the scenes at one of the world's true sporting cathedrals - Anfield, soaking up the peerless heritage of England's most successful football club.

Liverpool Metropolitan Cathedral

☐

Cathedral House, Mount Pleasant
Liverpool L3 5TQ
0151 709 9222
www.liverpoolmetrocathedral.org.uk
enquiries@metcathedral.org.uk

Architects throughout the world were invited in 1960 to design a Cathedral for Liverpool which would relate to the existing Crypt, be capable of construction within five years, cost at the current prices no more than one million pounds for its shell, and most important of all, express the new spirit of the liturgy then being radically reformulated by the Second Vatican Council. Of 300 entries from all over the world, Sir Frederick Gibberd's (1908-1984) design was chosen, and building began in October 1962.

Merseyside Maritime Museum

☐ ☐ ★

Albert Dock
Liverpool L3 4AQ
0151 478 4499
www.liverpoolmuseums.org.uk/maritime
press@liverpoolmuseums.org.uk

Set sail and drop anchor for a fun day out at Merseyside Maritime Museum - about the seafaring importance of Liverpool as a gateway to the world, including the city's role in the transatlantic slave trade and emigration. The Maritime Archive and Library contains one of the finest collections of merchant shipping records in the UK.

Museum of Liverpool

☐ ★

Pier Head, Liverpool Waterfront
Liverpool L3 1DG
0151 478 4545
www.liverpoolmuseums.org.uk/mol
sam.vaux@liverpoolmuseums.org.uk

The stunning Museum of Liverpool is the world's first national museum devoted to the history of a regional city, demonstrating Liverpool's unique contribution to the world. Showcasing popular culture while tackling social, historical and contemporary issues, it is a fantastic, free family day out and an exceptional learning and community resource.

National Museums Liverpool

☐

William Brown Street
Liverpool L3 8EN
0151 478 4597
www.liverpoolmuseums.org.uk
sara.parker@liverpoolmuseums.org.uk

National Museums Liverpool is a group of museums and galleries. Our diverse venues attracted over over 3 million visitors in 2011 Our collections are among the most important and varied in Europe and contain everything from Impressionist paintings to a lifejacket from the Titanic.

North West Museum of Road Transport

☐ ☐ £

Old Bus Depot, 51 Hall Street
St Helens WA10 1DU
01744 451681
www.nwmort.co.uk
email@hallstreetdepot.info

A unique and extensive collection of vintage buses, British trolleybuses and classic cars in the UK are the centrepiece of this regional transport museum formerly known as St Helens Transport Museum. Following its extensive and comprehensive refurbishment the North West Museum of Road Transport has joined the ranks of the top North West attractions and is open to the public every Saturday and Sunday.

Port Sunlight Museum

☐ ☐ ☐ £

23 King George's Drive
Port Sunlight, Wirral CH62 5DX
0151 644 6466
info@portsunlightvillage.com

Located in the heart of Port Sunlight, a world famous 19th century garden village, Port Sunlight Museum offers a unique insight into the origins and social history of one of Britain's finest and most intact model villages. Port Sunlight consists of over 900 Grade II Listed buildings and has one of the largest War Memorials outside of London. Discover within Port Sunlight Museum what it would have been like to live in this village during the late 1800s and early 1900s.

Prescot Museum

☐ ☐ ★

The Prescot Centre, Prescot Shopping Centre, Aspinall Street
Knowsley L34 5GA
0151 443 5617
www.prescotmuseum.org.uk
tina.ball@knowsley.gov.uk

Prescot Museum provides access to the cultural heritage of Knowsley through its local history collection, museum displays and educational and outreach programme. The museum presents a range of permanent and temporary exhibitions, celebrating the history of Prescot, including the town's watch-making past, former industries, local dignitaries, businesses and much more.

Sefton Park Palm House

Sefton Park
Liverpool L17 1AP
0151 726 2415
www.palmhouse.org.uk
info@palmhouse.org.uk

Sefton Park Palm House is a Grade II* listed Victorian palm house situated in leafy glades of Sefton Park, 2 miles from Liverpool City Centre. It was built in 1896 and gifted to the city by Henry Yates Thompson. It is managed by Sefton Park Palm House Preservation Trust and contains plants from around the world.

Smithy Heritage Centre

Kiln Lane, Eccleston
St Helens WA10 4RA
01744 730744
www.ecclestonpc.org.uk
smithyheritagecentre@hotmail.com

Located in an original blacksmith's forge that was still operating until the late 1970s, Eccleston Parish Council has transformed the smithy into a museum dedicated to the history of the area. Learn about the skills of local craftsmen including the farmer, the wheelwright, the farrier and the blacksmith, all of whom played a vital role in Eccleston's rural past.

Speke Hall, Garden & Estate - National Trust

The Walk
Liverpool L24 1XD
0151 427 7231
www.nationaltrust.org.uk/speke-hall
spekehall@nationaltrust.org.uk

Tudor half-timbered house with rich interiors and fine gardens. The atmospheric interior of this rambling house spans many periods.

St Helens Local History & Archives Library

First floor, Gamble Building
St Helens WA10 1DY
01744 676952
www.sthelens.gov.uk/history
localhistory&archivesservices@sthelens.gov.uk

The Local History & Archives Library is on the first floor of the Gamble Building. It holds the historic records of St Helens.

Sudley House

Mossley Hill Road, Aigburth
Liverpool L18 8BX
0151 724 3245
www.liverpoolmuseums.org.uk/sudley
sudley@liverpoolmuseums.org.uk

Sudley House is the former family home of the Holt family. George Holt founded the Liverpool shipping line Lamport and Holt and was a pioneer of trade with Brazil.

Collections: Sudley displays fine 18th and 19th century paintings from Holt's collection, together with works from the Walker Art Gallery. George Holt started collecting paintings in the late 1860s, specialising in contemporary British art, but later acquired portraits by Gainsborough, Romney and Raeburn, and two superb late paintings by Turner.

Unilever Archives

PO Box 69
Port Sunlight, Wirral CH62 4ZD
0151 641 4551
archives@unilever.com

The archivists are responsible for the collection and management of Unilever's archives which span several centuries – in fact, our oldest document dates from 1295. The archives contain original documents, printed sources, artefacts and artwork, images and films.

Collections: The Archive of the United Africa Company is of primary significance for the study of the evolution of British business and corporate organisations; the character of the transnational enterprise; the economic and political development of the main West African societies.

University of Liverpool, Museum of Dentistry

Edwards Building, School of Dental Surgery, Pembroke Place
Liverpool L3 5PS
0151 706 2000 x5279

The School's Museum of Dentistry was started in 1880 and has continued without interruption until the present day. Because of its long history, it contains many early dental artefacts, not least of these being the collection of early dentures, now thought to be one of the most important in the world.

Victoria Gallery & Museum

Ashton Street, off Brownlow Hill, University of Liverpool,
Liverpool, L69 3DR
Liverpool L69 3DR
0151 794 2348
www.vgm.liv.ac.uk
vgm@liv.ac.uk

The Victoria Gallery & Museum is home to the University's
unique art and museum collections donated to and created
by the University throughout its history. Paintings by JMW
Turner, sculpture by Jacob Epstein and a fascinating array
of Victorian bottled creatures are just some of the
highlights of this wonderful collection.

Western Approaches

1-3 Rumford Street, Near Town Hall
Liverpool L2 8SZ
0151 227 2008
www.liverpoolwarmuseum.co.uk

Set beneath the streets of Liverpool, re-live the times of
1940s Britain with an insight into the life and work of the
Wrens and Waafs working under constant pressure in the
original area command headquarters for the battle of the
Atlantic. Now open to the public, you can visit the
reconstruction of the 50,000 sq ft labyrinth of original
rooms which brings a dramatic period of history vividly to
life.

Williamson Art Gallery & Museum

Slatey Road
Birkenhead, Wirral L43 4UE
0151 652 4177
williamsonartgallery.org
williamsonartgallery@wirral.gov.uk

Located outside the centre of Birkenhead, the Williamson
Art Gallery & Museum was purpose-built and was opened
in December 1928. The Williamson has built a strong
regional reputation for the quality and variety of its
exhibitions and houses the vast majority of Birkenhead's
collection of art and history collections, some of which are
displayed in a series of varied and well proportioned
galleries. Always on show is the largest single display of
ship models in the area, focusing on Cammell Laird
shipbuilders and their contribution to marine history, the
Mersey Ferries and the variety of vessels that used the River
Mersey when it was at its busiest.

Wirral Transport Museum & Birkenhead Tramway

Wirral Transport Museum, 1 Taylor Street
Birkenhead, Wirral CH41 1BG
0151 647 2128
www.wirraltransportmuseum.org
birkenheadtram@tiscali.co.uk

Welcome to the Wirral Transport Museums. Birkenhead is
a town packed with transport heritage, it is the home of
Cammell Lairds shipyard and the home of the European
tramway.

Collections: Wirral Museums Historic Vehicle Collection is
a selection of vintage buses representing a variety of local
operators over a number of years. There is also a display of
cars,and motorcycles and a 1930s garage scene.

World Museum

William Brown Street
Liverpool L3 8EN
0151 478 4393
www.liverpoolmuseums.org.uk/wml
press@liverpoolmuseums.org.uk

Discover treasures from around the world, explore outer
space and meet live creatures. World Museum is the largest
and oldest of the National Museums Liverpool, founded in
1851 when the 13th Earl of Derby left his substantial
natural history collection to the city.

Collections: Its collections are worldwide in scope, and
world-class in quality. They cover archaeology, ethnology
and the natural and physical sciences.

World of Glass

Chalon Way East
St Helens WA10 1BX
01744 22766
www.worldofglass.com
info@worldofglass.com

Come along to The World of Glass and see our live
glassblowing demonstrations. Watch as our resident glass
artists take blobs of glowing glass from kilns many times
hotter than the oven in your kitchen. Be amazed how they
create beautifully shaped decorative pieces just by blowing
down a tube and using simple tools.

Norfolk

Norfolk, a maritime county in E. of England, bounded N.and E. by the North Sea, S. by Suffolk, and W. by Cambridgeshire; greatest length, 70 miles; greatest breadth, 43 miles; area, 1,356,173 acres, population 444,749. The coast line is about 90 miles in extent. All along the seaboard the land is low, and has suffered greatly from encroachments of the sea. Many thousands of acres however have been reclaimed from the waters of the Wash, and the work is still being prosecuted. A level surface characterises the appearance of the county, which is watered by the Yare, with its tributaries the Wensum, Waveuey, and Bure, and by the Ouse and its tributaries. Light sand and loam is the prevailing character of the soil, which generally has been rendered productive through the excellence of the system of farming that has been pursued during recent years. The barley of the county has especial celebrity. Great attention is paid to live stock, and the cobs and cart horses of the county are well known. Large numbers of geese and turkeys are supplied to city markets. Besides the great herring fishery of Yarmouth, there is all along the coast an important and valuable fishing industry, which employs many thousands of the people. Norfolk comprises 33 hundreds, 736 parishes, with parts of 9 others, the parliamentary and municipal boroughs of King's Lynn and Norwich, and most of the parliamentary and municipal borough of Great Yarmouth, and of the municipal borough of Thetford. It is mostly in the diocese of Norwich.

– John Bartholomew, *Gazetteer of the British Isles* (1887)

100th Bomb Group Memorial Museum

Common Road, Dickleburgh
Diss IP21 4PH
01379 740 708
www.100bgmus.org.uk

Housed in the original airfield control tower and other atmospheric buildings 100th Bomb Group Memorial Museum is a moving testament to the Americans who came to Thorpe Abbotts in Norfolk to fight alongside the allies during World War Two.

2nd Air Division Memorial Library

2nd Air Division Memorial Library, The Forum, Millennium Plain
Norwich NR2 1AW
01603 774747
www.2ndair.org.uk
2admemorial.lib@norfolk.gov.uk

During the Second World War over 6,700 young Americans, members of the 2nd Air Division of the 8th United States Army Air Forces, based in Norfolk and Suffolk England, lost their lives in the line of duty.

Collections: The purpose of the library is to house a collection of materials about American freedom, culture, and life, about the Second World War in the air, and about the special relationship between the people of the UK and the people of the United States.

448th Bomb Group Collection / Seething WWII USAAF Control Tower

448th BG Collection, Stanmare, Seething St, Seething; Seething Control Tower, Toad Lane, Seething .
Norwich NR151AL
01508 550288
www.seethingtower.org/448-grouphistory.php
p.everson448@btinternet.com

Seething Control Tower is a restored WWII control tower. The 448th Bomb Group flew B24 Liberator Bombers on 262 Mission and 500 men lost from November to June. We have lots of memorabilia, displays and the 448th BG collection consisting of large collection of photographs and albums of 448th veterans stories/war diaries.

93rd Bomb Group Museum

Station 104, Topcroft
Norwich NR15 2PP
https://sites.google.com/site/usaafhardwick/home

Located in original Nissen (Quonset) huts which formed part of the communal site for the 329th Bomb Squadron on the airfield, the museums exhibits range from displays of Second World War memorabilia to items of aviation archaeology. These include engines and sections of undercarriage.

Ancient House Museum of Thetford Life

21-23 White Hart Street
Thetford IP24 1AA
01824 752599
www.museums.norfolk.gov.uk
ancienthouse@norfolk.gov.uk

Thetford's Ancient House has recently benefited from a £1.6 million renovation, which has gone towards conserving the Grade I listed Tudor merchant's house and creating up-to-date displays. The atmospheric crooked house tells the remarkable story of Thetford and the Brecks. Discover rich collections alongside audio guides, films and animations. Meet local people from Thetford's past, from the revolutionary philosopher Thomas Paine to the Sikh hero Maharajah Duleep Singh and from rabbit warreners to railway workers.

Aviva Group Archive

8 Surrey Street
Norwich NR1 3NG
01603 682645
www.aviva.com/about-us/heritage
anna.stone@aviva.com

Our archive is acknowledged as the most important insurance industry archive in the UK. Discover some of the facts and stories from our 300-year history.

Binham Priory

Langham Road
Fakenham NR21 0DW
01328 830362
www.binhampriory.org
admin@binhampriory.org

The Priory church of St Mary and the Holy Cross in Binham, is a village parish church, but its ruins, precinct walls and gatehouse tell a different story. This was the site of a Benedictine monastery, founded in 1091 as a cell of St Albans Abbey by Peter de Valoines, a nephew of William the Conqueror. The Priory has had an amazing history.

Bishop Bonner's Cottage Museum

St Withburga Lane
East Dereham NR19 1ED
01362 853453 or 693969
www.derehamhistory.com
mus@suewhite.demon.co.uk

Housed in a beautiful timber-framed, reed-thatched early C16th cottage, with colourful pargetting. It is the oldest domestic building in the market town of Dereham.

Collections: Local Collection Rooms, with photographs and memorabilia from bygone Dereham. Local history exhibits include domestic and farm tools, Victorian clothing, toys, local personalities and trades.

Blickling Estate - National Trust

Blickling, Nr. Aylsham
Norwich NR11 6NF
01263 738030
www.nationaltrust.org.uk/blickling-estate
blickling@nationaltrust.org.uk

Blickling has been at the heart of this north Norfolk community since the 16th century. One of the most imposing and complete country estates in Norfolk, it offers you a glimpse into the lives of those who lived and worked above and below stairs. The estate is a treasure trove of romantic buildings, beautiful gardens, and landscaped park.

Brancaster Estate - National Trust

Brancaster Millennium Activity Centre, Dial House,
Brancaster Staithe
King's Lynn PE31 8BW
01485 210719
www.nationaltrust.org.uk/brancaster-estate
brancaster@nationaltrust.org.uk

Extensive coastal area around the fishing village of Brancaster Staithe, famous for wild birds. As well as the site of the Roman fort of Branodunum and Scolt Head Island (to which there is a private ferry service), there are tidal mud and sandflats and saltmarshes to explore.

Bressingham Steam Museum

Bressingham
Diss IP22 2AA
01379 686900
www.bressingham.co.uk
info@bressingham.co.uk

Take a step back in time to the power and romance of the age of steam. We have one of Europe's leading collections, including over 40 steam locomotives, traction and stationary engines and vehicles, all restored to their former glory - and each with its own story to tell.

Carrow House Costume & Textile Study Centre

301 King Street
Norwich NR1 2TN
01603 223870
www.museums.norfolk.gov.uk
museums@norfolk.gov.uk

Carrow House is a specialist study centre offering exceptional facilities for anyone interested in costume and textiles. Carrow is home to one of the UK's largest collections of period dress, textiles, accessories, needle crafts and home furnishings. The collection comprises over 25,000 items.

Castle Acre Priory - English Heritage

Castle Acre
Swaffham PE32 2XD
01760 755394
http://goo.gl/ds0Kap

One of the largest and best preserved monastic sites in England, the foundation of Castle Acre Priory in about 1090 sprang directly from a visit by William de Warenne II and his wife Gundrada to the great French monastery of Cluny. So impressed were they by its beauty and holiness that they vowed to introduce the Cluniac order of monks to England. There is much more to see at the priory, including the substantial remains of many of the buildings round the cloister.

Cathedral of St John the Baptist

Cathedral House, Unthank Road
Norwich NR2 2PA
01603 624615
www.sjbcathedral.org.uk
enq@sjbcathedral.org.uk

One of the finest examples of Victorian Gothic architecture in England. Norwich's Catholic Cathedral was gifted to the city of Norwich by Henry Fitzalan Howard, the 15th Duke of Norfolk, providing a new centre of worship for the Catholic community in Norwich.

Charles Burrell Museum

Minstergate
Thetford IP24 1BN
01842 751166
https://www.facebook.com/CharlesBurrellMuseum
burrell@thetfordtowncouncil.gov.uk

The Charles Burrell Museum opened in 1991 and is housed in the former Paint Shop on Minstergate in Thetford, Norfolk. The museum tells the stories of the Charles Burrell Works, the people who laboured there, and the machinery they produced. The past is captured through displays representing different areas of the works, such as the foundry, and the display of our collection of Burrell engines and other agricultural equipment.

City Hall

Norwich City Council, City Hall
Norwich NR2 1NH
01603 212212
www.norwich12.co.uk/city-hall
info@norwich.gov.uk

One of the finest municipal buildings of the inter-war period in England. During the 19th century the city's civic offices were housed in the medieval Guildhall and a range of old buildings located in what is now the Market Place. With developments in local government duties it became clear these premises were unsuitable.

City of Norwich Aviation Museum

Old Norwich Road, Horsham St Faith
Norwich NR10 3JF
01603 893080
www.cnam.co.uk
admin@cnam.co.uk

Aircraft and memorabilia relating to the history of aviation in Norfolk. The collection features a massive Vulcan bomber and some of the military and civil aircraft which have flown from Norfolk airfields.

Colman's Mustard Shop & Museum

15 The Royal Arcade
Norwich NR2 1NQ
01603 627889
www.mustardshopnorwich.co.uk
sales@mustardshopnorwich.co.uk

Colman's Mustard Shop & Museum is housed in the historic Royal Arcade and is a careful replica of a Victorian trade premises, where you can browse through original Colman's memorabilia whilst choosing from a wide range of unusual and exclusive mustard treats for your friends and family.

Cromer Museum

East Cottages, Tucker Street
Cromer NR27 9HB
01263 513543
www.museums.norfolk.gov.uk
cromer.museum@norfolk.gov.uk

Explore this cosy Victorian fisherman's cottage and imagine what it was like to live in Cromer at the end of the 19th century. Delve into the 'Old Cromer' Gallery and learn about the lost village of Shipden and Cromer's coal ships. Discover Cromer's history as a Victorian seaside resort with its fine hotels and scandalous mixed bathing.

Dad's Army Museum

The Old Fire Station, Cage Lane
Thetford IP24 2DS
01842 751975
www.dadsarmythetford.org.uk
information@dadsarmythetford.org.uk

The location shots for the Dad's Army TV series were filmed in and around the town of Thetford from 1968 to 1977. The museum celebrates this wonderful comedy.

Diss Museum

The Shambles, 4 Market Place
Diss IP22 4AB
01379 650618
www.disscouncil.com/museum.php
dissmuseum@lineone.net

Diss Museum is situated in the Market Place in a building called The Shambles, formerly two butchers' shops. There are a variety of displays, frequently changed, about the history of the town and area. Always on display are the Old Rectory Doll's House, old photos and jottings from the Memory Bank.

Dragon Hall

115-123 King Street
Norwich NR1 1QE
01603 663922
www.dragonhall.org
info@dragonhall.org

The City of Norwich is renowned for its wealth of historic buildings – from the Norman Castle and Cathedral to the Victorian railway station and Shire Hall to name but a few. Dragon Hall is a magnificent medieval trading hall, dating from around 1430, newly refurbished and restored.

Elizabethan House Museum - National Trust

4 South Quay
Great Yarmouth NR30 2QH
01493 855746
www.nationaltrust.org.uk/elizabethan-house-museum
yarmouth.museums@norfolk.gov.uk

Experience the lives of families who lived in this splendid 16th century quayside house from Tudor to Victorian times. Discover Victorian life 'upstairs and downstairs' and find out what it was really like to work in the kitchen and scullery. Decide for yourself if the death of Charles I was plotted in the Conspiracy Room.

Fakenham Museum of Gas & Local History

Hempton Road
Fakenham NR21 7LA
01328 863150
www.fakenhamgasmuseum.com
enquiries@fakenhamgasmuseum.com

The Fakenham Museum of Gas and Local History is the only surviving town gasworks in England and Wales, complete with all equipment used for the manufacture of gas from coal: retorts, condenser, purifiers, meter and gasholder. The museum is housed in the town's former gasworks, which ceased production of gas from the heating of coal in 1965 following the discovery of Natural Gas in the North Sea.

Felbrigg Hall, Gardens & Estate - National Trust

Felbrigg
Norwich NR11 8PR
01263 837444
www.nationaltrust.org.uk/felbrigg-hall
felbrigg@nationaltrust.org.uk

One of the finest 17th-century country houses in East Anglia. The Hall contains its original 18th-century furniture, one of the largest collections of Grand Tour paintings by a single artist, and an outstanding library.

Fishermen's Heritage Centre, The

West Cliff
Sheringham NR26 8JT
01263 821737
www.sheringhamsociety.com
secretary@sheringham-preservation.org.uk

The centre is housed in restored fishing sheds scenically situated at the top of the Fishermen's Slope, still used by fishing boats. It describes the lives led by the fishing community of Sheringham from the 19th century to the present day and contains the preserved lifeboat the Henry Ramey Upcher built in 1894 and presented to the fishing community by the Upcher family of Sheringham Hall.

Flying Eightballs Museum

67 Barton Street
Thetford IP25 7SB
01362 820709
www.shipdhamflyingclub.co.uk

Shipdham Flying Club is a group of flyers and friends who operate Shipdham Airfield for the benefit of the general aviation community. The airfield was the wartime base of the 44th Bombardment Group, known as the Flying Eightballs.

Great Hospital, The

Bishopgate
Norwich NR1 4EL
01603 622022
www.greathospital.org.uk
enquiries@greathospital.org

An exceptional set of medieval hospital buildings, in continuous use for more than 750 years. The Great Hospital was established when Bishop Walter de Suffield decided to found a hospital for elderly clergy, poor scholars and the sick poor.

Great Yarmouth Row of Houses & Greyfriars' Cloisters - English Heritage

No 8, Row 117, South Quay
Great Yarmouth NR30 2RG
01493 857900
http://goo.gl/oEx6cl
Simon.tansley@english-heritage.org.uk

Dating from 1603, this wealthy merchant's house with fine plaster ceilings was later divided into two tenements. It is displayed to show the living conditions of the Victorian families that occupied the house shortly after its division.

Gressenhall Farm & Workhouse, Museum of Norfolk Life

Gressenhall
Dereham NR20 4DR
01362 860563
www.museums.norfolk.gov.uk
gressenhall.museum@norfolk.gov.uk

Gressenhall brings together a museum, traditional farm, historic workhouse and beautiful grounds. Explore atmospheric shops and homes, stunning displays and a treasure trove of fascinating objects.

Grime's Graves Prehistoric Flint Mine - English Heritage

Brandon IP26 5DE
01842 810656
http://goo.gl/GNd8J7

Grime's Graves is the only Neolithic flint mine open to visitors in Britain. A grassy lunar landscape of over 400 shafts, pits, quarries and spoil dumps, they were first named Grim's Graves - meaning the pagan god Grim's quarries, or 'the Devil's holes' - by the Anglo-Saxons.

Guildhall, The

Gaol Hill
Norwich NR2 1JS
01603 305575
www.norwich12.co.uk/the-guildhall
info@heritagecity.org

England's largest and most elaborate provincial medieval city hall, Norwich Guildhall was the centre of city government from the early 15th century until its replacement by City Hall in 1938. The exterior provides an excellent example of the flint work that the city is so famous for. The east end of the building was reconstructed in the 16th century and is crafted from alternate squares of faced flint and ashlar stone, giving the building its chequered effect. As well as various courts, a prison and a chapel the building contained facilities for accounting and tax collection, accommodation for civic officials (it remains the

home of the Sheriff's parlour today) and storage space for records, money and civic regalia. The Assembly Chamber (or Sheriff's Court) was designed for meetings of the full medieval council.

History of Advertising Trust Archive

12 Raveningham Centre, Raveningham
Norwich NR14 6NU
01508 548623
www.hatads.org.uk
enquiries@hatads.org.uk

The History of Advertising Trust (HAT Archive) was established in the UK in 1974 by a small group of individuals who believed that the best of UK advertising should be preserved for posterity.

Collections: HAT Archive provides a vast and unique research resource. The collections consist of every kind of advertising and public relations material, including original artwork, posters, point of sale promotions, brochures, proofs, press and magazine cuttings, complete consumer magazines, direct mail, photographs, transparencies, audio and video tapes, TV and cinema commercials and campaign research.

Hungate Medieval Art

St Peter Hungate Princes Street
Norwich NR3 1AE
www.hungate.org.uk
HungateGlass@aol.com

Hungate Medieval Art is a centre for the appreciation of medieval art located in the heart of Britain's most complete medieval city, Norwich. Hungate Medieval Art aims to promote Norfolk's medieval heritage. In particular, the charity is concerned with the medieval art hidden in the county's parish churches.

Iceni Village Nature Reserve & Museums

Cockley Cley Iceni Village, Cockley Cley
Swaffham PE37 8AG
01760 721339
www.icenivillage.com

A reconstruction of the type of village occupied by Queen Boadicea and the Iceni tribe just before the invasion of the Romans around 2000 years ago. There is evidence that there was a settlement at Cockley Cley around the time of Christ.

John Jarrold Printing Museum

Norwich NR3 1SH
www.johnjarroldprintingmuseum.org.uk
enquiries@johnjarroldprintingmuseum.org.uk

One of the finest museums in the country dedicated to printing.

Litcham Village Museum

Fourways, Litcham
King's Lynn PE32 2NZ
01328 701383
www.litcham.org/Litcham/Museum.html

The museum is home to extensive collections of artefacts, photographs and records from the local area which date back several hundred years. .

Lynn Museum

Market Street
King's Lynn PE30 1NL
01553 775001
www.museums.norfolk.gov.uk
lynn.museum@norfolk.gov.uk

Visit the home of Seahenge - the astonishing Bronze Age timber circle uncovered on a Norfolk beach. Learn how these ancient timbers amazingly survived for 4,000 years and about the people who crafted them.

Mid-Norfolk Family History Society

104 Norwich Road, Dereham
Norwich NR20 3AR
www.tsites.co.uk/sites/mnfhs
sue.vickerage@ic24.net

Our local members have an interest in family history in general but do not necessarily have genealogical links to this part of Norfolk. However, we have a large number of distant members with interests in Mid-Norfolk and we aim to assist in their research by collecting and recording family history information from within an area of approximately 10 miles around Dereham.

Mo: Sheringham Museum, The

Lifeboat Plain
Sheringham NR26 8BP
01263 824482
www.sheringhammuseum.co.uk
enquiries@sheringhammuseum.co.uk

The Mo: Sheringham Museum is a stunning museum, located right on the seafront in Sheringham. The museum has a beautiful collection of fishing boats, crab boats and lifeboats.

Collections: Displays of local Sheringham history including boat building, lifeboats, fishing, the 'Weybourne Elephant' (1.5 million years old), leisure in Sheringham, the Upcher family, the war years, beach finds, the art of local people, art relating to the town, flint picking. In the museums research room we hold a digital copy of our photographic archive of around 2500 images and a collections database.

Muckleburgh Collection

Weybourne Military Camp
Weybourne NR25 7EG
01263 588210
www.muckleburgh.co.uk
info@muckleburgh.co.uk

The Muckleburgh Collection isthe UK's largest privately owned working military collection with 25 Tanks all in working order.

Museum of Norwich at the Bridewell

Bridewell Alley
Norwich NR2 1AQ
01603 629127
www.museums.norfolk.gov.uk
museums@norfolk.gov.uk

The Bridewell started life as a rich merchant's house in 1325. It became a prison for women and beggars (a 'Bridewell') in 1585 and in the mid 18th century became a conventional prison.

Collections: Highlights include an original Jacquard loom, Norwich shawls, shoes, the first wire netting machine, Shand Mason fire engine, printing presses, chemist shop, recreated pawnbrokers shop and Norwich City Football Club display.

Museum of the Broads, The

The Staithe
Stalham NR12 9DA
01692 581681
www.museumofthebroads.org.uk
info@museumofthebroads.org.uk

The Broads, one of England's unique landscapes, was formed by medieval peat diggings which became shallow lakes. Today they are a haven for both wildlife and holidaymakers, but behind the tourist industry lies a myriad of traditional ways of working and living.

Nelson Museum

26 South Quay
Great Yarmouth NR30 2RG
01493 850 698
www.nelson-museum.co.uk
curator@nelson-museum.co.uk

The Nelson Museum celebrates the life and times of Horatio Nelson, England's famous Naval hero. Explore Nelson's career, from his childhood through his famous battles to his tragic, heroic death, with our great displays and our hands-on activities.

Norfolk Family History Society

Headquarters, Library & Registered Office, Kirby Hall, 70 St Giles Street
Norwich NR2 1LS
01603 763718
www.norfolkfhs.org.uk
nfhs@paston.co.uk

The society welcomes people researching their Norfolk ancestors and family history. We currently have around 4,000 members researching their Ancestors in Norfolk, including members from as far afield as Papua New Guinea, Australia, U.S.A.

Norfolk Museums & Archaeology Service

Shire Hall
Norwich NR1 3JQ
www.museums.norfolk.gov.uk

There are approximately 3 million objects in the collections of the NMAS. Most of them have been catalogued on the databases and we have over 300,000 records in Collections Online for All, covering all subjects and museums. More work remains to be done however. The Costume and Textile collection (about 15,000 items) was recently added but Natural History collection at Norwich Castle (about 2 million specimens) is still being documented electronically.

Norfolk Record Office

The Archive Centre, Martineau Lane
Norwich NR1 2DQ
01603 222599
www.archives.norfolk.gov.uk
norfrec@norfolk.gov.uk

The Norfolk Record Office collects and preserves records of historical significance for the county of Norfolk and makes them accessible to as wide a range of people as possible. It is a joint service of the County and District Councils of Norfolk.

Norfolk Tank Museum

Bridge Farm, Station Road, Forncett St Peter
Norwich NR16 1HZ
01508 532650
www.norfolktankmuseum.co.uk
s.machaye@btinternet.com

The Norfolk Tank Museum is a small, independent museum of Cold War military vehicles, uniforms and artefacts. We are a not-for-profit organisation.

North Norfolk Railway

Sheringham Station, Station Approach
Sheringham NR26 8RA
01263 820800
www.nnrailway.co.uk
enquiries@nnrailway.com

The North Norfolk Railway is a working museum, providing an insight into railway transport in East Anglia over the last 130 years or so. Trains run, as per timetable, between Sheringham and Holt, a distance of 5 1/4 miles.

Collections: The working collection includes everything on the railway, including locomotives, coaches, wagons, signals and signalboxes, stations and other buildings, right down to the large collection of original signs.

Norwich 12

Norwich HEART, The Guildhall, PO Box 3130
Norwich NR2 1XR
01603 305575
www.norwich12.co.uk
info@norwich12.co.uk

Norwich 12 is the UK's finest collection of individually outstanding heritage buildings spanning the Norman, medieval, Georgian, Victorian and modern eras. The group consists of: Norwich Castle, Norwich Cathedral, The Great Hospital, The Halls - St Andrew's and Blackfriars', The Guildhall, Dragon Hall, The Assembly House, St James Mill, St John's Roman Catholic Cathedral, Surrey House, City Hall and The Forum. Individually each building is exceptional, but seen as a group they form an internationally important showcase of English urban and cultural development over the last millennium.

Norwich Castle Museum & Art Gallery

Norwich Castle
Norwich NR1 3JQ
01603 493636
museums.norfolk.gov.uk
museums@norfolk.gov.uk

One of the city's most famous landmarks, Norwich Castle was built by the Normans as a Royal Palace 900 years ago. Now a museum and art gallery, the castle is packed with treasures to inspire and intrigue visitors of all ages.

Norwich Cathedral

12 The Close
Norwich NR1 4DH
01603 218300
www.cathedral.org.uk
reception@cathedral.org.uk

For over 900 years the awesome beauty of this Norman building has reached out and touched people. The

Cathedral's architecture is justly famous, its history fascinating and its collection of art and objects outstanding.

Origins

🖾 £

The Forum, Millennium Plain, Bethel Street, Norfolk
Norwich NR2 1TF
01603 727922
theforumnorwich.co.uk/norfolkheritagecentre
origins@theforumnorwich.co.uk

Origins is an exciting exploration of 2000 years of Norfolk and Norwich history for you to take part in. Covering three floors within the stunning landmark Millennium project for the East of England Forum building, Origins has over 60 different exhibits - most with buttons to press, flaps to lift, levers to pull, games to play and challenges to take, there is information to read and listen to and artefacts to look at too, as well as the amazing panoramic film show.

Collections: The first floor works through Roman times through to WWII, including strong social history collections, artefacts from each period, information on language, architecture, cloth making and war-time recollections. The second floor is more hands-on, with information about dialect, famous personalities, agriculture, architecture and traditional myths and legends.

Oxburgh Hall - National Trust

🏰 £

Oxborough
nr King's Lynn PE33 9PS
01366 328258
www.nationaltrust.org.uk/oxburgh-hall
oxburghhall@nationaltrust.org.uk

15th-century moated manor house: * Secret doors and priest hole * Mary Queen of Scots embroideries * Bedingfeld family, still in residence after 500yrs * Magnificent Tudor gatehouse * French parterre.

RNLI Henry Blogg Museum

🖾 ★

The RNLI Henry Blogg Museum, The Rocket House, The Gangway
Cromer NR27 9ET
01263 511294
www.rnli.org.uk/HenryBlogg

Coxswain Henry Blogg (1876-1954) was the RNLI's most decorated lifeboatman. The museum illustrates the history of Cromer's lifeboats and tells the story of Henry Blogg's most famous rescues. For 37 years he served as Coxswain at Cromer and from 1935–45 his lifeboat was the legendary HF Bailey, which is the centrepiece of the museum.

Row 111 House (Great Yarmouth Row Houses) - English Heritage

Nos 6-8, Row 111, South Quay

Great Yarmouth NR30 2RG
01493 857 900
http://goo.gl/HIgQBC
Simon.Tansley@english-heritage.org.uk

An early 17th century Merchants House, later divided into three tenements. Displayed to show the living conditions of the last occupents in the late 1930s and early World War Two.

Royal Air Force Air Defence Radar Museum - RAFADRM

🏰 🖾 £

Royal Air Force Neatishead
Norwich NR12 8YB
01692 631485
www.radarmuseum.co.uk
curator@radarmuseum.co.uk

Discover the top secret world of Radar at the RAF Air Defence Radar Museum. Established in 1941 the base at Neatishead has remained pivotal in Air Defence from WWII right through the Cold War and it still remains an operational RAF station even today.

Collections: A unique collection of original, signed, RAF Sation and Unit Badges. The original 'Cold War' Operations Room used by the RAF until 1993.

Royal Norfolk Regimental Museum

🖾 £

Norwich Castle Museum, Castle Meadow
Norwich NR1 3JU
01603 493625
www.rnrm.org
museums@norfolk.gov.uk

The Royal Norfolk Regimental Museum (RNRM) looks after a wealth of objects relating to the regiment. Many of these objects are on display in Norwich Castle Museum, including army uniform, kit, personal letters and diaries that reflect the daily lives of soldiers in wartime and peace.

Sainsbury Centre for Visual Arts

🖾 ★

University of East Anglia
Norwich NR4 7TJ
01603 593199
www.scva.ac.uk
scva@uea.ac.uk

The Sainsbury Centre for Visual Arts is an inspirational public art museum where you can see outstanding world art for free.

Collections: The Robert and Lisa Sainsbury Collection is primarily found in a gallery known as the Living Area, where modern European art is interspersed with works from around the globe. The objects you'll find here span 5,000 years of human creativity. Objects from the UEA Collection of Abstract and Constructivist Art, Architecture and Design are also displayed.

Sheringham Park - National Trust

Sheringham Park
Upper Sheringham NR26 8TL
01263 820550
sheringhampark@nationaltrust.org.uk

Wander through Sheringham Park and you'll discover why it became the personal favourite of its designer, Humphry Repton. Visit the Repton exhibition to see the story of his 1812 design during a turbulent period of history.

Shrine of Our Lady of Walsingham, The

Education Department, The College, Knight street, Walsingham
Walsingham NR22 6EF
01328 824205
www.walsinghamanglican.org.uk
accom@olw-shrine.org.uk

The Shrine Church is situated in beautiful grounds close to the centre of the medieval village of Little Walsingham. Built in the 20th century, the Shrine Church is where the Holy House is located - a replica of the home in Nazareth of Joseph, Mary and Jesus (the Holy Family) - and where the Guardians of the Shrine have their stalls. This modern church reminds us of unbroken pilgrimage to the site for about a thousand years.

St Andrew's & Blackfriars' Halls

St Andrew's Plain
Norwich NR3 1AU
01603 628477
www.standrewshall.co.uk
thehalls@norwich.gov.uk

The only English friary to survive intact from the medieval period. The Halls were built over 600 years ago and were part of the medieval precinct of the Dominican or Black Friars. The layout is typical of a medieval English friary church, including a large nave (St Andrew's) used for preaching to congregations and a smaller chancel (Blackfriars'), where the friars held services. St Andrew's Hall has an impressive hammer beam roof, a gift of the Paston family, whose townhouse was in nearby Elm Hill.

St James Mill

Whitefriars
Norwich NR3 1SH
01603 677100
www.norwich12.co.uk/st-james-mill

The quintessential English Industrial Revolution mill. A Grade I listed building, St James Mill was built on a site originally occupied by the White Friars (or Carmelite Friars). The friars made many additions to their original site, building an impressive church of almost 68 metres (225 feet) in length.

St Seraphim

Station Rd
Walsingham NR22 6DG
01328 820610
iconpainter.org.uk

St Seraphim's Icon and Railway Heritage Museum incorporates St Seraphim's Chapel, which was founded in 1967 for the Orthodox community. It was converted in a former railway station, which opened in 1857.

Strangers' Hall

Charing Cross
Norwich NR2 4AL
01603 493625
www.museums.norfolk.gov.uk
museums@norfolk.gov.uk

Explore one of the oldest and most fascinating buildings in Norwich. Home to wealthy merchants and Mayors when Norwich was in its heyday, this beautifully preserved building dates back to 1320.

Swaffham Museum

Town Hall, 4 London Street
Swaffham PE37 7DQ
01760 721230
www.swaffhammuseum.co.uk
enquiries@swaffhammuseum.co.uk

A jewel of a museum set in a handsome townhouse on Swaffham's Georgian Market Place. Explore elegant rooms, rich collections and 21st century displays with lots for all the family to enjoy.

Collections: The museum focuses on the social history of the town and surrounding villages. The collections cover the many aspects of life including trade, industries, domestic life, from prehistoric times to the present day.

Time & Tide Museum of Great Yarmouth Life

Blackfriars Road
Great Yarmouth NR30 3BX
01493 743930
www.museums.norfolk.gov.uk
yarmouth.museums@norfolk.gov.uk

Come and explore this museum housed in a converted Victorian herring curing works and take an exciting journey into the past. Discover Great Yarmouth's fascinating history, its rich maritime and fishing heritage and some of the colourful characters who made their living from the sea. Wander through a Victorian 'Row' and see inside a fisherman's home.

Tolhouse, The

Tolhouse Street
Great Yarmouth NR30 2SH
01493 858900
www.museums.norfolk.gov.uk
yarmouth.museums@norfolk.gov.uk

Visit one of the oldest prisons in the country and explore Great Yarmouth's story of crime and punishment. Use the free audio guide to hear the gaoler and his prisoners describe their experiences.

True's Yard Museum

True's Yard, North Street
King's Lynn PE30 1QU
01553 770479
www.truesyard.co.uk
info@truesyard.co.uk

True's Yard is all that remains of King's Lynn's old fishing community, the North End, which existed for hundreds of years, and which was finally demolished in the clearances of the 1930s and the 1960s. Once hundreds of families lived within a stone's throw of their chapel of St Nicholas, which still dominates the area, and the North End had its own boat builders, chandlers, sail makers, pubs, bake houses and school.

University of East Anglia Library, Archives & Special Collections

Norwich Research Park
Norwich NR4 7TJ
01603 592 421
www.uea.ac.uk/is
library@uea.ac.uk

Collections: Apart from a core collection of University documents for public reference, the archives holds the following collections, among others: The Pritchard Papers and Isokon Trust (architecture, art and design of the 1930s); (Holloway Collection (printed ephemera on culture, 1960-2000); Zuckerman Archive (World War 2 operations and post-war science policy); Kenney Papers (suffragettes).

Walsingham Abbey Grounds & Shirehall Museum

Common Place
Little Walsingham NR22 6BP
01328 820510
www.walsinghamabbey.com
museum@walsinghamabbey.com

A place of pilgrimage since the 11th century, ruins of medieval priory, river and woodland walks leading into unspoilt woods and parkland famous for spectacular snowdrops in early spring. The Shirehall Museum houses an original Georgian courthouse, in use until 1971, displays on the history of Walsingham, local photographs and artefacts.

William Marriott Museum

c/o North Norfolk Railway, Holt Station, Cromer Road
Holt NR25 6QA
01263 710484
www.museumsnorfolk.org.uk/william-marriott-museum
enquiries@wmmuseum.org

The William Marriott Museum building houses many artefacts, documents and other bygones from the age of steam in East Anglia. Outside, the full 5 1/4 miles of the Poppy Line are packed with a multitude of working museum items, such as the buildings and general railway infrastructure, the locomotives and rolling stock and a truly historic signalling system. The museum has been created in a replica of a typical M&GN Goods Shed in Holt Station yard.

Wolterton & Mannington Estate

Mannington Hall
Norwich NR11 7BB
01263 584175
www.manningtongardens.co.uk
laurelwalpole@manningtongardens.co.uk

The gardens around this medieval moated manor house feature a wide variety of plants, trees (around 50 varieties) and shrubs in many different settings. Throughout the gardens are thousands of roses especially classic varieties. In the Heritage and Modern Rose Gardens are roses in areas with designs reflecting their date of origin from the 15th century to the present day.

Wymondham Heritage Museum

10 The Bridewell, Norwich Road
Wymondham NR18 0NS
01953 600205
www.wymondhamheritagemuseum.co.uk
info@wymondhamheritagemuseum.co.uk

This traditional and delightful museum brings together daily life and heroes and villains with great events from Wymondham's past. It also offers a lovely garden and a warm welcome.

North Yorkshire

Yorkshire, North-Riding, occupies the N. of the county, between the East-Riding and the county of Durham, and is separated from the West-Riding by the Ouse, the valley of the Ure, and the hills above Wharfedale; area, 1,361,664 acres, population 346,260. The principal rivers are the Derwent, which separates the North-Riding from the East-Riding, with its tributary the Rye; the Tees, which separates the North-Riding from Durham; and the Swale and the Ure, which unite to form the Ouse. The Vale of York, along the rivers Swale and Ouse, divides the eastern moorlands from the western. In the western moorlands the picturesque dells are mostly in pasture. The eastern moorlands contain several beautiful dales, including the Vale of Cleveland and the fertile Vale of the Rye. The best land is found in the Vale of York. The mountain lime-stone yields valuable lead deposits, and alum and jet are obtained at Whitby. Valuable beds of ironstone exist in the Cleveland Hills, and iron smelting and other allied industries are carried on on a vast scale at Middlesbrough, which is also a considerable seaport. Scarborough is one of the great watering-places, and Whitby is specially known for its manufacture of jet ornaments. The North-Riding comprises 11 wapentakes; 2 liberties; 554 parishes, and parts of 5 others; the parliamentary and municipal boroughs of York, Middlesbrough, and Scarborough; and the municipal borough of Richmond. It is almost entirely in the dioceses of York and Ripon.

– John Bartholomew, *Gazetteer of the British Isles* (1887)

2nd Infantry Divisional Kohima Museum

Imphal Barracks, Fulford Road
York YO1 4AU
01904 662 381
www.kohimamuseum.com

The Battle of Kohima in North East India, close to its border with Burma, took place between 4th April and 22nd June 1944 and marked the limit of the Japanese Army's advance into India. Here the enemy was stopped, defeated and forced into retreat. This museum tells the story.

Aldborough Roman Site - English Heritage

Aldborough
Boroughbridge YO51 9ES
01423 322768
http://goo.gl/WRvbP2
customers@english-heritage.org.uk

Among the northernmost urban centres in the Roman Empire, Aldborough was the 'capital' of the Romanised Brigantes, the largest tribe in Britain. One corner of the defences is laid out amid a Victorian arboretum, and two mosaic pavements can be viewed in their original positions. The site museum has an outstanding collection of Roman finds, a handling collection of Roman objects, and other hands-on aids for children and families.

Allied Air Forces Memorial & Yorkshire Air Museum

Halifax way Elvington
York YO41 4AU
01904 608595
www.yorkshireairmuseum.org
museum@yorkshireairmuseum.org

A Memorial Museum based on an authentic WWII Bomber Command Base, RAF Elvington, now the largest example of its type open to the public. Original buildings, including the Control Tower, now house some 15 fascinating exhibitions, including 'Against the Odds' the story of Bomber Command and 'Pioneers of Aviation', charting the work of Yorkshire aviation pioneers such as Sir George Cayley, the inventor of the aeroplane, Robert Blackburn and aviators such as Amy Johnson. The internationally renowned aircraft collection covers the birth of manned flight with the Cayley Glider, through WWI and WWII to the supersonic age.

Archaeology Live. Training Excavation

All Saints Church, North Street
York YO16JD
www.archaeologylive.wordpress.com
trainingdig@yorkat.co.uk

York Archaeological Trust offers numerous ways for people to engage with archaeology, none more hands on than our annual Archaeology Live. training excavations. Each year, we carry out an excavation in the heart of York, investigating sites that feature deeply stratified, highly complex archaeological deposits.

Bar Convent Museum, Library & Gallery

The Bar Convent, 17 Blossom Street
York YO24 1AQ
01904 643 238
www.bar-convent.org.uk
info@bar-convent.org.uk

The Bar Convent Museum outlines the early history of Christianity in the North of England and tells the story of Mary Ward, foundress of a religious congregation formerly known as the Institute of the Blessed Virgin Mary and now renamed the Congregation of Jesus. She was a pioneer both of women's education and apostolic religious orders for women.

Barley Hall
2 Coffee Yard, Off Stonegate
York YO1 8AR
01904 615505
www.barleyhall.co.uk
barleyhall@yorkat.co.uk

Barley Hall is a stunning medieval house, once home to the Priors of Nostell and the Mayor of York. Until the 1980s the house was hidden under the relatively modern facade of a derelict office block.

Beck Isle Museum of Rural Life
Bridge Street
Pickering YO18 8DU
01751 473653
www.beckislemuseum.org.uk
info@beckislemuseum.co.uk

The Beck Isle Museum is housed in a handsome Regency residence near the centre of Pickering, adjacent to the Pickering Beck, a stream that flows under a four-arched road bridge. One arch of this bridge (originally much narrower) is reputedly of mediaeval origin. Here William Marshall planned England's first agricultural institute in the early 1800s.

Bedale Museum
Bedale Hall
Bedale DL8 1AA
01677 422037
www.bedalemuseum.org.uk

The centre of this fascinating little museum is the hand drawn Bedale fire engine dated 1748. Old documents, toys, craft tools, clothing and household utensils give an absorbing picture of the life of ordinary people.

Beningbrough Hall & Gardens - National Trust

Shipton by Beningbrough
York YO30 1DD
01904 470666
www.nationaltrust.org.uk/beningbrough-hall
beningbrough@nationaltrust.org.uk

18th-century mansion with fine interiors and walled garden. York's 'country house and garden', this imposing Georgian mansion was built in 1716 and contains one of the most impressive baroque interiors in England.

Bolton Abbey
Estate Office, Bolton Abbey
Skipton BD23 6EX
01756 718009
www.boltonabbey.com

Bolton Abbey is in the heart of the Yorkshire Dales on the banks of the River Wharfe. With just under 30,000 acres of beautiful countryside, over 80 miles of footpaths and ample space to run around and enjoy the fresh air, there is something for all ages.

Borthwick Institute for Archives, University of York

Heslington
York YO10 5DD
01904 321166
www.york.ac.uk/library/borthwick
bihr500@york.ac.uk

The Borthwick Institute for Archives is one of the biggest archive respositories outside London. During our 50 year history we have collected archives from all around the world, from the 12th century to the present day. The Borthwick Institute originally specialised in ecclesiastical archives, but the past three decades or so have seen an enormous growth in the range and type of our holdings. Many of our archives have regional, national or international importance.

Byland Abbey - English Heritage
Nr Coxwold
Helmsley YO61 4BD
01347 868614
www.english-heritage.org.uk/visit/places/byland-abbey/
customers@english-heritage.org.uk

This beautiful ruin in a picturesque setting was once one of the great northern monasteries. A truly outstanding example of early Gothic architecture, Byland Abbey inspired the design for the famous York Minster Rose Window as well as influencing many other religious buildings throughout Europe.

Collections: The splendid collection of medieval floor tiles still in situ is the largest in Europe. The museum displays colourful interpretation panels together with archaeological finds from the site, giving an insight into monastic life.

Captain Cook & Staithes Heritage Centre

High Street, Staithes
Saltburn-By-The-Sea TS13 5BQ
01947 841454

As well as looking into the colourful history and heritage of Staithes itself, there is a tribute to the area most famous son, Captain James Cook.

Collections: A complete recreation of Sanderson's shop, where a young Captain Cook was once an apprentice as well as an enormous amount of information about the fishing and mining industries which were very important to Staithes, with its rich deposits of alum, iron ore and latterly, potash.

Captain Cook Birthplace Museum

Stewart Park, Marton
Middlesbrough TS7 8AT
01642 311211
www.captcook-ne.co.uk/ccbm
capt.cookmuseum@middlesbrough.gov.uk

At the Captain Cook Birthplace Museum you can discover why Captain Cook is the world's most famous navigator. Sail into uncharted waters to see Cook and his crew encounter new peoples, lands, plants and animals through a combination of original artefacts, films, computer interactives, and hands-on displays.

Collections: Ethnography, scientific instruments for navigation, natural history, life at sea, aboriginal art collection of over 500 items, some Cook and Cook family personalia, Cook postage stamps, coins and medals.

Captain Cook Memorial Museum

Grape Lane
Whitby YO22 4BA
01947 601900
www.cookmuseumwhitby.co.uk
cookmuseum@tiscali.co.uk

The museum is in the Grade-1-listed, 17c house on Whitby's harbourside which belonged to Captain John Walker. In 1746 the young Cook came here as Walker's apprentice.

Collections: The museum celebrates Cook's Whitby years and his later achievements. The collection includes period rooms restored faithfully following an inventory of 1752, models, maps and manuscripts, ship plans, artefacts from the Voyages, and many fine original paintings, drawings and prints.

Captain Cook Schoolroom Museum

101 High Street
Great Ayton TS9 7HB
01642 724296
www.captaincookschoolroommuseum.co.uk

The Schoolroom Museum in Great Ayton is housed in a building once used as a charity school which was founded in 1704 by Michael Postgate, a local landowner. It was here, between 1736 and 1740, that Captain James Cook received his early education.

Castle Howard

York YO60 7DA
01653 648 444
www.castlehoward.co.uk
house@castlehoward.co.uk

Built in 1699, Castle Howard is one of the country's finest historic houses and is still the private residence of the Howard family.

Collections: Indoors, art treasures include paintings by Canaletto, Holbein, Gainsborough and Reynolds, a collection of antique sculpture, and the porcelain collections include a spectacular Crown Derby botanical dessert service. Outdoors there are temples, lead statues and an array of monuments.

City of York & District Family History Society

26 Nursery Road, Nether Poppleton
York YO26 6NN
01904 794 973
www.yorkfamilyhistory.org.uk
secretary@yorkfamilyhistory.org.uk

The society covers the modern Archdeaconry of York which stretches from Coxwold, Hovingham and Sherburn in Harfordlythe in the North to Ledsham, Birkin, Selby and Drax in the South. As well as from Bramham, Bilton and Sherburn in Elmet in the West to Huggate and Bubwith in the East.

Clifford's Tower - English Heritage

Tower Street
York YO1 9SA
01904 646940
http://goo.gl/AmDfZl
customers@english-heritage.org.uk

With sweeping views of York and the surrounding countryside, it isn't hard to see why Clifford's Tower played such a crucial role in the control of northern England. The tower has a turbulent history, surviving 1,000 years of flood, fire and siege.

Courthouse Museum

Minster Road
Ripon HG4 1QP
01765 690799
www.riponmuseums.co.uk/courthouse.htm
info@riponmuseums.co.uk

The museum is housed in the former Quarter Sessions Courthouse built in 1830 to replace its medieval predecessor and the interior of the courtroom has not changed much since then. After Quarter Sessions ceased in 1953 the court continued as a Magistrates Court until it closed in 1998.

Craven Museum & Gallery

Skipton Town Hall, High Street
Skipton BD23 1AH
01756 706407
www.cravenmuseum.org
museum@cravendc.gov.uk

Craven Museum & Gallery, located in Skipton Town Hall, is a hidden gem in the market town of Skipton. This unique visitor attraction tells the story of Craven through the ages. Discover something different every time with changing exhibitions, workshops and family events.

Crimlisk Fisher Archive

Filey Town Council, Council Ofices, Queen Street
Filey YO14 9HE
www.exploringfileyspast.co.uk

In 1991 Filey Town Council started an archive of local heritage material. The basis for this now extensive collection were donations of material from Fred Fisher and also John Crimlisk. Fred had held the photographic collection of Filey photographer Walter Fisher, this collection is shared now between Filey Museum and The Crimlisk-Fisher Archive, both being located on Queen Street, Filey.

Dales Countryside Museum

Station Yard
Hawes DL8 3NT
01969 666210
www.dalescountrysidemuseum.org.uk
dcm@yorkshiredales.org.uk

This fascinating museum, managed by the Yorkshire Dales National Park Authority, tells the story of the people and landscape of the Yorkshire Dales past and present, and stimulates visitors to think about its future. Displays interpret the development of the Dales from prehistoric times to the present day.

DIG!

St Saviour's Church, St Saviourgate
York YO1 8NN
01904 615505
www.digyork.com
dig@yorkat.co.uk

At DIG. you will become an archaeological detective, and find out for yourself what York was really like through the ages, from Roman times to the present day. You will get the chance to excavate objects from the streets of York and then decide what they are, what they are made from, and why they got there. You will also have the chance to meet real archaeologists and talk to them about their work, see and handle artefacts from York and view recent exciting discoveries.

Dorman Museum

Linthorpe Road
Middlesbrough TS5 6LA
01642 813781
www.dormanmuseum.org.uk
dormanmuseum@middlesbrough.gov.uk

The Dorman Museum now has 8 permanent galleries to suit every taste from local history to dinosaurs, Ancient Egypt to 20th century Woman. Our water gallery is especially popular with children. In addition to our regular programme of exhibitions and events we are continuing to add to our permanent collections so visitors can be sure to see something new each visit.

Eden Camp Modern History Theme Museum

Malton YO17 6RT
01653 697777
www.edencamp.co.uk
admin@edencamp.co.uk

A visit to our unique museum at Eden Camp will transport you back in time to wartime Britain. You will experience the sights, sounds, even the smells of those dangerous years.

Embsay & Bolton Abbey Steam Railway

Bolton Abbey Station, Bolton Abbey
Skipton BD23 6AF
01756 710614
www.embsayboltonabbeyrailway.org.uk

Now you can travel on a train pulled by a steam locomotive from the historic station at Embsay, built in 1888, or Bolton Abbey Station. The culmination of a dream stretching back almost thirty years, the newly completed track extension and the opening of the award winning Bolton Abbey station offers a whole new experience for the visitor.

Fairfax House Museum

Fairfax House, Castlegate
York YO1 1RN
01904 655 543
www.fairfaxhouse.co.uk

Come and unlock the splendour within the finest Georgian town house in England. A classical architectural masterpiece of its age, Fairfax House was originally the winter home of Viscount Fairfax.

Filey Museum

8-10 Queen Street
Filey YO14 9HB
01723 515013
www.fileymuseum.co.uk

The museum building was originally two single storey cottages and is the oldest domestic building in Filey, 1696 being the date above the doors. The museum retains the original basic layout of rooms, each one dedicated to a different aspect of local life and work which was common place in Filey until comparatively recent times.

Fountains Abbey & Studley Royal Water Garden - National Trust

Fountains Abbey
Ripon HG4 3DY
01765 608888
www.nationaltrust.org.uk/fountains-abbey
fountainsenquiries@nationaltrust.org.uk

Cistercian abbey, Georgian water garden and medieval deer park.

Fulford Battlefield Society

Parish Hall, School Lane
York YO10 4LR
www.battleoffulford.org.uk
chas.j@writersservices.com

Fulford Battlefield Society formed to raise funds for research, to preserve the battle site and promote the Battle of Fulford to a wider audience. The battle took place 5 days before Stamford bridge and a few weeks before the clash at Hastings.

Gayle Mill

Mill Lane, Gayle
Hawes DL8 3RZ
01969 667320
www.gaylemill.org.uk
admin@gaylemill.org.uk

Gayle Mill began life as a Georgian cotton mill. Via wool and flax, it became a 19th century sawmill, and is fully restored complete with Victorian water-powered machinery.

Georgian Theatre Royal Museum

Victoria Road
Richmond DL10 4DW
01748 823 710
www.georgiantheatreroyal.co.uk
admin@georgiantheatreroyal.co.uk

The Georgian Theatre Royal, Britain's oldest working theatre in its original form, is both a thriving community playhouse and a living theatre museum. The theatre welcomes visitors of all ages to its hourly guided tours and museum.

Grassington Folk Museum

6 The Square
Grassington BD23 5AQ
www.grassingtonfolkmuseum.org.uk
grassingtonmuseum@live.com

The museum opened in its present building in 1979. Most items in its collection have been donated by local residents and businesses.

Grays Court

Chapter House Street
York YO1 7JH
01904 612613
www.grayscourtyork.com
enquiries@grayscourtyork.com

Grays Court is possibly the oldest continuously occupied house in the country. Dating back in part to 1080 and commissioned by the first Norman Archbishop of York to provide the official residence for the Treasurers of York Minster, the house has an unrivalled history. The Sterne Room was built above the original Medieval Magnesian Limestone wall (which can still be seen) by Jaques Sterne, Precentor and Canon Residentiary of the Minster and uncle of Laurence Sterne, author of Tristram Shandy, when he owned the house.

Green Howards Regimental Museum

Trinity Church Square
Richmond DL10 4QN
01748 826561
www.greenhowards.org.uk
museum@greenhowards.org.uk

The Green Howards Museum is Richmond, North Yorkshire. We tell the story of the regiment from its earliest times, through 300 years of conflict, service and sacrifice.

Guisborough Museum

Sunnyfield House, 36 Westgate
Guisborough TS14 6BA
01287 634595

This is a small volunteer-run museum showing the social, agricultural and commercial history of Guisborough. The museum displays a wealth of artefacts and photographs unique to the town and its people.

Gisborough Priory Gardens

Guisborough TS14 6PR
01287 637967
www.gisboroughprioryproject.co.uk

After the dissolution of the monasteries under Henry VIII the land next to Gisborough Priory was acquired by the Chaloner family. Eventually in the early 18th century a mansion house and magnificent garden was created on the site. This local volunteer-run charity aims to restore these gardens to provide a public green space and ensure the gardens' history is recorded for posterity.

Harrogate & District Family History Society

16 Swinborne Close
Harrogate HG1 3LX
www.hadfhs.co.uk
info@hadfhs.co.uk

We promote and encourage the public study of both family and local history in the Harrogate and surrounding areas. We also promote the preservation, security and accessibility of archive material.

Harrogate Museums & Arts

Royal Pump Room, Crown Place
Harrogate HG1 2RY
01423 556188
www.harrogate.gov.uk/museums
LG12@harrogate.gov.uk

Harrogate Museums & Arts serves the District of Harrogate within North Yorkshire. Our facilities include the Royal Pump Room Museum, Mercer Art Gallery, Knaresborough Castle and Museum, and St Robert's Cave.

Helmsley Castle - English Heritage

Castlegate
Helmsley YO62 5AB
01439 770442
http://goo.gl/BaCiRh
customers@english-heritage.org.uk

Towering over the attractive market town of Helmsley, and surrounded by spectacular banks and ditches, Helmsley Castle is an imposing site with a wealth of history. It has recently undergone a thorough makeover by English Heritage, making it more accessible to a wide range of visitors.

Henry VII Experience at Micklegate Bar

Micklegate
York YO1 6JX
01904 615505
www.henryviiexperience.com
info@henryviiexperience.com

Micklegate Bar, the iconic royal gateway of the City of York, invites you to discover The Henry VII Experience. Explore the life of the first Tudor King as he created a new era in British History, after defeating his rival Richard III.

JORVIK Viking Centre

15-17 Coppergate
York YO1 9WT
01904 615505
www.jorvik-viking-centre.co.uk
jorvik@yorkat.co.uk

At JORVIK Viking Centre travel back 1000 years and visit the Vikings of JORVIK. Explore York's Viking history exactly where our archaeologists found the remains of the original Viking-Age City of 'Jorvik'.

Collections: Everything in JORVIK Viking Centre is based on archaeological evidence unearthed during the Coppergate excavations undertaken between 1979 and 1981 by York Archaeological Trust. Archaeologists started digging on the site of an old sweet factory and unearthed remains of 10th century Viking-age buildings that were surrounded by moist, spongy layers of earth similar to that of a peat bog.

Kiplin Hall

Near Scorton
Richmond DL10 6AT
01748 818178
www.kiplinhall.co.uk
info@kiplinhall.co.uk

This hidden gem, situated between Richmond and Northallerton, was built in 1620 by George Calvert, Secretary of State to James I and Founder of Maryland, USA. Since then, the Calverts, Crowes, Carpenters and Talbots, all related by blood or marriage, have left their stamp on the house.

Kirkham Priory - English Heritage

Nr Malton YO60 7JS

01653 618768

www.english-heritage.org.uk/visit/places/kirkham-priory

customers@english-heritage.org.uk

These ruins of an Augustinian priory include an elaborate gatehouse and monkâ's washroom, all set in the peaceful Derwent valley, an area of outstanding natural beauty in the Yorkshire Wolds.

Collections: New interpretations include the story of the secret visit of Winston Churchill and the role of the site in preparation for D-Day during World War II.

Kirkleatham Museum

Kirkleatham

Redcar TS10 5NW

01642 479500

www.redcar-cleveland.gov.uk/museums

museum_services@redcar-cleveland.gov.uk

Kirkleatham Museum was opened in 1981. It is located in Kirkleatham Old Hall which was built in 1709 as a 'Free School' by the local Turner family.

Knaresborough Castle & Museum

Castle Yard

Knaresborough HG5 8AS

01423 556188

www.harrogate.gov.uk/museums

museums@harrogate.gov.uk

Knaresborough Castle and Museum is set beautifully towering over the River Nidd. Discover royalty and colourful local characters.

Malton Museum

Old Town Hall, Market Place

Malton YO17 7LP

01653 695136

www.maltonmuseum.co.uk

Malton Museum is Ryedale's major archaeological museum, located in the heart of Malton's market place and housed in an 18th century butter market. The museum houses an interesting array of Roman finds, from manicure sets to wall plaster paintings. Most of these have been discovered locally, the most recent find being a burial urn discovered by a local workman installing a new street light on a housing estate in nearby Norton.

Merchant Adventurers' Hall

Fossgate

York YO1 9XD

01904 654818

www.theyorkcompany.co.uk

enquiries@theyorkcompany.co.uk

The Merchant Adventurers' Hall is one of York's medieval marvels. Set in beautiful gardens, it is open to the public as a museum, wedding and hospitality venue and meeting place some 650 years after construction began in 1357.

Collections: The Hall contains fine collections of paintings, furniture and silver, all of which are on display to the public.

Middleham Castle - English Heritage

Leyburn DL8 4QG

01969 623899

http://goo.gl/XtVkMz

The childhood and favourite home of Richard III, Middleham Castle was a fortress of the mighty Neville family, Earls of Westmoreland and of Warwick. Around the massive 12th-century keep, they progressively constructed three ranges of luxurious chambers and lodgings, turning the castle into a fortified palace by the mid-15th century.

Mount Grace Priory - National Trust

Staddle Bridge

Northallerton DL6 3JG

01609 883494

www.nationaltrust.org.uk/mount-grace-priory

customers@english-heritage.org.uk

Set amid woodland below the escarpment of the North York Moors and the Cleveland Way National Trail, Mount Grace is a monastic ruin of an unusual kind. It is the best-preserved of the ten British 'charterhouses', whose Carthusian monks lived as hermits in cottage-like cells.

Museum of North Craven Life

The Folly, Victoria Street,

Settle BD24 9EY

www.ncbpt.org.uk/folly

curator@ncbpt.org.uk

The Folly is a beautiful 17th century Grade I listed building, in the heart of the pretty market town of Settle in the Yorkshire Dales. In 1996 The North Craven Building Preservation Trust purchased part of The Folly and completely restored the building and opened it to the public in 2001.

Museum of the Royal Dragoon Guards & the Prince of Wales's Own Regiment of Yorkshire

🖂 £

Military Museum, 3 Tower Street
York YO1 9SB
01904 662790
www.rdgmuseum.org.uk
hhq@rdgmuseum.org.uk

The Royal Dragoon Guards can trace its ancestry back to 1685, as it was formed by the amalgamation of four of the senior cavalry regiments in the British Army. The museum is well laid out in spacious surroundings and tells the story of the present day and former regiments from the late 17th century. Displays include uniforms, prints, paintings, weapons and standards, all housed in well lit, clearly labelled show cases.

Museum of the Wagoners Special Reserve

🖂 ★

The Estate Office, Sledmere, Driffield
Driffield YO25 3XQ
01377 236637
www.sledmerehouse.com/wagoners-museum.html

Possibly the smallest military museum anywhere. This remarkable museum tells the story of the Wagoners' Special Reserve.

Collections: Display includes photographs of wagoners in the first world war, memorabilia and some of the medals they were awarded. The exhibiton is of interest to the general visitor and historian alike.

Newby Hall & Gardens

🏛 £

Ripon HG4 5AE
0845 4504068
www.newbyhall.co.uk

Newby Hall is one of Britain's finest Adam Houses. Built under the guidance of Sir Christopher Wren in 17 century, the superb contents of the house, collected by William Weddell, ancestor of the Compton family, include the Gobelins Tapestry Room, a renowned gallery of classical statuary and some of Chippendale's finest furniture. The site also features 25 acres of award-winning gardens, full of rare and beautiful plants.

Nidderdale Museum

🖂 £

King Street
Pately Bridge HG3 5LE
01423 711225
www.nidderdalemuseum.com
info@nidderdalemuseum.com

Situated in the picturesque town of Pateley Bridge, North Yorkshire, this fascinating and friendly museum is housed in the former workhouse and is situated opposite St Cuthbert's Parish Church. Its 11 rooms illustrate the rural life of Nidderdale in the recent and more distant past.

Nidderdale Museum shows how ordinary people lived, in imaginative and realistic settings.

North East Film Archive

🏛 ★

School of Arts and Media, Teesside University
Middlesbrough TS1 3BA
01642 384022
www.northeastfilmarchive.com
NEFA@tees.ac.uk

The North East Film Archive (NEFA) is the public moving image archive for the North East of England. We hold over 36,000 hours of historical films and videos illustrating 20th century life and work in County Durham, Tyne & Wear, Northumberland and the Tees Valley.

North Yorkshire County Record Office

🏛 ★

Malpas Road
Northallerton DL7 8TB
01609-777585
www.northyorks.gov.uk/archives
archives@northyorks.gov.uk

The North Yorkshire County Record Office was established in 1949 and now occupies purpose-adapted premises, storing millions of documents in line with British Standard 5454, and making them available for a wide range of uses, from legal enquiries, to education and enjoyment. The Record Office offers a source of expertise in record keeping for the County Council and the people of North Yorkshire.

North Yorkshire Moors Railway

🏛 🖂 🏛 £

Pickering Station
Pickering YO18 7AJ
01751 472508
www.nymr.co.uk
info@nymr.co.uk

Britain's most popular heritage steam railway running through 18 miles of the North York Moors National Park.

Nunnington Hall - National Trust

🏛 £

Nunnington
York YO62 5UY
01439 748283
www.nationaltrust.org.uk/nunnington-hall
nunningtonhall@nationaltrust.org.uk

One of Ryedale's finest attractions, Nunnington Hall nestles on the banks of the picturesque River Rye. With period rooms, major exhibitons, an organic walled garden, a full events programme, peacocks and ghosts, this honey-coloured Yorkshire family manor house offers something for everybody to enjoy.

Collections: Period rooms displayed with a 1920s feel

reflecting the donor family's period of occupation with layers of history then going back to Tudor and Stuart times before that. There are some nice examples of needlework and paintings, among a varied and interesting collection of contents.

Ormesby Hall - National Trust

Ladgate Lane,
Ormesby TS3 0SR
01642 324188
www.nationaltrust.org.uk/ormesby-hall
ormesbyhall@nationaltrust.org.uk

Home of the Pennyman family for nearly 400 years, this classic Georgian mansion, with its Victorian kitchen and laundry, attractive gardens and estate walks, provides lively resources for local schools and community groups, and a unique venue.

Pickering Castle - English Heritage

Pickering YO18 7AX
01751 474989
http://goo.gl/TFxUPt
customers@english-heritage.org.uk

Pickering Castle is set in an attractive moors-edge market town. It is a classic and well-preserved example of an early earthwork castle refortified in stone during the 13th and 14th centuries, centred upon a shell-keep crowning an impressive motte.

Prince of Wales's Own Regiment of Yorkshire Regimental Museum

3 Tower Street
York YO1 9SB
01904 662790
www.pwo-yorkshire.museum
yorksregtaffairs@btconnect.com

The museum's collection spans three centuries of travel, campaigning and war. Artefacts and photographs of the Crimean War, the North-West Frontier of India, the Boer War and the two world wars form part of the vivid presentation of the regiment's story in both peace and war.

Prison & Police Museum

27 St Marygate
Ripon HG4 1LX
01765 690 799
www.ripon.co.uk/museums
info@riponmuseums.co.uk

The museum is housed in a building which formed part of the former House of Correction and Liberty Gaol and which is now an integral part of the overall attraction of the museum. The building's origins go back to the late 17th

century but the part now occupied by the museum was built as Ripon Liberty Prison in 1816 and continued to function as such until May 1878 when it, along with numerous other local prisons throughout the country, was closed as part of a government reform of prisons.

Quilt Museum & Gallery

St Anthony's Hall, Peasholme Green
York YO1 7PW
01904 613242
www.quiltmuseum.org.uk

The Quilt Museum & Gallery is owned and managed by The Quilters' Guild of the British Isles. The guild is an educational charity working to promote the understanding, appreciation and knowledge of the art, techniques and heritage of patchwork, quilting and applique.

Richard III Experience at Monk Bar

Monk Bar, Goodramgate
York YO1 7LQ
01904 615505
www.richardiiiexperience.com
info@richardiiiexperience.com

The JORVIK Group's newest attraction invites you to step foot into the historic Monk Bar to discover The Richard III Experience. Explore the life of the last Plantagenet King as he struggled for the throne and power during his short reign. Experience his mighty moments of battle, with multimedia presentations, and displays of the authentic medieval weapons and armour used to fight his opponents during the bloody War of the Roses.

Richmond Castle - English Heritage

Tower Street
Richmond DL10 4QW
01748 822493
http://goo.gl/1d5vpz
customers@english-heritage.org.uk

Breathtakingly sited on a rocky promontory above the River Swale, the great castle of Richmond is among the oldest Norman stone fortresses in Britain, begun in the decades after the Conquest. The story of conscientious objectors imprisoned in the keep during World War I is told in an interactive display exploring Richmond's nine centuries of development, and woven into the Cockpit Garden.

Richmondshire Museum

Ryders Wynd
Richmond DL10 4JA
01748 825 611
www.richmondshiremuseum.org.uk
info@richmondshiremuseum.org.uk

Richmondshire Museum was founded in 1974 by the Soroptimists of Richmond and the Dales; it opened its doors in 1978 in a former joiner's workshop, and has gradually grown ever since. Your visit begins in a reconstructed cruck house, with a collection of domestic bygones. The Leadmining Gallery details the industry which flourished in Swaledale until the end of the 19th century. The Transport Gallery, with its model of Richmond Station, leads to the Herriot Set from the BBC's All Creatures Great and Small, and Barker's Chemist's Shop. Next is the Wenham Gallery, which covers the history of Richmond and district, and contains a former village Post Office from just up the dale. The latest addition is a recreation of the Richmond grocer's shop, just round the corner in Frenchgate, where the founder of the Fenwick department store chain began his working life.

Rievaulx Abbey - English Heritage

Rievaulx
Helmsley YO62 5LB
01439 798228
http://goo.gl/DTmNHZ
customers@english-heritage.org.uk

Escape the crowds and experience the serenity and beauty of this impressive monastic site, situated in the middle of the North Yorkshire Moors National Park. Rievaulx Abbey was founded by St Bernard of Clairvaux in 1132 and become one of England's wealthiest monasteries before its dissolution by King Henry VIII in 1538.

Ripley Castle

The Ripley Castle Estate
Harrogate HG3 3AY
01423 770152
www.ripleycastle.co.uk
enquiries@ripleycastle.co.uk

In 2009 Ripley Castle has been the home of the Ingilby family for the last seven hundred years. The castle's history is one of political, military, religious and social turbulence, of plague and persecution, of renaissance, enlightenment and industrial revolution.

Ripon Cathedral

Kirkgate
Ripon HG4 1QS
01765 602075
www.riponcathedral.org.uk
postmaster@riponcathedral.org.uk

For over 1300 years people have been coming to worship and pray at Ripon. The cathedral building itself is part of this continuing act of worship, begun in the C7th when Saint Wilfrid built one of England's first stone churches on this site, and still renewed ever day.

RNLI Whitby Museum

Pier Road
Whitby YO21 3PU
01947 602001
http://goo.gl/HJF1If

Built in 1895, the double boathouse was used by the RNLI until 1957 when it was re-established as a museum. The museum has grown to contain an abundance of lifeboat material including models, paintings, medals, photographs, lifeboat kit and items from famous rescues.

RNLI Zetland Museum

The Esplanade
Redcar TS10 3AH
01642 494311
www.redcarlifeboat.org.uk/zetland/index.htm

The museum uses lifelike figures and models to bring to life the story of sea rescues on the north east coast. Upstairs is an extensive display of lifesaving equipment, past and present, and a reconstruction of a fisherman's sitting room.

Robin Hood's Bay & Fylingdales Museum

Fisherhead, Robin Hood's Bay
Whitby YO22 4TQ
museum.rhbay.co.uk
museum@rhbay.co.uk

On 31st July 1891, the building was purchased on a 1000 year lease by Rev. R.J.

Rotunda Museum

Vernon Road
Scarborough YO11 2NN
01723 353665
info@smtrust.uk.com

Explore modern interactive displays to learn about the fascinating geology of the Yorkshire coast. Find out about this unique geology that brought William Smith to the town and inspired him to design this fabulous iconic building in 1829.

Royal Pump Room Museum

Crown Place
Harrogate HG1 2RY
01423 556188
www.harrogate.gov.uk/museums
museums@harrogate.gov.uk

Visit the Royal Pump Room Museum to discover the intriguing story of how Harrogate became a spa town. Discover stories of Russian royalty and disappearing crime writers, marvel at the amazing spa treatments and join a tour to see the strongest sulphur well in Europe.

Ryedale Folk Museum

Hutton le Hole
Hutton le Hole YO62 6UA
01751 417367
www.ryedalefolkmuseum.co.uk
info@ryedalefolkmuseum.co.uk

Wander into 16th, 18th and 19th century thatched cottages, the Edwardian photographic studio, Iron Age roundhouse, working blacksmiths and many attractions of Ryedale Folk Museum's 5 acre site.

Scarborough Castle - English Heritage

Castle Road
Scarborough YO11 1HY
01723 372451
http://goo.gl/QchfRw
customers@english-heritage.org.uk

Scarborough Castle defends a prominent headland between two bays, with sheer drops to the sea and only a narrow landward approach. Specially contructed viewing platforms on the battlements offer panoramic views.

Scarborough Collections

Woodend, The Crescent
Scarborough YO11 2PW
01723 384503
info@smtrust.uk.com

Scarborough Collections is a unique facility housed in the Woodend Creative Workspace. It offers access to Scarborough's Collections which includes a vast array of social and natural history specimens that have been collected by the town over the years and include things like ammonites, beetles, paintings, prehistoric pots, even cuddly toys. These collections are now housed under one roof in a state of the art storage facility.

Collections: Scarborough.

Selby & District Family History Group

9 Larkfield Road
Selby YO8 9AS
www.selbydistrictfamilyhistory.btck.co.uk
sheila9@tiscali.co.uk

Formed in May 2001 from a short Workers Education Association Family History Course, it has developed into a group where experienced members offer help and advice to those that require it.

Shandy Hall

Coxwold
York YO61 4AD
01347 868465
www.laurencesternetrust.org.uk
shandyhall@dsl.pipex.com

The Laurence Sterne Trust was established as a registered charity in 1967 in order to promote the writings of Laurence Sterne, the 18th century novelist and vicar of Coxwold. Shandy Hall is where he lived and wrote The Life and Opinions of Tristram Shandy, Gentleman and A Sentimental Journey Through France and Italy. The Trust promotes Sterne's work and international reputation through exhibitions, events and public access to the property and its collection.

St Robert's Cave

St Robert's Cave, Abbey Road
Knaresborough HG5 8HX
01423 556188
www.harrogate.gov.uk/harrogate-1323

Sitting snugly beside the River Nidd on the outskirts of Knaresborough, Saint Robert's Cave is a rare survival of a medieval hermit's home. This site once attracted thousands of pilgrims to this North Yorkshire town. Robert of Knaresborough lived on this site in the late 12th and early 13th centuries.

Stewart's Burnby Hall Gardens & Museum

Burnby Hall Gardens, The Balk, Pocklington
York YO4 2QF
01759 302068
www.burnbyhallgardens.com

The magnificent and beautifully laid out gardens incorporate two lakes which contain a National Collection of hard water lilies, recognised as one of the largest displays found in a natural setting in Europe and are teeming with a vast collection of fish which can be hand-fed. Burnby Hall gardens provide nine acres of changing vistas which include a woodland walk, Victorian and secret garden, extensive rockeries and a fine collection of ornamental and indigenous trees. The Stewart Museum houses Major Stewart's remarkable range of cultural and religious exhibits collected on his 8 world tours in the early 20th century.

Swaledale & Arkengarthdale Archaeology Group

Hazel Brow House
Richmond DL11 6NE
01748 886542
www.swaag.org
info@swaag.org

SWAAG is a group of enthusiasts in the northernmost

Yorkshiredales who are contributing to the knowledge base of the history of our dales through archaeological and related activity. SWAAG, affiliated with the Swaledale Museum, work under the guidance and supervision of Tim Laurie, the leading expert on prehistoric landscapes in the area.

Swaledale Museum

Swaledale Museum, The Green, Reeth,
Richmond DL11 6QT
01748 884118
www.swaledalemuseum.org
museum@swaledale.org

The Swaledale Museum is an independent museum run by volunteers with the aims of collecting, displaying and making publicly accessible the local heritage of Swaledale and Arkengarthdale. Housed in the Methodist Day School built in 1836 the lively displays and hands-on exhibits explain the development of the area from its geological foundations, via early human occupation in the Iron Age, to the growth and decline of lead mining between the 1650s and1950s. You can learn how the stone walls were built, how local crafts flourished, and how people lived.

Teesside Archives

Exchange House, 6 Marton Road
Middlesbrough TS1 1DB
01642 248321
www.middlesbrough.gov.uk/teessidearchives
teesside_archives@middlesbrough.gov.uk

Teesside Archives collects and preserves archive material from churches, official and private sources in the areas served by the councils of Hartlepool, Middlesbrough, Redcar and Cleveland, and Stockton on Tees. We are able to offer a postal search service for members of the public who are unable to visit the department in person.

Thirsk Museum

70 Barton Street
Thirsk YO7 1PQ
01845 527707
www.homefrontthirsk.org.uk/museum

Thirsk Museum occupies the house where Thomas Lord, the founder of Lord's Cricket Ground, was born in 1755. There are eight rooms full of exhibits, featuring local life and industry, cricketing memorabilia, farming equipment, furniture, costumes and toys.

Transporter Bridge Visitor Centre

Ferry Road, St Hilda's
Middlesbrough TS2 1PL
01642 248566

This visitor centre is dedicated to the rich industrial

heritage of Middlesbrough. One of the powerhouses of the industrial northeast, the town was a major player in the Industrial Revolution, and especially shipping. The visitor centre promotes the history of the bridge and surrounding area through the use of graphic panels, video, computers, photographs, objects and models.

Treasurer's House, York - National Trust

Minster Yard
York YO1 7JL
01904 624247
www.nationaltrust.org.uk/treasurers-house-york
treasurershouse@nationaltrust.org.uk

Elegant town house dating from medieval times. Originally home to the treasurers of York Minster and built over a Roman road, the house is not all that it seems.

University of York - Institute for the Public Understanding of the Past

HRC, Berrick Saul Building University of York
York YO10 5DD
www.york.ac.uk/ipup
rq507@york.ac.uk

The Institute for the Public Understanding of the Past researches how narratives of the past function in our society and how identities are constructed in the present, using the past.

Upper Dales Family History Group

Croft House, Newbiggin in Bishopdale
Nr Leyburn DL8 3TD
01969 663738
www.upperdalesfhg.org.uk
glenys@bishopdale.demon.co.uk

The aim of the group is to support those members whose ancestors had their roots in Wensleydale and Swaledale. These ancestors often wandered far and wide so it is not surprising that our members' genealogical interests spread nationally and internationally.

Upper Wharfedale - National Trust

Upper Wharfedale
near Buckden BD23 5JA
01729 830416
upperwharfedale@nationaltrust.org.uk

Along the Upper Wharfe Valley the characteristic dry-stone walls and barns of the Dales, important flower-rich hay meadows, beautiful riverside and valleyside woodland combine to create a wonderful place to relax and explore the great outdoors.

Wharfedale Family History Group

Hideaway Cottage, Middle Lane, Kettlewell
Skipton BD23 5QX
www.wharfedalefhg.org.uk
membership@wharfedalefhg.org.uk

If your roots are in Wharfedale or further afield you will find help and encouragement in this fascinating hobby by joining the Wharfedale Family History Group.

Whitby Abbey - English Heritage

Whitby Abbey
Whitby YO22 4JT
01947 603568
www.english-heritage.org.uk/visit/places/whitby-abbey/
customers@english-heritage.org.uk

High on a cliff above the seaside town of Whitby are the gaunt, imposing remains of Whitby Abbey. Founded in 657 by St Hilda, Whitby Abbey has over the years been a bustling settlement, a kings' burial place, a home of saints and inspiration for Bram Stoker, author of Dracula.

Whitby Archives Heritage Centre

Flowergate
Whitby YO21 3BA
01947 821364
www.whitbyarchives.org.uk
info@whitbyarchives.freeserve.co.uk

A heritage centre containing historic photographs and artefacts from Whitby and North Yorkshire area. Family and local history departments, exhibition hall and heritage shop. Holders of the entire collection of the Whitby Gazette and home to the original West Cliff historic whalebone arch.

Whitby Museum

Pannett Park
Whitby YO21 1RE
01947 602908
www.whitbymuseum.org.uk
keeper@whitbymuseum.org.uk

Whitby Museum was started by local gentlemen in 1823 to preserve the fossils and other interesting artefacts existing in the area. It is owned by Whitby Literary and Philosophical Society and run entirely by volunteers from among the society's members.

Workhouse Museum

Sharow View, Allhallowgate
Ripon HG4 1LE
01765 690799
www.riponmuseums.co.uk
info@riponmuseums.co.uk

The Workhouse Museum is housed in the gatehouse building, part of the larger workhouse site (which visitors are welcome to explore), which contained the guardians' room, vagrants cells and receiving ward for inmates. we have also worked hard to recreate the original workhouse kitchen garden, located to the rear of the workhouse site which would have been tended by the inmates and been used to feed them.

World of James Herriot, The

23 Kirkgate
Thirsk YO7 1PL
01845 524 234
www.worldofjamesherriot.org
mail@worldofjamesherriot.com

The World of James Herriot is a unique tribute to vet and author James Herriot. Based in his original surgery at 23 Kirkgate, Thirsk, North Yorkshire - the 'skeldale House' of the Herriot books - it takes visitors on a journey back to the 1940s. When James Herriot died in 1995, Hambleton District Council bought the old surgery and set about painstakingly restoring it.

WR Mitchell Archive

Town Hall
Settle BD24 9EJ
01729 82229
www.settlestories.org.uk/wrmitchell
wrmitchellarchive@gmail.com

A collection of over 400 taped interviews of Yorkshire Dales Folk collected by WR 'Bill' Mitchell, editor of The Dalesman magazine.

York Archaeological Trust

47 Aldwark
York YO1 7BX
01904 663000
www.yorkarchaeology.co.uk
enquiries@yorkarchaeology.co.uk

York Archaeological Trust is a registered museum. Our professionally accredited team has over 30 years experience in investigating buildings, landscapes and buried remains.

York Archives & Local History

Archives and Local History, Acomb Explore, Front Street, Acomb
York YO24 3BZ
01904 552651
www.exploreyork.org.uk

Our collection contains thousands of unique documents, plans and photographs that tell the story of 800 years of York's history. Our oldest document dates from 1155, the most recent from 2012.

York Castle Museum

The Eye of York
York YO1 9RY
01904 687687
www.yorkcastlemuseum.org.uk
castle.museum@ymt.org.uk

Come and see hundreds of years of York's history in one place – from recreated Jacobean dining rooms to infamous Victorian criminals and all the way to the Space Age and the swinging Sixties. Kirkgate, the famous reconstructed Victorian Street that provides the core of the castle Museum, is a milestone in the history of museums.

York City Archives

Exhibition Square
York YO1 7EW
01904 551 878
www.exploreyork.org.uk
archives@york.gov.uk

The council minutes and accounts cover 500 years of civic life including the Mystery Plays and many references to Richard, Duke of Gloucester (later Richard III). They include some records of York City Courts. The 20th century collection includes housing clearance areas with an extensive collection of photographs and also sources for town planning and conservation.

York Cold War Bunker - English Heritage

Monument Close
York YO24 4HT
http://goo.gl/AcyVOp
01904 646940

The most modern and spine-chilling of English Heritage's properties, the York Cold War Bunker uncovers the secret history of Britain's Cold War. Enter the blast-proof doors and investigate the more unusual side of York's heritage. In active service from the 1960s–1990s the bunker was designed as a nerve-centre to monitor fall-out in the event of a nuclear attack.

York Mansion House

St Helens Square
York YO1 9QL
01904 552 036
www.mansionhouseyork.com
mansionhouse@york.gov.uk

Situated in the heart of the city in beautiful St Helen's Square, the Mansion House is an architectural masterpiece which plays host to an extensive collection of civic regalia and artefacts. The impressive collection of silver, paintings and furniture is unequalled by any other provincial city.

York Minster

York Minster
York YO1 7HH
0844 939 0011
www.yorkminster.org
info@yorkminster.org

York Minster provides a wealth of history for you to discover. The minster itself is an architectural masterpiece and a treasure house of stained glass.

York Museums Trust

St Mary's Lodge
York YO30 7DR
01904 687687
www.yorkmuseumstrust.org.uk
janet.bennett@ymt.org.uk

York Museums Trust is an independent charitable trust which manages York Castle Museum, Yorkshire Museum and Gardens, and York Art Gallery. The buildings and their contents are owned by the City of York Council, which has agreed to long-term funding of the Trust.

Yorkshire Air Museum

Halifax Way, Elvington
York YO41 4AU
01904 608 595
www.yorkshireairmuseum.co.uk
museum@yorkshireairmuseum.co.uk

A fascinating and dynamic museum, authentically based on a World War Two Bomber Command Station. The unique displays include the original control tower, air gunners' collection, barnes wallis' prototype 'bouncing bomb' and a superb airborne engineers display.

Collections: Historic aircraft collection covering aviation history from the Yorkshire aviation pioneer Sir George Cayley and his man-carrying glider of 1853, through to WWII aircraft including the unique Halifax bomber and to the supersonic age with frontline jets such as the Tornado. Significant collection of WWII air forces related artefacts, uniforms, records and vehicles.

Yorkshire Film Archive

York St John University, Lord Mayor's Walk
York YO31 7EX
01904 876550
www.yorkshirefilmarchive.com
yfa@yorksj.ac.uk

The Yorkshire Film Archive is the public access film archive for Yorkshire and the Humber. We hold over 14,000 items of film and video tape, dating from the earliest days of film making in the 1880s to the present day.

Yorkshire Museum & Gardens

York Museum Gardens
York YO1 7FR
01904 687687
www.yorkshiremuseum.org.uk
yorkshire.museum@ymt.org.uk

The Yorkshire Museum sits in the heart of York Museum Gardens, in the centre of York. The museum was opened in 1830 by the Yorkshire Philosophical Society and was one of the first purpose-built museums in the country. Housing some of the finest collections of archaeological and geological finds in Europe, the Yorkshire Museum is the ideal first port of call for any trip to York.

Collections: The collections cover numismatics, archaeological finds from Roman, Anglo-Saxon, Viking, and Medieval times, biology, geology and studio pottery.

Yorkshire Museum of Farming at Murton Park

Murton Park, Murton Lane
York YO19 5UF
01904 489966
www.murtonpark.co.uk

The museum opened in 1982 to house a range of exhibits from Burton Constable, collected by East Yorkshire Farm Machinery Preservation Society. The museum holds a fantastic regional agricultural collection.

Yorkshire Yeomanry Museum

Yorkshire Squadron, The Queen's Own Yeomanry, Yeomanry Barracks, Fulford Road
York YO1 4ES
01482 881974
Dominic.Peacock@hullcc.gov.uk

A small collection of artefacts and memorabilia from Yorkshire's Yeomanry Regiments. The museum can be visited by prior appointment with the Yorkshire Squadron Office of the Queen's Own Yeomanry which can be contacted on 01904 620320.

Northamptonshire

Northamptonshire (or Northampton), south-midland county of England, bounded N. by Leicestershire, Rutland, and Lincolnshire, E. by Cambridgeshire, Huntingdonshire, and Bedfordshire, S. by Bucks and Oxfordshire, and W. by Warwickshire; greatest length, NE. to SW., about 70 miles; greatest breadth, E. to W., about 26 miles; area, 629,912 acres, population 272,555. Although the surface appearance of the county is generally hilly there are no elevations of considerable altitude, the highest being near Daventry, where Arbury Hill reaches 804 ft. The NE. part of the county belongs to the Fen district. In some localities, particularly the W. and SW., the scenery is especially attractive; while here and there throughout the co. rich woods and well-watered vales afford pleasing aspects. The chief rivers are the Nen and the Weiland; the Avon forms a part of the N. boundary of the co., the Cherwell of the SW. boundary, and the Learn of the W. boundary; the Ouse has its rise near Brackley in the S. The canal system includes the Union and Grand Junction Canal, besides other similar waterways. On the uplands the soil is a fine brown loam, but the richest portion is found in the black mould of the Fen district. Throughout the whole county farming is successfully prosecuted, all kinds of cereal and green crops being raised; while upon the splendid pastures large numbers of cattle are reared, principally for the London market. Northampton is celebrated for its ash trees, old oaks, and elm avenues. Lias and oolite are the prevailing geological formations. Iron is largely found, and although worked as early as the time of the Roman occupation, its modern manufacture dates only from 1850, since which year remarkable progress has been made by the encouragement of the industry and its consequent productiveness. Apart from ironworking, the great industry of the county is centred in the manufacture of boots and shoes in the town of Northampton and the towns of the middle of the county. Northamptonshire contains 20 hundreds, 344 parishes, with parts of 4 others, the parliamentary and municipal borough of Northampton, part of the parliamentary and municipal borough of Peterborough, the municipal borough of Daventry, and part of the municipal borough of Stamford. It is almost entirely in the diocese of Peterborough.

– John Bartholomew, *Gazetteer of the British Isles* (1887)

78 Derngate

82 Derngate
Northampton NN1 1UH
01604 603407
www.78derngate.org.uk
info@78derngate.org.uk

The Charles Rennie Mackintosh House, 78 Derngate, is an important and award-winning historic house set in the heart of Northampton. Designed and remodelled by Charles Rennie Mackintosh in 1916, the house has been meticulously restored and opened to the public.

Abington Park Museum

Park Avenue South, Abington Park
Northampton NN1 5LW
01604 838110
www.northampton.gov.uk/museums
museums@northampton.gov.uk

A 15th century manor house, once the home of Shakespeare's granddaughter, Elizabeth Bernard, who is buried in the nearby church. It is now a museum including the history of the house.

Collections: Social history costume military history natural sciences egyptology leathercraft.

Althorp

Northampton NN7 4HQ
01604 771 07
www.althorp.com
mail@althorp.com

Family home of Diana Princess of Wales. House, gardens and exhibition open to the public for two months annually.

Boughton House

Boughton Park, Geddington
Kettering NN14 1BJ
01536 515731
www.boughtonhouse.org.uk
llt@boughtonhouse.org.uk

Boughton House, known as 'the English Versailles', is the Northamptonshire home of the Dukes of Buccleuch and Queensberry. Its transformation from a 15th century monastic building into one of the great houses of Europe 250 years later is a colourful story, best illustrated by the rich variety of the architecture and the superb quality of the contents.

Collections: Superb art treasures - paintings, furniture, tapestries, needlework, carpets, porcelain, arms and silver – and an incomparable armoury.

Burton Latimer Heritage Museum

Civic Centre, 120 High Street
Burton Latimer NN15 5RH
01536 722722
www.burtonlatimer.info
project@burtonlatimer.info

Burton Latimer Heritage Museum is situated in a former health centre now the Civic Centre. It is managed by Burton Latimer Heritage Society, which mounts two themed exhibitions each year.

Canons Ashby - National Trust

Canons Ashby
Daventry NN11 3SD
01327 860044
www.nationaltrust.org.uk/canons-ashby-house
canonsashby@nationaltrust.org.uk

A tranquil Elizabethan manor house set in beautiful gardens: * There are some beautiful Tudor/Jacobean wall paintings, Jacobean plasterwork and several tapestries with some excellent C17 needlepoint chairs * The kitchen and dairy offer an intimate view of life 'below stairs' * Colourful formal gardens, old orchard and sweeping parkland * St Mary's Church, the relic of an Augustinian priory * The park encompasses the deserted medieval village.

Carpetbagger Aviation Museum

Sunnyvale Farm, off Lamport Road, Harrington
Harrington NN6 9PF
01604 686608
www.harringtonmuseum.org.uk
enquiries@harringtonmuseum.org.uk

Displays and exhibits within the Carpetbagger Aviation Museum depict the history of the airfield and vividly show the work carried out by the 801st (Provisional) / 492nd Bomb Group of the US Eighth Air Force, especially during Operation Carpetbagger, and their secret missions to deliver agents and supplies to resistance groups in Occupied Europe during the Second World War. Other exhibits and displays include the secret work of the British Special Operations Executive from their RAF base at Tempsford; the cold war roles of the airfield at Harrington with the Thor rockets; and the Royal Observer Corps. Nearby in the former Paymaster nissen hut, and also forming part of the Harrington Aviation Museums, is the Northants Aviation Society Museum. This contains many other fascinating items of equipment and memorabilia.

Chichele College

Higham Ferrers NN10 8BH

01933 655401

angela-gaye.mallory-starks@culturalcommunitypartnerships.org.uk

Chichele College is an evocative mediaeval building situated in the centre of Higham Ferrers. The college was founded in the 15th century by Henry Chichele, Archbishop of Canterbury from 1414 to 1443.

Daventry Town Council Museum

Town Council Offices, 3 New Street
Daventry NN11 4BT

01327 301246

admin@daventrytowncouncil.gov.uk

The exhibition has some interesting displays of past Daventry artefacts including the old Borough Charter and a model of the railway station. Many displays are changed on a regular basis. At the present time the exhibition contains many interesting items of Daventry´s history donated or loaned or donated by local people of the town.

Earls Barton Museum of Local Life

Barkers Factory Complex, Station Road, Earls Barton
Northampton NN6 0DH

01604 811 735

Earls Barton Museum of Local Life offers visitors a chance to see just how the people of this area have lived through many stages in history. There is thought to have been a settlement in this area for a great deal of time, and this museum charts the development of people and practices through several stages.

Irchester Narrow Gauge Railway Museum

Irchester Country Park
Wellingborough NN29 7DL

01604 675368

https://sites.google.com/site/ingrmuseum/home

kadams7000@btinternet.com

Situated in Irchester Country Park, Northamptonshire, the Irchester Narrow Gauge Railway Museum is home to a collection of working steam and diesel locomotives.

Kelmarsh Hall & Gardens

Kelmarsh Hall, Kelmarsh
Northampton NN6 9LT

01604 686 543

www.kelmarsh.com

enquiries@kelmarsh.com

Kelmarsh is a 3,363 acre (1361ha) agricultural estate at the heart of which (physically and symbolically) stands the 18th century Kelmarsh Hall, surrounded by its pleasure gardens and parkland. Today the estate, hall and gardens are owned and managed by The Kelmarsh Trust whose principle aim is to preserve the Hall for the benefit of the nation together with its contents and surroundings, making them available for study and appreciation by the general public.

Kirby Hall - English Heritage

Corby NN17 3EN

www.english-heritage.org.uk/visit/places/kirby-hall/

01536 203230

Kirby Hall is one of England's greatest Elizabethan and 17th century houses, earlier owned by Sir Christopher Hatton, Lord Chancellor to Queen Elizabeth I. Although this vast mansion is partly roofless, the walls show the exceptionally rich decoration that proclaims that its successive owners were always in the forefront of new ideas about architecture and design.

Lamport Hall

Lamport
Northampton NN6 9HD (SAT NAV - NN6 9EZ)

01604 686272

www.lamporthall.co.uk

admin@lamporthall.co.uk

Lamport Hall is one of the finest Grade I listed buildings. It contains a wealth of outstanding furniture, books, china and paintings, many of which were brought back by the third Baronet's Grand Tour of Europe in the 1670s.

Lyveden New Bield - National Trust

Lyveden New Bield
near Oundle PE8 5AT

01832 205158

www.nationaltrust.org.uk/lyveden-new-bield

lyveden@nationaltrust.org.uk

Set in the heart of rural Northamptonshire, Lyveden is a remarkable survivor of the Elizabethan age. Begun by Sir Thomas Tresham to symbolise his Catholic faith, Lyveden remains incomplete and virtually unaltered since work stopped on his death in 1605. Discover the mysterious garden lodge and explore the Elizabethan garden with its spiral mounts, terracing and canals. Wander through the new orchard, containing many old varieties of apples and pears, or explore the Lyveden Way.

Manor House Museum

Sheep Street
Kettering NN16 0AN
01536 534219
www.kettering.gov.uk/museums
museumandgallery@kettering.gov.uk

Temporary exhibitions and regular activities make the Manor House Museum a lively and vibrant place to visit. Come along to explore Kettering's history and find out what makes the town unique.

Collections: The museum collects only those items, which were made or used within the geographical area of Kettering Borough for its permanent collections. The current size of the collections is thought to total circa 20,000 artefacts.

Museum of Leathercraft

c/o Central Museum & Art Gallery, Guildhall Road
Northampton NN1 1DP
01604 233 500
www.museumofleathercraft.org
neilmacgregor@museumofleathercraft.org

The museum of Leathercraft is internationally acknowledged as having one of the finest collections of leather artefacts in the world.

Museum of the Northamptonshire Regiment

Abington Park
Northampton NN1 5LW
01604 631454
www.northampton.gov.uk/info/200243/museums

The collection includes photographs acquired by the regiment over many years, some of which are the personal photograph albums of individual soldiers. Some of these photographs show life serving in a various number of places including Waziristan, India, Egypt, Iraq, China, Korea and other tours of various bases in Europe.

Naseby Battlefield Project

Glinton Cottage
Sibbertoft, Market Harborough LE16 9UJ
01858 880820
www.naseby.com
info@naseby.com

The battle of Naseby was fought on the morning of the 14th June 1645. In the open fields of that small Northamptonshire village, Parliament's New Model Army destroyed the main field army of King Charles I. It was the most important battle fought on British soil. The Naseby Battlefield Project aims to enhance visitor facilities at Naseby battlefield.

Northampton Museum & Art Gallery

Guildhall Road
Northampton NN1 1DP
01604 838111
www.northampton.gov.uk/museums
museums@northampton.gov.uk

Northampton Museum reflects the town's proud standing as both Britain's boot and shoe capital and the focus for history of the town through the ages.

Collections: The Boot and Shoe collection held at Northampton's Central Museum and Art Gallery is one of the most extensive collections of its kind in the world. It includes everything from Roman and medieval footwear to the work of contemporary designers and reflects the vital role of Northampton in the history of shoe making.

Northamptonshire Black History Project

Doddridge Centre, 109 St James Road
Northampton NN5 5LD
01604 590967
www.northants-black-history.org.uk
info@northants-black-history-project.org.uk

This community-led project aims to record and promote the histories and stories of Northamptonshire's Black communities over at least the past 500 years. It involves three main activities: (1) Historical research to reveal the Black presence by looking at newspapers, parish records, paintings, photographs, gravestones and other media; (2) community archiving to preserve the records of today's black communities and individuals for future generations; (3) Oral history interviews to document the stories and experiences of people living in Northamptonshire today.

Northamptonshire Family History Society

22 Godwin Walk, Ryehill Estate
Northampton NN5 7RW
www.northants-fhs.org
secretary@northants-fhs.org

Northants Family History Society for those interested in family history and genealogy in Northamptonshire.

Northamptonshire Ironstone Railway Trust

Hunsbury Hill Country Park, Hunsbury Hill Road, Camp Hill
Northampton NN49UW
01604 702031
www.nirt.co.uk
nirt@btinternet.com

Sited on the old ironstone quarry closed in the 1930s, this museum houses a collection of relics from the ironstone quarrying era of Northampton. Also on site is a 1.5 mile demonstration railway line in standard gauge.

Northamptonshire Record Office

Records Office, Wootton Hall Park
Northampton NN4 8BQ
01604 762129

The Northamptonshire Record Office holds over 800 years of the county's rich archival heritage, which can be accessed free of charge on-site. The archives cover all aspects of life in Northamptonshire, and the people who lived here.

Northamptonshire Yeomanry Section of Borough Combined Services Museum

Abington Park
Northampton NN1 5LW
01604 31454
www.northampton.gov.uk/museums

Learn about the history of the Northamptonshire Regiment and Yeomanry and about how we used to live.

Oundle Museum

The Courthouse, Mill Road
Oundle PE8 4BW
01832 272741
www.oundlemuseum.org.uk
oundle.museum@googlemail.com

Permanent exhibits include: local archaeological finds, brewing and malting, farming tools and machinery, remand cell.

Peterborough Cathedral

Cathedral Office, Minster Precincts
Peterborough PE1 1XS
01733 355315
www.peterborough-cathedral.org.uk
communications@peterborough-cathedral.org.uk

Peterborough Cathedral is the mother church of the Diocese of Peterborough which covers most of Peterborough City, Northamptonshire and Rutland.

Piddington Roman Villa Museum

Chapel End
Piddington, Northampton NN7 2DD
01604 870312
www.unas.org.uk

Housed in a former Wesleyan chapel, the museum displays some of the many finds made during the long running excavation of the Piddington Roman Villa over 25 years, and still on-going. Apart from the displays, the building houses stores for the many found objects.

Collections: Apart from significant archaeological material it houses displays interpreting 500 years of life at the settlement, including: a detailed model of the villa, as in the later 2nd century; a full-sized mannequin of a possible owner of the villa called Tiberius Claudius Severus, with an audio presentation; a full-scale reconstruction of sections of a typical roof and hypocaust, the Roman heating system.

Prebendal Manor & Tithe Barn Museum, The

Church Street, Nassington
Peterborough PE8 6QG
01780 782575
www.prebendal-manor.co.uk
info@prebendal-manor.co.uk

A 13th century manor dating from 1200 AD, overlaying and Anglo-Saxon hall. Included in the visit is the Tithe Barn Museum, a large recreated medieval garden, fish ponds and a 15th century dovecote.

Rothwell Arts & Heritage Centre

14-16 Bridge Street
Rothwell NN14 6JW
01536 711550
www.rothwellheritage.org.uk

Rothwell is a market town with many historic buildings and proud links to the past. The importance of Rothwell or Rowell in this context is recorded in the Domesday Book. The Arts and Heritage Centre was established in 2003 by Rothwell Museum Group and Rothwell and Desborough Market Towns Initiative.

Rushton Triangular Lodge - English Heritage

Rushton Road
Rushton NN14 1RP
http://goo.gl/dZeEBr
01536 710761

This delightful triangular building was designed by Sir Thomas Tresham (father of one of the Gunpowder Plotters) and constructed between 1593 and 1597. It is a testament to Tresham's Roman Catholicism: the number three, symbolising the Holy Trinity, is apparent everywhere.

Stoke Bruerne Canal Museum

Bridge Road, Stoke Bruerne
Towcester NN12 7SE
01604 862 229
brian.collings@thewaterwaystrust.co.uk

Housed in a restored cornmill in the picturesque village of
Stoke Bruerne on the Grand Union Canal, the museum
collection vividly portrays the heritage of 200 years of
inland waterways.

Collections: The collection includes objects painted by
boatmen in the traditional 'Roses and Castles' style,
costumes worn by boating families, waterways souvenirs
from the 1950s, a large collection of photographs and
extensive archive material such as canal company share
certificates.

Sulgrave Manor

Manor Road, Sulgrave
nr Banbury OX17 2SD
01295 760205
www.sulgravemanor.org.uk
enquiries@sulgravemanor.org.uk

Sulgrave Manor was set up in the 1920s as a symbol of the
rich network of links that bind the United Kingdom and
the United States together. It was built by George
Washington's direct ancestor in the middle of the 16th
century and is now restored to show how the gentry of the
period lived.

Collections: Carefully and sympahetically restored 16th
Great Hall and bedchamber and 18th century rooms
bedrooms, parlour and kitchen. Furniture, artefacts and
textiles of the period displayed as well as the largest
collection of George Washington memorabilia.

Wellingborough Museum

12 Castle Way
Wellingborough NN8 1XB
01933 276838
www.wellingboroughmuseum.co.uk
wellingboroughmuseum@msn.com

The Wellingborough Museum is housed in Dulley's Baths,
built in 1892 as an indoor swimming pool by David Dulley,
a brewer in the town. In 1920, the building was bought by
George Cox and converted into a shoe factory.

Collections: A typical market-town collection of mainly
social items relating to Wellingborough and district.

Northumberland

Northumberland, the most northerly county of England, bounded N. by the river Tweed, which separates it from Berwickshire, NW. by the Cheviot Hills, separating it from Roxburghshire, E. by the North Sea, S. by Durham, and W. by Cumberland; greatest length, N. to S., 70 miles; greatest breadth, E. to W., 53 miles; area, 1,290,312 acres, population 434,086. Somewhat triangular in outline, Northumberland possesses a varied surface, principally rugged, and rising gradually from the coast to the hill ranges of the Cheviots on the borders of Scotland and Cumberland. In the centre of the county the hills are undulating, and clad with green; in the W. and SW. they are bleak, and covered with moss and heather. On the coast are the Coquet, Fern, and Holy Islands. Allenhead, in the extreme S. of the county, is the highest inhabited district in England, its altitude being 1400 ft. Fertile valleys stretch from spurs of the Cheviots eastward towards the coast, and the county is well watered by several celebrated rivers, the Alne, Coquet, Wansbeck, Till, Tyne, and Tweed. In those localities where farming is most diligently pursued - i.e., near the coast and in the valleys - the soil is a rich clayey loam. Barley, wheat, and beans form the chief crops; and a considerable and lucrative employment is found in the rearing of the famous Cheviot sheep, also of short-horned Durham cattle. Among anglers the Northumberland rivers and their estuaries are held in high repute for the excellence of their sport, and their fisheries also have a high commercial value. A large number of boats are employed in the sea fisheries. Geologically the conspicuous feature of the co. is its immense coal formation, producing about 20,000,000 tons a year; other districts consist of various sandstones, and the porphyry, trap, and limestone of the Cheviots. The lead mining district is in the S., in S. Tynedale and Allendale, but of late the industry has suffered through foreign competition. In addition to coal and lead works, with their auxiliary employments, Northumberland has an enormous industrial system, shown most prominently by the ironworking, ship-building, ropemaking, chemical manufacture, glass making, pottery making, &c., on the Tyne. The county is divided into 9 wards and 541 parishes, and includes the parliamentary and municipal boroughs of Morpeth, Newcastle upon Tyne, and Tynemouth, and the municipal borough of Berwick upon Tweed.

– John Bartholomew, *Gazetteer of the British Isles* (1887)

Note: see Tyne & Wear for Newcastle, Tynemouth and North Shields.

Alnwick Castle

Alnwick NE66 1NQ
01665 511 100
www.alnwickcastle.com
info@alnwickcastle.com

Alnwick Castle is Britain's second largest inhabited castle; home to the Duke of Northumberland's family for over 700 years. Combining magnificent medieval architecture with sumptuous Italianate interiors, Alnwick Castle starred as Hogwarts in the Harry Potter films and more recently featured in ITV's Downton Abbey.

Aydon Castle - English Heritage

Corbridge NE45 5PJ
www.english-heritage.org.uk/visit/places/aydon-castle/
01434 632450

Aydon Castle is a wonderful family day out. Set in beautiful woodland surroundings the 13th century manor house has plenty to inspire children and is perfect for summer picnics.

Bailiffgate Museum & Gallery

14 Bailiffgate
Alnwick NE66 1LX
01665 605847
www.bailiffgatemuseum.co.uk
ask@bailiffgatemuseum.co.uk

Bailiffgate Museum depicts the history of Alnwick and the surrounding part of Northumberland in exciting and interactive displays as well as with traditional artefacts. Visitors can experience ten thousand years of history in one visit as well as enjoying the ever changing exhibitions in our gallery.

Bamburgh Castle

Links Road
Bamburgh NE69 7DF
01668 214515
www.bamburghcastle.com
administrator@bamburghcastle.com

Bamburgh Castle is probably the finest castle in England. It is perched on a basalt outcrop on the very edge of the North Sea at Bamburgh, Northumberland.

Belford & District Hidden History

Reading Room, 11 Market Place
Belford NE70 7NE
www.belfordhiddenhistory.co.uk
info@belfordhiddenhistory.co.uk

Small museum open to public since 2012. Our vision is to create a local museum to embody the spirit and history of Belford and the surrounding district, and through its welcoming and inspirational approach, to play an active role within the village, and to serve as a focus of attraction for visitors to the area.

Bellingham Heritage Centre

Station Yard, Woodburn Road
Bellingham NE48 2DF
01434 220 050
www.bellingham-heritage.org.uk
info@bellingham-heritage.org.uk

The Heritage Centre, Bellingham, is the local museum of the North Tyne and Redesdale areas of Northumberland, situated in the former railway station. We have exhibits on the Border Reivers, the Border Counties Railway, mining and farming.

Belsay Hall, Castle & Gardens - English Heritage

Belsay
Nr Ponteland NE20 0DX
01661 881636
http://goo.gl/kthQf2
customers@english-heritage.org.uk

There's something for everyone at Belsay. Explore a spectacular medieval castle, a Greek Revival 19th-century mansion and thirty acres of stunning Grade I gardens linking the two.

Berwick Museum & Art Gallery

The Clock Block, Berwick Barracks, Ravensdowne
Berwick-upon-Tweed TD15 1DG
berwickmuseum.org.uk
amoore@woodhorn.org.uk

A collection of local social history and fine and decorative art set in a historic barracks complex. The international art comes from the collection of Sir William Burrell.

Berwick Record Office

Berwick Record Office Council Offices Wallace green
Berwick-upon-Tweed TD15 1ED
01289 301865
www.experiencewoodhorn.com/berwick-record
lbankier@woodhorn.org.uk

The Berwick-upon-Tweed Record Office was established in 1980 as a branch of the then Northumberland County Archives Service. It holds records relating to the former Borough of Berwick-upon-Tweed which extended from Berwick, south to Ellingham, west to Ingram and north to Carham on the River Tweed.

Border Library

First Floor Moothall, Market Place, Hexham; All contact via:
Dept of Leisure & Tourism, Prospect House, Hexham NE46 3NH
Hexham NE46 3NH
01434 652351
museum@tynedale.gov.uk

Library collection housed in the Moothall courtroom. Books and music relating to the English-Scottish Borders area.

Brinkburn Priory - English Heritage

Longframlington
Morpeth NE65 8AR
0870 333 1181
http://goo.gl/qlX010

The beautiful 12th century church of the Augustinian priory of Brinkburn survives completely roofed and restored. Picturesquely set by a bend in the River Coquet, it is reached by a scenic ten minute walk from the car park.

Cherryburn - National Trust

Mickley
Stockfield NE43 7DD
01661 843 276
www.nationaltrust.org.uk/cherryburn
cherryburn@nationaltrust.org.uk

Cottage and farmhouse, the birthplace of Thomas Bewick: * Birthplace of Northumberland's greatest artist and engraver * Fascinating exhibition of Bewick's life and work * Demonstrations of old-fashioned woodblock engraving and hand printing.

Chesterholm Museum

Bardon Mill
Hexham NE47 7JN
01434 344277
www.vindolanda.com

Chesterholm Museum - Vindolanda is a Roman Frontier military and civilian site, which has been the location of extensive excavation for over 30 years with archaeologists on site. Vindolanda also offers an Open Air Museum featuring replicas of a Roman temple, Roman shop and house.

Chesters Roman Fort & Museum - English Heritage

Hexham NE46 4EU

01434 681379

http://goo.gl/7zgLzT

customers@english-heritage.org.uk

Chesters Roman Fort was built to guard the Roman bridge which carried Hadrian's Wall over the River North Tyne. The entire foundations of the headquarters building are visible and, down by the river, the bath house is extremely well preserved.

Chillingham Castle

Chillingham

Alnwick NE66 5NJ

01668 215359

www.chillingham-castle.com

enquiries@chillingham-castle.com

This remarkable castle with beautiful gardens and grounds has, since the twelve hundreds, remained in the same family line. You will see active restoration of complex masonry, metalwork and ornamental plaster as the state rooms are gradually restored. Steeped in the nation's history it occupied a strategic position as a fortress during Northumberland's bloody border feuds. Take a step back in time and relive the eerie atmosphere of the torture chamber and the chilling dungeon, not for the faint hearted.

Corbridge Roman Town - English Heritage

Corbridge NE45 5NT

01434 632349

http://goo.gl/PIVkNo

On the pivotal north side of the Tyne, Corbridge played a vital role in the Roman conquest of northern Britain. The fort dates from AD139, when the Emperor Antoninus Pius once more advanced the Roman frontier into Scotland.

Cragside - National Trust

Cragside

Rothbury NE65 7PX

01669 620333

www.nationaltrust.org.uk/cragside

cragside@nationaltrust.org.uk

Lord and Lady Armstrong used their wealth, art and science in a most ingenious way, and Cragside house was the first in the world to be lit by hydroelectricity.

Dunstanburgh Castle - National Trust

Craster

Alnwick NE66 3TT

01665 576231

www.nationaltrust.org.uk/dunstanburgh-castle

dunstanburghcastle@nationaltrust.org.uk

Built on the most magnificent scale, Dunstanburgh Castle stands on a remote headland. The castle was built at a time when relations between King Edward II and his most powerful baron, Earl Thomas of Lancaster, had become openly hostile. Lancaster began the fortress in 1313, and the latest archaeological research indicates that he built it on a far grander scale than was recognised, perhaps more as a symbol of his opposition to the king than as a military stronghold. The earl failed to reach Dunstanburgh when his rebellion was defeated, and was taken and executed in 1322.

Etal Castle - English Heritage

Etal TD12 4TN

01890 820332

www.english-heritage.org.uk/visit/places/etal-castle/

In 1341 Robert Manners was granted a licence to fortify his home to protect against the threat of attack from Scottish raiders. In 1513, when an army of 30,000 Scots led by James IV invaded England, Etal Castle fell to the Scots but the invaders were defeated in the bloody battle which ensued on Flodden Hill. An award-winning exhibition tells the story of the Battle of Flodden and of the border warfare which existed here before the union of the English and Scottish crowns in 1603.

Fusiliers Museum of Northumberland

The Abbot's Tower, Alnwick Castle

Alnwick NE66 1NG

01665 602152

www.northumberlandfusiliers.org.uk/index.php

The museum was founded to perpetuate the history of the Royal Northumberland Fusiliers and to show its continuation as part of The Royal Regiment of Fusiliers. The museum maintains a collection of uniforms, medals, weapons, paintings and memorabilia relating to the various historical campaigns in which the regiment has fought.

George Stephenson's Birthplace - National Trust

Street House

Wylam-on-Tyne NE41 8BP

01661 853 457

georgestephensons@nationaltrust.org.uk

Birthplace of the world-famous railway engineer: * Northumbria's smallest National Trust property * Furnished to reflect domestic living in 1781, the year Stevenson was born here * White stone miners cottage * Picturesque riverside path along the old Wylam Colliery wagon-way.

Hadrian's Wall & Housesteads Fort - National Trust

[icons]

Haydon Bridge
Hexham NE47 6NN
01434 344363
www.nationaltrust.org.uk/hadrians-wall
housesteads@nationaltrust.org.uk

Housesteads is the most complete example of a Roman fort in Britain, and one of the most popular sites on the Wall. Perched high on the exposed Whin Sill escarpment, it commands breathtaking views.

Heatherslaw Corn Mill

[icons]

Heatherslaw Mill, Ford Forge
Cornhill-on-Tweed TD12 4TJ
01890 820 338

On the banks of the River Till, this is the only working water-driven cornmill in Northumberland which continues a tradition that stretches back over 700 years on this site. The fully restored mill machinery still makes high quality, stoneground, wholemeal flour from wheat grown in the surrounding fields, and visitors can explore the building, watch the milling process from beginning to end and see our 21st century millers at work.

Hexham Moothall & Gallery

[icons]

Gilesgate
Hexham NE46 3NH
01434 658351

15th-century building with a gallery in the tunnel-vaulted basement. A variety of exhibitions mounted by local artists and crafts people.

Hexham Old Gaol

[icons]

Old Gaol, Hallgate
Hexham NE46 1XD
01670 624523
www.hexhamoldgaol.org.uk
oldgaol@woodhorn.org.uk

The Old Gaol is the earliest documented purpose-built prison in England. It was built by order of the Archbishop of York 1330-33.

Collections: Arms and armour from the C15th and C16th Items of local history (Tynedale) interest, photographs, documents and objects Border Library holds the Butler Collection, books, tapes and manuscript music relating to the culture of the Borders.

House of Correction

[icons]

Tyne Green Road
Hexham NE46 3NH
01434 652351
museum@tynedale.gov.uk

Remains of Hexham House of Correction (1783-1865), including men's day and night cells, cell doors, barbed windows, displays on history.

King's Own Scottish Borderers Regimental Museum

[icons]

Berwick Barracks, The Parade
Berwick Upon Tweed TD15 1DG
01289 307426
www.kosb.co.uk/museum.htm
kosbmus@milnet.uk.net

The history of the regiment from 1689 to 2006 is traced through displays of uniforms, badges, medals, weapons and relics from the various campaigns in which it has been involved. Tableaux and dioramas dramatically bring to life the regiment's battles and aspects of the soldier's profession.

Lady Waterford Hall

[icons]

c/o The Estate Office, Ford Village
Berwick-upon-Tweed TD15 2QA
01890 820 224

Lady Waterford Hall was commissioned in 1860 by Louisa Anne, Marchioness of Waterford, and owner of Ford Estate. The building served as a school until 1957 and in its heyday had as many as 134 local children on the register. As well as being a very generous lady who was concerned with the welfare of the estate workers and their children, Lady Waterford was also a keen amateur painter and spent 22 years decorating the interior of the Hall with Biblical scenes as a teaching aid for pupils.

Lindisfarne Castle - National Trust

[icons]

Holy Island
Berwick-upon-Tweed TD15 2SH
01289 389244
www.nationaltrust.org.uk/lindisfarne-castle
lindisfarne@nationaltrust.org.uk

Romantic 16th-century castle with spectacular views, transformed by Lutyens into an Edwardian holiday home. Dramatically perched on a rocky crag and accessible over a causeway at low tide only, the island castle presents an exciting and alluring aspect.

Lindisfarne Priory - English Heritage

Holy Island
Berwick Upon Tweed TD15 2RX
01289 389200
http://goo.gl/Yp0d11
customers@english-heritage.org.uk

Originally home to the Lindisfarne Gospels and the site of grisly Viking attacks, a visit to Lindisfarne Priory is a great day out in Northumberland. Sitting offshore on Holy Island and reached by a causeway at low tide, the peaceful atmosphere and beautiful views from the priory make a visit here well worth the effort. Lindisfarne Priory was an important centre of early Christianity, and the home of St Cuthbert.

Morpeth Chantry Bagpipe Museum

Bridge Street
Morpeth NE61 1PD
01670 500717
www.morpethbagpipemuseum.org.uk
amoore@woodhorn.org.uk

This unusual museum specialises in the history and development of Northumbrian small pipes and their music. They are set in the context of bagpipes around the world - from India to Inverness. An ingenious sound system brings the pipes to life - each visitor may listen to the music through personal headphones and learn the difference between a rant and a reel.

Norham Castle

Berwick-upon-Tweed TD15 2JY
01289 382329
www.english-heritage.org.uk

Commanding a vital ford over the River Tweed, Norham was one of the strongest of the border castles, and the most often attacked by the Scots. Besieged at least 13 times - once for nearly a year by Robert Bruce - it was called 'the most dangerous and adventurous place in the country'. But even its powerful 12th century keep and massive towered bailey walls could not resist James IV's heavy cannon, and it fell to him in 1513, shortly before his defeat at Flodden. The extensive 16th century rebuilding which followed, adapting the fortress for its own artillery, is still clearly traceable.

Northumberland Archives

Woodhorn, QEII Country Park
Ashington NE63 9YF
01670 528080
www.experiencewoodhorn.com/collections/

Now based within Woodhorn Museum in Ashington and providing free access to numerous records for local and family historians alike.

Northumberland County Libraries, Arts & Archives

County Library Headquarters, The Willows, Gas House Lane
Morpeth NE61 1TA
01670 534514
www.northumberland.gov.uk
reference@northumberland.gov.uk

Northumberland County Library seeks to collect all published items relating to Northumberland, its history, geography, customs, language and people, as well as materials by local authors or with a local setting. This collection provides invaluable source material for the student and serious researcher as well as pleasure for the general reader and information for the enquirer.

Prudhoe Castle - English Heritage

Prudhoe NE42 6NA
01661 833459
http://goo.gl/tVw53g

On a wooded hillside overlooking the River Tyne stand the remains of this formidable castle. Archaeological evidence reveals that a defended enclosure existed on the site as early as the mid-11th century.

RNLI Grace Darling Museum

Radcliffe Road
Bamburgh NE69 7AE
01668 214910
www.rnli.org.uk/gracedarling
askgracedarling@rnli.org.uk

The RNLI Grace Darling Museum was established by the RNLI in September 1938. It commemorates the life and times of Victorian heroine Grace Darling who, with her father, rescued 9 survivors from the shipwrecked SS Forfarshire in 1838.

Roman Vindolanda & The Roman Army Museum

Chesterholm Museum, Bardon Mill
Hexham NE47 7JN
01434 344277
www.vindolanda.com
info@vindolanda.com

Vindolanda is one of the premier sites on Hadrian's Wall. The home of the Vindolanda Writing tablets, voted Britain's Top Treasure by the British Museum.

Seaton Delaval Hall - National Trust

The Avenue Seaton Sluice
Whitley Bay NE26 4QR
0191 2379100
www.nationaltrust.org.uk/seaton-delaval-hall
seatondelavalhall@nationaltrust.org.uk

The romantic and partly-ruined Seaton Delaval Hall was built between 1718 and 1731 by Sir John Vanbrugh, architect of Blenheim Palace and Castle Howard, and is one of the most important historic houses in Britain. The Hall, its gardens and grounds in south Northumberland, near the coastal town of Blyth, was acquired by the National Trust in December 2009 after a tremendous fundraising effort by the local community. We hold regular arts, heritage and community events as well as children's craft and outdoor activities.

Wallington - National Trust

Cambo
Morpeth NE61 4AR
01670 773 600
www.nationaltrust.org.uk/wallington
wallington@nationaltrust.org.uk

The Wallington estate was laid out in the 18th century by Sir Walter Blackett, helped by William Joyce, Thomas Wright and Lancelot 'Capability' Brown, who went to school in the estate village. Original formality underlies the 'natural' landscape in which walks offer a variety of lawns, shrubberies, lakes and woodland enlivened with buildings, sculpture and water features.

Warkworth Castle & Hermitage - English Heritage

Warkworth NE65 0UJ
01665 711423
http://goo.gl/4zBWCP
customers@english-heritage.org.uk

The magnificent cross-shaped keep of Warkworth, crowning a hilltop rising steeply above the River Coquet, dominates one of the largest, strongest and most impressive fortresses in northern England.

Woodhorn Museum & Northumberland Archives

QE II Country Park
Ashington NE63 9YF
01670 624455
www.experiencewoodhorn.com
generalenquiries@woodhorn.org.uk

Woodhorn is a vibrant, exciting place to visit all year round with a great programme of activities and exhibitions for the whole family. Inspired by monster coal cutting machines once used deep underground, the stunning Cutter building and original listed colliery structures house fascinating, hands-on exhibitions and displays.

Collections: The Pitmen Painters were a group of mostly miners from Northumberland who founded the Ashington Art Group in the 1930s and who took as their subject everyday life in their mining community. Woodhorn museum holds the main Ashington Group collection of their work.

Wylam Railway Museum

Falcon Centre, Falcon Terrace
Wylam NE41 8EE
01661 852 174
www.northumberland.gov.uk/VG/wylam.htm#243

Wylam Railway Museum was opened in 1981, the bicentenary of the birth of 'The Father of Railways' George Stephenson who was born in Wylam, to commemorate Wylam's unique contribution to railway history. The museum is small, occupying a former classroom in the old village school, now known as the Falcon Centre. The displays focus on the famous local railway pioneers, George Stephenson, William Hedley, Timothy Hackworth and Nicholas Wood and the Wylam Colliery waggonway.

Nottinghamshire

*Nottinghamshire, Nottingham, or Notts,
north-midland county of England, bounded N. by
Yorkshire, E. by Lincolnshire, S. by Leicestershire, and
W. by Derbyshire; greatest length, N. to S., about 50
miles; greatest breadth, E. to W., about 25 miles; area,
527,752 acres, population 391,815. Towards the E.,
Nottinghamshire has a level surface; while westwards
it is marked by gentle hills of no great elevation,
which tend to impart some variety to the scenery. The
eastern portion comprises the vales of the Trent and
Belvoir; in the S., between the Soar and the Smite, are
the Wolds, consisting of level tracts of moor and
pasture; while in the W. are the remains of the royal
forest of Sherwood. The Trent flows through the
county from SW. to NE., and is navigable for river
vessels. All the other streams are tributaries of the
Trent; they include the Soar, Erwash, and Idle. By the
Nottingham and Grantham Canal, and the Fosse
Dyke Canal, there is connection between the Trent
and the Witham. The soil is varied, but cannot be
spoken of as being highly productive. Green crops are
the principal growth, and the common cereals are
cultivated. Hop plantations are numerous, while in
proximity to Nottingham and Newark there are many
market gardens. Magnesian limestone and old red
sandstone overlying coal prevail in the W.; in the
other districts are formations of marl, new red
sandstone, and lias, with quartz and gravel in the
Forest. In a few places coal is worked. The principal
manufactures are laces of various descriptions, in
recent years a great development being apparent in
the production of lace curtains. Hosiery
manufactures., woollen mills, cotton mills, and iron
foundries are also actively productive.
Nottinghamshire comprises 6 wapentakes, 273
parishes with parts of 5 others, the parliamentary
and municipal borough of Nottingham, and the
municipal boroughs of East Retford and Newark. It is
almost entirely in the diocese of Southwell.*

– John Bartholomew, *Gazetteer of the British Isles* (1887)

Bassetlaw Museum & Worksop Museum

Amcott House, 40 Grove Street
Retford DN22 6LD
01777 713749
www.bassetlawmuseum.org.uk
bassetlaw.museum@bassetlaw.gov.uk

Bassetlaw Museum is run by Bassetlaw District Council
which covers North Nottinghamshire, and includes the two
market towns of Retford and Worksop. The museum is
situated in Retford town centre in Amcott House, an 18th
century town house which retains many of its original
features.

Brewhouse Yard - Museum of Nottingham Life

Castle Boulevard
Nottingham NG7 1FB
0115 9153700
Judith.Edgar@nottinghamcity.gov.uk

The museum depicts the social history of Nottingham over
the last 300 years. Housed in five 17th century cottages
adjacent to the famous 'Trip to Jerusalem' public house.

Calverton Folk Museum

Main Street, Calverton
Nottingham NG14 6FG
www.calvertonvillage.com/CalMuseum.html
pressoc@ntlworld.com

A museum housing period furniture and clothing, fossils, a
framework knitting machine, Victorian Kitchen, living
room and bedroom and displays on the history of
framework knitting, invented by William Lee of Calverton.
There are also tapestry pictures of village buildings.

Clumber Park - National Trust

Clumber Park
Worksop S80 3AZ
0115 9772132
www.nationaltrust.org.uk/clumber-park
heritage@nottscc.gov.uk

Former site of Clumber House, Clumber Park is a perfect
example of Edwardian splendour with its bridges, temples,
Gothic chapel and walled kitchen garden.

Creswell Crags Museum & Education Centre

Creswell Heritage Trust, Crags Road, Welbeck
Worksop S80 3LH
01909 720378
www.creswell-crags.org.uk
info@creswell-crags.org.uk

Creswell Crags is a picturesque limestone gorge honeycombed with caves and smaller fissures. Stone tools and remains of animals excavated from the caves by archaeologists provide evidence for a fascinating story of life during the Ice Age between 60,000 and 10,000 years ago.

DH Lawrence Heritage Centre & Birthplace Museum

Mansfield Road
Eastwood NG16 3DZ
01773 717353
www.dhlawrenceheritage.org
culture@broxtowe.gov.uk

DH Lawrence Heritage is a multi-award winning visitor attraction celebrating one of the greatest writers of the 20th century.

East Midlands Museums Service

c/o Centre for Museum and Heritage Management, Nottingham Trent University, Clifton Lane
Nottingham NG11 8NS
0115 848 3562
www.emms.org.uk
emms@emms.org.uk

EMMS was founded in 1981, and incorporated as a company in 1992. We are a registered charity which serves museums of all types in the East Midlands region, operating in the historic counties of Derbyshire, Leicestershire, Lincolnshire, Northamptonshire, Nottinghamshire and Rutland. Formally an Area Museum Council, EMMS has operated as a membership network for museums in the region since April 2002, and provides its members with a wide range of services to support them in their work.

Flintham Museum

The Reading Room, Inholms Road
Flintham NG23 5LF
01636 525111
www.flintham-museum.org.uk
flintham.museum@googlemail.com

The Flintham Museum looks at rural life through the eyes of a 20th-century village shopkeeper. Fred White, Flintham's shop keeper from 1911-1949, was a keen amateur photographer.

Forum of East Midlands Military Museums

c/o RHQ WFR, Foresters House, Chetwynd Barracks
Chilwell NG9 5HA
0115 9465415
www.wfrmuseum.org.uk
rhqwfr-nottm@lineone.net

FEMMS' mission is to promote all military museums within the East Midlands and their links with the community.

Galleries of Justice Museum

High Pavement, Lace Market
Nottingham NG1 1HN
0115 952 0555
www.nccl.org.uk
learning@nccl.org.uk

The Galleries of Justice Museum is a heritage site housed in the old Shire Hall in Nottingham's Lace Market and made up of a range of Victorian courtrooms, an 18th century prison and Edwardian police station. For centuries citizens of the local community were locked up in the prison, stripped of their civil liberties in the courtroom and sometimes lost their lives, on the gallows of the front steps.

Green's Mill & Science Centre

Green's Windmill, Windmill Lane, Sneinton
Nottingham NG2 4QB
0115 9156878
www.greensmill.org.uk
greensmill@nottinghamcity.gov.uk

Once home of the mathematical physicist, George Green (1793-1841). Since we opened in 1985 thousands of people have enjoyed the opportunity to look around a working windmill, buy some award-winning flour, take part in an activity, get their hands on some fun science, admire the views over the Trent valley and enjoy a cup of coffee in the millyard.

Harley Gallery, The

The Harley Gallery, Welbeck
Worksop S80 3LW
01909 501700
www.harleygallery.co.uk
info@harleygallery.co.uk

Welcome to The Harley Gallery, where old and new come together. The Harley Gallery is home to the historic Portland Collection of fine and decorative art.

Hodsock Priory

Blyth
Nr Worksop S81 0TY
01909 591204
www.hodsockpriory.com
gb@hodsockpriory.com

The priory epitomises country house style, with fine furnishings and a distinct elegance. The ancient trees in the park provide the perfect back drop to the long drive which sweeps under the archway of the Tudor Gatehouse, bringing you to the secluded setting of Hodsock. We have renovated the house using traditional, period and heritage wall papers, paints, fixtures and fittings - the rooms reflect as closely as possible the original 1829 styles.

Holme Pierrepont Hall

Holme Pierrepont
Nottingham NG12 2LD
0115 933 2371
www.holmepierreponthall.com
rplb@holmepierreponthall.com

Early Tudor manor house and family home to the Brackenbury family.

Holocaust Centre, Beth Shalom

Laxton
Newark NG22 0PA
01623 836627
www.holocaustcentre.net
office@holocaustcentre.net

The historical museum and the centre is designed to tell a story of people and how their lives are affected by history. The centre also has an arts and culture programme showing concerts and other events related to the Holocaust.

Collections: The centre houses a permanent exhibition on the Holocaust detailing the unfolding of the history of the Final Solution. Outside memorial gardens provide places for quiet reflection.

Langwith Whaley Thorns Heritage Centre

Methodist Chapel, West Street, Whaley Thorns
Mansfield NG20 9BW
01623 747601
www.freewebs.com/lwtheritagecentre
heritagecentre@mail.com

Following a major refurbishment of the Methodist Chapel, the Langwith Whaley Thorns Heritage Centre is open to the public. A focal point of the village, the Heritage Centre tells the story of the area.

Collections: The John Hyatt Collection represents the life and history of the Langwith and Whaley Thorns citizens. It reflects the impact of the sinking of a coal mine in 1876

upon a rural farming community and provides a snapshot of a period of great social upheaval. There is also a strong local photographic collection.

Malt Cross Music Hall

16 St James' Street
Nottingham NG1 6FG
www.maltcross.com
info@maltcross.com

Malt Cross Music Hall.

Mansfield Museum

Leeming Street
Mansfield NG18 1NG
01623 463088
www.mansfield.gov.uk/museum
mansfieldmuseum@mansfield.gov.uk

The five galleries of Mansfield Museum contain a fascinating mix of contemporary and modern displays, from the exquisite Buxton watercolours and Pinxton porcelain to the hands-on XplorActive environment gallery. Images of Mansfield introduces the visitor to the social history of the area and a rolling programme of national and local temporary exhibitions ensures there is always something new to see.

Mattersey Priory - English Heritage

Mattersey DN10 5DT
http://goo.gl/YDEZtG

The remains of a small Gilbertine monastry, which was founded for six canons in 1185.

Mr Straw's House - National Trust

5 Blyth Grove
Worksop S81 0JG
01909 482 380
www.nationaltrust.org.uk/mr-straws-house
mrstrawshouse@nationaltrust.org.uk

Come explore our ordinary house, yet extraordinary home. An Edwardian semi-detached house, which the Straw family moved into in 1923, has remained virtually unchanged ever since. This life-sized time capsule has delighted guests for twenty years, providing a rare glimpse at treasured objects from times gone by.

Newark Air Museum

Drove Lane, Winthorpe
Newark NG24 2NY
01636 707170
www.newarkairmuseum.org
enquire@newarkairmuseum.org

The museum has been open to the general public since April 1973. The museum Archive is available for use via prior arrangement with the curator on 01636 705585.

Collections: The museum's collection currently stands at 68 aircraft and cockpit sections from across the history of aviation. These include transport, training and reconnaissance aircraft and helicopters and a diverse selection of jet fighters and bombers.

Newark Millgate Museum

48 Millgate
Newark NG24 4TS
01636 655730
www.newark-sherwooddc.gov.uk
museums@nsdc.info

Housed in a charming former mill and warehouse by the River Trent, Newark Millgate Museum displays the working, social and domestic life of Newark, covering the 19th and 20th centuries. In addition there are temporary exhibitions showcasing the work of contemporary local artists and designers.

Newark Town Hall Museum & Art Gallery

Town Hall, Market Place
Newark NG24 1DU
01636 680333
www.newarktownhallmuseum.co.uk
patty.temple@newark.gov.uk

One of the finest town halls in the country, it was designed in 1776 by John Carr of York. This Grade 1 listed building is still a working town hall, but also houses a museum, art gallery and temporary exhibition space in the Spotlight Gallery.

Newstead Abbey

Ravenshead
Nottingham NG15 8GE
01623 455900
www.mynottingham.gov.uk/newsteadabbey
newstead.abbey@nottinghamcity.gov.uk

Newstead Abbey is the ancestral home of the Poet Lord Byron. There is much to see including the poet's private apartments.

North Leverton Windmill

Mill Lane, North Leverton with Habblesthorpe
Retford DN22 0BA
01427 880254
www.north-leverton-windmill.co.uk/Home.html
info@north-leverton-windmill.co.uk

A unique windmill that has never stopped milling. Set in beautiful rolling countryside, the windmill grinds flour and animal feeds regularly. Built in 1813 by a group of local farmers, North Leverton Windmill is almost 200 years old.

Nottingham Castle Museum & Art Gallery

off Friar Lane
Nottingham NG1 6EL
0115 8761400
nottingham.castle@nottinghamcity.gov.uk

A vibrant museum and art gallery housing collections of contemporary, fine and decorative arts, plus fifteen centuries of Nottingham history. All housed in a magnificent 17th century ducal mansion built on the site of the original medieval castle with spectular views of the city.

Nottinghamshire Archives

County House, Castle Meadow Road
Nottingham NG2 1AG
0115 950 4524
www.nottinghamshire.gov.uk/archives
archives@nottscc.gov.uk

Nottinghamshire Archives houses archives for the county of Nottinghamshire, the city of Nottingham, the diocese of Southwell & Nottingham, and other local bodies, families and individuals.

Nottinghamshire Family History Society

26 Acorn Bank, West Bridgford
Nottingham NG2 7DU
www.nottsfhs.org.uk

The Nottinghamshire Family History Society exists to bring together all who are interested in family history research, to help in the preservation and indexing of local genealogical records, and in the copying and publishing of such records.

Nottinghamshire Local History Association

124 Churchill Drive, Ruddington
Nottingham NG11 6DG
0777 908 2085
www.nlha.org.uk
chairman@nlha.org.uk

Nottinghamshire Local History Association was formed in 1953 to bring together people and organisations interested in all aspects of local history in the county. Our aim is to keep members in touch with current developments in local history, to support local historians and heritage organisations and to promote the study of local history in Nottinghamshire.

Papplewick Pumping Station

Rigg Lane, off Longdale Lane
Ravenshead NG15 9AJ
0115 9632 938
www.papplewickpumpingstation.org.uk
director@papplewickpumpingstation.org.uk

Papplewick Pumping Station is regarded as the finest surviving fresh water pumping station in England. Now a Scheduled Ancient Monument, it is unique in retaining all of its original features including its six hand fired Lancashire boilers and two James Watt beam engines.

Queen's Royal Lancers & Nottinghamshire Yeomanry Museum, The

Thoresby Park, nr Perlethorpe
Nottingham NG22 9EP
0115 957 3295
www.qrlnymuseum.co.uk
qrlmuseum@btinternet.com

The UK's newest cavalry museum displays the historic collections of The Queen's Royal Lancers, the Sherwood Rangers Yeomanry and the South Nottinghamshire Hussars. These fascinating collections are of national importance and are displayed together for the first time in the newly renovated wing of Thoresby Courtyard.

Ruddington Framework Knitters Museum

Chapel Street
Ruddington NG11 6HE
0115 9846914
www.rfkm.org
rfwk-mus@btconnect.com

A working museum presenting all aspects of the lives of a Victorian knitting community. Comprises authentic cottage living accomodation and workshops set around a garden courtyard.

Ruddington Village Museum

St Peter's Rooms, Church Street
Ruddington NG11 6HA
0115 914 6645
www.ruddingtonlhs.org.uk/Village%20Museum.htm
info@ruddingtonlhs.org.uk

The Ruddington Village Museum occupies part of St Peter's Rooms, the former Ruddington Infant and Girls School.

Sherwood Foresters Regimental Museum

The Castle
Nottingham NG1 6EL
0115 946 5415
http://goo.gl/GcZy4V

The Sherwood Foresters Collection (Notts & Derby Regiment, 45th and 95th of Foot) is located in two separate galleries, one in Nottingham and one in Derby. Nottingham Castle has, since 1965 when the Collection had to move on the closure of Normanton Barracks in Derby, provided an excellent gallery to display artefacts of the regiment, along with its associated Nottinghamshire Militia and Rifle Corps. Derby City Museum and Art Gallery, The Strand, Derby has provided room to display artefacts of predecessor regiments, The Sherwood Foresters (Notts and Derbys), the 95th (Derbyshire) Regiment, Derbyshire Militia and Rifle Corps.

South Nottinghamshire Hussars Museum

TA Centre, Hucknall Lane, Bulwell
Nottingham NG6 8AQ
0115 9272 251
www.qrlnymuseum.co.uk/snh.htm

A small regimental collection which can be viewed by appointment only. There is no charge for entry but donations are gratefully received.

University of Nottingham Manuscripts & Special Collections

King's Meadow Campus, Lenton Lane
Nottingham NG7 2NR
0115 951 4565
www.nottingham.ac.uk/mss
mss-library@nottingham.ac.uk

Manuscripts and Special Collections is part of Information Services at The University of Nottingham and is located at King's Meadow Campus. Our printed, manuscript and archive collections together provide a rich resource for studies at all levels for a wide range of subjects. The Library has been collecting manuscripts since the early 1930s and now holds approximately 3 million documents, extensive holdings of printed collections, and the East Midlands Collection of local material.

William Booth Birthplace Museum

10-14 Notintone Place
Nottingham NG2 4QG
0115 979 3464
www.salvationarmy.org.uk/uki/wbbm
wbbm@salvationarmy.org.uk

The William Booth Birthplace Museum tells the story of the life and work of William Booth, Catherine Booth, their family and the legacy they left to the world – the founding of The Salvation Army – currently the largest provider of social care in the UK after the government. William Booth was born at 12 Notintone Place, 1829, the first of Booth's several childhood homes. The museum comprises three Regency era terraced properties, the middle one – 12 Notintone Place - being the birthplace of William Booth.

Wollaton Hall & Park

Wollaton Hall, Wollaton Park
Nottingham NG8 2AE
0115 915 3900
www.nottinghamcity.gov.uk/wollatonhall
wollaton.hall@nottinghamcity.gov.uk

Set in over 500 acres of historic deer park, Wollaton Hall is a spectacular Tudor building designed by Robert Smythson and completed in 1588. Following an extensive restoration programme, Wollaton Hall reopened with a number of new displays and refurbished rooms, including Tudor kitchens. Visitors touring the hall can now view the Prospect Room at the top of the hall, which gives spectacular views over Nottingham. The hall also houses Nottingham Natural History Museum. Wollaton Park's Courtyard Stables are home to Nottingham's Industrial Museum and Steam Engine House.

Workhouse, Southwell, The - National Trust

The Workhouse, Upton Road
Southwell NG25 0PT
01636 817262
www.nationaltrust.org.uk/theworkhouse
theworkhouse@nationaltrust.org.uk

Discover the most complete workhouse in existence. Built in 1824 the workhouse was a means of relief for the Victorian poor.

Oxfordshire

*Oxfordshire, south-midland county of England,
bounded N. by Warwickshire and Northamptonshire,
E. by Bucks, S. by Berks, from which it is separated by
the Thames, and W. by Gloucestershire; greatest
length, 60 miles; greatest breadth, 30 miles; area,
483,621 acres, population 179,559. Most of the
county is level, but there are gentle undulations of
surface, rising to 836 ft. at Broom Hill in the NW.,
which is the highest point of land. In the S. the
Chiltern Hills stretch across the co. from Bucks to
Berks. The chief rivers are the Windrush, Evenlode,
Cherwell, and Thame, all being tributaries of the
Thames, or Isis, which flows for about 70 miles along
the S. border of the county. The Oxford Canal, in
conjunction with the Coventry Canal, connects the
Thames with the Severn, Mersey, and Trent. The soil
is a light loam, which is exceedingly fertile and in a
high state of cultivation, agriculture receiving so
much attention that the county is justly held to be one
of the most productive districts in England. Excepting
the N. district, Oxfordshire may be considered a well
wooded county. It has many antiquities, and is
likewise noted for the beauty of its ecclesiastical
buildings and the number of its mansions. The
manufactures are not important. The county
comprises 14 hundreds, 292 parishes, with parts of 7
others, the greater part of the parliamentary and
municipal borough of Oxford, and the municipal
boroughs of Banbury and Chipping Norton. It is
almost entirely in the diocese of Oxford. .*

– John Bartholomew, *Gazetteer of the British Isles* (1887)

*Note: the Vale of the White Horse, now in
Oxfordshire, was in Berkshire until 1974.*

Abingdon County Hall Museum

The Market Place
Abingdon OX14 3HG
01235 523703
http://goo.gl/zbb0Ru
abingdon.museum@abingdon.gov.uk

Abingdon County Hall Museum is located in a Grade 1*
listed building in the centre of the town just opposite the
medieval abbey. This beautiful, perfectly-preserved
Restoration building overlooking the Market Place, is
considered to be one of the outstanding market buildings
in England.

Angus Library & Archive, The

Regent's Park College, Pusey Street
Oxford OX1 2LB
01865 288120
theangus.rpc.ox.ac.uk
angus.library@regents.ox.ac.uk

Leading collection of Baptist history and heritage. The
Angus Library and Archive has extensive archive
collections including manuscript collections from key
Baptist people such as William Carey, CH Spurgeon,
Joshua and Hannah Marshman and William Ward, EA
Payne, and JH Rushbrooke. It also holds manuscripts for
leading Baptist families such as Angus, Steele, Whitaker,
and Reeves.

Ashmolean Museum

Beaumont Street
Oxford OX1 2PH
01865 278000
www.ashmolean.org
education.service@ashmus.ox.ac.uk

Oxford's Ashmolean Museum is the country's oldest public
museum and home to one of the most important
collections of art and archaeology to be found anywhere.
The collections span the civilisations of east and west,
charting the aspirations of humankind from the Neolithic
era to the present day. Among its treasures are the world's
largest collection of Raphael drawings, the most important
collection of pre-Dynastic Egyptian material in Europe, the
only great Minoan collection in Britain, the finest
Anglo-Saxon collections outside the British Museum and
the foremost collection of modern Chinese art in the
Western world.

Banbury Museum

Spiceball Park Rd
Banbury OX16 2PQ
01295 259855
www.banburymuseum.org
banburymuseum@cherwell-dc.gov.uk

Welcome to Banbury Museum! We are a family friendly museum located in Banbury's town centre, next to the idyllic canal side. The Civil War, plush manufacturing, the Victorian market town, costume from the 17th century to the present day, Tooley's Boatyard and the Oxford Canal, are just some of the stories illustrated in the museum. There are also regularly changing exhibitions and activities to ensure that there is always something new to see and do.

Bate Collection of Musical Instruments

Faculty of Music, St Aldate's
Oxford OX1 1DB
01865 276139
www.bate.ox.ac.uk
bate.collection@music.ox.ac.uk

The Bate Collection celebrates the history and development of musical instruments of the Western Classical tradition from the medieval period until the present day. The collection is made available for study and judicious use by scholars, students, makers, and players, so as to enhance and increase the knowledge of the history of music as well as the enjoyment of historic performance for all.

Bishop's Palace

Mount House, Church Green
Witney OX28 4AZ
01865 300972
www.oxfordshire.gov.uk/cms/content/bishops-palace
museums.resource.centre@oxfordshire.gov.uk

The historic building known as the Bishop's Palace was built by the Bishop of Winchester in the 12th and 13th centuries and later became the Manor House. In 1757, the manor house was acquired by the Duke of Marlborough. The archaeological remains which are visible are protected from the elements under a modern roof cover.

Blenheim Palace

Woodstock OX20 1PP
0800 849 6500
www.blenheimpalace.com
operations@blenheimpalace.com

Set in the Oxfordshire Cotswolds, Blenheim Palace is considered to be one of the finest Baroque houses in the country. A gift from Queen Anne and a grateful nation to John Churchill, 1st Duke of Marlborough, in recognition of his famous victory over the French at the Battle of Blenheim in 1704. Sir Winston Churchill, arguably the greatest parliamentarian this country has ever seen, was born at Blenheim Palace.

Bloxham Village Museum

The Court House, Church Street, Bloxham
Banbury OX15 4ET
01295 721256
www.bloxhammuseum.com
peter.barwell@btinternet.com

Bloxham Village Museum was established in 1980 to celebrate the history of the small Oxfordshire village.

Bodleian Library

Catte Street
Oxford OX1 3BG
01865 277627
www.bodleian.ox.ac.uk
communications@bodleian.ox.ac.uk

The Bodleian Libraries of the University of Oxford form the largest university library system in the United Kingdom. They include the principal University library – the Bodleian Library – which has been a library of legal deposit for 400 years; major research libraries; and libraries attached to faculties, departments and other institutions of the University.

Buscot & Coleshill Estates, The - National Trust

Buscot Park
Faringdon SN7 8BU
01367 240786
www.nationaltrust.org.uk/buscot-coleshill-estates
buscotandcoleshill@nationaltrust.org.uk

The late 18th-century neo-classical house, set in parkland, contains the fine paintings and furniture of the Faringdon Collection Trust. The grounds include various avenue walks, and an Italianate water garden, designed in the early 20th century by Harold Peto, and a large walled garden.

Champ's Chapel Museum

Chapel Square
East Hendred OX12 8JX
www.hendredmuseum.org.uk
champschapel@googlemail.com

Besides the village war memorial stands a medieval building adjoining a half timbered priest's house. It was built in the 15th century by the Carthusian monks of Sheen (who owned Kings Manor) and is now often called Champs Chapel after the family who owned it once.

Charlbury Museum

Market Street
Charlbury OX7 3PN
01608 810060
www.charlbury.info/community/42

Museum displays illustrating the traditional crafts and industries of Charlbury, such as glovemaking, with maps and photographs.

Chastleton House - National Trust

Chastleton
Moreton in Marsh GL56 0SU
01608 674981
www.nationaltrust.org.uk/chastleton-house
chastleton@nationaltrust.org.uk

One of England's finest and most complete Jacobean houses, Chastleton House is filled with a mixture of rare and everyday objects, furniture and textiles collected since 1612. It was continuously occupied by one family and the trust has concentrated on conserving the house, rather than restoring it.

Chinnor & Princes Risborough Railway Association

Registered Office, Chinnor Station, Station Approach, Station Road
Chinnor OX39 4ER
01844 353535
www.chinnorrailway.co.uk

A standard gauge railway operating both steam and diesel hauled train services from our station at Chinnor in Oxfordshire. It operates part of the old Great Western Railway branch line which ran between Princes Risborough (Buckinghamshire) and Watlington (Oxfordshire).

Chipping Norton Local History Museum

Westgate, High Street
Chipping Norton OX7 5AD
01608 641712
www.chippingnortonmuseum.org.uk
pauline.watkins@tiscali.co.uk

A museum of local history including: prehistoric and Roman artefacts, From Saxon Manor to Market Town in pictures, Chippy at War - the Home Front, Chipping Norton Baseball Club (former All England Champions). More than one thousand postcards and photographs of local events and places. We are an independent museum run by the local history society.

Cogges Manor Farm

Cogges Manor Farm Museum, Church Lane
Witney OX28 3LA
01993 772602
www.cogges.org.uk
ops@cogges.org.uk

A beautiful Oxfordshire Cotswold farmstead with a 13th century manor house, 17th century rural barns and buildings, walled garden, orchard and moat set beside the Windrush River. Rare breed animals bring the site to life. At weekends and bank holidays see traditional cooking on the historic range.

Combe Mill

Blenheim Palace Sawmill, Combe
Long Hanborough OX29 8ET
01993 358694
www.combemill.org
events@combemill.org

Mid-19th century sawmill, with working steam beam-engine, original Cornish boiler (now out of service) and a working blacksmith's forge. Restored waterwheel.

Didcot Railway Centre

Great Western Society, Didcot Railway Centre
Didcot OX11 7NJ
01235 817200
www.didcotrailwaycentre.org.uk
info@didcotrailwaycentre.org.uk

Welcome to Didcot Railway Centre, home of the Great Western Society and its unique collection of Great Western Railway steam engines, coaches, wagons, buildings and small relics set in 22 acres alongside Didcot Parkway railway station. At its heart is the historic engine shed which is home to Great Western steam engines.

Dorchester Abbey

High Street, Dorchester-on-Thames
Wallingford OX10 7HH
01865 341192/01865 340007
www.dorchester-abbey.org.uk
education@dorchester-abbey.org.uk

Dorchester Abbey is a unique building, in an area of spiritual significance for 6000 years, offering visitors an inspiring and educational opportunity that is welcoming, engaging and inclusive. Built by Augustinian Canons(1140-1340)on the site of a Saxon Cathedral, the abbey is acclaimed for its outstanding architecture.

Dorchester Abbey Museum

Abbey Guest House, High Street, Dorchester-on-Thames
Wallingford OX10 7HR
01865 340054
www.dorchester-abbey.org.uk/museum.htm
museum@dorchester-abbey.org.uk

The museum is in two buildings on the Abbey site. The Old
Schoolroom is part of Dorchester Abbey's 14th-century former
Guest House and displays illustrations, maps and artefacts
reflecting the history of Dorchester and its locality which have
been continuously inhabited for over 6000 years. It also houses
an archive of Dorchester's history, available for inspection and
research by arrangement, and a souvenir and gift shop.

Greys Court - National Trust

Rotherfield Greys
Henley-on-Thames RG9 4PG
01491 628529
www.nationaltrust.org.uk/greys-court
greyscourt@nationaltrust.org.uk

This picturesque house, mainly Tudor in style, has a
beautiful courtyard and one surviving tower dating from
1347. The house was involved in Jacobean intrigue and has
a fascinating history.

Hook Norton Village Museum

Brewery Lane, Hook Norton
Banbury OX15 5NY
01608 730384
http://goo.gl/QoRmfN
heritage@hook-norton-brewery.co.uk

Hook Norton Village Museum is housed within Hook
Norton Brewery's Museum & Visitor Centre.

Collections: The village museum contains artefacts from
Hook Norton and the surrounding area with special
reference to the railway and ironstone quarrying.

Kelmscott Manor

Kelmscott
nr Lechlade GL7 3HJ
01367 252486
www.kelmscottmanor.org.uk
admin@kelmscottmanor.org.uk

Kelmscott Manor is a grade 1 listed Tudor farmhouse
adjacent to the River Thames, dating from about 1600 and
situated on the edge of the village of Kelmscott, near
Lechlade. William Morris (designer, writer and socialist)
chose it as his summer home, signing a joint lease with
Pre-Raphaelite painter Dante Gabriel Rossetti in 1871.
Morris loved the house as a work of true craftsmanship,
unspoilt, unaltered, and in harmony with the village and
the surrounding countryside.

Museum of Oxford

Town Hall, St Aldates
Oxford OX1 1BX
01865 252334
www.oxford.gov.uk/museumofoxford
museum@oxford.gov.uk

Visit the museum of Oxford's permanent Explore Oxford
galleries at the front of Oxford Town Hall to discover the
story of Oxford and its people.

Museum of the History of Science

Broad Street
Oxford OX1 3AZ
01865 277280
www.mhs.ox.ac.uk
museum@mhs.ox.ac.uk

The museum of the History of Science houses an unrivalled
collection of early scientific instruments in the world's
oldest surviving purpose-built museum building.

Museums Resource Centre

Cotswold Dene, Witney Road, Standlake
Witney OX29 7QG
01865 300972
http://goo.gl/huJcON
museums.resource.centre@oxfordshire.gov.uk

The centre houses the county's major reserve collections of
archaeology, social history, crafts and arts. It is a resource
for new and changing exhibitions countywide, for private
and academic research and local communities who are
interested in their local heritage.

Nuffield Place - National Trust

Nuffield Place
Huntercombe, near Henley-on-Thames RG9 5RY
01491 642857
www.nationaltrust.org.uk/nuffield-place
Nuffieldplace@nationaltrust.org.uk

The home of Britain's greatest philanthropist, William
Morris, Lord Nuffield, the founder of Morris Motor Cars
and one of the richest men in the world. The house and
collection provide a glimpse into the lifestyle of this modest
millionaire.

Oxford Bus & Morris Motors Museums

Station Yard, Main Road, Long Hanborough
Witney OX29 8LA
01993 883 617
www.oxfordbusmuseum.org.uk
busmuseum@googlemail.com

At the Oxford Bus Museum we tell the story of bus and coach travel around Oxfordshire over the last 130 years. Our exhibits include historic preserved horse-drawn vehicles, buses, coaches and a wide selection of artefacts (bus stops, ticket machines, timetables, posters, staff uniforms) and lots of fantastic photos illustrating our diverse public transport history. Since 2004 we've also been home to the Morris Motors Museum, which charts the story of how these classic British cars and commercial vehicles were produced at Cowley, in the city. Our impressive collection of vintage Morris vehicles represents those produced during William Morris's life. We also have a unique collection of 40 vintage bicycles, including a Penny Farthing.

Oxford Castle Unlocked

44-46 Oxford Castle
Oxford OX1 1AY
01865 260666
www.oxfordcastleunlocked.co.uk
info@oxfordcastleunlocked.co.uk

Visitors to 'Unlocked' will learn about the real people and events from the site's turbulent past: the first Oxford teachings, the owners, visionaries, activists and inmates. Visit St George's Tower and embark on a historical journey spanning the 10th to 16th centuries.

Oxford University Museum of Natural History

Parks Road
Oxford OX1 3PW
01865 272950
www.oum.ox.ac.uk
info@oum.ox.ac.uk

Founded in 1860 as the centre for scientific study at the University of Oxford, the museum of Natural History now holds the University's internationally-significant collections of geological and zoological specimens, as well as substantial archival material. Housed in a stunning example of neo-Gothic architecture, the museum's growing collections underpin a broad programme of natural environment research, teaching and public engagement.

Oxfordshire Family History Society

19 Mavor Close, Woodstock
Oxford OX20 1YL
01993 812258
www.ofhs.org.uk
secretary@ofhs.org.uk

The society caters for those with Oxfordshire or North Berkshire ancestry as well as those who live locally but with ancestors from elsewhere.

Oxfordshire Health Archives

The Warneford Hospital, Warneford Lane
Oxford OX3 7JX
01865 226308
www.oxfordshirehealtharchives.nhs.uk
enquiries@oxfordshire-health-archives.org.uk

Oxfordshire Health Archives selects and cares for the historic archives of NHS hospitals in Oxfordshire and provides advice on the management, care and disposal of recent records. We care for the archives of twenty two Oxfordshire hospitals, eight administrative bodies and several nurse training schools, as well as the collections of such related bodies as Leagues of Friends and Nurses' Alumni organizations.

Oxfordshire History Centre

St Luke's Church, Temple Road, Cowley
Oxford OX4 2HT
01865 398200
www.oxfordshire.gov.uk
archives@oxfordshire.gov.uk

Oxfordshire Record Office, Oxfordshire Studies and Oxfordshire Health Archives are now all in one building where you will find a variety of resources for researching family history, house history and local history.

Oxfordshire Museum, The

Fletcher's House, Park Street
Woodstock OX20 1SN
01993 811456
https://goo.gl/IzNmMJ
oxo.museum@oxfordshire.gov.uk

Situated in the heart of the historic town of Woodstock, the award-winning redevelopment of Fletcher's House provides a home for the new county museum.

Collections: Collections of local history, art, archaeology, landscape and wildlife as well as a gallery exploring the county's innovative industries from nuclear power to nanotechnology.

Pendon Museum

Long Wittenham
Abingdon OX14 4QD
01865 407365
www.pendonmuseum.com
webenquires@pendonmuseum.com

At Pendon we aim to recapture, in detailed and colourful miniature, scenes showing the beauty of the English countryside as it used to be in the years around 1930. Realistically modelled cottages, farms, fields and lanes recall the peaceful country ways of that period.

Pitt Rivers Museum

University of Oxford, South Parks Road
Oxford OX1 3PP
01865 270927
www.prm.ox.ac.uk
prm@prm.ox.ac.uk

The Pitt Rivers Museum is the University of Oxford's museum of anthropology and world archaeology. Founded in 1884 following a gift to the University from General Pitt-Rivers it retains its unique period atmosphere with dense displays of artefacts, many in the original wooden display cabinets.

River & Rowing Museum

Mill Meadows
Henley-on-Thames RG9 1BF
01491 415600
www.rrm.co.uk
museum@rrm.co.uk

The River & Rowing Museum has three galleries dedicated to rowing, rivers and the history of Henley on Thames. The museum is home to the magical Wind in the Willows exhibition, which brings to life the much-loved story with 3D models, lighting and music.

Soldiers of Oxfordshire

Access is via The Oxfordshire Museum, Park Street
Woodstock OX20 1SS
01993 810210
www.sofo.org.uk

Soldiers of Oxfordshire - Conflict and County focuses on the experience of local people affected by war at home and abroad, with displays and activities to engage families, schools, life-long learners and social and military researchers alike.

Swalcliffe Barn

Swalcliffe, Nr Banbury OX15 5DR
01295 788278
http://goo.gl/ku59LZ
jcdemmar@btinternet.com

Known locally as the Tithe Barn, Swalcliffe Barn was built for the Rectorial Manor of Swalcliffe by New College, who owned the manor. Constructed between 1400 and 1409, it is one of the dozen best barns in the country, with much of its mediaeval timber half-cruck roof intact. The Oxfordshire Buildings Trust owns it and repaired it with a grant from English Heritage.

Thame Museum

79 High Street
Thame OX9 3XE
01844 212801
www.thamemuseum.org
museum@ThameHistory.net

Located in what was previously the Magistrates Court, Thame Museum offers the visitor a wealth of local history - from the formation of New Thame in the 12th century to the modern 20th century developments. Items on display include a full set of 17th century trade tokens and a Saxon burial urn.

Tolsey Museum

126 High Street
Burford OX18 4QU
01993 823 236
www.thecotswoldgateway.co.uk/museums_tolsey.htm

The Tolsey Museum is midway along Burford's main street. The black and white timber fronted building erected on stone pillars was once the medieval meeting point for the wealthy wool merchants who also paid their tolls or tax here. The Tolsey now houses a collection of local artefacts depicting the social and industrial heritage of the Oxfordshire town and surrounding area.

Tom Brown's School Museum

Broad Street, Uffington
Faringdon SN7 7RA
01367 820259
museum.uffington.net
museum@uffington.net

Tom Brown's School Museum is housed in a Grade 1 listed building dated 1617. This small unique building was formerly a school room for '12 worthy boys'.

Collections: Includes archaeological material from The White Horse Hill and surrounding area. Reference material relating to Thomas Hughes and a collection of over 130 different editions of Tom Brown's Schooldays. Reference material relating to Sir John Betjeman who lived in the village. Local archives including photographs, video material, oral tapes and documentation.

Uffington Castle, White Horse & Dragon Hill - National Trust

Off the B4507
Woolstone SN7 7QJ
01793 762209
www.nationaltrust.org.uk/white-horse-hill
whitehorsehill@nationaltrust.org.uk

The internationally-renowned Bronze-Age Uffington White Horse can be seen for miles away leaping across the head of a dramatic dry valley in the Ridgeway escarpment. The horse is only part of the unique complex of ancient remains that are found at White Horse Hill and beyond, spreading out across the high chalk downland.

Vale & Downland Museum

The Old Surgery, Church Street
Wantage OX12 8BL
01235 771447
www.wantage.com/museum
museum@wantage.com

The Vale and Downland Museum and Visitor Centre is located in the busy market town of Wantage in Oxfordshire, UK.

Collections: Archaeology, social history, interactive relief map of the hinterland, specially produced films on the area narrated by David Attenborough, Wantage Tramway exhibit, rural arts and crafts, tanning and cloth making exhibits, agricultural machinery, Dean Butler and the Oxford Movement, Williams F1 racing car, discovery gallery for children.

Wallingford Museum

Flint House, 52 High Street
Wallingford OX10 0DB
01491 835065
www.wallingfordmuseum.org.uk
admin@wallingfordmuseum.org.uk

Wallingford Museum is a colourful and delightfully intimate local history museum, housed in a medieval oak-beamed hall-house opposite the Saxon banks in the Kinecroft and next to the public library.

Collections: Includes items from archaeological excavations in and around the town and artefacts from the Romans to the 20th century. Strong local social history emphasis focuses on the growth and decline of the vast Medieval Castle, one of the largest in the country, the government of the town under its unique 1155 Charter, and the more everyday nature of life in a Thames-side market town in later centuries.

Waterperry Gardens & Rural Museum

Waterperry Gardens, Waterperry
Nr Wheatley OX33 1JZ
01844 339254
www.waterperrygardens.co.uk
office@waterperrygardens.co.uk

A comprehensive and interesting collection of tools and implements is housed in the 18th century granary at Waterperry Gardens. This museum shows the skills required in making horticultural and agricultural tools and also the skills needed to use them, as for example to two man hedge cutter.

Witney & District Museum

75 High Street
Witney OX28 6JA
01993 775915
www.witneymuseum.co.uk
witney.museum@btconnect.com

The museum is situated in a traditional Cotswold stone building that was formerly the home of Malachi Bartlett, a prolific Victorian builder. The ground floor contains a large gallery containing local history displays, while the upper floor contains a large gallery used for temporary displays and two smaller rooms, one of which is furnished as a traditional Witney kitchen of circa 1953.

Collections: The collections reflect the social, industrial and military history of the township of Witney and the surrounding area. Local industries such as blanket-making and brewing are represented, and there are, in addition, large archive and photographic collections.

Rutland

Rutland (or Rutlandshire), inland county of England, bounded W. and N. by Leicestershire, NE. by Lincolnshire, and SE. by Northamptonshire; greatest length, N. and S., 18 miles; greatest breadth, E. and W., 17 miles; area, 94,889 acres, population 21,434. Rutland is the smallest county in England. The surface is diversified by gently rising hills and fine valleys, and is watered by the Eye Brook, the Chater, and the Gwash, flowing into the Welland, which forms the south-eastern boundary. The soil is in general loamy and fertile; in the east part it is chiefly in tillage, and in the west part under grass. The chief crops are wheat and barley. Great attention is paid to rearing choice breeds both of cattle and sheep. In the Vale of Catmose, round Oakham, are tracts of woodland, the remains of old forests. The prevailing rock is limestone. Rutland was made a county by Henry III, and gives the title of duke to the family of Manners. It contains 5 hundreds, 57 parishes, and part of another, and the market-towns of Oakham (where the assizes are held) and Uppingham; it has no parliamentary or municipal boroughs. It is in the diocese of Peterborough.

– John Bartholomew, *Gazetteer of the British Isles* (1887)

Lyddington Bede House - English Heritage

Bluecoat Lane
Lyddington LE15 9LZ
01572 822438
http://goo.gl/KH5sJ0

Lyddington Bede House is wonderful place to picnic and while away a few hours if you're looking for an interesting day out in the East Midlands. Origionally a wing of a medieval palace it was later converted into an almshouse.

Normanton Church Museum

Rutland Water
Oakham LE15 8PX
01780 686800.

This iconic church is Rutland's most famous landmark. It was saved from the water and is now open for guided tours that recount the history of this beautiful building and its surroundings and also provides a stunning location for civil weddings and classical concerts.

Oakham Castle

Market Place
Oakham LE15 6DX
01572 758440
www.rutland.gov.uk/castle

museum@rutland.gov.uk

The Norman Great Hall of Oakham Castle, a late 12th century fortified manor house, is one of the finest domestic buildings of the period. It stands within walled earthworks, and remains of an earlier motte and bailey castle are also visible.

Record Office for Leicestershire, Leicester & Rutland

Long Street
Wigston Magna LE18 2AH
0116 257 1080
www.leics.gov.uk/museums
museums@leics.gov.uk

The Record Office is a service provided by Leicestershire County Council in partnership with Leicester City Council and Rutland County Council. The Record Office exists to preserve and provide access to a wide range of Resources which can be used to research the history and culture of Leicestershire, Leicester and Rutland. Access to the collections is freely available to everyone and staff are on hand to help you find the information you need.

Rutland County Museum

Catmos Street
Oakham LE15 6HW
01572 758440
www.rutland.gov.uk/museum
museum@rutland.gov.uk

Rutland County Museum is the perfect introduction to England's smallest county. The museum is a guide to the history of Rutland and includes displays of local archaeology, history and an extensive rural life collection.

Collections: The museum has an extensive rural life collection, including tractors, farm equipment and waggons on display in the Riding School and in the adjoining Courtyard, where can be found the game larder of Lord Lonsdale, one of the famous Rutland characters whose stories can be found here. The collections include a wide range of rural tradesmen's tools, domestic and social history material, Rutland's standard weights and measures, and local archaeology.

Rutland Railway Museum

Ashwell Road, Cottesmore
Oakham LE15 7BX
01572 813203 recorded message when office closed
www.rutlandrailwaymuseum.org.uk
rrm.info@btinternet.com

The Rutland Railway Museum occupies an area of nearly 7 acres on part of the former Midland Railway mineral branch line. The branch line linked to the Melton Mowbray to Oakham main line at Ashwell Station.

Shropshire

Shropshire (or Salop), county in west-midlands of England, bounded N. by Cheshire and detached part of Flintshire, E. by Staffordshire, S. by Worcestershire, Herefordshire, and Radnorshire, and W. by Montgomeryshire and Denbighshire; area, 844,565 acres, population 248,014. The river Severn, running SE., divides the co. into 2 nearly equal parts. The northern, occupied by the new red sandstone, is generally level; the southern, belonging to the old red sandstone, is of a more elevated and rugged character, reaching in the Clee Hills a height of 1805 ft. The soil is various, but generally fertile and well cultivated; there are, however, considerable tracts of waste land. The principal crops are wheat, barley, oats, pease, beans, vetches, turnips, and potatoes. The co. is famous for its breed of sheep. Cattle-breeding and dairy-farming are carried on in the S. and W. The principal mineral products are coal and iron, with limestone, freestone, and lead. The manufactures, besides those connected with iron, include carpets, flannels, gloves, glass, stoneware, paper, and inalt. Shropshire is connected by the river with Gloucester and Bristol, and by canals with Chester and Liverpool, while Shrewsbury is a railway centre. The county contains 14 hundreds, 252 parishes, with parts of 6 others, the parliamentary and municipal borough of Shrewsbury, and the municipal boroughs of Bridgnorth, Ludlow, Oswestry, and Wenlock. It is in the dioceses of Hereford, Lichfield, and St Asaph.

– John Bartholomew, *Gazetteer of the British Isles* (1887)

Acton Scott Historic Working Farm

Wenlock Lodge, Acton Scott
Church Stretton SY6 6QN
01694 781307
www.actonscott.com
acton.scott.museum@shropshire.gov.uk

Acton Scott Historic Working Farm is one of Britain's leading working farm museums. We specialise in practical demonstrations of historic farming using traditional skills and period horse-drawn machines.

Battlefield Church - St Mary Magdalene

Battlefield Church
Shrewsbury SY1 1ED
http://goo.gl/bTMulr

Battlefield church (St Mary Magdalene church) was built on the site of the Battle of Shrewsbury in 1406. Visitors to Battlefield Church can see five newly installed panels describing the five main players in the Battle of Shrewsbury.

Blists Hill Victorian Town

Legges Way, Madeley
Telford TF7 5DU
01952 433 424
http://goo.gl/45drhX
tic@ironbridge.org.uk

Experience life as it was over 100 years ago through the sights, sounds, smells and tastes of a recreated Victorian Town. Victorian characters will give you a fascinating insight into Victorian life as they go about their daily lives in their cottages, shops and places of work.

Broseley Pipeworks - Clay Tobacco Pipe Museum

Duke Street
Broseley TF12 5NA
01952 433 424
http://goo.gl/vaAMZh
tic@ironbridge.org.uk

Few places are as evocative as Broseley Pipeworks. This abandoned factory once made millions of clay pipes - the kind that people smoked tobacco with - and exported them across the world.

Buildwas Abbey - English Heritage

Buildwas
Telford TF8 7BW
01952 433274
http://goo.gl/F3EJER

Impressive ruins of a Cistercian abbey, including its unusually unaltered 12th-century church, beautiful vaulted and tile-floored chapter house, and recently re-opened crypt chapel. In a wooded Severn-side setting, not far from the Iron Bridge and Wenlock Priory.

Clun Town Trust Museum

Town Hall, The Square
Clun SY7 8JA
01588 640681
www.clunmuseum.org.uk
clunmuseum@gmail.com

Houses a multitude of local historical & agricultural artefacts covering last 250 years reflecting the diversity of trades in this once self contained town in the centre of a large farming community. Unique noted collection of over 6,000 flints from Mesolithic period. Victorian smocks, uniforms and relics of 1st & 2nd World wars.

Coalbrookdale Museum of Iron

Coalbrookdale
Telford TF8 7DQ
01952 433 424
http://goo.gl/IEMDRr
tic@ironbridge.org.uk

Step inside the mighty Coalbrookdale Museum of Iron and discover the revolutionary techniques that made Coalbrookdale the most famous ironworks in the world. Explore the remains of the water powered blast furnace where Abraham Darby I perfected the smelting of iron with coke instead of charcoal.

Coalport China Museum

High Street, Coalport, Ironbridge
Telford TF8 7HZ
01952 433 424
http://goo.gl/JUXN8h
tic@ironbridge.org.uk

Coalport China Museum was home to the famous firm until 1926 and is filled with the finest examples of their work. The factory's unusual buildings contain colourful displays depicting a history of china-making, as well as demonstration workshops where, during school holidays, you'll be able to have a go yourself. The Coalport China Manufactory was the largest works of its kind in the mid 19th century.

Collections: The museum holds the most comprehensive collection of 18th century Caughley porcelain anywhere. The reference collection includes the pieces, several hundred sherds excavated at the factory site, and plaster moulds, together with a significant paper archive relating to the history and development of the factory and personnel associated with it.

Coleham Pumping Station

Longden Coleham
Shrewsbury SY3 7DN
01743 361196
www.shrewsburymuseums.com/coleham
museums@shrewsbury.gov.uk

The Pumping Station, resembling a Victorian chapel in style, was built in 1900 to house two massive steam-driven beam engines. The beam engines were built by Renshaws of Stoke to pump sewage as part of Shrewsbury's new sewerage system.

Darby Houses

Coalbrookdale
Telford TF8 7DQ
01952 433 424
http://goo.gl/9KyGnl
tic@ironbridge.org.uk

The Darby family's historic homes - Rosehill House and Dale House - are collectively known as the Darby Houses. See family objects, papers, plans and pictures which dot the rooms and give you a very real sense of how the family lived, as well as worked.

Dudmaston Estate - National Trust

Dudmaston Quatt
Bridgnorth WV15 6QN
01746 780866
www.nationaltrust.org.uk/dudmaston
ruth.watson@nationaltrust.org.uk

Dudmaston Hall, an 17th manor house is still very much today a family home, but with a surprise up its sleeve as although you will find some of the rooms expected in a house of this type, it also houses an important modern art collection assembled by Sir George Labouchere during his travels as an Ambassador to Spain.

Enginuity

Coach Road, Coalbrookdale
Telford TF8 7DQ
01952 433 424
www.ironbridge.org.uk/our_attractions/enginuity
tic@ironbridge.org.uk

Packed with hands-on experiences and interactive exhibits, a visit to this fun-filled science and technology centre is great fun for all ages. Investigate science and discover more about the power of technology at Enginuity.

Haughmond Abbey - English Heritage

[icons]

Off the B5062
Haughmond SY4 4RW
01743 709661
http://goo.gl/qUYDvV

The extensive remains of an Augustinian abbey, including its abbots' quarters, refectory and cloister. The substantially surviving chapter house has a frontage richly bedecked with 12th and 14th century carving and statuary, and a fine timber roof.

House on Crutches Museum

[icons]

Opposite Town Hall, High Street
Bishops Castle SY9 5AA
01588 630556
www.bchrc.co.uk
mail@bchrc.co.uk

First established in 1993, the House on Crutches Museum is situated in a remarkable timber framed building: an early 15th century house with crooked stairs, wonderful beams and sloping floors. This houses an extensive social history collection covering all aspects of this South Shropshire community. The story of this thriving market town is told through displays of local artefacts and memorabilia, temporary exhibits and the sharing of knowledge by our team of enthusiastic volunteers.

Iron Bridge & Tollhouse

[icons]

Ironbridge
Telford TF8 7JP
01952 433 424
http://goo.gl/PG42Qf
tic@ironbridge.org.uk

Step onto the Iron Bridge and follow in the footsteps of millions of tourists who, since 1779, have journeyed to marvel at the world's first cast-iron bridge. Built by Abraham Darby III and now recognised as one of the great symbols of the Industrial Revolution, the remarkable Iron Bridge still dominates the small town that bears its name. Discover the secrets of how and why the Iron Bridge was built in an exhibition within the original Tollhouse (the Tollhouse is open every weekend during the local school summer holidays or by prior arrangement for groups and school parties).

Ironbridge Gorge Museum, Library & Archives

[icons]

Long Warehouse, Coalbrookdale
Telford TF8 7DQ
01952 432 141
www.ironbridge.org.uk
library@ironbridge.org.uk

The museum has built up an extensive research library, which is based in the Long Warehouse, adjacent to the Coalbrookdale Museum of Iron. Collections include material on the history of the iron industry, bridge building, civil engineering, brick and tile manufacture, coal mining, the pottery and porcelain industries, railways, canals, the social history of the East Shropshire Coalfield and all other subjects represented at the museum's sites.

Jackfield Tile Museum

[icons]

Salthouse Road, Jackfield
Telford TF8 7LJ
01952 433 424
http://goo.gl/4erufr
tic@ironbridge.org.uk

The village of Jackfield was once the world centre of the tile industry, and Jackfield Tile Museum set in an immense Victorian factory, celebrates the decorative tiles that once graced the Empire. Room after room is filled with beautiful displays and room settings such as the pub, the tube station and the butchers.

Collections: The museum has an impressive collection of over 23,000 19th-century decorative tiles, with examples from most of the major Victorian factories in this country.

Land of Lost Content - Museum of British Popular Culture

[icons]

The Market Hall, Market Street
Craven Arms SY7 9NW
01588 676176
www.lolc.org.uk

A million memories from the 20th century. See all we enjoyed and all we endured, everything you, your parents, grandparents, sons and daughters owned, used, played with and threw away.

Lilleshall Abbey - English Heritage

[icons]

Oakengates
Nr Telford TF10 9HW
01216 256820
http://goo.gl/ZVFtAF

Extensive ruins of an Augustinian abbey, later a Civil War stronghold, in a deeply rural setting. Much of the church survives, unusually viewable from gallery level, along with the lavishly sculpted processional door and other cloister buildings.

Ludlow Castle

[icons]

Castle Square
Ludlow SY8 1AY
01584 873355
www.ludlowcastle.com
info@ludlowcastle.com

Walk through the castle grounds and see the ancient

houses of kings, queens, princes, judges and the nobility - a glimpse into the lifestyle of medieval society. The castle, firstly a Norman Fortress and extended over the centuries to become a fortified Royal Palace, has ensured Ludlow's place in English history - originally built to hold back unconquered Welsh, passing through generations of the de Lacy and Mortimer families to Richard Plantagenet, Duke of York.

Ludlow Library & Museum Resource Centre

7-9 Parkway
Ludlow SY8 2PG
01584 813 665
https://goo.gl/y2H97w

The Ludlow Library and Museum Resource Centre is situated at the end of Parkway off Corve Street, with a large public car park accessible from Upper Galdeford and Station Drive. Disabled parking and provision for bicycles is available adjacent to the entrance.

Ludlow Museum

Buttercross
Ludlow SY8 1AW
0345 678 9024
https://goo.gl/oQBm2L
shrewsburymuseum@shropshire.gov.uk

There's been a museum in Ludlow since 1833. The Resource Centre cares for some of Shropshire's most important collections. Find out about the town, its history, its archeology, its geology and its wildlife.

Market Drayton Museum & Resource Centre – The Story of Drayton

53 Shropshire Street
Market Drayton TF9 3DA
01630 654300
http://goo.gl/Cve4SW
ipictonr@talktalk.net

The story of Market Drayton and the surrounding area, from earliest times to today, told with things, pictures and words. Everything in it is associated with Drayton – either made here or with a special Drayton connection.

Much Wenlock Museum

High Street
Much Wenlock TF13 6HR
01952 727679
www.shropshire.gov.uk/museums
tim.king@shropshire.gov.uk

Much Wenlock Museum has been refurbished with financial assistance from the Heritage Lottery Fund and Shropshire Council. The new displays tell the story of the town and surrounding area, the links between Dr. William Penny Brookes and the Modern Olympic Games, and the geology of Wenlock Edge.

Museum of The Gorge

The Wharfage, Ironbridge
Telford TF8 7NH
01952 433 424
http://goo.gl/24Li7C
tic@ironbridge.org.uk

Understand more about the history of the Ironbridge Gorge and discover why, as a World Heritage Site, it ranks alongside the Pyramids and the Taj Mahal in its importance in world history. Located in a Gothic-style warehouse the museum of the Gorge provides a fascinating insight into the history of the Ironbridge Gorge and is a great place to start your visit to the area.

Mythstories Museum of Myth & Fable

The Morgan Library, Aston Street
Wem SY4 5AU
01939 235500
www.mythstories.com
info@mythstories.com

Mythstories is an actual and virtual museum of myths, fables and legends. Its focus is on storytelling and the oral tradition, every visitor gets to hear at least one verbal story. Group visits are tailored to their requirements - educational visits are always welcome, we cater from pre-school through to U3A. Given notice we can cater for most non-English speaking groups.

Northgate Museum

Northgate, High Street
Bridgnorth WV16 4ER
www.bridgnorthmuseum.org.uk

Visit the Northgate Museum in Bridgnorth, Shropshire. Packed full of treasures, the museum should be the first stop for anyone wanting to discover the history of the town and the local area.

Collections: It has over 4,500 objects in its collection. The earliest object on display at the museum dates back to the Saxon period.

Oswestry Transport Museum

Oswald Road
Oswestry SY11 1RE
01691 671 749
www.cambrian-railways-soc.co.uk

We are the Cambrian Railways Society, based in the Welsh-border market town of Oswestry. Formed in 1972, the group has spent the intervening period gathering an invaluable collection of artefacts from railways in the former Cambrian Railways Company (CR) area, which once covered a vast chunk of mid and north Wales, together with the Shropshire borderland; and ensuring the survival of many more.

Park Hall Countryside Experience

Park Hall Farm
Whittington SY11 4AS
01691 671123
www.facebook.com/parkhallfarmoswestry
info@parkhallfarm.co.uk

Park Hall near Oswestry in Shropshire is one of the region's most exciting all weather family visitor attractions. There are three museums: The Victorian School at Park Hall aims to offer a unique insight into the school life of the child born in the Victorian era; in 2009 a reproduction of an Iron Age roundhouse was built at Park Hall to compliment the development of the nearby Old Oswestry Iron Age Hillfort; we are proud to offer a permanent home to a magnificent collection of uniforms, artefacts and memorabilia which depicts the history of the life in the Welsh Guards.

Royal Air Force Museum Cosford

Cosford
Shifnal TF11 8UP
01902 376200
www.rafmuseum.org/cosford
cosford@rafmuseum.org

The Royal Air Force Museum at Cosford houses one of the largest aviation collections in the United Kingdom. It is home to 70 aircraft and war planes, missiles, transport & training and research and development collections. The National Cold War Exhibition with its interactive kiosks and hotspots offers visitors the opportunity to see what life was like behind the Iron Curtain.

Shrewsbury Castle & Shropshire Regimental Museum

Castle Street
Shrewsbury SY1 2AT
01743 358516
www.shropshireregimentalmuseum.co.uk

The oldest parts of the castle were built between 1066 and 1074, during the reign of William the Conqueror. There were additions over several centuries. The castle houses the spectacular collections of the Shropshire Regimental Museum Trust including pictures, uniforms, medals, silverware, weapons and other artefacts from the 18th Century to the present day. There is also a modern army display (including information on The Rifles), items from the collections of the Lords Lieutenant of Shropshire and a history of the castle itself.

Shrewsbury Museum & Art Gallery

The Music Hall, The Square
Shrewsbury SY1 1LH
01743 258885
www.shrewsburymuseum.org.uk
shrewsburymuseum@shropshire.gov.uk

The collections of Shrewsbury Museums Service comprise about 166,000 items including geology, natural history, archaeology, social history, fine and decorative arts.

Shropshire Archives

Castle Gates
Shrewsbury SY1 2AQ
01743 255350
www.shropshire.gov.uk/archives
archives@shropshire-cc.gov.uk

The archives and local studies centre for the historic county of Shropshire. We have 5 ½ miles of shelving holding local material from 12th century charters right up to yesterday's Shropshire Star.

Shropshire Family History Society

Larkrise, 16 Glentworth Avenue
Oswestry SY10 9PZ
01691 653 316
www.sfhs.org.uk
secretary@sfhs.org.uk

The Shropshire Family History Society was founded in 1979 to provide a meeting place in Shropshire for all those interested in family history. The society has around two thousand members from all round the world.

Stokesay Castle - English Heritage

Craven Arms SY7 9AH
01588 672544
http://goo.gl/iBB7au

Stokesay Castle is the finest and best preserved 13th-century fortified manor house in England. It offers visitors a unique glimpse into a distant age, when strength and elegance were combined. Set amid peaceful countryside near the Welsh border, Stokesay Castle forms an outstandingly picturesque group with its timber-framed gatehouse and the parish church. An audio tour will help you to imagine Stokesay as the centre of medieval life.

Tar Tunnel

Coalport
Telford TF8 7HT
01952 433 424
www.ironbridge.org.uk/our_attractions/tar_tunnel
tic@ironbridge.org.uk

Amongst the oldest tourist attractions in the Ironbridge Gorge is the Tar Tunnel, where miners digging in 1787 struck a spring of natural bitumen, a black treacle-like substance. The eerie brick-lined tunnel was a great curiosity in the 18th century and bitumen still oozes from its walls today.

Wenlock Priory - English Heritage

Bull Ring
Much Wenlock TF13 6HS
01952 727466
http://goo.gl/JKWlj4

Picturesque ruins of a large priory of Cluniac monks, whose love of decoration is reflected in the glorious carving of its 12th-century chapter house and rare 'lavabo' - a tiered washing fountain in a topiary bedecked cloister garden. Parts of the great church also stand, against the backdrop of the full-height infirmary wing. Set on the fringe of beautiful Much Wenlock, not far from Buildwas Abbey and the Iron Bridge.

Weston Park

Weston-under-Lizard
Nr Shifnal TF11 8LE
01952 852100
www.weston-park.com
enquiries@weston-park.com

The front door of the House at Weston conceals a world of fascinating and internationally significant treasures. From French Gobelin tapestries to Oriental ceramic works of art, furniture by royal makers Morel and Hughes and iconic paintings of old masters such as Van Dyck, Stubbs, Gainsborough, Constable; Weston has one of the greatest English country house collections.

Whitchurch Heritage Centre

12 St Mary's Street
Whitchurch SY13 1QY
01948 664577
www.whitchurch-heritage.co.uk
info@whitchurch-heritage.co.uk

The Heritage Centre opened in 1998 and includes a Tourist Information facility. Staff are able to offer a wealth of information on the town's history as well as giving invaluable advice on what to visit in the area and further afield. Displays in the Main Hall include local Roman archaeological finds and examples of Joyce's clocks. The Gallery contains paintings by Randolph Caldecott and displays of Edward German memorabilia - both previous inhabitants of Whitchurch.

Wroxeter Roman City - English Heritage

Wroxeter
Nr Shrewsbury SY5 6PH
01743 761330
http://goo.gl/m3a9gs

Wroxeter (or 'Viroconium') was the fourth largest city in Roman Britain. It began as a legionary fortress and later developed into a thriving civilian city, populated by retired soldiers and traders.

Somerset

Somerset, maritime county in SW. of England, bounded N. and NE. by the Bristol Channel and the estuary of the Severn, and from NE. round to S W. by the counties of Gloucester, Wilts, Dorset, and Devon; greatest length, N. and S., 43 miles; greatest breadth, E. and W., 67 miles; area, 1,049,812 acres, population 469,109. The coast line is generally low and marshy in the E., but lined with lofty slate cliffs in the W. The interior consists of ranges of hills separated by valleys, or by extensive low marshy flats. The principal ranges are the Mendip Hills, the Polden Hills, the Quantock Hills, the Brendon Hills, and Exmoor. The chief rivers are the Avon and the Parret (with its tributaries the Yeo or Ivel, Isle, and Tone), the former forming the boundary on the NE., the latter traversing the centre of the county; the other streams are the Yeo, Ax, and Brue. Both soil and climate are well adapted for agriculture, particularly in the low alluvial tracts; and in the Vale of Taunton heavy crops of the finest wheat are raised. The rich meadows rear large numbers of cattle, and the hilly grounds are pastured with numerous flocks of sheep. In the E. of the county are some small isolated coalfields, the most southerly in England, the quarries which furnish the famous Bath stone, and a large development of magnesian limestone; the W. of the county consists chiefly of slaty rocks, forming the wild moorlands of Exmoor. The chief minerals worked are lead, iron, and slate. The principal manufactures are woollen and worsted goods, gloves, lace, linen, crape, silk, paper, glass, and bath-bricks. There are salmon, herring, and other fisheries in the Bristol Channel. An important chain of internal communication is formed by the Yeo and Parret navigation and the Glastonbury Canal. The county contains 40 hundreds, 2 liberties, 489 parishes, with parts of 3 others, the parliamentary and municipal boroughs of Bath and Taunton, and the municipal boroughs of Bridgwater, Chard, Glastonbury, Wells, and Yeovil. It is nearly co-extensive with the diocese of Bath and Wells.

– John Bartholomew, *Gazetteer of the British Isles* (1887)

American Museum in Britain

Claverton Manor
Bath BA2 7BD
01225 460503
www.americanmuseum.org
info@americanmuseum.org

Founded in 1961, the museum has the finest collection of American decorative arts outside the United States. Displayed in a series of period rooms, the collection illustrates how early Americans lived between the 17th and 19th centuries.

Ashton Windmill

Chapel Allerton
Axbridge BS26 2PP
01278 435399
www.sedgemoor.gov.uk/index.aspx?articleid=5957
museums@sedgemoor.gov.uk

This unique 18th century flour mill stands on the 'Isle of Wedmore", a ridge giving commanding views of Cheddar Gorge, the Somerset Levels and Brent Knoll. A windmill is mentioned on this site as far back as 1317.

Bakelite Museum

Orchard Mill
Williton TA4 4NS
01984 632133
www.bakelitemuseum.co.uk
info@bakelitemuseum.co.uk

The largest collection of vintage plastics in Britain. Exhibits from the inter-war period and the smooth, stylish Art Deco styles that set the trends of the 20th century. Showcases hundreds of the domestic items which we all grew up with. Thousands of quirky and rare items on show, including spy cameras, monstrous perming machines and the Bakelite coffin. Housed within a historic watermill.

Barrington Court - National Trust

Barrington
near Ilminster TA19 0NQ
01460 241938
www.nationaltrust.org.uk/barrington-court
barringtoncourt@nationaltrust.org.uk

Discover the haunting echoes of the past at Barrington Court, a Tudor manor house free from collections and furniture. Explore using your imagination and your senses to discover a house full of memories, where light fills the rooms and you feel you can almost touch the past. The property was saved from ruin and restored by the Lyle family in 1920s, when the court house resembled a barn rather than the proud manor house that it is.

Bath Abbey

Bath

01225 422462

www.bathabbey.org

office@bathabbey.org

Bath Abbey stands at the heart of the city of Bath. During the past twelve and a half centuries, three different churches have occupied this site: an Anglo-Saxon Abbey Church dating from 757, pulled down by the Norman conquerors of England soon after 1066; a massive Norman cathedral begun about 1090; the present Abbey church founded in 1499, ruined after the dissolution of the monasteries in 1539 by order of Henry VIII, and completed in 1611.

Bath & North East Somerset Record Office

Guildhall, High Street

Bath BA1 5AW

01225 477421

www.batharchives.co.uk

archives@bathnes.gov.uk

Are you interested in the history of Bath? The record office collects, preserves and makes available to everyone historical records relating to Bath. These records include documents from the 12th century to the present day, reflecting all aspects of life in Bath.

Bath Museums Education Service

Heritage Services, Pump Room, Stall Street

Bath BA1 1LZ

01225 477757

http://goo.gl/Muelsq

romanbaths_bookings@bathnes.gov.uk

People learn at any age and at any time of their lives. The Heritage Services Learning and Programmes team enables this to happen in a range of fun, interactive and accessible ways.

Bath Postal Museum

27a Northgate Street

Bath BA1 1AJ

01225 460333

www.bathpostalmuseum.org

info@bathpostalmuseum.org

The Bath Postal Museum tells the history of 4000 years of communication from clay mail to e-mail. With colourful and frequently changing exhibitions, there is something for everyone. The story of Ralph Allen's revolutionary postal system and John Palmer's innovative mail coach organisation are told.

Beckford's Tower & Museum

Lansdown Road

Bath BA1 9BH

01225 460705

www.bath-preservation-trust.org.uk

beckford@bptrust.org.uk

Beckford's Tower was designed by Henry Edmund Goodridge in 1825 and completed in 1827 for William Beckford (1760-1844), one of the nation's most accomplished and interesting characters. The 120-foot neo-classical tower, which enjoys uninterrupted views of the countryside, was constructed as a study retreat and to house Beckford's precious collection of art and rare books. The tower is now home to a museum collection displaying furniture originally made for the tower, alongside paintings, prints and objects illustrating William Beckford's life as a writer, collector and patron of the arts.

Bishop's Palace, The

Wells BA5 2PD

01749 988111

www.bishopspalace.org.uk

More than simply an historic house and garden, this splendid medieval Palace has been the home of the Bishops of Bath and Wells for 800 years. There are 14 acres of gardens including the springs from which the city takes its name. Visitors can also see the Bishop's private Chapel, ruined Great Hall and the Gatehouse with portcullis and drawbridge beside which the famous mute swans ring a bell for food.

Blake Museum

Blake Street

Bridgwater TA6 3NB

01278 456127

www.bridgwatermuseum.org.uk

blake@bridgwatermuseum.org.uk

From the earliest settlements in the archaeology gallery to the hustle and bustle of the port, and from the drama of the Monmouth Rebellion to the glamour of Bridgwater's annual carnival – there is plenty to interest the whole family.

Bruton Museum

The Dovecote Building, 26 High Street

Bruton BA10 0AA

01935 462855

www.brutonmuseum.co.uk

This local history museum contains lots of historic artefacts from Bruton's past. On display is the table John Steinbeck wrote on when, close to Camelot, he started his book on King Arthur and his Noble Knights.

Building of Bath Collection

The Countess of Huntingdon's Chapel, The Vineyards
Bath BA1 5NA
01225 333895
http://goo.gl/E5krgG
admin@bptrust.org.uk

This unique collection interprets the rich architectural history of Bath and the men who transformed a provincial town into the world famous Georgian Spa. It demonstrates how classical design influenced the buildings and illustrates the construction of a house from the cellars to the rafters.

Cadbury Castle

South Cadbury
Yeovil BA22 7HA
www.britannia.com/history/arthur/cadcast.html

Cadbury Castle is an Iron Age hill fort in the civil parish of South Cadbury in the English county of Somerset. It is a Scheduled Ancient Monument and associated with King Arthur.

Castle Cary & District Museum

Market House, Market Place
Castle Cary BA7 7AH
01963 351334
www.castlecarymuseum.org.uk
castlecarymuseum@hotmail.co.uk

The museum in Castle Cary is found in the historic Market House, a splendid mid-Victorian building in the centre of town. We have a large collection of domestic and agricultural implements, archaeological and historical information and artefacts. Displays include: our geology section showing that this area of Somerset was once under the sea; the life of diarist Parson James Woodforde; Douglas Macmillan, the founder of Macmillan Cancer Support; T S Donne's Rope and Twine Works; and John Boyd's Horsehair Weaving factory.

Chard & District Museum

Godworthy House, High Street
Chard TA20 1QL
01460 65091
www.chardmuseum.co.uk
info@chardmuseum.co.uk

Chard Museum has displays illustrating the history of Chard and its surrounding area. Highlights include displays devoted to pioneers of powered flight (John Stringfellow) and the development of artificial limbs (James Gillingham).

Cheddar Gorge - National Trust

Cheddar Gorge
Cheddar BS27 3QF
01934 742 343
www.nationaltrust.org.uk/cheddar-gorge
caves@cheddarcaves.co.uk

Cheddar Man Museum of Prehistory explores 40,000 years of British pre-history, with demonstrations of Stone Age survival skills and beautiful cave art.

Claverton Pumping Station

Ferry Lane Claverton
Bath BA2 7BH
01225 483001
www.claverton.org

The Claverton Pumping Station is a rare example of the technology of the Late Georgian – Regency – period. Built in 1813, the year Jane Austen published Pride and Prejudice, this amazing pump uses the power of the River Avon to lift water up 48ft into the Kennet and Avon Canal above. Burning no fuel and making no waste it is the ultimate in environmentally friendly technology.

Cleeve Abbey - English Heritage

Old Cleeve, Abbey Road
Washford TA23 0PS
01984 640377
http://goo.gl/n1zXUG

In Washford lies one of the undiscovered jewels of Somerset, providing an interesting day out for families and budding historians alike. The Cistercian abbey of Cleeve is a haven of peace and tranquillity, said to contain the finest cloister buildings in England.

Clevedon Pier

The Toll House, The Beach
Clevedon BS21 7QU
01275 878846
www.clevedonpier.com
enquiries@clevedonpier.com

Clevedon Pier is the only fully intact, Grade 1 listed pier in the country. The pier has been beautifully restored and provides a lovely day out for all the family.

Community Heritage Access Centre

SSDC Lufton Depot, 7 Artillery Road, Lufton
Yeovil BA22 8RP
01935 462855
http://goo.gl/Y0Iyjm

Open by appointment the Community Heritage Access Centre houses the collection of the previous Museum of South Somerset. Major collections include gloving, firearms, textile and archaeology.

Crewkerne & District Museum

The Heritage Centre, Market Square
Crewkerne TA18 7JU
01460 77079
www.crewkernemuseum.co.uk

Newly opened in 2000, Crewkerne & District Museum is a small museum run by volunteers.It is contained in an historic house whose 18th century front conceals a much older dwelling behind. Many aspects of local history are explored in the museum - industries, commerce, religion, education and domestic life. Changing displays of photographs and other items from the collection or on loan are on view in the Exhibition Room.

Downside Abbey Library & Archives

Downside Abbey, Stratton on the Fosse
Radstock BA3 4RH
www.downside.co.uk
sparsons@downside.co.uk

Library and Archive of Downside Abbey in Somerset, we have recently begun our beacon of learning project. The school attached to the Abbey lost many ex pupils in the Great War and we want to recognise this sacrifice during the Centenary.

Dunster Castle & Gardens - National Trust

Dunster TA24 6SL
01643 821314
www.nationaltrust.org.uk/dunster-castle
dunstercastle@nationaltrust.org.uk

Ancient castle with fine interiors and sub-tropical gardens. Dramatically sited on a wooded hill, a castle has existed here since at least Norman times.

Dunster Dolls Museum

Memorial Hall, High Street
Dunster TA24 6SF
01643 822 315
www.dunstermuseum.co.uk
dunstermemorialhall@hotmail.co.uk

The Dolls Museum in Dunster is situated in the Memorial Hall. Mrs Mollie Hardwick began collecting dolls in 1957 and these were gifted to the Hall committee on her death in 1970 so that her collection could form a museum.

Farleigh Hungerford Castle - English Heritage

Farleigh
Hungerford BA2 7RS
01225 754026
http://goo.gl/VmPUz5

In a picturesque valley of the river Frome, on the border between Wiltshire and Somerset and nine miles from Bath stand the remains of Farleigh Hungerford Castle. Started in the 14th century it still has much for the visitor to enjoy.

Fashion Museum

Assembly Rooms, Bennett Street
Bath BA1 2QH
01225 477173
www.fashionmuseum.co.uk
fashion_enquiries@bathnes.gov.uk

A world class collection of contemporary and historical dress. Located in the magnificent Georgian Assembly Rooms, the Fashion Museum offers more than 150 figures dressed in original garments on display.

Collections: The collection at the Fashion Museum includes over 30,000 items of fashionable dress for men, women and children from the late 16th century to the present day.

Fleet Air Arm Museum

Royal Naval Air Station, Yeovilton
Ilchester BA22 8HT
01935 840565
www.fleetairarm.com
info@fleetairarm.com

The Fleet Air Arm Museum houses a very large and well presented collection of aircraft and memorabilia. Four display halls portray the development of naval aviation from World War I to the Gulf War.

Frome Museum

1 North Parade
Frome BA11 1AT
01373 454611
https://fromemuseum.wordpress.com
fromemuseum@tiscali.co.uk

Frome Museum aims to provide a modern museum with an industrial focus. It is housed in an elegant Italianate building in the centre of Frome.

Glastonbury Abbey

The Abbey Gatehouse, Magdalene Street
Glastonbury BA6 9EL
01458 832267
www.glastonburyabbey.com
info@glastonburyAbbey.com

Extensive ruins set in 36 acres of parkland in the centre of the town of Glastonbury. The abbey is believed to be one of the earliest recorded Christian foundations in the land, and the burial place of King Arthur as well as three Saxon Kings.

Glastonbury Lake Village Museum

The Tribunal, 9 High Street
Glastonbury BA6 9DP
01458 832954
http://goo.gl/b1UMPq
info@glastonburytic.co.uk

The fascinating story of the Glastonbury Lake Village can be viewed in the Tribunal, the 15th century merchant's house in Glastonbury High Street, that also houses the Tourist Information Centre. The Lake Village Museum presents an insight into everyday life in an Iron-Age settlement, dating from around 2000 years ago, when much of Somerset's landscape was covered by marshy sea.

Guildhall

Heritage Services, High Street
Bath BA1 1LZ
01225 477785
www.bathvenues.co.uk/venues/guildhall
romanbaths_bookings@bathnes-gov.uk

There has been a Guildhall on the present site in the heart of Bath since Tudor times. The current building was built by Thomas Baldwin in 1775 with its imposing façade it is a masterpiece of neo-classical decoration. It continues to house the Register Office, mayor's parlour and city archives.

Haynes International Motor Museum

Haynes Motor Museum
Sparkford BA22 7LH
01963 440804
www.haynesmotormuseum.co.uk
info@haynesmotormuseum.co.uk

Haynes International Motor Museum is Britain's biggest car collection with over 400 cars and motorcycles, dating from 1886 to the present day. Also a collection of memorabilia displayed in spectacular style.

Helicopter Museum, The

The Heliport, Locking Moor Road
Weston-super-Mare BS24 8PP
01934 635227
www.helicoptermuseum.co.uk
helimuseum@btconnect.com

This unique collection of over 70 helicopters and autogyros forms the world's largest dedicated rotorcraft museum and the only one in the United Kingdom.

Herschel Museum of Astronomy

19 New King Street
Bath BA1 2BL
01225 446865
www.bath-preservation-trust.org.uk
herschelbpt@btconnect.com

The Herschel Museum of Astronomy celebrates the achievements of William and Caroline Herschel who were brilliant astronomers and talented musicians. It was from the garden of this house, using a telescope of his own design that William discovered the planet Uranus in 1781.

Holburne Museum

Great Pulteney Street
Bath BA2 4DB
01225 388569
www.holburne.org
holburne@bath.ac.uk

This jewel in Bath's crown was once the Georgian Sydney Hotel, whose glittering society Jane Austen watched from her house opposite. It displays the treasures collected by Sir William Holburne: superb English and continental silver, porcelain, maiolica, glass and Renaissance bronzes. The Picture Gallery contains works by Turner, Guardi, Stubbs and others plus portraits of Bath society by Thomas Gainsborough.

Ilchester Museum

Town Hall and Community Centre, High Street, Ilchester
Yeovil BA22 8NQ
01935 841247
http://goo.gl/Lst8Yy

Ilchester has a small community museum in the Town Hall. It was a very important town in Roman times and this importance continued until the 19th century.

Jane Austen Centre

40 Gay Street, Queen Square
Bath BA1 2NT
01225 443000
www.janeausten.co.uk

The Jane Austen Centre at 40 Gay Street in Bath is a permanent exhibition which tells the story of Jane's Bath experience - the effect that living here had on her and her writing. Jane Austen is perhaps the best known and best loved of Bath's many famous residents and visitors. She paid two long visits here towards the end of the 18th century, and from 1801 to 1806 Bath was her home.

King John's Hunting Lodge - National Trust

The Square
Axbridge BS26 2WA
01934 732 012
www.nationaltrust.org.uk/king-johns-hunting-lodge
kingjohns@nationaltrust.org.uk

The museum aims to illustrate the history, geology and community of Axbridge and the surrounding area (the area of the old Axbridge Rural District Council, which included many neighbouring villages such as Cheddar, Wedmore, Mark and Winscombe).

Montacute House - National Trust

Montacute House
Montacute TA15 6XP
01935 823289
www.nationaltrust.org.uk/montacute-house
montacute@nationaltrust.org.uk

Magnificent Elizabethan stone-built house, with fine collections, garden and park. Built in the late 16th century for Sir Edward Phelips, Montacute glitters with many windows and is adorned with elegant chimneys, carved parapets and other Renaissance features, including contemporary plasterwork, chimneypieces and heraldic glass.

Muchelney Abbey - English Heritage

Muchelney
Langport TA10 0DQ
01458 250664
http://goo.gl/saOlhl

Muchelney, the atmospheric and once-remote 'great island' amid the Somerset Levels, has many rewards for visitors. Beside the clearly laid out foundations of the wealthy medieval Benedictine abbey (and its Anglo-Saxon predecessor) stands a complete early Tudor house in miniature.

Museum of Bath at Work

Camden Works, Julian Road
Bath BA1 2RH
01225 318348
www.bath-at-work.org.uk
mobaw@hotmail.com

This is the fascinating story of a local family firm. Mr Jonathan Burdett Bowler started his business in Bath in 1872 He described his trade as engineer, brass founder, gas-fitter, lock smith and bell hanger.

Museum of East Asian Art

12 Bennett Street
Bath BA1 2QJ
01225 464640
www.meaa.org.uk
info@meaa.org.uk

The museum of East Asian Art located in the heart of Georgian Bath offers visitors a wonderful insight into the art and culture of China and East Asia. This unique museum houses a fine collection of ceramics, jades, bronzes and much more from China, Japan, Korea and Southeast Asia.

Museum of Somerset, The

Taunton Castle, Castle Green
Taunton TA1 4AA
01823 255088
museumofsomerset.org.uk
museumofsomerset@somerset.gov.uk

An under-floor Plesiosaur, the largest collection of Roman coins ever discovered in Britain and a chilling recreation of the infamous Bloody Assizes – you'll find them all at the museum of Somerset. Set in the heart of Taunton, the museum of Somerset lies within the historic 12th century Taunton Castle.

Collections: Amongst the treasures on display for the first time is the Frome Hoard, the largest collection of Roman coins ever discovered in a single container in Britain, and which was saved for the nation following a national fundraising appeal. A shrunken head from South America and Judge Jeffreys' medical bill are a few of the many other exhibits to be discovered in the museum.

Museum of South Somerset

CHAC, SSDC Lufton Depot, 7 Artillery Road, Lufton
Yeovil BA22 8RP
01935 462855
http://goo.gl/Y0lyjm
heritage.services@southsomerset.gov.uk

The building which housed the museum of South Somerset closed in 2011. The items in the museum have been moved to the Community Heritage Access Centre (CHAC) at SSDC Lufton Depot, 7 Artillery Road, Lufton, Yeovil, Somerset, BA22 8RP which is open by appointment.

Collections: Includes archaeology from the many Roman Villa sites in South Somerset. Particular strengths of the collection are gloving and the Stiby firearm collection.

Nailsea Tithe Barn Trust

Nailsea Tithe Barn, Church Lane
Nailsea BS48 2BL
07749 563908
www.nailseatithebarn.co.uk
enquiries@nailseatithebarn.co.uk

Nailsea Tithe Barn dates from 1480 and with Holy Trinity Church is part of Nailsea's historic heart. A school for over 200 years, it is now fully restored to its medieval origins. The vaulted ceiling, stonework and owl & putlog holes are beautiful features along with the modern facilities you need.

No 1 Royal Crescent

c/o 1 Royal Crescent
Bath BA1 2LR
01225 428126
no1royalcrescent.org.uk
admin@bptrust.org.uk

No 1 Royal Crescent is a magnificently restored Georgian town house that creates a wonderfully vital picture of life in Georgian Bath. Built between 1767 – 1774 to the designs of the architect John Wood the Younger, the Royal Crescent is justly considered one of the finest achievements of 18th century urban architecture and represents the highest point of Palladian architecture in Bath. No 1 was the first house to be built in the Crescent and originally provided luxury accommodation for the aristocratic visitors who came to take the waters and enjoy the social season.

Prior Park Landscape Garden - National Trust

Ralph Allen Drive
Bath BA2 5AH
01225 833422
http://goo.gl/KBYwpf
priorpark@nationaltrust.org.uk

One of only four Palladian bridges of this design in the world can be crossed at Prior Park, which was created in the 18th century by local entrepreneur Ralph Allen, with advice from 'Capability' Brown and the poet Alexander Pope. The garden is set in a sweeping valley where visitors can enjoy magnificent views of Bath.

Radstock Museum

Waterloo Road, Radstock
Bath BA3 3EP
01761 437722
www.radstockmuseum.co.uk
info@radstockmuseum.co.uk

An award-winning museum that offers an insight into North Somerset life since the 19th century. Created and sustained by dedicated enthusiasts who live and work in the area, the museum is a gem for adults and children alike.

Roman Baths

Abbey Church Yard
Bath BA1 1LZ
01225 477785
www.romanbaths.co.uk
romanbaths_enquiries@bathnes.gov.uk

Bath was founded upon natural hot springs with the steaming water playing a key role throughout its history. Lying in the heart of the city the Roman Baths were constructed around 70 AD as a grand bathing and socialising complex.

Collections: Some of the best known finds from Roman Britain are to be found amongst the 50,000 objects in the Roman Baths Museum.

Sally Lunn's Historic Eating House & Museum

4 North Parade Passage
Bath BA1 1NX
www.sallylunns.co.uk
jon@sallylunns.co.uk

A must visit – the unique taste of Bath's history is open every day and evening. Right in the centre of the city, experience the traditional hospitality of Bath's oldest historic eating house.

Saltford Brass Mill

The Shallows
Saltford BS31 3EY
www.tcsafety.co.uk

Saltford Brassmill is situated on the banks of the River Avon in the village of Saltford, 5 miles west of the City of Bath in the South West of England. The Brassmill is the only surviving building still with a furnace and working water wheel remaining from a group of 18th century mills making brass and copper goods in the Avon Valley between Bristol and Bath.

Shoe Museum, The

40 High Street
Street BA16 0EQ
01458 842169
http://goo.gl/bhT0z1

IHeritage represents an important part of the Clarks brand and our extensive archive, spanning six generations of the family firm, has grown to reflect this. Now protected by the Alfred Gillett Charitable Trust, the archive preserves a varied assortment of objects and papers that remain a rich source of ideas and inspiration for the company, whilst acting as a resource to those interested in our business, economic, genealogical, local, religious or social history.

Somerset & Dorset Railway Trust Museum

The Railway Station, Washford
Watchet TA23 0PP
01984 640869
www.sdrt.org.uk
info@sdrt.org

The museum contains relics from the former Somerset & Dorset Joint Railway, which ran from Bath to Bournemouth with branchlines to Highbridge, Burnham on Sea, Wells and Bridgwater until closing in 1966. Artefacts on show include station nameboards, lamps, tools, signalling equipment, tickets, photographs, handbills, rolling stock and steam locomotives.

Somerset Archives & Local Studies

Somerset Heritage Centre, Brunel Way, Langford Mead, Norton Fitzwarren
Taunton TA2 6SF
01823 278805
www1.somerset.gov.uk/archives/

We exist to find, preserve and make available written records of Somerset's people and communities. We are based at the Somerset Heritage Centre in Taunton.

Somerset Brick & Tile Museum

East Quay
Bridgwater TA6 4AE
01823 320200
http://goo.gl/L3PVOK
county-museums@somerset.gov.uk

The museum is dedicated to the local industry of brick and tile making, one of the many labour-intensive coal based industries once found in Somerset. The core of the museum is the only remaining tile kiln in Bridgwater. It used to be one of six at the former Barham Brothers' Yard at East Quay.

Somerset County Museums Service

Taunton Castle, Castle Green
Taunton TA1 4AA
01823 320200
www.somerset.gov.uk/museums
county-museums@somerset.gov.uk

What we do: Collect, conserve, research, communicate and exhibit material evidence of human activity and the natural environment. Offer facilities at our museums in Taunton, Glastonbury and Bridgwater for visitors to discover, learn about and enjoy Somerset's fascinating history and heritage. Many of our collections are on public display whilst more are available for study by appointment.

Somerset Cricket Museum

7 Priory Avenue
Taunton TA1 1XX
01823 275893
www.indv.dreamhosters.com
somersetcricketmuseum@btconnect.com

Somerset Cricket Museum is located inside a medieval barn - one of the last remaining buildings of Taunton's Augustinian priory. It has exhibitions and displays about the history of Somerset County Cricket Club, Somerset cricket and cricket in general.

Somerset Military Museum

Taunton Castle, Castle Green
Taunton TA1 4AA
01823 355 504
www.sommilmuseum.org.uk
info@sommilmuseum.org.uk

The Somerset Military museum is located within the Museum of Somerset in Taunton Castle in the centre of the County Town. The museum features: The Somerset Light Infantry (Prince Albert's); The Somerset and Cornwall Light Infantry; The West Somerset Yeomanry; The North Somerset Yeomanry; Somerset Militia, Rifle Volunteers and Territorials; The Light Infantry and its successor regiment, The Rifles.

Somerset Rural Life Museum

Abbey Farm
Glastonbury BA6 8DB
01458 831197
www.somersetrurallifemuseum.org.uk
somersetrurallifemuseum@somerset.gov.uk

The Somerset Rural Life Museum is located on the outskirts of Glastonbury, not far from the famous abbey ruins, and was established in the 1970s to tell the story of rural life in the county. The museum is based at what was one of the principal dairy farms in the area and includes the magnificent 14th-century Abbey Barn, one of only four surviving barns which belonged to Glastonbury Abbey. The museum tells the story of Victorian domestic life, the farming year and local crafts and industries. The grounds contain a traditional cider apple orchard which is home to rare breeds of sheep and chickens. The museum is currently closed to the public for refurbishment.

Tyntesfield - National Trust

Tyntesfield
Wraxall BS48 1NX
0844 800 4986
www.nationaltrust.org.uk/tyntesfield
tyntesfield@nationaltrust.org.uk

See the spectacular Victorian Gothic house and chapel scaffolding free after extensive repairs and restoration works. Inside discover a family home lived in by four generations of the Gibbs family, all making their mark and never throwing anything away.

Victoria Art Gallery

Bridge Street, Pulteney Bridge
Bath BA2 4AT
01225 477233
www.victoriagal.org.uk
victoria_enquiries@bathnes.gov.uk

Wonderful display of British oil paintings from 17th century to the present day including works by Gainsborough, Barker and Sickert. Over 1,500 decorative arts treasures.

Watchet Boat Museum

Harbour Road
Watchet TA23 0AQ
01984 633117
www.wbm.org.uk
info@wbm.org.uk

In the museum can be seen many different types of flatner, plus nets and other items associated with their use. There are displays of maps, knotwork and boards showing the various uses of withy. The museum is housed in the historic Old Goods Shed, built in 1862 when Watchet was the terminus of the West Somerset railway.

Watchet Market House Museum

Market Street
Watchet TA23 0AN
01984 632266
www.watchetmuseum.co.uk
enquiries@watchetmuseum.co.uk

The museum houses many documents and artefacts charting Watchet's history through the ages. The museum

also develops studies on more detailed themes for those with a deeper interest in history.

Wells & Mendip Museum

8 Cathedral Green
Wells BA5 2UE
01749 673477
www.wellsmuseum.org.uk
Admin@wellsmuseum.org.uk

Wells & Mendip Museum is the home of Wells City Archives. The society was founded in 1888 to encourage the practical study of natural history, archaeology and kindred subjects in Wells and the surrounding countryside.

Wells Cathedral

Cathedral Green
Wells BA5 2UE
01749 674483
www.wellscathedral.org.uk
office@wellscathedral.uk.net

The present cathedral building was begun around 1175. It is one of the most impressive of the English cathedrals and has survived eight centuries with all its associated buildings still around it - the chapter house, vicars' hall, the cloisters and the unique vicars' close.

West Somerset Railway

The Railway Station
Minehead TA24 5BG
01643 704996
www.west-somerset-railway.co.uk
info@west-somerset-railway.co.uk

Our railway, a true country branch line of the old Great Western Railway is full of fascination whether you are looking for a nostalgic ride back in time through lovely countryside or to study the railway and industrial heritage which our line preserves. The historic steam locomotives, coaches and wagons, and the buildings of our ten unique stations linked by a twenty mile scenic journey will repay hours of exploration.

West Somerset Rural Life Museum

The Old School, Allerford
Minehead TA24 8HN
01643 862529
www.allerfordmuseum.org.uk
enquiries@allerfordmuseum.org.uk

The Rural Life Museum is housed in the old Village School leased from the National Trust. It was a school from 1821 to 1981 and opened as the Rural Life Museum in 1983.

Weston-super-Mare Family History Society

125 Totterdown Road
Weston-super-Mare BS23 4LW
www.wsmfhs.org.uk
secretary@wsmfhs.org.uk

If you have an interest in families in or from this area of
Somerset you will find plenty to help you here. Founded in
1984, we have a growing and active membership.

Weston-super-Mare Museum

Burlington Street
Weston-super-Mare BS23 1PR
01934 621028
westonmuseum.org
museum@wsm-tc.gov.uk

Family friendly museum featuring galleries of archaeology,
social and natural history. The Seaside Gallery and unique
Clara's Cottage make up the static displays.

Collections: archaeology of North Somerset, including
Worlebury Iron Age hill fort. Social history of North
Somerset: local industries including royal potteries, seaside
holidays, costume and domestic life.

Westonzoyland Pumping Station

Westonzoyland Pumping Station Museum, Hoopers Lane,
Westonzoyland, nr Bridgwater, Somerset
Westonzoyland TA7 0LS
01275 472385
www.wzlet.org
steamteam@wzlet.org

Westonzoyland Pumping Station is one of Somerset's
smallest and most isolated museums, housing a fascinating
collection of stationary steam-powered engines including a
restored and working 1861 Easton & Amos land drainage
machine. The original pumping house is a Grade 2* listed
building, built in 1830 and still in need of restoration. The
museum holds steaming days every month during the
tourist season.

Yeovil Railway Centre

Yeovil Junction Station Stoford
Yeovil BA22 9UU
01935 410420
www.yeovilrailway.freeservers.com
yeovilrailway@hotmail.com

Heritage railway centre with original Southern Railway 70ft
turntable. Visitors can see main line steam turned and
serviced from special viewing platform.

South Yorkshire

Sheffield, parliamentary and municipal borough, manufacturing town, parish, and township, S. division of West-Riding Yorkshire, on river Don, 157 miles NW. of London by rail, 42½ SE. of Manchester, and 53 SW. of York - township, 3028 acres, population 91,806; borough and parish, 19,651 acres, population 284,508. Sheffield has long been famous for its cutlery. It has also manufactures of almost every description, of iron, steel, and brass; and in connection with these it has numerous extensive iron and brass foundries, grinding, tilting, rolling, and slitting mills, &c. The branches of manufacture include steel, mostly made from Swedish iron; armour-plates for ships of war; rails, wheels, and all other castings for fixed or rolling stock; stoves, grates, fenders; plated goods; Britannia-metal goods; and optical instruments, including spectacles. Sheffield is picturesquely situated in an amphitheatre of wooded hills, traversed by the river Don. which here receives the Sheaf, Rivelin, Loxley, and Porter. The modern history of Sheffield is closely connected with that of Trades Unions.

Rotherham, municipal borough and market town, parish, and township - parish, 13,585 acres, population 38,997. Rotherham, which is practically by its nearness to Sheffield a suburb of that great town, has extensive iron and chemical works, manufactures of glass, soap, starch, and ropes, and exports of coal and lime.

Doncaster, municipal borough, market town, parish, and township; parish, 10,197 acres, population 25,887. Previous to the Reformation it was the seat of several monastic establishments. Its corn market is of considerable importance, and its trade is mainly agricultural; it has, however, manufactures of canvas, sacks, and ropes, some iron and brass foundries, and agricultural implement works, besides the extensive locomotive and carriage works of the Great Northern Railway.

Barnsley, township and borough, 2386 acres, population 29,790. Barnsley is one of the chief seats of linen manufacture, and is situated in a rich coal and iron mining district.

– John Bartholomew, Gazetteer of the British Isles (1887)

Note: South Yorkshire was formed in 1974, mostly from parts of the West Riding of Yorkshire, but also parts of Derbyshire and Nottinghamshire.

13th/18th Royal Hussar - Queen Mary's Own

Cannon Hall, Cawthorne
Barnsley S75 4AT
01226 790 270
www.lightdragoons.org.uk
mail@lightdragoons.org.uk

As with the regiment, The Light Dragoons Regimental Association was born from the amalgamation of two thriving Regimental Associations, 13/18H and 15/19H in December 1992. Centred around the administrative offices of Home Headquarters, its primary objectives are in maintaining contact between former members, fostering mutual friendship and providing for social gatherings.

Abbeydale Industrial Hamlet

Abbeydale Road South
Sheffield S7 2QW
0114 236 7731
www.simt.co.uk
postmaster@simt.co.uk

Abbeydale Industrial Hamlet is a unique 18th century industrial works. Catch a glimpse of life at home and at work at a rural scythe and steelworks dating back to the 18th century. Now a Grade 1 Listed Building and Scheduled Ancient Monument, 'Abbeydale Works' was once a main producer of agricultural scythe and edge tools, such as grass hooks and hay knives, and one of the largest water powered industrial sites on the River Sheaf. See worker's houses, waterwheels, tilit hammers, a grinding hull and workshops and the only intact crucible steel furnace surviving in the world today.

AeroVenture - South Yorkshire Aircraft Museum

AeroVenture, Dakota Way, Airborne Road, Doncaster Leisure Park
Doncaster DN4 7FB
01302 761616
www.southyorkshireaircraftmuseum.org.uk

Based at the former site of RAF Doncaster, AeroVenture is a treasure trove of aviation history, available to all from a short motorway journey. Most of our exhibits are under cover, ideal for sunny or rainy days.

Barnsley Archives & Local Studies

Barnsley Central Library, Shambles Street
Barnsley S70 2JF
01226 773950
http://goo.gl/j3jn5a

Our archives and local studies exist to preserve and make available historic records and printed material relating to the borough.

Barnsley Family History Society

11 Meadow Rise, Wadworthy
Barnsley DN11 9AP
www.barnsleyfhs.co.uk
secretary@barnsleyfhs.co.uk

The aim of the Barnsley Family History Society (BFHS) is to assist those who have connections with the Barnsley area to find out more about their family history and place it in its social context.

Bishops' House

Norton Lees Lane
Sheffield S8 9BE
0114 278 2600
www.bishopshouse.org.uk
enquiries@bishopshouse.org.uk

Museums Sheffield: Bishops' House is the best preserved timber–framed house in Sheffield. It is not known when it was built but the style of architecture suggests some time between 1460 and 1550.

Brodsworth Hall & Gardens - English Heritage

Brodsworth Hall and Gardens
Doncaster DN5 7XJ
01302 722598
http://goo.gl/2cihul
brodsworthhall@english-heritage.org.uk

Explore the changing fortunes of a wealthy Victorian family in this once opulent Yorkshire country home. Discover 150 years of family life documented at Brodsworth Hall: from silk and chandeliers, to the austerity of life during WWII.

Cannon Hall Museum

Bark House Lane, Cawthorne
Barnsley S75 4AT
01226 790270
www.barnsley.gov.uk
cannonhall@barnsley.gov.uk

For two hundred years Cannon Hall was home to the Spencer Stanhope family. From the 1760s the architect John Carr of York was commissioned to extend and alter the house while the designer Richard Woods was hired to landscape the parks and gardens.

Collections: Cannon Hall Museum contains collections of fine furniture, old master paintings, stunning glassware and colourful pottery. In addition it is home to 'Charge', the regimental Museum of the 13th/18th Royal Hussars (Queen Mary's Own).

Clifton Park Museum

Clifton Lane, Rotherham
Rotherham S65 2AA
01709 336633
www.rotherham.gov.uk/cliftonparkmuseum
cliftonparkmuseum@rotherham.gov.uk

The museum is located within Clifton House, a Grade II* listed building designed by John Carr. The house was built in 1783 as the home of Joshua Walker, son of the founder of Rotherham Ironworks, and it retains many period features.

Collections: The House has been a museum since 1893, and is the base of Rotherham Borough's Museums, Galleries and Heritage Service. Its collections aim to reflect the natural, social and industrial development of the town of Rotherham itself as well as the geographical area covered by the Rotherham Borough.

Conisbrough Castle

Castle Hill, Conisbrough
Doncaster DN12 3BU
01709 863329
www.conisbroughcastle.org.uk

The lofty 12th century keep of this very well-preserved building, now complete with its restored roof and floors, is a spectacular sight. It had a major role to play in the Wars of the Roses and was once owned by Richard of York. Conisbrough Castle featured in Sir Walter Scott's 'Ivanhoe', and with its many reminders of the golden age of knights in armour it makes a great value family day out near Doncaster.

Cusworth Hall Museum & Park

Cusworth Hall, Cusworth Lane
Doncaster DN5 7TU
01302 782342
www.cusworthhall.co.uk
museum@doncaster.gov.uk

Cusworth Hall has been described as the jewel in Doncaster's crown. A beautiful Grade 1 listed 18th century country house in acres of historic parkland with lakes, plantations and pleasure ground with dramatic views across the town and home to amazing social history collections, which illustrate the way people lived worked and entertained themselves over the last two hundred years.

Doncaster Archives

King Edward Road, Balby
Doncaster DN4 0NA
01302 859811
www.doncaster.gov.uk/doncasterarchives

Doncaster's Archives & Local Studies department holds historical borough information from the earliest times to the present day.

Doncaster Museum & Art Gallery

Chequer Road
Doncaster DN1 2AE
01302 734293
www.doncaster.gov.uk/museums
museum@doncaster.gov.uk

Doncaster Museum & Art Gallery is full of exciting collections depicting various aspects of natural history, archaeology, local history and fine and decorative art.

Elsecar Heritage Centre

Wath Road, Elsecar
Barnsley S74 8HJ
01226 740203
www.barnsley.gov.uk/tourism/elsecar/index.asp
elsecarheritagecentre@barnsley.gov.uk

The award winning Elsecar Heritage Centre is an exciting history and craft centre, set in the attractive conservation village of Elsecar and surrounded by beautiful South Yorkshire countryside. The centre is located within the former ironworks and colliery workshops of the Earls Fitzwilliam, where visitors can explore the attractively restored buildings and monuments. Features include the only Newcomen type engine, worldwide, to remain in its original location, a unique monument to the industrial age. Guided group tours available upon request.

Experience Barnsley Museum & Discovery Centre

Town Hall, Church Street
Barnsley S70 2TA
01226 773950
www.experience-barnsley.com
experiencebarnsley@barnsley.gov.uk

Experience Barnsley Museum and Discovery Centre is dedicated to the history and people of Barnsley. Visitors will uncover the incredible story of Barnsley told through centuries-old artefacts, documents, films and recordings that have been donated by people living and working in the borough. Unique, hands-on and interactive exhibits encourage visitors to explore the people and places of Barnsley.

Kelham Island Museum

Alma Street, Off Corporation Street
Sheffield S3 8RY
0114 272 2106
www.simt.co.uk
ask@simt.co.uk

The collections at Kelham Island Museum cover industries in Sheffield from 1750 up to the present. Major collections include the Iron & Steel Industry Collection, Cutlery

Industry Collection, Armament Industry Collection and the Tool Making Industry Collection.

Ken Hawley Collection Trust, The

c/o The University of Sheffield, West Court, 2 Mappin Street
Sheffield S1 4DT
0114 222 7100
www.shef.ac.uk/hawley
hawley.tools@sheffield.ac.uk

The Hawley Collection is an internationally important material record of tool making, cutlery manufacture and silversmithing from Sheffield, together with complementary material from Britain and the rest of the world. This collection is unique in that it combines finished artefacts and work in progress to illustrate how things were made. Together with published catalogues, archival material, pictures, photographs, tapes and films, it records the development of many of Sheffield's manufacturing processes and products and the skills of the workpeople involved.

King's Own Yorkshire Light Infantry Museum

Doncaster Museum and Art Gallery, Chequer Road
Doncaster DN1 2AE
01302 734 293
http://goo.gl/kXr2tF

Following extensive refurbishment the The regimental Gallery of the King's Own Yorkshire Light Infantry re-opened in 2010 in the Doncaster Museum and Art Gallery. The gallery displays an excellent collection of regimental memorabilia, uniforms, uniforms, pictures and silver dating from the raising of the regiment in 1755 to its amalgamation into The Light Infantry in 1968 and then into The Rifles in 2007. It includes a model of the Pontefract Barracks, the Roll of Honour of the 5th Battalion and one of the most extensive medal collections in this country.

Museums Sheffield: Millennium Gallery

Millennium Gallery, Arundel Gate
Sheffield S1 2PP
0114 278 2600
www.museums-sheffield.org.uk
info@museums-sheffield.org.uk

Step into one of Sheffield's architectural treasures, the award winning Millennium Gallery, an inspiring venue in the heart of the city centre.

Collections: The Metalwork Gallery collection is made up of cutlery, flatware and holloware made in the city, together with an outstanding selection of comparative material from Europe and many parts of Africa and Asia. It includes silver, pewter, stainless steel and Old Sheffield Plate and is the best collection of its kind in this country and almost certainly the world.

Museums Sheffield: Weston Park

Weston Park, Western Bank
Sheffield S10 2TP
0114 278 2655
www.museums-sheffield.org.uk
info@museums-sheffield.org.uk

At Museums Sheffield: Weston Park you can explore the world and its past, from millions of years ago to the present day. Children and adults will love the animated new displays, specially designed to delight even our littlest explorers.

Olde Smithy Museum, The

High Street, Owston Ferry
Doncaster DN9 1RE
01427 728169
http://goo.gl/NWISj0
davewilliams24@tiscali.co.uk

The Olde Smithy Museum is a village black smith shop that was closed during the 1980s. The smithy was never modernised and is today very much as it was in the early 1900s.

Roche Abbey - English Heritage

Maltby
Conisbrough S66 8NW
01709 812739
http://goo.gl/dDNm2R
customers@english-heritage.org.uk

Beautifully set in a valley landscaped by 'Capability' Brown in the 18th century, the most striking feature of this Cistercian abbey is the end of its church, built in the new Gothic style c1170. It has one of the most complete ground plans of any English Cistercian monastery, laid out as excavated foundations.

Rotherham Archives & Local Studies Service

Clifton Park Museum, Clifton Lane,
Rotherham S65 2AA
01709 336632
www.rotherham.gov.uk/Archives
archives@rotherham.gov.uk

The Archives and Local Studies Service holds over 700 archive collections in its secure and environmentally controlled strong rooms. We currently have over 4000 boxes of archives, which would fill over 8 double decker buses. The archival documents cover the history of the whole of Rotherham Borough from 1328 to the present day.

Sheffield & District Family History Society

12 Birchitt Road, Bradway
Sheffield S17 4QP
www.sheffieldfhs.org.uk
secretary@sheffieldfhs.org.uk

Sheffield and District Family History Society was founded in 1977 with the aims of promoting the study of genealogy, family history and local history in the area, for the benefit and education of the public.

Sheffield Archives

52 Shoreham Street
Sheffield S1 4SP
0114 203 9395
www.sheffield.gov.uk/archives
archives@sheffield.gov.uk

Sheffield Archives collects, preserves and lists written and other records relating to Sheffield and South Yorkshire, and makes them available for reference and research. The records date from the 12th century to the present day and include: business records, ecclesiastical records, family and estate records, local government records, local public records and records from individuals.

Sheffield Cathedral

Church Street
Sheffield S1 1HA
0114 275 3434
www.sheffieldcathedral.org

The cathedral is Sheffield's oldest building, the ancient heart of a great city. The life of this cathedral is rich and varied it is the seat of the Bishop and a centre of worship for the Diocese of Sheffield, serving the whole of South Yorkshire.

Shepherd Wheel

Whiteley Woods, off Hangingwater Road
Sheffield S7 2QW
0114 2722106
www.simt.co.uk
postmaster@simt.co.uk

A water powered grinding wheel set on a picturesque stretch of the river Porter. The site dates back to 1584.

Collections: Tools and equipment used in the cutlery industry.

South Yorkshire Archaeology Service

Development Services, Howden House, 1 Union Street
Sheffield S1 2SH
0114 273 6354

315

www.sheffield.gov.uk/syas
syorks.archservice@sheffield.gov.uk

The South Yorkshire Archaeology Service (SYAS) was established by the former South Yorkshire County Council in 1974. Since 1986 it has been maintained by the four districts of Barnsley, Doncaster, Rotherham and Sheffield and is administered by Sheffield City Council.

University of Sheffield, Turner Museum of Glass

Department of Engineering Materials, Sir Robert Hadfield Building, Mappin St
Sheffield S1 4DU
0114 275 4325
www.turnermuseum.group.shef.ac.uk
j.w.smedley@sheffield.ac.uk

The Turner Museum of Glass is one of the UK's most interesting and comprehensive collections of 19th and 20th century glass. The museum was founded in 1943 by Professor W.E.S. Turner.

Victoria Jubilee Museum

Taylor Hill, Cawthorne
Barnsley S75 4HQ
01226 790545
http://goo.gl/u0UDNu

This unique and exciting, small volunteer run museum can be found in the picturesque village of Cawthorne. The museum is a typical Victorian hotch potch. whichever way you turn there is something to catch the eye of both young and old.

Wentworth Castle Gardens

Lowe Lane
Stainborough, Barnsley S75 3ET
01226 776040
www.wentworthcastle.org
heritagetrust@wentworthcastle.org

Wentworth Castle and Stainborough Park is located approximately 3km south west of Barnsley in South Yorkshire. The estate's Grade 1 landscape and formal gardens are nationally significant for their extensive monuments, housing some of the earliest gothic follies in the country.

Worsbrough Mill Museum

Worsbrough Bridge
Barnsley S70 5LJ
01226 774527
www.worsbrough-mill.com/worsbrough-mill-museum
Worsbroughmill@barnsley.gov.uk

Worsbrough Mill is a 17th century working water powered corn mill set in over 200 acres of country park.

Staffordshire

Staffordshire, county in west-midlands of England; bounded NW. and N. by Cheshire, NE. and E. by Derbyshire, SE. by Warwickshire, S. by Worcestershire, and W. by Shropshire; greatest length, N. and S., 50 miles; greatest breadth, E. and W., 34 miles; area, 748,433 acres, population 981,013. Staffordshire lies in the basin of the Trent, which traverses the county from NW. to SE., receiving the Sow (with its tributary the Penk), Tame, Blythe, and Dove. Except in the north, which is chiefly wild moorland, the surface is generally level or gently undulating. About three-fourths of the surface is arable, but much of the soil is of a cold clayey nature; the best land is in the south. Along the banks of the streams are many rich meadows. The new red sandstone occupies the whole of the centre of the county, but in the N. and S. are 2 valuable coal fields - the Pottery coal field and the Dudley coal field, the latter of which is celebrated for the extraordinary thickness of one of its seams, for the excellence of its coal for ironmaking, and the number and richness of its iron ores. Its mineral wealth has given Staffordshire rank as the third county in England for manufacturing industry, North Staffordshire being the chief seat of the earthenware manufacture in the kingdom, and South Staffordshire one of the chief seats of the iron manufacture. The whole county is covered with a network of railways and canals. Staffordshire contains 5 hundreds, 247 parishes, and parts of 5 others, the parliamentary and municipal boroughs of Hanley, Newcastle under Lyme, Stafford, Stoke upon Trent, Walsall, West Bromwich, and Wolverhampton [Wolverhampton and Wednesbury became part of the West Midlands in 1974], the parliamentary borough of Wednesbury, the municipal boroughs of Burslem, Lichfield, and Longton, and parts of the municipal boroughs of Burton on Trent and Tamworth. It is mostly in the diocese of Lichfield.

– John Bartholomew, *Gazetteer of the British Isles* (1887)

Ancient High House

Greengate Street
Stafford ST16 2JA
01785 619131
www.staffordbc.gov.uk
mhartwell@staffordbc.gov.uk

Built in around 1595 for the wealthy Dorrington family, the ornate timber framed building is reputed to be the largest surviving timber framed town house in England from the Tudor period. In 1986 the house opened as a museum and now provides a fascinating glimpse into the lives of the people who have lived there over the centuries.

Apedale Valley Light Railway

Apedale Country Park, Loomer Road, Chesterton
Newcastle-under-Lyme ST5 7LB
0845 094 1953
www.avlr.org.uk
info@mrt.org.uk

The Trust currently operates the Apedale Valley Light Railway and is constructing a new museum to display its collection of industrial narrow gauge equipment.

Audley & District Family History Society

20 Hillside Avenue, Endon
Stoke-on-Trent ST9 9HH
www.acumenbooks.co.uk/audleynet/famhist/index.htm
famhist147@hotmail.co.uk

Audley parish is situated in the rolling hills of North Staffordshire and has a long and interesting history, including farming and a period of intensive coal mining. Since 1986 the Audley and District Family History Society has been working to make records available for Audley and its adjoining parishes.

Biddulph & District Genealogy & Historical Society

134 Mow Lane, Gillow Heath, Biddulph
Stoke-on-Trent ST8 6RJ
www.bdghs.org.uk
webmaster@bdghs.org.uk

Local and family history society. Meetings held once a month in local library.

Boscobel House & The Royal Oak - English Heritage

Brewood
Bishops Wood ST19 9AR
01902 850244

http://goo.gl/pfG1wv

Built in about 1632, Boscobel House, originally a timber-framed farmhouse, was converted into a hunting lodge by John Giffard of Whiteladies. The Giffard family were Roman Catholics, at a time when the religion suffered persecution, and tradition holds that the true purpose of Boscobel was to serve as a secret place for the shelter of Catholics in times of need. Following the execution of King Charles I in 1649, his eldest son made a brave though misguided attempt to regain the throne. In 1651 his hopes were crushed at Worcester in the final conflict of the Civil War. Young Charles was forced to flee for his life. He sought refuge at Boscobel, hiding first in a tree which is now known as The Royal Oak and then spending the night in a priest-hole in the house's attic. Boscobel remained a working farm and visitors today can also see the dairy, farmyard, smithy, gardens, and a descendant of The Royal Oak. White Ladies Priory, another of Charles's hiding places, is a short walk away.

Ceramica

Market Place, Burslem
Stoke-on-Trent ST6 3DS
01782 832001
www.ceramicauk.com
info@ceramicauk.com

Ceramica revitalises the Old Town Hall of Burslem into unique visitor attraction expoloring the past and future of the pottery industry in Stoke-on-Trent.

Cheddleton Flint Mill & Museum

Leek Road
Cheddleton Near Leek ST13 7HL
01782 502907
www.people.exeter.ac.uk/akoutram/cheddleton-mill

Cheddleton Flint Mill consists of a complex of buildings including two separate water mills, a miller's cottage, two flint kilns, a drying kiln and outbuildings. The Caldon Canal, which would have supplied the mill by narrow boat, passes by.

Churnet Valley Railway

Cheddleton Station, Station Road
Cheddleton ST13 7EE
01538 360 522
www.churnet-valley-railway.co.uk
enquiries@churnetvalleyrailway.co.uk

An Act of Parliament formed the North Staffordshire Railway in 1846. The Churnet Valley Railway takes you on a journey back to the classic days of railway travel on a rural line that passes through beautiful countryside known as Staffordshire's 'Little Switzerland'.

Claymills Pumping Engines Trust

Meadow Lane, Stretton
Burton upon Trent DE13 0DA
01283 509929
www.claymills.org.uk
enquiries@claymills.org.uk

Preserved Victorian sewage pumping station. We have 4 beam engines, 5 Lancashire boilers, steam driven workshop, Blacksmiths's forge, early electrical dynamo house and numerous small engines.

Erasmus Darwin House

Beacon Street
Lichfield WS13 7AD
01543 306260
www.erasmusdarwin.org
enquiries@erasmusdarwin.org

Erasmus Darwin, grandfather of Charles Darwin, was a philosopher and pioneer in science, technology and medicine. His work was of national and international significance but has been little known until recently.

Etruria Industrial Museum

Lower Bedford Street, Etruria
Stoke-on-Trent ST4 7AF
01782 233 144
www.stokemuseums.org.uk
etruria@stoke.gov.uk

Etruria Industrial Museum is the last steam-powered potters' mill in Britain. The mill is 'in steam' seven times a year when the 1903 boiler is fired and historic machinery can be seen working.

Ford Green Hall

Ford Green Road, Smallthorne
Stoke on Trent ST6 1NG
01782 233195
www.stokemuseums.org.uk
ford.green.hall@stoke.gov.uk

Ford Green Hall is a 17th century timber-framed farmhouse complete with period garden. An award-winning museum, the hall offers visitors a fascinating insight into the life of the 17th century.

Foxfield Steam Railway

Caverswall Road Station, Blythe Bridge
Stoke-on-Trent ST11 9EA
01782 396210
www.foxfieldrailway.co.uk
enquiries@foxfieldrailway.co.uk

The Foxfield Light Railway is one of the UK's earliest heritage railways. The line was built in the 1890s and unlike many lines which follow valleys, the Foxfield Railway maintains a 5½ mile round journey which boldly crosses open moorland, hills and woodland.

Gladstone Pottery Museum

Uttoxeter Road, Longton
Stoke on Trent ST3 1PQ
01782 237777
www.stokemuseums.org.uk/visit/gpm
angela.lee@stoke.gov.uk

As if frozen in time, Gladstone remains the only complete Victorian pottery factory from the days when coal-burning ovens made the world's first bone china. Traditional skills, original workshops, the cobbled yard and huge bottle kilns create an atmospheric time warp which has no equal.

Collections: 'Flushed with Pride': our sanitaryware gallery tells the story of the toilet from the 1840s slum to the toilets of the future. Tile Gallery: Gladstone is home to one of the finest collections of decorative tiles in Britain. Trace the development of tiles from medieval monasteries to the space shuttle. The Doctor's House: Hear some gruesome details of the illnesses and disease that plagued the Potteries.

Hanley Library

Bethesda Street
Stoke On Trent ST1 3RS
www.library.pitt.edu/bradford

Our reading room is open to all members of the public without charge. An Archive Service reader's ticket is required for use of the reading room.

Izaak Walton's Cottage

Worston Lane, Shallow Ford, Nr. Stone
Stafford ST15 0PA
01785 760278
www.staffordbc.gov.uk

Izaak Walton, author of the 'Compleat Angler', owned this charming cottage that nestles in the tiny hamlet of Shallowford, between Stafford and Eccleshall. His charming thatched 16th century half-timbered cottage will be of interest to anglers and non anglers alike. It offers a marvellous insight into the history of fishing and the literary talent of Stafford's famous son.

James Brindley Mill & Museum

Mill Street
Leek ST13
Tourist Information Centre 01538 483741
www.brindleymill.net

Brindley's Mill has all the charm associated with a building of the period and illustrates James Brindley's trademark design. The mill building houses a museum designed to enhance the interest of your visit. Displays illustrate the life and work of James Brindley and the history of milling, while preserving the atmosphere of a working corn mill.

Lichfield Cathedral

19A The Close
Lichfield WS13 7LD
01543 306100
www.lichfield-cathedral.org
enquiries@lichfield-cathedral.org

When Bishop Chad of Mercia died in 672, pilgrims began to come to his shrine in Lichfield. In 700, Bishop Hedda built a new church to house his bones.

Lichfield Heritage Centre

Market Square
Lichfield WS13 6LG
01543 256611
www.lichfieldheritage.org.uk/key_info.htm
info@lichfieldheritage.org.uk

Research into Lichfield's fascinating social history over the last 150 years through over 6000 photographs; negatives; newspapers; reports; leaflets and other interesting memorabilia from the past. Internet linked to Staffordshire County Council`s archives on www.staffspasttrack.org.uk which includes 100 photographs from our own collection relating to Lichfield.

Lichfield Record Office

The Friary
Lichfield WS13 6QG
01543 510720
www.staffordshire.gov.uk/archives
lichfield.record.office@staffordshire.gov.uk

Lichfield Record Office is part of the Staffordshire and Stoke on Trent Archive Service, and is the record office for the Diocese of Lichfield, the City of Lichfield and the surrounding area. Our collections include records of the Diocese of Lichfield, local government, nonconformist churches, public institutions such as courts and schools, charities, businesses, and local clubs and societies.

Middleport Pottery

Port Street Middleport, Stoke on Trent, Staffordshire ST6 3PE, United Kingdom
Stoke on Trent ST6 3PE
01782 499766
www.middleportpottery.co.uk
middleport@princes-regeneration.org

Middleport Pottery, home to Burleigh ware is the last working Victorian Pottery in the UK. It was acquired by The Prince's Regeneration Trust in June 2011 and is now a wonderful visitor attraction.

Mill Meece Pumping Station Preservation Trust

Mill Meece Pumping Station, Cotes Heath
Near Eccleshall ST21 6QU
01785 617171
www.millmeecepumpingstation.co.uk
millmeece@millmeecepumpingstation.co.uk

Mill Meece steam engines once pumped clean drinking water to the people of Stoke-on-Trent until they were retired from service in 1979. They are now steamed regularly for the public to enjoy. The two steam engines have been preserved in situ and are the only pair of their type still capable of being steamed.

Museum of Cannock Chase

Valley Road, Hednesford
Cannock WS12 1TD
01543 877666
www.wlct.org/museumofcannockchase
museumofcannockchase@wlct.org

The museum has five formal display galleries. The Local History Gallery - Tracing the Chase; The Miner's Cottage - depicting life at the turn of the 20th century; Toys and Games Past and Present - Relive your childhood memories; Seven Centuries of Coal - find out about Cannock's industrial heritage; The 1940s Room - domestic life during the Second World War.

Museum of the Staffordshire Yeomanry - Queen's Own Royal Regiment

Greengate Street
Stafford ST16 2HS
01785 240204
http://goo.gl/PaHkrS

The collection covers the history of this County Yeomanry Cavalry Regiment from its formation in 1794 to 1945. Special emphasis is laid on the World War 2 period where the Yeomanry fought at El Alamein and later took part in the D Day landings and the crossing of the Rhine (in swimming tanks).

Newcastle Borough Museum & Art Gallery

Brampton Park
Newcastle-under-Lyme ST5 0QP
01782 619705
www.newcastle-staffs.gov.uk/museum
nulmuseum@newcastle-staffs.gov.uk

Hidden in Brampton Park less than half a mile from the town centre lies Newcastle-under-Lyme's local history museum featuring over 800 years of borough history. Alongside our temporary exhibitions programme we have galleries depicting the rich and diverse history of the area using our amazing collections.

Potteries Museum & Art Gallery, The

Bethesda Street, Hanley
Stoke-on-Trent ST1 3DW
01782 232323
www.stokemuseums.org.uk
museums@stoke.gov.uk

Travel back in time and discover the history of the the Potteries, including the world's greatest collection of Staffordshire ceramics. See Reginald Mitchell's World War 2 Spitfire and all sorts of art and craft.

Raven Mason Collection of Porcelain & Ironstone China at Keele University

The Raven Trust at Keele University, John Raven Room, Keele Hall, Keele University
Keele ST5 5BG
01782 584169
www.keele.ac.uk/depts/uso/pr/RavenMason
j.kershaw@uso.keele.ac.uk

This important ceramic collection was lovingly created by brothers Ronald William and John Mason Raven; it is housed in Keele Hall within the University. It contains many important pieces outlining the development of Mason ceramics in Staffordshire from the beginning of the 19th century.

Redfern's Cottage: Museum of Uttoxeter Life

34-36 Carter Street
Uttoxeter ST14 8EU
01889 576176
redfernscottage.org
laura.wiggbailey@btinternet.com

This 17th century timbered framed cottage is situated in the historic market town of Uttoxeter. It offers visitors the opportunity to learn more about the town within the setting of an historic house with a beautiful courtyard garden.

Rudyard Lake Steam Railway

Rudyard Station
Nr Leek ST13 8PF
01538 306704
www.rlsr.org
info@rlsr.org

The Rudyard Lake Steam Railway is just North of Leek in Staffordshire. The lake railway uses miniature narrow gauge steam locomotives on its trains to give a 3-mile return trip along the side of Rudyard Lake.

Samuel Johnson Birthplace Museum

Breadmarket Street
Lichfield WS13 6LG
01543 264972
www.samueljohnsonbirthplace.org.uk
sjmuseum@lichfield.gov.uk

The museum stands in the centre of the historic city of Lichfield, which remained close to Johnson's heart throughout his life. Best known for his Dictionary of the English Language, Johnson spent the first 27 years of his life in the large, imposing house which overlooks Market Square, frequently returning until shortly before his death in 1784.

Shire Hall Gallery

Market Square
Stafford ST16 2LD
01785 278345
www.staffordshire.gov.uk/has
shirehallgallery@staffordshire.gov.uk

The Shire Hall Gallery is the largest venue in Staffordshire dedicated to visual arts and crafts. Situated in a fascinating Grade II listed building (formerly used as the Crown Court) the Shire Hall Gallery offers visitors a mixture of old and new. Stafford's Shire building has had several forms - the present building in the Market Square was constructed in 1793. As well as a permanent crime and punishment display in Court One, the gallery has a regularly changing programme of temporary exhibitions which focus on contemporary visual art and craft.

Shugborough Estate - National Trust

Milford, nr Stafford
nr Stafford ST17 0XB
01889 881388
www.nationaltrust.org.uk/shugborough-estate
shugborough.promotions@staffordshire.gov.uk

Leave the 21st century behind and step into the real working environments of the complete working historic estate. Shugborough is a rare example of the survival of a complete estate, with all major buildings including mansion house, servants' quarters, model farm and walled garden See, feel, hear and smell history as our costumed 'first person' characters take you on a journey into the inner workings of a large country estate and bring real working environments to life.

Stafford Castle

Newport Road
Stafford ST16 2DJ
01785 257698
www.staffordbc.gov.uk

This prominent vantage point and strategic site was quickly recognised by the Normans, who built a huge timber fortress here by 1100 AD. Originally built by Robert de Toeni (later known as Robert of Stafford), in the Norman period, Stafford Castle has dominated the local skyline for over 900 years. The visitor centre brings Stafford Castle to life.

Staffordshire & Stoke on Trent Archive Service

Staffordshire Record Office, Eastgate Street
Stafford ST16 2LZ
01785 278379
www.staffordshire.gov.uk/archives
staffordshire.record.office@staffordshire.gov.uk

Burton:

Burton Family and Local History Centre, Burton Library, Riverside, High Street
Burton upon Trent DE14 1AH
01283 239556

Lichfield:

Lichfield Record Office, The Friary
Lichfield WS13 6QG
01543 510720

Stoke on Trent:

Stoke on Trent City Archives, City Central Library, Bethesda Street, Hanley
Stoke on Trent ST1 3RS
01782 238420

William Salt Library:

Eastgate Street
Stafford ST16 2LZ
01785 278372

Archives & Heritage comprises the Staffordshire & Stoke on Trent Archive Service and the County Museum Service. Together we care for the historic archives of Staffordshire and Stoke and the museum collection for the County of Staffordshire. Our Archives Service can help you to find out more about the history of your family or your local community. The William Salt Library collections represent an outstanding resource for the study of local and family history in Staffordshire and are available for consultation by the public in our reading rooms free of charge.

Staffordshire Arts & Museum Service

Shugborough Estate, Milford
Stafford ST17 0XB
01889 881 388
www.staffordshire.gov.uk/sams

Staffordshire Arts and Museum Services is made up of The Shire Hall Gallery in Stafford and the County Museum housed at Shugborough Hall just outside Stafford centre. The Shire Hall Gallery is a contemporary art Gallery showing temporary exhibitions. The County Museum houses collections connected to Staffordshire.

Staffordshire County Museum

Staffordshire Arts and Museum Service, Shugborough
Milford ST17 0XB
01889 881388
http://goo.gl/Yb8z5G

Housed in the Servants' Quarters at the Shugborough Estate, the County Museum features the restored Victorian kitchen, laundry and brewhouse, as well as galleries and temporary exhibitions illustrating Staffordshire life over the past 200 years.

Staffordshire Regiment Museum

Whittington Barracks
Lichfield WS14 9PY
01543 434394
www.staffordshireregimentmuseum.com
curator@staffordshireregimentmuseum.com

Situated on the A51 between Lichfield and Tamworth, next to Whittington Barracks, the museum tells the story of the present day Staffordshire Battalion of the Mercian Regiment and its predecessors from 1705. There are frequent special exhibitions and events in the museum and/or its extensive grounds.

Tamworth Castle

The Holloway, Ladybank
Tamworth B79 7NA
01827 709626
www.tamworthcastle.co.uk
heritage@tamworth.gov.uk

A visit to Tamworth Castle takes you back in time and offers a perfect blend of fascinating history, regular live entertainment events and a stunningly complete building. As you explore the castle you can see for yourself the maze of intact rooms, halls and chambers that still echo with events from Saxon beginnings, Norman dynasties, Tudor grandeur and great family influences.

Tutbury Castle

Castle St Tutbury
Burton Upon Trent DE13 9JF
01283 812129
www.tutburycastle.com
info@tutburycastle.com

Situated in the heart of England, Tutbury Castle sits on wooded slopes overlooking the winding River Dove, with spectacular views across the plain of the Dove to the beautiful Derbyshire hills. Its commanding view and natural defensive position makes this an obvious site for a castle. Now the castle is host to a variety of events from theatre to ghost hunts.

Wall Roman Site

Watling Street
Nr Lichfield WS14 0AW
0870 333 1181
http://goo.gl/pTi3Vy

Wall was an important staging post on Watling Street, the Roman military road to North Wales. It provided overnight accommodation for travelling Roman officials and imperial messengers.

Wedgwood Museum & Visitor Centre

Wedgwood Drive, Barlaston
Stoke on Trent ST12 9ER
01782 371900
www.wedgwoodmuseum.org.uk
bookings@wedgwoodmuseum.org.uk

The Wedgwood Museum contains the world's greatest collection of Wedgwood ceramics, ranging from a unique collection of Josiah Wedgwood's original trials for the perfection of Queen's Ware, later delivered in the form of a 900+ piece dinner service to Catherine the Great of Russia in 1774, to a rare 5 foot high Exhibition Vase, decorated by Emile Lessore, the only one of its kind in Britain.

Suffolk

Suffolk, maritime county in E. of England, bounded N. by Norfolk, from which it is separated by the Waveney and Little Ouse, E. by the North Sea, S. by Essex, from which it is separated by the Stour, and W. by Cambridgeshire, from which it is separated by the Lark; area, 944,060 acres, population 356,893. The coast line (of about 50 miles), broken by the estuaries of the Stour, Orwell, Deben, and Aide, is generally low, and the sea has made great encroachments, particularly in the neighbourhood of Dunwich and Aldeburgh. The surface is generally level, and the soil is very varied - occasional fen, loam on the borders of the rivers, sand on the eastern and western borders, and clay in the centre. This last is fertile, and large crops are grown of wheat, barley, pease, and beans, the barley in particular being in high repute with brewers. Butter is extensively made for the London markets. Sheep are reared in the NW., which is hilly; and the Suffolk cart-horse, esteemed for its power of draught, is raised in considerable numbers. The manufactures – principally agricultural implements and artificial manure – are limited. Fine sea-salt is made on the coast. The trade of the seaports is chiefly in corn and malt. The herring and mackerel fisheries are extensively prosecuted at Lowestoft and other places, and oysters are found in the Orwell and Orford. Most of the towns have river communication, and the county is traversed in all directions by the railways of the Great Eastern system. It comprises 21 hundreds, 517 parishes, with parts of 7 others, the parliamentary and municipal boroughs of Bury St Edmunds and Ipswich, the municipal boroughs of Beccles, Eye, Lowestoft, and Southwold, and part of the municipal borough of Sudbury. It is mostly in the diocese of Norwich.

– John Bartholomew, *Gazetteer of the British Isles* (1887)

390th Bomb Group Memorial Air Museum & The British Resistance Organisation Museum

Parham Airfield, Parham
Framlingham IP13 9AF
01728 621373
www.parhamairfieldmuseum.co.uk

The 390th Bomb Group Memorial Air Museum is housed in an original wartime Control Tower. Associated Quonset (Nissen) Huts house The British Resistance Organisation Museum, Percy Kindred Library and tea room.

Collections: Exhibits include a unique and rare collection of recovered WWII aircraft engines, parts of allied and German aircraft, uniforms, documents, photographs and memorabilia relevant to the U.S. 8th Air Force, RAF and the German Luftwaffe of WWII.

Abbey Visitor Centre

Samson's Tower
Bury St Edmunds IP33 1RS
www.stedmundsbury.gov.uk

The extensive remains of the wealthiest and most powerful Benedictine monastery in England, and the shrine of St Edmund. They include the complete 14th century Great Gate and Norman Tower, and the impressive ruins and altered west front of the immense church.

Aldeburgh Museum, The Moot Hall

Aldeburgh
01728 454666
www.aldeburghmuseum.org.uk
enquiries@aldeburghmuseum.org.uk

16thC town hall which is a listed ancient building with a museum displaying items of local interest such as photographs and artefacts depicting life in Aldeburgh. The emphasis is on the fishing industry and the part played by the lifeboat and its crews.

Beccles & District Museum

Leman House, Ballygate
Beccles NR34 9ND
01502 715722
www.becclesmuseum.org.uk
museummanager@btconnect.com

Leman House was probably built about 1570 and was completely restored and modernised in the 1760s. Originally it was a timber frame structure, much of which disappeared when the brick facades were added.

Bentwaters Cold War Museum

Building 134, Bentwaters Parks
Rendlesham, Woodbridge IP12 2TW
07588 877020
www.bcwm.org.uk
info@bentwaters-as.org.uk

Museum is based in the United States Air Force (USAF) hardened command post on the former Bentwaters airbase which closed after the withdrawal of the USAF in 1993 and is believed to be the only such building open to the public in the UK and Europe. Visitors can experience the Cold War history with guides and talks about the operations of the base with detailed displays of the units stationed at both RAF Bentwaters and nearby RAF Woodbridge since WWII. Aircraft on display include English Electric Lightning, Hawker Hunter, BAC Jaguar, McDonnell Douglas Phantom & Harrier.

Brandon Heritage Centre

George Street
Brandon IP27 0BX
07882 891022
www.brandonheritagecentre.org

The Brandon Heritage Centre is a community-run independent museum with a permanent collection telling the story of Brandon from the Stone Age to the present day.

Bungay Museum

Council Offices, Broad Street
Bungay NR35 1EE
01986 892176
www.bungay-suffolk.co.uk/activities/museum.asp

Bungay Museum is situated in two small rooms of the Waveney District Council Office. It was established in 1963, and displays items relating to the heritage, society and businesses of the town.

Christchurch Mansion

, Soane Street
Ipswich IP4 2BE
01473 433554
www.cimuseums.org.uk
museums@colchester.gov.uk

This beautiful Tudor mansion is the jewel in the crown of Ipswich's historic past boasting over 500 years of history. Explore the period rooms from the Tudor kitchen to the sumptuous Georgian saloon and the beautifully detailed Victorian wing and much more. Gaze at the fine collection of art from Suffolk artists including the biggest collection of Thomas Gainsborough and John Constable paintings outside of London.

Clare Ancient House Museum

26 High Street, Clare
Sudbury CO10 8NY
01787 277572
www.clare-ancient-house-museum.co.uk
clareancienthouse@btinternet.com

Clare Ancient House is a Grade 1 Listed Building, dating in part to the 14th and, in part, the 15th century. It may have served as a shop, and has certainly been a bakery, a workhouse and a dwelling for the church sexton.

Clifford Road Air Raid Shelter Museum

Clifford Road Primary School, Clifford Road
Ipswich IP4 1PJ
01473 251605
www.cliffordroadshelter.org.uk
enquiries@cliffordroadshelter.org.uk

Hidden beneath a Suffolk school playground, among quiet residential streets, the shelter provides a vivid picture of life during World War Two. Hundreds of feet of substantial concrete tunnels were sealed up and forgotten in 1945. Thanks to their solid construction, they were in excellent condition when rediscovered over forty years later.

Dunwich Museum

St James' Street
Dunwich IP17 3EA
01728 648 796
www.dunwichmuseum.org.uk

Dunwich Museum is the perfect history experience for all the family. It tells the amazing story of a city lost to the sea through the narrative of its collection and the knowledge of its welcoming staff.

East Anglia Transport Museum

Chapel Road, Carlton Colville
Lowestoft NR33 8BL
01502 518 459
www.eatm.org.uk
eastangliatransportmuseum@live.co.uk

Here you can see a unique project; the creation of a museum of street transport designed to show the development of mechanical transport over the best part of a century. The essence of transport is movement, so we are building a living museum where vehicles of yesteryear can be seen in action, where half-forgotten sounds of the past are brought back to life and where visitors can journey back in time by travelling on a few of the exhibits along the museum's streets.

East of England Military Museum

Littleheath, Barnham
Thetford IP24 2SY
01842 890600
www.militarymuseumweb.org.uk

The museum is on the area where the very first 75 tank crews trained in World War I. We have a full size replica WWI tank on display.

Felixstowe Museum

Viewpoint, Landguard Point
Felixstowe IP11 7JG
01394 674355
www.felixstowe-museum.co.uk

Felixstowe Museum houses 14 galleries displaying the military and social history of this popular seaside resort. Even the building is of historical interest as it was once a submarine mining establishment. Felixstowe Museum is managed by our team of friendly, dynamic volunteers who are always happy to help.

Framlingham Castle - English Heritage

Framlingham IP13 9BP
01728 724189
http://goo.gl/aPDZFh

Framlingham is a magnificent example of a late 12th-century castle. Built by Roger Bigod, Earl of Norfolk, the castle, together with Framlingham Mere, was designed both as a stronghold and as a symbol of power and status - as befitted one of the most influential people at the court of the Plantagenet kings.

Gainsborough's House

46 Gainsborough Street
Sudbury CO10 2EU
01787 372958
www.gainsborough.org

Gainsborough's House is the birthplace museum of Thomas Gainsborough (1727-1788), one of the greatest artists in the history of British art. Gainsborough's House has the largest collection of his work on display at any one time in Britain. The house itself dates from around 1500 and retains many interesting architectural features.

Halesworth & District Museum

The Railway Station
Halesworth IP19 8BZ
01986 873030
halesworthmuseum.org.uk/wpress
office@halesworthmuseum.org.uk

This museum run by volunteers is in the railway station and is packed with displays, useful information about local families and local history and award winning archaeology and geology displays.

Haverhill & District Local History Centre

Town Hall Arts Centre, High Street
Haverhill CB9 8AR
01440 7149962
http://goo.gl/HtLa4d

Haverhill Local History Centre is a resource and study centre for Haverhill and surrounding villages. Haverhill has a long history; it is mentioned in the Domesday Book of 1086, and there have been archaelogical finds in the area dating from the Stone and Bronze ages. The town prospered during Victorian times with steam powered looms at the Gurteen factory and the coming of the railway.

Ickworth - National Trust

The Rotunda, Horringer
Bury St Edmunds IP29 5QE
01284 735270
www.nationaltrust.org.uk/ickworth
ickworth@nationaltrust.org.uk

Explore acres of space, woodland, wildlife, and a stunning architectural oddity, all with a story to match. See how one eccentric man's passion for art, Italy and for having a party led to the creation of this remarkable house and its renowned collection of paintings, portraits, furniture and other treasures. Through our Ickworth Lives project, learn about the servants and workers who kept this country estate running and share their memories.

Ipswich Museum

High Street
Ipswich IP1 3QH
01473 433550
www.cimuseums.org.uk
museums@colchester.gov.uk

This fascinating and unique museum gives you the opportunity to meet the famous woolly mammoth, the elegant towering giraffe and other wonderful curiosities from the natural world.

Ipswich Transport Museum

Old Trolleybus Depot, Cobham Road
Ipswich IP3 9JD
01473 715666
www.ipswichtransportmuseum.co.uk

The Ipswich Transport Museum has the largest collection of transport items in Britain devoted to just one town. Everything was either made or used in and around Ipswich, the county town of Suffolk.

Kentwell Hall

Long Melford
Sudbury CO10 9BA
01787 310207
www.kentwell.co.uk
enquiries@kentwell.co.uk

Kentwell Hall is a beautiful redbrick moated Tudor Manor House close to the historic village of Long Melford. Whilst not a stately home, this 'little great house' remains a lived-in and much-loved family home.

Lanman Museum

Framlingham Castle
Framlingham, Woodbridge IP13 9BP
01728 724189
www.thelanmanmuseum.onesuffolk.net/Lanman-Museum

Housed within Framlingham Castle, the collection is based round that of the late Harold Lanman. It includes artefacts relating to all aspects of daily life in the town over many centuries.

Lavenham Guildhall - National Trust

Market Place
Lavenham CO10 9QZ
01787 247646
www.nationaltrust.org.uk/lavenham-guildhall
lavenhamguildhall@nationaltrust.org.uk

Lavenham was once one of the wealthiest places in the country. Its famous blue cloth was exported across Europe and beyond. The village today is famed for its wealth of surviving timber-framed buildings, which make it one of the best-preserved medieval villages in England.

Laxfield & District Museum

The Guildhall, High Street, Laxfield
Woodbridge IP13 8DU
01986 798026
www.laxfieldmuseum.onesuffolk.net

The museum's collection includes early 20th century shop interiors together with window displays, artefacts, costumes; information on domestic life of the same period and the Mid Suffolk Light Railway, which terminated in Laxfield; farming and rural life in Suffolk; local 'field finds', including fossils; special exhibitions changed annually and displayed in the Marchant Room.

Little Hall Lavenham

[icons]

Little Hall, Market Place
Lavenham CO10 9QZ
01787 247 179
www.littlehall.org.uk
info@littlehall.org.uk

Step inside Little Hall, one of the oldest timberframed buildings in the best preserved of the Suffolk wool towns. Its history mirrors the changing fortunes of Lavenham. Built in the 1390s for the Causton family of clothiers, enlarged and improved in 1425-50, it was then 'modernised' in Tudor times by the addition of a fireplace and upper floor in the hall.

Long Shop Museum

[icons]

Main Street
Lieston IP16 4ES
01728 832189
www.longshopmuseum.co.uk

In the museum you will find a staggering collection of objects, ranging from full-size steam engines (the Richard Garrett & Sons engineering business made many hundreds of steam engines here) to touching mementoes of the lives of the working people of the town. The Long Shop itself – at the heart of the museum – is a Grade II* listed engineering workshop, thought to be one of the earliest purpose-built production lines in existence (made long before Henry Ford had the same idea.), and it's chock-full of fascinating exhibits.

Lowestoft Maritime Museum

[icons]

Whapload Road
Lowestoft NR32 1XG
01502 561963
www.lowestoftmaritimemuseum.org.uk
admin@lowestoftmaritimemuseum.org.uk

Lowestoft Maritime Museum is housed in a pretty flint cottage that sits between the North Sea and Lowestoft's Sparrow's Nest Park. The museum offers visitors an extensive series of displays, with many hands-on activities including lots for children and a small cinema where you can see wonderful archive film footage. If you haven't visited for a while, you'll be surprised to see how much there is.

Lowestoft Museum

[icons]

Broad House, Nicholas Everitt Park, Oulton Broad
Lowestoft NR33 9JR
01502 511457
www.lowestoftmuseum.org
info@lowestoftmuseum.org

Lowestoft Museum houses a collection of objects relating to the history of the area and its people, inside a grade 2 listed building situated within the grounds of Nicholas Everitt Park.

Mechanical Music Museum & Bygones

[icons]

Blacksmith Road, Cotton
Nr Stowmarket IP14 1QN
01449 613876
http://goo.gl/4bvvzF

Come visit a magical world where music was made not with computers or digital information but by mechanical movement. Our collection is literally an 'Aladdin's Cave' of musical items and memorabilia.

Melford Hall - National Trust

[icons]

Long Melford
Sudbury CO10 9AA
01787 379228
www.nationaltrust.org.uk/melford-hall
melford@nationaltrust.org.uk

Set in the unspoilt village of Long Melford, the house has changed little externally since 1578 when Queen Elizabeth I was entertained here, and retains its original panelled banqueting hall. It has been the home of the Hyde Parker family since 1786. There are a Regency library, Victorian bedrooms, good collections of furniture and porcelain and a small display of items connected with Beatrix Potter, who was related to the family.

Mid-Suffolk Light Railway Museum

[icons]

Wetheringsett IP14 5PW
01449 766899
www.mslr.org.uk
chairman@mslr.org.uk

Railway museum with demonstration running line, restored Middy buildings (corrugated iron cladding), appropriate rolling stock (all carriages are Victorian), extensive archive of photographs with some documents and artefacts. Event days usually themed around aspect of the railway's life and history.

Mildenhall & District Museum

[icons]

6 King Street, Mildenhall
Bury St Edmonds IP28 7ES
01638 716970
www.mildenhallmuseum.co.uk

Perhaps our building looks just a little austere and foreboding, but it holds a wealth of antiquities and other riches from Mildenhall and surrounding areas. In pride of place is the 4th century Roman hoard known as the Mildenhall Treasure. The museum provides excellent resources for the study of history, both recent and ancient, for the schools in our area.

Moyse's Hall Museum

Cornhill
Bury St Edmunds IP33 1DX
01284 757160
www.moyseshall.org
moyses.hall@stedsbc.gov.uk

Collections of local and social history alongside horology fine art and costumes housed in a rare example of 12th century Norman domestic architecture. Includes objects associated with the notorious Red Barn Murder. Also houses the Suffolk Regiment Gallery.

Museum of East Anglian Life

Iliffe Way
Stowmarket IP14 1DL
01449 612229
www.eastanglianlife.org.uk
enquiries@eastanglianlife.org.uk

The museum of East Anglian Life sits in over 70 acres of beautiful Suffolk countryside. The museum features historic buildings, farm animals, a nature walk and over 40,000 objects in its collection.

Norfolk & Suffolk Aviation Museum

Buckaroo Way, The Street, Flixton
Bungay NR35 1NZ
01986 896644
www.aviationmuseum.net
nsam.flixton@virgin.net

East Anglia's Aviation Heritage Centre, incorporating the museums of 446th Bombardment Group, RAF Bomber Command, Royal Observer Corps, No. 6 Group, Air Sea Rescue & Coastal Command.

Orford Castle - English Heritage

Orford
Woodbridge IP12 2ND
01394 450472
http://goo.gl/QD8a1y

The unique polygonal towerkeep of Orford Castle stands beside the pretty town and former port which Henry II also developed here in the 1160s. His aim was to counterbalance the power of turbulent East Anglian barons like Hugh Bigod of Framlingham, and to guard the coast against foreign mercenaries called to their aid. An 18-sided drum with three square turrets, and a forebuilding reinforcing its entrance, the keep was built to a highly innovative design.

Orford Museum

Orford Castle
Orford IP12 2ND
www.orfordmuseum.org.uk
mail@orfordmuseum.org.uk

Situated within Orford Castle, the museum includes some of the Orford Borough Regalia as well as archaeological finds from the surrounding area. These include rare coins, brooches and pottery dating from Roman and Anglo-Saxon times.

Ridgewell Airfield Commemorative Museum

c/o White Wings, Ashen Road, Ovington
Sudbury CO10 8JX
01787 277310
www.381st.com
jim.tennet@btinternet.com

We are a small, private collection of World War II memorabilia displayed in and around the old hospital buildings behind the U.S. 381st Bomb Group memorial. The site is dedicated to the brave men of the USAAF.

Rougham Tower Association

The Control Tower, Rougham Industrial Estate
Bury St Edmunds IP30 9XA
01359 271471
www.rougham.org
tower@rougham.org

Rougham Airfield is situated a couple of miles east of Bury St Edmunds, UK and was home to the USAAF 322nd and 94th Bomb Groups during the Second World War. This airfield is one of the few wartime bases to retain its control tower into current times.

Royal Naval Patrol Service Museum

RNPS Association, Sparrow's Nest Gardens, Whapload Road
Lowestoft NR32 1XG
01502 586250
www.rnps.lowestoft.org.uk/museum.html
rnps@lowestoft.org.uk

Thirty years after the end of World War 2 a handful of ex-members of the Royal Naval Patrol Service got together to form an Association to link not only those who had passed through HMS Europa, the stone frigate based at Sparrow's Nest Gardens, Lowestoft during the WW2 but also the widows of those who made the supreme sacrifice. The National Office and Museum are situated in Sparrow's Nest and a most attractive display of relics and memorablilia has been gathered together by members of the association who devote a great deal of their spare time in making this a unique and brightly-decorated meeting place.

Saxtead Green Post Mill - English Heritage

The Mill House, Saxtead Green, Saxtead
Woodbridge IP13 9QQ
01728 685789
http://goo.gl/UeMgqs

Saxtead Green Post Mill is perfect for those looking for a day out with a difference. Though milling ceased in 1947, it is still in working order. Climb the stairs to various floors, which are full of fascinating mill machinery.

Somerleyton Hall & Gardens

Somerleyton Hall
Lowestoft NR32 5QQ
01502 734901
www.somerleyton.co.uk

The grounds of Somerleyton Hall have been home to high status buildings since the post conquest Norman era. In 1240 the existing manorial Hall was rebuilt by Sir Peter Fitzosbert as a magnificent country house on the site of the original medieval Hall. Four centuries later the house was further enlarged and restyled by John Wentworth and transformed into an archetypal East Anglian Tudor-Jacobean mansion. The Hall's final and most drastic alteration took place in 1843 under new ownership of a wealthy Victorian entrepreneur Samuel Morton Peto who hired John Thomas, Prince Albert's favourite architect, to carry out extensive rebuilding.

Southwold Museum

9-11 Victoria Street
Southwold IP18 6HZ
01502 722 437
www.southwoldmuseum.org
southwold.museum@virgin.net

Southwold's unique cottage museum is dedicated to the local and natural history of this corner of Suffolk. Owned and managed by the Southwold Historical Society, this tiny building houses an astonishing collection of objects, paintings, photographs, models and wildlife exhibits.

St Edmundsbury Cathedral

Abbey House, Angel Hill
Bury St Edmunds IP33 1LS
01284 748720
www.stedscathedral.co.uk
cathedral@stedscathedral.co.uk

Welcome to St Edmundsbury Cathedral, the Mother Church of the Anglican Diocese of St Edmundsbury and Ipswich. For over 1,000 years the site of Suffolk 's Cathedral has been one of worship and pilgrimage. Established as a Benedictine foundation in 1020 by King Canute, the Abbey at Bury St Edmunds housed the body of Edmund, King of the East Angles, who was martyred in 869.

St Peter's by the Waterfront

St Peter's Church, College Street
Ipswich IP1 1XF
01473 225269
www.stpetersbythewaterfront.com
manager@stpetersbythewaterfront.com

St Peter's by the Waterfront is a heritage centre in one of the former mariner churches on the historic waterfront of Ipswich. The church is important in the history of Ipswich, and was once the chapel to the short lived Cardinal College set up by Cardinal Thomas Wolsey in the 16th century with major renovations taking place at this time and in the Victorian era. All that remains of the college is St Peter's and the 'Wolsey Gate", a water gate situated on the South perimeter wall of the church. The centre hosts historic artefacts from the Church's history and the locally commissioned Ipswich Charter hangings.

Suffolk Family History Society

2 Flash Corner, Theberton
Leiston IP16 4RW
www.suffolkfhs.org.uk
admin@suffolkfhs.org.uk

Founded at Lowestoft in 1975, we are a group of keen amateur genealogists whose objectives are to promote and encourage the study of family history, genealogy, heraldry and local history with particular reference to Suffolk; and to promote the preservation, security and accessibility of archive material.

Suffolk Punch Heavy Horse Museum

The Market Hill
Woodbridge IP12 4LU
01394 380643
www.suffolkhorsesociety.org.uk
sec@suffolkhorsesociety.org.uk

The Suffolk Punch Heavy Horse Museum is an exhibition devoted to the Suffolk Horse, more usually known as the Suffolk Punch breed of heavy working horse. The museum displays the history of the breed and its Society, the work of the blacksmith and the harness maker, the world of shows and showing, the work the horses did and the life of the horsemen.

Suffolk Record Office

www.suffolk.gov.uk/sro

Bury St Edmunds:

Suffolk Record Office, 77 Raingate Street
Bury St Edmunds IP33 2AR
01284 741212

Ipswich:

Suffolk Record Office, Gatacre Road

Ipswich IP1 2LQ
01473 263909
Lowestoft:
Suffolk Record Office, Clapham Road
Lowestoft NR32 1DR
01502 674680

Based in Bury St Edmunds, Ipswich and Lowestoft, the Suffolk Record Office holds an amazing range of information about the history of Suffolk and its people.

Suffolk Regiment Museum, The

The Keep, Gibraltar Barracks, Newmarket Road
Bury St Edmunds IP33 3RN
01284 752394
www.suffolkregiment.org/museum.html
suffolkregiment@taffmail.demon.co.uk

The Suffolk Regiment Museum was established, in the Officers Mess, for the 250th Anniversary of the regiment in 1935. The first acquisitions were items which belonged to even older collections of badges, medals and uniform items which had been displayed in the Mess since before The Great War.

Sutton Hoo - National Trust

Tranmer House
Sutton Hoo IP12 3DJ
01394 389700
www.nationaltrust.org.uk/sutton-hoo
richard.phillips@nationaltrust.org.uk

This hauntingly beautiful 255 acre estate, with far-reaching views over the river Deben, is home to one of the greatest archaeological discoveries of all time. Walk around the ancient burial mounds and discover the incredible story of the ship burial of an Anglo-Saxon king and his treasured possessions. Come face to face with your ancestors and explore our award-winning exhibition, the full-size reconstruction of the burial chamber, stunning replica treasures and original finds from one of the mounds, including a prince's sword. Look inside the Edwardian house or enjoy the beautiful seasonal colours on our estate walks.

Theatre Royal Bury St Edmunds - National Trust

6 Westgate street
Bury St Edmunds IP33 1QR
01284 769505
www.nationaltrust.org.uk/theatre-royal
booking@theatreroyal.org

The Theatre Royal is the last working Regency playhouse in Britain. Owned by Greene King brewery, it has been in the care of the National Trust since 1975 and is run by an independent theatre company.

Unseen Archive: 50 Years of Suffolk Life in Photographs, The

c/o The Unseen Archive, Press House, 30 Lower Brook Street
Ipswich IP4 1AN
01473 324874
services.eadt.co.uk/suffolk/content/unseenarchive

A photographic resource covering the last 50 years of Suffolk life. The Unseen Archive aims to be a valuable and accessible educational and heritage resource for all.

West Stow Anglo-Saxon Village

Icklingham Road
West Stow, Bury St Edmunds IP28 6HG
01284 728718
www.weststow.org
weststow@stedsbc.gov.uk

West Stow is the site of an Anglo-Saxon settlement occupied 420 – 650AD. Today there is a unique reconstructed Anglo-Saxon Village built on the original settlement site, giving visitors the opportunity to touch and experience Anglo-Saxon houses as we imagine them to have been.

Woodbridge Museum

5A, Market Hill
Woodbridge IP12 4LP
01394 380502
http://goo.gl/07tNE3

There is a permanent exhibit complementing the Anglo-Saxon site at Sutton Hoo and another for Burrow Hill. Displays reflect the history and life of Woodbridge and its townspeople - including the Elizabethan lawyer and benefactor Thomas Seckford, the painter Thomas Churchyard and the translator Edward FitzGerald.

Woolpit & District Museum

The Institute, The Street
Woolpit IP30 9RF
01359 240822
www.woolpit.org/museum

The museum first opened in 1985 and is run by volunteers. Woolpit Museum is said to be the smallest in Suffolk.

Surrey

Surrey, county in SE. of England, bounded N. by the Thames, which separates it from Bucks and Middlesex, E. by Kent, S. by Sussex, W. by Hants, and NW. by Berks; greatest length, N. and S., 26 miles; greatest breadth, E. and W., 40 miles; area, 485,129 acres, population 1,436,899. The county is traversed from E. to W. by the North Downs range, from which the surface slopes gently down towards the Thames on the N., while on the S. it descends into an extensive flat plain (partly also in the counties of Kent and Sussex) called the Weald. Except a small portion in the SW., and another small portion in the SE., the whole of the county is drained by the Thames and its tributaries, the Wey, Mole, and Wandle. There are many varieties of soil, including plastic and alluvial clays, rich vegetable loam, calcareous earth, and almost barren heath. On the plastic clays the crops are wheat and beans; the alluvial soils, particularly in the vicinity of the metropolis, are chiefly occupied by orchards, market gardens, and farms for the culture of medical and aromatic plants; on the loamy soils the crops are barley, oats, and pease, carrots and parsnips; while the chief products of the calcareous soils are hops and clover. There are some industries in oil, paper, calicoes, woollen goods, &c., and those places situated on the Thames share in the trade of the port of London, but (except in that part of the county included within the limits of the metropolis) the trade and manufactures are not of great importance. The amenities of climate and scenery, the vicinity of the metropolis, and the complete means of railway communication, have caused many parts of Surrey to be studded over with mansions and villas. The county contains 14 hundreds, 152 parishes with parts of 2 others, the parliamentary and municipal borough of Croydon, the parliamentary boroughs of Battersea and Clapham, Camberwell, Lambeth, Newington, Southwark, and Wandsworth; and the municipal boroughs of Godalming, Guildford, Kingston upon Thames, and Reigate. The county is in the dioceses of Canterbury, Rochester, and Winchester.

– John Bartholomew, *Gazetteer of the British Isles* (1887)

Note: The London boroughs of Lambeth, Southwark, Wandsworth, and parts of Lewisham and Bromley were in Surrey until 1889. The boroughs of Croydon, Kingston upon Thames, Merton, Sutton and Richmond upon Thames south of the River Thames were part of Surrey until 1965.

Archaeology Centre - Surrey Heath Archaeology & Heritage Trust

Surrey Heath Archaeology and Heritage Trust, 4-10 London Road
Bagshot GU19 5HN
07870 447810
www.shaht.co.uk
shaht.bagshot@gmail.com

We hold extensive collections of borderware pottery, clay pipes and coins. All the collections are available for viewing at the centre.

Ash Museum

Cemetery Chapel, Ash Cemetery, Ash Church Road
Ash GU12 6LX
01252 542341
bit.ly/ashmuseum
ash.museum@ntlworld.com

Local history museum for Ash, Ash Vale, Ash Green and Tongham.

Basingstoke Canal Visitors Centre

Mychett Place Road
Mychett GU16 6DD
01252 370073
http://goo.gl/RGjb2w
info@basingstoke-canal.co.uk

The Basingstoke Canal is declared by many to be Britain's most beautiful waterway. From the rolling North Hampshire hills to the dramatic flights of locks in Surrey, the tree-lined canal offers a variety of delights.

Bourne Hall Museum

Spring Street, Ewell
Epsom KT17 1UF
020 83941734
http://goo.gl/DyRe4L
Bournehall@epsom-ewell.gov.uk

Discover the fascinating past of Epsom & Ewell at Bourne Hall Museum. Based in the futuristic building of Bourne Hall, our free museum allows you to come face to face with the local past. With exhibits ranging from prehistoric times to the modern day, our permanent displays and regular exhibitions illustrate every aspect of local life and have something to interest all members of the family. The museum charts the borough's history through its collections of document and picture archives, fine art, costume, archaeology and social history. Highlights of our collection include Lord Rosebery's hansom cab, a 19th-century fire engine, extensive Derby memorabilia and significant Roman archaeology from local sites.

Brooklands Museum

Brooklands Museum Trust Limited, Brooklands Road
Weybridge KT13 0QN
01932 857381
www.brooklandsmuseum.com
info@brooklandsmuseum.com

Brooklands was the first purpose-built motor racing circuit in the world in 1907. It was also one of the most prolific aircraft production sites in Europe, with over 18,500 aircraft built or assembled at Brooklands by companies such as Vickers, Hawker, BAC and British Aerospace.

Collections: The 30 acre Museum site displays a wide range of Brooklands- related motoring and aviation exhibits reflecting many great engineering and technological acievements throughout the 20th century. These range from the 1933, 24-litre Napier-Railton racing car to a Wellington Bomber recovered from Loch Ness; a unique collection of Vickers/BAC-built aircraft and the only Concorde publically accessible in the South East.

Caterham & District Local History Centre

Caterham Valley Library, Stafford Road
Caterham CR3 6JG
01883 - 343580
www.surreycc.gov.uk/northtandridgelocalhistory
caterhamvalley.library@surreycc.gov.uk

Local history archive for the communities of Caterham, Chaldon, Chelsham, Farleigh, Warlingham, Woldingham, Whyteleafe, Tatsfield and Titsey. A collaboration between Surrey East Area Libraries, Surrey History Service, Tandridge District council, The Bourne Society, The East Surrey Family History Society, Parish Councils and local schools.

Collections: The centre holds printed publications, historic maps and prints of the area and a photographic collection, part of which has been digitised at www.exploringsurreyspast.org.uk.

Chertsey Museum

The Cedars, 33 Windsor Street
Chertsey KT16 8AT
01932 565764
www.chertseymuseum.org
enquiries@chertseymuseum.org.uk

We have fine collections, including history of the Runnymede area, local archaeology and history of Chertsey Abbey, fine art, decorative art, social history including many documents and photographs, local clocks and the nationally significant Olive Matthews Collection of dress and textiles.

Chobham Museum

Benhams Corner, Bagshot Road
Chobham GU24 8BP
01276 858322
www.chobham.org/museum
david@callnetuk.com

A small museum situated in a pretty Surrey village. SLocal items. Photographic catalogue of more than 200 old photographs of Chobham.

Clandon Park - National Trust

Clandon
Guildford GU4 7RQ
01483 222482
www.nationaltrust.org.uk/clandon-park
clandonpark@nationaltrust.org.uk

Grand 18th-century Palladian mansion: * Two-storey White Marble Hall * Superb collection of Chinese, Meissen and Sèvres Porcelain * Home to the Queens' Royal Surrey Regiment Museum.

Crafts Study Centre

University for the Creative Arts, Falkner Road
Farnham GU9 7DS
01252 891450
www.csc.ucreative.ac.uk
craftscentre@ucreative.ac.uk

The Crafts Study Centre, established in 1970, has an international standing as a unique archive and collection of 20th century British crafts.

Collections: The Crafts Study Centre's collection embraces ceramics, textiles, calligraphy and wood, accompanied by reference books.

Dorking Museum & Heritage Centre

The Old Foundry, 62 West Street
Dorking RH4 1BS
01306 876591
www.dorkingmuseum.org.uk
admin@dorkingmuseum.org.uk

Dorking Museum aims to preserve and present the heritage of Dorking and its surrounding villages and countryside by collecting, conserving, interpreting and displaying items of historic interest, and to provide facilities for study and research.

East Surrey Family History Society

10 Cobham Close
Wallington SM6 9DS
020 8642 6789
www.eastsurreyfhs.org.uk
secretary01@eastsurreyfhs.org.uk

The East Surrey Family History Society for parishes in the Eastern part of the ancient County of Surrey. This includes those London Boroughs south of the River Thames which are now in Greater London but which were originally Surrey.

East Surrey Museum

1 Stafford Road
Caterham CR3 6JG
01883 340275
www.eastsurreymuseum.org.uk
es@emuseum.freeserve.co.uk

The museum is situated on the ground floor of a flint and brick house, built about the turn of the 19th century. A local history museum with geological and archaeological displays, crafts, artefacts and other changing exhibitions. The permanent East Surrey Room charts the history of East Surrey from earliest times. The junior room has a permanent World War Two display along with handling artefacts, toys from the past and some changing displays.

Egham Museum

Literary Institute, High Street
Egham TW20 9EW
01483 543599
www.eghammuseum.org
libraries@surreycc.gov.uk

Egham Museum is an independent, community museum serving the communities of Egham, Egham Hythe, Thorpe, Englefield Green and Virginia Water.

Elmbridge Museum

Elmbridge Borough Council, Civic Centre, Esher, KT10 9SD
Esher KT10 9SD
01932 843573
www.elmbridgemuseum.org.uk
ebcmuseum@elmbridge.gov.uk

The museum displays absorbing pop-up exhibitions around the borough, illustrating the histories and mysteries of the area - a must for anyone seeking to understand what makes Elmbridge the Borough it is today.

Farnham Castle Keep - English Heritage

Farnham GU9 0AG
01252 713393
www.english-heritage.org.uk/server/show/nav.15093

The impressive motte and shell keep of a castle founded in 1138 by Bishop Henry of Blois. Long a residence of the wealthy bishops of Winchester, the accommodation in the keep was updated in the 1520s.

Gatwick Aviation Museum

Vallance By Ways, Lowfield Heath Road
Charlwood, Nr. Gatwick Airport RH6 0BT
01293 862915
www.gatwick-aviation-museum.co.uk
gpvgat@aol.com

This aviation museum has a unique collection of British Aircraft from the 'golden age' of British aircraft manufacture. From the end of WWII until the 1970s British aircraft designers produced some of the most innovative and advanced aircraft of the day.

Godalming Museum

109A High Street
Godalming GU7 1AQ
01483 426510
www.waverley.gov.uk/godalmingmuseum
godalming.museum@waverley.gov.uk

At Godalming you will find a friendly, welcoming museum in a listed medieval building dated to 1446. You can follow a trail to discover how the museum looked in medieval times and how it has changed over six centuries.

Guildford Castle

Castle Street
Guildford GU1 3SX
www.guildford.gov.uk/castle

The Great Tower is now open after extensive renovation, including new floors and a roof which has made the building more accessible to visitors. The Tower contains a model of the original castle circa 1300, and interpretation panels tracing its history to the present day.

Guildford Cathedral

Stag Hill
Guildford GU2 7UP
01483 547860
www.guildford-cathedral.org
reception@guildford-cathedral.org

Guildford Cathedral is the mother church of the Diocese of

Guildford, covering 500 square miles of Surrey, north east Hampshire, the London Borough of Kingston and a part of West Sussex. With a seating capacity of 1000, the cathedral provides both focus and resource for the whole community, a venue for concerts, art and education, a place of pilgrimage, as well as stillness, prayer and daily choral worship.

Guildford Museum

Castle Arch
Guildford GU1 3SX
01483 444751
www.guildford.gov.uk/museum
heritageservices@guildford.gov.uk

The museum was founded in 1898 and now houses the largest collection of archaeology, local history and needlework in Surrey.

Hampton Court Palace

Hampton Court
East Molesey KT8 9AU
0844 482 7777
www.hrp.org.uk/HamptonCourtPalace
hamptoncourt@hrp.org.uk

Hampton Court Palace was home to some of England's most famous kings and queens from Henry VIII (1509-47), its first royal resident, to George II (1727-60), its last. With 500 years worth of history to explore, Hampton Court Palace has been divided into a series of historical routes which help to explain how the palace was used when it was occupied by the monarch.

Haslemere Educational Museum

78 High Street
Haslemere GU27 2LA
01428 642112
www.haslemeremuseum.co.uk
enquiries@haslemeremuseum.co.uk

Haslemere Educational Museum is one of the largest natural history museums in central southern England with over 240,000 specimens, along with over 140,000 Human History artefacts from around the world. There are three large permanent galleries for geology, natural history and human history artefacts.

Hatchlands Park - National Trust

East Clandon
Guildford GU4 7RT
01483 222482
www.nationaltrust.org.uk/hatchlands-park
hatchlands@nationaltrust.org.uk

18th-century mansion with Adam interiors and collection of keyboard instruments, set in parkland.

Hearsum Collection

Pembroke Lodge, Richmond Park
Richmond TW10 5HX
www.hearsumcollection.org.uk
info@hearsumcollection.org.uk

Our charity collects and preserves the unique heritage of Richmond Park, the largest of London's Royal Parks, for all to enjoy. We have a diverse range of heritage material covering the last four centuries, with some 2,500 items including antique prints, paintings, maps, postcards, photographs, documents, books and press cuttings.

Homewood, The - National Trust

Portsmouth Road
Esher KT10 9JL
01372 476424
www.nationaltrust.org.uk/homewood
thehomewood@nationaltrust.org.uk

20th-century Modernist house and garden. The house and landscape garden, designed by architect Patrick Gwynne, reflect the style and ethos of the Modern Movement.

Leatherhead Museum of Local History

Hampton Cottage, 64 Church Street
Leatherhead KT22 8DP
01372 386348
http://goo.gl/uUQpGD

The Leatherhead Museum of Local History is in Hampton Cottage, a timbered 17th century house. It is the Leatherhead & District Local History Society's HQ as well as its showcase for many items of local interest.

Leith Hill - National Trust

Leith Hill
Dorking RH5 6LY
01306 712711
www.nationaltrust.org.uk/leith-hill
leithhill@nationaltrust.org.uk

Woodland and open heath with Leith Hill Tower commanding extensive views. The highest point in south-east England, the hill is crowned by an 18th-century Gothic tower, with panoramic views northwards to London and the English Channel to the south.

Lightbox, The

Chobham Road
Woking GU21 4AA
01483 737800
www.thelightbox.org.uk
info@thelightbox.org.uk

The Lightbox is the award winning gallery and museum in Woking, Surrey, where there is something for everyone. Whether you're passionate about the arts and history, want activities and fun, or would just like somewhere quiet to relax and think, you'll find it all at The Lightbox.

Merton Heritage & Local Studies Centre

2nd floor, Morden Library, Merton Civic Centre, London Rd, Morden, Surrey
Morden SM4 5DX
020 8545 3239
www.merton.gov.uk/localstudies
local.studies@merton.gov.uk

Merton Heritage & Local Studies Centre tells the story of Merton and its people through a changing programme of exhibitions and events. The centre also provides access to a wide range of local history resources from maps and photographs, to period newspapers, the census and a large collection of genealogical material.

Museum of Farnham

38 West Street
Farnham GU9 7DX
01252 715094
https://farnhammaltings.com/museum
museum@farnhammaltings.com

Farnham is a town of outstanding Georgian architecture and a designated town of craft with a lively and artistic atmosphere. The museum aims to reflect this in a varied programme of exhibitions and events for adults and children alike.

Oakhurst Cottage - National Trust

Hambledon
nr Godalming GU8 4HF
01483 208477
www.nationaltrust.org.uk/oakhurst-cottage
oakhurstcottage@nationaltrust.org.uk

Small 16th-century timber-framed cottage: * Restored and furnished as a simple labourer's dwelling * Fascinating artefacts reflecting 4 centuries of occupation * Delightful gardens with typical Victorian plants.

Polesden Lacey - National Trust

Polesden Lacey, Nr. Great Bookham
Dorking RH5 6BD
01372 452048
www.nationaltrust.org.uk/polesden-lacey
polesdenlacey@nationaltrust.org.uk

Nestled in the Surrey Hills, Polesden offers the perfect opportunity to unwind. Mrs Greville, an ambitious Edwardian hostess, chose it as the ideal place for entertaining and relaxing with friends.

Reigate District Family History Group

St Mark's Hall, Alma Road, Reigate
01737 766 135
www.surreycc.gov.uk/redhilllocalhistory
johnsonjackie@hotmail.com

Redhill Local and Family History centre is based in Redhill Library, and you can use the local history centre resources at any time that the library is open.

Reigate Hill & Gatton Park - National Trust

Reigate Hill, Wray Lane
Reigate RH2 0HX
01372 220640
http://goo.gl/3ravq8
reigate@nationaltrust.org.uk

This stretch of the North Downs is good walking country with flower-sprinkled grasslands and quiet shady woods. Sitting proud at the top of the Hill is the 19th-century Reigate Fort.

Reigate Priory Museum

Reigate RH2 7RL
01737 222550 afternoons
www.reigatepriorymuseum.org.uk

Reigate Priory is a grade 1 listed building set in 65 acres of open parkland with a pond, woodland and playing fields only a few hundred yards from the centre of Reigate town, which is situated at the foot of the North Downs. The building is home to Reigate Priory Museum and Reigate Priory School. The museum has a collection of local history and domestic items as well as period costumes.

RH7 History Group, Lingfield

Box Cottage, The Platt Dormansland
Lingfield RH7 6QU
www.rh7.org
jjbox@btinternet.com

The RH7 History Group aims to encourage and assist in the

study of local and family history. As our name suggests, we mainly focus on the RH7 postal district which covers the south-east Surrey communities of Lingfield, Blindley Heath, Crowhurst, Dormansland and Newchapel. Members are encouraged to undertake research of their area, house or any local history subject they choose (help is available when needed), and results may be published in the form of factsheets.

Royal Logistic Corps Museum

The Princess Royal Barracks, Newfoundland Road, Deepcut
Camberley GU16 6SQ
01252 833371
www.rlcmuseum.co.uk

The museum tells the story of British Army logistics from the 15th century to the present day. Exhibits include weapons, uniforms, medals and equipment relevant to the RLC (formed 1993) and its predecessors, whose collections are also held.

Rural Life Centre

Old Kiln Museum Trust, Reeds Road, Tilford
Farnham GU10 2DL
01252 795571
www.rural-life.org.uk
info@rural-life.org.uk

The collection documents the changes in rural life over the period between about 1750 and 1960 in an area roughly encompassing Surrey, east Hampshire, West Sussex and parts of Berkshire. Areas covered include all aspects of domestic and village life including agriculture, crafts and trades.

Shalford Mill - National Trust

Shalford Mill
nr Guildford GU4 8BS
01483 561389
www.nationaltrust.org.uk/shalford-mill
riverwey@nationaltrust.org.uk

18th-century watermill with well-preserved machinery. This large timber-framed mill on the River Tillingbourne was given in 1932 by a group of anonymous NT benefactors calling themselves 'Ferguson's Gang'.

Surrey Heath Museum

Knoll Road
Camberley GU15 3HD
01276 707284
www.surreyheath.gov.uk/leisure/museum
museum@surreyheath.gov.uk

A small, lively borough museum, based in the centre of Camberley. The museum's collections are particularly strong in 19th and 20th century domestic materials, 20th century costume, natural history and photographs.

Surrey History Centre

130 Goldsworth Road
Woking GU21 6ND
01483 518737
www.surreycc.gov.uk/surreyhistorycentre
shs@surreycc.gov.uk

Surrey History Centre collects and rescues archives and printed materials relating to Surrey's past and present, so that they can tell the story of the county and its people to future generations. We can help you discover your family history learn about famous Surrey people, buildings, businesses and organisations trace the history of your house, street, town or community or research a school or university project.

Surrey Infantry Museum, The

Clandon Park
Guildford GU4 7RQ
01483 223419
http://goo.gl/tGzCMG

Following the amalgamation of The Queen's Royal Regiment and the East Surrey Regiment in 1959, the ownership and management of museum artefacts and archives was vested in The Queen's Royal Surrey Regiment Museum Trust. Following the closure of Regimental Headquarters and Museum in the Keep at Kingston-upon-Thames the artefacts had to be put in store.

Undercroft, The

High Street
Guildford GU1 3HE
01483 444751
www.guildford.gov.uk/undercroft

The medieval Undercroft on Guildford High Street is one of the finest examples in the country. Dating from the end of the 13th century, this stone vaulted semi-basement is thought to have been a merchant's shop, selling wine or expensive cloths or silk. Undercrofts like this are a feature of towns engaged in the import and export trade, and the merchant who built this Undercroft must have expected to deal with prosperous clients who sought luxury goods.

Wanborough Barn

Nr Wanborough
Guildford GU3 2JR
www.wanboroughgreatbarn.co.uk

Wanborough Barn is located just off the A31 between Guildford and Farnham. Built by the Cistercian monks of Waverley Abbey in 1388, the large medieval barn is the most important in Surrey.

Wandle Industrial Museum

Vestry Hall Annexe, London Road
Mitcham CR4 3UD
020 8648 0127
www.wandle.org
curator@wandle.org

The museum works to preserve, store, and interpret the heritage and history of the industries and people of the River Wandle. We are proud to display the evidence which establishes that the River Wandle was, in its day, the most industrialised river in Europe.

West Surrey Family History Society

21 Sheppard Road
Basingstoke RG21 3HT
www.wsfhs.org
secretary@wsfhs.org

We cover the ancient County of Surrey, both Rural Surrey and the Metropolitan Surrey area, ie those parts of the old county of Surrey which are now in Greater London.

Tyne & Wear

Newcastle upon Tyne, parliamentary and municipal borough, city, seaport, market town, and county of itself, Northumberland, on river Tyne, 10 miles from its mouth, 117 miles SE. of Edinburgh and 276 miles NW. of London by rail, 5371 acres, population 145,359. Modern Newcastle, through the rich mineral products of the neighbourhood, and the industrial genius and activity of the inhabitants, has attained a first position among the great centres of British business enterprise. Being in the midst of one of the largest coalfields in England, it exports immense quantities of that commodity; also iron, chemicals, hardware, glass, earthenware, and machinery. Important industries are shipbuilding, the manufacture of locomotive and marine engines, cannon, patent shot, tools, fire-bricks, hemp and wire ropes, cables, anchors, sails, &c. The port (which is one of the Tyne Ports) has a very extensive traffic, greatly facilitated by the Northumberland and Tyne Docks. A bishopric was founded for Newcastle in 1882, and the place was created a city.

Gateshead, parliamentary and municipal borough, seaport, market town, and parish, N. Durham, on right bank of river Tyne, opposite Newcastle; borough, 3243 acres, population 65,803. The modern town is practically a part of Newcastle, and its industries are similar. Large quantities of coal are shipped from the almost inexhaustible coalfields of the district, and the other principal industries are ironworks (including foundries and the making of engines, boilers, cables, &c.), ship. building, glassmaking, chemical works, &c.

Sunderland – parliamentary and municipal borough, seaport town, and parish, Durham, at mouth of river Wear; municipal borough, 3306 acres, population 116,542. Sunderland rose into importance as a seat of trade and commerce about the middle of the 18th century, and is now one of the chief coal-shipping ports in the kingdom. After its coal trade and shipping, the town depends chiefly upon its ship-building; it has also large marine engineering works, works for heavy iron-forging, and for the manufacture of glass, cordage, earthenware, &c.

– John Bartholomew, *Gazetteer of the British Isles* (1887)

Note: Tyne & Wear was formed in 1974 from parts of Northumberland and County Durham.

Arbeia Roman Fort & Museum

Arbeia Roman Fort and Museum, Baring Street
South Shields NE33 2BB
0191 456 1369
www.twmuseums.org.uk/arbeia
info@arbeiaromanfort.org.uk

Four miles east of the end of Hadrian's Wall at South Shields, Arbeia Roman Fort played an essential role in the mighty frontier system. Originally built to house a garrison, Arbeia soon became the military supply base for the 17 forts along the Wall.

Bede's World

Church Bank
Jarrow NE32 3DY
0191 489 2106
www.bedesworld.co.uk
visitor.info@bedesworld.co.uk

Bede's World celebrates the extraordinary life and achievements of the Venerable Bede (AD 673 - 735) who lived and worked here in the monastery 1300 years ago. Visit: - Interactive permanent exhibition 'The Age of Bede' in the stunning new museum building - Historic site of the Anglo-Saxon monastery of St Paul and medieval monastery ruins - Rare breeds of animals, recreated Anglo-Saxon timber buildings and ancient varieties of crops and vegetables on Gyrwe, the Anglo-Saxon demonstration farm - Herb garden, based on Anglo-Saxon and medieval herbs, and laid out partly to a 9th century plan.

Bessie Surtees House

41-44 Sandhill, Newcastle
Newcastle & Gateshead NE1 3JF
0191 269 1200
www.english-heritage.org.uk

Two 16th- and 17th-century merchants' houses, one of which is a rare example of Jacobean domestic architecture. The house is perhaps best known as the scene of the elopement of Bessie Surtees and John Scott, who, in 1771, became Lord Chancellor of England.

Blackfriars

Friars Street
Newcastle-upon-Tyne NE1 4XN
0191 261 5945
www.blackfriarsrestaurant.co.uk

With its origins dating back to 1239 and a long and turbulent history that included a spell as a hostel to accommodate King Henry III, Blackfriars confidently lays claim to be the oldest dining room in the UK..

Bowes Railway Centre

Springwell Village
Newcastle & Gateshead NE9 7QJ
0191 416 1847
www.bowesrailway.co.uk

The only place in the world where rope haulage can be seen on a standard gauge railway system, Bowes Railway is a preserved colliery railway. On operating days, steam train rides are given to the hauler house for rope haulage demonstrations, but the fine examples of Victorian workshops and machinery can be seen during the week for free.

Castle Keep

Castle Garth
Newcastle & Gateshead NE1 1RQ
0191 2327938
www.oldnewcastle.org.uk

The castle Keep of Newcastle-upon-Tyne was built by Henry II between 1168-1178, it is one of the finest surviving examples of a Norman Keep in the country. It stands within a site that also contains: an early motte and bailey castle built by Robert Curthose, the son of William the Conqueror: an Anglo-Saxon cemetery and a Roman Fort (Pons Aelius). The castle Keep is a Grade 1 listed building, a Scheduled Ancient monument, and is open to the public 361 days of the year as a heritage visitor attraction. Owned by Newcastle City Council it is leased to and managed by the society of Antiquaries of Newcastle-upon-Tyne, the second oldest antiquarian society in the world.

Cathedral Church of St Nicholas

St Nicholas Churchyard
Newcastle & Gateshead NE1 1PF
0191 232 1939
stnicholascathedral.co.uk
office@stnicnewcastle.co.uk

The Cathedral Church of St Nicholas, Newcastle-upon-Tyne, is not like other northern cathedrals such as Durham and Carlisle.

Discovery Museum

Discovery Museum, Blandford Square
Newcastle & Gateshead NE1 4JA
0191 232 6789
www.twmuseums.org.uk/discovery
discovery@twmuseums.org.uk

Discover all about life in Newcastle and Tyneside, from the area's renowned maritime history and world-changing science and technology right through to fashion through the ages and military history. The museum is bursting with interactive displays, which makes it the perfect place to learn and have fun. Explore Newcastle's past from Romans to the present day; Tyneside inventions that changed the world; a fun approach to science and take a walk through fashion.

Fulwell Windmill

Newcastle Road, Fulwell
Sunderland SR5 1EX
0191 516 9790
www.fulwell-windmill.com
fulwell.windmill@sunderland.gov.uk

Fulwell Windmill started to appear on the Sunderland skyline in 1806 and became the familiar landmark we know today when it opened in 1808. 200 years on, the Mill is still the famous landmark it was and continues to be one of Sunderland's most treasured heritage sites.

Gateshead Libraries

Central Library, Prince Consort Road
Gateshead NE8 4LN
0191 433 8420
www.gatesheadlibraries.com
enquiries@gateshead.gov.uk

Our Local Studies section offers access to parish records, census returns, electors lists, newspapers, maps and a large collection of photographs about the Gateshead area. Our specialist staff are on hand to help.

Gibside - National Trust

nr Rowlands Gill, Burnopfield
Newcastle-upon-Tyne NE16 6BG
01207 541820
www.nationaltrust.org.uk/gibside
gibside@nationaltrust.org.uk

An 18th century landscape 'forest' garden once home to the Bowes-Lyons family. Now, owned and managed by the National Trust, Gibside is a magnificent 600 acre estate for you to venture, exploring our woodlands, riverside and parkland to discover some of our rare and beautiful wildlife.

Great North Museum: Hancock

Barras Bridge
Newcastle & Gateshead NE2 4PT
0191 222 6765
www.greatnorthmuseum.org
info@twmuseums.org.uk

The Great North Museum incorporates collections from the Hancock Museum and Newcastle University's Museum of Antiquities, the Shefton Museum and the Hatton Gallery. Highlights of the £26million museum include a large-scale, interactive model of Hadrian's Wall, major new

displays showing the wonder and diversity of the animal kingdom, spectacular objects from the Ancient Greeks and mummies from Ancient Egypt, a planetarium and a life-size T-Rex dinosaur replica skeleton.

Lit & Phil - The Literary & Philosophical Society

23 Westgate Road
Newcastle & Gateshead NE1 1SE
0191 232 0192
www.litandphil.org.uk
library@litandphil.org.uk

The Literary & Philosophical Society (Lit & Phil) is the largest independent library outside London, housing over 150,000 books. A wide selection of current fiction and non-fiction can be found alongside historical collections covering every field of interest.

Mining Institute

Neville Hall, Westgate Road
Newcastle-upon-Tyne NE1 1SE
0191 233 2459
www.mininginstitute.org.uk
librarian@mininginstitute.org.uk

The Mining Institute, a registered charity, is situated in the heart of Newcastle-upon-Tyne and is housed in Neville Hall, a Grade II* listed building. Outstanding gothic library richly decorated.

Monkwearmouth Station Museum

Monkwearmouth Station Museum, North Bridge Street
Sunderland SR5 1AP
0191 567 7075
www.twmuseums.org.uk
info@twmuseums.org.uk

This splendid Victorian railway station recreates a sense of rail travel in the past. Explore the ticket office as it would have looked in Victorian times, see the guard's van and goods wagon in the railway sidings and watch today's trains zoom past the Platform Gallery.

Newcastle Community Heritage Project

Ouseburn Regeneration Centre, Spiller
Newcastle & Gateshead
www.newcastlecommunityheritage.org

The Newcastle Community Heritage Project works with residents, local groups, schools and visitors to create opportunities for celebrating cultural heritage and community history.

North East Aircraft Museum

Washington Road
Sunderland SR5 3HZ
0191 5190662
www.neam.org.uk

The North East Aircraft Museum, formerly the Northumbrian Aeronautical Collection, began life in 1974 as a small group of vintage aircraft enthusiasts meeting very informally at Sunderland Flying Club to exchange views and information on their chosen interest. At this time, the North East was the only major area of the United Kingdom not covered by any form of vintage aircraft group.

North East Bus Museum

Postal address only: 8 Seaburn Hill
Sunderland SR6 8BS
www.nebpt.co.uk
events@nebpt.co.uk

The North East Bus Preservation Trust (NEBPT) is a group of over 130 bus and coach enthusiasts dedicated to preserving the vehicles and heritage of the North East of England. At the present time the North East Bus Preservation Trust has three buildings used for storage and workshop facilities. The North East Bus Preservation Trust currently owns 17 vehicles and we also maintain a list of preserved buses. During the Winter months we hold indoor meetings, with regular slide shows/videos and occasionally a guest speaker from within the transport industry. From Spring onwards we try to arrange evening trips in a preserved vehicle belonging to the trust, or a bus kindly offered by an owner member.

Northumberland & Durham Family History Society

2nd Floor, Bolbec Hall, Westgate Road
Newcastle-upon-Tyne NE1 1SE
0191 261 2159
www.ndfhs.org.uk
secretary@ndfhs.org.uk

The society, founded in 1975, promotes interest in family history amongst its members and the general public. We invite you to consider joining and to visit our Research Centre at Percy House with its library and search room.

Northumberland Hussars Museum

Discovery Museum, Blandford Square
Newcastle & Gateshead NE1 4JA
0191 232 6789
http://goo.gl/4UR8fh

The Northumberland (Hussars) could trace its origins to December 1819 when the Northumberland and Newcastle Volunteer Corps of Cavalry formed, under the command of Charles John Brandling, of Gosforth House. Justification

for its formation was attributed to the revolutionary spirit then especially prevalent in the North of England.

Ryhope Engines Museum

Ryhope
Sunderland SR2 0ND
0191 521 0235
www.ryhopeengines.org.uk

The Ryhope Engines Museum is based on the Ryhope Pumping Station which was built in 1868 to supply water to the Sunderland area. The station ceased operation in 1967 - after 100 years of continuous use. The museum is now regarded as one of the finest industrial monuments in the North East of England, and is in a Grade II (starred) listed building.

Segedunum Roman Fort, Baths & Museum

Buddle Street
Wallsend NE28 6HR
0191 236 9347
www.twmuseums.org.uk/segedunum
segedunum@twmuseums.org.uk

In AD122 the Emperor Hadrian ordered a mighty frontier system to be built across Britain to defend the Roman Empire from the barbarians to the North. The result was Hadrian's Wall, a 73 mile barrier stretching from the River Tyne in the east to the Solway Firth in the west. Segedunum, which means 'strong Fort', was built to guard the eastern end of the Wall, and housed 600 Roman soldiers.

Collections: The Roman collections at Segedunum relate to the more recent excavations of the 1970s, 80s and 90s, and are constantly being augmented by fresh archaeological fieldwork in the Wallsend area. Their particular significance lies in the fact that they represent a comparatively comprehensive span of both the 300 year occupation of the site, and of the assorted structures within it.

Shipley Art Gallery

Shipley Art Gallery, Prince Consort Road
Newcastle & Gateshead NE8 4JB
0191 477 1495
www.shipleyartgallery.org.uk
info@shipleyartgallery.org.uk

The Shipley Art Gallery is home to a collection of over 700 breathtaking pieces by the country's leading craft makers. A dazzling selection of this collection is on permanent show and includes studio ceramics, glass, metalwork, jewellery, textiles and furniture.

Souter Lighthouse & The Leas - National Trust

[icons]

Coast Road, Whitburn
Sunderland SR6 7NH
0191 529 3161
www.nationaltrust.org.uk/souter
souter@nationaltrust.org.uk

Opened in 1871 Souter remains an iconic beacon. Hooped in red and white and standing proud on the coastline midway between the Tyne and the Wear.

South Shields Museum & Art Gallery

[icons]

Ocean Road
South Shields NE33 2JA
0191 456 8740
www.twmuseums.org.uk/southshields
info@twmuseums.org.uk

This friendly venue explores the story of South Tyneside, including the lifetime achievement of the successful local author Catherine Cookson. Its major collections are in social history and art which are represented in the newly refurbished Changing Faces gallery.

St Mary's Heritage Centre

[icons]

St Mary's Church, Oakwellgate
Gateshead NE8 2AU
0191 433 4699
http://goo.gl/Q2ptsM
heritage@gateshead.gov.uk

St Mary's Church, which sits high above the River Tyne close to The Sage Gateshead, reopened on the 16th December 2008 following a £1.2m transformation, funded by Gateshead Council, the European Regional Development fund and the heritage lottery fund, into Tyneside's newest visitor attraction. The interior of the Grade 1-listed church has been completely stripped out to return it as far as possible to its former state, and is now open to the public with a programme of exhibitions and activities including a new family history section focusing on the church and the nearby area.

Stephenson Railway Museum

[icons]

Middle Engine Lane
North Shields NE29 8DX
0191 200 7146
www.twmuseums.org.uk/stephenson
info@twmuseums.org.uk

Re-live the glorious days of the steam railway at the Stephenson Railway Museum in North Shields. The museum is home to George Stephenson's 'Billy', a forerunner of the world-famous Rocket, and many other engines from the great age of steam including 'Jackie Milburn', named after the Newcastle United legend. Rides on a real steam train can be taken and the story of coal and electricity's impact on ordinary people's lives can be discovered.

Stephenson Works

[icon]

20 South St,
Newcastle upon Tyne NE1 3PE
0191 222 0905
www.robertstephensontrust.com/page16.html

In 1823 George and Robert Stephenson, along with three partners, opened the world's first purpose built locomotive works on Forth Banks, Newcastle upon Tyne. Part of these historic works has been rescued from near dereliction.

Sunderland Museum & Winter Gardens

[icons]

Burdon Road
Sunderland SR1 1PP
0191 553 2323
http://goo.gl/LIgFzH
museumwintergardens@sunderland.gov.uk

Exciting hands-on exhibits and interactive displays tell the story of Sunderland from its prehistoric past through to the present day. The Art Gallery features paintings by L S Lowry alongside Victorian masterpieces and artefacts from the four corners of the world.

Tanfield Railway - The World's Oldest Railway

[icons]

Marley Hill Engine Shed, Old Marley Hill
Gateshead NE16 5ET
0845 463 4938
www.tanfield-railway.co.uk
info@tanfield-railway.co.uk

Step aboard the world famous Tanfield Railway, a great day out for all the family. Join us for an unforgettable journey on a vintage steam train with unique Victorian carriages and lovingly restored locomotives, for a six mile round trip through beautiful rolling countryside and a spectacular wooded valley.

Trinity House

[icons]

Broad Chare
Newcastle & Gateshead NE1 3DQ
0191 232 8226
www.trinityhousenewcastle.org.uk
ncl_trinityhouse@hotmail.com

Trinity House, Newcastle, is a maritime organisation, dedicated to safe navigation and welfare of seamen. Established in 1492, the organisation was granted a Royal Charter of Incorporation in 1536 by King Henry VIII and has operated by Royal Charter ever since. The house also maintains the buildings and preserves the heritage and ancient traditions of this unique organisation. The buildings forming the Trinity House complex include the private Brethrens Chapel, 1505; the entrance hall, 1800; the Banqueting Hall and Board Room, 1721.

Tyne & Wear Archives

The Archives, Discovery Museum, Blandford Square
Newcastle & Gateshead NE1 4JA
0191 2772248
www.twmuseums.org.uk/archives
archives@twmuseums.org.uk

The Archives hold documents relating to Gateshead, Newcastle upon Tyne, north Tyneside, South Tyneside and Sunderland. The Archives preserve documents relating to the area from the 12th to the 21st century, and the service is free for everyone to use.

Collections: The Shipbuilding, Marine and Maritime Trade Collection in the Archives is a Designated Collection of national importance. This collection comprises material from over 20 Tyneside shipbuilding firms, including major companies such as Swan Hunter.

Tynemouth Priory & Castle - English Heritage

Pier Road
Tynemouth NE30 4BZ
0191 257 1090
http://goo.gl/tKYr7n

Once a monastery and a burial place of kings and saints Tynemouth Priory and Castle is an inspiring day out sure to capture the kids' imaginations. Explore the ruins, find tranquillity in the tiny chapel, take in the beautiful coastal views and enjoy a picnic in the grounds.

Tynemouth Volunteer Life Brigade Watch House

Spanish Battery
Tynemouth NE30 4DD
0191 257 2059
www.tvlb.org/TVLB%20Main%20Pages/Museum.htm
enquiries@tvlb.org

The Brigade Watch House Museum is packed full of fascinating and unique artefacts of the Brigade's history, including the ship's bell from one of the shipwrecks that led to the creation of the Brigade in 1864. Furthermore behind every picture and relic is a captivating story about how it links into both the Brigade's past and present role as a Voluntary Life Brigade on the North Tyneside Coastline.

Victoria Tunnel

Arch 6, Stepney Bank
Ouseburn Valley NE1 2NP
0191 2616 596
www.ouseburntrust.org.uk

clive.goodwin@ouseburntrust.org.uk

The Victoria Tunnel is a fully preserved 19th century waggonway under the city from the Town Moor to the Tyne, to transport coal from Spital Tongues (Leazes Main) Colliery to the river and operated between 1842 and the 1860s. The tunnel was converted into an air raid shelter to protect Newcastle citizens during World War 2. The tunnel was carefully repaired and opened for guided tours with funding from the Heritage Lottery Fund and TyneWear Partnership. Since 2010 the Ouseburn Trust has operated guided tours with fully trained volunteer guides.

Victoria Tunnel Education Project

FREEPOST NT623
Newcastle & Gateshead NE1 1BR
www.victoriatunnel.info
tunnelenquiries@newcastle.gov.uk

Welcome to the Victoria Tunnel Education Project. 766 yards (700m) of this old underground waggonway has been newly restored and includes audio-visual effects and 'Rainbow Code' – an exciting, interactive artwork. Part of the Victoria Tunnel, including the audio-visual displays, is wheelchair accessible and we are able to arrange tours to suit your access requirements. Tours are limited to 10 people so booking is essential. Please contact us for our current programme of public tours and a booking enquiries form.

Washington 'F' Pit Museum

Washington 'F' Pit Museum, Albany Way
Washington NE37 1BJ
0191 553 2323
www.twmuseums.org.uk/404.html
info@twmuseums.org.uk

Washington 'F' Pit's magnificent Victorian steam engine, engine house and headgear are preserved to mark the town's coalmining heritage that reaches back over 250 years. The industrial monument is the last of its type in the North East.

Washington Old Hall - National Trust

The Avenue
Washington NE38 7LE
0191 416 6879
www.nationaltrust.org.uk/washington-old-hall
washingtonoldhall@nationaltrust.org.uk

Washington Old Hall is a delightful stone-built 17th-century manor house, which incorporates parts of the original medieval home of George Washington's direct ancestors. It is from here that the family surname of Washington was derived.

Warwickshire

Warwickshire, county in west-midlands of England; bounded N. by Staffordshire, Derbyshire, and Leicestershire, E. by Northamptonshire, S. by Oxfordshire and Gloucestershire, and W. by Worcestershire; greatest length, N. and S., 52 miles; greatest breadth, E. and W., 32 miles; area, 566,271 acres, population 737,339. Warwickshire presents a pleasant undulating surface of hill and dale, watered by the Avon, Learn, and Tame. The climate is mild and healthy, and the soil, except some cold stiff clays on the higher grounds, is fertile. It consists chiefly of a strong red loam adapted for wheat and beans, or a sandy loam for barley and turnips. Much land is kept in permanent pasture for grazing. Formerly the county was thickly wooded (that part N. of the Avon being called the Forest of Arden), and fine timber is still abundant. Geologically it mainly belongs to the secondary formation. A coal field, 16 miles by 3 miles, extends from the neighbourhood of Coventry to the border of Staffordshire, E. of Tamworth. The principal minerals are coal, ironstone, limestone, freestone, blue flagstone, and fire-clay. The manufactures are carried on chiefly at Birmingham (hardware and silk goods) and Coventry (watches and ribbons). There are mineral springs at Leamington, Stratford on Avon, Umington, Southam, Willoughby, King's Newnham, &c. The county is traversed in all directions by canals and railways. Warwickshire comprises 4 hundreds, 256 parishes, with parts of 7 others, the parliamentary and municipal boroughs of Birmingham and Coventry, the parliamentary boroughs of Aston Manor and Warwick and Leamington, and the municipal boroughs of Leamington, Stratford on Avon, and Warwick. It is mostly in the diocese of Worcester.

– John Bartholomew, *Gazetteer of the British Isles* (1887)

Note: for Birmingham and Coventry, see West Midlands.

Anne Hathaway's Cottage

Cottage Lane, Shottery
Stratford-upon-Avon CV37 9HH
01789 292100
http://goo.gl/s0jTLD
reception@shakespeare.org.uk

Discover where the young William Shakespeare courted his future bride Anne Hathaway at her picturesque family home. Anne Hathaway's Cottage is a thatched farmhouse containing many original items of family furniture, including the Hathaway Bed. It is nestled within stunning grounds and gardens, overflowing with fragrant blooms and traditional shrubs..

Baddesley Clinton - National Trust

Baddesley Clinton Rising Lane
Baddesley Clinton B93 0DQ
01564 783294
www.nationaltrust.org.uk/baddesley-clinton
baddesleyclinton@nationaltrust.org.uk

From refuge to haven, this atmospheric moated house has been a sanctuary since the 15th century, hiding persecuted Catholics in its three priest holes, and was home to the Ferrers family for 500 years. The peaceful gardens include fish pools, a romantic lake and a walled garden filled with colours for every season.

Bedworth Society Parsonage Heritage Centre

All Saints Square
Bedworth CV12 8NR
024 7636 4446
www.bedworth-society.co.uk

The cellar of the Almshouses has been completely renovated to house changing exhibitions focusing on the cultural, industrial and agricultural history of the town.

Bosworth Battlefield Heritage Centre & Country Park

Sutton Cheney
Nuneaton CV13 0AD
01455 290429
www.bosworthbattlefield.com
bosworth@leics.gov.uk

Bosworth Battlefield Heritage Centre and Country Park is a unique day out for all the family. Relive this famous turning point in British history - the death of a King and the birth of the all powerful Tudor dynasty.

Charlecote Park - National Trust

Charlecote Park
Warwick CV35 9ER
01789 470277
www.nationaltrust.org.uk/charlecote-park
charlecote.park@nationaltrust.org.uk

The home of the Lucy family for over 700 years, the mellow brickwork and great chimneys of Charlecote seem to sum up the very essence of Tudor England. There are strong associations with both Queen Elizabeth and Shakespeare, who knew the house well - he is alleged to have been caught poaching the estate deer.

Chedham's Yard

All enquiries via 2 School Road
Wellesbourne CV35 9NH
01789 842770
www.chedhamsyard.org.uk
enquiries@chedhamsyard.org.uk

Discover this secret wheelwrights, blacksmiths and much more. Chedham's Yard is a prize-winning heritage site, restored and maintained by a hard working team of volunteers.

Compton Verney

Compton Verney
Warwick CV35 9HZ
01926 645500
www.comptonverney.org.uk
info@comptonverney.org.uk

Visitors of all ages are warmly welcomed to this award-winning art gallery. Housed in a grade I listed Robert Adam mansion and surrounded by stunning 'Capability' Brown landscaped parkland, Compton Verney offers a great day out. Be enthralled by our programme of exhibitions, explore art from around the world and stroll along our woodland walk.

Coughton Court - National Trust

National Trust, Coughton Court
Alcester B49 5JA
01789 400777
www.nationaltrust.org.uk/coughton-court
coughtoncourt@nationaltrust.org.uk

Coughton Court is a beautiful Tudor house set in 25 acres of landscaped gardens in Alcester, Warwickshire. Through its rich and varied history, the house has witnessed some of the most defining moments in British history – from the court of Henry VIII to the Gunpowder plot of 1605.

Falstaff Experience, The

40 Sheep Street
Stratford-upon-Avon CV37 6EE
01789 298070
www.falstaffexperience.co.uk
info@falstaffexperience.co.uk

The Falstaff Experience's Tudor World is an award-winning museum of Tudor life, gift shop and theatre set within one of Stratford's most historic buildings. It is the real life home of Shakespeare's famous comic character John Falstaff.

Hall's Croft - Shakespeare Birthplace Trust

Old Town
Stratford-upon-Avon CV37 6BG
01789 292 107
http://goo.gl/hbVR9Z

Wander through the elegant home of Susanna Shakespeare and her husband, Dr John Hall. Enjoy the luxurious rooms and beautiful decoration of this fascinating house, befitting a wealthy physician of Dr John Hall's status.

Harvard House & the Museum of British Pewter

Harvard House, High Street
Stratford-upon-Avon CV37 6AU
01789 204507
http://goo.gl/yIlCFo

An architectural gem, boasting an ornately carved timber framed frontage, Harvard House is a fine example of an Elizabethan town house, rebuilt in 1596 by master butcher Thomas Rogers. His daughter Katherine was the mother of John Harvard, who gave his name to the USA's Harvard University. The house is also the home of the museum of British Pewter.

Heritage Motor Centre

Banbury Road, Gaydon
Warwick CV35 0BJ
01926 641188
www.heritage-motor-centre.co.uk
enquiries@heritage-motor-centre.co.uk

The Heritage Motor Centre is home to the world's largest collection of British Cars; it boasts nearly 300 cars in its collection which span the classic, vintage and veteran eras and is a mecca for car enthusiasts.

Kenilworth Castle - English Heritage

Castle Green
Kenilworth CV8 1NE
01926 852078
http://goo.gl/jkFaiE
customers@english-heritage.org.uk

Enjoy a great day out in Warwickshire at Kenilworth Castle and Elizabethan Garden. One of the largest historic attractions in the West Midlands, the whole family will enjoy exploring the spectacular castle ruins. The ruins are best known as the home of Robert Dudley, the great love of Queen Elizabeth I.

Leamington Spa Art Gallery & Museum

Royal Pump Rooms, The Parade
Royal Leamington Spa CV32 4AA
01926 742700
www.warwickdc.gov.uk/royalpumprooms
prooms@warwickdc.gov.uk

Award winning Art Gallery and Museum with services on offer including: fine art collection, exhibition on the history of Royal Leamington Spa, cabinet of curiosities, restored Victorian Turkish baths room and more.

London & North Western Railway Society - Staff History Group

34 Falmouth Close
Nuneaton CV11 6GB
024 7638 1090
www.lnwrs.org.uk
secretary@lnwrs.org.uk

We aim to collect and disseminate information about the London and North Western Railway, its constituents and its successors. We are interested in the infrastructure of the railway, the men and women who made it work, as well as the engines and rolling stock which it built and used.

Lunt Roman Fort

Coventry Road
Baginton CV8 3AJ
024 76786142
www.luntromanfort.org
luntromanfort@coventry.gov.uk

Close to the Air Museum in Baginton, is the Lunt Roman Fort, once inhabited by the Roman Army. This ancient site provides a fascinating snapshot of Roman military life.

Market Hall Museum

Market Hall, Market Place
Warwick CV34 4SA
01926 412 500
www.warwickshire.gov.uk/museum
museum@warwickshire.gov.uk

Built in 1670 as a market place, it originally contained arches on all four walls (later converted to windows), to provide under-cover space for stalls. In the 19th century, the archways were railed off, and the space was used for stocks. The building is now a branch of Warwick County Museum, concentrating upon the history, natural history, archaeology and social history of Warwickshire. It also houses the world famous Sheldon Tapestry Map of Warwickshire.

Mary Arden's Farm

Station Road, Wilmcote
Stratford-upon-Avon CV37 9UN
01789 293455
http://goo.gl/tD00Qj
info@shakespeare.org.uk

Be surrounded by the sights, sounds and smells of a Tudor farm at Mary Arden's Farm. Discover the daily routine of a 16th century farm and marvel as the farmer, maid and labourer bring the farm to life. Home of Shakespeare's grandparents and childhood home of Shakespeare's mother, Mary Arden.

Midland Air Museum

Coventry Airport
Baginton CV8 3AZ
01203 301 033
www.midlandairmuseum.co.uk
midlandairmuseum@aol.com

Our exhibits range from the magnificent Avro Vulcan bomber through more than 30 other historic aircraft, both civil and military, aero engines and other artefacts, to a wide range of memorabilia. We're particularly proud of our collection of material relating to Sir Frank Whittle, the Coventry-born engineer who designed the jet engine which made modern high-speed aircraft and economical air travel possible.

New Place / Nash's House

Chapel Street
Stratford-upon-Avon CV37 6EP
01789 292 325
http://goo.gl/zR96fu

Nash's House was named after Thomas Nash, first husband of Shakespeare's granddaughter, and a wealthy local property owner. Today, it is a well preserved Tudor building and the ground floor is furnished as it would have been in Nash's day. Next door to Nash's House are the foundations of New Place. This was the house bought by William Shakespeare in 1597.

Nuneaton & North Warwickshire Family History Society

34 Falmouth Close
Nuneaton CV11 6OB
024 7638 1090
www.nnwfhs.org.uk
nuneatonian2000@aol.com

The NNWFHS started life as the Nuneaton Family History Group. Because of our rapidly increasing membership and the family interests that many of our members have in North Warwickshire we expanded our area and changed our name to reflect this in April 1998.

Nuneaton Museum & Art Gallery

Riversley Park, Coton Road
Nuneaton CV11 5TU
024 7635 0720
www.nuneatonandbedworth.gov.uk/museum
museum@nuneatonandbedworth.gov.uk

The museum and Art Gallery is set in the beautiful Riversley Park and has three galleries which house regularly changing temporary and touring art exhibitions. We also have galleries devoted to permanent displays of local author George Eliot, local history and our fine art collection.

Packwood House - National Trust

Packwood Lane
Lapworth B94 6AT
01564 782024
www.nationaltrust.org.uk/packwood-house
packwood@nationaltrust.org.uk

Much-restored Tudor house, park and garden with notable topiary. The culmination of a lifetime of dreams: salvaged objects and exotic pieces come together in a Jacobean meets Edwardian style.

Queen's Own Hussars Regimental Museum

Lord Leycester Hospital, High Street
Warwick CV34 4BH
01962 492035
www.qohmuseum.org.uk/index-2.htm
info@qohmuseum.org.uk

The collection is displayed to give a comprehensive history of the regiment from its foundation in the late 17th century up to the present, with emphasise on both horse and tank warfare.

Ragley Hall

Ragley
Alcester B49 5NJ
01789 768694
www.ragley.co.uk
zoeheal@ragley.co.uk

Country estate with a Palladian mansion, designed by Robert Hooke and open in summer, plus gardens.

Roman Alcester

Globe House
Alcester B49 5DZ
01789 7662216
www.romanalcester.org

Established around AD 47, the town of Alcester grew up around a fort located on the Roman road of Icknield Street, which stretched hundreds of miles from the North East to the South West of England. Thanks in part to being on the salt route from nearby Droitwich, Alcester developed into a town of bustling streets, temples and workshops.

Collections: Designed specifically to evoke everyday life in Roman Alcester, the museum displays many of artefacts discovered in the town. As well these items, there is an interactive area where visitors can handle and sort the archaeological evidence.

Royal Regiment of Fusiliers Museum - Royal Warwickshire

Royal Regiment of Fusiliers Museum, St John's House
Warwick CV34 4NF
01926 491653
www.warwickfusiliers.co.uk
rrfwarksmuseum@btconnect.com

The museum tells the story of one of the oldest Regiments in the country, the 6th Foot (Royal Warwickshire Regiment), from its raising in 1674 to the Fusilier of the present day.

RSC Collection

RSC, The Courtyard Theatre
Stratford-upon-Avon CV37 6BB
01789 296655
www.rsc.org.uk
collection@rsc.org.uk

The RSC Collection consists of several thousand items, not counting the large archive of photographs and documents held by the Shakespeare Birthplace Trust. It was first put together in the late 19th century and held in a purpose built section of the original Shakespeare Memorial Theatre.

Rugby Art Gallery & Museum

Little Elborow Street
Rugby CV21 3BZ
01788 533201
www.ragm.org.uk
ragm@rugby.gov.uk

Rugby Collection of 20th century and contemporary British art including prints and paintings by Stanley Spencer, Bridget Riley, L S Lowry and Lucian Freud. Tripontium Collection of Roman artefacts from an important Roman settlement near Rugby. Social History Collection reflecting Rugby's industrial history, impact of war and the changing pattern of family life.

Shakespeare's Birthplace & the Shakespeare Centre

Henley Street
Stratford-upon-Avon CV37 6QW
01789 204 016
www.shakespeare.org.uk
info@shakespeare.org.uk

The Shakespeare Birthplace Trust is an independent charity that cares for Shakespeare's heritage. It owns five Shakespeare Houses in and around Stratford-upon-Avon, all directly linked to Shakespeare.

Southam Heritage Collection

Basement, Vivian House 2, 1 Market Hill
Southam CV47 0HF
http://goo.gl/5hrWgE
cardallcollection@hotmail.co.uk

The Southam Heritage Collection (previously know as Southam's Cardall Collection) contains over 4,500 documents and items relating to the history of Southam and the surrounding villages. In addition it houses the Alan Griffin photographic archive consisting of over 1,000 unique local photographs plus 450 glass plate negatives from the early 20th century.

St John's House Museum

St John's
Warwick CV34 4NF
01926 412021
www.warwickshire.gov.uk/museum
museum@warwickshire.gov.uk

St John's House Museum occupies the ground floor of this 17th century historic house, with its gardens, a grassy picnic area and a nearby spacious car park. There is a Victorian school room and a kitchen, full of drawers to open and cupboards to explore; a real experience of how people lived in the past.

Stoneleigh Abbey

Stoneleigh Abbey
Kenilworth CV8 2LF
01926 858535
www.stoneleighabbey.org
enquire@stoneleighabbey.org

With humble beginnings as a Cistercian monastic house in 1154, Stoneleigh Abbey was converted at the Dissolution into a comfortable family home. One of the seats of the Leigh family, Stoneleigh has played host to several people of note, including King Charles I, Queen Victoria, and novelist Jane Austen.

Upton House & Gardens - National Trust

Upton House and Gardens
nr Banbury OX15 6HT
01295 670266
www.nationaltrust.org.uk/upton-house
uptonhouse@nationaltrust.org.uk

Outstanding art collections in a 17th-century mansion, with superb terraced gardens: outstanding collection of English and Continental Old Master paintings; important collections of English and French 18th-century porcelain; fascinating exhibition of Shell advertising posters from 1920s and 30s.

Warwick Castle

Castle Hill
Warwick CV34 4QU
0870 442 2000
www.warwick-castle.co.uk
customer.information@warwick-castle.com

Bursting to the towers with tales of treachery and torture, passion and power and above all fascinating people, times and events, Warwick Castle is so much more than simply a castle. Experience preparations for battle, feel the weight of a sword and get a soldiers eye view from beneath a battle helmet, see lavishly decorated State Rooms fit for Kings & Queens, watch as a Victorian household prepares for a Royal Weekend Party and discover how electricity was generated over 100 years ago to light up the castle.

Warwickshire County Record Office

Priory Park
Warwick CV34 4JS
01926 738959
http://goo.gl/bdBGrN
rowanfisher@warwickshire.gov.uk

Warwickshire County Record Office is involved in safeguarding, managing and developing Warwickshire's archives so that they can be accessed, interpreted and enjoyed by all those with an interest in Warwickshire's past and its people. We hold records dating from the 12th century up to the 21st to do with Warwickshire's history.

Warwickshire Family History Society

44 Abbotts Lane
Coventry CV1 4AZ
www.wfhs.org.uk
chairman@wfhs.org.uk

We were established in 1986 and our aim is to help people everywhere conduct research into their Warwickshire ancestors. We cover the entire county and are the only family history society devoted solely to the whole of Warwickshire.

Warwickshire Museum Field Services

The Butts
Warwick CV34 4SS
01926 412500
www.warwickshire.gov.uk/museum
fieldarchaeology@warwickshire.gov.uk

Warwickshire Museum Field Services, based at The Butts, Warwick, comprises the County's Archaeological and Ecological Teams.

Warwickshire Yeomanry Museum

The Court House, Jury Street
Warwick CV34 4EW
01926 494837
www.warwickshire-yeomanry-museum.co.uk

We are a regimental museum completely supported by volunteers and our aim is to safeguard the heritage and collective memory of those who have served with the Warwickshire Yeomanry so that both present and future generations may learn the importance of the past through its history.

West Midlands

Birmingham, parliamentary and municipal borough and parish, on NW. border of Warwickshire, 88 miles SE. of Liverpool and 113 NW. of London by rail – municipal borough (comprising also Edgbaston parish and part of Aston parish), 8400 acres, population 400,774. Birmingham is situated on the verge of a great coal and iron district, nearly in the centre of England, and built on a rising ground, the workshops and warehouses being in the lower parts of the city. It is the principal centre of metal manufactures, consisting of articles in iron, gold, silver, brass, steel, &c., valued at over £5,000,000 per annum. Of these the most important are the manufacture of fire-arms and swords, in some recent years as many as 500,000 gun-barrels being tested annually; the manufacture of boilers and engines, the largest works, founded in 1757, being at Soho; the steel pen manufacture, 900,000,000 pens being annually produced; the making of railway carriages and waggons; jewellery and electro-plate manufactures, which are continually on the increase; iron casting of all kinds; galvanised ironware; fancy-goods in leather, wood, papiér-maché, &c.

Wolverhampton, parliamentary and municipal borough and manufacturing town, parish, and township, Staffordshire; parliamentary borough, comprising also the townships of Bilston, Wednesfield, and Willenhall, and the parish of Sedgley, 18,888 acres, population 164,332. Wolverhampton stands on the summit of an eminence, amid a network of railways and canals. It is now the largest manufacturing town in the county, and is known as the Metropolis of the Black Country. Situated in the heart of the great midland mining district, with extensive beds of coal and ironstone in its vicinity, it possesses enormous iron foundries, where articles of every description of ironware are produced. Steel, brass, tin, papier mbche, and japanned wares are also extensively made, with galvanised ironware, chemicals, colours, varnishes, &c. Wolverhampton has long been noted for its locks and keys.

Coventry, parliamentary and municipal borough and market town; municipal borough, 1430 acres, population 42,111. In the 15th century it was noted for its woollens; then for its dyeing; then for its weaving of camlets, shalloons, &C. At present its staples are ribbons, silk, and watches; but it has also woollens, carpets, cotton, art metalwork, and ironfounding.

– John Bartholomew, *Gazetteer of the British Isles* (1887)

Note: West Midlands was formed in 1974 from parts of Warwickshire, Worcestershire and Staffordshire.

Aston Hall

🏛 🖾 £

Trinity Road, Aston
Birmingham B6 6JD
07842 029477
www.bmag.org.uk/aston-hall
astonhallmuseum@gmail.com

One of the last great homes to be built in the flamboyant Jacobean style, the mansion which was built between 1618 and 1635 for Sir Thomas Holte. In 1643 the house was badly damaged in an attack by Parliamentary troops. Today the house is displayed as a series of period rooms containing fine furniture, paintings, textiles and metal work from the collections of Birmingham Museum & Art Gallery.

Bantock House Museum

🏛 🖾 ★

Finchfield Road
Wolverhampton WV3 9LQ
01902 552195
www.wolverhamptonart.org.uk/bantock
bantockhouse@wolverhampton.gov.uk

Bantock House, once the home of the Bantock family, allows you to discover the secrets of Wolverhampton's history. As you wander through the house you can admire our exquisite decorative arts collection that includes enamels, steel jewellery and japanned ware.

Collections: The collections on display at Bantock House highlight local trades of the 1700 and 1800s, including Japanned ware, Enamels, Steel Jewellery and Locks.

Birmingham & Midland Society for Genealogy & Heraldry

👪

5 Sanderling Court, Spennells
Kidderminster DY10 4TS
01562 743912
www.bmsgh.org
jackie.cotterill1@btinternet.com

The Birmingham and Midland Society for Genealogy and Heraldry is the principal family history society for the counties of Staffordshire, Warwickshire and Worcestershire.

Birmingham Assay Office

🖾 £

Newhall Street
Birmingham B3 1SB
0121 236 6951
www.theassayoffice.co.uk
gem@theassayoffice.co.uk

Founded by an Act of Parliament in 1773, The Birmingham Assay Office houses a spectacular collection of historic silver and jewellery and a library containing many rare historic books on hallmarking, jewellery, precious metals, science and art.

Birmingham Back to Backs - National Trust

[icons]

50-54 Inge Street/55-63 Hurst Street
Birmingham B5 4TE
0121 666 7671
www.nationaltrust.org.uk/birmingham-back-to-backs
backtobacks@nationaltrust.org.uk

Carefully restored 19th-century courtyard of working people's houses. Birmingham's last surviving court of back to back housing - the story is told through the experiences of the people who lived and worked here. Covers four different periods, from 1840 to 1977.

Birmingham Cathedral

[icons]

Colmore Row
Birmingham B3 2QB
0121 262 1840
www.birminghamcathedral.com
enquiries@birminghamcathedral.com

Birmingham Cathedral has been a place of Christian worship since 1715 designed by the Baroque architect, Thomas Archer. Situated in the heart of the city we are open and staffed every day of the year.

Birmingham City University Art & Design Archives

[icons]

Parkside Building, 5 Cardigan Street
Birmingham B4 7BD
0121 331 6981
www.biad.bcu.ac.uk/research/archives
sian.vaughan@bcu.ac.uk

Birmingham City University Art and Design Archives contains both art and archival collections. There are 16 different archives and collections in the archives.

Birmingham Museum & Art Gallery

[icons]

Chamberlain Square
Birmingham B3 3DH
0121 303 2834
www.bmag.org.uk
enquiries@birminghammuseum.org.uk

Birmingham Museum and Art Gallery (BMAG) first opened in 1885. It is housed in a Grade II* listed city centre landmark building.

Collections: There are over 500,000 objects in Birmingham Museums and Art Gallery's collection. Our collection of Pre-Raphaelite paintings and drawings draws visitors from around the world.

Bishop Asbury Cottage

[icons]

Newton Road, Great Barr
West Bromwich B43 6HN
0121 553 0759
www.museums.sandwell.gov.uk

An 18th century cottage which was the boyhood home of Francis Asbury, the first American Methodist Bishop. Furnished in period style, and with memorabilia and information relating to Asbury's life both in West Bromwich and in America.

Black Country Living Museum

[icons]

Tipton Road
Dudley DY1 4SQ
0121 557 9643
www.bclm.com
info@bclm.com

Covering 26 acres of former industrial land, Black Country Living Museum is uniquely placed to tell the story of the creation of the world's first industrial landscape. Over fifty authentic shops, houses and workshops have been carefully reconstructed to preserve the character of the region when its manufacturers bought worldwide fame to Black Country towns. Explore the underground mine and experience the authentic sights, sounds, smells and tastes from the past.

Black Country Society

[icons]

44 Whitehall Road
Stourbridge DY8 2JT
01384 379972
www.blackcountrysociety.co.uk
rp1914bcs@virginmedia.com

The society exists to foster interest in the past, present and future of the Black Country through meetings, talks and the quarterly magazine, The Blackcountryman. Its membership serves not only the local area but also the rest of Britain.

Blakesley Hall

[icons]

Blakesley Road, Yardley
Birmingham B25 8RN
0121 464 2193
www.bmag.org.uk
blakesley_hall@birmingham.gov.uk

After painstaking and careful restoration, Blakesley Hall a stunning, Elizabethan yeoman's house in Yardley, has reopened its doors to the public. Blakesley Hall has undergone extensive renovations to reinstate the ground floor rooms, as closely as possible, to their original appearance.

Broadfield House Glass Museum

Compton Drive
Kingswinford DY6 9NS
01384 812745
www.dudley.gov.uk/see-and-do/museums/glass-museum
glass.museum@dudley.gov.uk

Situated in the historic Stourbridge glass quarter, Broadfield House Glass Museum is one of the best glass museums in the world. It has a magnificent collection of British glass, much of which was made in the Stourbridge area, from 18th century tableware to Victorian cameo vases, historic paperweights to modern sculptural pieces.

Coventry Cathedral

1 Hill Top
Coventry CV1 5AB
024 7652 1200
www.coventrycathedral.org.uk
visits@coventrycathedral.org.uk

Coventry has had three cathedrals in the past 1000 years: the 12th century Priory Church of St Mary, the Medieval Parish Church Cathedral of St Michael and the modern Coventry Cathedral, also named for St Michael.

Coventry Family History Society

12 Knoll Drive, Styvechale
Coventry CV3 5BT
0247 669 3904
www.covfhs.org
enquiries@covfhs.org

The society was formed in 1994 to fulfill a growing need and to promote and encourage the study of family history, genealogy and local history in relation to the City of Coventry and its environs.

Coventry History Centre

Jordan Well
Coventry CV1 5QP
02476 834060
www.theherbert.org/collections/archives

Coventry History Centre is the place to research local and family history, using large collections of historical material, including the city's archives.

Coventry Transport Museum

Millennium Place, Hales Street
Coventry CV1 1JD
024 7623 4270
www.transport-museum.com
enquiries@transport-museum.com

The museum displays the largest collection of British cars, cycles and motorcycles in the world and is designated as a collection of national importance. Visitors can explore over 150 years of unique history and there's something different round every corner.

Dudley Archives & Local History Service

Dudley Archives and Local History Centre, Tipton Road
Dudley DY1 4SQ
01384 812770
http://goo.gl/8CG42W
archives.centre@dudley.gov.uk

Our aim is to acquire, preserve and make available for public research any and all material relating to the present Dudley Metropolitan Borough area. This includes both manuscripts, such as parish records, council minutes and files, title deeds and maps, and also printed material, in the form of books, pamphlets, posters and newspapers, and audio visual material.

Dudley Museum & Art Gallery

St James's Road
Dudley DY1 1HP
01384 815575
www.dudley.gov.uk/see-and-do/museums
dudley.museum@dudley.gov.uk

Town centre museum and art gallery combining permanant art, geology and fossil collections with contemporary exhibitions, local interest shows and hands-on exhibitions related to the school curriculum. Home to the Brooke Robinson collection - a Victorian gentleman's collection of paintings, furniture, Greek and Roman pottery, Oriental and European ceramics, and enamel snuff boxes.

Edgbaston Museum

Warwickshire County Cricket Club, The County Ground, Edgbaston
Birmingham B5 7QU
0121 446 4422
www.thebears.co.uk
museum@thebears.co.uk

A museum dedicated to the famous test venue and home of Warwickshire County Cricket Club. From memorabilia commemorating one hundred years of test history including kit used by some of the greats, to the achievements and history of the Warwickshire side itself.

Electric Railway Museum

Rowley Road, nr Coventry Airport and the Air Museum
Coventry CV3 4LE
02476 997397

www.electricrailwaymuseum.co.uk

visiterm@electricrailwaymuseum.co.uk

Electric Railway Museum is a UK based charity which aims to promote the heritage of all electric trains in the UK through traction and rolling stock restoration, display and operation along with work in gathering historically relevant technical and photographic archives.

Galton Valley Canal Heritage Centre

Brasshouse Lane

Smethwick B66 1BA

0121 558 8195

www.museums.sandwell.gov.uk

Situated just off the Birmingham main line canals, the centre gives visitors an insight into some of the most important civil engineering feats in the area. As well as our displays and exhibitions at the main heritage centre site we also look after the New Smethwick Pumping Station and the original site of James Watt and Matthew Boulton's Smethwick Engine.

Haden Hill House

Halesowen Road

Cradley Heath B64 7JU

01384 569444

www.hadenhillhouse.sandwell.gov.uk

A Victorian gentleman's residence, furnished in period style, and surrounded by 55 acres of beautiful parkland.

Herbert Art Gallery & Museum

Jordan Well

Coventry CV1 5QP

024 7683 2386

www.theherbert.org

info@theherbert.org

We provide places for the people of Coventry and visitors to the City to meet, celebrate and explore their cultural and creative past, present and futures.

Himley Hall & Park

Himley Park, Himley

Dudley DY3 4DF

01384 817817

www.dudley.gov.uk/himleyhall

Himley Hall, situated between Kingswinford and Wombourne, started life in the 18th century when a medieval manor house on the site belonging to the Earl of Dudley was demolished to make way for a great Palladian mansion. The 180 acres of grounds were designed by Capability Brown to include a great lake fed by a series of waterfalls from a higher chain of smaller pools.

Jaguar Heritage

Browns Lane, Allesley

Coventry CV5 9DR

024 7640 1288

www.jdht.com

museumvisit@jdht.com

Established for the nation in 1983, The Jaguar Daimler Heritage Trust maintains a unique collection of motor vehicles and artefacts manufactured by Jaguar Cars Limited and the many other renowned marques associated with the company.

Lace Guild, The

The Hollies, 53 Audnam

Stourbridge DY8 4AE

01384 390739

www.laceguild.demon.co.uk

hollies@laceguild.org

The Lace Guild is the largest organisation for lacemakers in the British Isles, and our membership is international. Our aims are to provide information about the craft of lacemaking, its history and use; to promote a high standard of lacemaking; and to encourage design, development and professional presentation of lace.

Lapworth Museum of Geology

School of Earth Sciences, University of Birmingham, Edgbaston

Birmingham B15 2TT

0121 414 7294

www.lapworth.bham.ac.uk

lapworth@contacts.bham.ac.uk

The Lapworth Museum of Geology has the finest and most extensive collections of fossils, minerals and rocks in the West Midlands. Dating back to 1880, the museum is one of the oldest specialist geological museums in the UK.

Library of Birmingham

Centenary Square

Birmingham B1 2ND

0121 242 4242

www.libraryofbirmingham.com/archives

There are millions of individual items in the collections, dating from the 12th century to the present day. For safe keeping and preservation, these are stored in environmentally-controlled conditions inside the Library's 'golden box'.

Locksmith's House, The

54 New Road
Willenhall WV13 2DA
0121 557 9643
www.bclm.co.uk
info@bclm.com

The Locksmith's House shows the lifestyle and working conditions of the Hodson lockmaking family of Willenhall at the turn of the century. The Victorian house and lockmaking workshops are typical of the many small businesses which once flourished in the town which has been the heart of lockmaking since the Industrial Revolution - the Hodson family business was established in 1792.

Modern Records Centre, University of Warwick Library

Modern Records Centre, University Library, University of Warwick
Coventry CV4 7AL
024 7652 4219
www2.warwick.ac.uk/services/library/mrc
archives@warwick.ac.uk

The Modern Records Centre holds nationally important archives for the study of social, economic and political history, mainly from the mid 19th century onwards. The centre was founded in October 1973 with the principal objectives of locating and preserving primary sources for modern British social, political and economic history, with special concentration on the national history of industrial relations, industrial politics and labour history. The record centre contains the archives of national trade unions, employers.

Museum Collections Centre

25 Dollman St
Birmingham B7 4RQ
0121 303 0190
www.birminghammuseums.org.uk/bmag
bmag_enquiries@birmingham.gov.uk

The museums Collections Centre in Nechells has brought together 80 per cent of Birmingham Museums and Art Gallery's stored collections under one roof. The 1.5 hectare site, close to Duddeston Station, holds hundreds of thousands of objects. Among the collections are steam engines, sculptures, an entire collection of Austin, Rover and MG motor cars, a red phone box and even a Sinclair C5.

Museum of the Jewellery Quarter

75-80 Vyse Street, Hockley
Birmingham B18 6HA
0121 554 3598

www.bmag.org.uk/jewellery_quarter
bmag_enquiries@birmingham.gov.uk

Built around the preserved workshops and offices of Smith & Pepper, a Birmingham jewellery firm, the award-winning Museum of the Jewellery Quarter offers a fascinating insight into the city's historic jewellery trade. Visitors can enjoy a guided tour around the perfectly preserved 'time capsule' factory - little changed since the beginning of the century - and see demonstrations of jewellery making.

Oak House Museum

Oak Road
West Bromwich B70 8HJ
0121 553 0759
www.oakhouse.sandwell.gov.uk

Oak House is a delightful half timbered yeoman's house, furnished with contemporary furniture. The house is a ten minute walk from the centre of West Bromwich, and near to the Lodge Road metro stop.

Pen Museum, The

Unit 3 The Argent Centre 60 Frederick Street, Birmingham, West Midlands B1 3HS, United Kingdom
Birmingham B1 3HS
0121 236 9834
www.penroom.co.uk
penmuseum@penroom.co.uk

One of Birmingham's great attractions and centres of information about the city's fascinating history. Dedicated to steel pen making in Birmingham.

Collections: Current themes are Birmingham manufacturers; pen manufacturing processes supported by social history of workers; the history of writing and methods of communicating. The core collection comprises of items from Birmingham and the Birmingham pen-related trades.

Priory Visitor Centre

Coventry Arts and Heritage, Priory Row
Coventry CV1 5EX
024 7655 2242
www.theherbert.org
priory.visitorscentre@coventry.gov.uk

Discover Coventry's first cathedral at the Priory Visitor Centre and Undercrofts. For hundreds of years the ruins of Coventry's first cathedral lay hidden beneath the city centre. The 'Phoenix Initiative', Coventry's Millennium project, gave archaeologists the opportunity to excavate this important site.

Red House Glass Cone

High Street, Wordsley
Stourbridge DY8 4AZ
01384 812750
www.dudley.gov.uk/see-and-do/museums
redhousecone@dudley.gov.uk

The Red House Glass Cone lies in the heart of the Glass Quarter, Stourbridge, West Midlands. It was built at the end of the 18th century and used for the manufacture of glass until 1936.

Collections: Newly installed exhibition galleries tell the story of glassmaking in the area and the history of this unique glassworks. Glass and archive material from the Stuart Collection which spans over 100 years will also be on display.

Ruskin Glass Centre

Wollaston Road, Amblecote
Stourbridge DY8 4HE
01384 399400
http://goo.gl/JU1CDC

Situated in Stourbridge's historic glass quarter, the Ruskin Glass Centre houses a wide range of skilled craftspeople, including some of the leading British studio glass companies. Visitors can view the whole array of glassmaking processes including blowing, cutting, kiln work, stained glass and lampwork. There are also other craftspeople including photographers, printers and publishers and glass repairers.

Saint Nicolas Place

81 The Green, Kings Norton
Birmingham B38 8RU
0121 458 1223
www.saintnicolasplace.co.uk

The Tudor Merchant's House and the 17th century Old Grammar School are set either side of St Nicolas' Church, a place of worship much of which has stood here since Norman times. Together, they constitute the finest collection of mediaeval buildings in Birmingham. They were restored in 2004 and are owned and managed by Kings Norton Parish Church Council for all to enjoy and use.

Sarehole Mill

Colebank Road, Hall Green
Birmingham B13 0DB
0121 777 6612
www.birminghammuseums.org.uk/sarehole
bmag_enquiries@birmingham.gov.uk

A 250 year old idyllic watermill only four miles from Birmingham city centre. The original main waterwheel, mill gears and grinding stones can been seen in action on milling days, every Wednesday and Sunday during the open season. Explore Sarehole Mill's links with Tolkien. Signposts to Middle-Earth is a family-friendly exhibition explores the connections of JRR Tolkien with Sarehole Mill and the surrounding area.

Selly Manor

Corner of Maple and Sycamore Roads, Oak Tree Lane, Bournville
Birmingham B30 2AE
0121 472 0199
www.sellymanormuseum.org.uk
sellymanor@bvt.org.uk

Selly Manor and Minworth Greaves are two ancient timber-framed manor houses moved to Bournville in the early 20th century by the chocolate manufacturer George Cadbury. They are two of Birmingham's oldest houses and are beautiful examples of medieval and Tudor architecture, surrounded by an authentic period garden.

Smethwick Heritage Centre

Victoria Park Lodge, High Street
Smethwick B66 3NJ
0121 555 7278
www.smethwick-heritage.co.uk
info@smethwick-heritage.co.uk

Our aim is to collect, store, archive and display object and material connected with Smethwick.

Soho House Museum

Soho Avenue, Handsworth
Birmingham B18 5LB
0121 554 9122
www.bmag.org.uk/soho-house
bmag_enquiries@birmingham.gov.uk

Soho House Museum was the home of Matthew Boulton, one of Birmingham's most famous sons. Boulton is famous for his associations with James Watt and the Lunar Society and left his mark on industrial development in Birmingham.

Special Collections, University of Birmingham

Special Collections, Academic Services, Main Library, University of Birmingham, Edgbaston
Birmingham B15 2TT
0121 414 5839
www.special-coll.bham.ac.uk
special-collections@bham.ac.uk

The Special Collections & Archives of the University of Birmingham have been built up over a period of 120 years and consist of approximately 120,000 pre-1850 books dating from 1471 and some 3 million archives and manuscripts, all of which provide a rich resource for teaching and research.

St Chad's Cathedral

Queensway
Birmingham B4 6EU
0121 236 2251
www.stchadscathedral.org.uk
reception@rc-birmingham.org

St Chad's, the first Catholic cathedral erected in England since the Reformation, was built between 1839 and 1841 to serve the rapidly expanding Catholic population in Birmingham. It was designed in north German 13th century style by Augustus Welby Northmore Pugin (1812-1852), the world famous pioneer of Gothic revival architecture.

St Mary's Guildhall

Bayley Lane
Coventry CV1 5RN
02476 833328
www.stmarysguildhall.co.uk
guildhall@coventry.gov.uk

St Mary's Guildhall is one of the finest surviving medieval guildhalls in England.

Collections: The civic collection at St Mary's Guildhall includes a diverse range of items and artworks that have been amassed at the Guildhall over the centuries, some as donations and bequests, others as specific commissions by the guilds or civic leaders.

Thinktank: Birmingham's Science Museum

Millennium Point, Curzon Street
Birmingham B4 7XG
0121 202 2222
www.thinktank.ac
findout@thinktank.ac

Where can you explore deepest space, find out how doctors perform life-saving surgery and travel back in time to Birmingham's amazing industrial past, all under one roof? From steam engines to intestines, Thinktank has over 200 hands-on exhibits on science and discovery from the past, present and future.

Collections: The science and industry collections consist of around 40,000 objects, including James Watt's Smethwick engine of 1779, the oldest working steam engine in the world.

Tipton Community Heritage Centre

Tipton Community Heritage Centre, Tipton Library, Unit 19, Tipton Shopping Centre, Owen Street,
Tipton DY4 8QE
0121 522 3722
www.tiptonheritagecentre.sandwell.gov.uk

The centre features a small but informative display covering various aspects of Tipton's industrial and social history. One focus is on the development of the town following the construction of the first canal in 1769.

University of Birmingham, Research & Cultural Collections

University of Birmingham Collections, c/o University Curator, Main Library, The University of Birmingham, Edgbaston
Birmingham B15 2TT
0121 414 6750
http://goo.gl/OiCCs3
j.h.hamilton@bham.ac.uk

The University of Birmingham Collections is a cornucopia of extraordinary artefacts, from West African masks in the Danford Collection, to important 20th century paintings such as Peter Lanyon's mural in the Arts Building. The University owns, displays and teaches from groups of objects within seven distinct collections, including archaeology, physics and pathology.

Vintage Trains

670 Warwick Road, Tyseley
Birmingham B11 2HL
0121 707 4696
www.vintagetrains.co.uk
office@vintagetrains.co.uk

Tyseley Locomotive Works is the engineering subsidiary of the Birmingham Railway Museum Trust, which is a registered educational charity. The trust was established to preserve and demonstrate the steam locomotives in the Tyseley collection.

Walsall Leather Museum

Littleton Street West
Walsall WS2 8EQ
01922 721153
cms.walsall.gov.uk/leathermuseum

Discover why Walsall became the British leather goods capital in this fascinating working museum, housed in a restored leather factory. For two hundred years Walsall people have been making some of the world's finest saddles and leather goods.

Walsall Local History Centre

Essex Street
Walsall WS2 7AS
01922 721305
cms.walsall.gov.uk/localhistorycentre
localhistorycentre@walsall.gov.uk

The research room is open to all members of the public free of charge and you will receive a friendly welcome from helpful staff.

Walsall Museum

Lichfield Street
Walsall WS1 1TR
01922 653116
cms.walsall.gov.uk/museums
museum@walsall.gov.uk

Walsall Museum is a friendly and welcoming museum in the heart of Walsall, sharing a building with the town's central library.

Collections: Collection of social and industrial history from Walsall's past and present, ranging from 17th century firemarks to 21st century posters. Strong collection of costume and textiles, including the Hodson Shop Collection, a unique collection of unsold shop stock of working-class clothing from the 1920s to 1960s.

Warwickshire County Cricket Club Museum

County Ground, Edgbaston
Birmingham B5 7QU
0121 446 4422
www.thebears.co.uk/history/museum

A visit to the Warwickshire County Cricket Club Museum at Edgbaston is to take a unique journey through the last 113 years of first-class cricket played at this famous ground. Photographs, memorabilia, artefacts and articles are displayed in a way that captures the interest of the visitor .

Wednesbury Museum & Art Gallery

Holyhead Road
Wednesbury WS10 7DF
0121 556 0683
www.museums.sandwell.gov.uk

A Victorian Art Gallery, recently redecorated, housing collections which include fine art paintings, applied art, including one of the world's largest collections of Ruskin pottery, and geology.

Weoley Castle

Alwold Road, Weoley Castle
Birmingham B29 5RX
0121 464 2193
www.birmingham.gov.uk/weoleycastle
bmag_enquiries@birmingham.gov.uk

The ruins at Weoley Castle are over 700 years old and are the remains of the moated medieval manor house that once stood here. The site has been inhabited from the 12th century and, according to the Doomsday Book, was part of the estates of William Fitz Ansculf. Excavations have revealed the wealthy status of the castle's occupants. Finds have included glass from Syria and a range of kitchen equipment.

Wightwick Manor & Gardens - National Trust

Wightwick Bank
Wolverhampton WV6 8EE
01902 761400
www.nationaltrust.org.uk/wightwick-manor
wightwickmanor@nationaltrust.org.uk

One of only a few surviving examples of a house built and furnished under the influence of the Arts & Crafts Movement. The many original William Morris wallpapers and fabrics, Pre-Raphaelite paintings, Kempe glass and de Morgan ware help conjure up the spirit of the time.

Winterbourne House & Garden, University of Birmingham

58 Edgbaston Park Road, Edgbaston
Birmingham B15 2RT
0121 414 3003
www.winterbourne.org.uk
enquiries@winterbourne.org.uk

Winterbourne is a rare surviving example of an early 20th century suburban villa and garden. The house was built in 1903 for John and Margaret Nettlefold, of Guest, Keen & Nettlefold. Botanic gardens display collections of plants from all around the world.

Wolverhampton City Archives

Molineux Hotel Building, Whitmore Hill
Wolverhampton WV1 1SF
01902 552480
www.wolverhamptonart.org.uk
archives@wolverhampton.gov.uk

Wolverhampton Archives keeps documents, maps, books, photos, newspapers and more relating to the history of areas now within the city of Wolverhampton.

West Sussex

Sussex, maritime county in SE. of England, bounded N. and NE. by Surrey and Kent, SE. and S. by the English Channel, and W. and NW. by Hants; greatest length, N. and S., 27 miles; greatest breadth, E. and W., 76 miles; area, 933,269 acres, population 490,505. The county is traversed by the South Downs. The rivers are not important; they are the Arun, Adur, Ouse, and Rother, all flowing S. to the English Channel. The principal means of communication are the railways; these belong chiefly to the London, Brighton, and South Coast system. The most fertile soil is the low land along the coast, which yields heavy crops of grain and hay; the South Downs are chiefly pastoral, and support a well-known breed of sheep to which they give name. Ironstone is abundant, and so long as wood only was used for smelting the co. was one of the chief seats of the British iron trade. 'Sussex marble', a kind of limestone containing fresh-water shells, is worked near Petworth. The manufactures include woollens, paper, gunpowder, bricks and tiles, &c., but are not extensive. The seaports are now small and comparatively unimportant, but the mildness of the climate along the sea coast has led to the growth of numerous watering and bathing places and health resorts, including Brighton, Hastings, Eastbourne, Worthing, Seaford, Littlehampton, and Bognor. Sussex was the scene of much of the early history of the country, and is rich in archaeological remains. It is almost entirely in the diocese of Chichester.

– John Bartholomew, *Gazetteer of the British Isles* (1887) [The above description refers to East and West Sussex combined.]

Amberley Working Museum

Houghton Bridge, Amberley
Arundel BN18 9LT
01798 831370
www.amberleymuseum.co.uk

Amberley is a thirty-six acre open air museum set in the midst of the beautiful South Downs in West Sussex. Dedicated to the industrial heritage of the South East, exhibits include a narrow-gauge railway and bus service (both provide free nostalgic travel around the site), Connected Earth Telecommunications Hall, Milne Electricity Hall, Printing Workshop and much more. The museum is also home to traditional craftspeople, such as the blacksmith and potter.

Arundel Castle & Gardens

Arundel Castle and Gardens
Arundel BN18 9AB
01903 882173
www.arundelcastle.org
bryan.mcdonald@arundelcastle.org

There is nearly 1,000 years of history at this great castle, situated in magnificent grounds overlooking the River Arun in West Sussex and built at the end of the 11th century by Roger de Montgomery, Earl of Arundel.

Collections: The results of all this history are concentrated at the castle, which houses a fascinating collection of fine furniture dating from the 16th century, tapestries, clocks, and portraits by Van Dyck, Gainsborough, Mytens, Lawrence, Reynolds, etc. Personal possessions of Mary, Queen of Scots and a selection of historical, religious and heraldic items from the Duke of Norfolk's collection are also on display.

Arundel Museum & Heritage Centre

Arundel Museum, Mill Road
Arundel BN18 9PA
01903 885866
www.arundelmuseum.org

Arundel Museum is the south coast's newest museum, revealing the story of the historic town of Arundel. Exhibitions change regularly but focus on the life of the town of Arundel from Roman times to the 20th century.

Bignor Roman Villa

Bignor
Pulborough RH20 1PH
01798 869 259
www.bignorromanvilla.co.uk
enquiries@ bignorromanvilla.co.uk

Bignor Roman Villa is the stunning remains of a Roman home and farm with world-class mosaic floors in a spectacular downland setting. Learn why the Roman owners chose to develop such a magnificent settlement at Bignor in the 3rd century AD and how they acquired wealth from its location.

Bognor Regis Local History Museum

69 High Street
Bognor Regis PO21 1RY
01243 865636
www.bognormuseum.org

Bognor Regis Local History Society was formed in 1979 to promote research into, and recording of, the town's history.

Collections: Locally found fossils. Social history collections reflecting past local businesses from pawnbrokers to photography, toys to tobbaconist and chemists to cobblers.

Burgess Hill Museum

Cyprus Hall, Cyprus Road
Burgess Hill RH15 8DX
www.burgesshillmuseum.co.uk

The collection of artefacts includes roman and locally made pottery, Victoria Pleasure Gardens memorabilia, maps, photographs and many more items of interest.

Chichester Cathedral

West Street
Chichester PO19 1RP
01243 782595
www.chichestercathedral.org.uk
enquiry@chichestercathedral.org.uk

For 900 years Chichester Cathedral has stood at the heart of Chichester. Each generation has left its mark on the cathedral, so this magnificent building has unique architecture ranging from original Norman features to the towering Victorian Spire and newly restored Lady Chapel.

Christ's Hospital School Museum

The Counting House, Christ's Hospital
Horsham RH13 7YP
01403 211293
http://goo.gl/xkK9QV

Housed on the top floor of the infirmary, the museum has many artefacts from school life at London, Hertford and Horsham, as well as an original matron's kitchen from 1902. Christ's Hospital has a complete run of admission books, giving pupils' details from 1563 to present day, as well as many other records detailing life at the school.

Coultershaw Water Pump

Coultershaw Mill, Station Road
Petworth GU28 0JE
01798 865774
www.coultershaw.co.uk
rlwconsult@btinternet.com

This waterwheel-driven three-throw beam pump was installed in 1782 to pump water from the River Rother up to Petworth, 150ft higher. The machinery has been put in working order and a 100 year old barn from Goodwood erected over it to act as a reception and display centre.

Crawley Museum

Crawley Museum Centre, Goffs Park House, Old Horsham Road, Southgate
Crawley RH11 8PE
01293 539 088
www.crawleymuseums.org
office@crawleymuseums.org

This museum is run by Crawley Museum Society in the present location, but will move to a historic house in central Crawley in 2016/7. The displays show the life of the Crawley area from the Stone Age to the present day, and include a fine Bronze Age sword and a Rex Forecar of 1903 which featured regularly in the London-Brighton run.

Cuckfield Museum

Queen's Hall, High Street
Cuckfield RH17 5EL
01444 473630
www.cuckfieldmuseum.org
info@cuckfieldmuseum.org

Cuckfield Museum is a small volunteer run, independent museum, housed on the first floor of historic Queen's Hall situated on Cuckfield's medieval High Street.

Collections: The museum has a permanent exhibition of items from its collection illustrating various aspects of life in and around Cuckfield during the last two hundred years. The museum houses a local history reference library and document archive.

East Grinstead Museum

Old Market Yard, Cantelupe Road
East Grinstead RH19 3BJ
01342 302233
www.eastgrinsteadmuseum.org.uk
info@eastgrinsteadmuseum.org.uk

Interesting and varied displays trace the history of the town and surrounding area. Artefacts and memorabilia are interspersed with interactive touch screens and film.

Fishbourne Roman Palace

Roman Way, Fishbourne
Chichester PO19 2QR
01243 785859
www.sussexpast.co.uk
adminfish@sussexpast.co.uk

Explore this first-century home and outstanding archaeological site, get hands-on at our exciting family events and marvel at the largest collection of early Roman mosaic floors in Britain. Dating back to the beginning of Roman occupation of Britain this Roman Palace offers visitors of all ages a unique experience.

Guildhall Museum

Priory Park
Chichester PO19 1NH
Contact 01243 784683, Tuesday to Saturdaay
www.thenovium.org/index.cfm?articleid=20295
districtmuseum@chichester.gov.uk

The Guildhall was built in 1269 as the church for the Greyfriars. After the Dissolution of the monasteries in 1538 the church became the Town Hall.

Collections: Displays show the history of the area including the castle which was destroyed in 1217, the Greyfriars and William Blake. There is also information on Priory Park.

Henfield Museum

Henfield Hall, Cooper's Way, High Street
Henfield BN5 9DB
01273 492507
www.henfieldhub.com/henfield-museum
office@henfield.gov.uk

The museum is owned and run by Henfield Parish Council. The objects exhibited range from early fossils and flint implements, through the Medieval and Tudor era to the Georgian, Victorian and Edwardian periods. Household objects from these times recall Henfield in the past.

Horsham Museum & Art Gallery

Causeway House, 9 Causeway
Horsham RH12 1HE
01403 254959
www.horshammuseum.org
museum@horsham.gov.uk

Horsham Museum is situated at the head of the Causeway one of Sussex's and most picturesque streets of period buildings. The museum building itself dates back to the 1400s and is well worth a visit alone.

Ifield Watermill

Hyde Drive, Ifield
Crawley RH11 0PL
01293 539 088
www.crawleymuseums.org/watermill

Ifield Watermill is thought to be the only working Watermill in West Sussex still powered by its original water source, the Ifield millpond.

Littlehampton Museum

Manor House, Church Street
Littlehampton BN17 5EW
01903 738100
www.littlehampton-tc.gov.uk
museum@littlehampton-tc.gov.uk

Littlehampton Museum is in the heart of the town centre and offers a fascinating insight into the community's social history through a variety of exciting galleries, many with audio points and interactive elements to help guide you through the history of the town.

Collections: The collection includes a wealth of archaeological material from the surrounding area including Angmering Roman Villa, the Climping coin hoard and features Bronze and Iron Age exhibits.

Manor Cottage Heritage Centre

Manor Cottage, Southwick Street
Southwick BN42 4TE
01273 465164
www.southwicksociety.btck.co.uk/TheManorCottage
nigel.divers@unisonfree.net

The building dates from about the mid 15th century and was built as an open hall with an oak frame, wattle and daub walls and probably a thatched roof.

Marlipins Museum

36 High Street
Shoreham-by-Sea BN43 5DA
01273 462994 or 01273 405735 out of season
www.friendsofmarlipins.org.uk/museum.html
marlipins@sussexpast.co.uk

The medieval building in which Marlipins Museum presents its collections is of national importance (Grade II* Listed). It houses more than 2,500 exhibits reflecting the rich history of the area, its archaeology, maritime shipbuilding past, the two World Wars, and the Shoreham Beach nature reserve..

Novium, The

✉ £

Tower Street
Chichester PO19 1QH
01243 775888
www.thenovium.org
thenovium@chichester.gov.uk

The Novium offers intriguing stories from Chichester District connected with extraordinary artefacts in a brand new, state-of-the-art building. Alongside the commitment to preserve our rich local heritage, The Novium also provides visitors with a glimpse into the past 500,000 years.

Nymans - National Trust

🏛 ★

Staplefield Road, Handcross
Haywards Heath RH17 6EB
01444 405250
www.nationaltrust.org.uk/nymans
nymans@nationaltrust.org.uk

Nymans is one of the great gardens of the Sussex Weald and is internationally famous for its beauty and collection of rare plants. It is the achievement of three generations of the Messel family over a period of over a hundred years.

Pallant House Gallery

🏛 ✉ £

9 North Pallant
Chichester PO19 1TJ
01243 774557
www.pallant.org.uk
info@pallant.org.uk

Pallant House Gallery is a unique combination of a Grade 1 listed Queen Anne townhouse and an award-winning contemporary extension. It is based in the heart of Chichester and holds one of the best collections of Modern British art in the country.

Parham Park

🏛 £

Pulborough RH20 4HS
01903 742021
www.parhaminsussex.co.uk

THistoric manor house dating from the Elizabethan era, with rare art, gardens and 875-acre deer park.

Petworth Cottage Museum, The

✉ £

346 High Street
Petworth GU28 0AU
01798 342100
www.petworthcottagemuseum.co.uk
stevensonguk@yahoo.co.uk

The museum is a Leconfield Estate worker's cottage restored and furnished as it might have been in about 1910, when Mrs. Mary Cummings lived in No 346. The museum also has a rare collection of Petworth Goss China.

Petworth House & Park - National Trust

🏛 £

Petworth Park
Petworth GU28 0AE
01798 342207
www.nationaltrust.org.uk/petworth-house
petworth@nationaltrust.org.uk

Rebuilt in 1688 by the 'Proud Duke' (Charles Seymour, 6th Duke of Somerset) around the ancient manor house of the Percy family, Petworth today houses the largest collection of paintings and sculpture in the care of the National Trust. Petworth also features a 30-acre woodland garden, which forms part of the Pleasure Ground, and a majestic 700-acre landscaped park designed by 'Capability' Brown which is home to the largest herd of fallow deer in England.

Priest House & Garden, The

🏛 ✉ £

North Lane
West Hoathly RH19 4PP
01342 810479
www.sussexpast.co.uk
priest@sussexpast.co.uk

The only one of its kind open to the public, this beautiful 15th century Wealden hall house stands in a traditional cottage garden on the edge of the Ashdown Forest in picturesque West Hoathly. The house was owned in turn by Henry VIII, Thomas Cromwell, Anne of Cleves, Mary I and Elizabeth I. It is now furnished with 17th & 18th century country furniture and domestic objects while the garden is planted with over 170 culinary, medicinal & household herbs.

Royal Sussex Living History Group, The

⛺

07977 511134
www.royalsussex.org.uk
info@royalsussex.org.uk

The Royal Sussex Living History Group is a small group dedicated to recreating the Royal Sussex Regiment as it would have been in the Victorian period, keeping alive the days of scarlet tunics, buff leather equipment and bell tents.

Rustington Heritage Association Exhibition Centre

✉ ★

34 Woodlands Avenue
Rustington BN16 3HB
01903 788478
www.rustingtonmuseum.org
museum@rustingtonpc.org

Rustington Museum is housed in a newly renovated

thatched cottage in the heart of the village of Rustington. The museum tells the fascinating story of the village from prehistory right through to the present day.

Selsey Lifeboat Museum

Kingsway
Selsey PO20 0DL
01243 602387
www.selseylifeboats.co.uk/index.html
terry@kaytel.fsnet.co.uk

Today's lifeboat station at Selsey operates an all weather Tyne class lifeboat (AWL 47-031 'Voluntary Worker') and a D class inshore lifeboat (ILB D691 'Betty and Thomas Moore'). Over its 150-year history the crew have been presented with 10 awards for gallantry.

Shoreham Airport Historical Association & Archive

Terminal Building, Shoreham Airport
Shoreham-by-Sea BN43 5FF
01273 441 061
www.visitorcentre.info
saha.archive@btinternet.com

The services offered at the Visitor Centre include an introduction to the aviation world to anybody of any age and above all with any interest. For those wishing to experience the world of aviation we have regular airport guided tours and our Visitor Centre is full of interesting displays relating to Shoreham's history.

Collections: The Archive houses a massive collection of photographs and literature dating back 95 years. In addition, we also publish a quarterly journal which contains a large degree of research material.

Standen - National Trust

Standen, West Hoathly Road
East Grinstead RH19 4NE
01342 323029
www.nationaltrust.org.uk/standen
standen@nationaltrust.org.uk

Standen is a fine show-piece of the late 19th-century Arts & Crafts Movement, featuring rich William Morris textiles and wallpapers, complemented by contemporary furniture, ceramics and pictures of the time. Philip Webb, friend of William Morris, designed this family house in the 1890s.

Steyning Museum

The Museum, Church Street
Steyning BN44 3YB
01903 813333
www.steyningmuseum.org.uk
contact@steyningmuseum.org.uk

Steyning, Bramber and Upper Beeding are full of surprises. There has been a castle in Bramber since the time of William the Conqueror. Steyning church was founded by a Saxon saint - with a very strange story.

Storrington & District Museum

The Old School, School Lane
Storrington RH20 4LL
01903 740188
www.storringtonmuseum.org
info@storringtonmuseum.org

The museum houses local archaeology, articles from local churches, domestic history, details of local people and their memorabilia, artefacts of vanished local places, trades and services and articles from the two world wars.

Sussex Family History Group

8 Wythwood
Haywards Heath RH16 4RD
www.sfhg.org.uk
secretary@sfhg.org.uk

For all those interested in family history and genealogical research in Sussex, England.

Tangmere Military Aviation Museum

Tangmere
Chichester PO20 2ES
01243 790090
www.tangmere-museum.org.uk
info@tangmere-museum.org.uk

The museum was opened in 1982 with exhibits depicting 70 years of military aviation in Sussex, with special emphasis on the RAF at Tangmere and the air war over southern England from 1939 to 1945. There are full size replicas of a Hurricane and a Spitfire. The Tangmere Hall has exhibits illustrating the history of Tangmere from 1917 to 1970.

TimeMachineFun, The Clock Trust

Time Machine/Clocktrust Woodend Turning, Common Road,
Funtington/East Ashling
Chichester PO18 9DH
01243576890
www.clocktrust.com
contact@clocktrust.com

The building itself comes from the block work recovered
from the cathedral collapse in 1850. TimeMachineFun, a
museum with a difference, you get to explore and interact
with the exhibits, which are experiments. On display we
have a variety of weird and wonderful technology,
demonstrating how science and engineering has totally
changed the society we all enjoy. Instead of just looking at
the exhibits from a distance we have a hands-on approach
where we open items up, take them apart and explore the
science and engineering inside.

Uppark House & Garden - National Trust

South Harting
Petersfield GU31 5QR
01730 825 415
www.nationaltrust.org.uk/uppark
uppark@nationaltrust.org.uk

Late 17th-century house in an impressive setting. Fine late
17th-century house elevated upon the South Downs.
Renowned Grand Tour Collection. Impressive Georgian
doll's-house.

Wakehurst Place - National Trust

Ardingly RH17 6TN
01444 894066
www.nationaltrust.org.uk/wakehurst-place
wakehurst@kew.org

The 200 hectares (500 acres) at Wakehurst Place include
walled gardens, water gardens, a wetland conservation area,
woodland, lakes and ponds.

Weald & Downland Open Air Museum

Singleton
Chichester PO18 0EU
01243 811363
www.wealddown.co.uk
office@wealddown.co.uk

Our ancestors' homes and the way they built them, their
animals and the way they raised them, their crops and
flowers and the way they grew them…at the Weald and
Downland Open Air Museum visitors discover how the
people of south east England lived over the last 500 years.
At the heart of the museum's collection are 50 historic
homes, farms and workplaces that have been rescued and
restored as far as possible to their original form.

West Sussex Record Office

3 Orchard Street
Chichester PO19 1DD
01243 753602
http://goo.gl/ADxNp7

The record office acquires, preserves and makes publicly
available the documented and recorded heritage of the
county.

Worthing Museum & Art Gallery

Chapel Road
Worthing BN11 1HP
01903 221067
www.worthingmuseum.co.uk
museum@adur-worthing.gov.uk

Opened in 1908 this fine Edwardian building houses West
Sussex's largest museum. Permanent displays include
archaelogy, costume, local history and decorative art.

West Yorkshire

Yorkshire, West-Riding, in W. and SW. of county; area, 1,768,380 acres, population 2,175,314. The surface rises towards the W. and NW., reaching in Whernside Mountain an altitude of 2414 ft. The principal rivers are the Ribble, Nidd, Calder, Don, Aire, and Wharfe. The West-Riding is the seat of Yorkshire industrial enterprise. The great Yorkshire coalfield, on which all the staple mfrs. of the Riding are situated, is a space 45 miles by 20 miles, between the Aire and the Don. Some of the leading branches of national industry have long had their seat in the West-Riding – woollens at Leeds, Bradford, Halifax, Dewsbury, and Huddersfield; linens at Leeds and Barnsley; and hardware, cutlery, and plated goods at Sheffield. There are mineral waters at Harrogate, Knaresborough, and Ilkley Wells. On the N. and E. sides corn and other crops are largely grown; and in the NW., round Settle and Skipton, it is all grass and dairy land. The West-Riding comprises 9 wapentakes; 724 parishes, and parts of 6 others; the parliamentary and municipal boroughs of Bradford, Dewsbury, Halifax, Huddersfield, Leeds, Pontefract, Sheffield, and Wakefield; and the municipal boroughs of Barnsley, Batley, Doncaster, Morley, Ripon, and Rotherham. It is mostly in the dioceses of York, Ripon, and Manchester.

– John Bartholomew, *Gazetteer of the British Isles* (1887)

Note: parts of the West Riding of Yorkshire, including Sheffield, Rotherham, Doncaster and Barnsley, became South Yorkshire in 1974.

Abbey House Museum

Abbey Walk, Abbey Rd, Kirkstall, Leeds
Leeds LS5 3EH
0113 230 5492
www.leeds.gov.uk/abbeyhouse
abbey.house@leeds.gov.uk

Based in the heart of the Kirkstall community, Abbey House was once the gatehouse for Kirkstall Abbey. Displays in the museum enable you to steep yourself in the romantic history of the abbey.

Collections: The museum holds large and important social history collections. This includes an archive relating to the Suffragette campaigns of Mrs Leonora Cohen (b.1873) who was one of the first women in Leeds to start campaigning for votes for women. Leeds Museums have been collecting toys, dolls and games since at least the 1920s and now hold one of the major collections in the country.

Bagshaw Museum

Wilton Park
Batley WF17 0AS
01924 326155
www.kirklees.gov.uk/museums
bagshaw.museum@kirklees.gov.uk

Where can you meet a mummy from Ancient Egypt, hear a Shirley Bassey hit, and come face to face with a Ganges crocodile? Bagshaw Museum brings together fasinating objects from all over the world, in the magnificient Victorian gothic setting of 'Woodlands' a former mill owners house set in Wilton Park.

Bankfield Museum

Boothtown Road
Halifax HX3 6HG
01422 352334
http://goo.gl/t8iVJo
bankfield.museum@calderdale.gov.uk

With its internationally important collection of textiles, weird and wonderful objects from around the world, and a varied programme of exhibitions and events, there is much to see and enjoy. The historic house of the Akroyd family is also home to the Duke of Wellington's Regimental Museum and the Marble Gallery, a new selling space for contemporary craft.

Bolling Hall Museum

Bowling Hall Road
Bradford BD4 7LP
01274 723057
www.bradfordmuseums.org/venues/bollinghall

Bolling Hall offers visitors a fascinating journey through the lives and times of the Bradford families for whom it provided a home over five hundred years. Bolling Hall was for many years the seat of two important land-owning families, the Bollings and the Tempests. With parts of the building dating from the medieval, Bolling Hall is a rambling mixture of styles with every nook and cranny packed with history. Rooms are furnished and decorated to give an accurate taste of life at different periods of the house's history.

Bracken Hall Countryside Museum

Glen Road, Baildon
Shipley BD17 5EA
01274 584140
www.bradfordmuseums.org/brackenhall
brackenhallcc@btconnect.com

Bracken Hall Countryside Centre and museum is situated on the edge of Shipley Glen, a popular beauty spot. The centre has displays relating to the natural history, geology, archaeology and local history of the area.

Bradford 1 Gallery

Centenary Square
Bradford BD1 1SD
01274 437800
http://goo.gl/zPHTnv

Bradford 1 Gallery is the new city centre space for exhibitions of contemporary and historic art and craft. It will host shows from national and regional touring venues as well as drawing upon the major collections of the museums and galleries service.

Bradford Cathedral

1 Stott Hill
Bradford BD1 4EH
01274 777720
www.bradfordcathedral.co.uk
cathedral@bradford.anglican.org

There has been worship on this site in Bradford for over a thousand years. This beautiful building has been a place of peace, prayer, hope and worship for many over the centuries.

Bradford Family History Society

5 Leaventhorpe Avenue, Fairweather Green
Bradford BD8 0ED
www.bradfordfhs.org.uk
secretary@bradfordfhs.org.uk

Family history information for the Bradford area.

Bradford Industrial Museum

Moorside Road, Eccleshill
Bradford BD2 3HP
01274 435900
www.bradfordmuseums.org
neil.hinchliffe@bradford.gov.uk

Original Victorian worsted spinning mill complex built in 1875, now used to recreate life in Bradford at the turn of the 19th century.

Bradford Local Studies

Central Library, Prince⬚s Way
Bradford BD1 1NN
01274 433686
http://goo.gl/JssrTw

The Local Studies service offers family and local history resources for the Bradford Metropolitan District and the West Yorkshire region. We have a wide range of material including books and maps, plus free access to several genealogy and historical newspaper websites.

Bronte Parsonage Museum

Church Street, Haworth
Keighley BD22 8DR
01535 642323
www.bronte.org.uk

The Bronte parsonage and museum focuses on the life and work of the celebrated family of writers. It has an unrivaled collection of objects and archival material relating the lives and work of Emily, Charlotte and Anne.

Calderdale Family History Society

15 Far View, Illingworth
Halifax HX2 0NU
www.cfhsweb.co.uk
secretary@cfhsweb.co.uk

The society was formed in 1985 and now has a great many active members. Many live beyond the Calderdale area, both in the UK and further afield in Australia, New Zealand, Canada, USA and other countries.

Calderdale Museums & Art Service

The Piece Hall
Halifax HX1 1RE
01422 358087
www.calderdale.gov.uk/leisure/museums-galleries

Calderdale Council operates a variety of museums & galleries throughout the region. The museum service cares for over 80,000 objects relating to the heritage of the area.

Castleford Forum Museum

Carlton Street
Castleford WF10 1BB
01977 722084
http://goo.gl/p3AiVe
museums@wakefield.gov.uk

Castleford Forum Museum, located in the new Castleford Forum Library and Museum building in the centre of town, is testament to the rich and extraordinary history of the area. The displays include fascinating and unique objects that tell stories of Castleford and its people.

Cliffe Castle Museum

Spring Gardens Lane
Keighley BD20 6LH
01535 618231
http://goo.gl/UAjYF
daru.rooke@bradford.gov.uk

Cliffe Castle Museum was originally the spectacular mansion of the local Victorian millionaire and textile manufacturer, Henry Isaac Butterfield. It stands in attractive hillside grounds with greenhouses, aviaries and a children's play area. The house is now a large museum with a wide variety of displays.

Colne Valley Museum

Cliffe Ash, Golcar
Huddersfield HD7 4PY
01484 659762
www.colnevalleymuseum.org.uk
info@colnevalleymuseum.org.uk

Colne Valley Museum is housed in a row of weavers cottage of the mid 19C. The museum depicts the cottage textile industry and the social history of the area.

Dewsbury Museum

Crow Nest Park, Heckmondwike Road
Dewsbury WF13 2SG
01924 325100
www.kirklees.gov.uk/museums
Dewsbury.Museum@kirklees.gov.uk

Revisit your childhood and enjoy the popular toy gallery and recreated 1940s classroom. Explore the fascinating Discovering Dewsbury local history gallery.

Duke of Wellington's Regiment Museum

Bankfield Museum, Ackroyd Park
Halifax HX3 6HG
01422 354823 / 01422 352334
http://goo.gl/y8p0Qw
john.spencer@calderdale.gov.uk

Representing over 300 years of the Duke of Wellington's Regiment, since its raising in 1702, this museum tells the stories of the soldiers who served using their own words. The 'Iron Duke', Arthur Wellesley, was the Colonel of the 33rd which became, after his death, the only Regiment to be named after a person not of the Royal Blood. Displays include items relating to the Duke himself and to the rich and varied history of the regiment, including the campaigns of 33rd and 76th foot.

East Riddlesden Hall - National Trust

Bradford Road
Keighley BD20 5EL
01535 607075
www.nationaltrust.org.uk/east-riddlesden-hall
eastriddlesden@nationaltrust.org.uk

This National Trust owned property boasts an attractive 17th-century manor house, delightful gardens, tearoom and shop. There is a fine collection of Yorkshire oak furniture and pewter, together stunning examples of textiles and 17th-century embroidery.

Fulneck Moravian Museum

55-57 Fulneck
Pudsey LS28 8NT
0113 256 4862
www.fulneck.org.uk/?page_id=16

Two 17th century cottages, Victorian parlour and kitchen, weaving chamber, Moravian embroidery, folk exhibits, an 1822 hand-pulled fire engine and ethnographical exhibits.

Gibson Mill

Hardcastle Crags, Hollin Hall, Crimsworth Dean
Hebden Bridge HX7 7AP
01422 844518
http://goo.gl/He2j2n
hardcastlecrags@nationaltrust.org.uk

Gibson Mill is a 19th-century cotton mill that sits at the heart of Hardcastle Crags. The mill has been brought back into use as a facility for visitors and for the local community.

Harewood House

Harewood House Trust, Harewood
Leeds LS17 9LG
0113 2181010
www.harewood.org
info@harewood.org

One of England's greatest country houses, created by architect John Carr and designer Robert Adam, furnished by master cabinet-maker Thomas Chippendale and set in a landscape created by 'Capability' Brown. The House, renowned for its stunning architecture and exquisite Adam interiors, contains a rich collection of Chippendale furniture, fine porcelain and outstanding art collections from Italian Renaissance masterpieces and Turner watercolours to contemporary works. Lord Harewood's mother, HRH Princess Mary, Princess Royal, lived at Harewood for 35 years and much of her Royal memorabilia is still displayed.

Heptonstall Grammar School Museum

Church Yard Bottom
Heptonstall HX7 7LY
01422 843 738
http://goo.gl/DXXWd0

Heptonstall museum lies in the centre of the ancient village of Heptonstall, in the Old Grammar School building. Some of the original features of the school remain including the black oak desks. The displays focus on the changing importance of this charming village from prehistoric times to the present day and cover the compelling story of the infamous Cragg Vale Coiners and Heptonstall's part in the English Civil War.

Home Farm

Temple Newsam Estate
Leeds LS15 0AD
0113 264 5535
www.leeds.gov.uk/templenewsam
temple.newsam@leeds.gov.uk

Displays set in the original Georgian and Victorian farm buildings bring to life the stories of the past. Home Farm is now the largest working Rare Breeds Farm in Europe with over 400 animals, including cattle, pigs, sheep, goats and poultry.

Horsforth Village Museum

5 The Green, Horsforth
Leeds LS18 5JB
0113 281 9877
http://goo.gl/IOUyY9
horsforthmuseum@hotmail.com

Horsforth was once described as the largest village in England and has somehow managed to retain some of its village like identity, character and sense of community. The museum aims to reflect this heritage in its interesting exhibits which are drawn from all aspects of life in and around Horsforth and have a great nostalgia and educational value.

Huddersfield & District Family History Society

33a Green's End, Meltham
Holmfirth HD9 5NW
www.hdfhs.org.uk
secretary@hdfhs.org.uk

For family history research in the Huddersfield, Dewsbury and Mirfield areas.

Huddersfield Local Studies Library

Princess Alexandra Walk
Huddersfield HD1 2SU
01484 221965
http://goo.gl/my6Ebq

Local history is the story of your community. Whether you are wanting to trace the history of a local firm, undertaking a project for homework or wanting to begin researching your family tree, the Local Studies Library may be able to help.

Ilkley Toy Museum

Whitton Croft Road
Ilkley LS29 9HR
01943 603855
www.ilkleytoymuseum.co.uk
ilkleytoymuseum@supanet.com

The museum contains one of the finest private collections of toys in the North of England. The many exhibits feature dolls, dolls houses, teddy bears, tin plate toys, lead figures and a working model fairground.

Ingrow Museum of Rail Travel

Ingrow Railway Centre, South Street, Ingrow
Keighley BD21 5AX
01535 680425
www.vintagecarriagestrust.org
admin@vintagecarriagestrust.org

Over 60 television programmes and films have featured carriages from our award-winning museum. Sound and video presentations bring our collection to life.

Keighley & District Family History Society

2 The Hallows, Shann Park
Keighley BD20 6HY
01535 672144
www.kdfhs.org.uk
suedaynes@hotmail.co.uk

Keighley and District Family History Society was created in 1986 by a small group of individuals interested in researching family history.

Keighley & Worth Valley Railway - KWVR

The Railway Station
Haworth BD22 8NJ
www.kwvr.co.uk/guide/kwvr/kwvr.html

Britain's last remaining complete heritage branch line runs from Keighley to Oxenhope, along a rich seam of West Yorkshire's rail and cultural heritage. Travel via Ingrow, with its award-winning Museum of Rail Travel, and Damems, the country's smallest complete station (Ormston in BBC TV's Born & Bred series) to Oakworth, Haworth and Oxenhope.

Keighley Bus Museum Trust

Keighley Bus Museum Trust (not open to the public)
Keighley BD20 6LH
01282 413179
www.kbmt.org.uk
enquiries@kbmt.org.uk

The Trust's ultimate aim is to have a permanent home for the collection of around 30 vintage buses, lorries and military vehicles in or near the centre of Keighley. The collection is currently housed in central Keighley; unfortunately the building is not suitable to be opened as a real museum on a permanent basis. Our Riverside Depot is open to visitors throughout the year – contact us via email in advance of your visit.

Kirkstall Abbey

Abbey Walk, Kirkstall Road
Leeds LS5 3EH
0113 230 5492
www.leeds.gov.uk/kirkstallabbey
abbey.house@leeds.gov.uk

One of the best preserved abbeys in Britain, Kirkstall Abbey is a spectacular and picturesque ruin. Founded in the 12th centruy by Cistertain monks, it was closed down in 1539 by Henry VIII. This fascinating archeological site has been sought after as the subject matter for famous paintings by JMW Turner and Thomas Girton.

Leeds City Museum

Millennium Square
Leeds LS2 8BH
0113 224 3732
http://goo.gl/jFWGK
city.museum@leeds.gov.uk

Experience a world of discovery... explore four floors of interactive and exciting galleries. Come face-to-face with the Leeds tiger, step into Ancient Worlds to meet Nesyamun, the Leeds mummy and dig for fossils in the Life on Earth gallery.

Leeds Civic Trust

17-19 Wharf Street
Leeds LS2 7EQ
0113 243 9594
www.leedscivictrust.org.uk
info@leedscivictrust.org.uk

Leeds has a distinct and attractive built heritage, from its beginnings as a trading centre for cloth through its development as an industrial city to its current status as a regional capital. Its medieval origins, its Georgian, Victorian and Edwardian architecture, its streets and arcades, all contribute to that distinctive character. Leeds Civic Trust celebrates that heritage through its Blue Plaques scheme, its walks and events, its co-ordination of Heritage Open Days, and its list of Heritage at Risk.

Leeds Industrial Museum at Armley Mills

Canal Rd, Armley
Leeds LS12 2QF
0113 263 7861
www.leeds.gov.uk/armleymills
armleymills.indmuseum@virgin.net

Formerly the largest woollen mill in the world, Armley Mills is now a museum which explores Leeds' rich industrial past. Displays cover the local textiles and clothing industries, printing, cinematography, photography and engineering.

Leeds Museum Discovery Centre

Carlisle Road
Leeds LS10 1LB
0113 214 1548
www.leeds.gov.uk/discoverycentre
discovery.centre@leeds.gov.uk

Home to a million wonders.. Leeds Museum Discovery Centre is the city's purpose built museum storage and conservation facility. As only 5% of Leeds Museums and Galleries collections can be displayed at only one time, the Discovery Centre houses objects not on permanent display at other sites across the city. From elephant skulls to a medieval log boat, discover many more treasures with regular behind the scenes tours and family activities.

Lotherton Hall

🏠 £

Lotherton Lane, Aberford

Leeds LS25 3EB

0113 264 5535

www.leeds.gov.uk/lothertonhall

lotherton.hall@leeds.gov.uk

Lotherton Hall is a beautiful country house surrounded by historic gardens. Formerly the home of the Gascoigne family, it evokes a world of high Edwardian living.

Manor House Art Gallery & Museum

✉

Castle Yard

Ilkley LS29 9DT

01943 600066

www.bradfordmuseums.org/venues/manorhouse

Situated within the beautiful surroundings of the Wharfe Valley, one of Ilkley's oldest buildings, the Manor House, has been converted into an attractive museum and art gallery. On the ground floor visitors are given a glimpse into Ilkley's past while the first floor galleries provide the venue for a regularly changing programme of temporary exhibitions. While being a major exhibit in itself, the Manor House also stands on the remains of the Roman fort of Olicana.

Marks in Time Exhibition: Marks & Spencer Company Archive

🏠 ✉ 🏛 ★

Michael Marks Building, University of Leeds, off Clarendon Road

Leeds LS2 9LZ

020 87182800

www.marksintime.marksandspencer.com

company.archive@marks-and-spencer.com

Did you know M&S was born in Leeds? Discover our story and unlock the fascinating journey that has made M&S one of Britain's best loved retailers. Explore our Marks In Time Exhibition and uncover some fascinating facts from over 130 years of M&S history. From the clothes we wear to the food we eat the Marks In Time Exhibition showcases the M&S Company Archive collection, tracking the development of the business from 1884 to the present day.

Middleton Railway

🏠 ✉ £

Middleton Railway Trust Ltd, The Station, Moor Road, Hunslet

Leeds LS10 2JQ

0845 680 1758

www.middletonrailway.org.uk

info@middletonrailway.org.uk

Having been established by an Act of Parliament in 1758, the Middleton Railway, Leeds, can claim to be the oldest working railway in the world. It also played host to the first commercially successful, revenue earning, steam locomotives which entered service there in 1812.

Collections: Includes standard gauge industrial railway locomotives and some narrow gauge. The core collection is of Leeds-built locomotives, although other cities and indeed countries are represented.

Morley & District Family History Group

👥

1 New Lane, East Ardsley

Wakefield WF3 2DP

www.morleyfhg.co.uk

carol@morleyfhg.co.uk

We are a small and friendly group whose aims are to promote and encourage mutual help between like-minded people who are interested in their ancestors, who they were, what they did and what their lives may have been like.

Museum of the History of Science, Technology & Medicine, University of Leeds, The

✉ 🏛 ★

University of Leeds

Leeds LS2 9JT

0113 343 3460

www.leeds.ac.uk/collections

C.L.Jones@leeds.ac.uk

The University of Leeds has rare and signficant collections relating to its scientific and technological past. Areas represented include physics, chemistry, biology, medicine and geology.

Nostell Priory & Parkland - National Trust

🏠 £

Doncaster Road, Nostell

nr Wakefield WF4 1QE

01924 863892

www.nationaltrust.org.uk/nostell-priory

nostellpriory@nationaltrust.org.uk

Nostell Priory is an 18th century architectural masterpiece set in a landscape park. The house was built by the architect James Paine on the site of a medieval priory for Sir Rowland Winn, 4th Baronet.

Collections: The Priory houses one of the best documented collections of Chippendale furniture and furnishings which were designed especially for the house by the great cabinet maker. Other treasures include an outstanding art collection with works by Pieter Brueghel the Younger, Hogarth and Angelica Kauffmann, the remarkable 18th-century doll's house with its original fittings and the John Harrison longcase clock with its rare movement made of wood.

Oakwell Hall Country Park

Oakwell Hall and Country Park, Nutter Lane, Birstall
Batley WF17 9LG
01924 326240
www.kirklees.gov.uk/museums
oakwell.hall@kirklees.gov.uk

This beautiful Elizabethan manor house has delighted visitors for centuries. Visiting in the 19th century, Charlotte Brontë featured it as 'Fieldhead' - the home of the heroine in 'shirley'.

Otley Museum

Wellcroft House, Otley Cycle Club, Crow Lane
Otley LS21 1TZ
01943 468181
www.otleymuseum.org
otleymuseum@btconnect.com

A comprehensive collection of documents and photographs tells the story of this Wharfedale community from prehistoric times to the 20th century. A fascinating insight into Otley's heritage for the visitor and a key resource for both the amateur and professional researcher.

Peace Museum UK

10 Piece Hall Yard
Bradford BD1 1PJ
01274 780241
www.peacemuseum.org.uk
info@peacemuseum.org.uk

The Peace Museum UK occupies three small galleries in one of Bradford's many fine Victorian buildings. A member of the International Network of Museums for Peace, it is unique in that it is the only accredited museum of its kind in the UK.

Collections: The Peace Museum has a collection of some 6,000 items. They chart the history of peacemakers and peace-making, locally, nationally and globally.

Pontefract & District Family History Society

Eadon House, Main Street, Hensall
Goole DN14 0QZ
www.pontefractfhs.org.uk
secretary@pontefractfhs.org.uk

An active group of family historians who live in Pontefract and the surrounding area.

Pontefract Castle & Visitors Centre

Pontefract Castle, Castle Chain
Pontefract WF8 1QH

01977 723 440
www.wakefield.gov.uk/castles
castles@wakefield.gov.uk

Remains of medieval Royal Castle, which was one of the most important fortresses in Britain. The Visitors Centre has an education room which includes displays on the castle's history and a shop with gifts and refreshments.

Pontefract Museum

Salter Row
Pontefract WF8 1BA
01977 722 741
http://goo.gl/IFZGnO
museums@wakefield.gov.uk

Pontefract Museum is in a flamboyant Art Nouveau building with a wonderful tiled entrance hall and many original 1904 furnishings. Situated in the centre of town, the museum has new displays on the archaeology and history of Pontefract.

Red House Museum

Red House, Oxford Road, Gomersal
Nr Cleckheaton BD19 4JP
01274 335100
www.kirklees.gov.uk/museums
red.house@kirklees.gov.uk

This delightful, red-brick house, built in 1660, was home to the Taylor family who were cloth merchants and manufacturers. Mary Taylor, daughter of the house in the 19th century, was a close friend of Charlotte Bronte, who visited often, featuring the house as 'Briarmains' in 'shirley'.

Royal Armouries

Royal Armouries Museum, Armouries Drive
Leeds LS10 1LT
08700 344 344
www.royalarmouries.org
enquiries@armouries.org.uk

Home to Britain's national collection of arms and armour, the Royal Armouries Museum houses a world-renowned collection of over 75,000 objects. Check out the weapons and armour of warriors through the ages from early medieval knights to the modern-day soldier.

Collections: The collection consists of some 70,000 examples of arms, armour and artillery dating from antiquity to the present day. It includes royal armours of the Tudor and Stuart kings; arms and armour of the English Civil Wars; British and foreign military weapons from the Board of Ordnance and MOD Pattern Room collections; hunting and sporting weapons, as well as an exceptional collection of oriental arms and armour.

Sandal Castle & Visitors Centre

Manygates Lane, Sandal
Wakefield WF2 7DS
01924 249 779
www.wakefield.gov.uk/castles
castles@wakefield.gov.uk

Remains of 13th century stone castle and the fine motte and bailey. The Visitors Centre has an education room which includes displays on the castle's history and a shop with gifts and refreshments.

Second World War Experience Centre

1a Rudgate Court, Walton
Wetherby LS23 7BF
01937 541 274
www.war-experience.org
enquiries@war-experience.org

The Second World War Experience Centre collects, documents, preserves, exhibits and encourages access to the surviving material evidence and associated information of the men and women who participated in the war in whatever capacity, whether military, civilian or conscientious objector.

Shibden Hall

Lister's Road
Halifax HX3 6XG
01422 352246
http://goo.gl/p2kodg
shibden.hall@calderdale.gov.uk

For over 300 hundred years Shibden Hall was the home of the Lister family, but the house itself is even older, first built in about 1420. Many generations of people and their families have lived and worked here, and all have left their mark on its history.

Special Collections of the JB Priestley Library, University of Bradford

Bradford BD7 1DP
01274 235256
www.bradford.ac.uk/library/special-collections
special-collections@bradford.ac.uk

Special Collections at the University of Bradford: over 100 collections of rare books and archives, almost a kilometre in shelf length, relating to University or Yorkshire history, or University areas of excellence from archaeology to Yugoslavia.

Collections: Over 100 collections of archives and rare books, with particular strengths in modern history, peace, nonviolence, social change, politics, literature, religion, Quaker history, archaeology, Yorkshire and Bradford, textiles.

Special Collections, Leeds University Library

Leeds University Library, University of Leeds, Woodhouse Lane
Leeds LS2 9JT
0113 343 5663
www.leeds.ac.uk/library/spcoll
library@leeds.ac.uk

Free to all visitors, the Brotherton Library at the University of Leeds holds exceptional collections on a vast variety of subjects. We welcome you to research the area of your interest in the Fay and Geoffrey Elliott Reading Room, whether for formal academic study or personal interest.

Standedge Tunnel

Waters Road
Marsden, Huddersfield HD7 6NQ
01484 844298
https://canalrivertrust.org.uk/standedge-tunnel

Standedge Tunnel is the highest, longest and deepest canal tunnel in the UK, stretching for 5,029 metres (3.25 miles) through hard millstone grit. An engineering marvel worked on by Thomas Telford, the tunnel runs from Marsden in Yorkshire through to Diggle in Lancashire.

Stephen Beaumont Museum

Fieldhead Hospital, Ouchthorpe Lane
Wakefield WF1 3SP
01924 328654
http://goo.gl/gwgGXX

This unusual museum of mental health depicts the story of the West Riding Pauper Lunatic Asylum built in 1818. The exhibition includes restraining equipment, a padded cell, photographs dating from 1862 plus medical and surgical equipment and documents. There is also a scale model of the original 1818 building built by a former curator of the museum based on the original plans and drawings.

Temple Newsam House

Temple Newsam Rd, Off Selby Rd
Leeds LS15 0AE
0113 264 5535
www.leeds.gov.uk
temple.newsam.house@leeds.gov.uk

This magnificent Tudor-Jacobean house, was the birthplace of Lord Darnley, infamous husband of Mary Queen of Scots, and for 300 years the home of the Ingram family until it was bought by Leeds from Lord Halifax in 1922. Temple Newsam is home to outstanding collections of fine and decorative arts.

Thackray Museum

Near St James's Hospital, Beckett Street
Leeds LS9 7LN
0113 244 4343
www.thackraymuseum.org
info@thackraymuseum.org

Experience the sights, sounds and smells of a Victorian Leeds street and see brave developments in surgery and healthcare.

Collections: The museum collection has over 35,000 objects which, in particular, include a vast range of surgical instruments dating from the late 19th century to the present day. The collection also includes a unique collection of English pharmacy ceramics.

Thoresby Society Library & Archive Collection, The

Claremont, Clarendon Road
Leeds LS2 9SZ
0113 2457910
www.thoresby.org.uk/library.htm
library@thoresby.org.uk

The Thoresby Society is named after Ralph Thoresby (1658-1725), the first historian of the town. Since its foundation in 1889 the society has published books about Leeds, including the transcripts of the parish registers.

Thwaite Mills Watermill

Thwaite Mills, Thwaite Lane, Stourton
Leeds LS10 1RP
0113 2141914
www.leeds.gov.uk/thwaitemills
adrian.marshall@leeds.gov.uk

Thwaite Mills is one of the only fully restored working water-powered mills in Yorkshire. With over 300 years of industrial history, a tour of this early 19th century watermill presents a fascinating insight into life and times of the putty mill and its owners, the Horn family.

Tolson Museum

Ravensknowle Park, Wakefield Rd
Huddersfield HD5 8DJ
01484 223830
www.kirklees.gov.uk/museums
tolson.museum@kirklees.gov.uk

The history book of a typical Yorkshire town, Tolson Museum draws a vivid and intriguing picture of Huddersfield and its people, from the prehistoric to the present. Each layer of Huddersfield's past is revealed in its exciting displays.

ULITA - an Archive of International Textiles

University of Leeds International Textiles Archive, St Wilfred's Chapel, Maurice Keyworth Building, Moorland Road, The University of Leeds
Leeds LS2 9JT
0113 3433919
www.leeds.ac.uk/ulita
m.a.hann@leeds.ac.uk

ULITA - an Archive of International Textiles was founded in 1892, and includes textiles and other design material, particularly featuring European and Asian textiles. The collection was established as a research and teaching resource, but has always been available to a wider public.

University of Huddersfield Archives & Special Collections

Queensgate
Huddersfield HD1 3DH
01484 473168
https://goo.gl/NBe73d
h.a.stephens@hud.ac.uk

The Archives and Special Collections Service provides a rich source of research material for many disciplines. Detailed lists of the collections are found at http://www.hud.ac.uk/archives/.

Victoria Tower

Castle Hill, Almondbury
Huddersfield HD5
http://goo.gl/XCKssL
events@kirklees.gov.uk

The scheduled monument of Castle Hill comprises the remains of a late-Bronze Age or early Iron Age univallate hillfort with a single raised bank, a later Iron Age multivallate hillfort, a 12th-century motte and bailey castle and the site of a deserted medieval village. The grade II listed Victoria Tower on the summit of Castle Hill is by far the most conspicuous landmark in Huddersfield.

Wakefield & District Family History Society

101 Thornes Road
Wakefield WF2 8QD
01924 373014
www.wdfhs.co.uk

The objective of the society is to advance public education in family history and genealogy for the benefit of anyone living in the area of the Wakefield Metropolitan District Council or with interests or family in that area.

Wakefield Cathedral

Northgate
Wakefield WF1 1HG
01924 373923
wakefieldcathedral.org.uk
admin@wakefield-cathedral.org.uk

Wakefield Cathedral, or the Cathedral Church of All Saints in Wakefield, West Yorkshire, England, is one of three co-equal Anglican cathedrals for the Diocese of Leeds and a seat of the Bishop of Leeds. Originally the parish church, it has Anglo Saxon origins and after enlargement and rebuilding has the tallest spire in Yorkshire.

Wakefield Museum

Wakefield Museum, Wakefield One, Burton Street
Wakefield WF1 2EB
01924 305356
www.wakefield.gov.uk/museums
museums@wakefield.gov.uk

Wakefield Museum is a stimulating and vibrant part of the new and prestigious Wakefield One building in the heart of Wakefield. Discover the extraordinary, the oldest, the first, and the one and only in the Welcome to Wakefield display. See our local cultural treasures and learn surprising facts about the city. Explore the history of Wakefield in the Main Gallery and hear stories of wealth and power, hardship and hope, love and war, and passion and belief through the eyes of the people involved in shaping the city.

West Yorkshire Archive Service

www.archives.wyjs.org.uk

Bradford:
WYAS, Bradford Central Library, Prince⊠s Way
Bradford BD1 1NN
01274 435099

Calderdale:
WYAS, Central Library, Northgate House, Northgate
Halifax HX1 1UN
01422 392636

Kirklees:
WYAS, Central Library, Princess Alexandra Walk
Huddersfield HD1 2SU
01484 221966

Leeds:
WYAS, Nepshaw Lane South, Morley
Leeds LS27 7JQ
0113 393 9788

Wakefield:
WYAS, Registry of Deeds, Newstead Road
Wakefield WF1 2DE
01924 305980

The West Yorkshire Archive Service exists to preserve the county's heritage of historical documents and to help members of the public make use of them. Collecting and preserves historical records of all kinds dating from the 12th century to the present day.

Yorkshire Archaeological Society

Claremont, 23 Clarendon Road
Leeds LS2 9NZ
0113 245 7910
www.yas.org.uk/

Yorkshire Archaeological Society exists to promote the study of Yorkshire's historical past. It was founded in 1863 by a group of eminent citizens to study and preserve antiquities in the Huddersfield area.

Yorkshire Group of Family History Societies

101 Thornes Road
Wakefield WF2 8QD
01924 373014
www.yorksgroup.org.uk
cdgwelch@aol.com

The Yorkshire Group of Family History Societies is an umbrella organisation for the many societies that cover various areas within the pre-1974 three Ridings of Yorkshire.

Wiltshire

Wiltshire (or Wilts), county in SW. of England, bounded NW. and N. by Gloucestershire, E. by Berks and Hants, S. by Hants and Dorset, and W. by Somerset; greatest length, N. and S., 53 miles; greatest breadth, E. and W., 37 miles; area, 866,677 acres, population 258,965. The county is divided into 2 divisions by the Vale of Pewsey extending E. and W., the northern principally a fertile flat rising near the N. border in the direction of the Cotswold Hills, the southern a varied district broken by downs and intersected by fertile and well-watered valleys. To the northern division belong the Marlborough Downs, and in the southern division is Salisbury Plain. The principal rivers are the Upper Avon, flowing SW. to the Bristol Channel; the Lower Avon (with its tributaries the Wiley, Nadder, and Bourne), flowing S. to the English Channel; and the Kennet, flowing E. to the Thames. The greater part of the surface is kept in pasture, devoted in the northern division to grazing and dairy farming, and in the southern division to the rearing of sheep. Wiltshire is famous for its bacon and cheese. The geological strata are principally cretaceous, forming part of the central chalk district of England. Ironstone is abundant. The principal manufactures are woollens and carpets at Bradford, Trowbridge, Westbury, and Wilton; cutlery and steel goods at Salisbury; ironfounding at Devizes; and ropes and sacking at Marlborough. The locomotive and carriage works of the Great Western Railway are at Swindon, and near Downton is the College of Agriculture. Wiltshire is especially remarkable for the number and variety of the memorials of antiquity left by Britons, Romans, Saxons, and Danes, the chief of these being the megalithic remains of Stonehenge and Avebury. The county contains 29 hundreds, 340 parishes, and parts of 7 others, the parliamentary and municipal borough of Salisbury (1 member), and the municipal boroughs, of Calne, Chippenham, Devizes, and Marlborough. It is mostly in the diocese of Salisbury.

– John Bartholomew, *Gazetteer of the British Isles* (1887)

Alexander Keiller Museum

High Street, Avebury
nr Marlborough SN8 1RF
01672 529203
www.english-heritage.org.uk

Details the history of the stone circle at Avebury, particularly in regard to the archaeological excavations that have taken place there.

Collections: The collection is primarily archaeological and mainly of Neolithic and Early Bronze Age date, with a smaller component of Anglo-Saxon and later material. It includes a large excavation archive from excavations in the 1920s and 1930s.

Athelstan Museum

The Town Hall, Cross Hayes
Malmesbury SN16 9BZ
01666 829258
www.athelstanmuseum.org.uk
info@athelstanmuseum.org.uk

Malmesbury is a beautiful hilltop town on the southern edge of the Cotswolds, built to a Saxon road plan round a Norman abbey. Archaeological digs have shown there was a Neolithic fort here around 2,500 BC - people have lived here for four and a half thousand years, so Malmesbury may be the oldest town in the country.

Collections: The Athelstan Museum is noted for its costume collection and exhibition of Malmesbury Lace and lace making.

Atwell Wilson Motor Museum Trust

Downside, Stockley Lane
Calne SN11 0NF
01249 813119
www.atwellwilson.org.uk
awmmcalne@aol.com

Although the majority of the collection is cars, the museum also houses an impressive collection of lorries, motorcycles, mopeds, push bikes, and a large selection of vehicle manuals and other archive material, and a large collection of motor memorabilia.

Avebury - National Trust

Nr Marlborough SN8 1RF
01672 539250
www.nationaltrust.org.uk/avebury
avebury@nationaltrust.org.uk

One of the most important megalithic monuments in Europe and spread over a vast area, much of which is under National Trust protection. The great stone circle, encompassing part of the village of Avebury, is enclosed by a ditch and external bank and approached by an avenue of stones.

Bowood House & Gardens

Bowood Estate, Derry Hill
Calne SN11 0LZ
01249 812102
www.bowood.org
reception@bowood.org

Bowood House was built c1745 and the estate was purchased by the 1st Earl of Shelburne in the mid 18th century and has been in the family ever since.

Bradford on Avon Museum

Bridge Street
Bradford on Avon BA15 1BY
01225 863280
www.bradfordonavonmuseum.co.uk

Opened in 1990 the museum displays aspects of the natural and historical heritage of the town and the villages of the former Bradford Hundred. The centrepiece is a pharmacy shop which stood for over 120 years in the town and has been removed and carefully rebuilt.

Chippenham Museum & Heritage Centre

10 Market Place
Chippenham SN15 3HF
01249 705020
www.chippenham.gov.uk/museum
heritage@chippenham.gov.uk

Chippenham Museum & Heritage Centre is housed in a fine 18th century grade II listed building. The displays tell the story of the historic market town from prehistoric times up until the present day. Visitors can discover more about the history of the town, its villages and the local area through the extensive collections and by meeting some of the former residents as they guide you through history.

Cricklade Museum

16 Calcutt Street
Cricklade SN6 6BD
01793 750686
www.cricklademuseum.org
info@cricklademuseum.org

Cricklade Museum is home to a local collection including material on social and family history, Roman occupation, Saxon times, rotten borough elections and World War II. There is also an archive of 3000 photographs.

Fox Talbot Museum, The

Lacock
Chippenham SN15 2LG
01249 730 459
www.nationaltrust.org.uk/lacock
foxtalbotmuseum@nationaltrust.org.uk

The Fox Talbot Museum commemorates the life and work of William Henry Fox Talbot - one of the greatest figures of the 19th century - mathematician, physicist, classicist, philologist, and transcriber of Assyrian and Chaldean cuneiform texts. In late August 1835 he made the first photographic negative at Lacock Abbey and he is known as the Father of Photography.

Kennet & Avon Canal Museum, The

Devizes Wharf, Couch Lane
Devizes SN10 1EB
01380 721279
www.katrust.org
administrator@katrust.org.uk

The museum collections include artefacts, papers, photographs and memorabilia relating to the Kennet and Avon Canal along it's 87-mile length through Berkshire, Wiltshire and Somerset since the canal's inception over 200 years ago.

Lacock Abbey, Fox Talbot Museum & Village - National Trust

High Street Lacock
nr Chippenham SN15 2LG
01249 730 459
www.nationaltrust.org.uk/lacock
lacockabbey@nationaltrust.org.uk

Lacock Abbey is a house with over 800 years of history. Founded as an abbey in 1232, it has been a home to many different characters, each of whom has put their own unique stamp on the building.

Longleat House

Warminster BA12 7NW
01985 844400
www.longleat.co.uk
enquiries@longleat.co.uk

Longleat House is widely regarded as one of the best examples of high Elizabethan architecture in Britain and one of the most beautiful stately homes open to the public. Substantially completed by 1580 and now home to the 7th Marquess of Bath, Longleat House is set within 900 acres of stunning 'Capability' Brown landscaped parkland.

Lydiard House

Lydiard Park, Lydiard Tregoze
Swindon SN5 3PA
01793 770401
www.lydiardpark.org.uk
lydiardpark@swindon.gov.uk

Lydiard Park is the ancestral home of the Viscounts Bolingbroke. The ground floor state rooms of the Palladian house are open to visitors all year round.

Market Lavington Village Museum

15 Church Street
Market Lavington SN10 4AB
01380 816222
www.marketlavingtonmuseum.org.uk
curator@marketlavingtonmuseum.org.uk

The home of the museum is the Old Schoolmaster's House, built in 1846. The museum illustrates village life and work mainly from Victorian times to the present day.

Mere Museum

Barton Lane
Mere BA12 6JA
01747 860908
www.meremuseum.org.uk
info@meremuseum.org.uk

Mere museum is home to a local history collection with a good photographic archive. Displays are changed every few months.

Museum of Computing, The

6-7 Theatre Square
Swindon SN1 1QN
07834 375628
www.museumofcomputing.org.uk
info@museumofcomputing.org.uk

The first museum in Britain dedicated to computing opened in Swindon, February 2003. The museum holds a repository of artefacts and has active displays featuring retro and vintage games.

Collections: 1970s/1980s computing hardware, software, printed materials, namely: home computers; TV and handheld electronic games; portable computers; business systems; software; magazines, books and peripherals. Many rare items; regular magazine produced; regular lectures and events held.

Old Sarum - English Heritage

Castle Road
Salisbury SP1 3SD
01722 335398
http://goo.gl/AZoQx5

The great earthwork of Old Sarum stands near Salisbury on the edge of Wiltshire's chalk plains. Its mighty ramparts were raised in about 500 BC by Iron Age peoples, and later occupied by the Romans, the Saxons and, most importantly, the Normans. Today, the remains of the prehistoric fortress and of the Norman palace, castle and cathedral evoke memories of thousands of years of history, which are interpreted by graphic panels throughout the site.

Old Wardour Castle - English Heritage

Tisbury
Salisbury SP3 6RR
01747 870487
http://goo.gl/t7VU4u

Set in the peaceful Wiltshire countryside beside a lake, Old Wardour Castle, near Tisbury was once one of the most daring and innovative homes in Britain. It was built in the 14th century as a lightly fortified luxury residence for comfortable living and lavish entertainment.

Pewsey Heritage Centre

Whatleys Old Foundry, Avonside
Pewsey SN9 5AF
01672 562617
www.pewsey-heritage-centre.org.uk
info@pewsey-heritage-centre.org.uk

The Heritage Centre reflects many aspects of bygone life in the Pewsey Vale. Displays include Victorian industrial machinery, steam and agricultural models, commercial and domestic items.

Purton Museum

Purton Library, 1 High Street
Purton SN5 4AA
01793 770178
www.purtonmuseum.com
curator@purtonmuseum.com

Purton Museum is home to an interesting collection reflecting Purton's long heritage from Neolithic times to the modern day. Of particular note is a comprehensive collection of agricultural hand tools and dairy equipment - evidence of the village's past reliance on the land.

Collections: The collection includes objects relating to Purton and district under the following headings: Working Life Domestic Life Community Life Sports and Recreation Local Societies Militaria.

Rifles - Berkshire & Wiltshire Museum, The

⌂ £

The Wardrobe, 58 The Close
Salisbury SP1 2EX
01722 419419
www.thewardrobe.org.uk
curator@thewardrobe.org.uk

The collection and archives of the Royal Berkshire Regiment, the Wiltshire Regiment, the Duke of Edinburgh's Royal Regiment and the Royal Gloucestershire, Berkshire & Wiltshire Regiment (the latter shared with the Soldiers of Gloucestershire museum). Museum web site has over 2000 images on line of collection objects and photographs. Web site also has searchable transcripts of 13 battalion war diaries from the First World War (over 12,000 records).

Salisbury & South Wiltshire Museum

🏛 ⌂ £

The King's House, 65 The Close
Salisbury SP1 2EN
01722 332151
www.salisburymuseum.org.uk
museum@salisburymuseum.org.uk

A friendly museum in a Grade 1 listed building. The archaeology collections contain rich and varied material from major prehistoric and later excavations, including finds and archaeology from nearby Stonehenge and other villages in south Wiltshire.

Salisbury Cathedral

🏛 £

33 The Close
Salisbury SP1 2EJ
01722 555120
www.salisburycathedral.org.uk
visitors@salcath.co.uk

Discover over 750 years of history, including Britain's tallest spire, the world's best preserved original Magna Carta and Europe's oldest working clock, on a tour with one of our volunteer guides. Built between 1220 and 1258, in one architectural style, Salisbury is Britain's finest 13th century Gothic cathedral.

Science Museum at Wroughton, The

⌂ ★

Hackpen Lane, Wroughton
Swindon SN4 9LT
01793 846200
www.sciencemuseum.org.uk/wroughton
wroughton.enquiries@nmsi.ac.uk

On a site of breathtaking scale near Swindon we store the large and iconic objects from the National Collections of the Science Museum.. and we've got 18,000 of them, including aircraft, cars and tractors, fire-fighting appliances, industrial production machinery, large scientific instruments, machine tools, motorcycles, printing, and telecommunications.

Silbury Hill - English Heritage

🏛 ★

Avebury
http://goo.gl/1Qynts

The largest man-made mound in Europe, mysterious Silbury Hill compares in height and volume to the roughly contemporary Egyptian pyramids. Probably completed in around 2400 BC, it apparently contains no burial. Though clearly important in itself, its purpose and significance remain unknown.

STEAM - Museum of the Great Western Railway

⌂ 🏛 £

Fire Fly Avenue
Swindon SN2 2EY
01793 466637
www.steam-museum.org.uk/Pages/Home.aspx
steampostbox@swindon.gov.uk

STEAM tells the remarkable story of the men and women who built, operated and travelled on 'God's Wonderful Railway'. Hands on displays, world-famous locomotives, archive film footage and the testimonies of ex-railway workers bring the story to life.

Stonehenge - English Heritage

🏛 £

Stonehenge
Amesbury SP4 7DE
0870 333 1181
http://goo.gl/Mv9npY
stonecircleaccess@english-heritage.org.uk

Walk in the footsteps of your Neolithic ancestors at Stonehenge – one of the wonders of the world and the best-known prehistoric monument in Europe. Explore the ancient landscape on foot and step inside the Neolithic Houses to discover the tools and objects of everyday Neolithic life. Visit the world-class exhibition and visitor centre with 250 ancient objects and come face to face with a 5,500 year-old man.

Stourhead - National Trust

🏛 £

The Estate Office, Stourton
Warminster BA12 6QD
01747 841152
www.nationaltrust.org.uk/stourhead
stourhead@nationaltrust.org.uk

Stourhead is full of surprises. As well as the outstanding 18th century landscape gardens with their temples and grotto, there is also a Palladian Mansion with large painting collection.

Swindon Museum & Art Gallery

Bath Road, Old Town
Swindon SN1 4BA
01793 466556
www.swindon.gov.uk/museumandartgallery
SM&AG@swindon.gov.uk

Housed in a listed building in Swindon's Old Town, the Swindon Community Heritage Museum and Art Gallery displays exhibits of local history, archaeology and geology. It tells the story of Swindon's Jurassic past, its connections with the Roman Empire as well as the more recent social history of this thriving town.

Trowbridge Museum

The Shires, Court Street
Trowbridge BA14 8AT
01225 751 339
www.trowbridgemuseum.co.uk
clare.lyall@trowbridge.gov.uk

The museum is housed in a former woollen mill within the Shires shopping centre. Displays tell the history of the woollen industry, Trowbridge town and its people.

Village Museum, The

The Street
Castle Combe ST 847777
01249 782250
www.museum.castle-combe.com
villagemuseum@castle-combe.com

The museum's collection consists of artefacts, photographs and printed material associated with Castle Combe, Biddestone, Grittleton, Nettleton and North Wraxall. Artefacts in the collection date from pre-historical to the present time.

Warminster Museum

Warminster Public Library, Three Horseshoes Mall
Warminster BA12 9BT
01985 216022
www.warminstermuseum.org.uk
museum.warminster@gmail.com

In 1973 the History Society assumed the care of artefacts from the town council, including the Victor Manley collection of geology, the Harold Dewey Collection, and other items given for the benefit of the people of Warminster. The society set up a museum in the Sexton's cottage at the rear of the Chapel of St Lawrence. In 1982 the museum moved to the present library building where it has a display area, storeroom and offices. Only a proportion of its items can be on display at any one time, but items from the museum storeroom can be studied by arrangement with the museum staff.

West Kennet Long Barrow

Nr West Kennet
http://goo.gl/K8WVXw

One of the largest, most impressive and most accessible Neolithic chambered tombs in Britain. Built in around 3650 BC, it was used for a short time as a burial chamber, nearly 50 people being buried here before the chambers were blocked.

Wiltshire & Swindon History Centre

Cocklebury Road
Chippenham SN15 3QN
01249 705500
www.wshc.eu
heritageadmin@wiltshire.gov.uk

The History Centre brings together the archaeology, archive, buildings record, conservation, and museum advisory services together with the county local studies library to create a centre whose sum is much more than that of its parts.

Wiltshire College Museum of Agriculture & Rural Life

Wiltshire College, Lackham, Lacock
Chippenham SN15 2NY
01249 466800
www.lackhamcountrypark.co.uk
daviaj@wiltscoll.ac.uk

The museum originated as a collection of agricultural implements and machinery. Today its collections and displays are broadly focused upon the agricultural practices and the rural life of the County of Wiltshire.

Wiltshire Council Museums Advisory Service

Wiltshire and Swindon History Centre, Cocklebury Road
Chippenham SN15 3QN
01249 705526
www.wshc.eu
museums@wiltshire.gov.uk

The museums Advisory Service assists museum organisations across Wiltshire. There are 18 independent museums supported by the museums Advisory Service ranging from small voluntary community museums to large museums with internationally important collections.

Wiltshire Family History Society

Resource Centre, Unit 3 Bath Road Business entre

Devizes SN10 1XA

01380 724 379

www.wiltshirefhs.co.uk

secretary@wiltshirefhs.co.uk

The society's aim is to encourage the study of family history, including both Wiltshire ancestry of people worldwide and worldwide ancestry of Wiltshire residents.

Wiltshire Museum

41 Long Street

Devizes SN10 1NS

01380 727369

www.wiltshiremuseum.org.uk

hello@wiltshiremuseum.org.uk

The collections contain Early Bronze Age items, along with objects related to the World Heritage Sites of Avebury and Stonehenge including gold ornaments and jewellery made of various materials. The displays also include outstanding and Iron Age, Roman, Saxon and medieval collections.

Yelde Hall

Market Place

Chippenham SN15 3HL

01249 665970

www.chippenham.gov.uk/the-yelde-hall.9470.aspx

heritage@chippenham.gov.uk

The medieval Yelde Hall is Chippenham's most iconic building. Originally constructed as the town's main meeting place in the mid-15th century, the hall has seen several uses over time, not least as the town fire station. The hall is now part of the Museums and Heritage Service.

Worcestershire

Worcestershire, west-midland county of England, bounded N. by Shropshire and Staffordshire, E. by Warwickshire, S. by Gloucestershire, and W. by Herefordshire; greatest length (not including the detached parts), NW. and SE., 36 miles; greatest breadth, NE. and SW., 45 miles; area, 472,453 acres, population 380,283. Worcestershire lies almost entirely in the basin of the Severn, which receives the Stour, Teme, and Avon. The surface is a broad undulating plain, broken in the NE. by hills of moderate height, and in the SW. by the Malvern Hills, which reach an altitude of 1395 ft. The soil, chiefly clay and loam, is very fertile. Wheat is extensively grown, and there are numerous hop-gardens and orchards. Large quantities of cider and perry are made. There are several extensive and beautiful valleys (notably that of the Severn), with rich pastures, and great numbers of cattle and sheep are fattened. The strata consist for the most part of new red sandstone, lias, and oolite; other formations are visible in the Malvern Hills and some other districts. Coal and iron are found in the Dudley district, and the mfr. of iron and steel and of hardware is extensive. Carpets and rugs are made at Kidderminster, glass at Dudley and Stourbridge, gloves and porcelain at Worcester, and needles and fish-hooks at Redditch and Feckenham. Immense quantities of salt are obtained from the brine springs at Droitwich. The Birmingham and Worcester and other canals connect the Severn basin with those of the Trent and Mersey. The county contains 5 hundreds, 243 parishes, the parliamentary and municipal boroughs of Kidderminster and Worcester, part of the parliamentary and municipal borough of Dudley, and themunicipal boroughs of Bewdley, Droitwich, and Evesham. It is almost entirely in the diocese of Worcester.

– John Bartholomew, *Gazetteer of the British Isles* (1887)

Note: Parts of Worcestershire, including Dudley, formed the West Midlands in1974.

Almonry, The

Abbey Gate
Evesham WR11 4BG
01386 446944
www.almonryevesham.org

This 14th century building was once home to the Almoner of the Benedictine Abbey that was founded at Evesham in the 8th century. Today, the Almonry, two churches, bell tower and cloister arch are all that remain of what was reportedly the third largest abbey in England. The Almonry houses a collection that spans the prehistoric to the 20th century.

Ashmolean Museum Broadway, The

Tudor House, High Street
Broadway WR12 7DP
www.ashmolean.org

The Ashmolean has worked in close partnership with Worcestershire County Council, other local organisations, and the Keil family, to transform a historic building in the Cotswold village of Broadway, Worcestershire, into this new independent museum.

Avoncroft Museum of Historic Buildings

Stoke Heath
Bromsgrove B60 4JR
01527 831886
www.avoncroft.org.uk
admin@avoncroft.org.uk

Avoncroft Museum of Historic buildings is an award-winning museum spanning 700 years of Midlands' heritage set in a stunning rural location over 19 acres. Our collection includes a windmill, a Tudor town house and a fully furnished prefab. The museum was England's first ever open-air museum and is no home to 30 exhibits of architectural and historic significance that have been rescued from destruction or demolition and rebuilt at Avoncroft.

Bewdley Museum

Load Street
Bewdley DY12 2AE
0845 603 5699
www.wyreforestdc.gov.uk/museum
bewdley.museum@wyreforestdc.gov.uk

Objects associated with local crafts - pewter and brass, rope making, charcoal burning and woodland crafts. Social history objects,clothing and domestic implements.

Bordesley Abbey Visitor Centre & Forge Mill Needle Museum

Needle Mill Lane, Riverside
Redditch B98 8HY
01527 62509
www.forgemill.org.uk/index.htm

The Bordesley Abbey Visitor Centre, which is set in an original reconstructed 16th century barn, shows many of the finds that have been excavated over the years, and consists of a purpose built heritage centre with outer courtyard. The exhibits show what archaeologists have discovered about the life of the Cistercian monks of Bordesley - from how they worshiped, to the clothes they wore, and the illnesses they suffered.

Commandery, The

Sidbury
Worcester WR1 2HU
01905 361821
http://goo.gl/Gl1BRn
thecommandery@cityofworcester.gov.uk

Originally built as a monastic hospital, The Commandery boasts over a thousand years of history. A Royalist Headquarters at the Battle of Worcester in 1651, this stunning complex of buildings with its magnificent timber framed Great Hall, medieval wall paintings, period rooms, peaceful gardens and a unique atmosphere, ensures your visit is one not to forget.

Croome - National Trust

NT Estate Office, The Builders' Yard, High Green
Severn Stoke WR8 9JS
01905 371006
www.nationaltrust.org.uk/croome
croomepark@nationaltrust.org.uk

Magnificent landscape park being restored to its former glory: 'Capability' Brown's first complete landscape park. Lakeside garden with islands, bridges and grotto Wonderful Robert Adam park buildings, like the Temple Greenhouse and the Owl Seat Miles of walks through lakeland gardens, shrubbery and open parkland.

Droitwich Spa Heritage Centre

St Richard's House, Victoria Square
Droitwich Spa WR9 8DS
01905 774 312
http://goo.gl/wl1pJ1

The Droitwich Spa Heritage and Information Centre is housed on the former Brine Baths site, which was first established in the 1880s.

Elgar Birthplace Museum

Crown East Lane
Lower Broadheath WR2 6RH
01905 333224
www.elgarmuseum.org
birthplace@elgarmuseum.org

The Elgar Birthplace Museum gives a fascinating insight in to the life and music, family and friends, development and inspirations of Sir Edward Elgar, one of England's greatest composers. Visit the country cottage where he was born on 2nd June 1857 and the newly redeveloped Elgar Centre and Jubilee Family Garden.

Fleece Inn, The - National Trust

Bretforton
Nr Evesham WR11 5JE
01386 831173
www.nationaltrust.org.uk/fleece-inn
fleeceinn@nationaltrust.org.uk

The black-and-white half-timbered house, which originally sheltered a farmer and his stock under the same roof, is largely unaltered since first becoming a licensed house in 1848.

Forge Mill Needle Museum & Bordesley Abbey Visitor Centre

Needle Mill Lane, Riverside
Redditch B98 8HY
01527 62509
www.forgemill.org.uk
museum@redditchbc.gov.uk

The Forge Mill Needle Museum is an industrial museum of the Redditch needle making and fishing tackle industries, housed in the original mill buildings. It features water-powered working machinery in a unique needle scouring mill. The Bordesley Abbey Visitor Centre, which is set in an original reconstructed 16th century barn, shows many of the finds that have been excavated over the years, and consists of a purpose built heritage centre with outer courtyard. The exhibits show what archaeologists have discovered about the life of the Cistercian monks of Bordesley.

George Marshall Medical Museum

Charles Hastings Education Centre, Worcestershire Royal Hospital, Charles Hastings Way
Worcester WR5 1DD
01905 760 738
www.medicalmuseum.org.uk
louise.price@worcsacute.nhs.uk

The museum illustrates the history of medicine, nursing

and the associated health care professions, with particular reference to Worcester and the surrounding area. It contains 500 items of equipment including a reconstructed 19th-century operating theatre, apothecary's shop and death masks believed to be of hanged criminals.

Gordon Russell Design Museum

15 Russell Square
Broadway WR12 7AP
01386 854695
www.gordonrussellmuseum.org
grussellmuseum@btconnect.com

The Gordon Russell Museum is housed in the Grade-II-listed workshop used by Russell and his furniture company in Broadway, Worcestershire between 1920 and 2000. It charts the work, lives and success of the company throughout the 20th century and displays a unique collection of furniture, decorative art and archival material.

Hanbury Hall & Gardens - National Trust

School Road, Hanbury
Droitwich Spa WR9 7EA
01527 821214
www.nationaltrust.org.uk/hanbury-hall
hanburyhall@nationaltrust.org.uk

Built in 1701 by Thomas Vernon, a lawyer and whig MP for Worcester, Hanbury Hall is a beautiful country house. Inside, a mix of interiors await to be discovered, from the restored Hercules rooms and recreated Gothic corridor, to the recently re-decorated smoking room and stunning staircase wall-paintings by Sir James Thornhill.

Harvington Mill

Harvington
Nr Kidderminster DY10 4LR
01562 777846
https://goo.gl/OsqKz7

Harvington Mill is a beautiful example of a mill that would have once been an important part of the local industry in this area. No longer is it a commercial enterprise or needed by the people of the community, but that does not downplay its historical significance.

Hive, The

Sawmill Walk, The Butts
Worcester WR1 3PB
01905 822 866
www.thehiveworcester.org
HiveAdminTeam@worcestershire.gov.uk

The Hive has been 10 years in the making and came about due to the vision and commitment of two key partners; the University of Worcester and Worcestershire County Council. It is Europe's first joint university and public library. The Hive is home to a huge range of print and online resources, including Worcester City Archive and records of the Diocese of Worcester.

Infirmary, The

University Of Worcester, City Campus, Castle Street, Worcester, WR1 3AS, United Kingdom
Worcester WR1 3AS
01905 542373
www.facebook.com/TheInfirmaryWorcester
m.macleod@worc.ac.uk

An interactive exhibition at the University of Worcester's City Campus combining history, science, art and technology to explore the medical stories of one of England's oldest infirmaries.

Collections: Displays incorporate the collections of the George Marshall Medical Museum, also in Worcester, and include medical, surgical and nursing equipment, archives, photographs, uniforms and other associated paraphernalia of the last 250 years.

Kidderminster Railway Museum

Station Approach, Comberton Hill
Kidderminster DY10 1QX
01562 825316
www.krm.org.uk
krm@krm.org.uk

The Kidderminster Railway Museum houses a vast range of railway artefacts, most of which date back to the days of steam travel. From pen nibs to clocks, from signs to signalling equipment, from photographs to timetables and rolling stock, there is a vast amount to see. The collections are housed in a warehouse built by the Great Western Railway in 1878.

Lace Guild Museum, The

The Hollies, 53 Audnam
Stourbridge DY8 4AE
01384 390739
www.laceguild.org
hollies@laceguild.org

The Lace Guild's collection contains over 16,000 objects — lace of all kinds, bobbins, shuttles, netting needles, threads and much more — all recorded on a database. See the website for details of open days and exhibitions.

Malvern Museum

The Abbey Gateway, Abbey Road
Great Malvern WR14 3ES
01684 567 811
www.malvernmuseum.co.uk

We are a small, friendly museum, located in the centre of Great Malvern within 5 minutes walk of Malvern Priory and the Tourist information Centre. Dinosaurs, Victorian scenes, a Water Cure patient and an observation bee hive are just some of the experiences our visitors enjoy.

Museum of Carpet

Stour Vale Mill, Green Street
Kidderminster DY10 1AZ
01562 69028
www.museumofcarpet.org.uk
info@museumofcarpet.org.uk

A new museum looking at the world famous carpet industry of Kidderminster along side stories of wealth, poverty and ingenuity of the people who created the carpets. Come and visit us for a fantastic experience, lots for the family and a wonderful gift shop to browse.

Museum of Royal Worcester

Severn Street
Worcester WR1 2ND
01905 21247
www.museumofroyalworcester.org
info@museumofroyalworcester.org

The Worcester Porcelain Museum houses the world's largest collection of Worcester Porcelain. The ceramic collections, archives and records of factory production, form the primary resource for the study of Worcester porcelain and its history.

Museum of the Worcestershire Yeomanry Cavalry

City Museum and Art Gallery, Foregate Street
Worcester WR1 1DT
01905 25371
http://goo.gl/dM2wN9

The museum of the Worcestershire Yeomanry is housed within the City Art Gallery and Museum. The collections are the property of the Worcestershire Yeomanry Museum Trust, which maintains close links with the successor regiment, the Royal Mercian and Lancastrian Yeomanry, but are managed by Worcester City Museums.

Pershore Abbey

Church Street
Pershore WR10 1DT
www.pershoreabbey.org.uk

Pershore Abbey was an Anglo-Saxon abbey and is now an Anglican parish church.

Salt Museum

c/o 128 Worcester Road
Droitwich Spa WR9 8AW
http://goo.gl/l6R9Mb

The Droitwich Spa Heritage and Information Centre is housed on the former Brine Baths site, which was first established in the 1880s. The permanent exhibition shows the fascinating story of the town from pre-Roman times to modern day. Excavations in the town have revealed much about early Droitwich and its salt industry; many of these remains are in excellent condition. The salt industry is traced, using displays and many old photographs, through Roman, Saxon and medieval periods and finally the Victorian era.

Severn Valley Railway

The Railway Station
Bewdley DY12 1BG
01299 403816
www.svr.co.uk

The SVR is a full-size standard-gauge railway line running regular steam-hauled passenger trains for the benefit of visitors and enthusiasts alike between Kidderminster in Worcestershire and Bridgnorth in Shropshire, a distance of 16 miles. The Severn Valley Railway was in the transport business as a through route for 101 years, from 1862 until 1963.

Stourport Basins

Severn side
Stourport-on-Severn DY13 9EP
01299 822827
stourporttown.co.uk/?page_id=179
liz@stourportforward.co.uk

Stourport on Severn is an inland port, where exotic goods from the great seaports of Bristol and Gloucester were transferred and exchanged with manufactured goods and materials from Birmingham and the Black Country. Stourport on Severn developed where the Staffordshire & Worcestershire Canal joined the River Severn. Historic Georgian buildings and numerous bridges, locks and canal basins give a fascinating insight into the life of an 18th century inland port.

Tenbury Museum

Goff's School, Cross Street
Tenbury Wells WR15 8EF
07722 820983
www.tenburymuseum.org.uk

Tenbury and District Museum is housed in the old Goff's School building. In this single room we have numerous exhibits illustrating the local history and way of life.

Tenbury Wells Pump Rooms

Teme Street
Tenbury Wells WR15 8BA
www.teme-valley.co.uk/pumprooms2.htm

Tenbury Wells had the 'Wells' added to its name last century to help promote the mineral water wells that had been found in the town from 1840 onwards. The mineral waters brought about the building in 1862 of the now restored Tenbury Spa.

Transport Museum, Wythall, The

Chapel Lane
Wythall B47 6JX
01564 826 471
www.wythall.org.uk
enquiries@wythall.org.uk

The museum has three halls which accommodate one of the most significant collections of preserved buses in the country. It has the largest collection of preserved Midland Red buses and can probably make the same claim for Birmingham City Transport.

Tudor House

Friar Street
Worcester WR1 2NA
www.tudorhouse.org.uk
manager@tudorhouse.org.uk

Tudor House has had a varied life in the five centuries since it was built. It has been used as a work place for weavers, clothiers, tailors, bakers, painters, brewers and was used as lodgings, the Cross Keys Inn, a tearoom, a WW2 air raid wardens' post, a school clinic and a museum.

Witley Court & Gardens - English Heritage

Worcester Road
Great Witley WR6 6JT
01299 896636
http://goo.gl/6tuSqR

The vast and rambling remains of this palatial 19th century mansion, surrounded by magnificent landscaped gardens & containing huge stone fountains, provide a great day out in Worcestershire. The largest fountain, representing Perseus and Andromeda - now restored - was described as making the 'noise of an express train' when fired.

Worcester Cathedral

Chapter Office, 8 College Yard
Worcester WR1 2LA
01905 732900
www.worcestercathedral.co.uk

info@worcestercathedral.org.uk

Worcester Cathedral is a magnificent sight as it rises majestically above the River Severn. Worcester has been the seat of a bishopric since the 7th century, and the cathedral was served by monks until the Reformation.

Worcester City Art Gallery & Museum

Foregate Street
Worcester WR1 1DT
01905 25371
www.museumsworcestershire.org.uk
gallerymuseum@worcestershire.gov.uk

Housed in a beautiful Victorian building in the heart of Worcester, the City Art Gallery & Museum runs a lively programme of exhibitions, activities and events for all the family. The gallery presents a changing programme of contemporary art and craft exhibitions.

Worcestershire Archaeology Service

Woodbury, University College Worcester, Henwick Grove
Worcester WR2 6AJ
01905 855455
www.worcestershire.gov.uk/archaeology
archaeology@worcestershire.gov.uk

Worcestershire Archaeological Service provides planning and land management advice, maintains the principal database of archaeological discoveries in the county and has an active field section that undertakes the majority of field projects in the county. The service maintains and develops the reference collection of ceramics for the county. Part of this database has now been put on line at www.worcestershireceramics.org. A reference library is open to the public by appointment.

Worcestershire County Museum

Hartlebury Castle, Hartlebury
Kidderminster DY11 7XZ
01299 250416
http://goo.gl/oHlri
museum@worcestershire.gov.uk

Worcestershire County Museum is housed in historic Hartlebury Castle, home to the Bishops of Worcester for 1000 years.

Worcestershire Regiment Museum

Foregate Street
Worcester WR1 1DT
01905 25371
http://goo.gl/YIRBD9

On display are artefacts from the regiment, its predecessors the Worcestershire Regiment and the 29th and 36th of Foot along with the Militia and Volunteer Units of Worcestershire.

SCOTLAND

National

Archaeology Scotland

Suite 1a, Stuart House Eskmills, Station Road
Musselburgh EH21 7PB
0845 872 3333
www.archaeologyscotland.org.uk
info@archaeologyscotland.org.uk

Archaeology Scotland is a key centre for community archaeology in Scotland. We are a voluntary membership organisation that works to secure the archaeological heritage of Scotland for its people through education, promotion and support.

Museums Galleries Scotland

Waverley Gate, 2-4 Waterloo Place
Edinburgh EH1 3EG
0131 550 4100
www.museumsgalleriesscotland.org.uk
admin@museumsgalleriesscotland.org.uk

Museums Galleries Scotland is the National Development Body for the museum sector in Scotland. Our role is to work collaboratively to invest in and develop a sustainable museum and galleries sector for Scotland. We work with a sector of over 400 museums and galleries, supporting and enabling them to meet their objectives in a number of ways, including though strategic investment, advice, advocacy and skills development opportunities.

National Archives of Scotland (NAS)

The National Records of Scotland, HM General Register House, 2 Princes Street
Edinburgh EH1 3YY
0131 535 1314
www.nrscotland.gov.uk

We perform the registration and statistical functions of the Registrar General for Scotland, including responsibility for demographic statistics and census, and the archival functions of the Keeper including maintaining the archives as one of Scotland's five National Collections, and providing a leadership role for Scottish archive and record professionals. We are also responsible for the service for family history provided under the highly successful ScotlandsPeople brand.

National Library of Scotland

George IV Bridge
Edinburgh EH1 1EW
0131 226 4531
www.nls.uk
enquiries@nls.uk

Scotland's largest library and the world centre for the study

of Scotland and the Scots. Thanks to our UK legal deposit status, we are also a vast reference library.

Collections: 7 million printed books, 120,000 volumes of manuscripts, 1.6 million maps, and over 20,000 newspaper and magazine titles.

National Museum of Flight Scotland

East Fortune Airfield
East Fortune EH39 5LF
0300 123 6789
www.nms.ac.uk/flight
info@nms.ac.uk

Discover the extraordinary story of our human ambition to take to the skies. East Fortune played an important role as an airfield during two World Wars.

National Museum of Rural Life Scotland

Wester Kittochside, Philipshill Road
East Kilbride G76 9HR
0300 123 6789
www.nms.ac.uk/rural
info@nms.ac.uk

You'll find plenty to fill your day out at the National Museum of Rural Life. We've got pigs, sheep, cows, horses and hens, as well as an award-winning museum, historic farmhouse and wide open fields.

National Museum of Scotland

Chambers Street
Edinburgh EH1 1JF
0300 123 6789
www.nms.ac.uk
info@nms.ac.uk

From the age of dinosaurs to the technology of the future, our galleries contain treasures from around the world. From meteorites to monsters from the deep, our Natural World galleries tell the story of our planet, while our World Cultures gallery links people and possessions across the globe. Follow the story of Scotland from prehistory to the present day in our Scottish galleries, marvel at a spectacular array of over 800 objects in our Window on the World and meet the Scots whose ideas, innovations and leadership took them across the world in our Discoveries gallery.

National Piping Centre & Museum

The Piping Centre, 30-34 McPhater Street, Cowcaddens
Glasgow EH1 1JF
0141 353 0220
www.thepipingcentre.co.uk/museum-heritage
reception@thepipingcentre.co.uk

Now you can witness hundreds of years of Scottish

heritage, played out right before your eyes and ears at The museum of Piping in the Piping Centre. As a showcase for artefacts from the National Museums of Scotland, the museum of Piping houses the most authoritative display of its kind anywhere. Already, the Piping Centre's collection of archival material is an internationally respected resource for serious students and musicologists. Yet this priceless collection is presented in a lively audio-visual format that is as entertaining as it is enlightening.

National Records of Scotland - NRS

The National Archives of Scotland, H M General Register House, 2 Princes Street
Edinburgh EH1 3YY
0131 535 1314
www.nrscotland.gov.uk
enquiries@nas.gov.uk

In 2011, the General Register Office for Scotland merged with the NAS to become the National Records of Scotland (NRS). The NAS has been making the archives of Scotland available through its publications since the early 19th century. So whether you are studying history or reading it purely for your own pleasure, our range of publications can help bring the past alive.

National Trust for Scotland

Hermiston Quay, 5 Cultins Rd
Edinburgh EH11 4DF
0131 458 0200
www.nts.org.uk
information@nts.org.uk

The National Trust for Scotland is the conservation charity that protects and promotes Scotland's natural and cultural heritage for present and future generations to enjoy.

National War Museum Scotland

Edinburgh Castle
Edinburgh EH1 2NG
0300 123 6789
www.nms.ac.uk/war
info@nms.ac.uk

War and military service have touched the lives of countless Scots, leaving their mark on Scotland's history, image and reputation abroad. Here, in the magnificent setting of Edinburgh Castle, explore over 400 years of the Scottish military experience.

Royal Commission on the Ancient & Historical Monuments of Scotland - RCAHMS

John Sinclair House, 16 Bernard Terrace
Edinburgh EH8 9NX
0131 662 1456

www.rcahms.gov.uk
info@rcahms.gov.uk

The Royal Commission on the Ancient and Historical Monuments of Scotland (RCAHMS) collects, records and interprets information on the architectural, industrial, archaeological and maritime heritage of Scotland. We have been doing this for more than a hundred years, and our archive offers a unique insight into the special nature of Scotland's Places.

Scottish Archaeology & Heritage Festival

The Council for Scottish Archaeology, c/o National Museum of Scotland, Chambers Street
Edinburgh EH1 1JF
http://goo.gl/3jvhGC

A month-long festival celebrating Scotland's unique archaeological heritage. Under the co-ordination of the Council for Scottish Archaeology (CSA). Over 100 events are on offer each September.

Scottish Association of Family History Societies

77 Erskine Hill, Polmont
Falkirk FK2 0UH
01324 713037
www.safhs.org.uk

The Scottish Association of Family History Societies provides access to family history societies in Scotland and elsewhere, resources, and advice.

Scottish Council on Archives

General Register House, 2 Princes Street
Edinburgh EH1 3YY
www.scottisharchives.org.uk
k.orchard@scottisharchives.org.uk

We provide leadership for the archives and records management sector in Scotland. We build national and international partnerships, deliver strategic advice and research, and develop projects spanning stakeholder engagement, education, and quality improvement.

Scottish Fisheries Museum

St Ayles, Harbourhead
Anstruther KY10 3AB
01333 310628
www.scotfishmuseum.org
enquiries@scotfishmuseum.org

The Scottish Fisheries Museum, housed in a range of historic buildings on Anstruther's harbour front, tells the story of Scotland's fishing industry, and the people who took part in it, from the earliest times to the present. Our library and archive, containing much of interest to family historians and researchers into the industry, are open by appointment.

Scottish Football Museum

The National Stadium, Hampden Park
Glasgow G42 9AY
0141 616 6100
www.scottishfootballmuseum.org.uk
info@scottishfootballmuseum.org.uk

Opened in May 2001, the Scottish Football Museum is housed within the oldest national football stadium in the world, Hampden Park. The museum is now home to the world's oldest international match ticket (from Scotland v England, 1872), the world's oldest football trophy (the Scottish Cup) and the first ever World Championship trophy (won by Renton in 1888).

Scottish Genealogy Society

15 Victoria Terrace
Edinburgh EH1 2JL
0131-220-3677
www.scotsgenealogy.com
sales@scotsgenealogy.com

The society, based in Edinburgh and founded in 1953, helps with research into Scottish family and local history. Run by volunteers, we can advise you at all stages in your research. Members and visitors will always get a friendly welcome at our Library & Family History Centre.

Scottish Maritime Museum

The Linthouse Building, Laird Forge, Gottries Road
Irvine KA12 8QE
01294 278283
www.scottishmaritimemuseum.org
visitorservices@scotmaritime.org.uk

Scotland's influence on the maritime history of the world from the 18th century to the modern day has been enormous and out of all proportion to the size of the country. The two sites operated by the Scottish Maritime Museum contain the exhibitions and collections that tell the story of that great maritime tradition.

Scottish Mining Museum

Lady Victoria Colliery
Newtongrange EH22 4QN
0131 663 7519
www.scottishminingmuseum.com
visitorservices@scottishminingmuseum.com

The Scottish Mining Museum is housed within the Lady Victoria Colliery, one of Europe's finest examples of Victorian architecture and the last remaining colliery in Scotland. The visitor centre contains films, exhibitions, interactives, recreated underground and coalface, Scotland's largest winding engine and recently launched Big Stuff tours which all contribute to bringing the history of Scotland's coal mining industry to the forefront of people's minds.

Scottish National War Memorial

Edinburgh Castle
Edinburgh EH1 2YT
0131 226 7393
www.snwm.org
info@snwm.org

The National War Memorial for Scotland, established by Royal Charter to commemorate the sacrifice of Scots in the Great War, Second World War and subsequent conflicts. The Memorial within Edinburgh Castle houses and displays the Rolls of Honour of Scots servicemen and women from all the Armed Services, the Dominions, Merchant Navy, Womens' Services, Nursing Services and Civilian casualties of war from 1914 to date.

Scottish Printing Archival Trust

3 Zetland Place
Edinburgh EH5 3HU
www.scottishprintarchive.org
b.clegg@scottishprintarchive.org

The Scottish Printing Archival Trust was formed in 1988 to conserve 'knowledge and examples of Scotland's printing heritage for the benefit of the public and print/media education'. The Trust promotes interest in the history of the Scottish printing industry, which is one of Scotland's oldest. It does not hold any archival collections itself, but works with various institutions to ensure that printing archives and artefacts are not lost.

Scottish Rugby Union Library

Murrayfield Stadium
Edinburgh EH12 5PJ
0131 346 5100
www.scottishrugby.org

Join our knowledgable guides on a tour around
Murrayfield, the home of Scottish Rugby. Your visit
includes the Royal Box, pitchside, tunnel and dressing
rooms, President's Suite, TV studio and corporate boxes
(not all areas may be available).

Scottish Screen Archive

1 Bowmont Gardens
Glasgow G12 9LR
0141 337 7400
ssa.nls.uk
janet.mcbain@scottishscreen.com

The Scottish Screen Archive was established in 1976 and is
a department of Scottish Screen, a publicly funded
organisation. The main purpose of the archive is to locate,
preserve and provide access to Scotland's moving image
heritage.

Collections: Principally non-fiction, the collection
comprises some 32,000 reels and videotapes. The nature of
the holdings includes topical, documentary, educational,
promotional, industrial and amateur material as well as
Gaelic language productions.

Scottish Tartans Museum

The Institute Hall, Mid Street
Keith AB55 5BJ
01542 888 419
www.scottishtartans.org/gallery.html

The Scottish Tartan's Museum's main focus is on the history
and development of Scottish Highland Dress, namely
tartan and the kilt. The museum gallery features original
and replica kilts showing styles from the late 16th century
till today, with many original kilts dating back over 200
years.

Scottish Textile Heritage Online

www.scottishtextiles.org.uk
info@scottishtextiles.org.uk

Our website aims to provide a one-stop shop for anyone
wanting information about the richness and diversity of
Scottish Textile heritage collections. Users will be able to
browse through a database of some 4,000 descriptions of
archive and museum collections and objects with
supporting images.

Scran

John Sinclair House, 16 Bernard Terrace
Edinburgh EH8 9NX
0131 662 1456
www.scran.ac.uk
scran@scran.ac.uk

Scran is the award-winning learning website with over
360,000 images, videos and sounds from museums,
galleries, archives and the media.

Collections: Key holdings in the areas of art history,
photography, british history, archaeology, architectural
history, social history, industrial history, everyday life,
historic maps, scottish culture and local history. Collections
also include artefacts from other world cultures, including
Africa, the Far East and America.

Society for the Protection of Ancient Buildings in Scotland

The Glasite Meeting House, 33 Barony Street
Edinburgh EH3 6NX
0131 557 1551
www.spab.org.uk/scotland
info@spabscotland.freeserve.co.uk

Members of the SPAB living and working in Scotland
decided to form their own semi autonomous group in
1995. Scotland has her own buildings traditions,
architectural language and property laws, which are best
dealt with locally.

Aberdeenshire

Aberdeenshire, a maritime county in the NE. of Scotland; bounded N. and E. by the German Ocean; S. by the counties of Kincardine, Forfar, and Perth; and W. by the counties of Inverness and Banff. Greatest length, NE. and SW., 85 miles; greatest breadth, NW. and SE., 42 miles; coast-line, 60 miles. Area, 1955.4 square miles. Population 267,990, or 137 persons to each square mile. The coast is mostly bold and rocky, and with little indentation. The chief promontories are Kinnaird's Head, Rattray Head, and Buchan Ness, the last being the most easterly point of Scotland. The surface, on the whole, is hilly and mountainous. It is lowest in the districts bordering on the coasts; hilly in the interior, with much moor, but also with many slopes and hollows in a good state of cultivation; and grandly mountainous in the SW., where numerous summits, including Ben Macdhui (4296 ft.), rise above 3000 ft. Much of the country is well-wooded. The chief rivers are the Dee, Don, Ythan, Ugie, and Deveron. Granite is the principal rock, and is extensively quarried for exportation. The soil has been rendered highly productive under skilful farming. Large numbers of fat cattle are annually reared and sent to the principal markets of Scotland and England. The coast and river fisheries are extensive and valuable. The county comprises 76 parishes and 9 parts, the parliamentary burgh of Aberdeen, the parliamentary burghs of Inverurie, Kintore, and Peterhead (part of the Elgin Burghs). .

– John Bartholomew, *Gazetteer of the British Isles* (1887)

Aberdeen & North East Scotland Family History Society

158 - 164 King Street
Aberdeen AB24 5BD
01224 646323
www.anesfhs.org.uk
enquiries@anesfhs.org.uk

The Aberdeen & North-East Scotland Family History Society exists to assist and promote the study of genealogy and family history based on the North-East corner of Scotland. This area covers the old counties of Aberdeenshire, Banffshire, Kincardineshire and Morayshire.

Aberdeen City & Aberdeenshire Archives

Old Aberdeen House, Dunbar Street
Aberdeen AB24 3UJ
01224 481775
http://goo.gl/8gWjk7

Aberdeen City and Aberdeenshire Archives exists to collect and preserve historical records relating to the City of Aberdeen and its locality and to secure significant modern records for future generations.

Aberdeen Maritime Museum

Shiprow
Aberdeen AB11 5BY
01224 337700
http://goo.gl/EWMAo0
info@aagm.co.uk

The City's award-winning Maritime Museum brings the history of the North Sea to life. View multimedia displays and exciting exhibitions on the offshore oil industry, shipbuilding, fishing and clipper ships.

Aberdeen University, Zoology Museum

Department of Zoology, Zoology Building, Tillydrone Avenue, King's College
Aberdeen AB24 2TZ
01224 274330
www.abdn.ac.uk/museums
kingsmuseum@abdn.ac.uk

Aberdeen University has the only large, international collection of zoological specimens in the north of Scotland. The Zoology Museum's collections are worldwide in scope and cover more than 200 years of biological study at the University.

Aberdeenshire Farming Museum

Aden Country Park, Mintlaw
Peterhead AB42 5FQ
01771 622906
http://goo.gl/IUIfVU

Delightful country park location with children's play area and walks. Relive the story of our famous farming past in the beautiful surroundings of Aden Country Park. Start at the unique, semi-circular Home Farm steading by exploring the 'Aden Estate Story' and the 'Weel Vrocht Grun' exhibitions. Visit Hareshowe, a working farm set in the 1950s.

Arbuthnot Museum & Gallery

St Peter Street
Peterhead AB42 1QD
01779 477778
http://goo.gl/xltnrr

Discover the wealth of Peterhead's maritime history in one of Aberdeenshire's oldest museums.

Collections: See models showing the development of Peterhead fishing boats, an important collection of Inuit Artifacts, displays on Arctic animals and whaling, one of Northern Scotland's largest coin collections and temporary exhibitions with regularly changing programme of events.

Banchory Museum

Bridge Street
Banchory AB31 5SX
01330 823367
http://goo.gl/IcTHX3
claire.petty@aberdeenshire.gov.uk

Visit Banchory Museum - gateway to Royal Deeside - and learn about the life of Banchory-born musician and composer, J. Scott Skinner, the 'Strathspey King'.

Banff Museum

High Street
Banff AB45 1AE
01771 622906
www.pc.gc.ca/eng/lhn-nhs/ab/banff/index.aspx

Visit one of Scotland's oldest museums, founded in 1828. See an electro-type copy of the Deskford Carnyx, a unique 2000-year-old war trumpet, as well as an award-winning natural history display.

Blairs Museum

South Deeside Road
Aberdeen AB12 5YQ
01224 863767

www.blairsmuseum.com
manager@blairsmuseum.com

Housed in part of a former college, Blairs Museum gives a unique insight into Scotland's Catholic history and heritage with spectacular collections spanning more than 500 years.

Brander Museum

The Square
Huntly AB54 8AE
01771 622906
http://goo.gl/g6lGtu

See civic regalia, an extensive collection of communion tokens, displays on Huntly textile industry and learn about Huntly-born author George MacDonald, 19th century arms and armour from Sudan, and archaeological finds from Huntly Castle.

Castle Fraser - National Trust for Scotland

Sauchen
Inverurie AB51 7LD
01330 833463
http://goo.gl/ycB8JN

Approaching Castle Fraser down the Broad Walk, the granite walls rising up to the distinctive turrets make an imposing sight. This was the impression the lairds intended as the present castle took shape between 1575 and 1636 – a statement of pride for the Fraser family and a show of strength to any would-be detractors.

Craigievar Castle

Alford
Alford AB33 8JF
0844 493 2174
www.nts.org.uk/Property/Craigievar-Castle

Craigievar is an iconic tower house, amongst the best preserved and the most loved in Scotland. The large estate features woodland, parkland with magnificent specimen trees, and farmland with extensive views over the surrounding countryside to Bennachie. Extensive collection of mid-20th-century ceramics. Stunning 17th century plaster ceilings. Virtually unchanged since built in 1610.

Crathes Castle, Garden & Estate

Banchory
Banchory AB31 5QJ
0844 493 2166
http://goo.gl/Ci0ecr
crathes@nts.org.uk

One of the most beautiful and best preserved castles in Scotland set against a magnificent garden with its world-renowned June Border. Occupied by the Burnetts of leys for over 350 years the castle, garden and estate are a must see for any visitor to the north-east of Scotland.

Drum Castle, Garden & Estate

Drumoak
By Banchory AB31 5EY
0844 493 2161
www.nts.org.uk/Property/Drum-Castle-Garden-Estate
drum@nts.org.uk

The oldest intact building in the care of the National Trust for Scotland, Drum Castle was, from 1323 to 1975, the home of the Irvine family. Situated in the world-famous castle country of North East Scotland, the castle stands at the gates to Royal Deeside on a ridge overlooking the River Dee. Beautiful medieval chapel, 17th-century mansion house and 19th-century additions.

Duff House Country House Gallery

Banff AB45 3SX
01261 818181
www.duffhouse.org.uk
duff.house@aberdeenshire.gov.uk

Duff House is a treasure house and cultural arts centre operated by a unique partnership of Historic Scotland, the National Galleries of Scotland and Aberdeenshire Council. Storytellers, musicians and artists are at home here and Duff House organises a regular artistic programme of exhibitions, music and lectures.

Fordyce Joiners Workshop

Church Street
Fordyce AB45 2SL
01771 622906
http://goo.gl/cdsGZl

Discover the importance of the rural carpenter to the local community in the days before mass produced goods, with displays of early tools and audio-visual presentation.

Collections: See a craftsman working in wood, relax in a Victorian-style garden and view early workshop machinery.

Fraserburgh Heritage Centre

Quarry Road
Fraserburgh AB43 9DT
01346 512888
www.fraserburghheritage.com
heritage@fraserburghheritage.com

The heritage centre is leased by Fraserburgh Heritage Society and operated on a voluntary basis. The building was originally a barrel store, then the foundry of the Consolidated Pneumatic Tool Company Ltd, before being converted to a modern visitor centre which illustrates the history of Fraserburgh and its people.

Fyvie Castle - National Trust For Scotland

The National Trust for Scotland, Fyvie
Nr. Turriff AB53 8JS
01651 891266
http://goo.gl/zuVrdl

Ghosts, legends and folklore are all woven into the tapestry of Fyvie's 800-year history. Each tower of this magnificent Scottish Baronial fortress is traditionally associated with one of the castle's five successive families – Preston, Meldrum, Seton, Gordon and Forbes-Leith.

Garlogie Mill Power House Museum

Garlogie
SkeneWesthill AB32 6RX
01771 622 906
http://goo.gl/Er6OgW

Relive the early days of the industrial revolution at Garlogie Mill. See the rare beam engine - the only one of its type to have survived intact on its original location - which powered the woollen mill.

Gordon Highlanders Museum, The

St Luke's, Viewfield Road
Aberdeen AB15 7XH
01224 311200
www.gordonhighlanders.com
museum@gordonhighlanders.com

From the Napoleonic wars to the modern day, you can re-live the compelling and dramatic story of The Gordon Highlanders through our spectacular and interactive displays. The museum is housed in the former home and studio of prominent Scottish artist, Sir George Reid.

Collections: The museum houses the regimental treasures of The Gordon Highlanders collected over 200 years and includes medals, weapons, textiles, silver, ceramics, photography, art and an extensive archive.

Grampian Transport Museum

Grampian Transport Museum
Alford AB33 8AE
019755 62292
www.gtm.org.uk
info@gtm.org.uk

Dramatic displays, working exhibits and DVD presentations trace the history of road travel and transport in the North East of Scotland. Horse drawn, motor cars, motorcycles, pedal cycles, steam and commercial vehicles are represented. Approximately 50 motor vehicles and 50 motorcycles.

Haddo House

Methlick
Ellon AB41 7EQ
0844 493 2179
www.nts.org.uk/Property/Haddo-House
haddo@nts.org.uk

Designed by Scottish architect William Adam in 1732, Haddo House near Aberdeen is a magnificent example of an historic Scottish stately home. Originally Palladian in style, the house now has late Victorian interiors after a 19th-century refurbishment and is renowned for its stunning decorated ceilings. It also has impressive collections of period furniture, ceramics and art, including paintings by Sir Thomas Lawrence and James Giles. The house is open for guided tours only but the grounds are open all the time.

King's Museum, University of Aberdeen

Old Aberdeen Town House, High Street
Aberdeen AB24 3EN
01224 274330
www.abdn.ac.uk/museums
kingsmuseum@abdn.ac.uk

King's Museum lies at the heart of the University's Old Aberdeen campus. Its origins lie in a museum collection established in King's College in 1727. King's Museum has exhibitions changing every few months to display these collections, some involving students and academic staff collaborating with the museum to bring recent research to a wider audience.

Leith Hall Garden & Estate

Huntly AB54 4NQ
0844 493 2164
www.nts.org.uk/Property/Leith-Hall-Garden-Estate
leithhall@nts.org.uk

A typical Scottish laird's residence brimming with family treasures, Leith Hall is set in 286 acres of scenic estate containing 6 acres of wonderful garden that overlooks some of Aberdeenshire' finest rolling countryside. The House contains many tapestries, several interesting clocks, some fine china and a wonderful collection of family portraits and paintings.

Marischal Museum, University of Aberdeen

Marischal College, Broad Street
Aberdeen AB10 1YS
01224 274301
www.abdn.ac.uk/marischalmuseum
museums@abdn.ac.uk

In the centre of Aberdeen, the museum lies in the University of Aberdeen's Marischal College, the second-largest granite structure in the world. The museum was founded in 1786, with material that has been donated by generations of friends and graduates of the university.

Maud Railway Museum

Maud Railway Station
Maud AB42 5LY
01771 622807
http://goo.gl/fdBvIA

Relive the great days of steam trains at the former Maud Railway Station. Sound effects add to the nostalgia of varied displays of railway memorabilia.

Museum of Scottish Lighthouses, The

Museum of Scottish Lighthouses, Kinnaird Head
Fraserburgh AB43 9DU
01346 511022
www.lighthousemuseum.org.uk
info@lighthousemuseum.org.uk

Discover the skill, dedication, science and romance of Scotland's lighthouses in the only dedicated museum in the United Kingdom. In the company of our friendly guides, climb the 72 steps up the first lighthouse in Scotland.

Collections: The museum tells the story of the Stevenson family, lighthouse engineers to the world, the story of the lighthouse service in Scotland and the Keepers and their families who manned the Scottish lighthouses.

Peterhead Maritime Heritage

South Road, Aberdeenshire
Peterhead AB42 2YP
01779 473000
http://goo.gl/hycEZ6
macduffaquarium.ed@aberdeenshire.gov.uk

Visit one of Aberdeenshire's latest visitor attractions, built next to the shore on South Bay, Peterhead in an award-winning building. Experience Peterhead's maritime life past and present in picture and sound.

Provost Skene's House

Guestrow, off Broad Street
Aberdeen AB10 1AS
01224 641 086
http://goo.gl/s9Ffyj
info@aagm.co.uk

Dating from 1545, Provost Skene's House now houses an attractive series of period room settings, recalling the elegant furnishings of earlier times. Visitors can see an intriguing series of religious paintings in the Painted Gallery, changing fashions in the Costume Gallery and enjoy a light snack in Provost Skene's Kitchen.

Salmon Bothy

Links Road, Portsoy
Banff AB45 2SS
01261 842951
www.salmonbothy.org.uk
contact@salmonbothy.co.uk

The Salmon House was purpose built in 1834 by the Seafield Estate, which then owned the salmon fishing rights along the coast. The three-storey building provided an office, a bothy, an ice house, a fish preparation area, workshop and storage accommodation. The Salmon Bothy Museum is housed in what were the ground floor ice house chambers used in the salmon fishing operation.

Sandhaven Meal Mill

Sandhaven Meal Mill Visitor Centre, Sandhaven
Fraserburgh AB43 4EP
01771 622906
http://goo.gl/OSZczk

See how oatmeal used to be ground in this typical 19th century Scottish meal mill.

Session Cottage Museum

22 Westfield Road
Turriff AB53 7AF
01888 563 451
http://goo.gl/9e6OGD

A 250-year-old but 'n ben cottage furnished as a home of about a century ago. The collection focuses on social and domestic history and includes furniture, furnishings, household equipment, some clothing and personal possessions of local inhabitants of Turriff during the years 1880-1900.

Tolbooth Museum

Old Pier, The Harbour
Stonehaven AB39 2JU
01771 622906
http://goo.gl/VHtUvr

Visit Stonehaven's oldest building - the Earl Marischal's 16th-century storehouse which served as the County Tolbooth of Kincardineshire from 1600-1767 to discover why Episcopal priests were imprisoned here in 1748, Stonehaven's links with the sea, and local bygones.

University of Aberdeen Historic Collections: Special Libraries & Archives

Special Libraries and Archives, King's College
Aberdeen AB24 3SW
01224 272598
www.abdn.ac.uk/library/about/special
speclib@abdn.ac.uk

Aberdeen University's Special Libraries and Archives provides a unique and internationally significant range of printed, archival and other documentary sources for the benefit of the higher education community and beyond. The richness of these collections extends across all the disciplines of the medieval and early modern university curriculum and across the European world of learning.

University of Aberdeen Pathology & Forensic Medicine Collection

Department of Pathology, Medical School, Foresterhill
Aberdeen AB25 2ZD
01224 553792
www.abdn.ac.uk/museums
museums@abdn.ac.uk

The Pathology and Forensic Medicine Collection provides an important comprehensive and unique 20th century record of disease manifestations and traumatic pathology. It comprises of more than 2000 specimens and objects.

University of Aberdeen, Anatomy Museum

The Suttie Centre for Teaching & Learning in Healthcare, Foresterhill,
Aberdeen AB25 2ZD
01224 274320
www.abdn.ac.uk/museums
museums@abdn.ac.uk

The Anatomy Museum collection comprises specimens and objects that provide a comprehensive reference for normal anatomical conditions, which covers the range of functional body systems. The collection has over 2000 specimans and objects, including human tissue, osteological material, historical anatomical models and information relating to 19th century grave robbing.

University of Aberdeen, Geological Collections

Department of Geology and Petroleum Geology, Meston
Building, King's College
Aberdeen AB24 3UE
01224 273448
www.abdn.ac.uk/museums
museums@abdn.ac.uk

The Geological Collections are a repository for research
material of palaeontological, mineralogical and lithological
nature. Numbering around 32,000 specimens, worldwide in
scope.

University of Aberdeen, Herbarium

Department of Plant and Soil Science, Cruickshank Building,
St Machar Drive, King's College
Aberdeen AB24 3UU
01224 272705
www.abdn.ac.uk/museums
museums@abdn.ac.uk

The Herbarium is an internationally important collection. It
contains approximately 120,000 specimens and consists of
material that is worldwide in scope, with the British and
South-East Asian collections forming the core of the collection.

University of Aberdeen, Natural Philosophy
Collection of Historical Scientific Instruments

Fraser Noble Building, Aberdeen University, King's College
Aberdeen AB24 3UE
01224 272081
www.abdn.ac.uk/museums
museums@abdn.ac.uk

The Natural Philosophy Collection of Historical Scientific
Instruments is one of the most diverse collections in any
British University, covering some 250 years. The earliest
material dates from the mid-18th century and the most
recent from the 21st centruy.

University of Aberdeen, Photographic
Collections

Historic Collections, King's College,
Aberdeen AB24 3SW
01224 272598
www.abdn.ac.uk/historic/Catalogue_online.shtml
speclib@abdn.ac.uk

The University of Aberdeen has in its large and varying
photographic collection the George Washington Wilson
Collection, which consists of over 40,000 glass plate
negatives produced by the Aberdeen photographer's
company during the second half of the 19th century. These
range from all Britain covering the simple grandeur of
Fingal's Cave, to the bustle of London's Oxford Street.

Angus

Forfarshire (or Angus), maritime county in E. of Scotland; is bounded N. by the counties of Aberdeen and Kincardine, E. by the North Sea, S. by the Firth of Tay, and W. by the county of Perth; greatest length, 37 miles; greatest breadth, 27 miles; area, 560,087 acres, population 266,360. The surface presents great variety. In the NW. are the Braes of Angus, a group of spurs of the Grampians, intersected by romantic glens; in the SW., 8 miles from and parallel to the Firth of Tay, are the Sidlaw Hills; between the Braes of Angus and the Sidlaw Hills is the fertile valley of Strathmore (Great Valley) or Howe of Angus; from the Sidlaw Hills to the coast on the E. and S. the land is level and highly cultivated. From Dundee to Arbroath the coast consists of sand; from Arbroath to Lunan Bay it is formed of sandstone cliffs, culminating in the Red Head. The chief rivers are the Isla, a tributary of the Tay, and the North Esk and South Esk, which flow SE. to the North Sea. Agriculture has the advantage of the most approved methods, and cattle rearing is carried to great perfection; the polled Angus cattle, however, are now raised chiefly in the county of Aberdeen. Nearly the whole of the NW. of the county is either waste land, or is occupied as sheep-walks or deer-forests. Granite is the prevailing rock in the N. portion of the Grampians, and sandstone in the neighbourhood of the Sidlaw Hills; sandstone flags are quarried in the Carmylie district, and there are limeworks in the neighbourhood of Montrose. The principal industry is the manufacture of linen and jute, Dundee being the chief seat of those trades in Britain. The county contains 51 parishes, and 5 parts, the parliamentary burgh of Dundee, the parliamentary burghs of Montrose, Arbroath, Brechin, and Forfar (part of the Montrose Burghs).

– John Bartholomew, Gazetteer of the British Isles (1887)

Angus Archives

Hunter Library, Restenneth Priory
Forfar DD8 2SZ
01307 468644
www.angus.gov.uk/history/archives/default.htm

Angus Archives is a vast collection of items covering 800 years of the history of Angus and its people. The archives house and preserve the area's written, printed and photographic history.

Angus Folk Museum

Kirkwynd
Glamis DD8 1RT
01307 840288
www.nts.org.uk/Property/5

18th century cottages home to important collections, offering an insight into the domestic life of rural workers in Angus. The agricultural centre houses a reconstructed farm steading as part of a 'life on the land' exhibition. Museum highlights include a reconstructed farm steading with farmer's bothy as part of the exhibition, charming exhibitions housed in six 18th century cottages offering vivid insights into rural life in Angus, and a schoolroom, Victorian manse parlour and rural kitchen among the many displays.

Arbroath Signal Tower Museum

Signal Tower Museum, Ladyloan
Arbroath DD11 1PU
01241 435329
www.angus.gov.uk/history/museums/signaltower
signal.tower@angus.gov.uk

Beside Arbroath's harbour, on the sea front, stands an elegant complex of regency buildings built in 1813. The building formed the shore station for the families of the lighthouse keepers that served on the Bell Rock Lighthouse. Arbroath Signal Tower Museum collects artefacts, photographs and archive material relating to the history of Arbroath and District. The collections are especially representative of the Burgh.

Barry Mill

Barry
Carnoustie DD7 7RJ
0844 493 2140
www.nts.org.uk/Property/Barry-Mill
barrymill@nts.org.uk

Barry Mill is a magnificent example of Scotland's industrial heritage. It is set in a secluded area beside the Barry Burn, with a working mill, ladeside and burnside walks, and guided tours. Exhibition explaining the role of the mill in the rural economy. Milling demonstrations - normally on Sunday afternoons and for pre-booked groups. A working example of a traditional water-powered oatmeal mill.

Brechin Town House Museum

28 High Street
Brechin DD9 6ER
01307 461460
www.brechintownhouse.org.uk
brechin.museum@angus.gov.uk

The museum is located within the old Town House in the centre of Brechin. A tollbooth was first mentioned on this site in 1450 but was replaced in 1789-90 by the present building.

Broughty Castle Museum

Castle Approach, Broughty Ferry
Dundee DD5 2TF
01382 436916
www.leisureandculturedundee.com
broughty@leisureandculturedundee.com

Broughty Castle is a 15th century fort, housing fascinating displays on the life and times of Broughty Ferry and seashore life. Be intrigued by the armour in the military gallery and the history of the soldiers who were stationed in the building.

Camperdown House

Camperdown Country Park
Dundee DD2 4TF
01382 432084
www.camperdownpark.com

A neo-classical house built in 1828 and designed by the architect William Burn. It was named after the Battle of Camperdown, where Admiral Adam Duncan triumphed over the Dutch fleet in 1797.

Discovery Point & RRS Discovery

Discovery Quay, Riverside Drive
Dundee DD1 4XA
01382 309060
www.rrsdiscovery.com
admin@_dundeeheritage._co._uk

This is the story of Discovery from her beginnings in Dundee and Captain Scott's remarkable Antarctic expedition, through her long ocean-going career until her final journey home. Find out about life on board and the essential design features that allowed her to survive the extreme polar conditions.

Dundee City Archives

Archive and Record Centre, Support Services, 21 City Square
Dundee DD1 3BY
01382 434494
www.dundeecity.gov.uk/archive

Dundee City Archives holds the official records of Dundee City Council, of the former City of Dundee District Council, the former Corporation of Dundee and the former Tayside Regional Council. The centre also holds records retransmitted from the National Records of Scotland (NRS), such as kirk session minutes in the Presbytery of Dundee.

Frigate Unicorn

Victoria Dock
Dundee DD1 3JA
01382 200 900
www.frigateunicorn.org

His Majesty's Frigate Unicorn, of 46 guns, was built for the Royal Navy in the Royal Dockyard at Chatham and launched in 1824. She is now the world's last intact warship from the days of sail, one of the six oldest ships in the world and Scotland's only representative of the sailing navy.

Glenesk Folk Museum

The Retreat, Tarfside, Glenesk
Edzell DD9 7TA
01356 648070
www.gleneskretreat.co.uk
visit@gleneskretreat.co.uk

The Glenesk Folk Museum at the Retreat was set up in 1955 by Miss Greta Michie, a local farmer's daughter and school teacher, based on Scandinavian folk museums she had visited in Norway. The Retreat houses an extremely large collection of artefacts, some of which are now on display in the museum.

House of Dun - National Trust Scotland

Montrose DD10 9LQ
01674 810 264
http://goo.gl/DYhcOA
houseofdun@nts.org.uk

With so much history behind it, the rich character of the House of Dun is sure to keep you occupied all day. The Dun Estate was home to the Erskine family from 1375 until 1980, but archaeological evidence shows that people have lived here for at least 9,000 years.

J M Barrie's Birthplace

🏛️ £

9 Brechin Road
Kirriemuir DD8 4BX
01575 572646
http://goo.gl/W73T19

In this two-storeyed house J M Barrie (1860-1937), the creator of Peter Pan, was born. The upper floors are furnished as they may have been when Barrie lived there.

Kirriemuir Gateway to the Glens Museum

📷 ⭐

The Townhouse, 32 High Street
Kirriemuir DD8 4BX
01575 575479
http://goo.gl/A4Vx2L
kirriegateway@angus.gov.uk

Kirriemuir Gateway to the Glens Museum is situated in Kirriemuir Town House, a building that has been at the heart of Kirriemuir since its construction in 1604.

McManus, The: Dundee's Art Gallery & Museum

📷 ⭐

Albert Square, Meadowside
Dundee DD1 1DA
01382 307200
www.leisureandculturedundee.com
themcmanus@leisureandculturedundee.com

The McManus is a magnificent Victorian, Gothic building where art, history and the environment combine to offer a fascinating insight into Dundee.

McManus Collections Unit

📷 🏠 ⭐

Barrack Street
Dundee DD1 1PG
01382 307200
www.leisureandculturedundee.com
themcmanus@leisureandculturedundee.com

From birds to butterflies, coins to costumes and fossils to foreign artefacts, The Collections Unit offers visitors a fascinating behind-the-scenes glimpse of Dundee's museum collections. Tours of the facility are available on selected dates.

Meffan Museum & Art Gallery

📷 ⭐

20 West High Street
Forfar DD8 1BB
01307 464123
www.angus.gov.uk/history/museums/meffan
the.meffan@angus.gov.uk

Situated in the heart of Forfar's historic town centre is 'The

Meffan' built in 1898 as a bequest from the daughter of Provost Meffan. Originally Forfar's library and museum, the building is now a lively art gallery and museum.

Mills Observatory

📷 £

Glamis Road, Balgay Park
Dundee DD2 2UB
01382 435967
www.leisureandculturedundee.com
mills.observatory@leisureandculturedundee.com

Britain's first purpose-built public observatory. Gifted to the people of Dundee in 1935, with a bequest from John Mills, a linen and twine manufacturer and keen amateur scientist.

Collections: Victorian 10' Cooke refracting telescope (1871), providing breathtaking views of the Moon and Planets. Interesting displays of historic equipment and information of local importance.

Montrose Air Station Heritage Centre

🏛️ 🏠 £

Waldron Road
Montrose DD10 9BB
01674 678222
www.rafmontrose.org.uk
rafmontrose@aol.com

The earliest air station in Britain, established 1913 by the Royal Flying Corps, dating from a period of manned flight when planes were, quite literally, kites. The museum features a fascinating photographic archive and collection of aviation memorabilia, artefacts and vehicles relating to the flying history of Montrose.

Montrose Museum & Art Gallery

📷 ⭐

Panmure Place
Montrose DD10 8HF
01674 673232
www.angus.gov.uk/history/museums/montrose
montrose.museum@angus.gov.uk

Montrose Museum was built in 1842 with funds raised by the Montrose Natural History and Antiquarian Society. One of the oldest purpose-built museums in Scotland, it is an elegant building constructed from pink sandstone which overlooks the historic Mid Links parks.

Collections: Fine local historical collections including Pictish stones, the Baltic trade, whaling, Jacobite material, Marquis of Montrose, Montrose Silver, Lord Gray Agate Collection, local pottery, Stone & Iron Age. William Lamb Studio.

North Carr Lightship

c/o South Victoria Dock Road
Dundee DD1 3BP
01382 542516
www.northcarr-lightship.org
info@northcarr.org.uk

North Carr is the only remaining Scottish lightship. She protected shipping off Fife Ness until 1975 when she was briefly berthed as a tourist attraction in Anstruther Harbour.

Scotland's Jute Museum @ Verdant Works

West Henderson's Wynd
Dundee DD1 5BT
01382 309060
www.verdantworks.com
info@dundeeheritage.co.uk

Scotland's Jute Museum @ Verdant Works weaves the tale of jute with the life and work of old Dundee, from the incredible rise of the industry to its subsequent decline. At Scotland's Jute Museum @ Verdant Works the rattle and the roar of the orgininal restored machinery transport you back over 100 years to an era when jute was king and Dundee was its realm.

St Vigeans Sculptured Stones

Kirkstyle, St.Vigeans
Arbroath DD11 4RB
01241 878756
http://goo.gl/ZpKx1w

A fascinating and very important collection of over 30 Pictish carved stones housed in a cottage in the charming village of St Vigeans. In the village of St Vigeans 0.5m N of Arbroath off of the A92.

University of Dundee Museum Services

Hawkhill House, 5-7 Hawkhill Place, University of Dundee
Dundee DD1 4HN
01382 384 310
www.dundee.ac.uk/museum
museum@dundee.ac.uk

A fascinating University collection of art, science and nature. A superb collection of Scottish art from 18th century to contemporary work. Scientific instruments, natural history specimens, medical equipment, textiles and design pieces.

Argyll

Argyllshire, a maritime county in the W. of Scotland, including nearly all the islands of the Inner Hebrides. In extreme length the mainland extends about 112 miles S. from the boundary with Inverness-shire to the North Channel, and approaches the opposite coast of Ireland within a distance of 13 miles. Area, 3213.1 square miles. Population 76,468, or 24 persons to each square mile. The mainland is much indented by picturesque and far-reaching sea-lochs, which render its coast-line proportionately very great. The peninsula of Kintyre extends about 55 miles S. from the Crinan Canal to the Mull of Kintyre, and is from 5 miles to 10 miles broad. Ardnamurchan Point is the most westerly projection on the mainland of Scotland. The principal sea-lochs are Eil, Linnhe, Leven, Etive, and Firth of Lorne in the NW.; and Fyne, Striven, Long, and Goil branching from the Firth of Clyde. The sea views along the W. coast and among the islands are magnificent, while the loch and mountain scenery is everywhere grand and picturesque. The surface is nearly all rugged and mountainous, the low and arable land lying chiefly round the coasts. The highest summit is Ben Cruachan, altitude 3611 ft., in the NW. of the mainland. The largest lake is Loch Awe, which stretches for upwards of 20 miles S. from the base of Ben Cruachan. The arable land constitutes about one-eighth of the entire area. Slate is extensively quarried and exported. The fisheries are very important, especially the herring fishery on Loch Fyne. There are several large distilleries in Islay and at Campbeltown. Railway communication extends through Perthshire to Oban, on the NW. of Argyllshire. The county comprises the districts of Lochiel, Ardgour, Sunart, Ardnamuchan, and Morven in the NW. detached section; Lorn, Argyll, Cowal, Knapdale, and Kintyre in the main body; 37 parishes, parts of 3 other parishes, the parliamentary burghs of Campbeltown, Inveraray, and Oban (part of the Ayr Burghs).

– John Bartholomew, *Gazetteer of the British Isles* (1887)

Note: see Hebrides for islands in Argyll.

Argyll & Bute Council Archives

Manse Brae Area Office
Lochgilphead PA31 8QU
01546 604774
http://goo.gl/3yibxi

The Archives (records office) holds and preserves the official records of Argyll and Bute Council and also the records of the organisations whose functions the council inherited. These organisations include: the Commissioners of Supply, parish councils, burgh councils, schools, school boards, Argyll County Council and Bute County Council.

Auchindrain Museum

By Inveraray PA32 8XN
01499 500235
auchindrain.org.uk
manager@auchindrain-museum.org.uk

Farm townships like Auchindrain were once common throughout Scotland and indeed much of Europe. Today only Auchindrain survives as an exceptionally complete, evolved group of farm buildings, dating from the period 1750-1840.

Bute Museum

7 Stuart Street, (by Rothesay Castle), Rothesay
Isle of Bute PA20 0BX
01700 505067
www.butemuseum.org.uk
historycurator@butemuseum.org

In this busy museum, situated behind the castle, you can experience the archaeology, history, natural history and geology of the Isle of Bute. It offers an extensive display of birds and mammals etc found on the island, and a wild flower display throughout the summer.

Campbeltown Museum

Hall Street
Campbeltown PA28 6BJ
01586 552366
www.argyll-bute.gov.uk/node/32683
marij.vanhelmond@argyll-bute.gov.uk

Campbeltown Museum occupies a sizeable room in an A-listed building which also houses the local public library. The initiative to establish a library and museum was came in 1896 from the Kintyre Scientific Association, today still active as the Kintyre Antiquarian and Natural History Society.

Castle House Museum

🏛️ £

Castle Gardens

Dunoon PA23 7HH

01369 701422

www.castlehousemuseum.org.uk

info@castlehousemuseum.org.uk

The Castle House Museum, which has been open since 1998, is one of Dunoon's most historic locations. Dunoon became a holiday resort when Lord Provost Ewing of Glasgow bought the land around the ruined medieval castle and built himself a holiday home.

Glencoe & North Lorn Folk Museum

🏛️ 🏠 🏛️ £

Glencoe Village

Glencoe PH39 4HP

01855 811 664

www.glencoemuseum.com

admin@glencoemuseum.com

The Glencoe Folk Museum was co-founded in 1966 with the aim 'To collect, preserve and exhibit articles, costume, objects and information, relevant to the history and social conditions of the Glencoe and North Lorn district for the purposes of education and interest'.

Hill House, The

🏛️ £

The Hill House, Upper Colquhoun Street

Helensburgh G84 9AJ

0844 493 2208

www.nts.org.uk/Property/The-Hill-House

thehillhouse@nts.org.uk

The Hill House is considered to be Charles Rennie Mackintosh's finest domestic creation. Sitting high above the Clyde, it is home to original Mackintosh furniture and interior design and also has attractive formal gardens designed recognisably in the Mackintosh style.

Inveraray Jail & County Court

🏛️ £

Church Square, Inveraray

Argyll PA32 8TX

01499 302381

www.inverarayjail.co.uk

info@inverarayjail.co.uk

Inveraray Jail is a living museum and top Scottish visitor attraction where real people portray life in a 19th century prison. Interact with costumed characters, watch courtroom trials, talk to the prisoners, meet the Warder, go to jail and witness cell life, sample the punishments, browse the exhibition of prison artefacts, then make your escape.

Iona Abbey & Nunnery - Historic Scotland

🏛️ £

Island of Iona PA76 6SQ

www.historic-scotland.gov.uk/places

Founded by St Columba in 563, the restored abbey and monastic buildings retain their spiritual atmosphere, and house a superb collection of over 180 medieval carved stones, from high crosses to pillow stones.

Islay Family History Society

🏛️

Islay House Square, Bridgend

Isle of Islay PA44 7NZ

01496 810 187

http://goo.gl/mNPUdB

islayfhs@btconnect.com

From May to September, volunteers man the society's office at Highfield, High Street, Bowmore, Isle of Islay.

Kilmartin House Museum

🏛️ 🏠 🏛️ £

Kilmartin House Museum

Kilmartin PA31 8RQ

01546 510278

www.kilmartin.org

museum@kilmartin.org

There are more than 350 ancient monuments within a six-mile radius of the village of Kilmartin, Argyll: 150 of them are prehistoric. This extraordinary concentration and diversity of monuments distinguishes the Kilmartin Glen as an area of outstanding archaeological importance.

Lismore Museum & Heritage Centre

🏠 £

Port a' Charrain PA34 5UL

www.celm.org.uk

lismore-museum@btconnect.com

A stunning ecologically friendly building, opened in March 2007, housing a museum charting island life throughout the ages. On the same site is an award winning 19th century Cottar's Cottage, fully restored, a time warp of island life in the late 19th and early 20th centuries; a library/research and conference room; a gift shop and café.

MacDougall Collection

🏠

Dunollie House

Oban PA34 5TT

01631 570550

http://goo.gl/TNKCks

macdougallcollection.oban@virgin.net

Not yet a museum, but a museum collection with a vigorous outreach programme. The private collection of the late Miss Hope MacDougall, comprising some 5000 objects.

Mount Stuart

Isle of Bute PA20 9LR
01700 503877
www.mountstuart.com
contactus@mountstuart.com

The spirit of 19th-century invention is embodied in Mount Stuart – a feat of Victorian engineering, this neo-gothic mansion was one of the most technologically advanced houses of its age. Truly a house of firsts, we believe Mount Stuart was the first home in the world to have a heated indoor swimming pool, and the first in Scotland to be purpose built with electric light, central heating, a telephone system and a Victorian passenger lift – most of which are still in use today.

Museum of Islay Life

Port Charlotte
Isle of Islay PA48 7UA
01496 850 358
www.islaymuseum.org

The museum building is the former Free Church in Port Charlotte, and after restoration opened to the public in 1977. Since then, with the generous help of islanders donating material of all kinds, the museum has built up a main collection of over 2700 objects as diverse as stone implements used in the Mesolithic era, Victorian and Edwardian items from the Laird's house, farming implements, everything necessary for an illicit still, relics from shipping disasters, over 1200 books, very substantial paper archives, including much unique material, and nearly 5000 photographs, some dating back more than 100 years.

Oban War & Peace Museum

Old Oban Times Building, Corran Esplanade
Oban PA34 5PX
01631 570007
www.obanmuseum.org.uk
obanwarandpeacemuseum@aol.com

Oban War and Peace Museum boasts interesting collection of artefacts and photographs showing many aspects of life in Oban and the area through the years, including information on the strategic role played by the area during WWII when Oban Bay was home to Flying Boats. Find out about old Oban, the ferries, the fishing and maritime industries, the railway and local sport. There is a fine collection of Military badges and probably the largest Flying Boat model in Scotland.

Ross of Mull Historical Centre

Millbrae Cottage, Bunessan
Isle of Mull PA67 6DG
01681 700 659
www.romhc.org.uk
enquiries@romhc.org.uk

Museum relating to the history of the region. Includes geneaological resources, documentation on local issues, maps and information relating to the Ross of Mull.

Skerryvore Lighthouse Museum

Lower Square
Hynish, Isle of Tiree PA77 6UQ
01865 311468
http://goo.gl/e9PTta

Tisit the Story of Skerryvore Lighthouse exhibition to find out how the heroic engineers and keepers built and maintained Scotland's tallest lighthouse, Skerryvore, on one of Britain's most dangerous rocks, over 10 nautical miles out to sea. This exhibition records the fascinating account of the hazardous Skerryvore reef and the design and construction of the lighthouse by Alan Stevenson, uncle of Robert Louis Stevenson. It features unique examples of industrial archaeology, a scale model of the lighthouse and interpretation material of general and educational interest.

Strachur Smiddy Museum

The Clachan
Strachur PA27 8DG
01369 860565
www.strachursmiddy.org.uk
museum@strachursmiddy.org.uk

The building in which this small museum is housed has been owned and operated for four generations by the Montgomery family as the local blacksmiths. The contents have remained virtually untouched since the last iron was set down and the building was closed for commercial use. The museum therefore contains tools, clothing and equipment that would have been used as part of the blacksmiths day to day work.

Ayrshire

Ayrshire, a maritime county in the SW. of Scotland, adjoining the cos. of Renfrew, Lanark, Dumfries, Kirkcudbright, and Wigtown. It is in the shape of a crescent, with the concave side, measuring about 70 miles, adjacent to the Firth of Clyde. Its greatest breadth, across the middle, is 30 miles. Area, 1128.5 square miles. Population 217,519, or 193 persons to each square mile. The coast in the S. is rocky and destitute of natural harbours, but becomes row and sandy northwards from Ayr. The lofty islet of Ailsa Craig is comprised in this county. The surface slopes with slight undulations from the landward border, which is hilly in most parts, and is mountainous in the SE. The soil is various, sandy near the coast, of a rich clay in the middle parts, and moor in the uplands. The rivers are the Garnock, Irvine, Ayr, Doon, Girvan, and Stinchar. The largest lake is Loch Doon, on the SE. border. The minerals are coal, iron, limestone, and sandstone, all of which are extensively worked. The county is famous for dairy produce and a fine breed of cows. The mfrs. are valuable, and include woollen, cotton, iron, and earthenware. The county comprises 43 parishes and 3 parts, the parliamentary burghs of Ayr and Irvine (part of the Ayr Burghs -- 1 member), and Kilmarnock (part of the Kilmarnock Burghs -- 1 member).

– John Bartholomew, *Gazetteer of the British Isles* (1887)
Note: the Isle of Arran is included here with Ayrshire.

Bachelors' Club

Sandgate Street
Tarbolton KA5 5RB
01292 541 940
www.nts.org.uk

In this 17th-century thatched house, Robert Burns and friends formed a debating club in 1780. Burns attended dancing lessons, and was initiated into Freemasonry here, in 1781.

Baird Institute

3 Lugar Street
Cumnock KA18 1AD
01290 421701
bairdinstitute.org.au

The Baird Institute Museum lies in the centre of the town of Cumnock, and was opened in 1891. The museum holds a collection of Mauchline ware of world importance, complimented by many items of Cumnock pottery, mining equipment, and photographs and artefacts of local and social history. Works of traditional and contemporary art and crafts are also displayed here.

Balmacara Estate

Lochalsh House, Balmacara
Kyle IV40 8DN
0844 4932233 Email :
www.nts.org.uk/Property/Balmacara-Estate
balmacara@nts.org.uk

The Balmacara Estate is a diverse highland crofting estate of high nature conservation and cultural value. The land has been used for millennia, with the agricultural and woodland management of the last two centuries giving rise to a pleasing blend of built, crofted and natural environments in the landscape. Includes the historic village of Plockton and its open air church.

Brodick Castle

Brodick KA27 8HY
01770 302 202
www.nts.org.uk/Property/13/Contact
brodickcastle@nts.org.uk

Brodick Castle and Country Park is unique in being the only island country park in Britain. The castle offers 600 years of history, a fabulous collection of valuable artefacts, and stunning views over Brodick Bay to the Ayrshire Coast.

Burns Cottage Museum

Burns Cottage
Alloway KA7 4PY
01292 441215
www.burnsmuseum.org.uk
burns@nts.org.uk

Robert Burns Birthplace Museum offers a truly unique encounter with Scotland's favourite son. The museum comprises the famous Burns Cottage where the poet was born, the historic landmarks where he set his greatest work, the elegant monument and gardens created in his honour and a modern museum housing the world's most important collection of his life and works.

Culzean Castle & Country Park

Silver Ave
Maybole KA19 8LE
01655 760274
www.culzeanexperience.org/events.asp

TWith its dramatic clifftop setting, Robert Adam architecture, fascinating history and beautiful surroundings, it's easy to see why Culzean Castle is one of Scotland's most popular visitor attractions. Surrounded by Culzean Country Park, an extensive estate encompassing lush woodland, landscaped gardens and rugged coastline, this 18th-century Scottish castle couldn't be better placed for a family day out.

Darvel Telephone Museum

1b Burn Road
Darvel, Ayrshire KA17 0AJ
01560 320780
www.mflemmich.freeserve.co.uk
max@mflemmich.freeserve.co.uk

The Darvel Telephone Museum contains a unique display of telephone memorabilia dating from 1900s to the present day. At the moment there are no regular opening times. Please phone prior to visiting to ensure access.

Dean Castle

Dean Road, Off Glasgow Road
Kilmarnock KA3 1XB
01563 554734
www.deancastle.com
DeanCastle@east-ayrshire.gov.uk

The country park boasts beautiful woodland walks, adventure playground, urban farm, visitor centre, tearoom, shop and a fantastic 14th century castle housing world class collections including historic weapons, armour and musical instruments.

Dumfries House

Dumfries House
Cumnock KA18 2NJ
01290 425 959
dumfries-house.org.uk

Dumfries House is one of Britain's most beautiful stately homes. Set in 2,000 acres of land, this stunning estate and 18th-Century house with its unrivalled collection of original furniture has something for everyone.

East Ayrshire Archives

Burns Monument Centre, Kay Park Cottage, Kay Park
Kilmarnock KA3 7RU
01292 521819
http://goo.gl/MppfXA

Material held at Burns Monument Centre includes official records from the East Ayrshire burghs of Cumnock, Darvel, Galston, Kilmarnock, Newmilns and Greenholm and Stewarton, dating back to the 1600s. We have a significant collection of Church records from the Ayr and Irvine Presbyteries.

East Ayrshire Family History Society

c/o Dick Institute, Elmbank Avenue
Kilmarnock KA1 3BU
www.eastayrshirefhs.co.uk

enquiries@eastayrshirefhs.org.uk

East Ayrshire Family History Society was formed in 1997 and takes its name from the new local authority created around the same time. The area covered by East Ayrshire comprises the former districts of Kilmarnock & Loudoun and Cumnock & Doon Valley, however resources held by EAFHS cover all of Ayrshire.

Isle of Arran Heritage Museum

Rosaburn
Brodick, Isle of Arran KA27 8DP
01770 302 636
www.arranmuseum.co.uk
info@arranmuseum.co.uk

Originally the site of a small school, the present group of buildings were a croft and smiddy, and include a farmhouse, cottage, bothy, milk house, laundry, stable, coach house and harness room.

Largs & North Ayrshire Family History Society

Bogriggs Cottage, Carlung
West Kilbride KA23 9PS
01294 823690
www.largsnafhs.org.uk
membership@largsnafhs.org.uk

The Largs and North Ayrshire Family History Society was formed in 1988. Its aim is to promote the study of family history in Largs and the surrounding area of North Ayrshire.

Largs Museum

Kirkgate House, Manse Court
Largs KA30 8AW
01475 687 081
http://goo.gl/EcWC2Y

The museum has displays on the history of the town and the surrounding area, local family history, overseas links especially with Australia, the ship HMS Largs, and so on. Each year a special themed display is prepared for the museum's opening in June, July and August.

McKechnie Institute

Dalrymple Street
Girvan KA26 9AE
01465 713643
www.south-ayrshire.gov.uk/galleries/mckechnie

The McKechnie Institute opened in 1889 thanks to the benevolence of a local businessman, Thomas McKechnie. Its architectural style is Scottish Baronial with some Renaissance detailing. There are most often displays of items from the McKechnie Institute collection, in conjunction with a programme of temporary exhibitions in the downstairs and upstairs galleries.

Museum of the Cumbraes

Manse Street

Saltcoats KA21 5AA

01294 464 174

http://goo.gl/iQzXDf

Housed within Garrison House, the museum of The Cumbraes provides a fascinating glimpse into Cumbrae's past. From 4,000 year-old stone coffins – or 'cists' – found on the Cumbraes, through stories of smuggling in the 18th century to life during the second world war and indeed life on the island today.

North Ayrshire Heritage Centre

Manse Street

Saltcoats KA21 5AA

01294 464174

http://goo.gl/nh2odm

The Heritage Centre, in Saltcoats, has an extensive genealogy section for those wishing to trace their Ayrshire ancestry.

North Ayrshire Museum

Manse Street

Saltcoats KA21 5AA

01294 464174

http://goo.gl/zxnOIY

namuseum@north-ayrshire.gov.uk

The North Ayrshire Museum is the main museum in North Ayrshire and displays the social history of the area. It is housed in an old parish church dating from 1744. Changing displays and exhibitions of the area's social history, archaeology, transport and culture are on show.

Penkill Castle

Old Dailly

Girvan KA26 9TQ

01465 871219

www.culture24.org.uk/am18467

A small village of South Ayrshire, Penkill lies a mile (2 km) south of Old Daily and 3 miles (5 km) northeast of Girvan. To the south of the village lies the Penkill Castle, an imposing 15th century castle with additions dating through to 19th century.

Robert Burns Birthplace Museum

Murdoch's Lane, Alloway

Ayr KA7 4PQ

0844 493 2601

http://goo.gl/13GS1L

burns@nts.org.uk

The Robert Burns Birthplace Museum offers visitors a chance to experience the rich heritage of Burns within the environment that inspired his imagination. The late medieval Brig o' Doon, spanning the beautiful River Doon, was chosen by Burns for the climax of his tale in Tam o'shanter. Alloway Auld Kirk is the burial place for the poet's father. Burns Cottage, birthplace of Robert Burns, was built in 1757 by the poet's father, William Burness.

Rozelle House Galleries

Rozelle Park, Monument Road

Ayr KA7 4NQ

01292 445 447

www.south-ayrshire.gov.uk/galleries/rozellehouse

Rozelle.House@south-ayrshire.gov.uk

The Royal Burgh of Ayr held the Rozelle lands as part of the Barony lands of Alloway until an auction in 1754 to reduce the Burgh debt brought sale of the lands to Robert Hamilton for £2,000. The Hamilton family made their fortune in the sugar and tobacco industries in the West Indies. Rozelle House is now a major display venue, currently showing the significant collection, Tam O' Shanter, a series of 54 paintings, by Alexander Goudie. Rozelle House is also home to the Ayrshire Yeomanry museum,

Skelmorlie ROC Post

PA17 5AQ

www.roc-heritage.co.uk/scotland.html

info@nuclearburst.co.uk

Fifteen feet below the ground, a close-knit team of dedicated and highly trained volunteers waited for the message they hoped would never come. Throught the Cold War, the underground monitoring post of the Royal Observer Corps at Skelmorlie played an important role as part of the United Kingdom Warning and Monitoring Organisation.

Collections: Includes many items of post equipment including air raid siren, ground zero indicator, bomb power indicator, burndept radio, teletalk and fixed survey meter. the post is also lucky to have the only known example of an experimental air filtration system in Scotland.

Souter Johnnie's Cottage

Kirkoswald KA19 8JH

01655 760603

www.nts.org.uk/Property/Souter-Johnnies-Cottage

See Scottish literature come to life in this 18th-century thatched cottage in the heart of Kirkoswald, Ayr. The former home of cobbler – or souter – John Davidson, the real-life Souter Johnnie immortalised in the Robert Burns poem Tam o' Shanter, it features a thatched tavern in the garden, complete with life-sized sandstone statues of the poem's main characters. The house also offers a taste of how the Davidson family would have lived and worked – inside the cottage there is a reconstructed shoemaking workshop crammed with Souter Johnnie's original tools, as well as living quarters with period furniture.

South Ayrshire Archives

Carnegie Library, 12 Main Street, Ayr KA8 8EB

01292 286385

http://goo.gl/VEPHBd

The Scottish and Local History Library is located on the first floor of the Carnegie Library in Ayr. The department houses a unique collection of books, pamphlets, directories, maps, plans, local newspapers and photographs.

Troon @ Ayrshire Family History Society

c/o M.E.R.C., Troon Public Library, South Beach

Troon KA10 6EF

www.troonayrshirefhs.org.uk

E: info@troonayrshirefhs.org.uk

Troon @ Ayrshire Family History Society is one of the smaller societies in Scotland but still has the reputation of being very active, and we have a fairly strong attendance at the monthly meetings September - June.

West Kilbride Museum

Public Hall, 1 Arthur Street

West Kilbride KA23 9EN

01294 822102

www.westkilbridemuseum.org.uk

admin@westkilbridemuseum.org.uk

This local museum has a regular display which includes social history, trades and craft implements, dolls, toys and a large collection of Ayrshire lace embroidery and local Paisley weaving. There are also regular exhibitions held on specific topics.

Berwickshire

Berwickshire, a maritime county in the extreme SE. of Scotland, extending in extreme breadth about 20 m. between Haddingtonshire and the English border, and in extreme length about 33 miles between Roxburgshire and the German Ocean; coast-line about 20 miles; area, 460.6 square miles; population 35,392, or 77 persons to each square mile. The coast is high and rocky, and the few but important fishing harbs. are much exposed. St Abbs Head is the main projection. The Lammermuir Hills, to the average breadth of 7 miles, occupy all the N.; a bleak and mostly moorland tract of 5 miles in breadth, but somewhat diversified towards the E., succeeds; and the luxuriant and fertile district, called the Merse, slopes from this to the banks of the Tweed. The district of Lauderdale, on the W., is chiefly upland. The Tweed traces about half of the S. boundary, and receives the Leader, Eden, Leet, and the Whiteadder (with its affl. the Blackadder). The Eye enters the German Ocean at Eyemouth. The lands on Tweedside are in a very high state of cultivation; the rest of the county is chiefly pastoral. The fisheries, both on the coast and in the Tweed, are among the most important in Scotland. The county comprises 31 parishes and parts of 2 others.

– John Bartholomew, *Gazetteer of the British Isles* (1887)

Coldstream Museum

12 Market Square

Coldstream TD12 4BD

01890 882 630

www.holy-island.info/coldstream-museum

Atulloch@Scotborders.gov.uk

The story of the Coldstream Guards regiment. Colours, customs, duties and dramas spanning over 350 years.

Eyemouth Museum

Auld Kirk, Manse Road

Eyemouth TD14 5JE

01890 751701

www.eyemouthmuseum.org

enquiries@eyemouthmuseum.co.uk

Eyemouth Museum is based in the centre of the town and documents the fishing and social heritage of Eyemouth, brought to life in its exhibits and through stories from local people. Central to the museum is the famous Eyemouth Tapestry that commemorates the Great East Coast Fishing Disaster of 1881, known as Black Friday, when 129 Eyemouth men lost their lives at sea.

Jim Clark Room, The

44 Newtown Street
Duns TD11 3AU
01361 883 960
http://goo.gl/vJ5NQO

The museum Room is devoted to the career of Jim Clark, World Motor Racing Champion and Berwickshire farmer. It houses a fascinating display of trophies, awards, photographs, model cars, memorabilia and video presentation.

Manderston

Duns TD11 3PP
01361 882636
www.manderston.co.uk
palmer@manderston.co.uk

Manderston is the supreme country house of Edwardian Scotland; the swan-song of its era. A house on which no expense was spared with opulent staterooms, the only silver-staircase in the world and extensive 'downstairs' domestic quarters.

Visitors will find much to enjoy including Britain's first privately-owned Biscuit Tin Museum.

Paxton House

Berwick upon Tweed TD15 1SZ
01289 386291
www.paxtonhouse.co.uk
info@paxtonhouse.com

Built to the design of John Adam in 1758 for a dashing young Scottish laird, Patrick Home of Billie, Paxton House is perhaps the finest 18th century Palladian country house in Britain with 12 period rooms, interiors by Robert Adam and the pre-eminent collection of Chippendale furniture in Scotland. The magnificent picture gallery, the largest in a Scottish country house, exhibits over 70 paintings from the National Galleries of Scotland and the fully restored working Georgian kitchen is complete with active charcoal stoves and baking oven.

Thirlestane Castle

Thirlestane Castle Trust
Lauder TD2 6RU
01578 722430
www.thirlestanecastle.co.uk
admin@thirlestanecastle.co.uk

Thirlestane Castle is one of the oldest and finest castles in Scotland and holds a uniquely important place in Scottish History. The castle has its origins in the 13th century.

Caithness

Caithness-shire, a maritime county, in the extreme NE. of the mainland of Scotland. The side adjoining Sutherlandshire measures about 33 miles; the coast on the Pentland Firth about 41 miles; and the coast on the North Sea about 43 miles; area, 438,878 acres; population 38,865, or 57 persons to each square mile. The coast along the N. and partly on the E. is bold and precipitous; between Wick and the Ord of Caithness, in the SE., it is mostly low and sandy. The chief promontories are Duncansbay Head and Dunnet Head, the latter being the most northerly point of the mainland. The surface in general is slightly undulating, and is much interspersed with small lakes and tracts of morass. It rises into mountains along the landward border, the chief summit of which, Morven, has an altitude of 2313 ft. The streams are numerous, but small; the principal are the Berridale and the Wick Water, flowing to the North Sea, and the Thurso and the Forss, flowing to the Pentland Firth. Flagstone is extensively quarried for exportation. The soil, though generally poor, is well cultivated. The coast fisheries are among the most important in the country; great quantities of herrings are annually cured and exported. The river Thurso is famed for its splendid salmon-fishing. There is railway communication to Thurso, in the extreme N. The county comprises 9 parishes and part of 1 other, the parliamentary and royal burgh of Wick (part of the Wick Burghs).

– John Bartholomew, *Gazetteer of the British Isles* (1887)

Caithness Archive Centre

Wick Library, Sinclair Terrace
Wick KW1 5AB
01955 606432
www.highlandarchives.org.uk/caithness.asp

As part of the Highland Archive Service, the Caithness Archive Centre, Wick, is responsible for collecting, preserving and making locally accessible archives relating to the history of the county of Caithness.

Caithness Broch Centre

Northlands Viking Centre, The Old School House, Auckengill, Keiss
Wick KW1 4XP
01955 631377
www.caithnessbrochcentre.co.uk

Brochs, unique to Scotland, are amongst the most studied monuments in British prehistory. A broch is a drystone tower with cells or galleries contained within the thickness of the wall.

Caithness Family History Society

Dwarick Park
Dunnet KW14 8XD
01847 851 295
www.caithnessfhs.org.uk
b.l.hiddleston@btinternet.com

Caithness Family History Society was formed in September 1999 by a small group of enthusiasts and has already grown to some 350 members worldwide. Our aim is to promote an interest in genealogy and, wherever we can, to help others trace their roots - especially families originating from Caithness.

Caithness Horizons

Old Town Hall, High Street
Thurso KW14 8AJ
01847 896508
www.caithnesshorizons.co.uk
info@caithnesshorizons.co.uk

Caithness Horizons contains: 1) Permanent exhibitions which interpret the cultural and natural heritage of Caithness from prehistory to the present day 2) An audio-visual presentation which provides an overview of the natural and cultural heritage of Caithness.

Castle of Mey

Mey, Thurso
Caithness KW14 8XH
www.castleofmey.org.uk

Since 1952 the property of Queen Elizabeth The Queen Mother, the castle of Mey is situated on the north coast of Caithness, in the parish of Canisbay, about 15 miles east of Thurso and 6 miles west of John O'Groats. It stands on rising ground about 400 yards from the seashore, overlooking the Pentland Firth and the Orkney Islands.

Clan Gunn Heritage Centre & Museum

Old Parish Church
Latheron KW5 6DG
01593 721 325
www.clangunnsociety.org

The Clan Gunn Heritage Centre and Museum is housed in the old parish church, Latheron which was built in 1734. The centre tells the story of the clan from its Norse origins to the present day against the background of the history of the north of Scotland.

Dunbeath Heritage Centre

The Old School
Dunbeath KW6 6ED
01593 731233
www.dunbeath-heritage.org.uk/heritage.html
info@dunbeath-heritage.org.uk

The centre provides a focus for the work of Dunbeath Preservation Trust: Registered museum; archaeological exhibition, Neil M Gunn literary landscape, engaging approach to landscape interpretation through art installations, photography and unique floor map. Repository for research data, manuscripts, photographs and items of local material culture; venue for lectures, storytelling and workshops; gathering place for local people and visitors – young and old – alike.

Laidhay Croft Museum

Laidhay, Dunbeath
Dunbeath KW6 6EH
01593 731244
http://goo.gl/FGLkjJ

Typical rush thatched Caithness longhouse incorporating dwelling, stable and byre under one roof. House furnished and with artefacts common early 1900s.

Clackmannanshire

Clackmannanshire, the smallest county of Scotland, extending 10 miles N. and S. between the main body of Perthshire and the river Forth, and 11 miles E. and W. between the counties of Stirling and Fife; area, 30,477 acres; population 25,680, or 539 persons to each square mile. The surface rises from the Forth by an easy ascent, broken by gentle undulations and by the valley of the river Devon, to the Ochil Hills, which extend along the N. border. These hills afford excellent pasturage; the low grounds are well cultivated. Coal is raised in the Devon valley; the towns of Alloa and Tillicoultry have woollen manufacture. The county comprises 4 parishes and parts of 2 other parishes.

– John Bartholomew, *Gazetteer of the British Isles* (1887)

Alloa Tower

Alloa Park
Alloa FK10 1PP
01259 211701
www.nts.org.uk/Property/3

Ancestral home of the Earls of Mar, Alloa Tower is one of Scotland's largest surviving medieval tower houses with an important collection of portraits, silver and furniture; temporary exhibitions from family's private collections. Features of the tower, where Queen Mary once stayed, include a magnificent medieval oak beamed roof, dungeon and 11 ft thick walls, and stunning views from the tower's roof walk - the walkway goes all the way around the top of the tower.

Castle Campbell & Garden - Historic Scotland

Castle Campbell and Garden
Dollar Glen FK14 7PP
01259 742408
www.historic-scotland.gov.uk/places

Formerly known as the 'Castle of Gloom', this castle is beautifully sited. The oldest part is a well-preserved 15th-century tower around which other buildings were constructed, including an unusual loggia.

Clackmannanshire Archives

Information Librarian & Archivist, Library Services, Alloa Library, 26/28 Drysdale Street
Alloa FK10 1JL
01259 453600
www.clacksweb.org.uk/culture/archives/

Clackmannanshire Archives contains historical records relevant to the county, many of which were previously held in the Central Region Archives Department at Stirling.

Clackmannanshire Museum & Heritage Service

29 Primrose Street
Alloa FK10 1JJ
01259 216913
www.clacksweb.org.uk/culture/museumheritage

The Museum and Heritage Service can help you find out more about Clackmannanshire. The county, with its dramatic landscape of flat carseland on the north bank of the River Forth and dominant Ochil Hills, has a rich cultural history. There is archaeological evidence for prehistoric settlement, as well as some later occupation during the first millennium AD. Four impressive tower houses have survived at Alloa, Clackmannan, Castle Campbell in Dollar and Sauchie and, with Menstrie Castle, represent just a few of the great houses which once existed in the county. The Museum and Heritage Service has a fascinating collection of material, ranging from prehistoric items to industrial and social history objects, as well as an art collection.

Dollar Museum

Castle Campbell Hall, High Street
Dollar FK14 7AY
0159 742 895
home.btconnect.com/dollarmuseum
dollarmuseum@btconnect.com

Dollar Museum is an independent local museum dedicated to the history and heritage of the village of Dollar, in the county of Clackmannanshire, Scotland. Set up in 1988, it occupies two floors of an early 19th century woollen mill (now called the castle Campbell Hall), and has a wide-ranging collection illustrating all aspects of the history of Dollar.

Menstrie Castle

Castle Street
Menstrie FK11 7AY
0844 493 2130
www.nts.org.uk/Property/Menstrie-Castle

Menstrie Castle is a three-storey castellated house that was home to a branch of the Clan MacAlister and was the birthplace of Sir William Alexander, later 1st Earl of Stirling. The property is over 400 years old. Fell into steady decline from the middle of the 18th century. Museum dedicated to an exhibition about Nova Scotia and the Baronets of Nova Scotia.

Cromartyshire

Dumfriesshire

Cromartyshire, small county, in the N. of Scotland, consisting of 20 detached portions merged in Ross-shire, so that for political and most practical purposes it is treated as a component part of that county. See Ross-shire.

– John Bartholomew, *Gazetteer of the British Isles* (1887)

Cromarty Courthouse Museum

Church Street
Cromarty IV11 8XA
01381 600418
www.cromarty-courthouse.org.uk

This elegant former courthouse, built in 1773, now houses fascinating exhibitions about the historic town of Cromarty. The courtroom scene has life-like figures and audio enactment to tell the story of one trial, the other rooms tell the history of Cromarty and each year there are special exhibitions and displays.

Hugh Miller's Cottage - National Trust For Scotland

Church Street
Cromarty IV11 8XA
01381 600245
http://goo.gl/I5LECS

Here in this thatched cottage built c1698 by his great-grandfather was born Hugh Miller, on 10 October, 1802. Miller rose to international acclaim as a geologist, editor and writer.

Dumfries-shire, maritime county, on S. border of Scotland; adjoins the counties of Lanark, Peebles, and Selkirk on the N., and on the S. is washed by the Solway Firth; extends about 53 miles NW. and SE. between Ayrshire and Cumberland, and about 32 miles NE. and SW. between Roxburghshire and Kirkcudbrightshire; coast-line, about 20 miles; area, 680,217 acres, population 76,140, or 72 persons to each square mile. The surface in general is bare and hilly. The dales of the Nith, Annan, and Esk, however, are rich in beauty, and contain fine holms for pasture and some good arable land. The rivers are numerous, and yield splendid salmon and trout fishing. The coast and S. region is low and sandy; much of it is covered with morass, and lochs are numerous around Lockerbie; but there is also much excellent corn-growing land. The Lowther or Lead Hills along the N. boundary are upwards of 2000 ft. in height, and abound in lead ore. These and the other hills round the borders are mostly smooth in outline, and afford excellent pasturage. Red sandstone is a prevailing rock, and limestone, coal, and lead, are worked. The county comprises 41 parishes, with 2 parts, and the parliamentary burghs of Annan, Dumfries (greater part), Lochmaben and Sanquhar (part of the Dumfries Burghs).

– John Bartholomew, *Gazetteer of the British Isles* (1887)

Annan Museum

Bank Street
Annan DG12 6AA
01461 201384
www.dumgal.gov.uk/artsandmuseums
info@dumfriesmuseum.co.uk

Small and friendly local history museum. A regular programme of local history, archeology, photographic and arts and craft exhibitions.

Burns House Museum

Burns Street
Dumfries DG1 2PS
01387 255297
www.dumgal.gov.uk/artsandmuseums
elainek@dumgal.gov.uk

It was in this simple sandstone house in a quiet Dumfries street that Robert Burns, Scotland's national poet, spent the last years of his brilliant life. He died here in 1796 at the age of just thirty seven.

Collections: The desk and chair in the study where Robert Burns wrote his best known poems, the famous Kilmarnock and Edinburgh editions of his work, many original manuscripts and belongings of the poet and his family.

Caerlaverock Castle - Historic Scotland

Caerlaverock Castle
Caerlaverock, Near Dumfries DG1 4RN
01387 770244
www.historic-scotland.gov.uk/places

This is one of the finest castles in Scotland. Its most remarkable features are the twin-towered gatehouse and the Nithsdale Lodging, a splendid Renaissance range dating from 1638. Access to a children's adventure park and replica siege engines in front of castle and nature trail to the old castle is included.

Castle of St John

Charlotte Street
Stranraer DG9 7JP
01776 705544
http://goo.gl/s1GMO6

The castle of St John is a medieval tower house in the centre of Stranraer. It was built around 1500 by the Adairs of Kilhilt, one of the most powerful families in Wigtownshire.

Creetown Heritage Museum & Exhibition Centre

Creetown Heritage Museum, The Exhibition Centre, 16 St John Street
Newton Stewart DG8 7JE
www.creetown-heritage-museum.com

Surrounded by all the luscious green tranquility of the hills and forests of Galloway, here is to be found the fascinating history of a small town built on granite. Originally, Creetown was known as Ferrytown of Cree because up to three ferries took pilgrims across the Cree on their way to visit the shrine of St Ninian of Whithorn.

Dalbeattie Museum

Southwick Road
Dalbeattie DG5 4HA
www.dalbeattiematters.co.uk/features.asp?ID=229

The museum is an excellent record of Dalbeattie in Victorian and early 20th century times, right up to the 50s and 60s. There is an old fashioned 'shop' at the front of the museum, plus a 1920s kitchen, and a small viewing room to look at movies of old Dalbeattie.

Devil's Porridge Exhibition

Stansfield, Annan Road, Eastriggs
Annan DG12 6TF
01461 700021
www.devilsporridge.co.uk
devils-porridge@tiscali.co.uk

The Devil's Porridge Exhibition was founded in 1997 by Richard Brodie and tells the story of the greatest munitions factory on earth. 9 miles long and 2 miles wide HM Factory Gretna employed 30,000 people during the First World War, most of them women, and produced 1100 tons of cordite every week.

Drumlanrig Castle

ThornhilIDG3 4AQ
01848 331 555
www.drumlanrigcastle.co.uk
info@drumlanrigcastle.co.uk

The magnificent 17th century Drumlanrig Castle boasts over 40 acres of beautiful gardens and offers a range of of activities for the whole family. Set in the 120,000 acre Queensberry Estate, complete with a country park and Victorian gardens, this 17th century castle is one of the most important Renaissance buildings in the country. The Dumfriesshire home of the Duke and Duchess of Buccleuch, Drumlanrig Castle with its magnificent rooms and spectacular collections of silver, porcelain, French furniture and art - including Rembrandt's Old Woman Reading - is perhaps one of the most rewarding and romantic of Scotland's great houses.

Dumfries & Galloway Family History Society

Family History Research Centre, 9 Glasgow Street
Dumfries DG2 9AF
01387-248093
www.dgfhs.org.uk
secretary@dgfhs.org.uk

Dumfries and Galloway Family History Society was
founded in 1987 to encourage the study of family history,
genealogy and the local history of the South West of
Scotland.

Dumfries & Galloway Archives

33 Burns Street
Nithsdale DG1 2PS
01387 269254
www.dumgal.gov.uk/?articleid=2300

The Council keeps archives of documents relating to the
local area. These may include parish registers, maps and
plans, council minutes and other historic documents
providing an insight into the history of the area.
Information of local interest is often donated, bequeathed
or loaned to the archive service by local residents and
historians.

Dumfries & Galloway Aviation Museum

Heathhall Industrial Estate, Heathhall
Dumfries DG1 3PH
01387 251623
www.dumfriesaviationmuseum.com
info@dumfriesaviationmuseum.com

Based around the original control tower of the former RAF
Dumfries, the museum is a fascinating collection of aircraft
and memorabilia reaching back to the golden years of
flight. The museum is staffed and maintained entirely by
volunteers from the membership of the Dumfries &
Galloway Aviation Group.

Dumfries Museum & Camera Obscura

The Observatory
Dumfries DG2 7SW
01387 253374
www.dumgal.gov.uk/artsandmuseums
dumfriesmuseum@dumgal.gov.uk

A treasure house of history in Dumfries and Galloway
telling the story of the land and people of the region. The
Camera Obscura, installed in 1836, is on the top floor of
the old windmill tower. From it you can see a fascinating
panoramic view of Dumfries and the surrounding
countryside.

Collections: Look out for fossil footprints left by prehistoric
animals, the wildlife of the Solway, tools and weapons of
our earliest people, stone carvings by Scotland.

John Paul Jones Museum

John Paul Jones Cottage, Arbigland, Kirkbean
Dumfries DG2 8BG
01387 880613
www.jpj.demon.co.uk

The cottage is furnished in the style of the 1700s when John
Paul Jones, 'The Father of the American Navy', was born.
Through headsets his mother describes life in the cottage.

Moffat Museum

The Neuk, Church Gate
Moffat DG10 9EG
01683 220868
www.dumfriesmuseum.demon.co.uk/moffat.html

Originally established in Moffat's old Bakehouse, Moffat
Museum provides a fascinating insight into the town's
history: from early Roman times, the Border Reivers, the
heyday of its coaching era, to the discovery of the Well and
Moffat's popularity as a spa.

Newton Stewart Museum

The Museum, York Road
Newton Stewart DG8 6HH
01671 402472
http://goo.gl/W9IAkP
jmclaymus@btinternet.com

Housed in the former St John's Church, the museum
contains a wealth of historical treasures, some
pre-Victorian, with exciting and interesting displays of the
natural and social history of Galloway.

Old Bridge House Museum

Mill Road
Dumfries DG2 7BE
01387 656904
www.dumgal.gov.uk/artsandmuseums
elainek@dumgal.gov.uk

Built in 1660 into the sandstone of the bridge itself,
Dumfries' oldest house is now a museum of everyday life in
the town. A Museum trail brings the story alive.

Collections: Furnished room settings include a family
kitchen, nursery and bedroom of a Victorian home, and an
early dentist.

Robert Burns Centre

Mill Road
Dumfries DG2 7BE
01387 264808
www.dumgal.gov.uk/artsandmuseums
elainek@dumgal.gov.uk

Situated in the town's 18th century watermill on the west bank of the River Nith, the Robert Burns Centre tells the story of Robert Burns' last years spent in the bustling streets and lively atmosphere of Dumfries in the late 18th century. There are museum trails and fun activities, and visitor information to help you explore Dumfries and Galloway's Burns connections.

Sanquhar Tolbooth Museum

High Street
Sanquhar DG46BN
01659 50186
www.dumgal.gov.uk/artsandmuseums
elainek@dumgal.gov.uk

Discover Sanquhar's world famous knitting tradition and the story of the mines and miners of Sanquhar and Kirkconnel. What was it like to be a prisoner in Sanquhar jail? How did the ordinary people of Upper Nithsdale live and work in times past? All this and more can be found in the town's fine 18th century tolbooth. A free audio-visual presentation and museum trail takes you on a tour, revealing the fascinating story of Upper Nithsdale.

Savings Banks Museum

Ruthwell DG1 4NN
01387 870 640
www.savingsbanksmuseum.co.uk
enquiries@savingsbanksmuseum.co.uk

The museum houses a collection of early home safes, coins and bank notes from many parts of the world, including the first three lock box used in the Ruthwell Parish Bank. As well as bank memorabilia and records, the collection traces the life of the Rev Henry Duncan, the 'Father' of Savings Banks, demonstrating his many interests and accomplishments.

Stewartry Museum

St Mary Street
Kirkcudbright DG6 4AQ
01557 331643
www.dumfriesmuseum.demon.co.uk/stewmuse.html

Opened in 1893, the museum has a collection of remarkable range and quality, reflecting the human and natural history of the Stewartry - the eastern half of Galloway. The social history collections of the 18th and 19th century are particularly important.

Stranraer Museum

The Old Town Hall, 55 George Street
Stranraer DG9 7JP
01776 705088
http://goo.gl/nEDk0o

Stranraer's historic Old Town Hall, built in 1776, is the home of Stranraer Museum. Step inside and discover Wigtownshire's fascinating past.

Thomas Carlyle's Birthplace

The Arched House
Ecclefechan DG11 3DG
0844 4932247
http://goo.gl/6yW8li

In 1795 the great social historian Thomas Carlyle was born in this humble house. The three rooms of the museum contain many of Carlyle's possessions, providing a fascinating insight into 19th century life in a small Scottish town. The birthplace has been open to the public since 1883 and has changed very little in that time, giving an authentic look into a Victorian household. Fascinating collection of portraits and Thomas Carlyle's personal possessions.

Threave House - National Trust for Scotland

Castle Douglas DG7 1RX
01556 502575
www.nts.org.uk
threave@nts.org.uk

Threave House opened to the public for the first time in 2002 and have attracted great interest. The interiors have been restored to their appearance in the 1930s, and from the house visitors can enjoy impressive vistas of the Galloway countryside.

Whithorn Trust

45-47 George Street
Whithorn DG8 8NS
01988 500508
www.whithorn.com
enquiries@whithorn.com

The Whithorn Trust was set up in 1986 to explore the archaeology and history of Whithorn, and to examine its role in the evolution of Christianity in Scotland. The Trust was established as a direct consequence of an archaeological excavation at Whithorn in 1984. This project showed that remains had survived which dated back to the early centuries of Whithorn's development as a Christian centre.

Dunbartonshire

Dumbartonshire, county, partly maritime but chiefly inland, in W. of Scotland, comprising a main body and a detached portion; area, 154,542 acres; population 75,333, or 312 persons to each square mile. The main body is in the shape of a crescent, having the convex side adjacent to the estuary of the Clyde, and measures 1½ to 14 miles in breadth, and about 38 miles between its extreme points. The N. section (about two-thirds of the entire area), projecting between Loch Long and Loch Lomond, is wholly mountainous, and is celebrated for its picturesque and sublime scenery. Ben Vorlich and Ben Vane, in the extreme N., are 3092 and 3004 ft. high. The lower district along the Clyde is flat, and in general under excellent cultivation. The peninsular parish of Roseneath separates Loch Long and the Gare Loch, offshoots of the Firth of Clyde. The detached section (12 miles by 4 miles) lies 4½ miles E. of the nearest point of the main body. The rivers, besides the Clyde, are the Leven, Allander, Kelvin, and Endrick. The manufactures are very important; numerous bleachfields, dye, print, and other works line the banks of the Leven; and there are extensive shipbuilding yards along the Clyde. Dumbartonshire in former times formed part of the territory of Lennox. Vestiges of the Roman wall of Antoninus still exist. The county comprises 11 parishes, and a part, and the parliamentary and royal burgh of Dumbarton (part of the Kilmarnock Burghs).

– John Bartholomew, Gazetteer of the British Isles (1887)

Auld Kirk Museum

The Cross
Kirkintilloch G66 1AB
0141 775 1185
www.eastdunbarton.gov.uk

Auld Kirk Museum houses a rich collection of museum objects of local, national and international significance, interpreted in an innovative, exciting and educational way for visitors of all ages and abilities.

Clydebank Museum & Art Gallery

Town Hall, Dumbarton Road
Clydebank G81 1UE
0141 562 2400
http://goo.gl/f1Pz4e
clydebank.museum@west-dunbarton.gov.uk

Situated beside the shipyard where many of the famous liners of the Clyde were built. Local, social and industrial history collections including shipbuilding and engineering. Major collection of Singer sewing machines.

Denny Ship Model Experiment Tank

Castle Street
Dumbarton G82 1QS
01389 763444
http://goo.gl/XKsMa4

The Denny Ship Model Experiment Tank was built in 1882. It is one of the last reminders of the shipyard of the innovative and famous Company William Denny and Brothers.

Dumbarton Castle - Historic Scotland

Dumbarton Castle
Dumbarton G82 1JJ
01389 732167
www.historic-scotland.gov.uk/places

Spectacularly situated on a volcanic rock the castle is on the site of the ancient capital of Strathclyde. The most interesting features are the 18th-century artillery fortifications, with 19th-century guns.

East Dunbartonshire Archives

William Patrick Library, 2-4 West High Street
Kirkintilloch G66 1AD
0141 777 3142
www.edlc.co.uk
archives@eastdunbarton.gov.uk

East Dunbartonshire Archives collects and preserves the records of East Dunbartonshire for the benefit of the public. Our collections date back to the 15th century, and include manuscripts, photographs, maps, plans, films and sound recordings. Access to the archives is free and everyone is welcome to visit us to consult the historical records.

East Dunbartonshire Information & Archives

William Patrick Library, 2-4 West High Street
Kirkintilloch G66 1AD
0141 7773142
www.edlc.co.uk/heritage/archives.aspx

Explore the rich and fascinating history of East Dunbartonshire through its historical records. Our collections date back to the 15th century and include manuscripts, photographs, maps, plans, film and sound recordings.

Geilston Garden

🏛 £

Cardross
Dumbarton G82 5EZ
01389 841 867
www.nts.org.uk

A delightful garden, typical of the small country estates on the banks of the Clyde purchased by merchants and industrialists in the 18th and 19th centuries. Attractive features include a walled garden and a burn, winding through the wooded glen.

Motoring Heritage Centre

🏛 ✉ £

Loch Lomond Outlet Shopping Centre
Alexandria G83 0UG
01380 607862
www.motoringheritage.co.uk/html/the_centre.html

When it was built, this amazing Grade A listed building was the largest motor car factory in the world. Its marble and sandstone façade, reminiscent of an Edwardian town hall or railway station, is just part of a factory that originally covered 11 acres.

Titan Clydebank

🏛 £

Clydebank rebuilt, 1 Aurora Avenue
Clydebank G81 1BF
0141 951 3420
www.titanclydebank.com
emma.baxter@clydebankrebuilt.co.uk

The Titan Crane in Clydebank is one of the world's first giant cantilever cranes. Built by Sir William Arrol Brothers in 1907, this fabulous crane is all that remains of what was once the famous John Browns shipyard, where some of the world's most famous ships were launched including the Queen Mary, the Royal Yacht Britannia and the QE2.

East Lothian

Haddingtonshire (or East Lothian), maritime county in SE. of Scotland; is bounded NW., N., and NE. by the Firth of Forth and the North Sea, SE. and S. by Berwickshire, and W. by Edinburghshire (or MidLothian); greatest length, N. and S., 17 miles; greatest breadth, E. and W., 26 miles; seaboard, 31¾ miles; area, 173,298 acres, population 38,502. The coast along the Firth of Forth is flat and sandy; along the North Sea it is bold and rocky. In the S. are the Lammermuir Hills, whence the surface slopes gently to the sea, in a vast plain, watered by the river Tyne, and broken by the Garleton Hills, and by the isolated summits of Traprain Law and North Berwick Law. Of the cultivated part of the county – finely diversified by woods and plantations – the soil is mostly a clayey loam, and is generally fertile, and Haddington is one of the foremost agricultural counties of Scotland. Great numbers of sheep are fed on the Lammermuir Hills. The manufactures are unimportant; they consist of two or three foundries, breweries, potteries, brickworks, salt pans, a paper mill, a distillery, &c. The western part of the county forms the eastern margin of the Mid-Lothian coalfield, and is rich in coal and limestone, which are extensively worked. Fishing and fish-curing are carried on at Dunbar, Cockenzie, and other points. The county comprises 23 parishes, and parts of 2 others; and the royal burghs of Dunbar, Haddington, and North Berwick.

– John Bartholomew, Gazetteer of the British Isles (1887)

Coastal Communities Museum

School Road
North Berwick EH39 4JU
01620 894 313
www.coastalmuseum.org

The volunteer-run Coastal Communities Museum aims to bring to life the history of the towns and villages of the coastal ward. There is a varied programme of exhibitions and events throughout the year.

Dunbar Town House Museum & Gallery

High Street
Dunbar EH42 1ER
01368 863734
http://goo.gl/zZRrqn

The historic Dunbar Town House, built towards the end of the 16th century, contains what is considered Scotland's oldest functioning council chamber. Spanning a history of more than 400 years, the building has recently been given a 21st-century refurbishment and has a brand new museum and gallery exhibition space managed by the museums Service.

East Lothian Museum Service Headquarters

Dunbar Road
Haddington EH41 3PJ
01620 820600
http://goo.gl/DC0hOc
elms@eastlothian.gov.uk

The Museums Service operates museums at: John Gray Centre; Prestongrange; Dunbar Town House; John Muir's Birthplace. We also support the Musselburgh Museum and Heritage Group to operate Musselburgh Museum and the Coastal Communities Museum Trust to operate the Coastal Communities Museum.

John Gray Centre

15 Lodge Street
Haddington EH41 3DX
01620 820690
www.johngraycentre.org
jgc@eastlothian.gov.uk

The John Gray Centre Museum is located on the first floor of the centre. This 5-star museum tells the story of East Lothian from its earliest settlers to present-day communities.

John Muir's Birthplace

126 High Street
Dunbar EH42 1JJ
01368 865899
www.jmbt.org.uk
trust@jmbt.org.uk

Born in Dunbar in 1838, John Muir emigrated with his parents to the United States where he campaigned for the preservation of natural environments through his work as an environmentalist, geologist and botanist. John Muir's life and work has inspired people all over the world. Now the Dunbar birthplace of the pioneering conservationist has been transformed into a new visitor attraction. Our family-friendly interpretative centre explores the work and achievements of this remarkable man.

Musselburgh Museum

65 High Street
Musselburgh EH21 7BZ
0131 6656642
www.musselburghmuseum.org.uk

Musselburgh Museum is a fascinating visit for all ages. Discover the long and remarkable history of the Honest Toun through the changing displays and exhibitions, and have fun with the activities for children and families.

Newhailes

Newhailes Road
Musselburgh EH21 6RY
0844 493 2125
www.nts.org.uk/Property/Newhailes

An amazing survival of early 18th century decorative art and collections, surrounded by an 18th century designed landscape. 17th century villa, later significantly added to by the Dalrymple family, who were influential figures of the Scottish Enlightenment. Superb example of James Smith's domestic Palladian architecture.

Preston Mill & Phantassie Doocot

East Linton EH40 3DS
0844 493 2128
http://goo.gl/l2tYn7

Stunningly picturesque mill the present buildings being from the 18th century, though there has been a mill on this site since the 16th century. The mill was used commercially until 1959 and visitors can still experience the working machinery on a tour today. A working watermill in a picturesque setting. Exhibition on the history of milling and the millers at Preston Mill Short walk to Phantassie Doocot currently inhabited by birds.

Prestongrange Museum

Morrison's Haven
Prestonpans EH32 9RX
0131 653 2904
www.prestongrange.org
prestongrange@btconnect.com

Prestongrange is a site of major importance in the story of Scotland's Industrial Revolution. Visitors can discover the story of the harbour, glass works, pottery, colliery and brickworks.

Collections: East Lothian Museum Service collections comprise some 25,000 items, ranging from steam locomotives to fine art, and including local archaeology, ceramics, textiles and costume, natural history specimens, as well as objects illustrating domestic, working and community life. Those not on display are held at our store in Haddington.

Edinburgh

Edinburgh, ancient capital of Scotland, parliamentary and royal burgh, and county town of Mid-Lothian, 1½ mile from its seaport Leith on S. shore of Firth of Forth, 42 E. of Glasgow, and 3961 N. of London by East Coast route – parliamentary and municipal burgh, 17,028 acres, population 236,032. Edinburgh is one of the most picturesque of cities, and its beauties and historical associations attract a constant influx of visitors. It is built on 3 ridges running E. and W., and is surrounded on all sides, except the N., by lofty hills. The Old Town occupies the central ridge, terminated by the Castle on the W., and by Holyrood on the E.; the Castle Rock is 437 ft. high. The Castle was built in the 7th century by Edwin of Northumbria, on a site previously occupied, in all probability, by the Romans and the Southern Picts. Edinburgh was added to the kingdom of the Scots in the 10th century. The Old Town contains many buildings of historical interest, notably the ancient Parliament House and the collegiate church or cathedral of St Giles. The New Town presents a splendid assemblage of streets, squares, gardens, and monuments. The principal industries of Edinburgh are printing, type-founding, bookbinding, lithographing, and engraving; machine-making and brass-founding; coach-building; manufactures of glass and jewellery; tanning, brewing, and distilling. There are 3 distilleries. Edinburgh is the seat of the Government departments for Scotland, and is a garrison town. It is also the centre of the railway and the banking systems of Scotland. Edinburgh, however, depends for its prosperity chiefly on its courts of law, colleges, and schools, on its attractions for visitors, and its amenity as a place of residence.

– John Bartholomew, *Gazetteer of the British Isles* (1887)

Cockburn Museum of Geology at the University of Edinburgh

Geology and Geophysics, King's Building, West Mains Road
Edinburgh EH9 3JF
0131 650 8527
www.geos.ed.ac.uk/public/cockburn

The Cockburn Museum at King's Buildings holds a very extensive collection of geological specimens and historical objects which reflect Edinburgh's prominent position in geological sciences since the time of James Hutton (1726-1797) and its continuing activity today.

Corstorphine Heritage Centre, The

The Dower House, St Margaret's Park
Edinburgh EH12 7SX
0131 316 4246
www.corstorphine-trust.ukgo.com
corstorphine-trust@ukgo.com

The Corstorphine Trust is a local community association, based at The Corstorphine Heritage Centre (The Dower House) in St Margaret's Park, Corstorphine.

Collections: Our holdings include many images of the old village and adjoining area. These can be found in old photographs, postcards, slides, drawings and paintings.

Craigmillar Castle

Craigmillar Castle Road
Edinburgh EH16 4SY
0131 661 4445
http://goo.gl/r52U08
hs.website@scotland.gsi.gov.uk

A well preserved medieval castle, Craigmillar has a tower house, courtyard and gardens. Craigmillar's story is linked with that of Mary Queen of Scots.

Edinburgh Castle

Edinburgh EH3
0131 225 9846
www.edinburghcastle.gov.uk

This most famous of Scottish castles has a complex building history. The oldest part, St Margaret's Chapel, dates from the 12th century; the Great Hall was erected by James IV around 1510; the Half Moon Battery by the Regent Morton in the late 16th century; and the Scottish National War Memorial after the First World War.

Collections: The castle houses the Honours (Crown Jewels) of Scotland, the Stone of Destiny and the famous 15th-century gun Mons Meg.

Edinburgh City Archives

Level 1, City Chambers, 253 High Street
Edinburgh EH1 1YJ
0131 5294616
http://goo.gl/ILkzIv

We hold the official historical records of the council and its previous authorities. We also have records about the Edinburgh area created by individuals, businesses, societies, clubs and organisations.

Georgian House

7 Charlotte Square
Edinburgh EH2 4DR
0131 226 3318
www.nts.org.uk/Property/Georgian-House
thegeorgianhouse@nts.org.uk

The Georgian House is part of Robert Adam's masterpiece of urban design, Charlotte Square. It dates from 1796, when those who could afford it began to escape from the cramped, squalid conditions of Edinburgh's Old Town to settle in the fashionable New Town.

Gladstone's Land

477b Lawnmarket
Edinburgh EH1 2NT
0844 4932120
www.nts.org.uk/Property/Gladstones-Land

Step back in time to bustling and turbulent 17th century Edinburgh. Explore Thomas Gladstone's land to discover the lives of his tenants and experience what life was really like in Edinburgh's old town 400 years ago.

Holyrood Abbey & Abbey Strand - Historic Scotland

Edinburgh EH7 5TT
www.historic-scotland.gov.uk/places

The ruined nave of the 12th and 13th century abbey church, built for Augustinian canons. Abbey and palace administered by the Lord Chamberlain.

Holyrood Park

Holyrood Park Education Centre, 1 Queen's Drive
Edinburgh EH8 8HG
0131 652 8150
www.historic-scotland.gov.uk/ranger
hs.rangers@scotland.gsi.gov.uk

Holyrood Park sits in the centre of Edinburgh and encompasses numerous archaeological sites, an ancient volcano (Arthur's Seat) and a large diversity of wildlife.

Lauriston Castle

Cramond Road South
Edinburgh EH4 5QD
0131 336 2060
www.edinburghmuseums.org.uk
lauristoncastle@edinburgh.gov.uk

When you step inside Lauriston Castle, you see it just as it was in 1926, when it was left to the nation by the last private owner, Mrs Reid. The castle and the collections it contains is one of Scotland's greatest gifts.

Lloyds Banking Group Archives

12 Bankhead Crossway South
Edinburgh EH11 4EN
http://goo.gl/B1KK2p
silvia.gallotti@lloydsbanking.com

The Archive of Lloyds Banking Group is our corporate memory. It charts the expansion, development and innovations that have made us the company we are today.

Menzies Campbell Dental Museum

9 Hill Square
Edinburgh EH8 9RU
0131 527 1649
http://goo.gl/AW77lu

The Dental Museum incorporates the Menzies Campbell collection of dental instruments, artefacts and art. It is one of the largest dental collections in this country and demonstrates the development of dentistry from its early days to modern times.

Museum Collections Centre

10 Broughton Market
Edinburgh EH3 6NU
0131 556 9536
http://goo.gl/Kqhjvb

This centre houses the reserve collections of the city museums. There are many interesting objects on 'open storage' display, especially social history objects, decorative art and archaeology collections. Open for group and individual visits on the first Tuesday of the month at 2pm.

Museum of Childhood

42 High Street, Royal Mile
Edinburgh EH1 1TG
0131 529 4142
www.edinburghmuseums.org.uk

The museum of Childhood is a fun day out for the whole family. Young people can learn about the children of the past and see a fantastic range of toys and games, while adults enjoy a trip down memory lane.

Museum of Edinburgh

Huntly House, 142 Canongate
Edinburgh EH8 8DD
0131 529 4143
www.edinburghmuseums.org.uk

The museum of Edinburgh is the City's treasure box - a maze of historic rooms crammed full of iconic objects from the capital's past. Find out about the history of Edinburgh from the earliest times to the present day.

Museum of Fire

Lothian and Borders Fire Brigade, Brigade Headquarters, Lauriston Place
Edinburgh EH3 9DE
0131 228 2401
www.lbfire.org.uk

The museum of Fire tells the history of the oldest municipal fire brigade in the United Kingdom, formed in 1824. Housed in the historic Fire and Rescue Service Headquarters building at Lauriston, it shows the development of firefighting in an exciting and educational way. On display is a range of engines including manual, horse drawn, steam and motorised pumps dating from 1806, along with many other fire related items from as far back as 1426.

Museum on the Mound, The

HBOS plc, The Mound
Edinburgh EH1 1YZ
0131 243 5464
www.museumonthemound.com
info@museumonthemound.com

Treasures from the HBOS collections. Opened in 2006, this fascinating museum takes a fresh look at money – and much, much more. Art and design, technology, crime, trade and security – all feature in the story of money.

Nelson Monument

Calton Hill
Edinburgh EH1 3BJ
www.edinburghmuseums.org.uk

The Nelson Monument was built in memory of Admiral Lord Nelson, who died at the Battle of Trafalgar in 1805. Weather permitting, the Trafalgar flag signal 'England expects that every man will do his duty' is still flown on Trafalgar Day (21 October).

Palace of Holyroodhouse & The Queen's Gallery, The

The Palace of Holyroodhouse, Canongate
Edinburgh EH8 8DX
020 7766 7300
www.royalcollection.org.uk
familylearning@royalcollection.co.uk

The Palace of Holyroodhouse, the official residence in Scotland of Her Majesty The Queen, stands at the end of Edinburgh's Royal Mile against the spectacular backdrop of Arthur's Seat. This fine baroque palace is closely associated with Scotland's rich history. The Palace is perhaps best known as the home of Mary, Queen of Scots, and as the setting for many of the dramatic episodes in her turbulent reign.

People's Story Museum

Canongate Tolbooth 163 Canongate
Edinburgh EH8 8BN
0131 529 4057
www.edinburghmuseums.org.uk

The People's Story explores the lives of Edinburgh's ordinary people at work and play from the late 18th century to today. Visitors can see displays showing a bookbinder's workshop, a wartime kitchen and much more, all packed with real objects.

Real Mary King's Close, The

2 Warriston's Close, High Street
Edinburgh EH1 1PG
0845 070 6244
www.realmarykingsclose.com
info@realmarykingsclose.com

Underneath the Royal Mile lies Edinburgh's deepest secret; a warren of underground streets and houses that has remained frozen in time since the 17th century. In the company of an expert guide, you can explore the site and experience what it was really like for people who lived, worked and died here.

Reid Concert Hall Museum of Instruments at the University of Edinburgh

Reid Concert Hall, Bristo Square
Edinburgh EH8 9AG
www.music.ed.ac.uk/euchmi/rch/index.html

On display are 1000 items including stringed, woodwind, brass and percussion instruments from Britain, Europe and from distant lands. the instrumental history of the orchestra, the wind band, theatre, dance, popular music, parlour music, brass bands, etc.

Royal Observatory Visitor Centre

Blackford Hill
Edinburgh EH9 3HJ
0131 668 8404
www.roe.ac.uk/vc
vis@roe.ac.uk

Your window into the world of astronomy. The Royal Observatory, Edinburgh is housed in a bold Italianate building located on Blackford Hill two miles south of the city.

Royal Scots Dragoon Guards Museum

The Castle
Edinburgh EH1 2YT
0131 310 5100
www.scotsdgmuseum.com/pages/museum.php
scotsdgmuseum@gmail.com

Visit the museum of the famous Royal Scots Dragoon Guards in Edinburgh Castle. Experience over 300 years of history from Scotland's only cavalry regiment.

Royal Scots Regimental Museum

The Castle
Edinburgh EH1 2YT
0131 310 5016
www.theroyalscots.co.uk/museum.html

The museum is situated in Edinburgh Castle. It is a private one and, as we do not receive any part of the admission charge to the castle, it is financially dependent on voluntary contributions.

Scott Monument

East Princes Street Gardens
Edinburgh EH2 2HG
www.edinburghmuseums.org.uk

The Scott Monument is the largest monument to a writer in the world. It commemorates Sir Walter Scott.

Sir Jules Thorn Historical Exhibition

9 Hill Square
Edinburgh EH8 9RU
0131 527 1649
-library.aspx

The Sir Jules Thorn Exhibition, adjacent to the Playfair Hall, is a display illustrating the scope of modern surgery. It includes examples of the surgical specialties.

South Side Museum

Nelson Hall Community Centre, 5 Spittalfield Crescent
Edinburgh EH8 9QZ
0131 667 8838
www.southside.edin.org
keith.smith@ea.edin.sch.uk

The legacy of Thomas Nelson Jnr built the hall in 1913 to be used as a place 'to which persons of the working class and others can go to sit, read, write, converse and otherwise occupy themselves'. The South Side Museum is located in the Gray Room and displays artefacts from the South Side's industrial past, school mementoes and old local photographs.

St Cecilia's Hall Museum of Instruments at the University of Edinburgh

St Cecilia's Hall, Niddry Street, Cowgate
Edinburgh EH1 1LJ
0131 650 2805
www.music.ed.ac.uk/euchmi/sch/index.html

On display are some 50 of the world's most important and best-preserved early keyboard instruments: harpsichords, virginals, spinets, organs and fortepianos from the period of their first construction to around 1840, many in playing order, and a new display of harps, lutes, citterns and guitars.

Surgeons' Hall Museum

Royal College of Surgeons of Edinburgh, 18 Nicolson Street
Edinburgh EH8 9DW
0131 527 1711
www.museum.rcsed.ac.uk
museum@rcsed.ac.uk

Surgeons' Hall houses one of the largest and most historic collections of surgical pathology in the world. Developed as a teaching museum for students of medicine, its fascinating collections, including bone and tissue specimens, artefacts and works of art, have also been open to the public since 1832, making it Scotland's oldest museum.

University of Edinburgh, Anatomy Museum

🖼 ⭐

Teviot Place
Edinburgh EH8 9AG
0131 242 9300
www.anatomy.mvm.ed.ac.uk/museum/index.php
mvm@ed.ac.uk

The Anatomical Museum, founded and developed by the Monro dynasty, flourished under Sir William Turner, Professor of Anatomy from 1867 to 1903, and Principal of the University from 1903 to 1917. Turner had broad interests in evolution and comparative anatomy and built up the impressive collections displayed. The splendid museum hall was at the heart of the new Medical School designed by the architect Robert Rowand Anderson.

University of Edinburgh, Natural History Collections

🖼

The Ashworth Laboratories, King's Buildings, West Mains Road
Edinburgh EH9 3JT
0131 650 5477
www.nhc.ed.ac.uk

The University has been collecting zoological specimens for teaching and research for over three hundred years. The invertebrate and vertebrate specimens are displayed within a taxonomic framework to illustrate the diversity of the animal kingdom.

Water of Leith

🖼 £

Water of Leith Visitor Centre, 24 Lanark Road
Edinburgh EH14 1TQ
0131 455 7367
www.waterofleith.org.uk
admin@waterofleith.org.uk

Explore Edinburgh's hidden natural asset, the Water of Leith, visit our fantastic interactive exhibition at the Visitor Centre and discover the river's wildlife and heritage. The information panels surrounding the unique video well describe the walkway, the river's past, its bridges, its industry, and its people.

Writers' Museum

🖼 ⭐

Lady Stair's House, Lady Stair's Close, Lawnmarket
Edinburgh EH1 2PA
0131 529 4901
http://goo.gl/gB3X5Q

Visitors can see portraits, rare books and personal objects including Burns' writing desk, the printing press on which Scott's Waverley Novels were first produced, and Scott's own dining table and rocking horse. We have Robert Louis Stevenson's riding boots and the ring given to him by a Samoan chief, engraved with the name 'Tusitala', meaning 'teller of tales'.

Fife

Fife (or Fifeshire), maritime county in E. of Scotland; is bounded N. by the Firth of Tay, E. by the North Sea, S. by the Firth of Forth, and W. by the counties of Perth, Kinross, and Clackmannan; greatest length, 43 miles; greatest breadth, 18 miles; area, 314,952 acres, population 171,931. Fife forms the peninsula between the Firths of Forth and Tay. The coast is varied and picturesque; that part of it bordering on the Firth of Forth is lined with a succession of towns and villages, for the great number of which Fife is remarkable. The surface is pleasantly undulating. A ridge of high ground, commencing with the Lomond Hills, runs from W. to E.; to the N., between the Lomonds and a spur of the Ochils, lies an extensive plain called Strath Eden, or the Howe of Fife; to the S. is another stretch of low land, broken by Saline Hill, Knock Hill, the Hill of Beath, and the Cullalo Hills. The principal rivers are the Eden and the Leven. In the NW. the soil is moss, moor, and rock; in the NE. it consists of wet clay; the most fertile tracts are the Howe of Fife and the belt of loam which fringes the Firth of Forth. The formation is chiefly Carboniferous, and Fife is the third largest coal-producing county in Scotland. Limestone and freestone abound. Blackband ironstone is worked at Lochgelly and Oakley (where there are smelting furnaces); oil shale is worked near Burntisland. The principal manufacture is linen – damasks and diapers at Dunfermline, checks and ticks at Kirkcaldy. The county comprises 61 parishes and 2 parts, the Kirkcaldy Burghs, the St Andrews Burghs, and the parliamentary burghs of Dunfermline and Inverkeithing (part of the Stirling Burghs).

– John Bartholomew, *Gazetteer of the British Isles* (1887)

Abbot House Heritage Centre

🏛 🖼

Abbot House, Maygate
Dunfermline KY12 7NE
01383 733 266
www.abbothouse.co.uk
dht@abbothouse.fsnet.co.uk

Abbot House Heritage Centre is a charity, dedicated to protecting and preserving the fabric of this atmospheric medieval building, and helping our visitors to learn about Dunfermline's early and medieval past through the exploration of our collections. Sited within a beautiful walled garden, and featuring heritage displays and a replica 17th century brew house.

Andrew Carnegie Birthplace Museum

Moodie Street
Dunfermline KY12 7PL
01383 724302
www.carnegiebirthplace.com
info@carnegiebirthplace.com

In 1895 the Birthplace Cottage was bought as a surprise 60th birthday present for Andrew Carnegie by his wife Louise and then let out to tenants. With the creation of the Carnegie Dunfermline Trust in 1903, a caretaker was installed and in 1908 it was first opened to the public.

Collections: Strong social historic artefacts that reflect past local crafts and trades including cloth making. A series of gifts presented to Andrew Carnegie in return for his generous donations.

Balmerino Abbey

Balmerino Village
Newport-on-Tay DD6 8SB
0844 4932185
www.nts.org.uk/Property/Balmerino-Abbey
robrown@nts.org.uk

The ruins of Balmerino Abbey are a fine example of a 13th century Cistercian monastery, which became a dwelling house of the lords Balmerino after secularisation in 1603. Connected with the Abbey are historical figures such as William the Lion, Mary of Guise, Mary Queen of Scots and even Bonnie Prince Charlie. The abbey is situated in the award winning hamlet of Balmerino where examples of medieval farm buildings can be seen.

Bell Pettigrew Museum of Natural History

Bute Medical Building, School of Biology, University of St Andrews
St Andrews KY16 9TS
01334 461660
www.st-andrews.ac.uk/museum/bellpettigrew
bellpett@st-andrews.ac.uk

The Bell Pettigrew Museum of Natural History was founded, and most specimens acquired, during the heyday of the Victorian age, when collecting was all the rage.

British Golf Museum

Bruce Embankment
St Andrews KY16 9AB
01334 460046
www.britishgolfmuseum.co.uk
kathrynbaker@randagc.org

Our collection tells the fascinating story of British golf, through material dating from the 17th century to the present day. It is the most comprehensive golf collection in Britain, and one of the finest worldwide, celebrating golf

from grass roots to international level. Over 16,000 items cover equipment (clubs, balls, manufacturing and clothing), prizes (trophies and medals), decorative art (artworks, ceramics, silverware and ephemera), film, photographs and archives (books, periodicals, programmes and patents). The displays and archives are enhanced by unique loan collections from The Royal and Ancient Golf Club of St Andrews and The Women Golfers' Museum.

Buckhaven Museum

College Street (above Library)
Buckhaven KY8 1LD
01592 412 860
http://goo.gl/tFFpgX

A small local museum in a town once described as a full-flavoured fisher town. Buckhaven's past importance in the East Coast Fisheries is reflected in the displays housed above Buckhaven Library.

Burntisland Museum

192 High Street
Burntisland KY3 9AS
01592 412860
www.fifedirect.org/museums
kirkcaldy.museum@fife.gov.uk

Burntisland Museum has recreated a walk through the sights and sounds of the town's fair in 1910, based on a painting of the scene by local artist Andrew Young. See rides, stalls and side shows of the time and view the local history gallery.

Crail Museum & Heritage Centre

62-64 Marketgate
Crail KY10 3TL
01333 450869
www.crailmuseum.org.uk

The museum provides insight into the past life of this ancient royal burgh, its kirk, seafaring tradition, 220 year-old golf club and Airfield history (HMS Jackdaw, Fleet Air Arm Station, HMS Bruce Boys Training School and Joint Services School for Linguists).

Culross Palace Townhouse & Study

Culross Palace, Culross
Dunfermline KY12 8JH
01383 880358
http://goo.gl/Rq92sd

Everywhere you look in Culross you're surrounded by the past. Close your eyes and you can almost hear the calls of medieval street vendors selling their wares and the clang of hammers on metal as the Hammermen of Culross fashioned the famous girdles.

Dunfermline Abbey

Dunfermline KY12 7PE

01383 724586

www.dunfermlineabbey.co.uk/wwp

The Abbey, whose foundation goes back to 1072, was built by King David I of Scotland in honour of his mother the saintly Queen Margaret.

Dunfermline City Chambers

City Chambers, Kirkgate

Dunfermline KY12 7ND

01383 312734

http://goo.gl/7wfcMe

Information is available on request about the history of the City Chambers, as well as the works of art housed within the building. Magnificent works of religous fairy painter Sir Joseph Noel Paton and impressive portraits displaying great figures of Scottish history.

Falkland Palace, Garden & Old Burgh

Falkland Palace, Falkland

Cupar KY15 7BU

01337 857397

www.nts.org.uk

The Royal Palace of Falkland was the country residence of Stuart kings and queens when they hunted deer and wild boar in the Fife forest. Mary, Queen of Scots spent some of the happiest days of her tragic life here.

Fife Archive Centre

Fife Council,Carleton House,The Haig Business Park,Balgonie Road Markinch

Glenrothes KY7 6AQ

01592 583352

http://goo.gl/zT5w3u

The Archive Centre looks after documents covering the last 500 years of history in Fife.

Fife Council Museums East Headquarters

County Buildings, St Catherine Street

Cupar KY15 4TA

01334 412934

http://goo.gl/DlZ5ow

Management and administration centre for Fife Libraries & Museums.

Fife Family History Society

Glenmoriston, Durie Street

Leven KY8 4HF

01333 425321

www.fifefhs.org

membership@fifefhs.org

Fife Family History Society, which was formed in 1989, aims to join together people with an interest in the research of their Fife ancestors.

Fife Folk Museum

High Street, Ceres

Nr Cupar KY15 5NF

01334 828180

www.fifefolkmuseum.org

info@fifefolkmuseum.org

The Fife Folk Museum's collections are housed in beautiful, listed buildings, including the original tollbooth and adjacent weavers' cottages. Ceres itself is a charming village with a communal green and a burn running through its centre.

Fife Museums

Cupar

Fife KY15 4TA

01334 412934

www.fifedirect.org.uk/museums

Each venue has its own unique character, with fascinating permanent displays such as an A-Z of St Andrews and the stunning Scottish Art on show at Kirkcaldy Museum & Art Gallery.

Hill of Tarvit Mansionhouse & Garden

Cupar KY15 5PB

01334 653127

www.nts.org.uk

hilloftarvit@nts.org.uk

The present house was remodelled in 1906 by Sir Robert Lorimer for Mr F B Sharp to form a suitable setting for his notable collection which includes French, Chippendale-style and vernacular furniture, Dutch paintings and pictures by Raeburn and Ramsay, Flemish tapestries and Chinese porcelain and bronzes. The interior is very much in the Edwardian fashion.

Kellie Castle & Garden

Pittenweem KY10 2RF

01333 720271

www.nts.org.uk

Kellie Castle is a very fine example of the domestic architecture of Lowland Scotland. The oldest part is believed to date from 1360, but the building in its present form is mainly 16th- and early 17th-century and was completed about 1606.

Kirkcaldy Museum & Art Gallery

War Memorial Gardens
Kirkcaldy KY1 1YJ
01592 412860
www.fifedirect.org.uk/themes/index.cfm
kirkcaldy.museum@fife.gov.uk

Kirkcaldy Museum & Art Gallery, set in the attractive garden grounds of the town's War Memorial Gardens, houses a collection of fine and decorative arts of local and national importance. The museum owns what is probably the largest public collection of the works of William McTaggart and Scottish Colourist SJ Peploe existing outside the National Galleries of Scotland. The collection also includes a significant number of works by the Glasgow Boys. The ground floor features an award winning permanent local history display.

Laing Museum

High Street
Newburgh KY14 6DX
01337 840223
http://goo.gl/eR2iMg
museums.east @fife.gov.uk

A small local history museum with displays about this interesting town and local historian and benefactor Alexander Laing.

Methil Heritage Centre

272 High Street
Methil KY8 3EQ
01333 422100
www.methilheritage.org.uk

Methil Heritage Centre is a small local history museum and exhibition venue, situated in the coastal town of Methil in Central Fife.

MUSA Collections Centre

87 North Street
St Andrews KY16 9AE
01334 461662
www.st-andrews.ac.uk/museum/musacollectionscentre
museumenquiries@st-andrews.ac.uk

Explore behind the scenes to discover some of the fascinating treasure from the University of St Andrews' collections. From fine art to furniture, intricate sculptures to coffee pots, the Collections Centre is the home to many of the thousands of fascinating objects.

Museum of Communication Foundation Trust

131 High Street
Burntisland KY3 9AA
01506 823424
www.mocft.co.uk
mocenquiries@tiscali.co.uk

The Trust was set up to preserve communications technology for future generations. It is currently developing a major facility at Burntisland in Fife which will educate visitors in an entertaining way, showing them how past technologies have shaped their own lives.

Museum of the University of St Andrews (MUSA)

7a The Scores
St Andrews KY16 9AR
01334 461660
www.st-andrews.ac.uk/musa
museumenquiries@st-andrews.ac.uk

MUSA tells the story of the history of the University of St Andrews. On display you can see highlights from the University's collection of over 112,000 artefacts.

Pittencrieff House Museum

Pittencrieff Park
Dunfermline KY12 8QH
01383 722 935
http://goo.gl/ZRZn6T

From the outside you can see that Pittencrieff House was once a private residence. In fact it was a home for nearly 300 years until Andrew Carnegie bought the grounds in 1903.

Scotland's Secret Bunker

Crown Buildings, Troywood
Nr St Andrews KY16 8QH
01333 310301
www.secretbunker.co.uk
mod@secretbunker.co.uk

For 40 years Scotland kept a secret. Hidden beneath an innocent Scottish farmhouse lies Scotland's Secret Bunker. We invite you to take the journey down the 450 foot tunnel and through the blast doors to discover the secrets of the bunker, which was built to help safeguard Scotland during the Cold War in the event of a nuclear attack.

St Andrews Cathedral & St Rule's Tower - Historic Scotland

St Andrews Cathedral And St Rule's Tower
St Andrews G1 4ER

01334 472563
www.historic-scotland.gov.uk/places

The remains of the largest cathedral in Scotland, and of the associated domestic ranges of the priory. The precinct walls are particularly well preserved.

St Andrews Museum

Kinburn House, Kinburn Park, Doubledykes Road
St Andrews KY16 9DP
01334 412690
http://goo.gl/3zNHWd
StAndrews.Museum@fife.gov.uk

St Andrews Museum is situated in a beautiful Victorian mansion within the grounds of Kinburn Park. The long term display, St Andrews A-Z, is housed in the downstairs gallery.

St Andrews Preservation Trust Museum

12 North Street
St Andrews KY16 9PW
01334 477629
www.standrewspreservationtrust.co.uk
curator@standrewspreservationtrust.org.uk

The St Andrews Preservation Trust Museum is a small, independent museum situated in a lovely 17th century house in the heart of the town's old fisher quarter, a stone's throw from both the castle and the cathedral. The museum contains a wealth of fascinating information and objects pertaining to the history of St Andrews and its people.

St Margaret's Cave

Glen Bridge Car Park, Chalmers Street
Dunfermline KY12 8DF
http://goo.gl/RIALU9

Queen Margaret came here to pray over 900 years ago. Then there was only a wooded path by a stream at the bottom of the valley with a short climb up to the small cave. Now there's a tunnel with 87 steps leading deep underground. When you descend into the earth, with the haunting sound of monks singing, you can feel the weight of centuries of Dunfermline's history.

University of St Andrews Library

University Library, University of St Andrews
St Andrews KY16 9TR
01334 462283
www.st-andrews.ac.uk/library/

The Special Collections Department houses over 120,000 rare printed books, a world-class collection of early photography, plus significant manuscript holdings ranging from Greek papyri of the second century to modern business records.

Glasgow

Glasgow, parliamentary and royal burgh, partly in Renfrewshire but chiefly in Lanarkshire, on river Clyde, 14 miles SE. of Dumbarton (at the commencement of the Firth of Clyde), 47½ (by rail) W. of Edinburgh, and 401½ (by West Coast route) NW. of London; parliamentary and municipal burgh, population 511,415; town (municipal and suburban), population 674,095. Glasgow is the commercial and industrial metropolis of Scotland, and claims to be the second city of the British Empire. The commercial importance of Glasgow is of comparatively modern date. At the Reformation the population was about 5000, at the Union about 12,000, and at the beginning of the 19th century about 77,000; it is now. including the neighbouring burghs, which are essentially parts of Glasgow, about 750,000. The chief natural cause of the rapid growth of Glasgow is its position within the richest coal and ironstone field in Scotland, and on the banks of a river which has been rendered, by almost incredible labour, navigable for vessels of the largest tonnage. Its industries, which are characterised by their immense variety, include textile manufactures (principally cotton, woollen, and carpets): bleaching, printing, and dyeing; chemical mfrs.; the iron manufacture., engineering, and shipbuilding. All the iron trade of Scotland is controlled by Glasgow, which is also the headquarters of the great shipbuilding industry of the Clyde. Glasgow has 4 distilleries and 6 paper mills. It is one of the three principal seaports of the United Kingdom. The harbour extends along the river for over 2 miles, and includes 2 tidal docks, one of them (the Queen's Dock) the largest in Scotland. The foreign trade is with all parts of the world, but chiefly with India, the United States, Canada, and South America, Belgium, France, and Spain. Glasgow contains terminal stations of the 3 great trunk lines of Scotland; and its railway communications are assisted by the City Union Railway and the Underground Railway.

– John Bartholomew, *Gazetteer of the British Isles* (1887)

Cumbernauld Museum

North Lanarkshire Council, Buchanan Business Park, Stepps
Glasgow G33 6HR
0141 304 1975
http://goo.gl/irVkYO

Situated within the town's main library, the museum tells the story of Cumbernauld and surrounding area from pre-history to the Romans and on through the 19th century, to the development of the new town in the 1960s. A studies area allows for more in-depth research or browsing of photograph albums.

Glasgow & West of Scotland Family History Society

Unit 13, 32 Mansfield Street, Partick
Glasgow G11 5QP
0141 339 8303
www.gwsfhs.org.uk
publicity@gwsfhs.org.uk

The Glasgow & West of Scotland Family History Society is a charity and is run entirely by volunteers, who give their time and talents to provide a service to assist others interested in researching their family history.

Glasgow City Archives

Mitchell Library, North Street
Glasgow G3 7DN
http://goo.gl/qNmRfx

Glasgow City Archives is part of Culture and Sport Glasgow which delivers cultural services on behalf of Glasgow City Council.

Glasgow Museums

200 Woodhead Road
Glasgow G53 7NN
www.glasgowlife.org.uk/museums/Pages/home.aspx

Glasgow Museums manages a collection of over a million objects and operates 9 museum venues - Kelvingrove, the Burrell Collection, Riverside, the Gallery of Modern Art, The People's Palace, Scotland Street School Museum, St Mungo Museum of Religious Life and Art, Provand's Lordship and Glasgow Museums Resource Centre - on behalf of Glasgow City Council.

Glasgow Museums Resource Centre

200 Woodhead Road, South Nitshill Industrial Estate
Glasgow G53 7NN
0141 276 9300
www.glasgowmuseums.com/venue/index.cfm?venueid=8
museums@cls.glasgow.gov.uk

Glasgow Museums Resource Centre is the first publicly accessible store for the city's museum service. It is a new purpose-built museum storage facility and visitor centre in the south side of Glasgow. Glasgow Museums Resource Centre also houses the outreach service for Glasgow Museums which offers handling and reminiscence kits for loan, and temporary exhibits for display.

Glasgow Police Museum

First Floor, 30 Bell Street, Merchant City
Glasgow G1 1LG
0141 552 1818
www.policemuseum.org.uk
curator@policemuseum.org.uk

At the Glasgow Police Museum you have the unique opportunity to step into the compelling and dramatic history of the United Kingdom's oldest police force. Telling the stories of the people who served in the Glasgow Police is the principal theme of the museum. Painstaking research has uncovered interesting, little-known facts concerning the lives, careers and personalities of the characters who policed the city during 200 years of its history. Complementary to the historical exhibits, our vibrant display of worldwide police uniforms, headgear, badges and insignia is the largest in Europe.

Glasgow University Archive Services

Archive Services, University of Glasgow, 13 Thurso Street
Glasgow G11 6PE
0141 330 5515
www.gla.ac.uk/services/archives

Glasgow University Archive Services is a unique learning and corporate heritage resource that is an inspiration for all. We hold the records that document the history of the University and its management, staff and students from its foundation in 1451 to the present day. We also have one of the largest collections of historical business records in Europe and it includes much of the archive of Scottish industries such as banking, retail, distilling and shipbuilding.

Glasgow Vintage Vehicle Trust

76-136 Fordneuk Street, Bridgeton
Glasgow G40 3AH
www.gvvt.org
info@gvvt.org

The Glasgow Vintage Vehicle Trust was formed at the end of 2002. There are five Trustees, each having considerable experience of large vehicle preservation.

Glasgow Women's Library

23 Landressy Street, Bridgeton
Glasgow G40 1BP
0141 550 2267
www.womenslibrary.org.uk
info@womenslibrary.org.uk

Glasgow Women's Library is a provider of information by and about women. The library collection comprises information broadly in the following sections: reference, reports, work, education, politics, feminist theory, history, violence against women, abuse, pornography issues, prostitution, lesbian lives and cultures, young women, women of colour, women in global contexts, myth, goddesses and religion, travel, peace and war, sport, fiction, poetry, literary theory, autobiographies and biographies, drama, art, architecture and older women.

Heatherbank Museum of Social Work

Glasgow Caledonian University, City Campus, Cowcaddens Road
Glasgow G4 0BA
0141 331 8637
www.gcu.ac.uk/_library/heatherbank/

Heatherbank Museum of Social Work was founded in 1975 by Colin and Rosemary Harvey. The museum exists to increase public awareness of the social welfare needs of society, particularly those who are disadvantaged. It is the only museum entirely dedicated to social work and welfare in Europe.

Holmwood House

76-136

61-63 Netherlee Road
Glasgow G44 3YG
01416 372 129
www.nts.org.uk

Holmwood House is Alexander 'Greek' Thomson's finest domestic design. This family home was built in 1857-8 for James Couper who, with his brother Robert, owned Millholm Paper Mills on the banks of the River Cart.

Hunterian Museum & Art Gallery, The

University of Glasgow
Glasgow G12 8QQ
0141 330 4221
www.hunterian.gla.ac.uk
m.douglas@museum.gla.ac.uk

The University of Glasgow's Hunterian Museum and Art Gallery is home to one of the top five collections in Scotland, with over a million items ranging from meteorites to Mackintosh and mummies. The Hunterian is the legacy of Dr William Hunter, a pioneering obstetrician and teacher. His passion for collecting was legendary.

Collections: The Hunterian collections are extensive and wide-ranging with just over one million objects.

Kelvingrove Art Gallery & Museum

Argyle Street
Glasgow G3 8AG
0141 276 9599
http://goo.gl/5lEapd
info@glasgowlife.org.uk

One of the finest civic collections in Europe is housed within this Glasgow landmark. Here you can explore collections that include everything from fine and decorative arts to archaeology and the natural world. Among its many treasures is the earliest near-complete field armour in the world (the famous 'Avant' armour, made in Milan c1440).

Martyrs' School

Parson Street
Glasgow G4 0PX
0141 552 2356
http://goo.gl/Cclmdd

Martyrs' School is a hidden architectural gem that deserves to be better known. It is one of the earliest buildings by Glasgow's most famous and influential architect and designer, Charles Rennie Mackintosh (1868-1928). When the school was commissioned in 1895 Mackintosh was a junior assistant with Honeyman and Keppie, having just completed his apprenticeship.

Maryhill Burgh Halls

10-24 Gairbraid Avenue
Glasgow G20 8YE
0845 860 1878
www.maryhillburghhalls.org.uk
info@mbht.org.uk

The restored Burgh Halls recaptures the splendid historic beauty of this treasured building, and now provides the local community with a modern public hall, a cafe and heritage exhibition space.

Mitchell Library Family History Centre

Family History Centre, Level 3, The Mitchell Library, North Street
Glasgow G3 7DN
0141 2872937
http://goo.gl/CB5xHE

We can help you discover and learn lots of information and skills to help you trace your family history.

Museum of Transport

1 Bunhouse Road
Glasgow G3 8DP
0141 287 2720
www.glasgowmuseums.com

The museum uses its collections of vehicles and models to tell the story of transport by land and sea, with a unique Glasgow flavour. Here you will find the oldest surviving pedal cycle and the finest collection in the world of Scottish-built cars, including such world famous makes as Argyll, Arrol Johnson and Albion.

People's Palace & Winter Gardens

Glasgow Green
Glasgow G40 1AT
0141 554 0223
http://goo.gl/N7nzmL
museums@glasgowlife.org.uk

The People's Palace is Glasgow's social history museum and a chance to see the story of the people and city of Glasgow from 1750 to the present. You can see paintings, prints and photographs displayed alongside a wealth of historic artefacts, film and computer interactives.

Pollok House

Pollok Country Park, 2060 Pollokshaws Road
Glasgow G43 1AT
0844 493 2202
www.nts.org.uk/Property/Pollok-House
jmurray@nts.org.uk

Pollok House is the ancestral home of the Maxwell family. The present house dates from around 1750 and contains one of the finest collections of Spanish art in the United Kingdom together with furniture and furnishings appropriate to an Edwardian country house.

Provand's Lordship

3 Castle Street
Glasgow G4 0RB
0141 552 8819
www.glasgowmuseums.com/venue/index.cfm?venueid=11

At Provand's Lordship you can step back into Glasgow's past in the only house to survive from the medieval city. Now open to the public, Provand's Lordship has been extensively restored to give a real flavour of life in medieval Glasgow.

Riverside Museum

100 Pointhouse Place
Glasgow G3 8RS
0141 287 4350
http://goo.gl/Md6PHZ
info@glasgowlife.org.uk

The multi-award winning Riverside Museum is home to over 3,000 objects that detail Glasgow's rich past from its days as maritime powerhouse to a glimpse into daily Glasgow life in the early to mid 20th century. Amongst the objects on display are everything from skateboards to locomotives, paintings to prams, velocipedes to voiturettes, vintage cars to a stormtrooper.

Royal College of Physicians & Surgeons of Glasgow Library & Archives

Royal College of Physicians and Surgeons of Glasgow, 232-242 St Vincent Street
Glasgow G2 5RJ
0141 227 3234
www.rcpsg.ac.uk/library
library@rcpsg.ac.uk

Founded in 1599, the RCPSG enjoys a history spanning four centuries.

Collections: The collection spans the 15th to the 20th Centuries, and includes many of the key medical, anatomical and surgical texts of the 16th and 17th centuries, being particularly strong in the areas of anatomy, medicine, surgery, botany and materia medica in the 18th, 19th and early 20th centuries.

Royal Highland Fusiliers Regimental Museum

518 Sauchiehall Street
Glasgow G2 3LW
0141 332 0961
http://goo.gl/6m5MUX

The building at 518 Sauchiehall Street has been the HQ of the RHF since 1960. However, the earliest part of it dates from 1825 and originally formed part of Albany Place, a terrace of townhouses extending from Garnet Street to

Charing Cross. In 1903 the architect, in partnership with Charles Rennie Macintosh, was commissioned by Glasgow photographer Thomas Annan, to design an extension to the building.

Scotland Street School Museum

225 Scotland Street
Glasgow G5 8QB
0141 287 0500
www.glasgowmuseums.com/venue/index.cfm?venueid=12
museums@cls.glasgow.gov.uk

Scotland Street School Museum presents the history of education in Scotland as a genuine school experience. The museum, designed by Charles Rennie Mackintosh between 1903 and 1906, is also an essential destination for Mackintosh enthusiasts and all those interested in the history of design.

Collections: The three classroom reconstructions show the changing face of the schoolroom from the Victorian era through the Second World War to the classroom of the fifties and sixties. The barrel vaulted cookery room, cloakrooms, and ceramic-tiled drill hall are restored to Mackintosh's original 1906 designs.

Shotts Heritage Centre

North Lanarkshire Council, Buchanan Business Park, Stepps
Glasgow G33 6HR
0141 304 1975
http://goo.gl/4VFg35

The displays include the area's covenanting history, as well as the era of the industrial revolution and the rise and fall of local heavy industries such as mining, the railways and iron production. A rare surviving 19th century lamp post from the Shotts Ironworks has been installed at the front of the library.

Springburn Local History Centre

Springburn Leisure Centre, Kay Street, Springburn
Glasgow G21 1JY
0141 276 9357
http://goo.gl/LiaLon

Established in May 2003, Springburn Local History Centre (formerly known as Springburn Museum) was formed by a Glasgow Open Museum Project in partnership with former staff of Springburn Museum and local volunteers. It is dedicated to the people and history of Springburn, and showcases objects from the Glasgow Museums Collections alongside those created by students from North Glasgow College and collections owned by local people.

St Mungo Museum of Religious Life & Art

2 Castle Street
Glasgow G4 0RH
0141 553 2557
www.glasgowmuseums.com/venue/index.cfm?venueid=13
museums@glasgowlife.org.uk

This unique museum explores the importance of religion in people's lives across the world and across time.

Collections: Displays occupy three floors and are divided into four exhibition areas: the Gallery of Religious Art, the Gallery of Religious Life, the Scottish Gallery and a temporary exhibition space.

Summerlee Heritage Park

Heritage Way, Coatbridge
Glasgow ML5 1QD
01236 431261
www.northlanarkshire.gov.uk/summerlee
museums@northlan.gov.uk

Summerlee Heritage Park it is situated around the site of the 19th century Summerlee Ironworks and a restored section of a branch of the Monklands Canal.

Tall Ship at Glasgow Harbour, The

100 Stobcross Road
Glasgow G3 8QQ
0141 222 2513
www.thetallship.com
info@thetallship.com

The Tall Ship operates a programme of year-round maritime themed events and activities, with specially devised talks and tours, school visits and costumed volunteer days. Explore every nook and cranny of the Glenlee, including the refurbished Captain's cabin, with our brand new audio guide facility, a fun way to learn the history of the ship.

Tenement House, The

145 Buccleuch Street, Garnethill
Glasgow G3 6QN
0844 493 2197
www.nts.org.uk
tenementhouse@nts.org.uk

The Tenement House provides a rare glimpse into life in Glasgow in the early 20th century, in the faithfully restored four-room house lived in by Miss Agnes Toward for over half a century. This first-floor flat is a typical late Victorian example, consisting of four rooms and retaining most of its original features such as its bed recesses, kitchen range, coal bunker and bathroom. The furniture, furnishings and personal possessions of Miss Agnes Toward, who lived here for over fifty years, present a fascinating picture of domestic life at the beginning of the 20th century.

Hebrides

Hebrides, The (or Western Islands), the collective name of the islands on the W. coast of Scotland; area, (about) 1,800,000 acres; population 82,335. About 100 of them are inhabited. They are geographically divided into the Inner Hebrides, comprising the 3 groups of Islay, Mull, and Skye, and extending from The Aird, in N. of Skye, to the Mull of Islay, a distance of 150 miles; the Outer Hebrides (separated from the Inner Hebrides by the Minch), or The Long Island, comprising Lewis, Harris, North Uist, Benbecula, South Uist, Barra, &c., and extending from the Butt of Lewis to Barra Head, a distance of 130 miles; and the small St Kilda group, about 60 miles W. of the Outer Hebrides. Anciently they comprehended also the islands in the Firth of Clyde, the peninsula of Kintyre, the island of Rathlin, and the Isle of Man. They are politically divided between the shires of Ross, Inverness, and Argyll. The principal towns are Stornoway, in Lewis; Tobermory, in Mull; Bowmore, in Islay; and Portree, in Skye. The humid climate of the Hebrides is unsuitable for corn crops, and only a comparatively small portion of the soil is arable. The principal crops are oats, barley, and potatoes. Much of the surface is occupied by sheep-farms and moors. Besides the raising of cattle and sheep, and distilling (principally in Islay), the only important industry is the fisheries, of which Stornoway is the chief seat on the W. coast of Scotland. The manufacture of kelp, which was at one time extensively carried on, is now almost extinct. The Hebrides are visited by great numbers of tourists, and have regular steamboat communication with Oban and Glasgow. There are lighthouses at the Butt of Lewis, Stornoway, Monach islands, Scalpay island, Ushenish, and Barra Head.

– John Bartholomew, *Gazetteer of the British Isles* (1887)

Barra & Vatersay Historical Society

Barra Heritage and Cultural Centre, Castlebay
Isle of Barra HS9 5XD
01871 810 352
www.barraheritage.com

The Comunn Eachdraidh (Historical Society) was formed in 1995 to conserve and promote the culture and heritage of the islands of Barra and Vatersay. The society collects artefacts, documents and photographs, and has built up extensive archives and collections.

Bernera Museum

Bernera
Bernera, Isle of Lewis HS2 9LF
01851 612 331
http://goo.gl/UBDMhz
cesb@zoom.co.uk

The collection comprises some 500 artefacts which illustrate the domestic, economic, cultural and religious life of Bernera district. Its strengths lie mainly in the fields of domestic, social life, fishing and the sea. A room is dedicated to the Iron Age village at Bostadh.

Calanais Visitor Centre

Calanais
Isle of Lewis HS2 9DY
01851 621422
http://goo.gl/EIJ2nG
calanais.centre@btinternet.com

A cross-shaped setting of standing stones, unique in Scotland and outstanding in Great Britain. Dates to around 2,900-2,600BC.

Comunn Eachdraidh Nis

Cross School, North Dell, Ness
Isle of Lewis HS2 0SN
01851 810377
https://goo.gl/ya4WMB
office@cenonline.org

Since being established in 1977, the society has managed to research and record a wealth of material, largely based on the oral tradition of the isles, that documents the unique social history of the Gaelic speaking communities of Ness and northern Lewis. Over that period, hundreds of hours of audio and videotape have been recorded and transcribed, as well as thousands of photographs that have been collected, to produce one of the finest and most important archives in Scotland of life in rural Lewis during the 19th and 20th century.

Dell Mill

North Dell
Ness, Isle of Lewis PA86 0SN
www.galsontrust.com/web/?page_id=507

Muileann Dhail (Dell Mill), mid-19th century part of an enclosed quadrangle beside the River Dell, one of the island's few substantial farm complexes that were usually operated by mainland farmers. The intact mill in the eastern range extends north, incorporating a large, all-iron internal water wheel.

Dualchas: Skye & Lochalsh Area Museums Service

Skye and Lochalsh Archive Centre, Elgin Hostel, Dunvegan Road
Portree, Isle of Skye IV51 9EE
01478 613857
www.highlandarchives.org.uk/skye-and-lochalsh.asp

As part of the Highland Archive Service, the Skye and Lochalsh Archive Centre, Portree, is responsible for collecting, preserving and making available archives relating to the history of the Skye and Lochalsh area. The archives date from the 17th century to the present, and consist of documents in different formats including minute books, correspondence, maps, plans, photographs, drawings and sound recordings.

Mingulay, Berneray & Pabbay

Mingulay, Berneray And Pabbay
0844 4932237
http://goo.gl/rr3WLu

Wandering among the abandoned settlements on this remote group islands is an evocative reminder of those who once lived here. The last of the inhabitants left in 1912, leaving behind a precarious existence based on crofting, fishing and fowling.

Mull Museum

Clumba Buildings, Main Street
Tobermory, Isle of Mull PA75 6NY
01688 302208
www.mullmuseum.org.uk
enquiries@mullmuseum.org.uk

The history of the Isle of Mull is captured in the Mull Museum - a small museum crammed with information about Mull in the past. From early people living in duns and brochs, through the times of warring clans and their castles, to more recent events. Exhibits of crofting, farming, fishing and everyday objects show what life was like in Mull in the past.

Museum nan Eilean

Francis Street
Stornoway, Isle of Lewis HS1 2NF
01851 822746
www.cne-siar.gov.uk//museum/index.asp
museum@cne-siar.gov.uk

Museum nan Eilean was established in 1983 by Comhairle nan Eilean, the Western Isles Islands Council, as it was then, to provide the first professional museum service for the Western Isles.

Museum of the Isles

Clan Donald Skye, Armadale
Ardvasar, Isle of Skye IV45 8RS
01599 534454
www.clandonald.com
museum@clandonald.com

This award winning accredited museum was opened in 2002 to house our growing collection of artefacts and paintings. Six interconnecting galleries take you through 1500 years of the history and culture of the area once known as the Kingdom of the Isles. A seventh gallery is the venue for special exhibitions that change each year.

Ness Heritage Centre

Sgoil Chrois
Ness, Isle of Lewis HS2 0TG
http://goo.gl/DNYtK4

An impressive archive of documents, genealogical records, photographs, video and audio recordings and artefacts; contributed over the years by a willing and generous community that cherishes its own history and heritage. This collection comprises some 500 artefacts illustrating the social, economic, cultural and religious life of Ness. Its strengths lie mainly in the fields of domestic life, social life, fishing and the sea. The material dates from the 19th and 20th centuries.

Raasay Heritage Trust Museum

Isle of Raasay IV40 8PB
01478 660207
www.angelfire.com/il2/raasayheritagetrust
osgaig@lineone.net

The Island of Raasay is located off the east coast of the Isle of Skye in the Scottish Inner Hebrides. Raasay Heritage Society was formed to preserve and promote the language and culture of the island for future generations and to show visitors all aspects of the island's unique past and its unusual geological and botanical features.

Skye & Lochalsh Archive Centre

Elgin Hostel, Dunvegan Road
Portree, Isle of Skye IV51 9EE

01478 614078

www.highlandarchives.org.uk/skye-and-lochalsh.asp

As part of the Highland Archive Service, the Skye and Lochalsh Archive Centre, Portree, is responsible for collecting, preserving and making available archives relating to the history of the Skye and Lochalsh area.

Staffin Museum, The

6 Ellishadder, Staffin
Isle of Skye IV51 9JE

www.skyecomuseum.co.uk

The Staffin Museum is a small community-based museum located in the village of Ellishadder, on the eastern coast of the Trotternish peninsula, Isle of Skye. The Staffin Museum contains excellent collections of local geological and fossil specimens, as well as representative artefacts illustrating prehistory and social history on the Trotternish.

Taigh Chearsabhagh

Lochmaddy
Isle of North Uist HS6 5AA

01876 500293

www.taigh-chearsabhagh.org

admin@taigh-chearsabhagh.org

Museum and two gallery spaces with regularly changing exhibitions. Photo archive room with over 2,000 local photographs & reference books relating to Gaelic language, local & Scottish history and genealogy.

Uig Heritage Trust

Uig Community Centre
Timsgarry, Isle of Lewis HS2 9JT

01851 672 476

www.ceuig.com/about/uig-museum

sarah@ceuig.com

The Comann Eachdraidh runs a small registered museum situated in the community centre in Timsgarry. We have a number of displays covering different aspects of local history. We also have a good archive of background material available for browsing and a large collection of old photographs.

Inverness-shire

Inverness-shire, maritime county in NW. of Scotland; is bounded N. by Ross and Cromarty and the Inner moray Firth, NE. by Nairnshire and Elginshire, E. by Banffshire and Aberdeenshire, SE. by Perthshire, S. by Argyllshire, and W. by the Atlantic; area, 2,616,498 acres; population 90,454. Inverness-shire is the largest county in Scotland. It consists of 2 portions, insular and mainland. The insular portion embraces the island of Skye, the St Kilda group, and the whole chain of the Outer Hebrides, except Lewis. The mainland portion - intersected NE. and SW. by Glen More nan Albin and the Caledonian Canal - consists almost entirely of mountain, loch, and glen. Ben Nevis (4406 ft.), in the SW., at Fort William, is the highest mountain in Great Britain. The principal lochs are Loch Ness, Loch Arkaig, Loch Lochy, Loch Laggan, and Loch Ericht. The W. coast is indented by Loch Hourn, Loch Nevis, and Loch Moidart. The principal rivers are the Spey, the Ness, and the Beauly, on all of which are valuable salmon fisheries. With the exception of the northern seaboard, the glens contain nearly all the fertile land, and only about one-twentieth of the total acreage is under tillage, all the rest being wood and forest, heath, and stony waste. There are nearly 300,000 acres of deer forests, and about 1,700,000 acres of heath, one-half of which affords pasturage for sheep; the other half serves only for grouse shooting. Inverness-shire is traversed by splendid military roads (constructed in the 18th century), by the Caledonian Canal, and in the N. and E. by the Highland Railway. The prevailing language is Gaelic. The county (insular and mainland) contains 26 parishes and parts of 10 others; the parliamentary and royal burgh of Inverness (part of the Inverness Burghs).

– John Bartholomew, *Gazetteer of the British Isles* (1887)

Note: see Hebrides for islands in Inverness-shire.

Clan Cameron Museum

Achnacarry PH34 4EJ
01397 712090
www.clan-cameron.org/museum.html
museum@achnacarry.fsnet.co.uk

The history and artefacts of the Clan Cameron. Also included in the museum are artefacts, photographs and information about the Commandos who trained at Achnacarry during the 1939/45 War and who frequently return here to visit their old training grounds.

Clan Grant Museum

Duthil
by Carrbridge PH23 3ND
www.clangrant.org
info@clangrant.org

The home of our Society - of the Clan Grant Worldwide - is the old Church at Duthil, close to Grantown-on-Spey. Inside, two glass display cabinets dedicated to the Métis and the Cherokees have recently been installed, as well as many paintings, photos and other clan memorabilia displayed on the walls. Important and valuable weapons and artefacts of the clan are held in storage by the National Museums of Scotland, and we have begun to display some of these items in the centre.

Clan Macpherson Museum

Laggan Road
Newtonmore PH20 1DE
01540 673 332
www.clan-macpherson.org/museum

Interested in Highland history? Want to discover the role of a clan in the Highlands? Then this is the place for you. Are you a Macpherson, Ellis, Pearson, Clarkson, Lees, Currie, Carson, Gillespie, Gillies, McLeish or McClair? Then we have your clan story

Culloden Battlefield & Visitor Centre

Culloden Moor
Inverness IV2 5EU
0844 493 2159
www.nts.org.uk/culloden
culloden@nts.org.uk

The course of British, European and world history was changed here at Culloden on 16 April 1746. It was here that the Jacobite army fought to reclaim the throne of Britain from the Hanoverians for a Stuart king.

Fort George - Historic Scotland

Fort George
Ardersier IV2 7TD
01667 462777
www.historic-scotland.gov.uk/places

A vast site and one of the most outstanding artillery fortifications in Europe. It was planned in 1747 as a base for George II's army and was completed in 1769.

Glenfinnan Monument

NTS Information Centre
Glenfinnan PH37 4LT
01397 722250
http://goo.gl/Zo3yal
glenfinnan@nts.org.uk

Glenfinnan Monument, set amid superb Highland scenery at the head of Loch Shiel, was erected in 1815 by Alexander Macdonald of Glenaladale in tribute to the clansmen who fought and died in the cause of Prince Charles Edward Stuart. It was designed by the eminent Scottish architect James Gillespie Graham.

Glenfinnan Station Museum

Glenfinnan Railway Station, Glenfinnan
Fort William PH37 4LT
01397 722 295
www.glenfinnanstationmuseum.co.uk
enquiry@glenfinnanstationmuseum.co.uk

Glenfinnan Station Museum is situated in the famous and beautiful village of Glenfinnan on the Road to the Isles between Fort William and Mallaig. The Glenfinnan Experience not only includes the Station Museum but also has the added attractions of the Monument to Bonnie Prince Charlie at the head of Loch Shiel, the adjacent National Trust Visitor Centre and the Loch Shiel Eagle Watch Cruises. Towering above and behind, set in the mountain backdrop, stands the Glenfinnan Railway Viaduct, initially famous as the largest concrete viaduct in this country but now internationally acclaimed as a key location in the Harry Potter Films.

Highland Aviation Museum

9 Dalcross Industrial Estate, By Inverness Airport
Inverness IV1 7XB
01463 831459
www.highlandaviationmuseum.org.uk
JamesACampbell@highlandaircraft.fsnet.co.uk

We are situated just a few minutes walk away from the terminal building of Inverness Airport. At our museum you'll find an outdoor exhibition of aircraft and an Airport Fire Tender.

Highland Council Archive Service

Highland Archive and Registration Centre, Bught Road
Inverness IV3 5SS
01463 256444
www.highlandarchives.org.uk/

The Highland Archive Service is responsible for locating, preserving and making accessible archives relating to all aspects of the history of the geographical area of the Highlands.

Highland Family History Society

Highland Archive & Registration Centre, Bught Road
Inverness IV3 5SS
www.highlandfamilyhistorysociety.org
info@highlandfamilyhistorysociety.org

Researching ancestors in the Highlands of Scotland and connecting their descendants around the world.

Highland Folk Museum

Kingussie Road
Newtonmore PH20 1AY
01540 673551
www.highlandfolk.com
Maureen.robinson@highlifehighland.com

This award winning museum has recreated a thriving township from the 1700s with heather thatched roofs and open turf fires, a working croft with cattle, sheep,ducks and hens and an old tin school from the 1930s. Costumed interpreters bring history to life.

Inverness Museum & Art Gallery

Castle Wynd
Inverness IV2 3EB
01463 237114
inverness.highland.museum
mailto:enquiries@invernessmuseum.com

Located in the heart of Inverness, we re-opened in January 2007 after a full refurbishment of all our displays and facilities. Visit us to explore the past and learn about the people, environment and traditions of the Highlands.

Lochaber Archive Centre

West Highland College, An Aird
Fort William PH33 6FF
01397 701942
www.highlandarchives.org.uk/lochaber.asp

As part of the Highland Archive Service, the Lochaber Archive Centre at Fort William is responsible for locating, preserving and making accessible documents relating to all aspects of Highland history.

Mallaig Heritage Centre

Station Road
Mallaig PH41 4PY
01687 462085
www.mallaigheritage.org.uk

Local history museum for Mallaig, West Lochaber and the
Small Isles, housing a comprehensive range of displays and
exhibitions covering fishing, railway, steamers and ferries,
Knoydart Clearance, agriculture and other themes.

Regimental Museum of The Queen's Own Highlanders

Regimental Headquarters, The Highlanders, Cameron
Barracks
Inverness IV2 3XD
01463 224380
www.thehighlandersmuseum.com

The Regimental Museum Collection of the Queen's Own
Highlanders is the private collection of a regiment with
over 200 years association with Fort George.

Urquhart Castle - Historic Scotland

Urquhart Castle
Loch Ness, near Inverness IV63 6XJ
01456 450551
www.historic-scotland.gov.uk/places

Magnificently sited, overlooking Loch Ness. Urquhart is
one of the largest castles in Scotland, with a long and
colourful history, built in the 1230s, seized by the English
in 1296, sacked by the MacDonald Lord of the Isles in 1545
and left to fall into decay after 1689.

West Highland Museum

Cameron Square
Fort William PH33 6AJ
01397 702169
www.westhighlandmuseum.org.uk
info@westhighlandmuseum.org.uk

The West Highland Museum's collections tell the story of
the region and its history. Our most renowned and unusual
collection relates to Bonnie Prince Charlie and the Jacobite
cause. But we also hold a wealth of curious and fascinating
collections relating to less well-known aspects of the lives of
the people of the West Highlands.

Lanarkshire

*Lanarkshire, inland county in SW. of Scotland; is
bounded N. by Dumbartonshire and Stirlingshire, E.
by Linlithgowshire, Edinburghshire, and Peeblesshire,
S. by Dumfriesshire, and W. by Ayrshire and
Renfrewshire; greatest length, NW. and SE., 52 miles;
greatest breadth, NE. and SW., 34 miles; area, 564,284
acres, population 904,412. Lanarkshire is often called
Clydesdale, occupying, as it does, the valley of the
Clyde, which traverses the county from SE. to NW.,
and receives numerous tributary streams, including the
Douglas, Avon, and Calder. The surface rises towards
the S., where the Lowther or Lead Hills reach an alt. of
2403 ft. The Upper Ward is chiefly hill or moorland,
affording excellent pasture for sheep; the Middle Ward
contains the orchards for which Clydesdale has long
been famous; and in the Lower Ward are some rich
alluvial lands along the Clyde; but all over the county a
considerable proportion of the soil is moist, marshy,
and barren. Dairy-farming is prosecuted with success.
The minerals are very valuable; coal and iron are
wrought to such an extent that Lanarkshire is one of
the principal seats of the iron trade; lead is mined in
the Upper Ward. The county comprises 40 parishes
and 4 parts, the parliamentary and municipal burgh of
Glasgow, the parliamentary burghs of Airdrie,
Hamilton, and Lanark (part of the Falkirk Burghs),
and the parliamentary burgh of Rutherglen (part of the
Kilmarnock Burghs).*

– John Bartholomew, *Gazetteer of the British Isles* (1887)

Note: see the separate entry for Glasgow.

Bothwell Castle

Uddingston Road
Bothwell G71 8TD
01698 816894
http://goo.gl/1dlJvf

Bothwell is Scotland's largest and finest 13th century castle.
Part of the original circular keep survives.

Bothwell Parish Church

48 Main Street
Bothwell G71 8EX
www.bothwellparishchurch.org.uk
bothwellparishoffice@btconnect.com

Bothwell Parish Church is the oldest Collegiate Church in
Scotland in which worship is still held. It is one of the most
ancient, historic, beautiful and worshipful church buildings
in Scotland.

Brownsbank Cottage

c/o Biggar Museum Trust, Moat Park
Biggar ML12 6DT
01899 221050
www.brownsbank.org.uk/cottage2.htm

Few people would question the key role of Christopher Murray Grieve ('Hugh MacDiarmid') in the Scottish Literary Renaissance of the 1920s. His rebelliously controversial statements about Scottish culture and identity gave a dynamic new perspective on the nation's arts, politics, education and philosophy. His cottage, as it is now, retains many of its original artefacts: portraits, wallie dugs, memorabilia.

Colzium Museum

Colzium House, Colzium-Lennox Estate
Kilsyth G65 0PY
01236 735077
http://goo.gl/Kgr9BC

Colzium House Museum is situated within the historic mansion house for the Colzium Lennox estate. The house was once the seat of the Edmonstone family but became the property of the Burgh of Kilsyth after the Second World War.

David Livingstone Centre

165 Station Road
Blantyre G72 9BT
01698 823140
www.nts.org.uk/Property/David-Livingstone-Centre

Scotland's most famous explorer and missionary was born here in 1813, in a single-roomed house in Shuttle Row - today a Grade A listed tenement. It is now part of the museum that tells the story of Livingstone's explorations in Africa and is home to a wide range of his personal belongings and travel aids. The museum also gives a fascinating insight into the harsh conditions endured by industrial workers in the 19th century.

Douglas Heritage Museum

Bells Wynd
Douglas ML11 0QH
01555 851 243
www.douglasheritagemuseum.co.uk

TThe Museum was originally a chapel named after St Sophia. It is believed Mary Queen of Scot's spent the night here, and to show her gratitude she gifted the village with the oldest working clock in Scotland in 1565.

Gladstone Court Victorian Street Museum

Moat Park, Kirkstyle
Biggar ML12 6DT
01899 221050
www.biggarmuseumtrust.co.uk/home/gladstone-court
info@biggarmuseumtrust.co.uk

Gladstone Court Museum began as a private venture in 1964, and opened its doors to the public in 1968. Here you can visit 'real' Victorian streets and visit the various small shops and business premises.

Greenhill Covenanter's House

Burn Braes
Biggar ML12 6DT
01899 221497
www.biggar-net.co.uk

This 17th century house was rescued from its original location at Wiston about 13km away. On visiting Greenhill you return to the troubled century of the signing of the National Covenant and of the 'Killing Times', when people were hunted down for worshipping in open fields, rather than attending state controlled churches.

Hunter House Museum

Maxwelltown Road, Calderwood
East Kilbride G74 3LW
01355 261 261
www.southlanarkshire.gov.uk
lowparksmuseum@southlanarkshire.gov.uk

Hunter House in East Kilbride is a museum with a difference. The building itself was the birthplace of William and John Hunter, the famous medical pioneers, and now houses interactive displays telling the story of their lives and their medical discoveries.

John Hastie Museum

Threestanes Road
Strathaven ML10 6DX
01357 521257
www.southlanarkshire.gov.uk
lowparksmuseum@southlanarkshire.gov.uk

John Hastie Museum in Strathaven is small, but very popular, local history museum on the edge of picturesque Strathaven Park. Founded originally in 1889 by local grocer, John Hastie, to benefit the people of the town, the museum tells the story of local life and industry, with displays featuring the Covenanters and textile weaving, as well as changing temporary exhibitions.

Kilsyth's Heritage

Kilsyth Library, Burngreen
Kilsyth G65 0HT
01236 823147
www.northlan.gov.uk
Museums@Northlan.gov.uk

Situated on the upper level of Kilsyth Library, this small display of local heritage offers a chance to gain an insight into the history of the Burgh of Kilsyth. Of particular note to researchers is the map and photographic archive.

Lanark Museum

8 Westport
Lanark ML11 9HD
01555 666680
www.lanarkmuseum.org

Lanark Museum houses a collection of items which illustrate the ancient and varied history of the town. Lanark is one of Scotland's oldest burghs, and from the time of King William the Lion was a favoured hunting area of the Kings of Scotland.

Lanarkshire Family History Society

c/o Local History Room, Motherwell Heritage Centre, High Road
Motherwell ML1 3HU
www.lanarkshirefhs.org.uk
society@lanarkshirefhs.org.uk

We're here to help people research their family history primarily in Lanarkshire's parishes, in addition we also hold information on other areas of Scotland.

Low Parks Museum

129 Muir Street
Hamilton ML3 6BJ
01698 328232
www.southlanarkshire.gov.uk
lowparksmuseum@southlanarkshire.gov.uk

Low Parks Museum is housed in beautiful and historically significant buildings which were once part of the Duke of Hamilton's estate. The 18th century Assembly Room, with its original plasterwork and musician's gallery, forms a striking centrepiece to the buildings.

Moat Park Heritage Centre

Moat Park, Kirkstyle
Biggar ML12 6DT
01899 221050
http://goo.gl/HZ2oul

Geology displays explain how the Clyde and Tweed valleys were formed millions of years ago, and splendid models portray early dwellings, mottes, castles and bastle houses, all accompanied by archaeological exhibits. Among many other colourful characters from history you will encounter an Iron Age family and one of the invading Roman soldiers from around 1900 years ago.

Museum of Lead Mining

Wanlockhead, By Biggar
Lanarkshire ML12 6UT
01659 74387
www.leadminingmuseum.co.uk

Welcome to Scotland's Museum of Lead Mining, situated in the Lowther Hills at Wanlockhead, Scotland's highest village. We offer guided tours down a former working lead mine.

North Lanarkshire Council Archives

NLC Archives and Records Centre, Records Manager, Learning and Leisure Services, 10 Kelvin Road
Cumbernauld G67 2BA
01236 638980
http://goo.gl/CXezWe

Explore the historical records of North Lanarkshire.

North Lanarkshire Heritage Centre

High Road
Motherwell ML1 3HU
www.northlanarkshire.gov.uk/index.aspx?articleid=15875

Our six-level tower is a permanent exhibition space where you will be able to explore the history of the Motherwell area from pre-history to the present. Visitors who wish to research their local or family history can do so in our friendly local history room on the first floor.

Midlothian

Edinburghshire (or mid-Lothian), maritime county in SE. of Scotland; is bounded E. by Haddington (or East-Lothian), Berwick, and Roxburgh; S. by Selkirk and Peebles; SW. by Lanark; and NW. by Linlithgow (or West-Lothian); coast-line, 12 miles; 231,724 acres, population 389,164. The surface is finely diversified. The Moorfoot Hills, a continuation of the Lammermuirs, occupy the SE.; the Pentland Hills stretch across the co. from the SW. All the streams, with the exception of the Tyne and Gala, in the E. and the SE., run to the Firth of Forth; the principal are the North Esk, the South Esk, the Water of Leith, and the Almond; the North Esk especially is noted for its picturesque scenery. The lowlands towards the Forth are the most fertile; the hilly parts of the S. are chiefly under pasture; in the W. are dairy-farms; in the vicinity of the city of Edinburgh are extensive nursery grounds and market gardens. The principal crops are oats and barley, turnips and potatoes. The county consists chiefly of carboniferous strata; and coal, shale, ironstone, limestone, and freestone, are extensively worked. There are valuable herring fisheries in the Firth of Forth. The manufactures are limited; but (beyond Edinburgh and Leith) there are numerous paper mills, oil-works, and several iron foundries and brick and tile works. Gunpowder is made at Roslyn. The county is traversed by the North British and Caledonian Railways, and by the Union Canal. It contains 28 parishes, and 4 parts, the parliamentary burgh of Edinburgh, and the Leith Burghs.

– John Bartholomew, *Gazetteer of the British Isles* (1887)

Note: see the separate entry for Edinburgh.

Cousland Smiddy

Hadfast Road, Cousland
Dalkeith EH22 2NZ
0131 663 8118
www.cousland.net/smiddyhistory.asp
info@couslandsmiddy.co.uk

In its heyday, the Smiddy was at the centre of the village social life. On long summer evenings, the smith worked late and folk came to watch the work and have a crack; games of quoits were played (throwing horse shoes at a marker post) and even boxing matches were sometimes held. The 18th century Smiddy is a treasure trove of old tools and agricultural and metal working artefacts.

Lothians Family History Society

c/o Lasswade High School Centre, Eskdale Drive
Bonnyrigg EH19 2LA
www.lothiansfhs.org.uk
lothiansfhs@hotmail.com

Whether you are a novice or an accomplished researcher the LFHS is here to help you. If you live locally or at a great distant our Society is committed to help you in your quest for knowledge about your family tree.

Midlothian Local Studies & Archives

Local Studies and Archives, 2 Clerk Street
Loanhead EH20 9DR
0131 2713976
http://goo.gl/swT5fB
Local history and heritage resources in Midlothian.

Rosslyn Chapel

Chapel Loan
Roslin EH25 9PU
0131 440 2159
www.rosslynchapel.org.uk
mail@rosslynchapel.com

Rosslyn Chapel is a Category A listed building and Scheduled Ancient Monument, located in the village of Roslin, approximately 7 miles south of Edinburgh. Built between 1446 and 1484, practically every surface of Rosslyn Chapel is covered with carvings of individual figures and scenes.

Moray

Elginshire (or Morayshire), maritime county, in NE. of Scotland; is bounded N. by the Moray Firth, E. and SE. by Banff, SW. by Inverness, and W. by Nairn; coast-line, 30 miles; 304,606 acres; population 43,788. Along the sea-coast the surface is mostly low and sandy; inland it consists of fertile valleys, divided by low hills, which gradually rise to the mountains on the S. border. In the S. a large portion of the surface is still covered by forest. The principal rivers are the Spey, Lossie, and Findhorn; the Spey and the Findhorn have salmon and grilse, and in the lochs there is abundance of trout; large quantities of haddock, cod, and ling are caught in the Moray Firth. In the lower part of the co. farming and stock-raising are prosecuted with great success. The principal crops are wheat, oats, potatoes, and turnips. Granite occurs in the S., and red sandstone in the N. There are large quarries of freestone and a few slate quarries; whisky is distilled; and there is some shipbuilding at the mouth of the Spey; but otherwise the industries, besides agriculture and fishing, are unimportant. Corn, timber, salmon, and whisky are the chief exports. The county comprises 15 parishes, and 7 parts, the parliamentary and royal burgh of Elgin (part of Elgin Burghs), and the parliamentary and royal burgh of Forres (part of Inverness Burghs).

– John Bartholomew, *Gazetteer of the British Isles* (1887)

Brodie Castle

Forres
Forres IV36 2TE
0844 493 2156
www.nts.org.uk/Property/Brodie-Castle
brodiecastle@nts.org.uk

Set in peaceful parkland, this fine 16th-century tower house is packed with enough art and antiques to keep connoisseurs happy all day. It contains fine French furniture English, continental and Chinese porcelain and a major collection of paintings, including 17th-century Dutch art, 19th-century English watercolours, and early 20th-century works.

Dufftown Museum

The Tower, The Square
Dufftown AB55 4AD
01340 820507
www.whisky.dufftown.co.uk/whisky_museum.php

The Dufftown Whisky Museum provides a unique opportunity to discover the secrets of whisky making in days gone. It also gives a fascinating insight into the lives and times of whisky smugglers. Many of the exhibits were provided by local distillers as well as HM Custom and Excise.

Elgin Cathedral - Historic Scotland
Elgin
King St, IV30 1HU
01343 547171
www.historic-scotland.gov.uk/places

The superb ruin of what many think was Scotland's most beautiful cathedral. Much of the work is in a rich late 13th-century style, much modified after the burning of the church by the Wolf of Badenoch in 1390.

Elgin Museum
1 High Street
Elgin IV30 1EQ
01343 543675
www.elginmuseum.org.uk
curator@elginmuseum.org.uk

Possibly the oldest independent museum in Scotland. Established in 1836, with the purpose built museum opening in 1842.

Collections: World famous fossil collection, Romano-Celtic collection, Pictish Stones, and the 'People & Place' exhibition.

Falconer Museum

Tolbooth Street
Forres IV36 1PH
01309 673701
falconermuseum.co.uk
museums@moray.gov.uk

Established in Victorian era by the Falconer family to offer the town of Forres a museum and library facility.

Collections: Includes many local artefacts, both archaeological and from Victorian age donated by residents since the founding in 1871. A portion of Dr Hugh Falconer's fossils together with his library and personal papers are held in our store.

Grantown Museum & Heritage Centre

Burnfield House, Burnfield Avenue
Grantown-on-Spey PH26 3HH
01479 872478
www.grantownmuseum.co.uk

Grantown Museum tells the story of the town's beginnings and is a source of great pride to the people of Grantown. The museum houses the archives of the Grantown Society. It provides research facilities for genealogy and local history. Grantown is the traditional home of the Clan Grant and the museum receives frequent visits and enquiries from Grants across the world.

Knockando Woolmill

The Woolmill, Knockando
Aberlour AB38 7RP
01340 810 345
www.knockandowoolmill.org.uk
mail@knockandowoolmill.co.uk

Set deep in the Spey Valley, Knockando Woolmill is a district mill, serving the needs of the local community and processing wool into yarn and woven cloth on historic machinery and looms, in continuous production for over 200 years.

Moray & Nairn Family History Society

www.morayandnairnfhs.co.uk
info@morayandnairnfhs.co.uk

Moray & Nairn Family History Society was established in February 2009, for people researching their ancestry in these old counties. The society has members throughout Britain and overseas.

Moray Council Museums Service

Falconer Museum, Tolbooth Street
Forres IV36 IPH
01309 696261
www.moray.gov.uk/museums
museums@moray.gov.uk

The Moray Museums Service manages three cultural sites; Falconer Museum and Nelson Tower in Forres and the Tomintoul Museum. Please contact us with any questions or queries you may have relating to our museums or other aspects of Moray culture.

Moray Local Heritage Services

Local Heritage Officer, Moray Local Heritage Centre, Institution Road
Elgin IV30 1RP
01343 569011
www.moray.gov.uk/moray_standard/page_1537.html

The Local Heritage Centre for Moray offers a fascinating insight into Moray's history and ancestry searches.

Tomintoul Museum

The Square
Tomintoul AB37 9ET
01807 580285
www.moray.gov.uk/moray_standard/page_627.html
museums@moray.gov.uk

On the margin of the Cairngorm Mountains, situated in the highest village in Britain. Reconstructed crofter's kitchen. Reconstructed village blacksmith's shop (the 'Tomintoul Smiddy'). The sounds and smells of rural working life. Displays on local wildlife. The history of Tomintoul and Glenlivet.

Tugnet Ice House

Tugnet, Spey Bay
Fochabers IV32 7DU
01249 449500
www.wdcs.org/connect/wildlife_centre/spey_bay.php

Recently acquired by the Whale and Dolphin Conservation Society, please call for details ahead of making any plans to visit. Reputedly the largest industrial ice house in Scotland, Tugnet Ice House nestles between the River Spey and the Moray Firth at the mouth of the Spey. This spectacular building is open to the public free of charge, and you are welcome to walk through its six chambers and appreciate the spectacular vaulted brick ceiling.

Nairnshire

Nairnshire, a maritime county in the NE. of Scotland, bounded N. by the Moray Firth, E. by Elginshire, and S. and W. by Inverness-shire; consists of a main body and 5 detached portions, 3 of which are in Elginshire, 1 in Inverness-shire, and 1 in Ross and Cromarty; the main body has an extreme length, N. and S., of 18 miles, and an average breadth, E. and W., of 11 miles; the coast, which is flat and sandy, has an extent of 10 miles; area, 127,905 acres; population 10,455. The low ground near the coast is fertile and well-wooded, the soil consisting of a rich free loam over sand or gravel. The surface gradually rises thence into mountains in the S. Granite is abundant, and is quarried. The rivers are the Nairn and the Findhorn. Agriculture and the fisheries are the chief industries. The county comprises 3 pars, and 7 parts, and the parl. and royal burgh of Nairn (Inverness Burghs). It unites with Elginshire in returning 1 member to Parliament.

– John Bartholomew, *Gazetteer of the British Isles* (1887)

Moray & Nairn Family History Society

▦

www.morayandnairnfhs.co.uk

info@morayandnairnfhs.co.uk

Moray & Nairn Family History Society was established in February 2009, for people researching their ancestry in these old counties. The society has members throughout Britain and overseas.

Nairn Museum

🖼 £

Viewfield House, Viewfield Drive

Nairn IV12 4EE

01667 456791

www.nairnmuseum.co.uk

manager@nairnmuseum.freeserve.co.uk

Since 1858 Nairn Museum has fascinated generations of visitors and locals alike of all ages. Located in a Georgian House set in parkland, the museum tells the story of Nairnshire and the families who had lived and worked in burgh or country.

Orkney Islands

Orkney, insular county of Scotland, separated from Caithness by the Pentland Firth (6½ to 8 miles broad); area, 240,476 acres, population 32,044; population of Pomona, or Mainland, 17,165. The Orkneys comprise 67 islands, 28 of which are inhabited, besides a large number of rocky islets or skerries. They are divided into 3 groups - the South Isles, comprising the large islands of Hoy, South Ronaldshay, and many smaller ones; Pomona, or Mainland, the largest island of the Orkneys; and the North Isles, comprising Rousay, Shapinshay, Westray, Papa Westray, Eday, Stronsay, Sanday, and North Ronaldshay. Except on the S. and W. sides, where the cliffs are bold and precipitous, the coasts of the islands are extremely irregular, abounding in bays and headlands. The surface - most elevated in Hoy, which is hilly - is generally low, and much interspersed with rocks, swamps, and lochs. The climate, prevailingly moist, is mild and equable for the latitude. The soil mostly consists of peat or moss, but is either sandy or of a good loam where the land is arable. The farms are usually of small size; oats, barley, and turnips are grown. Live stock, poultry, and eggs are largely exported. There is regular steam communication between Leith and Kirkwall, an active trade being kept up. Orkney forms one of the great Scottish fishery districts. Fishing and agriculture are the chief industries. There are two distilleries in Pomona. The Orkneys were known to the Romans as the Orcades, and seem to have been originally peopled by Celts. About the beginning of the 4th century the islands were visited by the Norse sea-rovers, who ultimately settled upon them. They were annexed to Norway in the latter part of the 9th century, and in 1468 were attached to Scotland as a pledge for the dowry of the Princess of Denmark who married James III. The people still retain some traces of their Scandinavian descent. Orkney comprises 18 parishes, and the parliamentary burgh of Kirkwall (part of the Wick Burghs).

– John Bartholomew, *Gazetteer of the British Isles* (1887)

Corrigall Farm Museum

c/o Broad Street
Kirkwall KW15 1DH
01856 771411
http://goo.gl/ShTVLY
customerservice@orkney.gov.uk

Opened to the public in 1980, Corrigall Farm Museum is a traditional 'but and ben' house. It portrays a typical Orkney farmhouse and steading in Victorian times - late 19th century.

Kirbuster Farm Museum

c/o Broad Street
Kirkwall KW15 1DH
01856 77268
http://goo.gl/noNg6a

Kirbuster Museum was opened to the public in 1986. It is the last un-restored example of a traditional 'firehoose' in Northern Europe.

Lyness Interpretation Centre

Lyness, Hoy
Kirkwall KW16 3NU
01856 791 300
www.scapaflow.co.uk/sfvc.htm

Sometimes known as the Scapa Flow Visitor Centre, the Lyness Interpretation Centre houses an important record of the role the Royal Navy played in Orkney during both World Wars. Situated at Lyness on the island of Hoy, the centre is run by Orkney Islands Council Museums Service, which has converted the former pump house to provide a comprehensive series of interpretative displays, as well as being home to a fascinating outside collection of military equipment such as vehicles and guns.

Maeshowe Chambered Cairn - Historic Scotland

Orkney
01856 761606
www.historic-scotland.gov.uk/places

The finest megalithic tomb in the British Isles, with a large mound covering a stone-built passage and a large burial chamber with cells in the walls. Of Neolithic date, broken into in Viking times by people who carved extensive runic inscriptions on the walls.

Orkney Family History Society

Orkney Library and Archives, 44 Junction Road
Kirkwall KW15 1AG
01856 879 207
www.orkneyfhs.co.uk
secretary@orkneyfhs.co.uk

The Orkney Family History Society has an office in the Orkney Library & Archive, and is usefully located next to the Archives. Our office is staffed by volunteers, and visitors, whether members or not, are assured of a friendly welcome.

Orkney Library & Archive

44 Junction Road
Kirkwall KW15 1AG
01856 873166
www.orkneylibrary.org.uk/

Orkney Library & Archive provides a wide range of services, many of them free of charge, and welcomes everybody, whether a resident of Orkney or just visiting.

Orkney Museum

c/o Broad Street
Kirkwall KW15 1DH
01856 3191
http://goo.gl/oDgOz6

The Orkney Museum tells the story of Orkney, from the Stone Age, to the Picts and Vikings, right through to the present day. There is a large collection of old photos and activities to amuse younger visitors.

Orkney Wireless Museum

Kiln Corner
Kirkwall KW15 1LB
01856 871400
www.owm.org.uk
sfirth@owm.org.uk

The museum came about because of the love of wireless sets of its founder, the late Jim MacDonald. During his lifetime he gathered together an extensive and varied collection of domestic and defence wireless equipment.

Skaill House

Breckness Estate
Sandwick KW16 3LR
01856 841501
www.skaillhouse.co.uk

Skaill House is the finest mansion in Orkney, a family home steeped in 5000 years of history. Situated in the parish of Sandwick overlooking the spectacular Bay of Skaill, the house is surrounded by spacious lawned gardens and stands in a peaceful secluded spot between the Loch of Skaill and the sea.

Skara Brae Prehistoric Village - Historic Scotland

🏛 ✉ £

Skara Brae Prehistoric Village
Orkney
01856 841815
www.historic-scotland.gov.uk/places

When a wild storm on Orkney in 1850 exposed the ruins of ancient dwellings, Skara Brae, the best preserved prehistoric village in northern Europe, was discovered. The excavated farming settlement dates back 5000 years.

Stones of Stenness Circle & Henge - Historic Scotland

🏛 ★

Stones of Stenness Circle and Henge
Stenness
01856 841815
www.historic-scotland.gov.uk/places

Standing at a maximum height of six metres (around 19 feet), the sheer scale of the megaliths that make up the Stones o' Stenness makes the monument visible for miles around. Located by the south-eastern shore of the Loch o' Stenness, only four of the ring's stones remain. These are considerably larger than those found in the nearby Ring o' Brodgar, approximately one mile to the north-west.

Stromness Museum

✉

52 Alfred Street
Stromness KW16 3DF
01856 850025
www.scbf.co.uk/museum.html

Stromness Museum was founded in 1837 with the creation of the Orkney Natural History Society. The building dates from 1858.

Westray Heritage Centre

🏛 ✉ £

Westray KW17 2BZ
01857 677414
www.westrayheritage.co.uk
enquiries@westrayheritage.co.uk

We are situated in the centre of Pierowall village in Westray next door to the Pierowall Hotel. Inside we have an annual display plus permanent exhibition panels on walls, and GEO with model seabirds and sounds.

Peeblesshire

Peeblesshire (or Tweeddale), an inland county in the SE. of Scotland, bounded N. and NE. by Edinburghshire, E. and SE. by Selkirkshire, S. by Dumfriesshire, and W. by Lanarkshire; greatest length, N. and S., 29 miles; greatest breadth, B. and W., 21 miles; area, 226,890 acres, population 13,822. From the narrow central valley of the Tweed the surface rises into hills and mountains, with fertile valleys or deep gorges between the ridges. The hills for the most part are grassy and softly rounded. The highest summit is Broad Law, 2723 ft., near the S. border. The streams in the glens and valleys afford good angling. Blue clay slate has been extensively worked, limestone is abundant, and coal is mined to some extent in the N. of the county. Sheep-farming is the main industry. The woollen manufacture is carried on at Peebles, Innerleithen, and Walkerburn. The county comprises 12 parishes, with parts of 4 others.

– John Bartholomew, *Gazetteer of the British Isles* (1887)

John Buchan Story

□ ⌂ £

The Chambers Institution, High Street

Peebles EH45 8AG

www.johnbuchanstory.co.uk

John Buchan is a national figure within both a Scottish and UK context. Through his prolific writing and by his many and varied contributions to public life, he was a highly influential figure, particularly during the inter-war period.

Robert Smail's Printing Works

 £

7/9 High Street

Innerleithen EH44 6HA

0844 4932259

http://goo.gl/VCb24Q

smails@nts.org.uk

A unique example of our industrial heritage in the form of a fully operational Victorian letterpress printing works in the Borders town of Innerleithen. See printing as it was at the turn of the last century. Records of the Smail's time as a shipping agent in the town. An archive of business records dating from the start of the printing business in 1866 until 1986.

St Ronan's Wells Interpretation Centre

⊞ □

c/o Chambers Institute, High Street

Peebles EH45 8AP

01721 724820

http://goo.gl/NPaBQ2

museums@scotborders.gov.uk

St Ronan's Wells is an historic spa, built in 1828, which houses displays telling the story of the site and its links with the great Scottish writers Walter Scott and James Hogg, the legend of St Ronan and the history of Innerleithen.

Traquair House

⊞ £

Innerleithen EH44 6PW

01896 830323

www.traquair.co.uk

enquiries@traquair.co.uk

Dating back to 1107, Traquair was originally a hunting lodge for the kings and queens of Scotland. Later a refuge for Catholic priests in times of terror – the Stuarts of Traquair supported Mary Queen of Scots and the Jacobite cause without counting the cost. Today, Traquair is a unique piece of living history welcoming visitors from all over the world.

Tweeddale Museum & Gallery

□ ★

c/o Chambers Institute, High Street

Peebles EH45 8AJ

01721 724820

http://goo.gl/nQIXRi

Tweeddale Museum was established by William Chambers, the founder of the famous publishing house. His aim was to create a centre of learning in his home town. It houses a museum and gallery which present a lively programme of exhibitions throughout the year. The Chambers Room houses the extraordinary plasterwork friezes commissioned by William Chambers and exhibitions on the history of Peebles and the surrounding area.

Perthshire

Perthshire, east-midland county of Scotland, bounded N. by Inverness-shire and Aberdeenshire, E. by Forfarshire, SE. by Fife and Kinross-shire, S. by Clackmannanshire and Stirlingshire, SW. by Stirlingshire and Dumbartonshire, and W. by Argyllshire; greatest length, E. and W., 72 miles; greatest breadth, N. and S., 60 miles; the detached portion (lying along the upper reach of the Firth of Forth, and separated from the main body by a belt of Fife and Clackmannanshire) is 6½ miles by 4½ miles; area, 1,617,808 acres; population 129,007. Perthshire includes some of the grandest and most beautiful scenery in Scotland, combining features characteristic both of the Highlands and the Lowlands. The ranges of the Ochils and the Sidlaw Hills, which are parted by the estuary of the Tay, occupy the SE.; while the N. and NW. districts, to the extent of more than one-half of the entire county, are occupied with the mountains of the Grampian system, this Highland region being intersected by numerous lochs and glens. The principal rivers are the Forth and the Tay. The soils of this county are of the most varied character, - rich deep clay or loam in the straths, a light sandy or gravelly soil in the hill valleys, and moorland on the higher lands. Coal and ironstone are wrought in the detached section of the county; roofing slate is obtained near Alyth, Comrie, and Dunkeld; and limestone is quarried at various places. Agriculture and sheep-farming are the chief industries. There are extensive deer forests, and the fisheries on the Tay are of very considerable value. The manufactures of woollen and tartan stuffs, cotton, and coarse linens are carried on to some extent. The ancient divisions of Perthshire, now only of local significance, were Athole, Breadalbane, Gowrie, Menteith, Methven, Perth, and Stormont. The county comprises 68 parishes, with parts of 13 others, the parliamentary burgh of Perth, and the parliamentary burgh of Culross (part of the Stirling Burghs).

– John Bartholomew, *Gazetteer of the British Isles* (1887)

Alyth Museum

Commercial Street
Alyth PH11 8AF
01738 632488
http://goo.gl/hix8U6

Alyth Museum overlooks the countryside of Strathmore, an area rich in farming which is an inspiration and resource for the displays you will find here. Enjoy a wealth of pictures and objects reflecting life as it was, in and around Alyth.

Black Watch Castle & Museum, The

Balhousie Castle, Hay Street
Perth PH1 5HR
01738 638 152
www.theblackwatch.co.uk
museum@theblackwatch.co.uk

The Black Watch Museum is housed in the dramatic and historic Balhousie Castle. The castle is set in its own beautiful gardens and grounds.

Blair Castle

Blair Atholl
Pitlochry PH18 5TL
01796 481207
www.blair-castle.co.uk

Discover Blair Castle and go on a journey into the fascinating past of the Dukes and Earls of Atholl. Unique amongst Scottish castles, the story told here will take you from a visit by Mary Queen of Scots to the Civil War, and from the Jacobite cause to the disaster of Culloden following Bonnie Prince Charlie's own stay in the castle. You'll hear how the lucky inheritance of a smuggler-infested island helped turn the castle into a comfortable home, and learn how Queen Victoria's famous stay led to the creation of Europe's only private army, the Atholl Highlanders.

Central Scotland Family History Society

11 Springbank Gardens
Dunblane FK15 9JX
01786 823937
www.csfhs.org.uk

The society was formed in 1990 to serve the needs of those interested in family history who lived in what was then Central Region. This means that as well as the old counties of Clackmannanshire, Stirlingshire and West Perthshire, the society covers the parishes of Bo'ness and Carriden which were in West Lothian.

Clan Donnachaidh Museum

Bruar
Pitlochry PH18 5TW
01796 483 296
www.donnachaidh.com

Clan Donnachaidh Museum is dedicated to the clan which bears its name. The name Donnachaidh means 'children of Duncan'.

Dunblane Museum

The Cross
Dunblane FK15 0AQ
01786 823440
www.dunblanemuseum.org.uk
curator@dunblanemuseum.org.uk

Founded in 1943 the Dunblane Museum is situated right at the heart of the Cathedral City of Dunblane. Few museums can boast that the building in which they are housed is a museum piece itself. Dunblane Museum houses a collection of artefacts, paintings, prints and photographs about the cathedral and Dunblane, and it has one of the largest collections of Communion tokens.

Dunkeld Cathedral Chapter House Museum

Dunkeld Cathedral
Dunkeld PH8 0AW
01350 727 249
www.dunkeldcathedral.org.uk
art@dunkeldcathedral.org.uk

The Cathedral Chapter House was built in 1457, and served as a sacristy and meeting place for 100 years. After the Reformation, when the Dukes of Atholl became responsible for the upkeep of the church they used the Chapter House as their Mausoleum and it still contains some magnificent monuments and memorials.

Hamilton Toy Collection, The

11 Main Street
Callander FK17 8BQ
01877 330004
www.thehamiltontoycollection.co.uk
info@thehamiltontoycollection.co.uk

A celebration of toys from the last hundred years. Open from March until the end of October.

Museum of Abernethy

Mornington Stables, School Wynd
Abernethy PH2 9JJ
01738 850889
www.museumofabernethy.co.uk
secretary@museumofabernethy.co.uk

The building, which stands within the lands of the old Culdees monastery, dates from the 18th century. Find out about our Round Tower, mythically built by the Picts. Find out the truth about Abernethy biscuits. Discover more about the local 3000 year old logboat.

Muthill Museum

Station Road
Muthill PH5 2AR
https://goo.gl/w08OGl

Amongst the many fascinating exhibits, have a look downstairs at the wooden brose bowl and horn spoon which was given to the twelve year old William Ross by his parents in 1869 when he left home to work on a farm. Close by is another ubiquitous cooking utensil of the times; a porridge spirtle which has very obviously seen a lifetime of stirring the old national dish.

Perth & Kinross Council Archive

AK Bell Library, York Place
Perth PH2 8EP
01738 477012
www.pkc.gov.uk/archives

Find information about over 800 years of council records and community collections.

Perth Museum & Art Gallery

78 George Street
Perth PH1 5LB
01738 632488
www.pkc.gov.uk/museums
museum@pkc.gov.uk

We are one of the oldest museums in the UK, with more than half a million objects in our large, varied collections.

Scottish Crannog Centre, The

Kenmore, Loch Tay
Aberfeldy, PH15 2HY
01887 830583
www.crannog.co.uk
info@crannog.co.uk

A crannog is a type of ancient loch-dwelling found throughout Scotland and Ireland dating from 5,000 years ago. Many crannogs were built out in the water as defensive homesteads and represented symbols of power and wealth. The Scottish Crannog Centre features a unique reconstruction of an early Iron Age loch-dwelling.

Stanley Mills

7.4m North Perth off the A9PH1 4QE
01738 828268
http://goo.gl/4LY03Q

Enjoy our new hi-tech interactive visitor experience at the spectacular 18th-century water mill complex beside the River Tay. The visitor centre tells the stories of those who worked there and the products they made.

Renfrewshire

Renfrewshire, maritime county, in SW. of Scotland, bounded N. by the river Clyde and Dumbartonshire, E. by Lanarkshire, S. by Ayrshire, and W. by the Firth of Clyde; greatest length, NW. and SE., 31 miles; greatest breadth, NE. and SW., 14 miles; area, 150,785 acres, population 263,374. The principal streams, all flowing to the Clyde, are the Black Cart, the White Cart, and the Gryde. The surface in the S. and SW. parts of the county is hilly, and somewhat bleak and moorish; it thence undulates to the banks of the Clyde, along which there is some rich and lowlying land. Coal, ironstone, and lime-stone are abundant; copper ore occurs near Gourock and Lochwinnoch. The principal industries, besides mining and agriculture, are the manufacture of cotton and thread, sugar-refining, and shipbuilding. The county comprises 20 parishes, with parts of 4 others, and the parliamentary burghs of Greenock, Paisley, and Port Glasgow and Renfrew (part of the Kilmarnock Burghs).

– John Bartholomew, *Gazetteer of the British Isles* (1887)

Mclean Museum & Art Gallery

15 Kelly Street
Greenock PA16 8JX
01475 715624
http://goo.gl/QTe0Yh
museum@inverclyde.gov.uk

The McLean Museum and Art Gallery is one of the best municipal museums in Scotland. The museum has served as the main museum in the Inverclyde area since it opened in 1876 and has many wonderful collections for the visitor to discover and explore. In addition to outstanding collections of local material from the Inverclyde area, the museum offers displays and collections drawn from many cultures across 3,000 years of human history.

Paisley Museum including the Coats Observatory

High Street
Paisley PA1 2BA
0300 300 1210
http://goo.gl/LR97Pb
museums.els@renfrewshire.gov.uk

Paisley Museum opened in 1871. The building was designed by the well-known Glasgow architect John Honeyman and was paid for by Sir Peter Coats of the famous Coats thread manufacturing family. Coats Observatory has astronomical equipment and displays, weather and earthquake recording equipment.

Renfrew Community Museum

The Brown Institute, 41 Canal Street
Paisley PA4 8QA
0141 886 3149
www.renfrewshire.gov.uk
museums.els@renfrewshire.gov.uk

The museum opened in 1997 to commemorate 600 years of Renfrew as a Royal Burgh. It houses local history collections and also has changing exhibitions.

Renfrewshire Central Library

68 High Street
Paisley PA1 2BB
0141 889 2360
http://goo.gl/BsBqAg

Information about local and family history resources in Renfrewshire.

Renfrewshire Family History Society

c/o Museum and Art Galleries, High Street
Paisley PA1 2BA
renfrewshirefhs.co.uk
webmaster.rfhs@ntlworld.com

Renfrewshire Family History Society exists to promote the study of family history, based on the County of Renfrewshire.

Sma' Shot Cottages

11-17 George Place
Paisley PA1 2HZ
0141 889 1708
www.smashot.co.uk

An opportunity to see two distinct periods in Paisley's weaving history. From Shuttle Street you will enter the Weaver's Cottage and be transported back in time by nearly 250 years. You will then cross a yard behind the cottage and jump forward in time by 70 years to experience life in the town during the early to mid 1800s.

Weaver's Cottage

The Cross
Kilbarchan PA10 2JG
01505 705 588
www.nts.org.uk

This restored historic 18th-century cottage near Glasgow vividly recreates the living and working conditions of a typical handloom weaver.

Ross-shire

*Ross and Cromarty, maritime county, in NW. of
Scotland; area, 2,003,065 acres, population 78,547. It
consists of a mainland portion which comprises all
the detached sections of Cromarty, and an insular
portion properly called Ross-shire which includes
Lewis island (excluding Harris) and a number of
smaller islands in the Outer Hebrides. The mainland
portion extends 67 miles N. and S. between
Sutherland and Inverness-shire, and 75 miles E. and
W. between the Moray Firth and the Atlantic Ocean.
On the E. coast, which affords good harbours, are the
Dornoch Firth, Cromarty Firth, and Beauly Firth;
and of numerous indentations along the W. coast the
largest are Loch Broom, Gruinard Bay, Loch Ewe,
Loch Torridon, Loch Carron, and Loch Alsh. The
largest streams are the Oykell, the Alness, and the
Conon, which flow to the Moray Firth. The chief
inland lochs are Maree, Fannich, Luichart, Sheallag,
and Bosyne. Of the 3 great divisions of the county,
Easter Ross, including all the low land between the
Dornoch and Cromarty Firths, is fertile and well
cultivated; Mid. Ross, including the district (known as
the Black Isle) between the Cromarty Firth and the
Moray and Beauly Firths, is mostly under good
cultivation; while Wester Ross, including by far the
greater portion of the county, is altogether of a
highland character, and abounds in rugged
mountains, beautiful lochs, and wild glens. Sheep
farming and cattle grazing are extensively pursued.
The distilling of whisky is the sole mfr. The fisheries,
coast and inland, are extensive and valuable. The
county comprises 31 parishes, with parts of 2 others,
and the parliamentary burghs of Cromarty,
Dingwall, Tain (part of the Wick Burghs) and
Fortrose (part of the Inverness Burghs).*

– John Bartholomew, *Gazetteer of the British Isles* (1887)

Dingwall Museum

Town Hall, High Street
Dingwall IV15 9RY
01349 865366
http://goo.gl/tPtLG3
enquiries@dingwallmuseum.co.uk

Dingwall Museum presents many local artefacts and
fascinating tales of human exploits which are unique to
Dingwall within a landmark building, once the centre of
local government. Over the years members have designed
displays to create pictures of the past for visitors to study
and enjoy.

Eilean Donan Castle

Dornie
by Kyle of Lochalsh IV40 8DX
01599 555202
www.eileandonancastle.com

You can explore almost every part of the castle from the
Banqueting Hall to the bedrooms. You'll be following in the
footsteps of many a warrior - from the Vikings to James
Bond, from Jacobites to Hollywood's 'Highlander'.

Gairloch Heritage Museum

Achtercairn
Gairloch IV21 2BP
01445 712287
www.gairlochheritagemuseum.org
info@gairlochheritagemuseum.org

An award-winning museum with displays recreating a croft
house interior, schoolroom, village shop, parlour and
others. Also on display is the light from Rhu Reidh
lighthouse, one of the largest lenses assembled by the
Northern Lighthouse Board.

Groam House Museum

High Street
Rosemarkie IV10 8UF
01381 620961
www.groamhouse.org.uk
admin@groamhouse.org.uk

Groam House Museum is situated in the Black Isle village
of Rosemarkie, occupying an 18th-century building. Our
lovely museum is an outstanding centre for Pictish and
Celtic Art in Ross-shire. The unique display is focused on
15 carved Pictish stones which all originated in the village,
an important centre of early Christianity. The sculptures are
amongst the works of Pictish Art that inspired George
Bain, the 'father of modern Celtic design', most of whose
surviving artwork is in the care of the museum.

Highland Council Museum Service

Ross and Cromarty Area, Council Offices, High Street
Dingwall IV15 9QN
01349 868460
www.museumsinthehighlands.com
lorna.cruickshank@highland.gov.uk

Council service that is set up to help and inform members
of the public regarding the museums and art galleries in
operation in Highland.

Highland Museum of Childhood

The Old Station
Strathpeffer IV14 9DH
01997 421031
www.highlandmuseumofchildhood.org.uk

The museum is located in Strathpeffer's charming old Victorian station where trains brought visitors in the village's heyday as a spa. The museum tells the story of childhood in the Highlands of Scotland, recording tales of childhood amongst hardworking crofters and townsfolk, where money and luxuries were scarce, and life followed the satisfying rhythm of the seasons.

Tain & District Museum

Tower Street
Tain IV19 1DY
01862 894089
www.tainmuseum.org.uk
info@tainmuseum.org.uk

Tain Through Time opens the door to the history of Tain, an ancient royal burgh in the north of the Highlands of Scotland. It is set in a complex of three buildings in an atmospheric churchyard: a medieval collegiate church, a museum, and a visitor centre in an old schoolhouse, each of which offers a different perspective on Tain's long and eventful past.

Tarbat Discovery Centre

Tarbatness Road, Portmahomack
Tain IV20 1YA
01862 871351
www.tarbat-discovery.co.uk
info@tarbat-discovery.co.uk

Tarbat Discovery Centre is a Museum situated in an old church in the beautiful coastal village of Portmahomack, 42 miles North East of Inverness. Having been abandoned in 1946 the dilapidated building was saved from ruin in 1980, when it was purchased by the newly formed Tarbat Old Parish Church Preservation Trust. You can find out how the archaeologists have slowly uncovered the ancient treasures at Tarbat.

Ullapool Museum & Visitor Centre

7-8 West Argyle Street
Ullapool IV26 2TY
01854 612 987
www.ullapoolmuseum.co.uk
info@ullapoolmuseum.co.uk

Housed within a restored Thomas Telford Parliamentary Church, originally built in 1829, the museum tells the story of Lochbroom - the land and its people, through a blend of traditional and multimedia displays. The audiovisual presentation tells the story of the people who have made this challenging environment their home, from the first settlers after the ice age to the present day.

Roxburghshire

Roxburghshire, inland county, in S. of Scotland, bounded N. by Berwickshire, NE. and SE. by Northumberland and Cumberland, SW. by Dumfriesshire, and NW. by Selkirkshire and Edinburghshire; greatest length, N. and S., 42 miles; greatest breadth, E. and W., 30 miles; area, 425,657 acres, population 53,442. The main body of the county, or three-fourths of the whole area, belongs to the basin of the Teviot; hence the general name of Teviotdale is sometimes used for Roxburghshire. The upper portions of Teviotdale and its tributary vales, rising by gently sloping and well rounded ridges from the banks of the streams to the watershed of the Cheviots, are chiefly bare and pastoral, but the lower portions consist of rich and well wooded valleys. Every vale abounds in rich and lovely scenery, and there is scarcely a spot without some interesting historical association. The principal streams which flow to the Teviot are the Borthwick, Ale, Slitrig, Rule, Jed, Oxnam, and Kale. The Liddel joins the Esk before it enters the Solway Firth. Farming is the great industry, and is in a highly advanced state. The woollen manufacture is extensively carried on at Hawick. The county comprises 29 parishes, with parts of 6 others, and the parliamentary burgh of Hawick (part of the Hawick Burghs).

– John Bartholomew, *Gazetteer of the British Isles* (1887)

Abbotsford House

Abbotsford
Melrose TD6 9BQ
01896 752043
www.melrose.bordernet.co.uk/abbotsford

Abbotsford is the house built and lived in by Sir Walter Scott, the 19th century novelist, and author of timeless classics such as Waverley, Rob Roy, Ivanhoe and The Lady of the Lake. In 1811 Sir Walter bought the property which was to become Abbotsford, set in the heart of the Scottish Borders, on the banks of the River Tweed.

Borders Family History Society

30 Elliot Road
Jedburgh TD8 6HN
www.bordersfhs.org.uk

Borders FHS promotes genealogy and family history in the counties of Roxburghshire, Berwickshire, Selkirkshire and Peeblesshire in SE Scotland.

Drumlanrig's Tower

1 Tower Knowe
Hawick TD9 9EN
01450 377615
http://goo.gl/Zkze3d

Drumlanrig's Tower was originally a 16th century stone L-plan tower house, founded by the Douglas family. Of three storeys and a garret, the basement in the main block was vaulted and the hall stood on the first floor.

Dryburgh Abbey - Historic Scotland

Dryburgh Abbey
near St Boswells TD6 0RQ
www.historic-scotland.gov.uk/places

Dryburgh sits by the Tweed River. Its remarkably complete medieval ruins makes it easy to appreciate the attractions of monastic life.

Friends of Kelso Museum

c/o The Secretary, c/o Maxwellheugh Cottage, Jedburgh Road
Kelso TD5 8AZ
01573 224753
http://goo.gl/153RX2

The Friends of Kelso Museum continue to work towards the re-establishment of a Museum in Kelso. The Friends promote eight public lectures on local history themes, four in November and four in March.

Harmony Garden

St Mary's Road
Melrose TD6 9LJ
0844 493 2251
www.nts.org.uk/Property/Harmony-Garden

Elegant Regency town house available as a holiday let, set within three acre walled garden which is open to the public.

Hawick Museum & the Scott Art Gallery

Wilton Lodge Park
Hawick TD9 7JL
01450 373457
http://goo.gl/WGZsBV

Discover passionate collectors, racing legends, famous painters and local history in a historic house within a beautiful Victorian park. There is always something new to see with a lively programme of changing art and museum exhibitions throughout the year.

Jedburgh Castle Jail & Museum

Castlegate
Jedburgh TD8 6QD
01835 864750
http://goo.gl/BCY8IG
museums@scotborders.gov.uk

Jedburgh Castle Jail gives visitors a taste of what life was like in an 1820s prison, whilst also telling the story of the Royal Burgh of Jedburgh. The main building of Jedburgh Castle Jail is home to the museum collection of the town of Jedburgh, focusing on traditions, industries and important individuals of this historic Scottish town.

Mary Queen of Scots' House & Visitor Centre

Queen Street
Jedburgh TD8 6EN
01835 863331
http://goo.gl/7zgy1S

This fine example of a 16th century bastel house is set in a beautiful garden of pear trees. Displays tell the story of Scotland's tragic queen.

Melrose Abbey - Historic Scotland

Melrose Abbey
Melrose TD6 9LG
01896 822562
www.historic-scotland.gov.uk/places

One of Scotland's most famous ruins, the abbey was founded by David I in 1136 for the Cistercian Order, it was largely destroyed by Richard II's English army in 1385. The surviving remains of the church are largely of the early 15th century.

Scottish Borders Archive & Local History Centre

Heritage Hub, Heart of Hawick, Kirkstile
Hawick TD9 0AE
01450 360699
www.scotborders.gov.uk/info/428/archives

Find out about the resources available to find out about local and family history in the Scottish Borders.

Trimontium Museum

c/o D Gordon, Cockleroi, Newstead
Melrose TD6 9DE
01896 822651
www.trimontium.org.uk/wb/pages/museum.php

The Three Hills Roman Heritage Centre housing the Trimontium Museum, is based in The Ormiston, The Square, Melrose and tells the story of a Roman frontier post and its people.

Selkirkshire

Selkirkshire, an inland county in the SE. of Scotland; is bounded N. by Edinburghshire, E. by Roxburghshire, S. by Dumfriesshire, and W. by Peeblesshire; greatest length, NE. and SW., 28 miles; greatest breadth, NW. and SE., 17 miles; area, 164,545 acres, population 25,564. The surface, rising in a succession of verdant uplands or heath-clad hills, is from 300 to 2433 ft. above sea-level. The country in early times was covered with woods, and, known as Ettrick Forest, was long a royal hunting-ground. Selkirkshire is more pastoral than agricultural, and has a light soil on the arable land. The woollen manufacture is the great industry of Selkirk and Galashiels. The county comprises 2 parishes, with parts of 9 others, the parliamentary burgh of Selkirk and the greater part of the parliamentary burgh of Galashiels.

– John Bartholomew, *Gazetteer of the British Isles* (1887)

Halliwell's House Museum

Halliwell's Close, Market Place
Selkirk TD7 4BC
01750 20096
http://goo.gl/IMUkR6

The museum is situated in the very atmospheric Halliwell's Close. The narrow, cobbled lane with outhouses, which was formerly gas-lit and was typical of many such closes in Selkirk, has a compelling history dating back over 400 years. The museum building itself dates from the end of the 18th century and is part of what is probably the oldest surviving row of dwellings in the historic town of Selkirk.

Old Gala House Museum

Scott Crescent
Galashiels TD1 3JS
01750 720096
http://goo.gl/aYxVOF

Old Gala House is an impressive and unusual building, its history and fortunes spanning five centuries. Visitors can discover the story of Old Gala House, its inhabitants and the early development of the town of Galashiels.

Sir Walter Scott's Courtroom

Market Place
Selkirk TD7 BT
01750 20096
http://goo.gl/xw6lzP

Built in 1803 as the Sheriff Court this is where Sir Walter Scott dispensed justice to the people of Selkirkshire. Explore Scott's life, his writings and his time as Sheriff. Displays on 'The Ettrick Shepherd' James Hogg and explorer Mungo Park.

Shetland Islands

Shetland, insular county of Scotland, 50 miles NE. of Orkney, 352,876 acres, population 29,705; Mainland, population 20,821; it consists of about 100 islands, 29 of which are inhabited - Mainland, Yell, Unst, Fetlar, Whalsay, and Bressay being the largest. Mainland, comprising more than half the area of the whole group, extends N. and S. for 54 miles, and has an extreme, breadth of 21 miles, but the coast-line is so irregular and deeply indented that no spot is 4 miles from the sea. The surface of Shetland is generally bleak and moorish, and rises to a maximum altitude of 1475 ft., but only in a few places higher than 500 ft. The rock scenery around the coasts is exceedingly grand and interesting. The climate is humid and comparatively mild, but severe storms are frequent. Large numbers of cattle and sheep of native breeds are reared, and the small Shetland ponies are remarkable for their strength and hardiness. Barley, oats, turnips, and potatoes are grown. The fisheries, especially the herring fishery, are of the greatest importance, and afford the chief employment. The knitting of woollen articles is also a great industry. Shetland comprises 12 parishes.

– John Bartholomew, *Gazetteer of the British Isles* (1887)

Bayanne House

Sellafirth
Yell ZE2 9DG
01957 744219
www.bayanne.co.uk
tony.gott@mac.com

Bayanne House was originally at the centre of a small estate created in the late 18th century by the Hoseason family of Yell. Many changes in fortune and ownership have resulted in its present extent of only 4.5 acres on the shores of Basta Voe.

Bod of Gremista & Shetland Textile Working Museum

Gremista
Lerwick ZE1 0PX
01595 694 386
http://goo.gl/q7AA9m
info@shetlandmuseumandarchives.org.uk

This 18th century fishing böd was the birthplace of Arthur Anderson, co-founder of the P&O shipping company. Two rooms are restored to how they looked 200 years ago and contain displays explaining the history of the whitefish industry at that time. The rest of the building houses the Shetland Textile Working Museum, specialising in the beautiful textiles that have become synonymous with the Shetland name.

Fetlar Interpretive Centre

Beach of Houbie
Fetlar ZE2 9DJ
01957 733206
www.fetlar.com
info@fetlar.com

We are a small community-run museum on the remote island of Fetlar in Shetland where you can walk through many exhibitions on history, archaeology, folklore and wildlife.

George Waterston Memorial Centre & Museum

Auld Skoll, Utra
Fair Isle ZE2 9JU
01595 760244
http://goo.gl/Eg6QL8

George Waterston OBE (1911 1980), the former Scottish Director of the Royal Society for the Protection of Birds, was a much loved figure who had massive and positive influence on Fair Isle. He bought the island after World War II and co-founded the Bird Observatory in 1948.

Old Haa Trust

Altona
Mid Yell ZE2 9BT
01957 702252
http://goo.gl/YclRKj

Museum with local history, natural history and art and craft exhibitions, shop, garden and genealogical resources.

Scalloway Museum

Castle Street, Scalloway
Shetland ZE1 0TP
01595 880734
www.scallowaymuseum.org
curator@scallowaymuseum.org

Scalloway was once the capital of Shetland. Fishing features in the museum, yet the unique story concerns 'The Shetland Bus' – the name given to clandestine operations to and from occupied Norway during the war.

Shetland Crofthouse Museum

Voe, Boddam
Dunrossness ZE2 9JG
01950 460 557
members/south-mainland/the-croft-house-museum
info@shetlandmuseumandarchives.org.uk

Located in a delightful setting, this typical thatched crofthouse has been restored to how it would have looked in the 1870s.

Shetland Family History Society

6 Hillhead
Lerwick ZE1 0EJ
01595 692276
www.shetland-fhs.org.uk
secretary@shetland-fhs.org.uk

Shetland Family History Society brings together those studying genealogy and family history in Shetland.

Shetland Museum & Archives

Hay's Dock
Lerwick ZE1 0WP
01595 695057
www.shetlandmuseumandarchives.org.uk
info@shetlandmuseumandarchives.org.uk

Set on the waterfront within a restored 19th century dock the Shetland Museum and Archives tells Shetland's story. As well as housing the museum and archive collections there are learning and research rooms.

Tangwick Haa Museum

Eshaness ZE2 9RS
01806 503389
www.tangwickhaa.org.uk

Different aspects of life in Northmavine through the years are illustrated by using a mixture of artefacts and photographs. Part of the display has a new theme every year. An important part of the museum are its parish records and census records.

Unst Boat Haven

Haroldswick ZE2 9ED
01957 711528
www.unstheritage.com
info@unstheritage.com

The Unst Boat Haven, part of the Unst Heritage Trust, is dedicated to the maritime history of Shetland boats. We have 17 boats, mainly traditional Shetland, but also from Faroe, Norway and Wales.

Unst Heritage Centre

Haroldswick ZE2 9ED
01957 711528
www.unstheritage.com
info@unstheritage.com

Unst's permanent link to its rich history, through a fine collection of artefacts and items donated to the centre from residents past and present. These depict an island full of tradition.

451

Stirlingshire

Stirlingshire, west-midland county of Scotland; consists of a main portion and two detached sections to the NE. included in Perthshire and Clackmannanshire; is bounded N. by Perthshire, NE. by Clackmannanshire and a detached portion of Perthshire, E. by the Firth of Forth and Linlithgowshire, S. by Linlithgowshire, Lanarkshire, and detached part of Dumbartonshire, and W. by Dumbartonshire; greatest length, NW. and SE., 46 miles; greatest breadth, NE. and SW., 22 miles; area, 286,338 acres, population 112,443. The E. part of the co. is flat, finely wooded, and well cultivated; and the valley of the Forth along the N. boundary includes some of the finest land in Scotland. The middle and S. are occupied with hills and valleys - the principal ridges being the Campsie Fells and Kilsyth Hills, and the Fintry Hills and Gargunnock Hills. On the W. a long projection extends north-wards, including a mountainous district in which Ben Lomond rises to an alt. of 3192 ft., and parts of Loch Lomond and Loch Katrine. Besides the Forth, the chief streams are the Avon, Carron, Bannock, Allan, Endrick, and Blane. Coal and ironstone are extensively worked; limestone and sandstone are abundant. There are important manufactures of woollens, cotton, and iron; and there are several large chemical works and distilleries. The county comprises 21 parishes, with parts of 5 others, and the parliamentary burghs of Stirling (part of the Stirling District of Burghs) and Falkirk (part of the Falkirk District of Burghs).

– John Bartholomew, *Gazetteer of the British Isles* (1887)

Battle of Bannockburn, The

Glasgow Road
Stirling FK7 0LJ
0844 493 2139
www.battleofbannockburn.com
bannockburn@nts.org.uk

Take your place on the battlefield. Stand face-to-face with fearless medieval warriors. Witness two opposing kings – Robert the Bruce and Edward II – whose tactics in 1314 changed the path of Scotland's history, forever. Harnessing state-of-the-art 3D technology, visitors can experience medieval combat like never before to learn about this crucial event in Scottish history.

Callendar House

Callendar Park
Falkirk FK1 1YR
01324 503770
http://goo.gl/fbZe6p
callendar.house@falkirk.gov.uk

Have a grand day out at Callendar House in Falkirk. Situated in magnificent park and woodland, Callendar House tells stories of 600 years of Scottish history.

Collections: Visit our two permanent exhibitions: 'William Forbes's Falkirk', a major state of the art exhibition which will take you on a journey through time from the days of the Jacobites to the advent of the railway; and 'The Story of Callendar House' which traces the story of the house and its occupants from the 11th century to the modern day and the part they played in shaping our nation's history.

Moirlanich Longhouse

Near Killin FK21 8TS
0844 493 2136
www.nts.org.uk/Property/Moirlanich-Longhouse

Visit this perfectly preserved cruck frame cottage and get a glimpse of Scottish village life in the 19th century. Moirlanich was home to at least three generations of the Robertson family, with the last member leaving in 1968.

Museum of the Argyll & Sutherland Highlanders

Museum of the Argyll and Sutherland Highlanders, The Castle
Stirling FK8 1EH
01786 475165
www.argylls.co.uk

The museum traces the history of the 91st Argyllshire Highlanders and the 93rd Sutherland Highlanders up to the time of their amalgamation in 1881 when they became the 1st and 2nd Battalions of The Argyll and Sutherland Highlanders Regiment and thereafter to the present day.

Museum Workshop & Stores - Falkirk Museums Service

7-11 Abbotsinch, Abbotsinch Industrial Estate
Grangemouth FK3 9UX
01324 504 689
www.falkirkcommunitytrust.org/venues/museum-store
niamh.conlon@falkirk.gov.uk

The museum Workshop, located in Grangemouth, is a storage facility that cares for the 30,000 objects belonging to Falkirk Council museums. Covering 1,150 square metres of floorspace, the workshop stores everything from large objects like a 1930s tramcar and heavy machinery from Falkirk's industrial past, to much smaller items like winged insects, 1970s platform shoes and Roman archaeology.

Stirling Archives

5 Borrowmeadow Road
Stirling FK7 7UW
01786 450745
http://goo.gl/PRZcn5

Are you interested in: learning more about the past of your local area? searching for your ancestors? finding out the history of your house? If so, the Archives is the place to come.

Stirling Castle - Historic Scotland

Stirling Castle
Stirling FK8 1EJ
01786 450000
www.historic-scotland.gov.uk/places

Without doubt one of the grandest of all Scottish castles, both in its situation on a commanding rock outcrop and in its architecture. The Great Hall and the Gatehouse of James IV, the marvellous Palace of James V, the Chapel Royal of James VI and the artillery fortifications of the 16th to 18th centuries are all of outstanding interest.

Stirling Smith Art Gallery & Museum

Dumbarton Road
Stirling FK8 2RQ
01786 471917
www.smithartgalleryandmuseum.co.uk
museum@smithartgalleryandmuseum.co.uk

Founded with the Bequest of Thomas Stuart Smith (1814-1869), the Stirling Smith Art Gallery & Museum opened in 1874. Built in the Italianate style & designed by John Lessels, the museum stands within its own grounds below Stirling Castle. The Smith provides Stirling with a museum service and a focus for the historical and cultural life of its people.

Sutherland

Sutherland, maritime county in the extreme N. of Scotland; is bounded W. and N. by the Atlantic Ocean, E. by Caithness and the Moray Firth, and S. by the Dornoch Firth and Ross and Cromarty; greatest length, NW. and SE., 63 miles; greatest breadth, NE. and SW., 60 miles; area, 1,297,846 acres, population 23,370. The surface consists chiefly of mountainous moorland, varied by numerous straths or narrow valleys which open towards the sea. The highest summit is Ben More Assynt, alt. 3273 ft. The angling in the lochs and streams is good, especially for trout. The coast fisheries are considerable. The amount of arable land is comparatively very small. There are extensive deer forests, and sheep are grazed in great numbers. The county comprises 13 parishes, with part of 1 other, and the parliamentary burgh of Dornoch.

– John Bartholomew, *Gazetteer of the British Isles* (1887)

Historylinks Museum

The Meadows
Dornoch IV25 3SF
01862 811275
www.historylinks.org.uk
enquiries@historylinks.org.uk

The museum is dedicated to the history of Dornoch parish. The permanent exhibition shows the cathedral, feuding clans, the shameful burning of Scotland's last condemned witch and the treachery and violence of Picts and Vikings.

Strathnaver Museum

Clachan
Bettyhill Thurso KW14 7SS
01641 521418
www.strathnavermuseum.org.uk
info@strathnavermuseum.org.uk

Journey from Strathnaver's mystical past, through the emergence of the Clan Mackay to the tragedy of the Highland Clearances.

Timespan Heritage Centre & Art Gallery

Dunrobin Street
Helmsdale KW8 6JX
01431 821327
www.timespan.org.uk

Timespan Museum offers a journey through the colourful historical themes of the area. It provides the visitor with a wealth of information about past ways of life and some of the more turbulent events in Sutherland's history.

West Lothian

Linlithgowshire (or West Lothian), maritime county in SE. of Scotland; is bounded N. by Firth of Forth, SE. by Edinburghshire, and W. by Lanarkshire and Stirlingshire; greatest length, NE. and SW., 19 miles; greatest breadth, E. and W., 14 miles; area, 76,806 acres, population 43,510. The coast is low; the surface is varied, but there are few hills of any height; the chief rivers are the Avon on the W. and the Almond on the E. border. Much of the soil is fertile, and agriculture is in an advanced condition. Linlithgowshire is one of the richest mineral counties in Scotland, coal, shales, ironstone, freestone, limestone, &c., being very abundant. Paraffin oil is largely manufactured at Bathgate, Broxburn, and Uphall. The county contains 12 parishes, and 2 parts, and the parliamentary and royal burghs of Linlithgow (Falkirk Burghs) and Queensferry (Stirling Burghs).

– John Bartholomew, *Gazetteer of the British Isles* (1887)

Almond Valley Heritage Centre

Millfield, Livingston Village
Livingston EH54 7AR
01506 414957
www.almondvalley.co.uk
info@almondvalley.co.uk

Almond Valley welcomes you to a great family day out with friendly farm animals, green countryside, play areas and child friendly museum displays. Crawl through tunnels, hunt for fossils, explore secret works and invest your savings in Scotland's famous shale oil industry.

Annet House Museum & Garden

143 High Street
Linlithgow EH49 7EJ
01506 670677
www.annethousemuseum.org.uk
enquiries@annethousemuseum.org.uk

On the upper floor the displays tell the story of the trades of the town, which includes textiles, leatherworking, distilling and chemicals. There is a video presentation telling the process of linen manufacture, an industry once important to Linlithgow. The garden extends over three terraces behind the house. It has been developed to show the uses of the garden when Annet House was first built with examples of some of the fruits, vegetables and herbs that might have been grown.

Bennie Museum

9-11 Mansefield Street
Bathgate EH48 4HU
01506 634944
www.benniemuseum.org.uk

The Bennie Museum opened in 1989 as a museum of Bathgate's history and life. Special exhibitions are mounted on a regular basis, covering subjects as diverse as the annual Newlands Day Procession, local anniversaries, and subjects of general interest, such as toys.

Blackness Castle - Historic Scotland

Blackness Castle
nr Linlithgow EH49 7NH
01506 834807
www.historic-scotland.gov.uk/places

Built in the 15th century by one of Scotland's most powerful families, the Crichtons, Blackness was never destined as a peaceful lordly residence; its enduring roles were those of garrison fortress and state prison.

Blackridge Community Museum

Blackridge Library, Craig Inn Centre
Blackridge EH48 3RJ
01506 776 347
http://goo.gl/4gDA6A
museums@westlothian.gov.uk

A community museum housed in the stable block of an old coaching inn. Open during library times, the museum relates the story of Blackridge's coaching and travelling past.

Bo'ness & Kinneil Railway

Bo'ness Station, Union Street
Bo'ness EH51 9AQ
01506 825855
www.bkrailway.co.uk
museum@srps.org.uk

This hidden gem, only 40 minutes drive from Glasgow and Edinburgh, is located in the historic town of Bo'ness. Our friendly staff will welcome you aboard one of our heritage steam or diesel-hauled trains and wish you a pleasant journey.

Collections: The collection is representative of Scottish railways from 1870 to the present day. There are 25 steam locomotives, 23 diesel locomotives, one electric locomotive, one electric and one diesel multiple units, 67 carriages and over 100 wagons.

Cairnpapple Hill - Historic Scotland

Torphichen
Linlithgow
01506 634622
www.historic-scotland.gov.uk/places

One of the most important prehistoric monuments on the mainland of Scotland, Cairnpapple was used as a burial and ceremonial site from about 3000 to 1400 BC. Good views of east central Scotland may be had from the hill.

House of the Binns

Linlithgow EH49 7NA
0844 4932127
www.nts.org.uk/Property/House-Of-The-Binns
houseofthebinns@nts.org.uk

The House of the Binns stands as a living monument to one of Scotland's oldest families, the Dalyells, who have lived here since 1612.

Kinneil Museum

Duchess Anne Cottages, Kinneil Estate
Bo'ness EH51 0PR
01506 778530
http://goo.gl/KcRvtR
callendar.house@falkirk.gov.uk

Kinneil Museum is located in the 17th century stable block of Kinneil House and acts as an interpretative centre for Kinneil Estate. The exhibition '2000 years of history' tells the story of the park from Roman times to the present day. Antoninus Pius, St Serf, Mary, Queen of Scots and James Watt are among the many historical characters associated with the estate.

Linlithgow Palace - Historic Scotland

Linlithgow Palace
Linlithgow EH49 7AL
01506 842896
www.historic-scotland.gov.uk/places

The magnificent ruin of a great Royal Palace set in its own park and beside Linlithgow Loch. A favoured residence of the Stewart kings and queens from James I (1406-37) onward.

Linlithgow Story

Annet House, 143 High Street
Linlithgow EH49 7EJ
01506 670677
www.linlithgowstory.org.uk
enquiries@linlithgowstory.fsnet.co.uk

Pleasure palace of the royal Stewarts. The majestic royal palace of the Stewarts at Linlithgow today lies roofless and ruined. Yet the visitor still feels a sense of awe on entering its gates.

Collections: The collection is representative principally of the social history of the town with photographs and objects largely from the 19th and early 20th century.

Queensferry Museum

53 High Street
South Queensferry EH30 9HP
0131 529 4139
www.cac.org.uk/venues/queensmuse.htm

Situated in the historic former royal burgh of Queensferry, the museum commands magnificent views of the two great bridges spanning the Forth. Its collections trace the history of the people of Queensferry and Dalmeny, the historic ferry passage to Fife, the building of the road and rail bridges, and the wildlife of the Forth estuary.

West Lothian Archives

Archives and Records Centre, 9 Dunlop Square, Deans Industrial Estate
Livingston EH54 8SB
01506 773770
www.westlothian.gov.uk/article/2052/Archives

West Lothian Council Archives and Records Centre preserves and makes accessible records relating to the history of West Lothian.

West Lothian Local History Library

Heritage and Information Centre, County Buildings, High St
Linlithgow EH49 7EZ
01506 282491
http://goo.gl/QNDMwJ

For information on West Lothian's history or heritage, visit the West Lothian Local History Library. The library holds tens of thousands of items relating to every aspect of West Lothian and its heritage.

Whitburn Community Museum

Whitburn Library, Union Road
Whitburn EH47 0AR
01506 776 347
http://goo.gl/4QS6sX
museums@westlothian.gov.uk

The history of Whitburn and its coal mining past are recreated in a permanent exhibition that can be accessed through the library. Temporary exhibitions are also held throughout the year.

WALES

National

Association of Family History Societies of Wales

c/o Menna Evans, Adran Casgliadau, National Library of Wales

Aberystwyth SY25 3BU

www.fhswales.org.uk

secretary@fhswales.info

The association was formed in 1981 as a grouping of the family history societies which then existed within Wales. Its constitution states that its Aims and Objectives are: to promote the study of family history and genealogy of Wales; to co-ordinate and support the activities of the family history societies in Wales; to promote and secure publication of material of particular interest and usefulness to family historians researching Welsh ancestry; to liaise with its affiliate members and other appropriate bodies in order to represent the interests and needs of its member societies.

Big Pit: National Coal Museum

Big Pit: National Coal Museum

Blaenafon NP4 9XP

01495 790 311

www.museumwales.ac.uk

bigpit@museumwales.ac.uk

Big Pit is a real colliery. It was the place of work for hundreds of men, women and children for over 200 years - a daily struggle to extract that precious mineral that stoked the furnaces and lit the household fires of the world.

Black History Association Wales

4 Dock Chambers, Bute Street

Cardiff CF10 5EQ

02920 256757

www.bhmwales.org.uk

coordinator@bhmwales.org.uk

BHAW aims to be the 'go to hub' for black history information, raising awareness of black history in Wales, establishing a sustainable education programme and training the trainers and facilitators across Wales to confidently deliver black history modules as part of the national curriculum all year round.

CyMAL: Museums Archives & Libraries Wales

Welsh Assembly Government, Rhodfa Padarn

Aberystwyth SY23 3UR

0300 062 2112

www.cymru.gov.uk/cymal

cymal@wales.gsi.gov.uk

CyMAL: Museums Archives and Libraries Wales (CyMAL)

represents a significant investment by the Welsh Government in the development of local museums, archives and libraries services which meet 21st century needs.

MOMA Wales

Y Tabernacl, Heol Penrallt

Machynlleth SY20 8AJ

01654 703355

www.momawales.org.uk

info@momawales.org.uk

The museum of Modern Art, Wales (MOMA WALES) has grown up alongside The Tabernacle, a former Wesleyan chapel which in 1986 reopened as a centre for the performing arts. MOMA WALES has six beautiful exhibition spaces which house, throughout the year, modern Welsh art, The Tabernacle Collection and The Brotherhood of Ruralists.

National Cycle Collection

The Automobile Palace, Temple Street

Llandrindod Wells LD1 5DL

01597 825531

www.cyclemuseum.org.uk

cycle.museum@care4free.net

How big is a Penny Farthing's wheel? And just how uncomfortable were those early bikes compared with today's hi-tec versions? Journey through the lanes of cycle history and see bicycles from 1819, such as the Hobby Horse, Boneshakers and Penny Farthings up to the most modern Raleigh cycles of today. See historic shop replicas including early lamp collections.

National Library of Wales / Llyfrgell Genedlaethol Cymru

National Library

Aberystwyth SY23 3BU

01970 632 800

www.llgc.org.uk

The National Library of Wales is one of the great libraries of the world. Its home is in the seaside town of Aberystwyth in Ceredigion.

Collections: As a Legal Deposit Library The National Library of Wales has a legal right to all UK publications. Its collections include ancient Welsh and Celtic manuscripts and items of particular interest to Wales and the Celtic nations.

National Museum Cardiff

Cathays Park
Cardiff CF10 3NP
029 20397951
www.museumwales.ac.uk/en/cardiff
post@amgueddfacymru.ac.uk

Discover art, archaeology, natural history and geology. With a busy programme of exhibitions and events, we have something to amaze everyone, whatever your interest – and admission is free.

Collections: The Welsh national archaeology, art, geology, botany and zoology collections. Highlights include one of the finest Impressionist art collections in Europe and the 'Evolution of Wales' exhibition - the history of Wales from the Big Bang until today, complete with dinosaurs and woolly mammoth.

National Museums & Galleries of Wales

Cathays Park
Cardiff CF1 3NP
029 2039 7951
www.nmgw.ac.uk
post@nmgw.ac.uk

Through our outstanding collections, curatorial excellence and learning expertise, Amgueddfa Cymru – National Museum Wales is ideally placed to strengthen tolerance, citizenship and mutual respect for the diverse communities of Wales and the world.

National Roman Legion Museum

High Street
Caerleon NP18 1AE
01633 423 134
www.museumwales.ac.uk/en/roman
post@nmgw.ac.uk

Almost 2000 years ago, the Roman Empire dominated the civilised world. Britain was its furthest outpost and, in AD 75, a fortress was founded at Caerleon which would guard the region for over 200 years.

National Screen & Sound Archive of Wales

The National Library of Wales
Aberystwyth SY23 3BU
01970 632828
www.screenandsound.llgc.org.uk
agssc@llgc.org.uk

The National Screen and Sound Archive of Wales is home to a comprehensive and unequalled collection of films, television programmes, videos, sound recordings and music relating to Wales and the Welsh. The National Screen and Sound Archive of Wales is responsible for safeguarding and celebrating Wales' rich audio-visual heritage.

National Slate Museum

Welsh Slate Museum, Padarn Country Park
Llanberis LL55 4TY
01286 870630
www.nmgw.ac.uk
slate@museumwales.ac.uk

The museum building is sited in the Victorian workshops built in the shadow of Elidir mountain, site of the vast Dinorwig quarry. Not so much a museum as a pocket of history, it is as though the quarrymen and engineers put down their tools and left the courtyard for home, just hours before. Civilised close-up exploration of the largest working waterwheel in mainland Britain. Slate-splitting demonstrations by hand-craftsmen revealing the skills and artistry of generations of quarry workers. The perilous ups and downs of a 19th century incline plane, a unique restoration of the machinery which transported slate.

National Waterfront Museum

Oystermouth Road, Maritime Quarter
Swansea SA1 3RD
02920 573600
www.museumwales.ac.uk/en/swansea
waterfront@museumwales.ac.uk

The National Waterfront Museum tells the story of industry and innovation in Wales, now and over the last 300 years. The Industrial Revolution in Wales had a tremendous effect on People, Communities and Lives as well as that of the rest of the World. Visitors can soak up the history with a breathtaking mix of old and new in the city's rapidly developing maritime quarter.

National Wool Museum

Dre-fach Felindre
Llandysul SA44 5UP
01559 370929
www.museumwales.ac.uk/en/wool
post@nmgw.ac.uk

Wool was historically the most important and widespread of Wales' industries. The picturesque village of Dre-fach Felindre in the beautiful Teifi valley was once the centre of a thriving woollen industry earning the nickname 'The Huddersfield of Wales'.

St Fagans: National History Museum

Cardiff CF5 6XB
029 2057 3500
www.museumwales.ac.uk/en/stfagans
post@museumwales.ac.uk

One of Europe's biggest and most exciting open-air museums. Here you will find centuries of Welsh social history gathered together in 100 acres of beautiful countryside.

Anglesey

Anglesey – an insular county of N. Wales, separated from the mainland by the Menai Strait, over which a suspension bridge was thrown in 1826, and a tubular railway bridge in 1850. The island is about 20 miles long, 16 broad, and 76 in circumference, and is the only county in Wales that is not mountainous. Area, 193,511 acres: population 51,416. The soil is moderately fertile. The rearing of cattle is one of the chief occupations. A considerable trade is also carried on in butter, cheese, hides, honey, wax, and tallow. It contains valuable minerals, and furnishes copper, lead, silver, marble, limestone, coal, and marl. The chief copper mines are at Parys. There are no important manufactures. The Chester and Holyhead Railway, a part of the main route between London and Dublin, traverses the S. of the county for 23 miles. The distance from Holyhead to Dublin is about 60 miles. Anglesey is generally believed to have been the chief seat of the Druids of the ancient Britons. It was called Mona by the Romans, and Anglesey, or Angle's Eye (that is, island) by the Saxons. Anglesey comprises 6 hundreds, 77 parishes, the municipal borough of Beaumaris, and the towns of Amlwch, Holyhead, and Llangefni. It is in the diocese of Bangor.

– John Bartholomew, *Gazetteer of the British Isles* (1887)

Anglesey Archives Service

Industrial Estate Road, Bryn Cefni Industrial Estate
Llangefni LL77 7JA
01248 751930
www.anglesey.gov.uk/leisure/records-and-archives
archives@anglesey.gov.uk

Anglesey Archives collects and preserve historical documents relating to the island of Anglesey and makes them available to anyone who wishes to use them. The Anglesey Archives Service operates a booking system.

Beaumaris Castle

Castle Street
Beaumaris LL58 8AP
01248 810361
www.beaumaris.com

Beaumaris Castle on the Island of Anglesey is the great unfinished masterpiece. It was built as one of the 'iron ring' of North Wales castles by the English monarch Edward I, to stamp his authority on the Welsh.

Beaumaris Gaol & Courthouse Museum

Steeple Lane
Beaumaris LL58 8EP
01248 724444
http://goo.gl/Yd7qHz

This Victorian Gaol was built by Hansom (famous for the Hansom Cab) in 1829. The gaol features the only original tread wheel in situ in Britain, and a gibbet is still fixed to the outer wall. Beaumaris Gaol will live in your memory for a long time.

Haulfre Stables

Haulfre Garden Unit
Llangoed LL58 8RY
01248 490709
http://goo.gl/7SWQ52

This modest, but fascinating small equestrian museum and restored stables has an interesting collection of Victorian harness and saddlery, carts and carriages and other equestrian and transport material, housed in an historic stable block. The equipment on display dates from an earlier age when horses were vital for transport, agriculture and haulage of heavy goods. Haulfre was the country house of the Chadwick family.

Holyhead Maritime Museum

🖼️ £

Newry Beach, Beach Road
Holyhead LL65 1YD
01407 769745
www.holyheadmaritimemuseum.co.uk
maritimemuseumholyhead@gmail.com

The museum is a fascinating experience for the whole family. Step back in time at the oldest lifeboat station in Wales.

Llynnon Mill

🖼️ £

Llanddeusant
Holyhead LL65 4AB
01407 730797
http://goo.gl/cLH4sk

The only working windmill in Wales. Operates as an agricultural museum, and produces stoneground wholemeal flour using organic wheat. There are also two roundhouses, 10m in diameter, built from timber with wattle and daub walls and a thatched roof - providing a unique insight of the life of Iron Age farmers over 3000 years ago.

Moelfre RNLI Seawatch

🖼️ 🖼️ ★

R.N.L.I. Gwylfan Moelfre Seawatch Centre
Moelfre LL728HY
01248 850976
http://goo.gl/l1cVYY
elizabeth.hampson@tiscali.co.uk

We have an Oakley Lifeboat inside the building and loads of history about the Moelfre Lifeboat and ship wrecks that are local to the village.

Oriel Ynys Môn

🖼️ ★

Rhosmeirch
Llangefni LL77 7TQ
01248 724 444

As a purpose built museum, arts and events gallery, Oriel Ynys Môn has so much to offer. Visitors who wish to learn about the cultural history of Anglesey can enjoy the centre's atmospheric Heritage Gallery which presents a vivid account of the island's past through sound, imagery, reconstructions and real artefacts.

Swtan Heritage Museum

🖼️ £

Dilwyn, Church bay, Holyhead
Anglesey LL65 4EY
01407 730186
www.swtan.co.uk
swtan@hotmail.co.uk

Swtan is a fully restored 17th century thatched cottage, situated in the scenic coastal AONB of Porth Swtan (Church bay). It is presented to tell the story of rural Welsh life circa 1900.

Brecknockshire

Brecknockshire, or Brecon, an inland county of S. Wales, bounded N. by Radnorshire, E. by Herefordshire and Monmouthshire, S. by Monmouthshire and Glamorgan, and W. by Carmarthenshire and Cardiganshire; greatest length, N. and S., 38 miles; greatest breadth, E. and W., 33 miles; area, 460,158 acres, population 57,746. Brecknockshire is one of the most mountainous of the Welsh counties, abounding in grand and picturesque scenery. A range of mountains, running E. and W., culminates about 4 miles S. of the centre of the county in the Van or Beacon (2862 ft.), the highest summit of South Wales; its rocks belong to the old red sandstone or Devonian system. Part of the S. lies within the great Welsh coal-field, where ironstone is also abundant; limestone occurs in the W. Less than one-half of the surface is under cultivation, and the mountain land is generally bare. The river Wye traces nearly the whole of the N. boundary, and the Usk flows in an easterly direction through the central valley. There are manufactures of coarse woollens and worsted hosiery. The Brecon Canal, 33 miles long, extends to the Monmouth Canal at Pontypool. The county comprises 6 hundreds, 91 parishes, with part of one other, and the municipal borough of Brecknock. It is mostly in the diocese of St David's.

– John Bartholomew, *Gazetteer of the British Isles* (1887)

Brecknock Museum & Art Gallery

Captain's Walk
Brecon LD3 7DW
01874 624121
www.powys.gov.uk/brecknockmuseum
brecknock.museum@powys.gov.uk

Brecknock Museum & Art Gallery is funded and administered by Powys County Council. First established in 1928 by the Brecknock Society, it occupies an historic building at the heart of an outstandingly attractive area with a rich and varied past.

Powys Family History Society

13 Swan Court, Woodchurch Road, Prenton
Birkenhead CH43 0RX
07977 631 132
www.powysfhs.org.uk
helen.brick1@virgin.net

The Powys Family History Society was formed in 1980, is a member of the Federation of Family History Societies, the Association of Family History Societies of Wales and Capel, the Welsh Chapels heritage society.

Howell Harris Museum

Coleg Trefeca, Trefeca
Brecon LD3 0PP
01874 711423
www.trefeca.org.uk
post@trefeca.org.uk

This small museum depicts the life and work of Howell Harris, the first Methodist (converted 1735) and the self-sufficient Christian community (Teulu Trefeca - the Trefeca family) founded on the site in 1752.

Collections: Furniture, scientific instruments and books made, adapted or used on the site; a scene of Howell Harris preaching; information about the 18th century Methodist revival and the subsequent development of Trefeca.

Regimental Museum of The Royal Welsh, The

The Barracks
Brecon LD3 7EB
01874 613310
www.royalwelsh.org.uk
info@royalwelsh.org.uk

The museum tells the fascinating story of four of the British army's most famous regiments. This long history, dating back to the 1680s, is told through many kinds of objects including uniforms, medals, weapons and models.

Tretower

Crickhowel NP8 1RD
01874 730279
http://goo.gl/UDJfic
tretowercourt@wales.gsi.gov.uk

For over 900 years Tretower Court and Castle have been altered, adjusted and adapted to keep up with the style and tastes of the time. Now you can see what the kitchen and great hall may have looked like around 1470.

Caernarfonshire

Carnarvonshire, a maritime county of North Wales, having the Irish Sea on the N., Denbighshire on the E., Merioneth and Cardigan Bay on the S., and on the W. Carnarvon Bay and the Menai Strait, which separates it from Anglesey; extreme length, NE. and SW., 53 miles; extreme breadth, NW. and SE., 23 miles; average breadth, 9 miles; coast-line, 95 miles; area, 369,477 acres; population 119,349. The surface is grandly mountainous. About the centre of the county rises Snowdon (3571 ft.), the loftiest mountain in Wales and England. Several other summits are from 1500 to 3000 ft. high. There are fine sea-views along the N. coast, while the interior abounds in grand lake and mountain scenery. A bleak upland peninsula extends from the Snowdon group about 20 miles to the SW., terminating in the prom. of Braich-y-Pwll, off which is Bardsey island. The river Conway flows N. along the E. boundary. The soil in the valleys and along the N. and S. coasts is productive of good crops of oats and barley. Slate is extensively quarried at Penrhyn, Llanberis, and Bethesda. The county comprises 10 hundreds, 74 parishes, with part of 1 other, the Carnarvon Boroughs (Bangor, Carnarvon, Conway, Criccieth, Nevin, and Pwllheli), and the municipal boroughs of Carnarvon, Conway, and Pwllheli. It is in the dioceses of St Asaph and Bangor.

– John Bartholomew, *Gazetteer of the British Isles* (1887)

Bangor Cathedral

The Diocesan Centre, Cathedral Close
Bangor LL57 1RL
www.facebook.com/bangorcathedral
comms@bangorcathedral.org.uk

The site of the present building of Bangor Cathedral has been in use as a place of Christian worship since the 6th century. The cathedral is built on a low-lying and inconspicuous site, possibly so as not to attract the attention of Viking raiders from the sea.

Caernarfon Castle

Castle Ditch
Caernarfon LL55 2AY
01286 677617
www.cadw.wales.gov.uk/default.asp?id=6&PlaceID=19
caernarfoncastle@Wales.gsi.gov.uk

With its seven polygonal towers (including the great Eagle Tower), two gatehouses, and walls of colour-banded stone, King Edward I intended the castle to be a royal residence and seat of government for north Wales. Begun in 1283 under the direction of Master James of St George, the King's mason-architect, and continuously in Crown possession since.

Conwy Castle

Rose Hill Street
Conwy LL32 8LD
01492 592358
www.conwy.com

Conwy castle is a gritty, dark stoned fortress which has the rare ability to evoke an authentic medieval atmosphere. Conwy was constructed by the English monarch Edward I between 1283 and 1289 as one of the key fortresses in his 'iron ring' of castles to contain the Welsh.

Criccieth Castle

Castle Street
Criccieth LL52 0DP
01766 522227
www.cadw.wales.gov.uk/daysout/criccieth-castle
cricciethcastle@wales.gsi.gov.uk

Beguiling from afar, this castle is perched on a headland with the sea pounding below. Get close however and its gatehouse intimidates prospective attackers.

Dinorwic Quarry & Quarry Hospital

Gilfach Ddu
Llanberis LL55 4TY
01286 870 892
http://goo.gl/S4yDo7

Covering more than 700 acres, Dinorwic was one of the largest slate quarries in the world. One of its inclines has now been restored to pristine working condition. Since 1972 Dinorwic has been home to the National Slate Museum, Llanberis. The Vivian Slate Quarry is now home to a rock-climbing and diving centre, but visitors today may still see the huts or gwaliau (literally 'lairs') where blocks of slate were split and dressed. Another site of interest is the old Quarry Hospital, built in 1860 to offer quarrymen medical care. Now open to the public, it features a display of the innovative equipment used there, including amputation tools and an X-ray machine.

Ffestiniog & Welsh Highland Railways

Harbour Station
Porthmadog LL49 9NF
01766 516024
www.festrail.co.uk
info@festrail.co.uk

The Ffestiniog Railway is the oldest independent railway company in the world. On our trains you can travel by steam through the spectacular scenery of the Snowdonia National Park, between Porthmadog and Blaenau Ffestiniog.

Ffestiniog Railway Museum

Harbour Station
Porthmadog LL49 9NF
01776 512 340
www.festrail.co.uk
enquiries@festrail.co.uk

A bustling and busy narrow gauge slate-carrying railway between Portmadoc and Blaenau Ffestiniog that pioneered narrow gauge steam and passenger services in the 19th. century and demonstrated the utility of such railways to the world.

Great Orme Bronze Age Copper Mines

Great Orme
Llandudno LL30 2XG
01492 870447
www.greatormemines.info
info@gomines.co.uk

Uncovered in 1987 during a scheme to landscape an area of the Great Orme, the copper mines discovered below the ground represent one of the most astounding archaeological discoveries of recent times. Dating back 4,000 years to the Bronze Age, they change our views about the ancient people of Britain and their civilized and structured society 2,000 years before the Roman invasion. Over the past 21 years mining engineers, cavers and archaeologists have been slowly uncovering more tunnels and large areas of the surface landscape to reveal what is now thought to be the largest prehistoric mine so far discovered in the world.

Gwynedd Archives

Caernarfon Record Office, Swyddfa'r Cyngor
Caernarfon LL55 1SH
01286 679095
www.gwynedd.gov.uk/archives

Gwynedd Archives Service welcomes the public to visit its Record Offices to use and enjoy the wide range of documents, photographs, maps and newspapers that are kept. .

Gwynedd Family History Society

12 Long Street, Gerlan
Bangor LL57 3SY
01248 600 102
www.gwyneddfhs.org
david.roberts10@homecall.co.uk

The society was founded in 1980 to bring together the many people interested in Family History. It caters for those with Gwynedd ancestry and we would be happy to help anyone in need of assistance with their research.

Gwynedd Museum & Art Gallery

Ffordd Gwynedd
Bangor LL57 1DT
01248 353368
www.gwynedd.gov.uk/museums
gwyneddmuseum@gwynedd.gov.uk

Gwynedd Museum & Art Gallery boasts a collection formed since 1884 by Bangor University. Now run by Gwynedd Council, the museum and Gallery is located near the cathedral in a Grade II listed building that was the Old Canonry dating to the 1870s.

Llandudno Museum

Llandudno Museum, 17-19 Gloddaeth Street
Llandudno LL30 2DD
01492 876517
www.conwy.gov.uk/doc.asp?cat=776&doc=1582
llandudno.museum@lineone.net

Llandudno Museum was established in 1927 following the bequest of FE Chardon (an artist) to the town of his magnificent collection of paintings and objets d'art from around the world.

Lloyd George Museum & Highgate Cottage

Llanystumdwy
Criccieth LL52 0SH
01766 522 071
www.gwynedd.gov.uk/museums
amgueddfeydd-museums@gwynedd.gov.uk

The Lloyd George Museum portrays the life and times of David Lloyd George, Britain's first modern Prime Minister, who led the country during the First World War. A visit to Highgate, the Victorian cottage where he spent his childhood, is included which features a Victorian garden and shoemaker's workshop.

Llyn Historical & Maritime Museum

Old St Mary's Church, Stryd Llan
Nefyn LL53 6LB
01758 720 270.
www.penllyn.com/1/gallery/nefyn/2a.html

Learn about maritime history at the Llyn Historical and Maritime Museum. It is located at St Mary's Church, Nefyn, whose tower supports a sailing ship weathervane. Through painting, photographs and artefacts is shown the local maritime history including ship building, coasting vessels, herring industry and also everyday life at the turn of the 19th century.

Nant Gwrtheyrn

Canolfan Iaith Genedlaethol, Nant Gwrtheyrn, Llithfaen
Pwllheli LL53 6PA

01758 750334

www.nantgwrtheyrn.org

This museum is based at the heart of the community. It brings together a collection of maps, documents and artefacts from across the region and has placed them in such an order as to be able to concisely tell the story of the foundations of the community.

Penmaenmawr Museum

4, New York Cottages
Penmaenmawr LL34 6LE

01492 575571

www.conwy.gov.uk/doc.asp?cat=776&doc=1584

Built in the 1840s these were amongst the first properties built in Penmaenmawr to house quarry workers. Recently restored, the ground floor of No. 4 houses a small museum on the quarrying industry and the growth of Penmaenmawr in the 19th century.

Penrhyn Castle - National Trust

Penrhyn Castle
Bangor LL57 4HN

01248 353 084

www.nationaltrust.org.uk/penrhyn-castle

penrhyncastle@nationaltrust.org.uk

This enormous neo-Norman castle sits between Snowdonia and the Menai Strait. Built by Thomas Hopper between 1820 and 1845 for the wealthy Pennant family, who made their fortune from Jamaican sugar and Welsh slate, the castle is crammed with fascinating things such as a one-ton slate bed made for Queen Victoria.

Plas yn Rhiw - National trust

Rhiw
Pwllheli LL53 8AB

01758 780219

www.nationaltrust.org.uk/plas-yn-rhiw

plasynrhiw@nationaltrust.org.uk

The house was rescued from neglect and lovingly restored by the three Keating sisters, who bought it in 1938. The views from the grounds and gardens across Cardigan Bay are among the most spectacular in Britain. The house is 16th-century with Georgian additions, and the garden contains many beautiful flowering trees and shrubs, with beds framed by box hedges and grass paths.

Porthmadog Maritime Museum

Oakley Wharf No.1, The Harbour
Porthmadog LL49 9LU

www.porthmadog.org.uk.

Discover the story of the world famous topsail schooners and other vessels, their builders, voyages and the men who sailed in them.

Royal Welch Fusiliers Regimental Museum

Caernarfon Castle
Caernarfon LL55 2AY

01286 673362

www.rwfmuseum.org.uk

rwfmuseum1@btconnect.com

The museum, situated within two towers of Caernarfon Castle, tells the exciting story of over 300 years of our history using film, sound, models and exhibits. You can learn how the regiment won 14 Victoria Crosses and hear the words of famous writers who served with the Royal Welch during the First World War, such as Siegfried Sassoon, Robert Graves, David Jones, Frank Richards and Hedd Wyn.

Segontium - National Trust

Beddgelert Road
Caernarfon LL55 2LN

01286 675625

www.nationaltrust.org.uk/segontium

mus@segontium.org.uk

The Segontium Roman fort was an auxiliary fort built by the Romans when they spread their conquest of Britain into Wales, and dates back to 77 AD. Although it was a remote outpost, it is one of the most well known Roman sites in Britain and attracts thousands of visitors each year.

Welsh Highland Heritage Railway

Welsh Highland Railway Ltd, Gelert's Farm Works, Madoc Street West
Porthmadog LL49 9DY

01766 513402

www.whr.co.uk

info@whr.co.uk

The Welsh Highland Heritage Railway is a small, friendly railway where the train ride is just part of the experience. Our vintage train also stops at the sheds, where you can get off for a free guided, hands on tour.

Cardiff

Cardiff, municipal and parliamentary borough, seaport, and county town of Glamorgan, at the mouth of the river Taff and on the estuary of the Severn 29 miles W. of Bristol by water and 170 miles W. of London by rail – parliamentary and municipal borough, population 82,761. In 1801 the population was only 1018; in 1841 it was 10,077; and 59,494 in 1871. The rapid prosperity of the town is due to the abundance of minerals in the district. Its exports of coal and iron from the valleys of Taff, Rhymney, &c., are among the most important in the kingdom. The docks have become very extensive, and a tidal harbour and low-water pier have been constructed. There are also very large iron foundries, tin-plate works, and iron-shipbuilding yards. The South Wales University College was opened at Cardiff in 1883. Cardiff Castle, originally founded in 1080, is the property of the Marquis of Bute, who has converted part of it into a modern seat. On the pier-head, Bute Dock, is a lighthouse, with fixed light (Cardiff) seen 10 miles.

– John Bartholomew, *Gazetteer of the British Isles* (1887)
[Note: Cardiff only became capital of Wales in 1955.]

Butetown History & Arts Centre

5 Dock Chambers, Bute Street (opposite the Baltimore Arms), Cardiff Bay
Cardiff CF10 5AG
029 2025 6757
bhac.org.c31.sitepreviewer.com
info@bhac.org

BHAC collects, preserves and presents the lived history of old Cardiff Bay. The exhibits, books and other materials that we produce draw on the photographs, documents and memories of local people.

Cardiff Castle

Castle Street
Cardiff CF10 3RB
029 2087 8100
www.cardiffcastle.com
cardiffcastle@cardiff.gov.uk

Cardiff Castle is situated in the heart of the capital. The castle's enchanting fairytale towers conceal an elaborate and splendid interior.

Cardiff Story, The

The Cardiff Story, The Old Library, Trinity Street,CF10 1BH
029 2078 8334
www.cardiffstory.com
cardiffstory@cardiff.gov.uk

In our fun, free and interactive galleries, discover how Cardiff was transformed from the small market town of the 1300s, to one of the world's biggest ports in the 1900s, to the cool, cosmopolitan capital we know today. The museum, in the beautiful and historic Old Library building, is rich in stories, objects, photographs and film telling the history of Cardiff through the eyes of those who created the city – its people.

Firing Line: The Cardiff Castle Museum of the Welsh Soldier

The Interpretation Centre, Cardiff Castle, Cardiff
Cardiff CF10 3RB
029 20 873 623
www.cardiffcastlemuseum.org.uk
admin@cardiffcastlemuseum.org.uk

The museum is housed within the fully accessible Interpretation Centre of Cardiff Castle and tells the story of the Welsh Soldier through the history of two of Wales' oldest and most distinguished regiments, 1st The Queen's Dragoon Guards and The Royal Welsh.

Cardiganshire

Cardiganshire, a maritime county of S. Wales, bounded on the W. by Cardigan Bay, and landward from N. to S. by the cos. of Merioneth, Montgomery, Radnor, Brecknock, Carmarthen, and Pembroke. Its seaboard is in the form of a crescent; coast line, 48 miles; extreme breadth, 22 miles; area, 443,387 acres; population 70,270. Rugged mountains and deep valleys occur in the N. and E. of the county. The summit of Plinlimmon, on the border of Montgomeryshire, has an altitude of 2469 ft. In the SW. the surface is less elevated. The largest streams are the Teifi, Aeron, and Ystwith. The prevailing rocks of the mountains are clay-slate and shale. The soil is either peaty or a sandy loam. The principal crops are oats and barley. Cattle and sheep are reared in great numbers. Lead ore is worked. The co. comprises 5 hundreds, 97 parishes, the municipal borough of Aberystwith, and the greater part of the municipal borough of Cardigan. It is entirely in the diocese of St David's.

– John Bartholomew, *Gazetteer of the British Isles* (1887)

Aberystwyth Castle

Aberystwyth SY23 2AG
www.discoverceredigion.co.uk/Pages/Splash.aspx

In the marvellous sweep of Cardigan Bay stand the ruins of one of Edward I's late 13th century castles. Of the seven major English strongholds he established in Wales, Aberystwyth has fared least favourably in the survival stakes.

Aberystwyth University School of Art Gallery & Museum

Aberystwyth University, School of Art, Buarth Mawr
Aberystwyth SY23 1NG
01970 622 460
www.aber.ac.uk/museum
museum@aber.ac.uk

The School of Art promotes its art collection as a public resource. It offers primary research material for public reference and in its galleries a regular programme of public exhibitions.

Collections: Our superb collection of 20th century British ceramics from pioneer studio pottery to contemporary, together with Welsh slipware and porcelain, is housed and displayed in the Ceramics Gallery at Aberystwyth Arts Centre on the University campus. The School of Art houses other ceramic collections that are available for study by appointment, most notably 18th-century British Delft, Art Pottery, and Japanese ceramics that include Satsuma and Bizenware.

Cardiganshire Family History Society

c/o Menna Evans, Adran Casgliadau, National Library of Wales
Aberystwyth SY25 3BU
www.cgnfhs.org.uk
ymholiadau@cgnfhs.org.uk

Cardiganshire Family History Society was formed in 1995 to encourage the study of genealogy and family history in Cardiganshire by those having family connections with the county wherever they may live.

Ceramic Collection & Archive, Aberystwyth University

School of Art, Buarth Mawr, Aberystwyth
Aberystwyth SY23 1NG
01970 622 192
www.ceramics-aberystwyth.com
contact@ceramics-aberystwyth.com

The ceramic collection was started in the early 20th century and revived in the 1970s. The gallery houses a seminal collection of studio pottery.

Ceredigion Archives

School of Art crest

County Offices, Marine Terrace
Aberystwyth SY23 2DE
01970 633697
www.archifdy-ceredigion.org.uk

Ceredigion Archives is the record office for the county formerly known as Cardiganshire or (in Welsh) Sir Aberteifi. We collect and preserve documents about the history of Cardiganshire and make them available for research.

Ceredigion Museum

Terrace Road
Aberystwyth SY23 2AQ
01970 633088
www.ceredigion.gov.uk/index.cfm?articleid=197
museum@ceredigion.gov.uk

Ceredigion Museum is housed in a restored Edwardian Theatre. It has been described as 'one of the most beautiful museum interiors in Britain'.

Collections: The museum displays objects of all ages from the county of Ceredigion (Cardiganshire). Most of the displays are of the Victorian period and later.

Cilgerran Castle

Cilgerran
Cardigan SA43 3SF
01239 621339
www.cadw.wales.gov.uk/daysout/cilgerran-castle
catherine.collins@wales.gsi.gov.uk

Perched on the edge of a steep gorge above the river Teifi, the Normans first built and earth-and-timber castle here around 900 years ago. Lost and won several times over, it was the Marshal family, earls of Pembroke, who raised the imposing stone castle seen today.

Internal Fire, Museum of Power

Castell Pridd
Tanygroes SA43 2JS
01239 811212
www.internalfire.com
paul@semidiesel.com

The museum is dedicated to the history of the internal combustion engine in industry over the last 100 years and aims to display all exhibits in working order. The displays change on a yearly basis and the museum now runs over twenty engines on a daily basis throughout the summer.

Collections: The collection covers early oil engines through to gas turbines but with the emphasis on diesel power from the 1920s to the 1960s.

Llanerchaeron - National Trust

Ciliau Aeron
near Aberaeron SA48 8DG
01545 570200
www.nationaltrust.org.uk/llanerchaeron
llanerchaeron@nationaltrust.org.uk

This rare example of a self-sufficient 18th-century Welsh minor gentry estate has survived virtually unaltered. The villa, designed in the 1790s, is the most complete example of the early work of John Nash. It has its own service courtyard with dairy, laundry, brewery and salting house, and walled kitchen gardens (with all its produce for sale when in season).

Llywernog Silver-lead Mine Museum, The

Ponterwyd
Aberystwyth SY23 3AB
01970 890 620
www.silvermountainexperience.co.uk
silverrivermine@aol.com

A restored water-powered silver-lead mine dating from the 18th and 19th centuries. A seven-acre site with working machinery and underground mine tours.

Strata Florida

Pontrhydfendigaid SY25 6ES
01974 831261
http://goo.gl/n4ioCd

This most remote and tranquil abbey was home to Welsh literature and learning for almost 400 years.

University of Wales Trinity Saint David: Roderic Bowen Library & Archive

Roderic Bowen Library and Archives, University of Wales Trinity Saint David, College Street
Lampeter SA48 7ED
01570 424716
www.uwtsd.ac.uk/rbla
rodericbowenlibrary@tsd.uwtsd.ac.uk

The Roderic Bowen Library & Archives, RBLA, houses the Special Collections of the University of Wales Trinity Saint David, the University's oldest printed books, manuscripts and archives and is one of the principal resources for academic research in Wales. Acquired over the last 200 years, largely by bequest and donation, the Special Collections include over 35,000 printed works, 8 medieval manuscripts, around 100 post medieval manuscripts, and 69 incunabula. Material from the Archives includes the early student registers and photographs from the mid 19th century onwards.

Welsh Quilt Centre, The

High Street
Lampeter SA48 7BB
01570 422088
www.welshquilts.com
quilts@jen-jones.com

This is the venue to see, enjoy and participate in Wales' rich quilt making heritage. The centre includes an annual quilt exhibition, gallery shop and workshops.

Carmarthenshire

Carmarthenshire, a maritime county of S. Wales, and the largest of all the Welsh counties; is bounded N. by Cardiganshire, E. by Brecknockshire and Glamorgan, S. by the Bristol Channel, and W. by Pembrokeshire; greatest length, NE. and SW., 50 miles; greatest breadth, E. and W., 42 miles; the coast, which is marshy, measures about 35 miles; area, 594,405 acres; population 124,864. The surface generally is upland or mountainous, much of it being waste. The Black Mountains rise on the NE. border, the chief summit, Carmarthen Van, having an altitude of 2596 ft. The vale of the river Towy extends in length about 30 miles NE. and SW. through the middle of the county. The uplands consist chiefly of slate or limestone; old red sandstone occurs about the estuary of the Towy; coal and ironstone are worked in the SE. Good crops of oats, barley, and wheat are produced in the valleys, but the principal industry is stock-raising. The fisheries are of some importance. The county comprises 5 hundreds, 3 commots [a secular division of land in mediaeval Wales], 81 parishes, with part of 1 other, the Carmarthen Boroughs (Carmarthen and Llanelly), and the municipal boroughs of Carmarthen and Llandovery. It is entirely in the diocese of St David's.

– John Bartholomew, *Gazetteer of the British Isles* (1887)

Bro Aman Museum

Ammanford Library
Ammanford SA18 3DN
01267 228696
http://goo.gl/wYPZsZ
museums@carmarthenshire.gov.uk

In the late 19th century, large-scale industry transformed the Amman Valley. Rich natural resources, especially the famous anthracite coal, brought coal mines, iron and tinplate works, railways and people to work them.

Carmarthen Town Museum & Gallery

Carmarthen Library, St Peter's Street
Carmarthen SA31 1LN
01267 228696
http://goo.gl/HCTHxl
museums@carmarthenshire.gov.uk

Carmarthen's new Town Museum and Gallery is located in Carmarthen Regional Library. The Library's listed facade once formed part of Furnace House, home to the Morgan dynasty of iron masters.

Collections: Carmarthen has been a centre of government, trade, industry and culture since Roman times. In the displays you can find pottery imported in Roman and medieval times, a collection of official weights and measures, and a Columbia printing press from when Carmarthen was the printing capital of Wales.

Carmarthenshire Archives

Parc Myrddin, Richmond Terrace
Carmarthen SA31 1HQ
01267 228232
http://goo.gl/mcOcrj

The Archives Service has in its care documents which date from the 14th to the 21st century. These unique records are the raw material for evidential historical and family research.

Carmarthenshire County Museum

Abergwili
Carmarthen SA31 2JG
01267 228 696
http://goo.gl/uXe3su
museums@carmarthenshire.gov.uk

The County Museum presents many aspects of Carmarthenshire's rich and varied past. Displays include local geology, archaeology, Welsh furniture, ceramics, portraits, landscape paintings, costume, a Victorian schoolroom, life on the farm and the Homefront in World War 2.

Dylan Thomas Boathouse

Dylan's Walk
Laugharne SA3 4SD
01994 427 420
www.dylanthomasboathouse.com

Dylan Thomas was one of the greatest writers from Wales and a giant in the 20th century. The most renowned in a school of Anglo-Welsh writers that flourished during that period. He worked in the writing shed above the Boathouse with its remarkable and inspiring views of four estuaries.

Kidwelly Castle

Castle Street
Kidwelly SA17 5BQ
01554 890104
www.cadw.wales.gov.uk/daysout/kidwellycastle
kidwellycastle@wales.gsi.gov.uk

Kidwelly is everything a castle should be - steep earthworks, high towers, tall walls and a great gatehouse which took at least a century to complete.

Kidwelly Industrial Museum

Broadford
Kidwelly SA17 4LW
01554 891078
www.kidwellyindustrialmuseum.co.uk
museums@carmarthenshire.gov.uk

Kidwelly Tinplate Works was established in 1737 and operated with varying success until its closure in 1941. Rescued by the Kidwelly Heritage Centre and Tinplate Museum Trust in 1982, the old works now interprets not only the tinplate industry, but also coal mining and brick manufacture in the area.

Laugharne Castle

King Street
Laugharne SA33 4SA
01994 427906
www.cadw.wales.gov.uk/daysout/laugharnecastle
tara.brown@wales.gsi.gov.uk

Think Laugharne, think Dylan Thomas, but think castle too. Both Dylan Thomas and author Richard Hughes put pen to paper in the castle's garden summer house. Built in the 13th century by the de Brian family, probably atop an earlier Norman ringwork castle, the solid mansion we see before us is the lasting legacy of Sir John Perrot. It didn't fare too well during the Civil War. Once captured by Parliamentary forces after a siege, it was partially dismantled.

Museum of Speed

Pendine
Pendine Sands SA33 4NY
01994 453488
http://goo.gl/AnH5p3
museums@carmarthenshire.gov.uk

Opened in 1996, the museum interprets the Pendine area, focusing on the use of the sands at Pendine for land speed attempts and racing. The main exhibit for the summer season is 'Babs', the motor car used by Parry Thomas on his fatal attempt at the record in 1927.

Parc Howard Museum & Art Gallery

Felinfoel Road
Llanelli SA15 3LJ
01554 772029
www.parchoward.org.uk
museums@carmarthenshire.gov.uk

Parc Howard houses a renowned collection of Llanelli Pottery (1839 - 1921), an art collection and material related to the history of the town. Parc Howard was built by the Buckley family in 1885, a family with a long association of brewing in the town. The mansion, with its 27 acre park, was given to the town of Llanelli in 1912 by Sir Stafford and Lady Howard.

West Wales Museum of Childhood

Pen-ffynnon
Llangeler SA44 5EY
01559 370428
www.toymuseumwales.co.uk
info@toymuseumwales.co.uk

Take a stroll down memory lane, see toys from your past, relax in the tea-room, or browse the souvenir shop.

Denbighshire

Denbighshire, maritime county of N. Wales; bounded N. by the Irish Sea, E. by Flintshire, Cheshire, and Shropshire, S. by Montgomeryshire and Merioneth; and W. by Carnarvonshire; length, NW. and SE., 42 miles; breadth, NE. and SW., from 7 to 27 miles; coast-line, about 9 miles; area, 425,038 acres; population 111,740. There is some level ground along the N.; the E. is hilly; and the mountains on the S. and W. rise from 1000 to 2500 ft. high. The principal streams are the Clwyd, Conway, and Dee; their vales are beautiful and fertile. Oats, barley, and rye are grown in the uplands, and wheat in the low grounds of the valleys. Ponies, and small but hardy sheep, are reared on the hills. The manufacture of woollen goods is carried on to some extent, but the chief industry, besides agriculture, is the mining of coal, iron, lead, and slate. The county comprises 6 hundreds, 90 parishes, with parts of 6 others, the Denbigh Boroughs (Denbigh, Holt, Ruthin, and Wrexham), and the municipal boroughs of Denbigh, Ruthin, and Wrexham. It is entirely in the diocese of St Asaph.

– John Bartholomew, *Gazetteer of the British Isles* (1887)

Bodelwyddan Castle & Park

Bodelwyddan
Near Rhyl LL18 5YA
01745 584060
www.bodelwyddan-castle.co.uk
enquiries@bodelwyddan-castle.co.uk

Bodelwyddan Castle is a Victorian country house museum with acres of parkland, gardens, family-friendly galleries and events throughout the year. We are a regional partner of the National Portrait Gallery with beautifully restored Victorian rooms providing a spectacular setting for enjoying the 19th century displays.

Caer Drewyn Hillfort

Corwen
http://goo.gl/Ic3FeA

Caer Drewyn was built around 2500 years ago. Unlike other hillforts in the area Caer Drewyn doesn't have earthen banks or ditches (ramparts), but a large dry stone wall, the remains of which can still be seen today. The hillfort interior would probably have contained roundhouses constructed of stone and wood, providing shelter and safety for the occupants. It is also believed to be the site where Owain Glyndwr gathered his troops after he proclaimed himself King of Wales in 1400.

Chirk Castle - National Trust

Chirk Castle
Chirk LL14 5AF
01691 777701
www.nationaltrust.org.uk/chirk-castle
chirkcastle@nationaltrust.org.uk

Magnificent 14th-century fortress of the Welsh Marches. Completed in 1310, Chirk's rather austere exterior belies the comfortable and elegant state rooms inside, with elaborate plasterwork, superb Adam-style furniture, tapestries and portraits.

Clwyd Family History Society

The Laurels, Dolydd Road, Cefn Mawr
Wrexham LL14 3NH
01978 822218
www.clwydfhs.org.uk
secretary@clwydfhs.org.uk

The Clwyd Family History Society was founded in 1980 to encourage the study of genealogy and family history in north-east Wales, and to provide a forum for people who are interested in these subjects to meet, and to help each other. It now has approximately 1000 members worldwide.

Denbigh Castle

Castle Lane
Denbigh LL16 3NB
01745 813385
www.denbighshire.gov.uk
susan.dalloe@denbighshire.gov.uk

Denbigh Castle was built as part of Edward I's 13th-century campaigns against the Welsh. Its finest feature is its striking triple-towered great gatehouse.

Denbigh Museum

Grove Road
Denbigh LL16 3UU
http://goo.gl/6Ldnur

The museum interprets the history of Denbigh showing its origins as a mediaeval settlement and its development as a cultural and industrial centre. Items featured include the town's mediaeval charters, interpretation of the castle and town.

Denbighshire Archives

The Old Gaol, 46 Clwyd Street
Ruthin LL15 1HP
01824 708250
http://goo.gl/Xc5CZZ

We collect historical records relating to Denbighshire, and preserve them for future generations. We also encourage the public to come and use our records.

Erddig - National Trust

Erddig
Wrexham LL13 0YT
01978 355 314
www.nationaltrust.org.uk/erddig
erddig@nationaltrust.org.uk

Atmospheric house and estate, vividly evoking its family and servants. Erddig is one of the most fascinating houses in Britain, not least because of the unusually close relationship that existed between the family of the house and their servants.

JAMES - Joint Area Museums Service

Office, Bodelwyddan Castle
Bodelwyddan LL18 5YA
01745 586700
http://goo.gl/12Yko9
adda.james@lineone.net

We were established in October 1999 to promote the educational potential of the museums and collections in Conwy, Denbighshire and Flintshire.

Llangollen Museum

Parade Street
Llangollen LL20 8PW
01978 862862
www.llangollenmuseum.org.uk
enquiries@llangollenmuseum.org.uk

Discover a little of the fascinating history of this unique area in the borderlands of Wales. Llangollen Museum will guide you through some of the different aspects of the heritage of the region, from the Stone Age, through the Romans and the Normans and on into the last two centuries.

Llanrwst Almshouses & Museum

1 - 12 Church Street, Ancaster Square
Llanrwst LL26 0BP
01492 642 550
http://goo.gl/GwE0VT
info@llanrwstalmshouses.wanadoo.co.uk

The Llanrwst Almshouses were constructed in 1610 by Sir John Wynn of Gwydir to house twelve poor men of the parish. For four hundred years they continued to provide shelter until 1976 when the buildings closed.

Collections: The Trust currently holds a collection of over a hundred items relating largely to the rural Conwy Valley – a number of items are associated with the renowned Llanrwst Bards of the late 19th century.

Minera Lead Mines

Wern Road
Minera LL11 3DU
01978 297 460
http://goo.gl/e59j6A
museum@wrexham.gov.uk

Do you know what kibbles, buddles and jigs are? Find out at Minera Lead Mines Visitor Centre, where you can learn more about the lives of the miners and explore where they worked at the remains of the 19th century lead processing works.

Nantclwyd Y Dre

Castle Street
Ruthin LL15 1DP
01824 709822
www.denbighshire.gov.uk/en-gb/DNAP-762LM7
nantclwydydre@denbighshire.gov.uk

Each of the 'seven Ages' of Nantclwyd's history is evoked by recreated and fully-furnished rooms. Visitors start in the 1942 hall, then the 1916 rector's study and 1891 schoolroom, to the splendid panelled and Chinese-wallpapered Georgian bedroom suite.

Plas Newydd, Llangollen

Hill Street
Llangollen LL20 8AW
01978 862834
www.denbighshire.gov.uk/en-gb/DNAP-73FFMH
heritage@denbighshire.gov.uk

At the turn of the 18th century Llangollen was well-known for being the home of the Ladies of Llangollen: Lady Eleanor Butler and Miss Sarah Ponsonby. The romantic story of their elopement from their families in Ireland, their journey to Wales and their setting up home at Plas Newydd captured the imagination of Regency society.

Rhuddlan Castle

Castle Street
Rhuddlan LL18 5AD
01745 590777
www.cadw.wales.gov.uk/daysout/rhuddlancastle
rhuddlancastle@wales.gsi.gov.uk

Another of Edwars I's North Wales fortresses not be to missed. Here he straightened the river Clwyd to make sure there was easy access to the sea.

Rhyl Library Museum & Arts Centre

Church Street
Rhyl LL18 3AA
01745 353814
www.denbighshire.gov.uk
sanantha.williams@denbighshire.gov.uk

Rhyl Museum displays a history of the town and its people. Walk along the pier and view the mural of Rhyl in the Edwardian period.

Ruthin Gaol

Clwyd Street
Ruthin LL15 1HP
01824 708259
www.ruthingaol.co.uk
samantha.williams@denbighshire.gov.uk

Ruthin Gaol opened in May 2002. The building was a prison from 1654 to 1916 and you can now see how prisoners lived their daily lives and how the prison worked.

Sir Henry Jones Museum

Y Cwm, Llangernyw
Abergele LL22 8PR
01492 575571
http://goo.gl/tl4TKH

Visit this fascinating museum of Welsh rural life and find out about Henry Jones and the story of his struggle for educational reform. Wander through the tiny kitchen and bedroom where the family of six ate and slept, and see the displays on Victorian life in a typical Welsh community.

Valle Crucis

Llangollen LL20 8DD
01978 860326
www.cadw.wales.gov.uk/daysout/vallecrucisabbey

Cistercian monks sought the most wild and remote places to build their abbeys they were often the most beautiful too. Nestling below the stunning Horsehow Pass, Valle Crucis ticks all the boxes.

Wireless in Wales Museum

Canolfan Iaith Clwyd Pwll Y Grawys
Denbigh LL16 3LF
01745 812287
www.gwefrhebwifrau.org.uk/index.php/en
info@wirelessinwales.org.uk

The Gwefr Heb Wifrau - Wireless in Wales - is a small radio museum with a difference. With its emphasis on the history of broadcasting in Wales, the influence of broadcasting on our national identity and the contribution of the Welsh to the development of wireless technology this museum is unique.

Wrexham County Borough Museum & Archives

County Buildings, Regent Street
Wrexham LL11 1RB
01978 297 460
http://goo.gl/zDmwq3
museum@wrexham.gov.uk

Wrexham County Borough Museum & Archives was originally the barracks for the Royal Denbighshire Militia; later the building became the town's police station and court house. The museum has three galleries: the main gallery is a family friendly space which introduces visitors to the history of Wrexham and displays some of the star items in the museum's collection.

Collections: Archives and local history of Wrexham and the Borderlands. Highlights of the collection include: brick, tiles and terracotta collection from local manufacturers, clocks made locally, bakelite ware collection and the Welsh Football Collection.

Flintshire

Flintshire, maritime county of N. Wales; is bounded N. by the Irish Sea, NE. by the estuary of the Dee, E. by Cheshire, and S. and SW. by Denbighshire; is 26 miles long, and from 10 to 12 miles broad; the detached hundred of Maelor (8 miles to the SE. of the rest of the county, and surrounded by Cheshire, Shropshire, and Denbighshire) is 9 miles long and 5 miles broad; area, 161,807 acres, population 80,587. Flintshire is the smallest county of Wales, and, next to Glamorgan, the most populous in proportion to its extent. Agriculture is advancing. Wheat and oats are grown in the plains and valleys; the uplands afford excellent pasture, and considerable quantities of butter and cheese are made. Flintshire is situated chiefly on the Coal Measures and other members of the Carboniferous rocks group, and is rich in minerals. There are numerous collieries, and the lead mines are the most productive in Britain. Copper, zinc, calamine, and limestone are also worked, and there are some coarse clay potteries. The Chester and Holyhead Railway runs all along the coast, which is lined by works for coal, iron, copper, lead-smelting, chemicals, shipbuilding, &c. Flintshire comprises 5 hundreds, 37 parishes, and parts of 4 others, and the Flint Boroughs (Caergwrle, Caerwys, Flint, Holywell, Mold, Overton, Rhuddlan, and St Asaph), and the municipal borough of Flint. It is mostly in the diocese of St Asaph.

– John Bartholomew, *Gazetteer of the British Isles* (1887)

Buckley Library, Museum & Gallery

The Precinct
Buckley CH7 2EF
01244 549210
www.flintshire.gov.uk
buckley.library@flintshire.gov.uk

The museum, located on the first floor of the public library, tells the story of Buckley's place as a major centre for the pottery and brick industries from medieval times through to the 20th century. Extensive local history reference resources.

Flintshire County Council Museum Service

County Hall
Mold CH7 6NB
01352 752121
http://goo.gl/CuxodJ
museums@flintshire.gov.uk

The museums Service aims to assist Flintshire residents and visitors in enjoying and exploring the history of the county. On our website you will find information about the museums in Buckley, Mold and the Greenfield Valley Heritage Park.

Flintshire Record Office

The Old Rectory, Rectory Lane
Hawarden CH5 3NR
01244 532364
http://goo.gl/5NRsWu

Discover your local and family history records at Flintshire Record Office.

Gladstone's Library

Gladstone
Hawarden CH5 3DF
01244 532350
www.gladstoneslibrary.org
enquiries@gladlib.org

Gladstone's Library is a unique institution. Founded by the great Victorian statesman, William Gladstone, following his death in 1898, it became the nation's tribute to his life and work and is today Britain's finest residential library and its only Prime Ministerial library. It has a unique collection of more than 250,000 printed items.

Greenfield Valley Museum & Farm

Greenfield Valley Heritage Park
Holywell CH8 7QB
01352 715 159
www.greenfieldvalley.com

An attractive collection of original and reconstructed local buildings which provide a fascinating insight into times past. Situated in the beautiful 70 acre Greenfield Valley Heritage Park, the Greenfield Valley Museum offers a glimpse of how we used to live.

Mold Museum

Museum & Gallery, Earl Road
Mold CH7 1AP
01352 754791
www.flintshire.gov.uk

The museum traces the fascinating history of Mold. You can see Bronze Age treasures including axes, jewellery and a replica of the famous gold cape.

St Winefride's Well Museum

Holywell CH8 7PN
www.saintwinefrideswell.com

The museum is housed in Well House which is part of a pilgrimage site that attracts thousands of visitors every year. It is open every Wednesday, Saturday and Sunday during the season April to October and at other times on request.

Glamorgan

*Glamorgan, a maritime county of South Wales,
bounded N. by Carmarthen, Brecknock, and
Monmouth, E. by Monmouth and the estuary of the
Severn, S. by the Bristol channel, and W. by
Carmarthen and Carmarthen Bay; greatest length,
N. and S., 28 m.; greatest breadth, E. and W., 48
miles; area, 516,959 acres, population 511,433.
Glamorgan is, commercially, the most important
county in Wales, chiefly owing to its great mineral
resources, the fertility of its soil, and the extent and
convenience of its seaboard. The surface of the county
in the N. is mountainous; but towards the S. it
becomes more level, especially in the fertile expanse
known as the Vale of Glamorgan. It is watered by
various rivers, of which the more important are the
Taff, Taw, Neath, and Rhymney; all the streams flow
S. to the Bristol Channel. Mining is the principal
industry, the county having one of the largest
coalfields in Britain, while its supply of ironstone and
limestone is said to be inexhaustible. The soil yields
abundant and excellent crops of the usual cereals,
and large quantities of dairy produce are exported.
Some of the largest ironworks in the world are in
Glamorgan, notably those at Merthyr Tydfil and
Dowlais; and the co. likewise contains very important
copper, tin, and lead works. Glamorgan comprises 10
hundreds, 166 parishes, the parliamentary and
municipal borough of Swansea, the greater part of the
parliamentary borough of Merthyr Tydfil, the Cardiff
Boroughs (Cardiff, Cowbridge, and Llantrisaint), and
the municipal boroughs of Aberavon, Cardiff, and
Neath. It is mostly in the diocese of Llandaff.*

– John Bartholomew, *Gazetteer of the British Isles* (1887)

[See also separate entry for Cardiff.]

Aberdulais Tin Works & Waterfall - National Trust
🖼 ✉ £

Aberdulais
Neath SA10 8EU
01639 636674
http://goo.gl/Gkj7Ss
aberdulais@nationaltrust.org.uk

Famous waterfall and fascinating industrial site with tin
workers' exhibition Set in a steep gorge, this place
demonstrates the power of water and its impact on
industry. Our film 'Reflections on Tin' traces its 400-year
history, from 1584, including a visit by the famous artist
JMW Turner. An early water-powered tin works was the
last industry here. Today the waters of the River Dulais are
used to make Aberdulais Falls self-sufficient in
environmentally friendly energy.

Caerphilly Castle
🖼 £

Castle Street
Caerphilly CF83 1JD
02920 883143
www.cadw.wales.gov.uk/default.asp?id=6&PlaceID=39

One of the largest medieval fortresses in Britain, begun in
1268 by the Anglo-Norman marcher lord, Gilbert de Clare.
Concentrically planned, the rings of stone and water
defences are formidable even today.

Castell Coch
🖼 £

Tongwynlais CF15 7JS
02920 810101
www.cadw.wales.gov.uk/daysout/castell-coch
castellcoch@wales.gsi.gov.uk

While resting on ancient foundations, Castell Coch (Red
Castle) is relatively modern, the by-product of a vivid
Victorian imagination, assisted by untold wealth. The
'eccentric genius' William Burges was given free rein by his
paymaster, John Patrick Crichton-Stuart, the 3rd marquess
of Bute, to create a High Gothic rural retreat to
complement the opulence of his main residence, Cardiff
Castle. Dazzling ceilings, over-the-top furnishings and
furniture were liberally applied.

Cefn Coed Colliery Museum
🖼 ✉ ★

Blaenant Colliery Site, Neath Road, Crynant
Neath SA10 8SN
01639 750556
http://goo.gl/W4PFgl
colliery@npt.gov.uk

Located near the village of Crynant in the Dulais Valley five
miles north of Neath, Cefn Coed Colliery Museum tells the
story of coal mining at Cefn Coed pit, once the deepest
anthracite coal mine in the world. Cefn Coed was one of
the most dangerous coalmines in Wales, gaining the
nickname 'The Slaughterhouse'.

Cowbridge & District Museum

Town Hall Cells, Town Hall
Cowbridge CF71 7DD
01446 775139
cowbridgeguide.co.uk/museums/cowbridgemuseum

A former house of correction, this historic building still retains many interesting features. The Mayor's Parlour contains the well which was used to supply male prisoners with water. The Council Chamber has a facsimile of the 1421 Charter, an oil painting of the Cowbridge Seal used from 1762 to 1887, a copy of the Grant of Arms of 1888 and boards listing past Mayors, Town Clerks and Honorary Freemen.

Cyfarthfa Castle Museum & Art Gallery

Brecon Road
Merthyr Tydfil CF47 8RE
01685 727371
http://goo.gl/RhQjdh
museum@merthyr.gov.uk

The 'Ironmaster' William Crawshay commissioned Cyfarthfa Castle in 1824. This grand castellated mansion overlooked his immensely successful ironworks and has been called, 'the most impressive monument of the Industrial Iron Age in South Wales'. At the castle you can admire the extensive fine and decorative art collections, including Swansea, Nantgarw and Wedgwood porcelain.

Cynon Valley Museum & Gallery

Depot Road, Gadlys
Aberdare CF44 8DL
01685 886729
www.cvmg.co.uk
cvm@rhondda-cynon-taf.gov.uk

Cynon Valley Museum & Gallery opened in 2001 and is situated on the outskirts of Aberdare in the South Wales valleys. Developed with the support of the Heritage Lottery Fund, the museum and gallery are situated on the site of the 19th century Gadlys Ironworks. Discover two hundred years of the valley's history – take an interactive journey through the 'Footprints through Time' gallery to see how the lives of the people of the Cynon Valley have changed.

Drenewydd Ironwork's Cottage

No 26/27 Lower Row, Butetown
Rhymney NP2 5HQ
01443 412248
www.culture24.org.uk/mw235

The ironworks would have once been the most important industry in this area of Wales and, although it is no longer in service, the heritage that is associated with it, and the way that it shaped the community, is still of significant importance. This cottage shows the way that a typical worker would have once lived, close to the main works: a simple existence, and a fascinating insight into social history.

Dyffryn Gardens - National Trust

Dyffryn Gardens
St Nicholas CF5 6SU
02920 593328
www.nationaltrust.org.uk/dyffryn-gardens
dyffryn@nationaltrust.org.uk

Dyffryn Gardens are an exceptional example of Edwardian garden design, covering more than 55 acres featuring a stunning collection of intimate garden rooms, formal lawns and seasonal bedding. There is also a statuary collection, and an arboretum featuring trees from all over the world. Within the gardens, Dyffryn House, a grand Victorian mansion overlooks the key aspects of the gardens.

Egypt Centre

Swansea University, Singleton Park
Swansea SA2 8PP
01792 295960
www.egypt.swansea.ac.uk
c.a.graves-brown@swansea.ac.uk

The Egypt Centre houses an important collection of Egyptian antiquities. The museum, officially opened in September 1998, has a collection of over 3,000 Egyptian antiquities once owned by the manufacturing pharmacist Sir Henry Wellcome (1853-1936).

Gelligroes Mill

Gelligroes
Pont Llansraith NP2 2HY
01495 222322
http://goo.gl/YmJlzA
tourism@caerphilly.gov.uk

The Old Mill, Gelligroes was built in the 17th century and was once a favoured source of grain milling for the local crop farmers. The mill now has a radio museum and a candle-making workshop, which has a Royal Warrant to make candles for Prince Charles. The Mill is also home to the Arthur Moore Amateur Radio Society.

Glamorgan Archives

Clos Parc Morgannwg, Leckwith
Cardiff CF11 8AW
0292 0872200
www.glamarchives.gov.uk/

Glamorgan Archives collects, preserves and makes accessible documents relating to the geographical area it serves, as detailed in its collection policy, and maintains the corporate memory of its constituent authorities.

Glamorgan Family History Society

44 Hendrecafn Road, Penygraig
Rhondda CF40 1LL
01443 434547
www.glamfhs.org
secretary@glamfhs.org

Glamorgan Family History Society is not just for those whose roots are in Glamorgan. Many members live within the historic county, but equally, many live far beyond its boundaries.

Glamorgan Gwent Archaeological Trust

Heathfield House
Swansea SA1 6EL
01792 655208
www.ggat.org.uk
outreach@ggat.org.uk

GGAT is the Welsh Archaeological Trust covering the Welsh counties of Glamorgan and Gwent. We currently hold about 25,000 records of archaeological and historical interest and make this information available to all those who have an involvement in the past whether as researchers, developers, school children or farmers.

Gower Heritage Centre

Parkmill, Gower
Swansea SA3 2EH
01792 371206
www.gowerheritagecentre.co.uk
reception@gowerheritagecentre.co.uk

The centre is based around a historic 12th century water-powered corn and saw mill, with craft workshops, daily tours and demonstrations. It caters for individual visitors, school and group visits, with an extensive programme of special events throughout the year.

Collections: The centre has a large collection of rural crafts machinery from the 19th century.

Joseph Parry's Cottage & Museum

4 Chapel Row, Georgetown
Merthyr Tydfil CF48 1BN
01685 383 704
http://goo.gl/D0NxEd
museum@cyfarthfapark.freeserve.co.uk

4 Chapel Row is a fine example of a typical ironworker's cottage. Built in the 1820s for the workers of the Cyfarthfa Ironworks, the cottage was the birthplace in 1841 of Joseph Parry, Wales best known composer.

Llancaiach Fawr Manor

Plas Llancaiach Fawr, Nelson
Treharris CF46 6ER
01443 412248
www.caerphilly.gov.uk/llancaiachfawr
llancaiachfawr@caerphilly.gov.uk

The peaceful, rural setting of Llancaiach Fawr Manor gives no clue to the turmoil of its early years nor to the exciting living history it now portrays. Built in 1530 for Dafydd ap Richard it was designed to be easily defended during the turbulent reigns of Tudor kings and queens. By the start of the Stuart dynasty the Prichards had prospered and the house was extended in 1628 to demonstrate their status.

Merthyr Tydfil Heritage Trust

Civic Centre, Castle Street
Merthyr Tydfil CF47 0DF
01685 725000
www.mtht.co.uk/HeritageTrusthomepage.html

Our mission: to preserve for the benefit of the residents of Merthyr Tydfil and of the nation at large whatever of the historical, architectural and constructional heritage may exist in and around Merthyr Tydfil in the form of buildings and artefacts.

Nantgarw China Works Museum

Tyla Gwyn
Nantgarw CF15 7TB
01443 841 703
www.nantgarwchinaworksmuseum.co.uk
info@sallystubbings.co.uk

The museum is housed in Nantgarw House where a collection of Nantgarw China is on display. While visiting the museum you can find out where this now world famous porcelain was made.

Pontypridd Museum & Art Gallery

Bridge Street
Pontypridd CF37 4PE
01443 490748
www.pontypriddmuseum.org.uk/en/home/about
enquiries@pontypriddmuseum.org.uk

Housed in a converted chapel built in 1861, the centre tells the story of the town and its people. A new audio-visual programme explains the origins of the chapels and traces the influence of Welsh Dissent at home and overseas.

Porthcawl Museum

Old Police Station, John Street
Porthcawl CF36 5DT
01656 782211
www.porthcawlandthegreatwar.com
porthcawlmuseum@hotmail.co.uk

Porthcawl Museum is located in the Old Police Station, which was used as a working police station from 1877 to its closure in 1974. Our collections include social, maritime and military history (particularly that of the 49th Recce Regiment, formed in Porthcawl in 1942), Victorian costumes and artefacts, railway history (of the DLPR, dating from 1825, and the GWR).

Rhondda Heritage Park

Lewis Merthyr Colliery, Coed Cae Road
Trehafod CF37 2NP
01443 682036
www.rhonddaheritagepark.com
info@rhonddaheritagepark.com

The Rhondda Heritage Park based at the former Lewis Merthyr Colliery, Trehafod, is one of the top heritage and cultural visitor attractions in South Wales and provides a fun and interesting day out for individuals, groups, school children and students. The Black Gold Tour features a fully guided tour with ex-miner guides and involves multimedia presentations, a tour of the pit head buildings and a trip 'underground' to experience the life of a coal miner.

Royal Mint Museum

Llantrisant
Pontyclun CF72 8YT
www.royalmintmuseum.org.uk

The Royal Mint Museum's aims are to advance the education of the public in the history of coins and medals, and the history of the Royal Mint.

South Wales Miners' Museum

Afan Forest Park, Cynonville
Port Talbot SA13 3HG
01639 850564
www.south-wales-miners-museum.co.uk

Visit the museum and find yourself being taken on a historical journey back in time. The Museum portrays the working life of a miner and the hardship adults and children had to endure. The Museum is made up of both indoor and outdoor exhibits. Outdoor exhibits include a the Blacksmith Shop, Lamp Room and an Engine House.

South Wales Police Museum

Police Headquarters, Cowbridge Road

Bridgend CF31 3SU
01656 303 207
www.south-wales.police.uk/museum
laura.pearcey@south-wales.pnn.police.uk

We tell the story of policing in South Wales from the Celts right through to the present day and hold one of the largest collections of police memorabilia outside London. Virtual tour includes the Edwardian charge room and our resident inmate Isaac Martin in his cell. See a glimpse of some of the fascinating objects on display in their original setting.

Swansea Museum

Museum Square, Victoria Road, Maritime Quarter
Swansea SA1 1SN
01792 653763
www.swanseamuseum.co.uk
karl.morgan@swansea.gov.uk

Swansea Museum is the oldest museum in Wales. The collections contain all kinds of objects from the past of Swansea, Wales and the rest of the world. We have everything from an Egyptian mummy to a Welsh Kitchen, displayed in six galleries.

West Glamorgan Archive Service

Civic Centre, Oystermouth Road
Swansea SA1 3SN
01792 636589
www.swansea.gov.uk/westglamorganarchives
westglam.archives@swansea.gov.uk

We are a local authority archive service for the people of Swansea and Neath Port Talbot.

Winding House

Cross Street
New Tredegar NP24 6EG
01443 822666
www.windinghouse.co.uk
windinghouse@caerphilly.gov.uk

The Winding House is the museum for Caerphilly County Borough. Inside the striking new building you can unearth the hidden history of Caerphilly County Borough, explore our latest exhibition, research your family's past, take part in one of our many events, discover the Victorian Winding Engine, eat, drink and shop.

Merioneth

*Merioneth, maritime county, N. Wales, bounded N.
by Carnarvonshire and Denbighshire, SE. by
Denbighshire, Montgomeryshire, and Cardiganshire,
and W. by Cardigan Bay; greatest length, NE. to SW.,
45 miles; greatest breadth, NW. to SE., 30 miles; area,
384,717 acres, population 52,038. The coast-line is
alternately cliffs and stretches of sand, and the co.
generally is the most mountainous in Wales, although
some of the mountains of Carnarvonshire rise to
greater elevations. Merioneth abounds in wild and
romantic mountain scenery, beautiful and fertile
valleys, and fine views of sea and lake and river. The
greatest heights are Aran Mowddwy (2970 ft.) and
Cader Idris (2929 ft.). The chief rivers are the Dee,
the Mawddach, and the Dovey. Waterfalls and small
lakes are numerous, the largest of the latter being
Bala Lake (4 miles long and 1 mile broad). Having
generally a poor soil, with large stretches of moor
quite beyond a profitable cultivation, Merioneth does
not appear as a successful agricultural county, except
in the valleys, where there are many fertile tracts.
Reclamation of land has been successful in some parts
of the co. Manufactures are insignificant, excepting
woollen and flannel goods, which are made chiefly at
Dolgelly. Considerable quantities of slate and
limestone are quarried, and there is a fair output of
lead and copper. Some years ago gold was found to
some extent, but the workings proving unprofitable
were stopped. Merioneth contains 5 hundreds, 33
parishes, and parts of 4 others, and the towns or
villages of Aberdovey, Bala, Barmouth, Corwen,
Dolgelly, Festiniog, and Harlech.*

– John Bartholomew, *Gazetteer of the British Isles* (1887)

Harlech Castle

🏰 💷

Twtil
Harlech LL46 2YH
01766 780552
www.cadw.wales.gov.uk/default.asp?id=6&PlaceID=78

Spectacularly sited Harlech Castle seems to grow naturally
from the rock on which it is perched. Like an all seeing
sentinel, it gazes out across land and sea, keeping a
watchful eye over Snowdonia.

Meirionnydd Archives

Ffordd y Bala
Dolgellau LL40 2YF
01341 424682
www.gwynedd.gov.uk/archives

Gwynedd Archives Service welcomes the public to visit its
Record Offices to use and enjoy the wide range of
documents, photographs, maps and newspapers that are
kept.

Narrow Gauge Railway Museum

📷 ⭐

Wharf Station
Tywyn LL36 9EY
0165 471 0472
www.ngrm.org.uk
curator@ngrm.org.uk

The Narrow Gauge Railway Museum was started in the
1950s and the first collections were displayed by 1956. A
new building was opened as part of the Wharf Station of
the Talyllyn Railway in 2006.

Collections: Over seventy railways are represented from
over 200 years of narrow gauge railway development in
Britain and Ireland. Locomotives, wagons, signals and
many items needed to operate railways are on show.

Quaker Heritage Centre

🏰 📷

Ty Meirion, Sgwar Eldon Square
Dolgellau LL40 1PU
01341 424442
http://goo.gl/ZZq8gB

Discover the story of the Quaker community that once
lived here and of the persecution which forced them to
emigrate to Pennsylvania. Includes an audio visual
presentation.

Monmouthshire

Monmouthshire, maritime county, in W. of England, bounded N. by Herefordshire and Brecknockshire, E. by Gloucestershire, S. by the Bristol Channel, and W. by Glamorgan; greatest length, N. to S., 32 miles; greatest breadth, E. to W., 27 miles; area, 370,350 acres; population 211,267. On the coast-line (22 miles) the only indentation is that formed by the mouth of the Usk. The county has a hilly appearance in the N. and NW., and culminates in the Sugar Loaf (1954 ft.). The chief rivers are the Wye and Usk; the latter is navigable for large vessels as far as Newport. Wheat and rye are the chief crops produced in the fertile valleys of the Usk; oats and barley are grown in the uplands. While farming and grazing are leading employments, there are in the W. large industries connected with coal mines, iron mines, and iron mfrs. The mineral district of the county contains over 100 coal mines. Monmouthshire has a powerful interest for antiquaries. It has many remains of ancient feudal castles, and amoug its ecclesiastical ruins are the splendid remains of the abbeys of Llanthony and Tintern. The co. contains 6 hundreds, 147 parishes, the Monmouth Boroughs (Monmouth, Newport, and Usk), and the municipal boroughs of Monmouth and Newport. It is entirely in the diocese of Llandaff.

– John Bartholomew, *Gazetteer of the British Isles* (1887)

[Note: Monmouthshire only officially became a part of Wales in 1974.]

Abergavenny Museum

The Castle
Abergavenny NP7 5EE
01873 854 282
www.abergavennymuseum.co.uk
abergavennymuseum@monmouthshire.gov.uk

Housed in a Regency hunting lodge, which is known as 'the keep', Abergavenny Museum is set within the ruins of a Norman castle. The museum presents the story of this historic market town from prehistoric, Roman and Norman times through to the present day.

Bedwellty House & Park

Morgan Street
Tredegar NP22 3XN
01495 353370
www.bedwelltyhouseandpark.co.uk
info@bedwelltyhouseandpark.co.uk

Bedwellty House is a listed Regency villa in the town of Tredegar in South Wales. It is surrounded by a historic garden that was established in the early 19th century for the Master of Tredegar Iron Works. Bedwellty House and Park are intimately linked with the early social history of Industrial Wales. Its relevance continued when the house and park were given to the people of Tredegar and consequently became a centre of the labour movement in Wales, and Britain at large. Probably the most famous name associated with Bedwellty House and Park is Aneurin Bevan, credited as the founder of the National Health Service

Blaenavon Ironworks

North Street
Blaenavon NP4 9RQ
01495 792615
http://goo.gl/CpLOoF
Blaenavon.Ironworks@BTopenworld.com

Blaenavon Ironworks, which commenced production in 1789, is the best preserved blast furnace complex of its period and type in the world and is one of the most important monuments to have survived from the early part of the industrial revolution. Today you can view the extensive remains of the blast furnaces, the cast houses and the impressively restored Water Balance Tower. Through exhibitions, advanced interpretation features and reconstructions, you can learn about the international significance of the iron industry and the scientific processes involved in the production of iron. A fascinating insight into the social history of industrial Britain can be gained by glimpsing into the past at the reconstructed company shop and the refurbished workers' cottages, at Stack Square and Engine Row.

Blaenavon World Heritage Centre

Church Road
Blaenavon NP4 9AE
01495 742333
www.visitblaenavon.co.uk
blaenavon.tic@torfaen.gov.uk

Visit a modern attraction in the first school in Wales built (in 1816) by ironmasters for their workers. Inside you will find interactive exhibitions telling the story of the Blaenavon World Heritage Site and its residents through history - it should be your first port of call to understand the World Heritage Landscape.

Caerleon

High Street
Caerleon NP18 1AE
01633 422518
http://goo.gl/FJjtvm
caerleonfortressbaths@wales.gsi.gov.uk

With over 50 acres to explore, you can spend a whole day at the Roman military base of Isca, the home of the Second Augustan Legion for mora tha 200 years. Up to 5,500 soilders could be stationed here at any time.

Caldicot Castle Country Park

Caldicot Castle, Church Road
Caldicot NP26 4HU
01291 420 241
www.caldicotcastle.co.uk
caldicotcastle@monmouthshire.gov.uk

Immerse yourself in the atmosphere of the castle's exciting past. The castle was developed as a fortress by Royal hands in the Middle Ages and restored as a Victorian family home.

Collections: The Cobb Collection includes furniture, fittings and other decorative objects which the family used to furnish the castle when it was their home (1880s to 1940s). This collection also includes costume with some fine 18th century clothing.

Castle & Regimental Museum

The Castle
Monmouth NP25 3BS
01600 772175
www.monmouthcastlemuseum.org.uk
curator@monmouthcastlemuseum.org.uk

This small volunteer-run museum, with free admission, tells the story of the Royal Monmouthshire Royal Engineers - the only present-day regiment to have survived from the Militia. From a muster in 1539 it evolved into a Posse Comitatus and, after enduring sieges in the Civil War, was a Militia Regiment for two centuries.

Chepstow Castle

Chepstow Castle, Bridge Street
Chepstow NP16 5EZ
01291 624065
www.cadw.wales.gov.uk/default.asp?id=6&PlaceID=50

Substantial remains of one of the earliest stone-built castles in Britain - the centre of the medieval Marcher lordship of Chepstow. The castle was modified and developed in successive stages throughout the Middle Ages and saw further action during and after the Civil War.

Chepstow Museum

Gwy House, Bridge Street
Chepstow NP16 5EZ
01291 625981
http://goo.gl/YDiFVm
chepstowmuseum@monmouthshire.gov.uk

Chepstow Museum reveals the rich and varied past of this ancient town, once an important port and market centre. Wine trade, shipbuilding and salmon fishing are among Chepstow's many industries featured in displays with atmospheric settings.

Gwent Archives

Steelworks Road, Ebbw Vale
Blaenau NP23 6DN
01495 353363
www.gwentarchives.gov.uk
enquiries@gwentarchives.gov.uk

Gwent Archives was established in 1938 as the Monmouthshire Record Office, serving the 'old' county of that name. In 1974, it became the Gwent County Record Office.

Gwent Family History Society

11 Rosser Street, Wainfelin
Pontypool NP4 6EA
www.gwentfhs.info
secretary@gwentfhs.info

Our Society exists to encourage an interest in both family history and genealogy amongst the people of Gwent, and amongst those living elsewhere who may have ancestral connections with the historic county of Monmouthshire.

Llanyrafon Farm

Llanfrecha Way, Llanyrafon
Cwmbran NP44 8HT
01633 861 810
www.llanyrafonmanor.org/en/Home.aspx

Llanyrafon Manor, called Llanyrafon Farm by some, has hugged the banks of the Afon Llwyd since the mid 1550s - yet many residents of Cwmbran have no idea that there is such an important building with a diverse heritage right in the middle of their community.

Nelson Museum & Local History Centre

New Market Hall, Priory Street
Monmouth NP25 3XA
01600 710630
http://goo.gl/a2SVCW
nelsonmuseum@monmouthshire.gov.uk

The Nelson Museum was founded in 1924, based on a collection of material relating to the famous admiral. The local history centre, in the same building, deals with Monmouth and its people, including Charles Rolls of Rolls-Royce fame and Henry V.

Newport Museum & Art Gallery

John Frost Square
Newport NP20 1PA
01633 656656
www.newport.gov.uk/museum
museum@newport.gov.uk

481

The history of the people who lived in this area is traced from the earliest evidence 250,000 years ago through to the 20th century. Themes covered by the social history collections range from domestic and personal life to local industrial developments and agriculture. The most significant collections are the Transporter Bridge archive and the Chartist collection; weapons, broadsheets, silver and prints from the 1839 Chartist protest in Newport.

Pontypool Museum

Park Buildings
Pontypool NP4 6JH
01495 752036
www.pontypoolmuseum.org.uk
pontypoolmuseum@hotmail.com

The museum collects artefacts from the history, archaeology, geology, social and industrial histories, art, craft and ecology of the Torfaen Valley (including the towns of Blaenafon, Pontypool and Cwmbran).

Raglan Castle

Raglan Castle
Raglan NP15 2BT
01291 690228
www.cadw.wales.gov.uk/daysout/raglancastle
raglancastle@wales.gsi.gov.uk

Raglan Castle was one of the last medieval castles to be built in England and Wales. Although it was designed with comfort and luxury in mind, the castle was pretty formidable too. It held off Oliver Cromwell's forces for 13 weeks in one of the last sieges of the Civil War.

Tredegar House - National Trust

Tredegar House
Newport NP10 8YW
01633 815880
www.nationaltrust.org.uk/tredegar-house
tredegar.house@newport.gov.uk

Set in a beautiful 90 acre park, Tredegar House is one of the best examples of a 17th century Charles II mansion in Britain. The earliest surviving part of the building dates back to the early 1500s.

Usk Rural Life Museum

The Malt Barn, New Market Street
Usk NP5 1AU
01291 673777
uskmuseum.org/blog
uskrurallife.museum@virgin.net

Based in the historic town of Usk, the museum aims to conserve and display aspects of the history, heritage and traditions of rural life in the county of Monmouthshire. .

Montgomeryshire

Montgomeryshire, inland county of North Wales, bounded N. by Denbighshire, E. and SE. by Shropshire, S. by Radnorshire, SW. by Cardiganshire, and W. and NW. by Merioneth; greatest length, 37 miles; greatest breadth, 30 miles; area, 495,089 acres, population 65,718. Montgomeryshire is almost wholly mountainous and bare, but on the Shropshire side there are some fertile and beautiful valleys. The principal rivers are the Severn (with its affluents the Vyrnwy, Tanat, and Rhiw) and the Dovey. Excellent harvests of wheat, oats, barley, &c., are gathered in the valleys; but in the higher districts the soil is poor, consisting mostly of moorland and sheep-walks. A superior breed of sheep is raised, also the fine description of Welsh ponies known as 'Merlins'. The principal mineral product is slate. Welsh flannel is the staple manufacture. Montgomeryshire contains 9 hundreds, 68 parishes, with parts of 3 others, the Montgomery Boroughs, and the municipal boroughs of Llanidloes and Welshpool. It is in the dioceses of Bangor, Hereford, and St Asaph.

– John Bartholomew, *Gazetteer of the British Isles* (1887)

Brynmawr & District Museum

First Floor, Carnegie Building, Market Street
Brynmawr NP23 4AJ
01495 313900
http://goo.gl/fKhkPh
museum@brynmawrscene.co.uk

Brynmawr Museum boasts many items of the unique Brynmawr Furniture, made solely at the Brynmawr Furniture Factory. The various artefacts donated by the community reflect the social and industrial history of Brynmawr and its surrounding areas.

Llanfyllin Workhouse

The Workhouse
Llanfyllin SY22 5LD
01691 649062
www.llanfyllinworkhouse.org
events@llanfyllinworkhouse.org

Llanfyllin Workhouse is owned and run by the community for the community as an arts and education centre. The Workhouse History Group is carrying out research into the history of the building and of the Llanfyllin Poor Law Union. Historical exhibitions have been held and it is planned to develop further educational resources and ultimately a Workhouse History Centre.

Llanidloes Museum

Town Hall, Great Oak Street
Llanidloes SY18 6BN
01686 413777
www.llanidloes.com/llanidloes_museum
powysland@powys.gov.uk

A local museum consisting of three themes - the social and industrial history of the town and surrounding area during the past 300 years; the museum's Victorian collection displayed in two recreated areas of a kitchen and a parlour; and the exhibition 'If you go down to the woods..", which looks at the importance of trees and man's influence on the forests of Britain including the nearby Hafren Forest.

Montgomeryshire Genealogical Society

24 Dysart Terrace, Canal Road
Newtown SY16 2JL
01686 627916
www.montgomeryshiregs.org.uk
monica.woosnam@btinternet.com

The Montgomeryshire Genealogical Society was founded in 1994 to provide a forum for people with family history interests in the historical county of Montgomeryshire and its borders.

Newtown Textile Museum

5-7 Commercial Street
Newtown SY16 2BL
01686 622024
http://goo.gl/U6gHzg
powysland@powys.gov.uk

The Textile Museum is situated at 5-7 Commercial Street in Newtown.The building is a fine example of a typical early 19th century weaving shop. It consists of two floors of back-to-back cottages.

Old Bell Museum

Arthur Street
Montgomery SY15 6RH
01686 668313
www.oldbellmuseum.org.uk
curator@oldbellmuseum.org.uk

The Old Bell, a 16th century inn, has been converted into a local history museum by Montgomery Civic Society. Eleven rooms house displays illustrating the long social and civic history of the ancient County Town of Montgomeryshire.

Old Parliament House & Owain Glyndwr Centre

Old Parliament House
Machynlleth SY20 8EE
01654 702932
www.canolfanglyndwr.org
glyndwr.enquiries@canolfanglyndwr.org

The low, stone built 16th century townhouse known as Old Parliament House on a site in Machynlleth traditionally associated with Owain Glyndŵr. The adjoining timber framed building on the right was built as the Owain Glyndŵr Institute in 1911 by Lord Davies of Llandinam.

Powis Castle & Garden - National Trust

Powis Castle
Welshpool SY21 8RF
01938 551920
www.nationaltrust.org.uk/powis-castle
powiscastle@nationaltrust.org.uk

A magnificent collection of paintings, sculpture, furniture and tapestries reflects the changing needs and ambitions of the Herbert and Clive families. A superb collection of treasures from India is displayed in the Clive Museum.

Powysland Museum

The Canal Wharf
Welshpool SY21 7AQ
01938 554656
http://goo.gl/OaeEcA
access.powysland@powys.gov.uk

Powysland Museum is a local museum with three permanent galleries depicting the archaeology and social history of the old county of Montgomeryshire. The museum also has a temporary exhibition gallery with changing exhibition throughout the year.

Robert Owen Museum

The Cross, Broad Street
Newtown SY16 2BB
01686 623340
robert-owen-museum.org.uk
info@robert-owen-museum.org.uk

The museum tells the remarkable story of social reformer Robert Owen, born in Newtown (Powys) in 1771. A village boy who hobnobbed with royalty, and created the New Lanark mill community in Scotland.

Collections: The museum is intriguingly laid out in a domestic style, which suits the large numbers of pictures on display. Portraits of Robert Owen and prints of New Lanark are strongly represented.

Pembrokeshire

Pembrokeshire, a maritime county of South Wales, washed by the sea on all sides excepting the NE. and E., where it is bounded respectively by Cardiganshire and Carmarthenshire; greatest length, N. to S., about 30 miles; greatest breadth, E. to W., about 25 miles; area, 391,181 acres, population 91,824. The coast line, which on the S. is rugged and inhospitable, shows several indentations of more or less importance to mariners; they include St Bride's Bay and Milford. Haven in the S., and Newport and Fishguard Bays in the N. Inland the surface of the co. displays a succession of green hills, with fertile valleys intervening. Among the Preseley Hills the highest elevation (1764 ft.) is reached. The chief rivers are the Teifi, which separates the co. from Cardiganshire in the NE., the East Cleddau, and the West Cleddau. Considerable variety characterises the soil; in the S. it is very productive, and in the NW. it is excellently suited for barley growing; but in the hilly and coal districts it is very poor. Owing to the violence of the SW. wind there is comparatively little timber, excepting in sheltered spots. Oats, barley, and potatoes are the chief crops, all being raised under very careful farming. Coal, lead, iron, and slate are the only minerals of the co. having a commercial value. From the number of English-speaking people in Pembrokeshire (chiefly through the settlement of a colony of Flemings, who adopted the English tongue), the county has been called 'Little England beyond Wales'. It comprises 7 hundreds, 153 parish, with part of 1 other, the Pembroke District of Parliamentary Boroughs (Pembroke, Milford, Tenby, Wiston, Haverfordwest, Fishguard, and Narberth), and the municipal boroughs of Haverfordwest, Pembroke, and Tenby.

– John Bartholomew, *Gazetteer of the British Isles* (1887)

Carew Castle & Tidal Mill

Carew Castle, Carew
Nr Tenby SA70 8SL
01646 651782
www.carewcastle.com
enquiries@carewcastle.com

The magnificent Carew Castle has a history spanning 2000 years. Set in a stunning location, overlooking a 23 acre millpond, the castle displays the development from a Norman fortification to an Elizabethan country house. Carew Castle still belongs to the Carew family.

Carew Cheriton Control Tower

near Tenby SA70 8PD
www.carewcheritoncontroltower.co.uk
martin@carewcheritoncontroltower.co.uk

An old WW2 airfield, renovated by volunteers. RAF Carew Cheriton was first used during the First World War as a Royal Naval Air Station.

Castell Henllys Iron Age Fort

Meline
Nr Crymych SA41 3UT
01239 891319
castellhenllys.pembrokeshirecoast.org.uk

Castell Henllys is a prehistoric promontory forts dating to around 600BC, the site of excavations for twenty years and home to several re-constructed thatched Iron Age buildings.

Haverfordwest Town Museum

Castle House
Haverfordwest SA61 2EF
01437 763087
www.haverfordwest-town-museum.org.uk

The museum seeks to give a flavour of the great heritage of Haverfordwest, a rich history from the Norman times to the present day. Using artefacts, photography and touch screen multimedia presentations the past is interpreted in an interesting and innovative way.

Lamphey Bishop's Palace

Lamphey SA71 5NT
01646 672224
http://goo.gl/wgs065

Now, as in the past, this is a place to seek solice from the stresses of everyday life. The medieval bishops of St Davids chose just the right place for a lavish sanctuary.

Milford Haven Heritage & Maritime Museum

The Old Custom House, The Docks
Milford Haven SA73 3AF
01646 694 496
http://goo.gl/AJHBd8

Housed in the old custom house on the quayside, the museum recreates Milford's colourful past focusing, naturally, on its maritime history.

Narberth Museum

The Bonded Stores, Church Street, Narberth
Narberth SA67 7BH
01834 860500
www.narberthmuseum.co.uk
info@narberthmuseum.co.uk

Narberth Museum has recently re-opened in the historic Bonded Stores. Here you can discover more about the people and places that define this ancient market town.

Pembroke Dock Sunderland Trust

1 The Terrace, Royal Dockyard
Pembroke Dock SA72 6YH
01646 684220
www.sunderlandtrust.com
enquiries@sunderlandtrust.org.uk

Heritage group which has two established visitor attractions in the former military town of Pembroke Dock and is leading heritage initiatives.

Pembrokeshire Record Office

The Castle
Haverfordwest SA61 2EF
01437 763707
http://goo.gl/X1oHde

Are you interested in your ancestors, the history of your house, the story of your village, parish, town, church, chapel or any aspect of Pembrokeshire's history? Pembrokeshire Archives holds historical sources ranging from a document from 1272 to last week's local newspaper.

Penrhos Cottage

Llanycefn
Clunderwen SA66 7XT
01437 731328
www.pembrokeshire.gov.uk/content.asp?id=5877&d1=0
Mark.Thomas@Pembrokeshire.gov.uk

This tiny cottage was built as a ty un nos (house built in one night) around 1800 and last occupied in 1967. It is the last thatched cottage in Pembrokeshire.

Picton Castle & Gardens

The Rhos
Haverfordwest SA62 4AS
01437 751326
www.pictoncastle.co.uk
info@pictoncastle.co.uk

A spectacular forty acre garden surrounding a 13th century fairy tale castle, with an ever changing pattern of colours and scents throughout the seasons, which never fails to enchant the visitor. A Royal Horticultural Society partner garden.

Scolton Manor Museum

Pembrokeshire Museums Service, Scolton Manor, Spittal
Haverfordwest SA62 5QL
01437 731328
http://goo.gl/0LGbXb

A traditional Victorian country house, Scolton Manor was home to successive generations of the Higgon family, until it was bought by Pembrokeshire County Council in 1972. The house has been sympathetically restored in order to provide visitors with a taste of Victorian society and style, both above and below stairs. The site also provides a home for the County Museum collection which includes fine art, photographs, costume and agricultural collections.

St David's Bishop's Palace

St Davids SA62 6PE
01437 720517
http://goo.gl/v4HuZ1

High walls, high carved stone human heads and mystical beasts. Only the striking chequerboard stonework hints at what lies within what was once the fabulous palace of the medieval bishops of St David's, built a stone's throw from the cathedral.

Tenby Museum & Art Gallery

Castle Hill
Tenby SA70 7BP
01834 842809
www.tenbymuseum.org.uk
info@tenbymuseum.org.uk

Tenby Museum was founded in 1878 by a group of interested gentlemen; it is now the oldest independent museum in Wales. The building is Grade II listed and situated in part of the old town castle.

Radnorshire

Radnorshire, inland county of South Wales, bounded N. by Montgomeryshire and Shropshire, E. by Herefordshire, S. and SW. by Brecknockshire, and W. by Cardiganshire; greatest length, N. and S., 30 miles; greatest breadth, E. and W., 34 miles; area, 276,552 acres, population 23,528. Radnorshire is the smallest of the 6 counties of South Wales. In the E. and S. are some comparatively level tracts, including the Vale of Radnor, but the greater portion of the surface is hilly, or even mountainous, the Forest of Radnor reaching in its highest summit an elevation of 2163 ft. Oats and wheat are grown in the lower parts, but attention is chiefly directed to the rearing of stock; the higher parts serve only for the feeding of sheep and the breeding of Welsh ponies. Butter is made in large quantities. The minerals are of little value, except the limestone which underlies the Vale of Radnor. The mfrs. are very limited, chiefly flannel. The forests, which at one time were of great extent, have long disappeared. There are several medicinal mineral springs, those of Llandrindod being in great repute. None of the rivers (Wye, Elan, Ithon, &c.) are navigable, but the railway communication is good. Radnorshire was made a county by Henry VIII. It comprises 6 hundreds and 60 parishes, with part of 1 other. It is in the dioceses of St David's and Hereford.

– John Bartholomew, *Gazetteer of the British Isles* (1887)

Judge's Lodging

Broad Street
Presteigne LD8 2AD
01544 260650
www.judgeslodging.org.uk
info@judgeslodging.org.uk

Explore the fascinating world of the Victorian judges, their servants and felonious guests. From the stunningly restored judge's apartments to the dingy servants' quarters below, wander through their gaslit world. Additional collections include photographs and objects relevant to the Radnorshire Constabulary and the building's life as a court.

Powys Archives

County Hall
Llandrindod Wells LD1 5LG
01597 826088
http://goo.gl/1SR4R6

Powys Archives is located in Llandrindod Wells, and serves as the official repository for the records of the county of Powys. Our collections date from the 14th century and can be used for all types of research.

Powys Heritage Online

history.powys.org.uk

The history of mid-Wales from photographs, documents, maps and museum exhibits.

Radnorshire Museum

Temple Street
Llandrindod Wells LD1 5DL
01597 824513
www.powys.gov.uk/index.php?id=613&L=0
radmus@powys.gov.uk

Radnorshire Museum is in the middle of one the prettiest spa towns in Wales. Llandrindod Wells has been visited by people wishing to taking the waters for medical problems since Dr Linden's famous treatise in 1756.

Rhayader Museum & Art Gallery

CARAD, East Street
Rhayader LD6 5ER
01597 810561
www.carad.org.uk
museum@carad.org.uk

Our museum gallery explores how landscape, culture and the social and economic environments shape our community. Our exhibition gallery has a changing programme of exhibitions.

NORTHERN IRELAND

National

FLAME. the Gasworks Museum of Ireland

44 Irish Quarter West
Carrickfergus BT38 8AT
028 9336 9575
www.flamegasworks.co.uk
info@flamegasworks.co.uk

Carrickfergus boasts Ireland's sole surviving coal gasworks and is one of only three left in the British Isles. Visit this unique site and see how gas was made from coal in Europe's largest set of hoizontal retorts. You'll also get a great view of the town from the top of the gasholder.

Collections: Besides the gasworks, FLAME also has an extensive collection of gas appliances and a library on the gas industry.

General Register Office for Northern Ireland (GRONI)

Oxford House, 49 - 55 Chichester Street,
Belfast BT1 4HL
0300 200 7890
http://goo.gl/q16ah4
gro.nisra@dfpni.gov.uk

The General Register Office for Northern Ireland administers marriage law and the registration of births, deaths, marriages, civil partnerships and adoption in Northern Ireland.

Irish Heritage Association

A.204 Portview, 310 Newtownards Road
Belfast BT4 1HE
028 90455325
http://goo.gl/C7FC9b

This association is involved in the Rally of Settler Families as well as several clann gatherings.

Irish Linen Centre & Lisburn Museum

Market Square
Lisburn BT28 1AG
028 92 663377
www.lisburnmuseum.com
irishlinencentre@lisburn.gov.uk

The Irish Linen Centre and Lisburn Museum houses a major exhibition of the history of Irish Linen, an interactive gallery with hands on participation in linen manufacturing processes; an audio-visual presentation on the lives of workers in a Victorian factory setting and hand loom weavers producing linen on restored 19th century looms.

National Museums Northern Ireland

Cultra
Holywood BT18 0EU
0845 608 0000
www.nmni.com
info@nmni.com

Across three unique sites, we care for and present the inspirational collections that reflect the creativity, innovation, history, culture and people of Northern Ireland.

North of Ireland Family History Society

Graduate School of Education, Queen⊠s university of Belfast, 69 University Street
Belfast BT7 1HL
www.nifhs.org
web@nifhs.org

The objective of the society is to foster an interest in family history with special reference to families with roots in the North of Ireland and their descendants, wherever they may be.

Northern Ireland Museums Council

6 Crescent Gardens,
Belfast BT7 1NS
028 9055 0215
www.nimc.co.uk
astdir@nimc.co.uk

The Northern Ireland Museums Council is a company with charitable status that was established under Ministerial order in 1993. It is managed by a Board, composed of representatives from the regional and national museums in Northern Ireland.

Northern Ireland War Memorial

21 Talbot Street
Belfast BT1 2LD
www.niwarmemorial.org
info@niwarmemorial.org

It is the mission of NIWM to enrich people's understanding of the contribution of the people of Northern Ireland in two world wars by preserving and displaying a unique collection. We deliver a programme of engaging displays and enjoyable events to visitors and tourists from around the world and reach out to everyone in Northern Ireland through a programme of learning and education.

Public Record Office of Northern Ireland (PRONI)

2 Titanic Boulevard

Belfast BT3 9HQ

028 9025 5905

www.proni.gov.uk

proni@dcalni.gov.uk

PRONI holds a diverse range of archives from official and private sources, including church and school registers, court records, wills, land valuation and landed estate records.

Railway Preservation Society of Ireland

Whitehead Excursion Station, Castleview Road

Whitehead BT38 9NA

028 2826 0803

www.steamtrainsireland.com

rpsitrains@hotmail.com

The RPSI was formed in 1964 to preserve in working order steam locomotives and other rolling stock built for the Irish railway system, from 1850 to the present day. The RPSI maintains a museum at Whitehead and operates steam-hauled excursions over the present day Irish railway network for families and enthusiasts.

Society of Genealogists Northern Ireland (SGNI)

www.sgni.net

secretary@sgni.net

The society of Genealogists Northern Ireland (SGNI) comprises commercial genealogists based in the six counties of Northern Ireland (Antrim, Armagh, Down, Fermanagh, Londonderry (Derry), Tyrone) who adhere to our Code of Practice.

Ulster Historical Foundation

49 Malone Road

Belfast BT9 6RY

028 9066 1988

www.ancestryireland.com

enquiry@uhf.org.uk

Discover your Irish and Scots-Irish Ancestry with Ulster Historical Foundation. The Foundation has online records and publications available to help you discover your Irish and Scots-Irish ancestors.

Belfast

Belfast, parliamentary and municipal borough, manufacturing and seaport town, and the principal town of Ulster, chiefly in Shankill parish, county Antrim, but partly also in Holywood and Knockbreda parishes, county Down, at the influx of the Lagan to Belfast Lough, 113 miles N. of Dublin by rail, 129 from Glasgow, and 160 from Liverpool – municipal borough, 5991 acres, population 208,122. On the land side the city is bounded and sheltered by a lofty and picturesque ridge of hills, which ends abruptly in the basaltic eminence of Cave Hill (1185 ft.). It presents a clean, prosperous, and business-like appearance, and possesses wide and regular streets, elegant and substantial buildings, and beautiful environs. An insignificant vil. in 1612, when Scottish and English colonists first settled there, Belfast is now the chief seat of the trade and manufactures of Ireland, and the second port next to Dublin. Of its numerous educational institutions, the most important is Queen's College, opened in 1849; it has professorships in arts, law, medicine, and science, including engineering and agriculture. The staple manufactures are linen and cotton; and bleaching, dyeing, and calico-printing are extensively carried on. Some of the flax-mills are very large. There are flour and oil mills; chemical works; iron foundries; breweries, distilleries; alabaster and barilla mills; shipbuilding (on Queen's island), rope, and sailcloth yards. Pork curing is an important branch of trade. The docks and wharfage have become very extensive. Steamers sail daily to and from Liverpool, Glasgow, Fleetwood, Barrow, and Ardrossan; and once or twice a week to Dublin, Cork, Bristol, London, Havre, &c.

– John Bartholomew, *Gazetteer of the British Isles* (1887)

36th (Ulster) Division Memorial Association

209 Woodstock Road
Belfast BT6 8PQ
www.ulsterdivision.com
ulsterdivision@yahoo.co.uk

Community based organisation established to recall with dignity and pride the actions of our forefathers. Secondly we wish to educate as much as possible using the arts, publications and exhibitions.

Fernhill House: the People's Museum

Glencairn Road, Glencairn
Belfast BT13 3PT
01232 715599
www.fernhillhouse.co.uk

Fernhill House was finished in 1864 by John Smith, the first resident and the house has little changed since than. The house is traditional in its Irish mid-Victorian appearance; it is a mixture of the Classical and Italian Renaissance architectural styles.

Linen Hall Library, The

17 Donegall Square North
Belfast BT1 5GB
028 9032 1707
www.linenhall.com
info@linenhall.com

The Linen Hall Library is a truly unique institution. Founded in 1788, it is the oldest library in Belfast and the last subscribing library in Ireland. It has a radical and 'enlightenment' foundation, and ever since has prized its independence and has maintained the principle that its resources are owned by the community for the community.

Collections: Library holdings range from its comprehensive collection of early Belfast and Ulster printed books to the 250,000 items in the Northern Ireland Political Collection, the definitive archive of the recent troubles.

Police Museum

Police Service of Northern Ireland Headquarters, Brooklyn, Knock Road
Belfast BT5 6LE
0845 600 8000 ext. 22499
http://goo.gl/ELGjLm
museum@psni.police.uk

The police museum was set up in the 1980s to explain and illustrate Northern Ireland's unique and often contentious policing history. Our collection includes police uniforms, equipment, medals and archives from the early 1800s to the present day and also weapons used against the police over the years. The police museum is located in a former sergeant's married quarters at Police Headquarters, Brooklyn.

Royal Ulster Rifles Museum

5 Waring Street
Belfast BT1 2EW
028 9023 2086
http://goo.gl/6d7wA0
rurmuseum@yahoo.co.uk

The museum houses an extensive collection of uniforms, badges, medals and regimental memorabilia covering the history of the regiment and the campaigns in which it has fought since its formation in 1793.

Schomberg House Cultural Heritage Centre

368 Cregagh Road
Belfast BT6 9YE
028 9070 1122
http://goo.gl/SsgCC5
info@grandorangelodge.co.uk

Schomberg House welcomes organised parties for tours and talks. You can also view the many interesting artefacts, some dating back to the 1690s and also access a unique documentary resource in our library. The heritage centre tells the story of Orangeism and its role in society not only in Northern Ireland but across the world and has on display artefacts from the Williamite period together with such diverse items as the ceremonial robe of the famous 'Grand Old Duke of York' of nursery rhyme fame and stone carvings by Native American members of the Orange Order in Canada.

Sentry Hill Historic House & Visitor Centre

Sentry Hill, 40 Ballycraigy Road
Newtownabbey BT36 8SX
028 9083 2363
www.sentryhill.net
sentry.hill@btconnect.com

Sentry Hill is a 19th century farmhouse in the Parish of Carnmoney, County Antrim. The house and its contents provide a rare insight into life in rural Ulster during the 19th and early 20th centuries. Sentry Hill was the home of the McKinney family, who came to Ireland from Scotland in the early 1700s.

Titanic Belfast

1 Olympic Way, Queen's Road, Titanic Quarter
Belfast BT3 9EP
028 9076 6386
www.titanicbelfast.com
welcome@titanicbelfast.com

Titanic Belfast extends over nine galleries, with multiple dimensions to the exhibition, drawing together special effects, the Shipyard Ride, full-scale reconstructions and innovative interactive features to explore the Titanic story in a modern and insightful way. Explore the shipyard, travel to the depths of the ocean and uncover the true legend of Titanic, in the city where it all began.

Ulster Museum

Botanic Gardens
Belfast BT9 5AB
0845 608 0000
www.nmni.com/um
info@nmni.com

Northern Ireland's treasure house of the past and present. Take 8,000 square metres of galleries, add rich collections of art, archaeology, local history and natural sciences, mix them with a constantly changing programme of temporary exhibitions and events, and you have all the ingredients for a fascinating voyage of discovery. From ancient Ireland to the South Pacific, from masterpieces of modern art to rare flowers, the museum is a window to the north of Ireland and a window on the world.

County Antrim

Antrim – a maritime county in extreme NE. of Ireland, prov. Ulster; bounded N. by the Atlantic, E. by the N. Channel, SE. and S. by Belfast Lough and county Down, and W. by Lough Neagh and the river Bann, which separate it from counties Tyrone and Londonderry. Greatest length, N. and S., 56 miles; greatest breadth, E. and W., 30 m.; coast-line, 90 miles. Area, 762,080 acres (709,832 acres of land and 52,248 of water). Population 421,943, of whom about 190,746 were Presbyterians, 108,344 Roman Catholics, 98,161 Protestant Episcopalians, and 11,842 Methodists. Off the N. coast are Rathlin island and the Skerries; off the E. are the Maiden rocks with 2 lighthouses. The chief headlands are Bengore Head, Fair Head, Garron Point, and Ballygalley Head. The surface consists chiefly of a tableland of basaltic trap, broken by numerous valleys, and presenting on the N. coast the most wonderful columnar formations (the Giants' Causeway); chief summit, Trostan, 1817 ft. The fisheries on the coast are important. Fine salt is obtained in the district of Carrickfergus. The cultivation of flax and the mfrs. of linen, cotton, and coarse woollens give employment to most of the people. The county comprises 15 baronies, 71 parishes, the greater part of the parliamentary and municipal borough of Belfast, and the towns of Antrim, Ballymena, Ballymoney, Carrickfergus, Larne, and Lisburn (part of).

– John Bartholomew, *Gazetteer of the British Isles* (1887)

Andrew Jackson & US Rangers Centre

2 Boneybefore
Carrickfergus BT38 7EQ
028 9335 8049
http://goo.gl/XFkaFp
touristinfo@carrickfergus.org

The Andrew Jackson Cottage highlights Carrickfergus' strong American and Ulster-Scots connections as well as telling the story of Andrew Jackson, the 7th president of the USA, whose parents emigrated to America from Carrickfergus in 1765. Located less than a mile from the town centre off the Larne Road, this single storey building has been restored to its original state.

Ballycastle Museum

59 Castle Street
Ballycastle BT54 6AS
01265 762942
www.moyle-council.org/tourism/attractions/?id=5

Ballycastle Museum houses the Irish Home Industries Workshop collection. This is a remarkable collection of the Arts and Crafts movement in Ireland from the early 1900s.

Ballymoney Museum

Ballymoney Town Hall, Townhead Street
Ballymoney BT53 6BE
028 2766 0245
www.visitballymoney.com
museum@ballymoney.gov.uk

The exhibition galleries include everything from Mesolithic archaeology to motorcycle road racing. On display are rare finds from the Bronze Age and Medieval period as well as exhibits associated with the political upheaval of the late 18th century and the United Irish Rebellion.

Braid, The - Mid-Antrim Museum

The Braid, 1-29 Bridge Street
Ballymena BT43 5EJ
028 2565 7161
www.thebraid.com
noreen.mullan@ballymena.gov.uk

The Mid-Antrim Museum at The Braid features galleries showcasing an impressive collection of fascinating artefacts of both local and national significance, alongside an exciting range of changing exhibitions. The use of interactive media brings history to life - as visitors are enticed to step back in time in a multi-sensory experience - while adjoining displays of artefacts are complimented by dramatic images of the local landscape.

Carrickfergus Castle

Marine Highway
Carrickfergus BT38 7BG
028 9335 1273
http://goo.gl/ZW9Zxs

A striking feature of the landscape from land, sea and air, Carrickfergus Castle greets all visitors with its strength and menace. It represents over 800 years of military might.

Carrickfergus Museum

Carrickfergus Museum and Civic Centre, 11 Antrim Street
Carrickfergus BT38 7DG
028 9335 8049
www.carrickfergus.org
visitorinfo@carrickfergus.org

Local museum interpreting the long and distinguished history of the town and surrounding area, with artefacts of treasure excavated in Carrickfergus. There are multi-media and audio-visual presentations.

Causeway School Museum

52 Causeway Road
Bushmills BT57 8SU
028 207 32142
www.northantrim.com/causewayschoolmuseum.htm
eleanor.killough@neelb.org.uk

The Causeway School Museum, situated beside the Giant's Causeway, was built in 1915 and designed by the architect Clough Williams-Ellis of Portmeirion fame. Clough Williams-Ellis was employed by the MacNaghten family who instructed that the school be built in memory of Lord Edward MacNaghten.

Dunluce Castle

87 Dunluce Road
Portrush BT57 8UY
028 2073 1938
http://goo.gl/0f5X9t

This late-medieval and 17th-century castle is dramatically sited, on a headland dropping sheer into the sea on the north Antrim Coast. It creates an exciting image of danger and adventure backed up by its history.

Larne Museum & Arts Centre

2 Victoria Road
Larne BT40 1RN
028 2827 9482
http://goo.gl/0fxtxM
Caldwellj@larne.gov.uk

TThis historic building, beautifully restored and renovated, with many of its original features remaining intact, houses Larne Museum with its modern and attractive displays, reflecting the distinctive history and heritage of the area. The port of Larne is the principal gateway into Northern Ireland and the strong maritime links of this east Antrim coastal community are portrayed through a variety of exhibits relating to the first roll-on, roll-off ferries, the Royal Navy and the Princess Victoria disaster.

Mid-Antrim Museums Service

Mid-Antrim Museum, The Braid, 1-29 Bridge Street
Ballymena BT43 5EJ
www.thebraid.com

Local Authority Partnership established in 1998 to provide enhanced museum services covering four Borough Councils within County Antrim of Ballymena, Larne, Newtownabbey and Carrickfergus with the flagship museum being Mid-Antrim Museum at The Braid, Ballymena.

Museum of the Royal Irish Regiment

Headquarters, The Royal Irish Regiment, St Patrick's Barracks
Ballymena BT43 7BH
028 2566 1383
www.royalirish.easynet.co.uk/Museum/museum.html

The Royal Irish Regiment is the last Irish Infantry Regiment. Born at midnight on 1st July 1992, the history of the regiment dates back to 1689 when the 'Inniskillingers' were raised at the castle in Enniskillen.

County Armagh

Armagh – an inland county, province Ulster, bounded N. by county. Tyrone and Lough Neagh, E. by co. Down, S. by Louth, and W. by counties Monaghan and Tyrone. Greatest length N. and S., 32 miles; greatest breadth E. and W., 20 miles. Area, 328,086 acres (311,048 acres land and 17,038 water). Population 163,177, of whom 75,709 were Roman Catholics, 53,390 Protestant Episcopalians, 26,077 Presbyterians, and 4884 Methodists. The surface rises with gentle undulations from the shores of Lough Neagh to the hilly districts of the S. and SE.; chief summit Slieve Gullion, 1893 ft. The rivers are the Bann, Blackwater, Callan, and Newry. The soil is generally fertile, and there is much bog. Linen is the staple manufacture; there is also cotton. The county comprises 8 baronies, 28 parishes and parts of parishes, part of the parliamentary borough of Newry, the city of Armagh, and the towns of Lurgan, Portadown, and Tanderagee.

– John Bartholomew, *Gazetteer of the British Isles* (1887)

Ardress House - National Trust

64 Ardress Road, Annaghmore
Portadown BT62 1SQ
028 8778 4753
www.nationaltrust.org.uk/ardress-house
ardress@nationaltrust.org.uk

This charming 17th-century farmhouse, elegantly remodelled in Georgian times, offers fun and relaxation for all the family. Set in 40 hectares (100 acres) of countryside there are apple orchards, charming woodland and riverside walks. The atmosphere of a working farmyard has been rekindled with the return of small animals.

Argory, The - National Trust

Derrycaw Road, Moy
Dungannon BT71 6NA
01868 784753
www.nationaltrust.org.uk/argory
argory@nationaltrust.org.uk

Built in the 1820s, this handsome Irish gentry house is surrounded by its 130-hectare (320-acre) wooded riverside estate. The former home of the MacGeough Bond family, a tour of this neo-classical masterpiece reveals it is unchanged since 1900 – the eclectic interior still evoking the family's tastes and interests.

Armagh Ancestry

38a English Street
Belfast BT61 7BA
028 3752 1800
www.armagh.co.uk/place/armagh-ancestry
researcher@armagh.gov.uk

Armagh Ancestry is the Irish Family History Foundation designated research centre for genealogical research in County Armagh. It is a member of the Irish Family History Foundation, a 32 county, cross border foundation, appointed by both the Church and State to create a national genealogical archive for the whole of Ireland.

Armagh County Museum

The Mall East
Armagh BT61 9BE
02837 523070
www.armaghcountymuseum.org.uk
acm.um@nics.gov.uk

Armagh County Museum is located on the Mall, an area of urban parkland in the centre of the city. The unique character of the museum's architecture makes it one of the most distinctive buildings in Armagh, similar in appearance to a little Greek temple. The oldest county museum in Ireland, its extensive collections are based on specimens gathered by the Armagh Natural History and Philosophical Society.

Armagh Observatory

College Hill

Armagh BT61 9DG

028 3752 2928

star.arm.ac.uk

lfy@star.arm.ac.uk

The Armagh Observatory is a modern astronomical research institute with a rich heritage. Founded in 1790 by Archbishop Richard Robinson, the Observatory is one of the UK and Ireland's leading scientific research establishments.

Craigavon Museum Services

Lough Neagh Discovery Centre, Annaloiste Road

Lurgan BT66 6NJ

028 3831 1669

https://www.facebook.com/CraigavonMuseumServices

museum@craigavon.gov.uk

Craigavon Museum Services is based at the Lough Neagh Discovery Centre. The museum collection includes over 150 vintage radios, ranging from the 1920s to the 1980s, along with many social history items and photographic material of the local area. T

Palace Stables Heritage Centre

Palace Demesne

Armagh BT60 4EL

028 3752 9629

http://goo.gl/zTAiTN

stables@armagh.gov.uk

Restored 1770 Georgian stables block set in the Palace Demesne. The Heritage Centre is located beside the Primate's Palace, formerly the home of the Archbishop of the Church of Ireland until the 1970s.

Royal Irish Fusiliers Museum

Sovereigns House, Mall East

Armagh BT61 9DL

01861 522911

https://goo.gl/fXuaAV

fusiliersmuseum@yahoo.co.uk

The museum is in Sovereign's House, a Grade B listed building. The collection contains the uniforms, medals, regalia and the two Victoria Crosses won by the regiment. The regimental archive and library may be viewed by appointment.

County Down

Down – a maritime county of Ulster province, in the NE. of Ireland, having county Antrim on the N., county Armagh on the W., and the sea on all other sides; greatest length, NE. and SW., 50 miles; greatest breadth, NW. and SE., 35 miles; average breadth, 24 miles; coast-line, about 67 miles (or 139 miles including all the inlets); area, 612,399 acres (3004 water), or 2.9 per cent, of the total area of Ireland; population 272,107, of whom 29.8 per cent, are Roman Catholics, 23.4 Episcopalians, 40.1 Presbyterians, and 1.9 Methodists. The coast is deeply indented by the spacious inlets of Belfast Lough, Strangford Lough, Dundrum Bay, and Carlingford Lough. There are numerous islands in Strangford Lough, and Copeland Island lies off the entrance to Belfast Lough. The surface on the whole is irregular and hilly. The Mourne Mountains occupy the S., the highest summit of which is Slieve Donard, altitude 2796 ft. The prevailing rock is clay slate; trap and limestone are abundant in the N., and granite occurs among the Mourne Mountains. Mineral springs are numerous. The principal rivers are the Lagan and the Upper Bann. Good crops of oats, wheat, flax, and potatoes are raised. The manufacture of fine linen fabrics, such as muslin, forms a leading industry. The fisheries are extensive. The county comprises 12 baronies – Ards (Lower and Upper), Castlereagh (Lower and Upper), Dufferin, Iveagh (Lower and Upper), Kinelarty, Lecale (Lower and Upper), Mourne, and Newry lordship; 70 parishes: part of Belfast; the greater part of the parliamentary borough of Newry; and the towns of Banbridge, Bangor, Downpatrick, Dromore, Holywood, Lisburn (part of), Newtownards, &C.

– John Bartholomew, Gazetteer of the British Isles (1887)

Castle Ward - National Trust

Strangford
Downpatrick BT30 7LS
028 4488 1204
www.nationaltrust.org.uk/castle-ward
castleward@nationaltrust.org.uk

Explore this exceptional 332-hectare (820-acre) walled demesne dramatically set overlooking Strangford Lough and marvel at the quirky mid Georgian mansion, home of the Ward family since the 16th century. An architectural curiosity, it is built inside and out in the distinctly different styles of classical and gothic.

Down County Museum

The Mall
Downpatrick BT30 6AH
028 4461 5218
www.downcountymuseum.com
museum@downdc.gov.uk

Welcome to Down County Museum where the rich heritage of County Down is brought to life in fascinating exhibitions, lively events, hands-on activities and award winning education programmes. The museum is located in the historic buildings of the 18th century County Gaol of Down. In addition to walking through the restored complex complete with cells, visitors can learn more about 9000 years of human history in County Down in the newly launched exhibitions Down Through Time.

Downpatrick & County Down Railway

The Railway Station, Market Street
Downpatrick BT30 6LZ
01396 615779
www.downrail.co.uk
downtrains@yahoo.co.uk

Downpatrick & Co Down Railway is Northern Ireland's only standard gauge heritage railway. The museum features locomotives and carriages painstakingly restored with guided tours of the exhibitions and workshops.

Newry & Mourne Museum

1a Bank Parade
Newry BT35 6HP
01693 66232
www.bagenalscastle.com/museum
museum@newryandmourne.gov.uk

The museum's diverse collections currently include material relating to prehistoric history; Newry's Cistercian foundations; Ulster's Gaelic Order and relationship with the English Crown; the building of a merchant town and the first summit level canal in the British Isles; the working life and folk traditions of rural and mountain areas; fishing, trade and migration by sea; renowned local personalities and businesses; folklore, storytelling and music; and modern experiences of a Border area.

North Down Heritage Centre

Bangor
028 9127 1200
www.northdownmuseum.com
heritage@northdown.gov.uk

Pieces from our Bronze Age, Early Christian, Plantation and Jordan Collections are all on display in our permanent exhibitions. Further temporary exhibitions are arranged from time to time to bring lesser seen items out of our stores, including pieces from the Percy French Collection.

Portaferry & Strangford Trust

30, the Square, Portaferry
Newtownards BT22 1LR
028 4272 9895
http://goo.gl/HwWK1X
eleanor.brown2301@gmail.com

PAST aims to celebrate and promote the maritime and built heritage of Portaferry, Strangford and the surrounding area by regenerating buildings and landscape and developing a maritime centre to promote the rich past present and future of the area.

Saint Patrick Centre

53a Lower Market Street
Downpatrick BT30 6LZ
028 4461 9000
www.saintpatrickcentre.com
director@saintpatrickcentre.com

The centre is a new and exciting interpretative exhibition which tells the fascinating story of Ireland's patron saint. Through Patrick's own words a light is shone on the arrival of Christianity in Ireland and its development through his mission.

Somme Heritage Centre

233 Bangor Road
Newtownards BT23 7PH
01247 823 202
www.irishsoldier.org

The Somme Heritage Centre is The Somme Association's flagship project. Situated adjacent to the Clandeboye Estate outside Newtownards, the centre is a unique visitor attraction of international significance showing the awful reality of the Great War, and its effects on the community at home.

Ulster Folk & Transport Museum

Cultra
Holywood BT18 0EU
028 90 428428
www.uftm.org.uk
uftmmarketing@btinternet.com

Take time to explore one of Ireland's foremost visitor attractions, recapturing a disappearing way of life, preserving traditional skills and celebrating transport history.

At the open air Folk Museum 60 acres are devoted to illustrating the way of life of people of the north of Ireland in the early 1900s.

County Fermanagh

Fermanagh, inland county of Ulster, Ireland; is surrounded by counties Donegal, Tyrone, Monaghan, Cavan, and Leitrim; greatest length, NW. and SE., 45 miles; greatest breadth, NE. and SW., 27 miles; average breadth, 18 miles; area, 457,369 acres (46,431 water), or 2.2 per cent. of the total area of Ireland; population 84,879, of whom 55.8 per cent. are Roman Catholics, 36.4 Episcopalians, 2.0 Presbyterians, and 5.7 Methodists. The surface rises into numerous abrupt eminences of no great elevation; the chief summit is Belmore Mountain, altitude 1312 ft. The great feature of the county is Lough Erne, which (with the river Erne joining its lower and upper parts) bisects the county throughout its entire length. The loughs are studded with verdant islands, and the whole scenery is picturesque. There is abundance of sandstone and limestone; coal and iron occur. The soil is only of middling quality, and there is much bog. The manufacture of coarse linens is carried on. The county comprises 8 baronies – Clanawley, Clankelly, Coole, Knockinny, Lurg, Magheraboy, Magherastephana, and Tirkennedy; 23 parsishes; and the town of Enniskillen.

– John Bartholomew, *Gazetteer of the British Isles* (1887)

Castle Coole - National Trust

Castle Coole
Enniskillen BT74 6JY
028 6632 2690
www.nationaltrust.org.uk/castle-coole
castlecoole@nationaltrust.org.uk

Castle Coole is one of the finest neo-classical houses in Ireland and is surrounded by a stunning landscape park on the edge of Enniskillen. Built to impress by the first Earl of Belmore 1789- 97, it still has the ability to leave people in awe.

Devenish Monastic Site

Lower Lough Erne, near Enniskillen
http://goo.gl/SHq2p

The most important of Lough Erne's many island church settlements, Devenish was founded in the 6th century by St Molaise. It was raided by Vikings in 837 and burned in 1157, but in the Middle Ages flourished as the site of the parish church and St Mary's Augustinian Priory. There are extensive low earthworks on the hillside, but the earliest buildings are St Molaise's House (a very small church) and the fine round tower close by, both with accomplished Romanesque decoration of the 12th century.

Fermanagh County Museum at Enniskillen Castle Museums

Enniskillen Castle, Castle Barracks
Enniskillen BT74 7HL
028 6632 5000
www.enniskillencastle.co.uk
castle@fermanagh.gov.uk

Enniskillen Castle, situated beside the River Erne in County Fermanagh, was built almost 600 years ago by Gaelic Maguires. Guarding one of the few passes into Ulster, it was strategically important throughout its history.

Collections: The museum collects artefacts from Co. Fermanagh relating to archaeology, local history, folklife fine art, applied arts, oral history and photographs.

Florence Court - National Trust

Florence Court
Enniskillen BT92 1DB
028 6634 8249
www.nationaltrust.org.uk/florence-court
florencecourt@nationaltrust.org.uk

There is something for all the family at the warm and welcoming 18th-century former home of the Earls of Enniskillen. The house enjoys a peaceful setting in west Fermanagh, with a startlingly beautiful backdrop of mountains and forests.

Headhunters Barber Shop & Railway Museum

🏛

5 Darling Street
Enniskillen BT74 7DP
028 6632 7488
www.headhuntersmuseum.com
info@headhuntersmuseum.com

A trip to Headhunters Barber Shop & Railway Museum is like taking a remarkable journey into the past bringing the golden age of the railway vividly to life. Visitors start their journey of discovery at the reconstructed Railway Booking Office where the ticket collector invites you to step on board and enjoy the evocative nostalgia, social heritage and amazing artefacts associated with the railways which operated throughout Fermanagh and the Border Counties until their closure in 1957.

Royal Inniskilling Fusiliers Regimental Museum

🏛 £

The Castle
Enniskillen BT74 7HL
02866 323142
www.inniskilling.com
museum@inniskilling.com

Enniskillen Castle is the splendid location of The Royal Inniskilling Fusiliers Regimental Museum. The castle - once the medieval stronghold of the Maguires - is located on the banks of the picturesque River Erne and presents an array of 19th century barrack buildings surrounding the Keep.

Collections: The collections trace the history of the regiment from its formation in 1689 to amalgamation in 1968. It is illustrated by a large and well laid out collection of uniforms, weapons, medals, photographs, silver, standards, badges and other regimental memorabilia.

Sheelin Irish Lace Museum

🏛 £

Bellanaleck, Enniskillen
Enniskillen BT92 2BA
028 6634 8052
www.irishlacemuseum.com
rosemarycathcart1@gmail.com

The Sheelin Antique Irish Lace Museum is located in the scenic village of Bellanaleck in Fermanagh's Lakelands. The museum houses approximately 400 exhibits, illustrating all the five main types of lace made in Ireland. On display are an irish crochet wedding dress, wedding veils, shawls, parasols, collars, baby bonnets, christening gown, flounces, jackets and many more items.

County Londonderry/Derry

Londonderry – a maritime county, Ulster province; bounded N. by Lough Foyle and the Atlantic Ocean, E. by co. Antrim and Lough Neagh, S. by co. Tyrone, and W. by county Donegal; greatest length, N. and S., 40 miles; greatest breadth, E. and W., 35 miles; average breadth, 20 miles; coast-line, about 30 miles; area, 522,315 acres (9480 water), or 25 per cent, of the total area of Ireland; population 164,991, of whom 44.4 per cent are Roman Catholics, 19.1 Protestant Episcopalians, 33.2 Presbyterians, and 0.9 Methodists. The surface is low along the N. and E. for a width of about 6 miles, hilly in the middle, and mountainous in the S., where the highest summit, Sawel, rises to an altitude of 2236 ft. The rivers from W. to E. are - Foyle, Faughan, Glen, Roe, Claudy, Moyola, and Bann, the last tracing nearly the whole of the E. boundary. The soil is for the most part fertile; the sub-strata consist of mica-slate, basalt, limestone, and sandstone. The chief crops are flax, oats, barley, and potatoes. The staple manufacture is linen. The fisheries on the coast and inland are important. About three-fourths of the whole county are owned by the Irish Society and the Twelve Trades' Companies of the City of London. The county comprises 6 baronies - Coleraine, Keenaght, Loughinsholin, North-East Liberties of Coleraine, North-West Liberties of Londonderry, and Tirkeeran; 43 parishes; the parliamentary and municipal borough of Londonderry, and the towns of Coleraine and Limavady.

– John Bartholomew, Gazetteer of the British Isles (1887)

Amelia Earhart Cottage

Ballyarnett Country Park
Ballyarnett BT48 7UF
028 7135 4040
http://goo.gl/5lg4cf
museums@derrycity.gov.uk

The Amelia Earhart Cottage is a small interpretative centre, built on the site where Amelia Earhart landed in 1932 when she completed her pioneering solo flight across the Atlantic. The cottage is located on the outskirts of Londonderry within the Ballyarnett parklands and is accessible by appointment.

Causeway Museum Service

Coleraine BC Headquarters, 66 Portstewart Road
Coleraine BT52 1EY
028 7034 7234
www.niarchive.org
cms@colerainebc.gov.uk

Causeway Museum Service provides museum services across Coleraine, Limavady and Moyle council areas.

Coleraine Museum

Coleraine Town Hall, The Diamond
Coleraine BT52 1EY
028 7034 7234
www.colerainebc.gov.uk/show.php?id=253
Sarah.Carson@colerainebc.gov.uk

Causeway Museum Service is developing and providing museum services within the four local authorities of Coleraine, Ballymoney, Moyle and Limavady. In Coleraine the Causeway Museum Service provides temporary exhibitions in Coleraine Town Hall.

Derry City Heritage & Museum Service

Harbour Museum, Harbour Square
Derry BT48 6AF
028 7137 7331
http://goo.gl/OlE8yJ
museums@derrycity.gov.uk

The aim of our Heritage & Museum Service is to promote greater awareness and education of the history and cultural heritage of the Derry City Council area. Our museums also provide a forum for the understanding of the diverse cultural traditions that exist within the area.

Ebrington Barracks & Square

Derry

http://goo.gl/PG6znS

Ebrington is a 26-acre site with 19 remaining buildings, 14 of which are listed. The site features a 19th century star fort, connected to the historic walled city by the iconic Peace Bridge, an Ilex project which was opened to the public in June 2011. Ebrington Square has been transformed as a new public realm and a multi-purpose event space.

Foyle Valley Railway Museum

Foyle Road

Derry BT48 6SQ

01504 265234

http://goo.gl/RQ07Yv

museums@derrycity.gov.uk

Foyle Valley Railway Centre is dedicated to telling the rich railway history of the city and surrounding area. At the heart of the exhibition is a recreated railway station platform and within the displays visitors can find out about the various railway companies which once operated out of the city.

Garvagh Museum & Heritage Centre

142a Main St

Garvagh BT51

garvaghmuseum.com

info@garvaghmuseum.com

Garvagh Museum is unique in Northern Ireland in that it is a rural folk museum in the Bann Valley. It had its origins when artefacts collected from the town and district were housed in a small building adjoining Garvagh Secondary School.

Limavady Museum

24 Main Street

Limavady BT49 0FJ

www.facebook.com/limavadymuseum

information@rvacc.co.uk

Limavady Museum's collections are displayed at the Roe Valley Arts and Cultural Centre in Limavady as well as Green Lane Museum in Roe Valley Country Park. The Roe Valley Arts & Cultural Centre has a dedicated heritage space- the Ritter Gallery- where temporary exhibitions of local and regional significance run throughout the year. The centre also has a purpose-built museum store, where the majority of the collection is now housed.

Springhill - National Trust

20 Springhill Road, Moneymore

Magherafelt BT45 7NQ

028 8674 8210

www.nationaltrust.org.uk/springhill

springhill@nationaltrust.org.uk

An atmospheric 17th-century 'plantation' home, and one of the prettiest houses in Ulster. The house tour takes in the exceptional library, Conyngham family furniture, gun room, nursery, resident ghost and the unusual and colourful costume exhibition which has some fine 17th-century Irish pieces.

Tower Museum

Union Hall Place

Derry BT48 6LU

02871 372411

www.derrycity.gov.uk/museums

towerreception@derrycity.gov.uk

The Tower Museum contains two permanent exhibitions and hosts a number of touring exhibitions throughout the year. The 'story of Derry' exhibition outlines the city's history from its earliest formation to the present day.

County Tyrone

Tyrone, an inland county of Ulster province, Ireland; is bounded NE. by county Londonderry, E. by Lough Neagh, SE. by county Armagh, S. by county Monaghan, SW. by county Fermanagh, and NW. by county Donegal; greatest length, NW. and SE., 48 miles; greatest breadth, NE. and SW., 38 miles; average breadth, 28 miles; area, 806,658 acres (31,403 water), or 379 per cent of the total area of Ireland; population 197,719, of whom 55.75 per cent, are Roman Catholics, 22.74 Episcopalians, 19.75 Presbyterians, and 1.78 Methodists. The surface in general is hilly and irregular; it rises into mountains of about 2000 ft. on the NE. border, and becomes level towards Lough Neagh on the E. The soil in the lower districts is very fertile and highly cultivated. Coal is worked near Lough Neagh and in the neighbourhood of Dungannon; marble is quarried near the boundary with Monaghan; old red sandstone occurs in the district around Omagh; mica slate and limestone prevail among the mountains. The chief mfrs. are linens, woollens, and coarse earthenware. The principal rivers are the Foyle, the Blackwater, the Mourne, and the Ballinderry. The county comprises 8 baronies - Clogher, Dungannon (Lower, Middle, and Upper), Omagh (East and West), Strabane (Lower and Upper); 46 parishes; and the towns of Omagh (the capital), Strabane, Dungannon, Cookstown, and Aughnacloy.

– John Bartholomew, *Gazetteer of the British Isles* (1887)

Gray's Printing Press - National Trust

🏠 ✉ £

49 Main Street
Strabane BT82 8AU
028 7188 0055
www.nationaltrust.org.uk/grays-printing-press
grays@nationaltrust.org.uk

An 18th-century printing press, where John Dunlap, the printer of the American Declaration of Independence, and James Wilson, grandfather of President Woodrow Wilson, learnt their trade. There is a collection of 19th-century hand-printing machines, as well as an audio-visual display.

Ulster American Folk Park

🏠 ✉ ★

Mellon Road, Castletown
Omagh BT78 5QY
028 8224 3292
www.folkpark.com
info@uafp.co.uk

The Ulster American Folk Park tells the story of emigration from Ulster to America in the 18th and 19th centuries. Here you will find fully furnished Old and New World buildings with costumed demonstrators going about their everyday tasks.

Collections: The museum's collection consists of original and replica Ulster and American dwelling houses and shops with original furniture and fittings from the 18th, 19th and early 20th centuries. There is a substantial social history collection of domestic, craft and agricultural objects in storage and on display in the exhibit buildings and permanent exhibition, including a small textile collection of Ulster and American patchwork and various miscellaneous costume and linen items.

CROWN DEPENDENCIES

Bailiwick of Guernsey

Guernsey, the most westerly, and in point of size the second of the Channel Islands; situated in the Bay of St Michael in the Gulf of Avranches at the entrance to the English Channel, 68 miles S. of Weymouth, 81 SE. of Plymouth, and 108 SW. of Southampton; on the French side the island is 42 miles SW. of Cherbourg; it is 9 miles long and 5 miles wide; 16,005 acres, population 32,607. On the coast the scenery of Guernsey is very impressive, but the interior is flat and thinly wooded. Commerce is represented chiefly by the working of the granite quarries, which supply excellent road material. There are very fair fisheries, and a little shipbuilding. Cows are reared for the English markets, and a profitable trade exists in the exportation of grapes, pears, and other fruits. St Peter Port in the SE. is the chief town. There are fixed lights (Guernsey Island), seen 3 and 9 miles respectively, at the old and new harbours of St Peter Port, and a revolving light (Guernsey Island) is displayed on SW. rock of Hanois, or Hanoveaux, seen 12 miles.

Alderney, one of the Channel Islands, about 7 miles from the coast of Normandy and 50 miles SE. from Portland Bill, Dorset; separated from Cape La Hague in France by the Race of Alderney. Area, 1962 acres, population 2048. The island is about 4 miles long, 1¼ mile broad, and 12 miles in circumference. The soil is rich and well cultivated, and the island is famous for its breed of cows. On the N. side an extensive breakwater and harbour of refuge have been constructed.

Sark (or Serq), one of the Channel Islands, consisting of 2 parts, Great Sark and Little Sark, 8½ miles NE. of Guernsey - Great Sark, 1035 acres, population 526; Little Sark, 239 acres, population 45. Great Sark and Little Sark are connected by a narrow neck of land called the Coupee. The island is almost entirely surrounded by inaccessible rocks; but a fine pier has recently been erected. Fishing is the principal occupation, but agriculture is also carried on; and there are some manufactures of stockings, gloves, and Guernsey jackets.

– John Bartholomew, *Gazetteer of the British Isles* (1887)

Alderney Museum

The Alderney Society, The Museum, High Street
Alderney GY9 3TG
01481 823222
www.alderneysociety.org/museum.php
alderneymuseum@alderney.net

TThe museum collection on display reveals an island community changing over the years to both external and internal pressures. Alderney has a fascinating history starting with extensive Stone, Bronze and Iron Age activity, with object evidence of historically important Roman activity at Longy. The Victorian era brought huge change to Alderney and the landscape it still dominated by Queen Victoria's interest in the island as a defence harbour from the French. Most recently the Second World War had an extreme effect on Alderney when all but a few of the island's inhabitants were evacuated and the island occupied by German forces for the duration of the war.

Castle Cornet & Museums

Castle Emplacement
St Peter Port GY1 1AU
01481 721657
www.museums.gov.gg
info@museums.gov.gg

Castle Cornet is Guernsey's ancient harbour fortress, which was isolated upon a rocky islet until the construction of a breakwater and bridge in the 19th century. Dating from the 13th century it was periodically upgraded, withstanding sieges during the Hundred Years War and English Civil Wars.

Collections: Substantial collections of maritime art, weapons, medals, militaria, uniforms, ship models, Roman and medieval archaeology, ship-building and privateering.

Family History Section of La Société Guernesiaise

PO Box 314, St Peter Port GYI 3TG
www.societe.org.gg/sections/familyhistory.php
societe@cwgsy.net

Guernsey's local research, natural history and conservation society.

Fort Grey & Shipwreck Museum

c/o Guernsey Museums & Galleries, Candie Gardens,
Guernsey
St Peter Port GY1 1UG
01481 265036
www.museums.gov.gg
info@museums.gov.gg

Fort Grey is located on Guernsey's rocky west coast, near the infamous Hanois reefs and the site of many historic shipwrecks. The small martello tower contains a museum about Guernsey shipwrecks, with many salvaged artefacts and related illustrations.

Guernsey Folk & Costume Museum

Saumarez Park, Route de Cobo
Castel GY5 7UJ
01481 255384
www.nationaltrust-gsy.org.gg
folkmuseumntgsy@cwgsy.net

The museum's collection of costumes and artefacts is unique in that it consists of material from within the Bailiwick of Guernsey only; that is, Guernsey, Alderney, Sark and Herm. It includes men's, women's and childrens' clothes for all occasions and every accessory imaginable - hats, bags, gloves, shoes, scarves, muffs, tippets, galoshes, spats and some items whose use we can but guess.

Guernsey Museum in Candie Gardens

Candie Gardens
St Peter Port GY1 1UG
01481 726518
www.museums.gov.gg
info@museums.gov.gg

Located in the beautiful Candie Gardens, a late 19th century pleasure garden in St Peter Port (Guernsey's main urban area), this is the headquarters of the museum service. The building houses the Story of Guernsey gallery, which tells the story of the island and its people from prehistoric times.

Hauteville House

38 Hauteville
St Peter Port GY1 1DG
01481 721911
www.victorhugo.gg/hauteville-house
hugohouse@cwgsy.net

Hauteville House is where Victor Hugo lived in exile for 15 years (from 1856 to 1870). An enthusiastic collector of secondhand furniture and bric-à-brac, he brought back a profusion of chests, sideboards, carpets, mirrors, crockery, figurines and other objects from his excursions around the island.

Bailiwick of Jersey

Jersey, the largest and most important of the Channel Islands, 15 miles N. of the French coast, 17 SE. of Guernsey, and 123 W. of Southampton, area 28,717 acres, population 52,445. Jersey is the most southerly of this group of islands, and is oblong in form; greatest length, E. to W., 12 miles; greatest breadth, N. to S., 7½ miles; circumference about 40 miles. In the N. the appearance of the island is rugged and precipitous, the cliffs rising sheer from the sea. Towards the S. and E. the land slopes, and terminates in fine stretches of shore. The interior may be described as beautifully wooded table-land, comprising many lovely valleys, and watered by a number of small streams. Numerous bays indent the coast on the W., S., and E., and small rocky islets abound on the N. The usual cereals grow in abundance, and large quantities of fruit of almost every description are exported. On the coast the fisheries are successfully prosecuted. St Helier is the chief town, and there is regular communication by steamer with both England and France.

– John Bartholomew, *Gazetteer of the British Isles* (1887)

Elizabeth Castle

St Aubin's Bay, St Helier
Jersey JE2 3NF
01534 723971
en.wikipedia.org/wiki/Elizabeth_Castle

An explorer's dream castle. Built across two islets in the Bay of St Aubin, Elizabeth Castle defended Jersey for over 300 years.

Hamptonne

Rue de la Patente
St Lawrence JE3 1HS
01534 863 955
http://goo.gl/gtrKQi

Let us transport you back to the turbulent era of the English Civil War, courtesy of one of our Goodwyfs, each with a different story to tell – or just enjoy the fresh country air and tranquility of rural Jersey. There is much to see in this unique collection of lovingly restored farm houses, gardens, meadows and orchard including a small museum, an environmental trail, farm animals and children's play area.

Jersey Archive

Clarence Road
St Helier JE2 4JY
01534 833300
www.jerseyheritage.org
archives@jerseyheritagetrust.org

The Jersey Archive was established in 1993 to collect and preserve the records, no matter what their physical form, of the States of Jersey, States Committees and Departments, the Royal Court, HE Lieutenant-Governor, parishes, churches, businesses, societies, and individuals relating to the Island.

Jersey Heritage

The Weighbridge
St Helier JE2 3NF
01534 633300
www.jerseyheritage.org

Jersey Heritage protects and promotes the island's rich heritage and cultural environment. We aim to inspire people to nurture their heritage in order to safeguard it for the benefit and enjoyment of everyone.

Jersey Museum

The Weighbridge
St Helier JE2 3NF
01534 633300
www.jerseyheritage.org
info@jerseyheritagetrust.org

The bright and spacious Jersey Museum offers hours of interest and enjoyment. It is the gateway to the island, its people, its customs and industries both past and present.

Jersey War Tunnels

Les Charri
St Lawrence JE3 1FU
01534 860808
www.jerseywartunnels.com
info@jerseywartunnels.com

Jersey War Tunnels - preserving, recording and presenting the story of Jersey's Occupation by German Forces from 1940 –1945. At its centre is Höhlgangsanlage 8 (Ho8), the German Underground Hospital, built by forced labourers.

La Hougue Bie Museum

La Route De La Hougue Bie
St Saviour JE2 7UA
01534 853 823
www.jerseyheritage.org

Deep inside the 6,000-year-old mound lies one of the finest Neolithic dolmens in Europe. Older than the pyramids of Egypt, the 13m high mound is topped by a medieval chapel to make a picturesque vantage point in the island.

Maritime Museum

New North Quay
St Helier JE2
01534 811043
www.jerseyheritage.org
info@jerseyheritagetrust.org

The Maritime Museum has so much to see, do and experience that you need to allow yourself plenty of time – especially if you have children with you. Since its grand opening in July 1997, this hands-on attraction has delighted visitors, both young and old and has received a great deal of media acclaim.

Mont Orgueil Castle

Gorey, St Martin
Jersey JE2 3NF
01534 853292
www.jerseyheritage.org

This jewel in Jersey's crown is one of the best preserved castles in Britain and one of the most photographed sites in the Channel Islands. Built from the 13th century onwards to protect Jersey against the French, this dramatic castle towers over Gorey harbour and gives spectacular views over the island and across the sea to France.

Moulin de Quetivel

St Peter JE3 1HU
01534 745408
www.nationaltrust.je/place/le-moulin-de-quetivel

Set amid beautiful woodland surroundings, Le Moulin de Quétivel is Jersey's last remaining working watermill and gives a unique insight into the 18th century when milling was at its peak.

Isle of Man

Man, Isle of, situated in the Irish Sea, 16 miles S. of Burrow Head, Wigtownshire, 27 miles SW. of St Bees Head, Cumberland, and 27 miles W. of Strangford Lough, county Down; greatest length, NE. to SW., 33 miles; greatest breadth, E. to W., 12½ miles; area, 145,325 acres, population 54,089. A precipitous islet, called the Calf of Man, is situated off the SW. extremity, and contains about 800 acres. On the Isle of Man itself a range of mountains runs NE. to SW.-from Maughold Head to the Calf - occupying the greater part of the island, the highest elevation being Snaefell (2034 ft). Amidst the mountains are the sources of the Sulby, Neb, Douglas, and other streams. The island contains no lakes. The coast on the SW. is rugged and precipitous, the cliffs in some places rising sheer from the sea to a height of over 1400 ft.; on the SE. it is generally low, with gradual elevations towards the mountains. On the E. are numerous creeks and bays, including Douglas Bay and Laxey Bay. Clay slate is the formation of the greater part of the island; granite and other eruptive rocks have burst through in one or two localities. Lead, copper, zinc, and iron are the principal minerals; the lead ore especially is rich and plentiful, yielding about 4000 tons a year. The land generally is in a high state of cultivation, scientific farming having greatly increased its richness and fertility. All along the coast sea fishing is actively prosecuted, and gives employment to several thousands of fishermen. For anglers the various streams present exceptional attractions, being well stocked with trout, &c. The shipping is almost wholly connected with coasting trade, which shows a considerable amount of activity. Manufactures are inconsiderable, and in the main consist of Manx cloth, cordage, nets, and canvas. Railway communication exists between the various towns, and there are numerous excellent roads. The island has a distinct bishopric, with the designation of Sodor and Man; the former name being derived from the Sudoreys, or Southern Islands, which were at one time politically connected with them. The island has a government and constitution of its own, also laws, law officers, and courts. The House of Keys, which controls its legislature, is very ancient, and consists of 24 members. Man is divided into 6 sheadings, having 17 parishes, which are subdivided into treens and quarterlands. The principal towns are Douglas, Castletown, Ramsey, and Peel. Castletown is the ancient capital, but Douglas is the chief town and the seat of government.

– John Bartholomew, *Gazetteer of the British Isles* (1887)

Castle Rushen

Castle Street
Castletown IM9 1LD
01624 648000
http://goo.gl/vSRRt6
enquiries@mnh.gov.im

Situated at the heart of the Isle of Man's ancient capital, Castletown, this impressive limestone fortress was the seat of the former Kings and Lords of Mann, with the castle's oldest parts dating to the time of Magnus, last Norse King of Mann, who died in 1265. Later the castle served as an administrative centre, a mint, a law court, and for over 100 years until the late 19th century, as a prison. Today, spectacular displays illustrate the castle at various times in history, with figures in period costume, historical furnishings, wall hangings, realistic food, contemporary music and speech brining the castle's medieval and 17th century periods to life.

Great Laxey Wheel & Mines Trail, The

Mines Road
Laxey IM4 7NL
01624 648000
http://goo.gl/HXWzfB
enquiries@mnh.gov.im

Built in 1854 to pump water from the Laxey mines, the Laxey Wheel is the world's greatest industrial water wheel. Known as 'Lady Isabella', a climb to the top of the Wheel is rewarded with breathtaking views across the valley, while the 'mines trail' displays the remains of a once thriving industrial complex and offers a pleasant walk through Glen Mooar.

Grove, The: Museum of Victorian Life

Andreas Road
Ramsey IM8 3UA
01624 648000
http://goo.gl/JfCmc9
enquiries@mnh.gov.im

Originally developed as the summer retreat for a wealthy Victorian merchant, The Grove tells the story of the Gibbs - a wealthy Victorian family in the Isle of Man. The period rooms in this modest sized Victorian villa display sumptuous original furnishings, costumes and a wealth of accumulated possessions, while the small complex of outbuildings shows the early farm vehicles and equipment that would have been used.

House of Manannan

Peel Quayside
Peel IM5 1TA
01624 648000
http://goo.gl/bosg1A
enquiries@mnh.gov.im

The mythological sea god, Manannan, guides you through the island's rich Celtic, Viking and maritime past, over 2000 years of unique Manx heritage. Step inside splendid reconstructions of a Manx Celtic roundhouse and a Viking longhouse.

Isle of Man Family History Society

4 Eleanoa Gardens
Douglas IM2 3NR
www.iomfhs.im
paminmans@manx.net

The Isle of Man Family History Society was formed in January 1979 to encourage the study of genealogy and family history.

Manx Aviation & Military Museum

Ronaldsway Airfield
Nr Ballasalla IM9 2AS
01624 829294
www.maps.org.im/museum
airmuseum@manx.net

The museum is dedicated to the Manx men and women who served their island in the cause of freedom; to those people of other nations who were brought to our shores by wartime service and to all those who, in war and peace, have lost their lives in the Isle of Man in aviation accidents.

Manx Museum

Kingswood Grove
Douglas IM1 3LY
01624 648000
http://goo.gl/ou38Gk
enquiries@mnh.gov.im

The island's treasure house provides an exciting introduction to the 'story of Mann' where a specially produced film portrayal of Manx history compliments the award winning displays. Galleries depict natural history, archaeology and social development of the island.

Manx National Heritage

Manx Museum, Kingswood Grove
Douglas IM1 3LY
01624 648000
www.storyofmann.com
enquiries@mnh.gov.im

Manx National Heritage is the national heritage agency for the Isle of Man, operating integrated cultural and natural heritage services and museums on behalf of the Manx people under the banner of the Story of Mann.

National Folk Museum at Cregneash, The

Arbrory Road
Cregneash IM9 5PT
01624 648000
www.storyofmann.com
enquiries@mnh.gov.im

Cregneash is the living, working illustration of 19th and 20th century Manx crofting life. Visitors can see traditional farming methods and skills in action, including the fields being worked with horse-drawn equipment, the processing of Manx loghtan wool, and woodturning in the Turner's Shed.

Nautical Museum

Parliament Square
Castletown IM9 1LA
01624 648000
www.storyofmann.com
enquiries@mnh.gov.im

Home of George Quayle's 18th century armed yacht 'The Peggy', this fascinating building perserves Quayle's mysterious architectural designs, and houses a replica sailmaker's loft. In the fishing gallery, you'll find a collection of boat models, equipment and photographs which reflect the importance of the Manx fishing industry.

Old Grammar School

St Mary's Chapel
Castletown IM9 1LE
01624 648000
http://goo.gl/vmxEn3
enquiries@mnh.gov.im

Built around 1200 as the first town church, St Mary's Chapel changed its role from 1570 to become the Grammar School, which closed in 1930. Rows of bench desks with ink wells are reminders of early Victorian school days.

Old House of Keys, The

🏛️ £

Parliament Square

Castletown IM9 1LA

01624 648000

http://goo.gl/kn6LSe

enquiries@mnh.gov.im

Inside the finely restored 19th century home of the Manx Parliament, visitors become members of the House of Keys through the ages, debating and deciding upon momentous issues from Manx political history. Should women be given the vote? Should motor racing be allowed on Manx public roads? Listen to the arguments for and against and then cast your vote..

Peel Castle

🏛️ £

St Patrick's Isle

Peel IM5 1TB

01624 648 000

www.storyofmann.com

enquiries@mnh.gov.im

One of the island's principle historic centres, this great natural fortress with its imposing curtain wall set majestically at the mouth of Peel Harbour is steeped in Viking heritage. The sandstone walls of Peel Castle enclose an 11th century church and the Round Tower, the 13th century St German's Cathedral and the later apartments of the Lords of Mann.

Rushen Abbey

🏛️ £

Mill Road

Ballasalla IM9 3DB

01624 648000

http://goo.gl/wxTIGX

enquiries@mnh.gov.im

Located in Ballasalla, Rushen Abbey is the Isle of Man's most substantial and important religious site, the highlight of a 'Christian Heritage' route around the island which includes ancient kiells and the carved stone crosses which can be found at parish churches and chapels throughout the Isle of Man. Explore the roots of Manx Christianity, the work of the Cistercian monks and life within the Abbey, before its closure in 1540.

COUNTY GUIDE

There have been many changes to county boundaries, particularly (but not exclusively) in 1844, 1889 and 1974. This book primarily uses 'ceremonial counties', many of which are based on 'historic counties', but in some cases there are variations and it may still not be clear where one should look. This appendix contains a list of most names of counties, islands and other significant land divisions (including modern unitary authorities) and indicates under which 'county' heading(s) in this book relevant places may be found. Entries in **bold** show counties or areas with their own specific sections in this book. (For further information see the introduction.)

Aberdeen (City) ....Aberdeenshire
Aberdeenshire
Abertawe...............................Glamorgan
Alderney ....Bailiwick of Guernsey
Anglesey
Angus
Antrim..........................County Antrim
Antrim & Newtownabbey
................................County Antrim
Argyll
Argyll & Bute ....Argyll
Argyllshire......................................Argyll
Armagh.......................County Armagh
Armagh, Banbridge & Craigavon
................................County Armagh
Arran, Isle of ....Ayrshire
Avon ....Gloucestershire/
..............................Somerset/Bristol
Ayrshire
Bailiwick of Guernsey
Bailiwick of Jersey
Banffshire.......................Aberdeenshire
Barra, Isle of ....Hebrides
Bath & North East Somerset..Somerset
Bedford ....Bedfordshire
Bedfordshire
Belfast
Berkshire
Berneray, Isle of ....Hebrides
Berwickshire
Blackburn with Darwen......Lancashire
Blackpool............................Lancashire
Blaenau Gwent............Monmouthshire
Borders......Berwickshire/Peeblesshire/
...........Roxburghshire/Selkirkshire/
................................Midlothian
Bournemouth ....Dorset
Bracknell Forest.....................Berkshire
Brecknockshire
Breconshire..................Brecknockshire
Bridgend ....Glamorgan
Brighton & Hove ....East Sussex
Bristol
Bro Morgannwg..................Glamorgan
Buckinghamshire
Bute ....Argyll
Buteshire.......................................Argyll
Caerdydd....................................Cardiff
Caerffili ....Glamorgan

Caernarfonshire
Caerphilly.............................Glamorgan
Caithness
Cambridgeshire
Cardiff
Cardiganshire
Carmarthenshire
Casnewydd.................Monmouthshire
Castell-nedd Port Talbot ....Glamorgan
Causeway Coast & Glens
................................County Antrim/
.......................County Londonderry
Central ....Clackmannanshire/
................................Stirlingshire
Central Bedfordshire ......Bedfordshire
Ceredigion......................Cardiganshire
Cheshire
Cheshire East ....Cheshire
Cheshire West & Chester ....Cheshire
Clackmannanshire
Cleveland
..North Yorkshire/County Durham
Clwyd ....Denbighshire/Flintshire/
................................Merioneth
Comhairle nan Eilean Siar .....Hebrides
Conwy...Caernarfonshire/Denbighshire
Cornwall
County Antrim
County Armagh
County Down
County Durham
County Fermanagh
County Londonderry
County Tyrone
Cromartyshire
Cumberland ....Cumbria
Cumbria
Darlington ....County Durham
Denbighshire
Derby.....................................Derbyshire
Derbyshire
Derry..................County Londonderry
Derry & Strabane
.......................County Londonderry
Devon
Dorset
Down ....County Down
Dumbarton ....Dunbartonshire
Dumbartonshire ....Dunbartonshire

Dumfries & Galloway ...Dumfriesshire
Dumfriesshire
Dunbartonshire
Dundee...Angus
Durham......................County Durham
Dyfed ....Cardiganshire/
....Carmarthenshire/Pembrokeshire
East Ayrshire ....Ayrshire
East Dunbartonshire ..Dunbartonshire
East Lothian
East Renfrewshire...........Renfrewshire
East Riding of Yorkshire
................................East Yorkshire
East Suffolk ....Suffolk
East Sussex
East Yorkshire
Edinburgh
Edinburghshire...................Edinburgh
Elginshire..................................Moray
Ely, Isle of ....Cambridgeshire
Essex
Falkirk ....Stirlingshire
Fermanagh............County Fermanagh
Fermanagh & Omagh
.........................County Fermanagh/
................................County Tyrone
Fife
Flintshire
Forfarshire ....Angus
Glamorgan
Glasgow
Gloucestershire
Grampian...........Aberdeenshire/Moray
Greater London
Greater Manchester
Guernsey...........Bailiwick of Guernsey
Gwent..........................Monmouthshire
Gwynedd....Anglesey/Caernarfonshire/
.................Denbighshire/Merioneth
Haddingtonshire ....East Lothian
Halton ....Cheshire
Hampshire
Harris, Isle of..........................Hebrides
Hartlepool..................County Durham
Hebrides
Hereford & Worcester
.........Herefordshire/Worcestershire
Herefordshire
Hertfordshire

Highland ...Inverness-shire/Ross-shire/
...............Cromartyshire/Caithness/
...................Nairnshire/Sutherland/
.................................Argyll/Moray
Hull ....East Yorkshire
Humberside...................East Yorkshire/
...........West Yorkshire/Lincolnshire
Huntingdon & Peterborough
...............................Cambridgeshire
Huntingdonshire.........Cambridgeshire
Inner Hebrides.......................Hebrides
Inverclyde.......................Renfrewshire
Inverness-shire
Iona, Isle of....................................Argyll
Islay, Isle of...................................Argyll
Isle of Man
Isle of Wight
Isles of Scilly ....Cornwall
Jersey.......................Bailiwick of Jersey
Jura, Isle of................................Hebrides
Kent
Kincardineshire ....Aberdeenshire
Kinross-shire ....Perthshire
Kirkcudbrightshire ....Dumfriesshire
Lanarkshire
Lancashire
Leicester............................Leicestershire
Leicestershire
Lewis, Isle of.............................Hebrides
Lincolnshire
Linlithgowshire................West Lothian
Lisburn & Castlereagh
........County Antrim/County Down
London.......................Greater London
Londonderry/Derry
.......................County Londonderry
Lothian ....East Lothian/Midlothian/
....West Lothian
Luton ....Bedfordshire
Man, Isle of...........................Isle of Man
Manchester...........Greater Manchester
Medway...Kent
Meirionnydd ....Merioneth
Merioneth
Merionethshire ....Merioneth
Merseyside
Merthyr Tydfil/Tudful ....Glamorgan
Mid & East Antrim......County Antrim
Mid Glamorgan ....Glamorgan
Mid-Ulster ....County Londonderry/
.....County Tyrone/County Armagh
Middlesbrough...........North Yorkshire
Middlesex....................Greater London
Midlothian
Milton Keynes ....Buckinghamshire
Mingulay, Isle of ....Hebrides
Monmouthshire
Montgomeryshire
Moray
Morayshire...................................Moray
Morgannwg.......................Glamorgan
Mull, Isle of...................................Argyll
Na h-Eileanan Siar ....Hebrides
Nairnshire
Neath Port Talbot ....Glamorgan
Newport.....................Monmouthshire
Newry, Mourne & Down
......County Down/County Armagh
Norfolk

North Ayrshire.........................Ayrshire
North Down & Ards......County Down
North East Lincolnshire...Lincolnshire
North Humberside
.....North Yorkshire/West Yorkshire
North Lanarkshire ....Lanarkshire
North Lincolnshire ....Lincolnshire
North Riding of Yorkshire
...............................North Yorkshire
North Somerset......................Somerset
North Uist, Isle of ....Hebrides
North Yorkshire
Northamptonshire
Northumberland
Nottingham................Nottinghamshire
Nottinghamshire
Orkney Islands
Outer Hebrides.......................Hebrides
Oxfordshire
Pabbay, Isle of.........................Hebrides
Peeblesshire
Pembrokeshire
Pen-y-bont ar Ogwr............Glamorgan
Perth & Kinross....................Perthshire
Perthshire
Peterborough..............Cambridgeshire
Plymouth ....Devon
Poole..Dorset
Portsmouth.........................Hampshire
Powys....................Montgomeryshire/
.........Radnorshire/Brecknockshire/
...................................Denbighshire
Raasay, Isle of.........................Hebrides
Radnorshire
Reading...................................Berkshire
Redcar & Cleveland....North Yorkshire
Renfrewshire
Rhondda Cynon Taf...........Glamorgan
Ross & Cromarty................Ross-shire/
....................................Cromartyshire
Ross-shire
Roxburghshire
Rutland
Sark.....................Bailiwick of Guernsey
Scottish Borders...............Berwickshire/
..........Peeblesshire/Roxburghshire/
...................Selkirkshire/Midlothian
Scottish Highlands......Inverness-shire/
..............Ross-shire/Cromartyshire/
.....................Caithness/Nairnshire/
................Sutherland/Argyll/Moray
Selkirkshire
Shetland Islands
Shropshire
Sir Aberteifi ....Cardiganshire
Sir Benfro ....Pembrokeshire
Sir Ddinbych ....Denbighshire
Sir Drefaldwyn...........Montgomeryshire
Sir Faesyfed ....Radnorshire
Sir Feirionnydd ....Merioneth
Sir Fôn.......................................Anglesey
Sir Forgannwg....................Glamorgan
Sir Frycheiniog............Brecknockshire
Sir Fynwy....................Monmouthshire
Sir Gaerfyrddin ....Carmarthenshire
Sir Gaernarfon ....Caernarfonshire
Sir Gâr......................Carmarthenshire
Sir Morgannwg ....Glamorgan
Sir y Fflint ....Flintshire

Skye, Isle of.............................Hebrides
Slough ....Berkshire
Soke of Peterborough...Cambridgeshire
Somerset
South Ayrshire ....Ayrshire
South Glamorgan ....Glamorgan
South Gloucestershire...Gloucestershire
South Humberside............Lincolnshire
South Lanarkshire ....Lanarkshire
South Uist, Isle of ....Hebrides
South Yorkshire
Southampton.......................Hampshire
Southend-on-Sea ....Essex
Staffordshire
Stirling ....Stirlingshire
Stirlingshire
Stockton-on-Tees.......County Durham
Stoke-on-Trent ....Staffordshire
Strathclyde.................Glasgow/Ayrshire/
.........Dunbartonshire/Lanarkshire/
...Renfrewshire/Argyll/Stirlingshire
Suffolk
Surrey
Sussex ....East Sussex/West Sussex
Sutherland
Swansea.................................Glamorgan
Swindon....................................Wiltshire
Tayside ....Angus/Perthshire
Telford & Wrekin ....Shropshire
Thurrock ....Essex
Tiree, Isle of.....................................Argyll
Torbay ....Devon
Torfaen.....................Monmouthshire
Tyne & Wear
Tyrone ....County Tyrone
Vale of Glamorgan ....Glamorgan
Warrington............................Cheshire
Warwickshire
West Berkshire......................Berkshire
West Dunbartonshire...Dunbartonshire
West Glamorgan.................Glamorgan
West Lothian
West Midlands
West Riding of Yorkshire
......West Yorkshire/South Yorkshire
West Suffolk ....Suffolk
West Sussex
West Yorkshire
Western Isles ....Hebrides
Westmorland..........................Cumbria
Wight, Isle of ....Isle of Wight
Wigtownshire.................Dumfriesshire
Wiltshire
Windsor & Maidenhead........Berkshire
Wokingham...........................Berkshire
Worcestershire
Wrexham/Wrecsam ....Denbighshire
Ynys Môn..................................Anglesey
York ....North Yorkshire
Yorkshire ....North Yorkshire/
...................................East Yorkshire/
......South Yorkshire/West Yorkshire
Yorkshire, East Riding...East Yorkshire
Yorkshire, North Riding
...................................North Yorkshire
Yorkshire, West Riding
......West Yorkshire/South Yorkshire
Zetland.......................Shetland Islands

INDEX

B

M

XYZ

Lightning Source UK Ltd.
Milton Keynes UK
UKOW06f2002230615

254011UK00016B/541/P